KU-454-892

Sex Before the Sexual Revolution

Famously, at least for Philip Larkin, sexual intercourse did not begin until 1963. So what did sex mean for ordinary people before the sexual revolution of the 1960s and 1970s? They have often been pitied by later generations as repressed, unfulfilled and full of moral anxiety. This book provides the first rounded, first-hand account of sexuality in marriage in the early and mid-twentieth century. These award-winning authors look beyond the conventions of silence among the respectable majority to challenge stereotypes of ignorance and inhibition. Based on vivid, compelling and frank testimonies from a socially and geographically diverse range of individuals, the book explores a spectrum of sexual experiences, from learning about sex and sexual practices in courtship, to attitudes to the body, marital ideals and birth control. It demonstrates that while the era's emphasis on silence and strict moral codes could for some be a source of inhibition and dissatisfaction, for many the culture of privacy and innocence was central to fulfilling and pleasurable intimate lives.

SIMON SZRETER is Professor of History and Public Policy at the University of Cambridge, and a Fellow of St John's College, Cambridge. His previous publications include *Fertility, Class and Gender in Britain 1860–1940* (Cambridge 1996) and *Changing Family Size in England and Wales 1891–1911: place, class and demography* (co-author, 2001). In 2009 he was awarded the Arthur Viseltear Prize of the American Public Health Association for distinguished contributions to the history of public health. He is also a founding member of the History and Policy Network at www.historyandpolicy.org.

KATE FISHER is Senior Lecturer in History at the University of Exeter. Her highly acclaimed first book, *Birth Control, Sex and Marriage in Britain, 1918–1960* (2006), won national and international awards including the RHS Whitfield Prize. In 2007 she was shortlisted for the Times Higher Education Young Academic Author of the Year Award.

Sex Before the Sexual Revolution

Intimate Life in England 1918–1963

Simon Szreter and Kate Fisher

CAMBRIDGE UNIVERSITY PRESS
Cambridge, New York, Melbourne, Madrid, Cape Town, Singapore,
São Paulo, Delhi, Tokyo, Mexico City

Cambridge University Press
The Edinburgh Building, Cambridge CB2 8RU, UK

Published in the United States of America by Cambridge University Press, New York

www.cambridge.org
Information on this title: www.cambridge.org/9780521149327

© Simon Szreter and Kate Fisher 2010

This publication is in copyright. Subject to statutory exception
and to the provisions of relevant collective licensing agreements,
no reproduction of any part may take place without the written
permission of Cambridge University Press.

First published 2010
Reprinted 2011

Printed in the United Kingdom at the University Press, Cambridge

A catalogue record for this publication is available from the British Library

Library of Congress Cataloguing in Publication data
Szreter, Simon.
Sex before the sexual revolution : intimate life in England 1918–1963 /
Simon Szreter, Kate Fisher.
p. cm. – (Cambridge social and cultural histories ; 16)
ISBN 978-0-521-76004-1 (hardback) – ISBN 978-0-521-14932-7 (paperback)
1. Sex–England–History–20th century. 2. Sex role–England–History–20th century. 3. Intimacy (Psychology) 4. England–Social life and customs–20th century. I. Fisher, Kate. II. Title. III. Series.
HQ18.G7S97 2010
306.70942'0904–dc22
2010033388

ISBN 978-0-521-76004-1 Hardback
ISBN 978-0-521-14932-7 Paperback

Cambridge University Press has no responsibility for the persistence or
accuracy of URLs for external or third-party internet websites referred to in
this publication, and does not guarantee that any content on such websites is,
or will remain, accurate or appropriate.

Contents

Acknowledgements

This book is the culmination of many years of work, and as a consequence we owe more debts of gratitude than can be acknowledged here. Our first and greatest is to the men and women who generously, candidly and with good humour shared their personal and intimate stories with us. We have been moved and inspired by their lives. Local authorities' social services departments, residential homes, day centres and homecare professionals provided invaluable assistance in making contact with potential respondents, and helped to create a supportive environment for our work. We are grateful to all our transcribers, especially Jenny Attoe, to Debbie Palmer for help checking proofs and also to Jacqui Cahif for selflessly assisting us in preparing the final manuscript. Additionally we extend our thanks to Chloe Howell, Liz Davey, the production team at Cambridge University Press, and our commissioning editors, Michael Watson and Liz Friend-Smith, for their efficiency, to Auriol Griffiths-Jones for indexing, and to Julene Knox for meticulous copy-editing.

The work on which this book is built has benefited from funding from a number of sources, including an ESRC project grant, an ESRC Fellowship and a Wellcome Trust project grant. We are also most grateful for additional financial support from the AHRC and Exeter University, and for the stimulating and sustaining intellectual environments we have enjoyed among our colleagues and students in Exeter and Cambridge.

We are indebted to Pat Thane for reading an early version of the text, and we benefited from perceptive and thought-provoking comments from our anonymous reviewers. We thank others who have read parts of the text, or provided helpful comments or support, particularly Nick and Sarah Fisher, Rebecca Langlands, Nic Bilham, Richard Smith, Tessa Stone, Sian Pooley, Ben Griffin; and the late Joe and Olive Banks for their encouragement from the earliest stages of formulating the research project. Many other colleagues, whom we have consulted or who have heard presentations at seminars and conferences, have assisted us with their critical insights, encouragement and enthusiasm, and we are grateful to each of them.

Above all, we would like to thank our partners, Hilary Cooper and James Mark, whose unstinting support and generosity has sustained our work, and whose incisive comments have added to it immeasurably.

The long gestation period of this work is pointed up by the number of pregnancies it has outlasted. Two sons extant at the start of this project have been joined by a further four, and it is to these six boys – Simon's Sam, Ben and Zack, and Kate's Edmund, Isaac and Kit – that this book is dedicated.

Earlier, shorter versions of Chapters 5 and 6 have been published, respectively, as: Simon Szreter and Kate Fisher, 'Love and Authority in Mid-twentieth Century Marriages: Sharing and Caring', ch. 6 in *The Politics of Domestic Authority in Britain since 1800*, eds. Lucy Delap, Ben Griffin and Abigail Wills (Basingstoke: Palgrave Macmillan, 2009), 132–54; and Simon Szreter and Kate Fisher, '"We Weren't the Sort that Wanted Intimacy Every Night": Birth Control and Abstinence in England, c.1930–60', *The History of the Family* 15 (2010): 139–60.

1 Introduction

Going back to your marriage, when you had sex, who made the first move?

ELMA (laughs) I'm not telling. (laughs) No, I think we were both of the same mind. No, I don't think – I don't think there was anything like that. If, if he wanted something he'd tell me, in a nice kind of a way.

How did you know that he was feeling amorous?

(laughs) I didn't; I just had to guess.

What were the signs?

Pardon?

What were the signs?

Well, the usual, two arms round me instead of one. (laughs)[1]

Oral history and private lives

This book addresses sexuality and intimacy, especially within the context of marriage, among ordinary people in England during the mid-twentieth century, approximately 1918–63. It presents evidence from an oral history study which solicited first-hand accounts from eighty-nine men and women, drawn from both the middle and the working classes, whose adolescence, marriage and childrearing occurred during the interwar and immediately post-war decades.[2] In adopting oral history as the prime research tool for this book we hope to provide a sophisticated and empirically based portrait of sexuality and intimacy within marriages during the interwar and early post-war decades of the twentieth century.[3] The interviewees were asked how they had learned about

[1] Elma msf/jm/bl/#42, born in working-class Rotherham in 1909 (her father was a shunter on the railways). In 1933 she married a Manchester policeman two years older than her, who died in 1972. One child born 1934. She worked throughout her marriage as a cook in company canteens. All names of respondents and of persons mentioned in the interviews are pseudonyms. In the text dates in brackets after interviewees' names indicate their year of birth.

[2] Through an oversight, one never-married individual was interviewed, Pearl (1915) msf/kf/bl/#40. Thus, throughout we refer to eighty-eight married interviewees and eighty-nine informants altogether.

[3] The collection of eighty-nine oral histories took place between 1998 and 2001 and was funded by an ESRC grant to Simon Szreter, Grant Number R000236621. Kate Fisher was the project's Research Officer. The research was given further support through a Wellcome Project Grant

sex in childhood and youth, how they had approached sex in adolescence and courtship, what sex had meant to them as adults and what part it played in their marriage relationships, particularly during their childbearing years when the issues of birth control and family planning would have had to be addressed. The central conclusion is the importance of privacy to intimacy within marriage especially in relation to the expression of sexuality.

Individuals presented marriages as private places where sex in particular was not part of an ongoing, reflective discussion, even between husband and wife.[4] In this context, it would appear to be a particular challenge systematically to collect first-hand oral history testimony on a topic which (as we conclude) many felt – and still feel – ought to be kept private:[5]

awarded to K. Fisher, Grant Ref: 059811/2/JM/HH/SW, an ESRC Fellowship to Simon Szreter, Award Number R000271041 and an AHRC Research Leave Term in 2006. Both authors conducted all aspects of the research and analysis together and should be regarded as equal and joint authors of this book. We undertook the construction of the text as a fully collaborative and joint exercise. Each author has had primary responsibility for four substantive chapters and produced the first draft (Simon chapters 2, 5, 6 and 7 and Kate chapters 3, 4, 8 and 9), but all chapters were subsequently edited and reworked by both authors innumerable times. See this section, immediately below, and the Appendices for fuller information about the research design, the interviewing process and the interviewees.

[4] This broadly conforms with the insightful, historically informed contemporaneous views of Norbert Elias in *The Civilizing Process*, transl. Edmund Jephcott, revised edition, eds. Eric Dunning, Johan Goudsblom and Stephen Mennell (Oxford: Blackwell, 2000), esp. 158–60 (first published in German in 1939). This construction of privacy in marital sexuality corresponds to valuing privacy of the person, privacy of 'personal space' and privacy in personal relations, which are three of the six dimensions of privacy which Brian Harrison sees as significant for thinking about the history of the shifting relationship between the public and the private in modern British history since 1800 (Brian Harrison,'The Public and the Private in Modern Britain', ch. 19 in *Civil Histories: Essays Presented to Sir Keith Thomas*, eds. Peter Burke, Brian Harrison, Paul Slack (Oxford: Oxford University Press, 2000), 338). For a detailed enquiry into representations of the public and the private during the prior, early modern period, see Michael McKeon, *The Secret History of Domesticity: Public, Private and the Division of Knowledge* (Baltimore: Johns Hopkins University Press, 2005).

[5] Previous oral histories have often only asked women about 'family life', and have been more limited in scope, or else focused on illicit, extra-marital sexual experiences, rather than the complex codes, norms and expectations of sex within marriage. See for example, Paul Thompson, *The Edwardians: The Remaking of British Society* (2nd edn, London: Routledge, 1992, first published 1975), Diana Gittins, *Fair Sex: Family Size and Structure, 1900–39* (London: Hutchinson, 1982), Elizabeth Roberts, *A Woman's Place: An Oral History of Working-Class Women 1890–1940* (Oxford: Blackwell, 1984), Steve Humphries, *A Secret World of Sex: Forbidden Fruit, the British Experience 1900–1950* (London: Sidgwick & Jackson, 1988), Jacqueline Sarsby, *Missuses and Mouldrunners: An Oral History of Women Pottery-Workers at Work and at Home* (Milton Keynes: Open University Press, 1988), Maureen Sutton, *We Didn't Know Aught: Study of Sexuality, Superstition and Death in Women's Lives in Lincolnshire During the 1930's, 40's and 50's* (Stamford: P. Watkins, 1992), Elizabeth Roberts, *Women and Families: An Oral History, 1940–1970* (Oxford and Cambridge, MA: Blackwell, 1995), Lucinda McCray Beier, *For Their Own Good: The Transformation of English Working-Class Health Culture, 1880–1970* (Columbus: Ohio State University Press, 2008), ch. 5. Slater and Woodside's study was an early contemporary enquiry about marriage relationships which did interview both men and women – indeed, they separately interviewed 102 sets of (hospitalised), mostly working-class (some had come from clerical work) servicemen and their wives from the London area (Eliot Slater and

ENID No, I am a very private person… [the] warden… asked me, 'Was it alright?' I said, 'Yes', but, erm, having said that, I never tell anybody my business. I keep myself to myself; that's the way I've been all my life.[6]

Despite the importance of privacy for the individuals whose life stories form the basis of this book, many were prepared to discuss sex, marriage and intimacy with us.[7] These interviews contest the widespread assumption that the subject of sex within marriage is too sensitive for such study.[8] Other researchers see the construction of interview narratives about sex as exercises in the breaking of a taboo: 'The interviews themselves were transgressions of the silencing in which women had been trained.'[9] We are less convinced that our interviews represent moments in which taboos were broken, making us party to secret sexual narratives. Rather, in response to skilled interviewing, respondents chose what aspects of their life histories to reveal and discuss on their own terms, and for their own reasons.

In part the obtaining of detailed interview material on the private lives of respondents reflects the sensitive and careful approach adopted. Various strategies were employed to ensure that those interviewed were not simply a select minority prepared to talk openly about sex, whose experiences and attitudes were not broadly typical of their generation.[10] We did not advertise

Moya Woodside, *Patterns of Marriage: A Study of Marriage Relationships in the Urban Working Classes* (London: Cassell and Co., 1951)). Their findings are of special comparative interest as the birth dates of those interviewed, 1896–1922, were very similar to those questioned by us for this book.

6 Enid msf/kf/bl/#49. Born in 1909 and married in 1939 to a trainee mill manager three years her junior, lower-middle-class Enid had three live-births and herself worked part-time as a secretary when her children were older.

7 In the late 1940s Mass Observation was 'startled… at the friendliness and willingness of all whom they met [on the street] to talk about sex subjects'. Mass Observation, File Report 3110 'General Attitudes to Sex', April 1949, 'Article One: Sex Attitudes', 1.

8 Richard C. Lewontin, 'Sex, Lies, and Social Science', *New York Review of Books* 42, no. 7 (1995). See also, Valerie Raleigh Yow, *Recording Oral History: A Practical Guide for Social Scientists* (Thousand Oaks, CA: Sage Publications, 1994), 128–9. Lewontin reported that in interviews with mill-women in Carboro, North Carolina, '[m]y co-researchers and I decided it would be useless of me to ask male narrators about sexual practices or for them to ask women. But even the women I talked to were unable to discuss the topic.' For a broader discussion of the problems see O. O. Dare and J. G. Cleland, 'Reliability and Validity of Survey Data on Sexual Behaviour', *Health Transition Review* 4, no. 2 (1994).

9 Patricia Zavella, '"Playing with Fire": The Gendered Construction of Chicana/Mexicana Sexuality', in *The Gender/Sexuality Reader: Culture, History, Political Economy*, eds. R. N. Lancaster and M. D. Leonardo (New York: Routledge, 1997), 393. For a successful and insightful study of courtship, marriage and sexuality based on life-story interviews conducted with twenty-six Mexican and Mexican-American women, see Jennifer S. Hirsch, *A Courtship after Marriage: Sexuality and Love in Mexican Transnational Families* (Berkeley: University of California Press, 2003).

10 Claus Adolph Moser and Graham Kalton, *Survey Methods in Social Investigation* (New York: Basic Books, 1972), 127–44, Humphries, *A Secret World of Sex*, 10–11, Raymond M. Lee, *Doing Research on Sensitive Topics* (London: Sage Publications, 1993), Roy Porter and

for participants, but instead asked local authorities for access to day centres and social groups where a short presentation was made and initial contacts with respondents could be established, trust gained and the aims of the project explained. This provided potential interviewees with the opportunity to meet researchers in an entirely unpressurised context, ask questions and to decide at their leisure whether or not to be interviewed.[11] Moreover, that contact was made through the local authority helped to legitimise the project and reassure respondents that we could be trusted with personal stories. Although certainly not all those who had heard our presentation subsequently volunteered to be interviewed, this approach led to significant numbers agreeing to take part once they understood the purpose of the study, how it was being conducted and once the first few interviewees reported back favourably to others about the experience. To a lesser extent, contact was made through the local authorities' home help systems and at residential care homes.

A flexible, unstructured and free-flowing interview process was chosen, usually taking place in the informant's home so as to be as informal as possible, and consequently interviews were frequently long, often involving multiple visits.[12] The two authors conducted most of the interviews.[13] These typically involved three to four hours of conversation, with some lasting considerably longer (the minimum was around an hour and a half in one or two cases). The interviews were completed between 1998 and 2001 with most of the interviewees aged from their mid-seventies to their mid-nineties at the time of the interview. Wide licence was given to respondents to present their memoirs and stories at length, in order to allow material of relevance to their sexual attitudes

Lesley A. Hall, *The Facts of Life: The Creation of Sexual Knowledge in Britain, 1650–1950* (New Haven: Yale University Press, 1995), 248.

[11] Little difference in response rate has been found between sex surveys and those on apparently more neutral topics. See, for example, Dare and Cleland, 'Reliability and Validity of Survey Data on Sexual Behaviour', 94, L. R. England, 'Little Kinsey: An Outline of Sex Attitudes in Britain', *Public Opinion Quarterly* 13, no. 4 (1950): 589.

[12] On the advantages of unstructured interviews see Janet Finch, '"It's Great to Have Some-One to Talk to": The Ethics and Politics of Interviewing Women', in *Social Researching: Politics, Problems, Practice*, eds. C. Bell and H. Roberts (London: Routledge & Kegan Paul, 1984), 73, Lee, *Doing Research on Sensitive Topics*, Sue Lees, *Sugar and Spice: Sexuality and Adolescent Girls* (London: Penguin, 1993), 11. The opposing view that 'censored behaviour' is more willingly revealed in 'self-administered questionnaires than in face-to-face interviews' is maintained by B. Laslett and R. Rapoport, 'Collaborative Interviewing and Interactive Research', *Journal of Marriage and the Family* 37, no. 4 (1975): 973–4, Dare and Cleland, 'Reliability and Validity of Survey Data on Sexual Behaviour', 101.

[13] Those wishing to know the identity of interviewers should examine the interview codes: *srss* in any code refers to interviews conducted by Simon Szreter, who is married and was in his early forties at the time of the interviews, those *kf* by Kate Fisher, who was at the time unmarried, childless and in her late twenties, and those *jm* by James Mark, an oral historian who was at the time unmarried and childless, also in his late twenties. In one case of a joint interview, Betty and Horace msf/kf/ht/#31, a first interview was conducted by Kate Fisher and a subsequent one by Simon Szreter. In all other cases, a single interviewer was involved.

and practices to emerge as much as possible from its proper context as the respondents saw it, and not from the analytical context of the interviewers' agenda.[14] Many interviewees welcomed the chance to reminisce about their lives for as long as they wished and claimed to have enjoyed the experience. The use of unstructured interviews, which gave interviewees some control over the format of the discussion, allowed them to direct the conversation to a considerable extent. Many were surprised that they chose to talk openly about their sex lives but nevertheless did not regret having done so and indeed several, like June (1914), recommended the experience to her friends:

> JUNE You are crafty, aren't you, asking all these questions? ... when she [a friend] mentioned it on Monday ... I said ... 'Well, I've enjoyed it.' I says, 'It's been nice talking about.' I just put it like that; it's been nice going back and thinking about the old times. I said, 'You don't have to answer any questions you don't want to answer' (laughs) ... I said, 'Anything personal if you don't want to discuss', I said, 'you don't discuss.' I thought I'd better put her mind at rest. She sounded as though she was a bit – didn't know what you'd ask her. So I just sort of said, 'Well, I'm comfortable [with what] I said and I've enjoyed it.' I said, 'I've enjoyed her company and I've enjoyed going back in time', you see, which is nice.[15]

Long, unstructured interviews also minimised the possibility that respondents systematically concealed significant or important aspects of their lives. Although certain sexual experiences might easily be isolated and left unmentioned, many other events were difficult to conceal without creating inconsistencies or anomalies in testimony which could be sensitively probed. Rose (1928) explicitly acknowledged that she had been trying to hide the fact that she had had an affair with the man who was to become her second husband before she invited him to become her lodger, and before her husband asked for a divorce. It was the need to tell a consistent life story which made this concealment unsustainable. The story was revealed with humour and without intrusive questioning:

> ROSE And then I met (pause) round ... this pub just down there. This fellow kept sayin' ''Ello, sweet'art'; I mean, I didn't know he were married, so, we started goin' out even tho' I were married. Hmm. Anyway, me ex-husband (pause). Y'know, I'm, I'm scrappin' that part ...
> *So you left your first husband, because ... ?*

[14] See below, next section, for a discussion of the ways in which the agenda of interviewees was likely to have been shaped by contemporary sexual discourses and assumptions about changing sexual behaviour.

[15] June msf/kf/ht/#27. Born 1914, the daughter of a bank manager in Barnsley, in 1936 she married a Liptons-trained grocery manager and lived most of her married life in Brighouse, Yorkshire, where she had two children (and one miscarriage). She did some work for her husband who owned his own grocery business.

Well, I can't remember whether he left – he must, oh, I know, uh, it's the part I'm tryin' not to tell ya (laughs). He [first husband] were going back t-…his mother or somewhere, and I said, 'Oh, go on then'; so I got a lodger! But we had been a bit friends before that! So when he [first husband] come back, he couldn't move in 'cos there was a lodger in! Ha! So, like I said, 'e's dead now, 'e's the only one that's dead now.
So did, then, did he divorce you for that?
He did, love, yeah…
So, the second husband…
Yeah.
Where did you meet him?
I tell ya, that Turner's pub 'ere, down 'ere; it's all circled round 'ere.
Hmm mm.
'Cos me first husband lived near Montague Street.
And how soon after your first marriage had broken up was it that you met your second husband?
Well, I met 'im before it, actually…
(overlapping) Right, it was…
(overlapping) you know, outside the pub
it was, and he became the lodger.
Yeah.
(laughs)[16]

The recollection of sensitive, shameful or socially unacceptable experiences was often disclosed as a result of the confiding relationship of trust that was built up. This included, for instance, painful memories of child sex abuse from some interviewees, including Rose.[17] In other cases sexual indiscretions were revealed. Lucy (1907), a weaver and a grocer's wife from Blackburn, almost inadvertently let slip the fact that she had had a brief affair:

LUCY Frank, I mean, he was my first. I always loved Frank. I loved Frank from the very beginning. Sometimes we 'ad a quarrel; we 'ad a row now and then, but still 'e were Frank. I didn't, yeah, but, I'd bin with somebody else – I've not been, yeah – I did go with someone else, during a bit, but anyway, I didn't like him, no, but Frank, there was nobody like Frank, nobody like Frank, no, no.
So when did you go with somebody else?
Well, I did once, twice. I 'ave been, yes, I've bin with someone else, yeah.
Was that before you were married?
No, after I was married, no. Just an odd time; I don't know whether I'd 'ad too much to drink or what, I don't know, but I did go with somebody else, but only once, yes.
And that was after you were married?

[16] Rose msf/kf/bl/#21. One of the poorest interviewees, Rose had a very difficult life: abused as a child, married four times, she had six children and undertook a range of jobs including being a winder in a woollen mill and a dinner lady. See also below, 153–4.

[17] Others recounting first-hand incidents of sexual abuse by adults when they were children were: Reg (1919) msf/kf/ht/#36 and Hubert (1911) msf/kf/ht/#32.

(overlapping) … but I didn't want, no, no, but Frank, Frank was mine. Yes, 'e was mine. I'm not grumblin' – I'm not grumblin' about my life, love, no.
So tell me, tell me about this other one, when was that?
Oh, oh, sometime during – it's a long, long while ago, but it were just someone. I must 'ave 'ad a drink, I don't know how it, how it happened but I just went once, once with him and that was all. It was when I was getting older like – I weren't young, but after that I never spoke to him again, no … It was just one of them things, as I slipped up at.
Yes.
I wouldn't do it again.
No.
No. No. Frank were my partner, that were right, yeah.
And did you tell Frank?
Pardon?
Did you tell Frank about it?
No. Oh, no, no, no. 'E'd 'ave gone after him (laughing); 'e'd 'ave murdered him – no 'e'd 'ave murdered me 'n all – no, no, I mean to say, no, but 'e were alright, I, yeah, I miss him though.[18]

Dougie (1919), a gardener from Berkhamsted, showed no reluctance in recalling his wartime brothel experiences:

DOUGIE When we were stationed in Brussels I used to go down and see this woman who used to own this little pub, and she was a brothel-owner; she owned two. And while I was going with her, she offered [me] her half, her bankbook if I'd got a divorce and married her.
Really?
Yeah, she'd al-, she was already married. 'Cos the one night when I slept with her, her husband was in the next room and I didn't know that and he come in with a four-legged stool … then we went, had a week's leave in Brussels and me and me mate went down, round that one, for, see if we could see her and one of the brothel women. She said, 'Don't you come in here, Dougie', she said, 'For God's sake, go!'; she said, 'She's got a revolver round her', she says, 'She'll shoot you if she gets a bloody chance'. So we went out and went into another one (chuckle).
So why did she have it in for you?
Well, I, I'd been in her other brothel, and I'd been upstairs with one of the girls, and that was her sister-in-law kept that one and she had already told her that, what I'd done.
And what had you done?
I'd been upstairs with one of the women who worked there. I, and I didn't know she was her sister-in-law, otherwise I worn't have gone in the bloomin' pub (laugh). Aah.
Describe what it was like.
Aah, just like an ordinary little pub where you get your drink and then these women come out and sit with you, and buy them a drink; you were soon nearly

[18] Lucy msf/kf/bl/#10.

broke by the time you bought them drinks, and then paid for going upstairs with them (laugh).[19]

Interviews were conducted with both men and women and by male and female interviewers.[20] Despite the sociological assertion that men respond 'best' to male interviewers and women to female investigators we did not assign interviews according to gender.[21] This is not to argue that we saw gender as irrelevant to the interview process, but rather that gender differences as well as similarities could be productive.[22] Merlin (1908) joked about the difficulties in talking to a young female interviewer about sex and compared this with the respect he was used to showing women. In part, however, this was clearly also an element of the flirtatious rapport that had built up, which contributed to the construction of an extraordinarily detailed and rich life story, while at the same time providing important insights into the ways in which beliefs about gender structured sexual conversations between men and women, including husbands and wives:

MERLIN No, her favourite position – I, I shouldn't talk to you like this, you're only a girl!
(Laugh)
The, the best way was, was from the back …
So it seems that there are very different ways in which you would talk to girls and to women than if you were talking to men friends.
Of course, yeah. Who told you, Judy [an acquaintance of Merlin's]?
Yes.
I'll, I'll kill her!

19 Dougie msf/kf/ht/#5. In contrast it is sometimes assumed that male interviewees will not talk to women about sexual matters let alone 'risqué sex' (Yow, *Recording Oral History*, 129). Dougie was one of eight children – the son of a Watford-based bus conductor – and his mother took in washing for extra money. He married in 1941 and had a sequence of low-paid jobs after the war. His wife had two children and also one abortion, which he said he had insisted on, as she acknowledged it was not his child.

20 On questions of gender and the importance of interviewing both men and women see, Caroline Daley, '"He Would Know, but I Just Have a Feeling": Gender and Oral History', *Women's History Review* 7 (1998): 343–59, Caroline Gatrell, 'Interviewing Fathers: Feminist Dilemmas in Fieldwork', *Journal of Gender Studies* 15, no. 3 (2006): 237–51.

21 See, for example, Ann Cartwright and Joanna Moffett, 'A Comparison of Results Obtained by Men and Women Interviewers in a Fertility Survey', *Journal of Biosocial Science* 6, no. 3 (1974), Yow, *Recording Oral History*, Maureen Padfield and Ian Procter, 'The Effect of Interviewer's Gender on the Interviewing Process: A Comparative Enquiry', *Sociology* 30, no. 2 (1996): 355–66.

22 See also, Patrick Branigan, Kirsti Mitchell and Kaye Wellings, 'Discomfort, Discord and Discontinuity as Data: Using Focus Groups to Research Sensitive Topics', *Culture, Health & Sexuality* 2, no. 3 (2000): 255–67, on the productive use of mixed-gender focus groups in exploring sexual attitudes and practices. On the complexities of gender and interviewing and the need to look beyond a simplistic focus on the gender of the interviewer and interviewee, see Barbara Pini, 'Interviewing Men: Gender and the Collection and Interpretation of Qualitative Data', *Journal of Sociology* 41, no. 2 (2005): 201–16.

[...]
So is the language you use with girls and with men very different?
Of course, yeah.
So you would swear with men, would you?
Of course, yeah.
And would you ever swear in front of your wife?
No. It wasn't the done, the done thing. You wouldn't even say damn. Because, uh, in, in those days things were much different than they are now. You, you respected women more than they do now.[23]

Although some were not concerned, all interviewees were of course guaranteed anonymity.

SARAH I should hate – I should hate my daughter to, uh, know that I'd, uh, discussed my private life ... I wouldn't like my daughter – that's what I said, I, that's the main thing ... I've really had, had serious thought, and I thought, 'Oh have I done the right thing?' ... Oh yes, my daughter would hate it. (pause) But on the other hand, she doesn't live in Blackburn, she, she lives and, and they wouldn't be any connection because her name is quite, is different than mine.
Well, your name is not going to be there ...
I have had quite serious doubts about it and I thought 'Oh dear ...'
Oh, have you? Oh.
'Have I, have I done the right thing?' Uh, anyway, it's done now isn't it? I don't (chuckle) ...
Well, I mean if you're, you know, if you're seriously doubting then I won't use what you told me because it did – you know, it's got to be up to you.
(interrupting) Well, you can use excerpts out of it (giggle) but, but, which you probably will, you'll pick what you want out of it, won't you?
But I promise you, everything is completely private, everybody is completely anonymous, everybody has to be for this sort of research ...
Yes, as long as no names (chuckle).[24]

What's in it for them?

It was not only through skilled interviewing that informants agreed to reveal details of their private lives. Other factors influenced the decision to break with the convention of remaining silent about marriage and sexuality. In some cases it was the existence of alternative social conventions which prompted detailed and frank disclosure. For instance, many politely and generously simply wished to be helpful and accommodating. As a result it was generally only the bolder

[23] Merlin msf/kf/bl/#35. Married in 1940, he was a Corporation bus and tram driver in Blackburn; his wife died in 1977.

[24] Sarah msf/kf/bl/#30, born in 1906, married an upholsterer in 1928 and they lived in Bolton before moving to Blackburn in 1944. She had two live-births in the early 1930s but one child was born with spina bifida and died after ten days.

and more forthright interviewees who refused to answer certain questions or openly objected to some themes.

Respondents sought to be helpful, then, despite sometimes finding the subject matter difficult. Felicity (1919), the wife of a claims assessor for British Rail, who had lower-middle-class origins (her father had been a grocer who ran a shop and her mother a weaver), got dressed up for the occasion. She was sometimes uncomfortable discussing sex and surprised at the interviewer's interest in the subject. She endeavoured, however, to provide an honest response. When faced with a discussion she was not entirely easy with she did not close the conversation down but answered directly, albeit curtly:

FELICITY Well, I've a bit of make-up on today. Have you noticed? 'Cos you were coming – didn't know who was coming.
(laughs) You did that for me?
Yes, and me hair's going to get done this afternoon. I generally have it done Wednesday but I've done that for you, you see. Having me hair done this afternoon.
[...]
So how important was sex in your, in your marriage?
Well, they do say it's the most important and the least important thing. And I think that's pretty accurate.
Right. What do you mean by that?
Well, if you haven't got it I think you need it to keep your man together in some way. But it's not absolutely – shouldn't be the focus – it shouldn't be the whole being of your life.
Um-hmm. So you said you had – you talked to other women who said that they didn't enjoy sex as much as the men...
Very difficult to talk about. Is it going to – there's going to be a lot of sex in your book, isn't there? Well, that's all you've asked me today: sex, sex, sex.
[...]
And did you always do the same things or did you have an adventurous sex life?
Pass.
And how of-, how long did sex last?
I didn't have me watch on. (laughs) Well, I suppose it was average; don't know.
Did you ever feel dissatisfied with sex?
...I don't think so.
And did it change after you had children?
No.
Was it difficult to find time to have sex after the children?
Sometimes.
Did you wait until they were in bed?
Oh yes. What else can you do?
And did you ever talk about sex with your husband?
Not a lot.[25]

[25] Felicity msf/kf/bl/#37.

It also became clear that many interviewees had their own reasons for discussing sexual matters and that many were interested in the subject. Many felt strongly about the changes in sexual behaviour and attitudes in recent times and were keen to have the opportunity to discuss them. It is a common accusation that oral history provides one with modern attitudes rather than access to attitudes from the past. However, the dialogue with the present, which is inevitably part of an oral history interview, should be seen as productive rather than distorting. Admittedly the present had a strong impact on many individuals and indeed some respondents now hold different (usually more permissive) views on sex than they had in the past; many also revealed a strong desire to compare past and present attitudes, values, experience and mores. Yet such changes in perspective and their presence in interviews was not necessarily problematic, especially as many respondents were fully aware of the ways in which their own views have been challenged and have been transformed during their lifetime. They used the interview process to reflect constructively and informatively on such changes.

Roger (1910) was one of the most frank and forthright interviewees. The son of a naval commander, he had a very loving and sensual relationship with his wife – a hairdresser. Yet he acknowledged that early in his marriage and prior to his marriage he and his wife did not talk about sex. The fact that sexual discourses are now no longer private gave him both the freedom and the language to discuss his sex life in extraordinary detail and with astonishing vigour and enthusiasm:

ROGER when I look back, she's often told me… 'I'd have done it [had sex before marriage]', but she said, 'Quite frankly, I thought you didn't want it!' 'Yes', she said, 'and it was that damn silly time we were in'; she said, 'We should have talked it through more.'

[…]it's a different world and it, it takes, sometimes, a lot of thinking on our parts, of my age and that, to realise… – as we would say – where it all went wrong… Sometimes we old men get together and we say, 'Well, I don't know', say, 'Did you read' – as someone said to me some time ago – 'about that girl Pamela Anderson?' I said, 'No', he said, 'Oh!'. He said, 'I've got the paper; I'll let you read it'. So I read it and when I gave him it back he said, 'What did you think?' I said, 'Do you know?' I said, 'I've come to a conclusion.' He said, 'What's that?' I said 'You and I and the others of our age group were born far too early!' […]

I've often said, 'I wonder what my dear old Dad would say if he came back today', because I have two step-grandchildren, both of them have had babies on what I call the wrong side of the blanket. I've seen the babies, lovely babies and that, and I love my two step-grandchildren, but you see, it's a hell of a thing for one generation to accept, the same as we've had to accept so much. And I look out and I think, 'Well, it doesn't seem as if we're on the same planet!', you see? – on the same planet. […]

I think today women… turn round and say, 'Oh, yes, he's a gorgeous hunk! I'll have something with him. I'll take him home and give him a good time for the night and then forget him the next morning.' I think that women are coming round to that but when I was young it was not so. How could a man ever go with a prostitute? Biological. I never went with one. I'm saying that truthfully – believe it. I was tempted once but I didn't... I just thought I would and then I looked and I saw the horrible man that she'd just left so I said, 'No thank you!' I didn't say it to her – I just thought, 'No, I'm not interested in this', and I went off. I thought after all, uh, you've got to be careful where you're going (laugh).[26]

Roger's ambivalent attitude to changing public articulation of sexual matters was not unusual, though few interviewees were as frank and bold in their articulation of their memories. Alongside joking that he had been born too soon to enjoy it, Roger, like many interviewees, stressed a continued valuation of the privacy and discretion that surrounded the discussion of sex during the first half of their lives, despite the tensions and stresses that this caused, and some were dismayed by the public visibility of sexual matters in modern popular culture. Moreover, this was a crucial factor behind the willingness on the part of many respondents to talk to interviewers about their sexual experiences. For interviewees the very perception that sexual attitudes had been transformed during recent decades provided both a justification and an inspiration to talk. Many wished to discuss and debate such changes with interviewers, who were seen as representatives of a younger generation with different attitudes. Lyn (1907) was a thoughtful and politically informed respondent, whose parents had been active in the trade-union movement and the Independent Labour Party (her mother had also been a prominent suffragette in Blackburn).

LYN [W]hen I watch a wedding... I never think they're a virgin, no I don't. 'Cos I don't believe them as they are... I think about my granddaughter, 16 and... I bet she's more sexual experience now, although I don't know, than I ever had with the freedom that she's allowed, you know. And I don't, um, I don't say it's wrong; I don't say it's right, neither. I think they should be taught a bit more values than what they are, nowadays, and I think they should be taught a little more self con [*sic*]; it should not be the permissiveness there is. It's gone from one extreme to the other.[27]

Angela (1924), born in Preston, the daughter of an iron moulder, who, after an incapacitating industrial accident, could not afford to send her to grammar school after she passed the entrance exam, nonetheless became sufficiently educated to develop a career doing clerical office work and to enjoy a lower-middle-class lifestyle. She also acknowledged the benefits of some aspects of changing sexual cultures, identifying the availability of reliable contraception as a particular bonus, while nevertheless criticising other aspects of

[26] Roger msf/kf/ht/#10. [27] Lyn msf/kf/bl/#1.

sexual freedom she saw as increasingly acceptable, such as adultery and wife-swapping parties:

ANGELA The Pill was a blessing but in my opinion it's gone too much the other way ... someone was saying at one of our church meetings that adultery is accepted as commonplace nowadays ... I think that's [wife-swapping] distasteful. I do, there we go (pause).[28]

Indeed for some of those particularly concerned with privacy there was a moral imperative to inform a younger generation of some of the advantages of their different approach to sex and marriage. Middle-class Bernard (1907) became frustrated with the interviewer following a question asking him what he knew of abortion. He crossly reiterated that he had had no interest in other people's lives because sex was private, while his wife Diana (1910) added that sex was not central to their lives:

BERNARD It didn't come into your life like you're making it come into people's lives today. Didn't come into our lives at all. You didn't bother; you'd no interest in it. Let them live their own life ... all these sort of things you're putting to us now – no – didn't come into our lives.

DIANA There's so many other things that were of interest and enjoyment. But they didn't all revolve on sex. That's my attitude.[29]

Similarly, the motivation behind Daphne's (1912) testimony was to contrast the innocence of her youth and the shame of illegitimacy with the lack of morals in modern society:

DAPHNE There wasn't the sex in those days ... we were innocent, very innocent. I mean to me this, too – the morals have gone out of life nowadays ... they're living together before they're married; they're sleeping together; they're carrying on and I don't approve of it. Might be narrow-minded, I don't know, but, er ... if a girl got in trouble it was a disgrace. But now, I mean, they flaunt it and get mother's support and – No – if a girl got in trouble it was really a disgrace.[30]

In this sense the changes in public discourses around sex provided respondents with both a reason and an ability to talk about sex. We did not primarily find oral history interviewees willing to discuss their private lives because their own attitudes to sex had changed and become less private, but because strong feelings on the differences between contemporary society and the lives they had lived induced them to talk. In order to debate and consider the changes and

[28] Angela msf/kf/ht/#18.

[29] Bernard and Diana msf/jm/bl/#45. They were both born into middle-class families in Oldham and were married there in 1936, moving to Blackburn in 1937, where he took up a senior management post; Diana did not work and they had one child in 1939.

[30] Daphne msf/jm/bl/#38. Married in 1937 and had two children. Daphne's father (a foreman overlooker in the mills) bought a baker's and confectioner's shop for her in the 1930s, which she later ran with her husband, whose butcher's business had collapsed.

issues raised by modern sexual culture, they were required to articulate and describe the details of their own lives. What we discovered, then, was privacy but not taboo.

The finding of interviewees prepared to talk about sex and at the same time concluding that for this generation sex was intensely private and rarely discussed is not, therefore, a paradox. Nor is it a reflection of disingenuousness on the part of our informants. Respondents talked about the privacy of their own approach to sex in the context of comparing modern openness, and were prepared to participate in this openness during an interview in order that this comparison might be made and their response made clear. Sarah (1906) was one of the older interviewees, born in Blackburn and working-class:

SARAH You didn't want others knowing your private affairs. There – they – private things were private things in those days … we didn't discuss our bedroom life at all … 'Well, sex is the be-all and end-all of everything today!' (chuckle) It didn't used to be, did it? No! (laugh) (pause) No, it, it, it's just (chuckle) how it is, you see, it, it, it … and I, I, I don't think children should know about things, about a lot of things too early because, well, they're not little children these days – they're little old fellas and little old women aren't they? (chuckle) (pause) No, children are not as nice as they used to be, any longer, they're not … you didn't, you didn't, uh, hug and kiss in front of everybody else, you didn't … you were very private – it's a very … it was a private thing. It's, it's, it's made, it's made dirty today because they make silly jokes about it and they, they do; it's a private thing, and it's not a dirty thing like they make it out, it's not! … I think it's, uh, it's private and it should be kept private.[31]

Maureen (1920), also born in Blackburn, was fourteen years younger and (lower-) middle-class:

MAUREEN I mean it's overdone now. I mean, everything … television, it stinks of sex; it stinks. It's horrible, it's vulgar, you know, and really it's ruined, it's ruined everything; it's ruined people's lives … I mean you can see too much. It's just – well, it's just unnecessary, you know, this – you need some … everybody needs some privacy, you know, don't they? I think so. And it's something that's private between you and your husband.[32]

The interviews which form the basis of this book, therefore, represent an extraordinary moment; respondents were prepared to talk openly about sex, sometimes (they claimed) for the first time. Despite the silence that surrounded sex earlier in their lives, despite retaining the belief that sex ought to be a private matter, concern about and interest in contemporary society's values motivated many to engage fully and frankly with the interviews. The ways in which these testimonies reflected the honest and frank discussion of sexual matters that had, until the interview, been rarely discussed or debated, even in private,

[31] Sarah msf/kf/bl/#30. [32] Maureen msf/kf/bl/#46.

and even between husband and wife, were particularly apparent in interviews with couples.

Here we found remarkable exchanges between married partners discussing how they had not talked to each other in their marriage. The genuineness of what they were saying about the private nature of sex between them was itself borne out during the interviews.[33] Yet in some cases the frankness and openness apparent in interviews with people on their own was unsustainable when in the presence of a spouse, in front of whom the need to maintain the privacy of the relationship was overriding.[34] The interview with Betty (1922) and Horace (1915), who had both been teachers, was extremely good humoured, jolly and relaxed. Horace used a few jokes to hide behind during some of the discussions of sex and maintained that he and his wife did not need or want to discuss sexual matters. Betty was more straightforward in her answers but asked for the interview to change direction when she felt Horace was upset by the detail of some of the questions:

HORACE Enjoy sex? Oh, we don't talk about that sort of thing. There's no need for it.
Did you enjoy sex?
BETTY Usually.
Usually, yeah.
HORACE You speak for yourself my girl.
Is this – is this his banter?
BETTY Um.
And what did you, um, did Horace – were, were you happy for Horace to touch all parts of your body or was, was it better that he didn't?
BETTY I didn't mind where he touched me.
Did you feel able to touch his body?
BETTY Um.
And did you enjoy doing that?
BETTY Yes.
All over?
HORACE (sighs)
BETTY I think this is upsetting Horace.
Okay.[35]

[33] While most interviews were conducted with single widows and widowers, ten pairs of married partners were interviewed together. In one case, Peter (1921) and Elizabeth (1923) msf/kf/bl/#26, this was a remarriage later in life (in 1998) and so much of the interview material taken from each of the partners in fact related to separate marriages they had had with somebody else (in fact Peter had been married twice previously in 1940 and 1948). In one case, two close neighbours in Harpenden, Grace (1922) and Dora (1923), msf/srss/ht/#38, both widows, were interviewed together initially (and then also separately), about their respective marriages.

[34] Many sociologists argue that couples should not be interviewed together for this reason: Julia Brannen, 'The Study of Sensitive Subjects', *Sociological Review* 36, no. 3 (1988): 557–8.

[35] Betty and Horace msf/kf/ht/#31.

In some instances, interviewees engineered single interviews arranged at later dates. Doreen (1922) asked to be interviewed alone on a day when her husband was out of the house (though this was primarily because she wanted the opportunity to complain about his negative attitude towards her working). She also sensitively decided to leave the room when Larry (1917) was discussing his early sexual experiences:

When did you first find out about sex?
LARRY It'd be 14 or 15 when you first started fiddling (laughs)…
DOREEN Do you want me to go out of your way while you tell tales? (laughs)
LARRY No.
DOREEN No?
LARRY I don't think that'll make any difference.
DOREEN Speak now or forever hold your peace.
I'd better go away…You've gone quiet, ha'n't he?
LARRY No.
DOREEN I'll not stop you talking.[36]

In other instances, far from impeding open revelation as some other researchers have claimed, interviewing couples together provided an opportunity for a pair to reconsider together their past privacy.[37] The idea that Angela (1924), a typist originally from Preston, was innocent and Hugh (1926), a chartered electrical engineer born in Trowbridge, more worldly and sexually informed was a recurrent dynamic in their interview; Hugh would contrast his knowledge with her ignorance and illustrate the ways in which he had preserved her naïvety and protected her from sordid sexual details. Their discussion of homosexuality provided a good illustration of this:

HUGH She's that innocent. Makes no difference but that's what makes her so special… she's so innocent and naïve with regarding sex. I accept, I pull her leg about it but that's it. We don't discuss our sexual relations just like we're discussing now; [it's] something we don't normally do with anybody else, alright. Um, I don't discuss any sexual things with my friends I go out – that goes on between me and her…
Mmm. So what did you feel about homosexuality? What was your attitude?
HUGH Well I think there's one along the road actually. And I mean Angela waves to him – Mr Tootucks, she says and I says.
ANGELA He waves to me.
HUGH You don't realise. 'He's a homo' … 'He's not' … 'Jolly well is; must be' (laughs). No, it's not somebody I would crave their, um, relationship really, but, um, whether that's right or wrong I don't know. It's a prejudice I suppose…
ANGELA Mmm, and I, I think that, um, I've heard, er, there's a doctor in our house group and he once said, 'If you had seen the physical damage that's done to the

[36] Doreen and Larry msf/kf/bl/#20. They married in 1946, had two children (and had one miscarriage) and lived in Blackburn.
[37] Branigan, Mitchell and Wellings, 'Discomfort, Discord and Discontinuity', esp. 259–60.

male, well, some of the male parts', he said, 'it would make you cry'. You would not go along with it and so, um, I don't – to me, I think it's distasteful, I do. (pause) And I think it's a great pity because I think that ordinary relationships between boy and girl are suffering. There's lots of girls who don't marry and lots of boys and I think, I think society in general is losing out, I do.

HUGH I'm against it in general but when you say about the law ... I think people need protecting and you can only protect them up to they're an adult, really. To criminalise it above 18 when it's not done in public; but when it's done in public I would criminalise it still now – probably is, I can't remember. But, er, done in private, consenting adults, I don't think you can do anything about it ...

ANGELA And, er, we, we haven't been in company where that, that had been talked about or practised, have we dear? I don't know anyone.

HUGH Well not – nobody would talk about sex of any sort in your presence dear – they, they know you, not as well as I do, but they know you and they respect you for it so they wouldn't talk about it.

ANGELA But to the best of my knowledge there's no strange relationships amongst any of our friends.

HUGH Oh no, oh no.[38]

Some respondents directly commented that the way in which they found themselves talking about sex during the interview was unfamiliar to them and not how they were used to seeing themselves, such as Dora (1923), one of the younger interviewees, who had been born in working-class Bethnal Green, happily married in Radlett since 1945 and was bereaved in 1998, two years before the interview:

DORA I've heard girls talk but I never spoke like how they used to speak. I'm rather surprised I'm talking to you like it really.[39]

Many found it difficult to discuss sexual matters, having been unaccustomed to doing so in the past. It initially appeared that Emma (1906), married in 1936 to a research scientist with whom she had three children and who had died in 1988, was avoiding addressing questions about sex, deflecting them with comments about her teacup, but she herself chose to come back to the issue. However, she struggled to express her views, despite being highly articulate, intellectual and intelligent – one of the very few university-educated informants. The struggle was clearly linked to the modest approach to sexual matters that characterised her relationship with her husband:

EMMA He wasn't a man who really discussed very personal things very much ... I think we were both a bit modest about things. I don't think we wanted to talk about it. We'd plenty of other things to talk about, you know.
And what was good about your sex life?

[38] Hugh and Angela msf/kf/ht/#18. [39] Dora msf/srss/ht/#38.

(pause) I don't know. I don't know.
Was anything bad about it?
No. No, I've got coffee – tea in my – it's alright; it's always underneath you see. They nearly always do that: they spill it into the saucer. Spill it in the saucer and then you always have drips down your clothes. That's why I put it on the paper because the paper absorbs the wet and I can safely put it back in there. Erm, now what did you say? What was good about our sex life? (laughs) I don't know how to tell you. I've no idea. It was just – um, we were in love you know; so I mean it, um – we were, I think we were, I think we were very pleased when we finally were married and living together – we'd been dodging about [with] no place to be together and at last we were living together.[40]

Although some were embarrassed and some were reticent, the frankness and determination to provide honest, clear and detailed accounts was in most cases astonishing. Far more than embarrassment we found an inability to find the words to express their views. Indeed, as many, such as Lucy (1907), married with one child from 1931 until her husband died in 1980, or Dora (1923), acknowledged, this was the first time they had ever discussed these matters.

LUCY Yes, and I'll bet you 'aven't been, been with anybody like me talking like me!
Oh, I have, yes!
(Laughs) I've spoken more to you than really I would 'ave done ordinary, no![41]

DORA It [sex] was never mentioned. I never heard my mum and dad mention anything. Nothing you know.
Right.
No. I don't think they did in them days, did they? I mean to tell the truth, to be honest, I never thought I could talk to somebody like you, Simon. You're the first person I've ever talked to like this in fact.[42]

The unfamiliarity with this kind of discussion and the absence of a clearly developed vocabulary all underscored the central finding of the privacy of sex. The attitudes expressed in this set of oral history interviews are perhaps uniquely tied to the beliefs and ideas developed early on in the respondents' lives. Rather than obtaining narratives and stories developed, honed and constructed over a long period,[43] we obtained sometimes fumbling and unrehearsed accounts of sexual experiences previously unarticulated and perhaps even relatively unformulated psychologically. Without a public language to discuss sexual matters, without even having discussed sex in private with a spouse or other intimate, the silent history here uncovered is, for many, that of a private and personal interior world.

[40] Emma msf/kf/ht/#37. [41] Lucy msf/kf/bl/#10. [42] Dora msf/srss/ht/#38.
[43] See also, Branigan, Mitchell and Wellings, 'Discomfort, Discord and Discontinuity'.

The interviewees and their historical contexts

The oral history testimony at the heart of this book reflects the recollections of a group of individuals predominantly born in the twenty-year period 1905–24, with thirty-eight born 1905–14 and forty-three born 1915–24.[44] Thus, for most of the informants their testimony relates to their lives and their marriages in the era after the Great War but before the cultural impact of 'the sixties', hence the indicative dates of the book's title, spanning these interwar and immediately post-war decades. Of course, this half-century was one of significant change for all the individuals involved and their testimony often reflects their different experiences of the consequences for their family life as children and adults of the Great War, the Great Depression, the Second World War and the coming of the welfare state, for instance.

Most of the interviewees for this study married in either the 1930s or 1940s (thirty-four first marriages were contracted in the 1930s and forty-five in the 1940s).[45] They experienced the Second World War as late teenagers or adults in their twenties or thirties, many of the men serving in the armed forces and many women employed in war work of various kinds. Although their lives were lived through much of the twentieth century, they represent a group who grew up in specific and formative historical circumstances, born too early for their values to have been formed by the cultural changes of the 1960s (or even by those of the 1950s),[46] but too late to be Victorians, or even Edwardians. They were socially and culturally formed as children and adolescents in the interwar years in a country much less sure of its imperial destiny and of moral and religious certainties than their parents' generation had been. It was more fearful for its prosperity and security than either the preceding or succeeding generations. However, these interviewees also approached and commenced

[44] Thus, just over 90 per cent (eighty-one) of the eighty-nine interviewees were born between 1905 and 1924. Four were born between 1901 and 1904; six between 1925 and 1928; and one, Judith msf/kf/ht/#33, in 1931. See Appendix C.

[45] Thus, of the eighty-eight interviewees who had ever been married, 90 per cent (seventy-nine) had first married between 1930 and 1949, with three doing so in the 1920s and six in the 1950s (all in the early 1950s except Judith msf/kf/ht/#33, who married in 1958, aged 27). See Appendix C.

[46] While there has been a general tendency in the historiography to confirm that an important cultural revolution in popular norms relating to love, sex and marriage swept through British society during 'the sixties' – meaning the years 1963–9 – research has also shown that there was a 'long 1960s' of associated significant cultural and legal change encompassing half a decade either side of this, 1958–74: Martin P. M. Richards and B. Jane Elliott, 'Sex and Marriage in the 1960s and 1970s', in *Marriage, Domestic Life and Social Change: Writings for Jacqueline Burgoyne (1944–88)*, ed. David Clark (London: Routledge, 1991), 47; Arthur Marwick, *The Sixties: Cultural Revolution in Britain, France, Italy, and the United States, c.1958–c.1974* (Oxford: Oxford University Press, 1998); Hugh McLeod, *Religious Crisis of the 1960s* (New York: Oxford University Press, 2007); Frank Mort, *Capital Affairs: The Making of the Permissive Society* (London: Yale University Press, 2010).

adulthood as members of the first democratic generation as of right, with full and equal voting rights for all, regardless of property, income or sex, granted by the 1918 and 1928 Representation of the People Acts.

It was a deliberate feature of the research for this book that interviewees were drawn from two economically contrasting regions of the country. One set had lived throughout their lives in or near Blackburn in the heartlands of the industrial north of Lancashire. The other 'Hertfordshire' group were interviewed primarily in affluent Home Counties Harpenden in north-west Hertfordshire and some in the neighbouring town of Berkhamsted. These two regions experienced particularly divergent economic fortunes during the first half of the respondents' lives.[47] In 1921, as soon as the short, post-war boom was spent, the over-capitalised Lancashire textiles industry was hit by the first of a series of severe economic dislocations, with world trade faltering and then imploding in the 1930s. In common with Britain's other long-established, export-oriented staple industries, notably ship-building and engineering, coal-mining and the other branches of the mechanised textiles industry, Lancashire's cotton mills and its proletarian workforce, including several of those interviewed here, suffered short-time working, unemployment and reduced earnings during both the 1920s and 1930s.[48] Subsequently rearmament, wartime orders and the post-war government's historic commitment to full employment brought back relative prosperity to the region from the late 1930s through to the 1960s.

The whole London region encompassing the Home Counties, by contrast, became the primary growth pole of employment in the economy after the Great War and was able to sustain this position through the 1930s and on into the post-war decades. Its unique concentration of upper-income, middle-class households provided the major source of mass demand in the interwar economy for a widening range of new consumer products. New companies like Hoover, Gillette, Aspro, Mars, Black and Decker, producing these electrical appliances, white goods, confectionery, cosmetic and pharmaceutical products, often preferred to locate their new production plants in the Home Counties,

[47] On the economic history of this period and the different regional experiences of the economy, see C. H. Lee, 'Regions and Industries in Britain', ch. 3 in *Twentieth-Century Britain: Economic, Social, and Cultural Change*, ed. Paul Johnson (London and New York: Longman, 1994), 38–56, Alan Booth and Sean Glynn, *Modern Britain: An Economic and Social History* (London and New York: Routledge, 1996), Martin Daunton, *Wealth and Welfare: An Economic and Social History of Britain, 1851–1951* (Oxford and New York: Oxford University Press, 2007), chs. 3–4, Francesca Carnevali, Paul Johnson and Julie Marie Strange, eds. *Twentieth-Century Britain: Economic, Cultural and Social Change* (London: Longman, 2007), chs. 9–10.

[48] There is of course a contemporary literature documenting and reflecting this experience. The two most celebrated examples are Walter Greenwood's *Love on the Dole* and George Orwell's *Road to Wigan Pier*, published in 1933 and 1937 respectively. The experience in Blackburn itself, from the perspective of a very poor working-class family, has also been the subject of a classic of the genre of personal memoir: William Woodruff, *The Road to Nab End: A Lancashire Childhood* (London: Abacus, 2002).

where unskilled and semi-skilled labour was non-unionised and where they could stay in close touch with the metropolitan advertising industry and the national and magazine press, which drove forward the marketing and fashions for these new products.[49] Some of our Hertfordshire interviewees were managers of these companies, others among the employees.

During this period, in addition to region, the social distinctions referred to by contemporaries through the language of 'class' were also highly significant in interviewees' lives.[50] Numerically the middle classes throughout this period 1918–63 never amounted to much more than 20 per cent of the population nationally and, because of their heavy preponderance in the metropolitan south-east, their proportionate presence everywhere else, including the industrial north, was rather less than this.[51] Nevertheless, class relations, though varying in their precise form in every community, were of ubiquitous importance. This oral history study was designed to engage directly with issues related to social class, while also taking into account what has been learned from recent studies of changing fertility in British society which have found that both place and communication communities influenced relationships of class and gender.[52]

[49] Mike Savage, 'Trade Unionism, Sex Segregation, and the State: Women's Employment in "New Industries" in Inter-War Britain', *Social History* 13, no. 2 (1988): 209–30. On the press and consumerism, see Adrian Bingham, *Gender, Modernity, and the Popular Press in Inter-War Britain* (Oxford and New York: Clarendon; Oxford University Press, 2004).

[50] The word 'class' was used by contemporaries in all sections of society and by journalists and other commentators throughout this period to denote both social status distinctions among individuals and affiliations of social identity. From the 1940s it was also increasingly deployed by social scientists and by historians, influenced by the writings of Marx and Weber, as both an analytical and a descriptive term for studying the politics and economics of inequality in British history from the era of industrialisation to the present time. See Dennis Dworkin's excellent recent guide to the main outlines of the subsequent historiographic inheritance: Dennis L. Dworkin, *Class Struggles* (Harlow and New York: Pearson Longman, 2007). Also see, Jon Lawrence, 'The British Sense of Class', *Journal of Contemporary History* 35, no. 2 (2000): 307–18. For the best recent general study of class during the period addressed here, see Ross McKibbin, *Classes and Cultures: England, 1918–1951* (Oxford: Oxford University Press, 1998). For the working classes, see Stephen Brooke, 'Gender and Working Class Identity in Britain During the 1950s', *Journal of Social History* 34, no. 4 (2001): 773–95, Andrew August, *The British Working Class, 1832–1940* (Harlow and New York: Pearson Longman, 2007), Part III.

[51] Taking a wide definition of the middle classes as all higher- and lower-grade professionals, all employers and proprietors, and all administrators and managers, this amounted to 14 per cent of the economically active male workforce in 1921 and 20.8 per cent by 1961 (A. H. Halsey, *Change in British Society*, 4th edn (Oxford and New York: Oxford University Press, 1995), Table 2.1).

[52] Communication communities comprise the social networks through which persons acquire, reproduce and negotiate their social and gender identities. An individual may identify with multiple communication communities with varying influences during their lifetimes in addition to those into which they are socialised. During the period of modern British history encompassing the fertility decline, c.1870–1950, the most powerful of such communication communities were often strongly related to the unique characteristics of specific towns and other geographical localities, lodged in distinctive industrial regions with their diverse histories of gendered labour relations, resulting in distinctive sets of family and work roles for those living there. On communication communities and fertility behaviour see Simon Szreter, *Fertility, Class, and*

Consequently both middle-class and working-class respondents of both sexes were interviewed in each of the contrasting locations. In Blackburn a total of fifty persons were interviewed (thirty-eight working-class and twelve middle-class), while in Hertfordshire twenty-two of the thirty-eight interviewees were classified as middle-class and sixteen as working-class.[53]

The influence of social class on individuals' perceptions was significantly mediated through their varying experiences of education. All the interviewees passed through the nation's education system during the period between the Balfour Act of 1902 and the Butler Act of 1944. Before the universal, free, secondary education provided by the 1944 Act, most children of working-class parents acquired only an elementary education, leaving school at age 14 (the minimum school-leaving age mandated by the 1918 Fisher Act). To attend secondary education was the highly socially selective marker of middle-class status.[54] Hence this was a national education system that has been described as recently as 1997 as one of 'educational apartheid'.[55] Although there were a small number of 'free place' scholarships to be won at secondary schools, only a small proportion of working-class children went to such schools even if they passed the 'Eleven Plus' entrance exam.[56] Otherwise they stayed in the 'senior' section of the elementary schools until leaving on their fourteenth birthday. Laura (1923), one of the Blackburn working-class informants in this study, confessed she was still 'mad I didn't pass me exams'.[57] Angela (1924), a working-class informant interviewed in Hertfordshire, passed the Eleven Plus but did not go to grammar school because her parents could not afford the incidental costs of books and uniform.[58] Eva (1911) was an excellent pupil but had to go to the mill in Blackburn at 14 because her mother was a war widow.[59] Maud (1912), the only child of a steel worker and a weaver, said that she refused to go to Blackburn High School because she saw this as a bid to

Gender in Britain, 1860–1940 (Cambridge and New York: Cambridge University Press, 1996), esp. 546–58. On place, locality and fertility behaviour, Eilidh Garrett et al., *Changing Family Size in England and Wales: Place, Class, and Demography, 1891–1911* (Cambridge and New York: Cambridge University Press, 2001), chs. 5–7.

[53] For further details on the social classification methods used, see Appendix B; and for individuals' designated social class attributions see Appendix C.

[54] On the history of the educational system during this period, see Gillian Sutherland and Stephen Sharp, *Ability, Merit, and Measurement: Mental Testing and English Education, 1880–1940* (Oxford and New York: Clarendon Press; Oxford University Press, 1984), Gillian Sutherland, 'Education', in *The Cambridge Social History of Britain, 1750–1950*, ed. F. M. L. Thompson (Cambridge and New York: Cambridge University Press, 1990), Brian Simon, *Education and the Social Order, 1940–1990* (London: Lawrence & Wishart, 1991).

[55] Andrew Adonis and Stephen Pollard, *A Class Act: The Myth of Britain's Classless Society* (London and New York: Hamish Hamilton; Penguin Books, 1997), xv.

[56] A very similar pattern emerged from Slater and Woodside's working-class interviews (Slater and Woodside, *Patterns of Marriage*, 35, 65, 269).

[57] Laura msf/kf/bl/#6. [58] Angela msf/kf/ht/#18. [59] Eva msf/kf/bl/#9.

leave the working class and she wanted to remain within her own social class.[60] In 1938 less than 7 per cent of the whole population aged 15–18 attended secondary schools – these were in the main children of the middle and upper classes; and even by 1951, by which time the youngest interviewee had long passed the age of 18, the proportion was still only 13 per cent.[61]

It had long been recognised by the middle classes that superior educational credentials were necessary for access to the most secure sources of prestigious and salaried employment in government and the professions. Nevertheless, in the social competition for access to such desirable forms of employment, even they found the costs of such education straightening. More was spent on sons' educations than daughters' and over the half-century before 1918 the middle classes had dramatically reduced their family size as a necessary adjustment to cope with the steeply rising educational outlays required.[62] Higher education was an even greater rarity at this time. During the interwar years only 1.6 per cent of the age group progressed to university and fewer than 3 per cent in total attended any form of further or higher education, including the 1 per cent or so who went to teacher training colleges.[63] These national class patterns in higher educational participation are almost exactly mirrored in the range of personal experiences found among the group of interviewees drawn from these two contrasting communities of Blackburn and Hertfordshire.[64]

The regional economic disparity which opened up after the Great War is reflected in the life-course patterns of many of the interviewees. Those interviewed in the north had been much less geographically mobile during their lifetimes, whether working-class or middle-class. With the disproportionate growth of the service sector in the south, there was a tendency for those

[60] Maud msf/kf/bl/#18.

[61] This was due to the fact that although from 1944 working-class children at age 11 could enter free secondary schools, most left to get jobs at the national minimum leaving age of 15 (A. H. Halsey, *Trends in British Society since 1900: A Guide to the Changing Social Structure of Britain* (London and New York: Macmillan; St. Martin's Press, 1972), Table 6.1, 163).

[62] The classic study of this is J. A. Banks, *Prosperity and Parenthood: A Study of Family Planning among the Victorian Middle Classes* (London: Routledge & Kegan Paul, 1954).

[63] Halsey, *Trends in British Society*, Table 7.2, 206.

[64] Thus, among the respondents only one (Emma) went to university when young – a northern redbrick where she had met her husband; while another's (Judith's) deceased husband had also been university educated; also Hugh had subsequently completed an Open University degree in the 1970s and Antonia took a BA in English in 1983; two others had attended further education courses when younger (Hilda at Victoria College, Manchester; and Gill took a non-degree Certificate in Social Administration at Manchester University); and three had attended teacher training college (Pearl and both Betty and Horace), while Norman had completed the Emergency Training Programme for teachers after the Second World War; and Judith had completed nursing training at St Bartholomew's in London. Emma msf/kf/ht/#37; Judith msf/kf/ht/#33; Hugh msf/kf/ht/#18; Antonia msf/kf/ht/#35; Hilda msf/kf/bl/#50; Gill msf/kf/bl/#48; Pearl msf/kf/bl/#40; Betty and Horace msf/kf/ht/#31; Norman msf/kf/ht/#17.

qualified for middle-class jobs to migrate from north to south during the twentieth century, rather than vice versa. While there are four examples of this north-to-south movement found among the twenty-two Hertfordshire interviewees classified as 'middle-class', there were no genuine examples of reverse south-to-north lifetime mobility found among the Blackburn middle-class interviewees, who had been much less geographically mobile during their lives than the Hertfordshire sub-group.[65] Nearly half (five) of the northern middle-class respondents were born and bred in Blackburn and had lived in the area all their lives, and most others, though not born in Blackburn, had spent all their marriages in the region – mostly in Lancashire itself.

By contrast, although Harpenden was certainly not a new town, all the middle-class individuals interviewed there had moved into it. Indeed, they had all moved place of residence not just once but at least twice in their lives and most of them had moved several times.[66] Their places of birth were very varied. While eight of the twenty-two were born in London, the birthplaces of the rest are almost randomly scattered across the map of Britain from Plymouth to Edinburgh, from Tenby in South Wales to Rothbury in Northumberland. Despite these diverse origins, over three-quarters (seventeen out of twenty-two middle-class interviewees) lived either in Hertfordshire or in the extra-metropolitan Home Counties throughout all or virtually all their married lives. They therefore constitute a group, not so much of Hertfordshire middle-class residents, but of those of the middle classes who, while originating in various parts of Britain, had chosen from early adulthood to make their living in and around the dynamic metropolitan economy and to bring up their families in the affluent commuter dormitory towns of the Home Counties: a communication community.

The divergence in the economic history of the two regions had significant class-related implications for gendered opportunities for employment, which were also reflected in interviewees' life stories. One of the distinctive features of all the various branches of the textiles industry in Britain, since

[65] The only ostensible exception was Gill msf/kf/bl/#48. She was born in Shropshire but her parents, who were both Blackburnites, had had to move to rural Shropshire for her father's health (he was gassed in the First World War). Gill in fact spent all her teenage and early adulthood in educational institutions in Lancashire (boarding school and college) and also maintained continuous contact with Blackburn throughout this period through her relatives living there, who also provided her with the introduction to the man she married – a Blackburn mill owner.

[66] These regionally distinct patterns of geographical mobility among the middle-class interviewees bear out the validity of McKibbin's thesis of the geographical bifurcation of the middle classes during this period, from 1918 through to the 1950s. He has argued that the expansion of new executive and service sector jobs, providing for a more career-mobile and geographically mobile 'new' middle class in the south, increasingly contrasted with the more 'traditional' and stable middle class of the northern industrial cities and towns, occupying a relatively unchanging and limited number of either industrial managerial or community professional roles, such as solicitors and surveyors, pharmacists and doctors (McKibbin, *Classes and Cultures: England 1918–1951*, 90–105).

initial mechanisation in the early nineteenth century, was the long-established place of female factory work at wage levels comparable with male rates.[67] Blackburn respondents therefore came from a community in which waged work for working-class women outside the home, including after marriage, was considered normal – something which was not true of most other working-class communities outside textiles regions.[68] With married female employment established as a community norm, married women also worked in other industries in Blackburn, such as at the new Mullards valve factory that opened in the late 1930s.

In the southern, metropolitan regional economy, by contrast, domestic service, shop work and dress-making were the three long-standing main possibilities providing mass female employment still in the 1920s, all mostly performed by young, unmarried women or domestically in the home.[69] There was a general increase in female work opportunities, especially during the 1950s and 1960s, including in manufacturing. The proportion of economically active women aged 20–64 rose throughout the economy from just over one-third in 1951 to just over one-half by 1971.[70] However, this trend was, of course, also in the context of a return to full employment for their husbands in these decades, perhaps therefore resulting in less impact on the overall pattern of gender relations in marriage, with women still preferring part-time work to complement

[67] On this feature of the Lancashire cotton textiles industry, see Patrick Joyce, *Work, Society and Politics: The Culture of the Factory in Later Victorian England* (Brighton: Harvester Press, 1980), Mike Savage, 'Women and Work in the Lancashire Cotton Industry, 1890–1939', in *Employers and Labour in the English Textile Industries*, eds. Tony Jowitt and Arthur McVicor (London: Routledge, 1988), 203–23, Jutta Schwarzkopf, *Unpicking Gender: The Social Construction of Gender in the Lancashire Cotton Weaving Industry, 1880–1914* (Aldershot and Burlington, VT: Ashgate, 2004).

[68] The potteries in the six towns of the Stoke-on-Trent conurbation being the principal other English exception to this generalisation (Richard Whipp, *Patterns of Labour: Work and Social Change in the Pottery Industry* (London and New York: Routledge, 1990)).

[69] On the notorious dress and clothing trade, the classic sweated work, see J. A. Schmeichen, *Sweated Industries and Sweated Labour: The London Clothing Trades, 1860–1914* (Urbana, IL: University of Illinois Press, 1984) and Sonya O. Rose, *Limited Livelihoods. Gender and Class in Nineteenth-Century Britain* (London: Routledge, 1992); on domestic service, see P. Horn, *The Rise and Fall of the Victorian Servant* (Dublin: Gill and Macmillan, 1975) and E. Higgs, 'Domestic Service and Household Production', in *Unequal Opportunities: Women's Employment in England 1800–1918*, ed. A. V. John (Oxford: Basil Blackwell, 1986), 125–50. As Angela John noted, by 1914 there were close to half a million shop assistants in England and Wales, many of them daughters of the middle classes working in the big London stores, but there seems to have been no dedicated study of this group of female workers (A. V. John, 'Introduction', in *Unequal Opportunities: Women's Employment in England 1800–1918*, ed. A. V. John (Oxford: Basil Blackwell, 1986), 17–18.

[70] B. Jane Elliott, 'Demographic Trends in Domestic Life, 1945–87', in *Marriage, Domestic Life and Social Change: Writings for Jacqueline Burgoyne (1944–88)*, ed. David Clark (London: Routledge, 1991), 102. Facilitated by the abandonment in 1946 of the marriage bar by the civil service and other employers, the balance also shifted strongly towards the majority of working women now being married, a group who increasingly occupied part-time jobs

their home-making duties if possible.[71] There was also a growing number of respectable, relatively well-paid 'white blouse' job opportunities for women in the metropolitan service sector: as clerks, receptionists and other office workers in commerce, business and government – a trend that had begun in the late nineteenth century.[72] Indeed, rising female competition for clerical work in the south was so strong in the interwar decades that a number of contemporary studies identified male 'white collar' work as a particular sector of the workforce that was witnessing 'status-decline' because of the 'feminisation' of the occupation.[73]

These regional differences in forms of available employment for women meant that while most working-class people in Blackburn viewed the possibility of a wage-earning wife as a realistic option, which was quite often taken up, most middle-class interviewees from Blackburn assumed that only husbands, not wives, would have respectable income-earning opportunities. By contrast among those interviewed in the south, many female middle-class interviewees in Hertfordshire reported having taken office-based jobs after marriage and were more likely to view this as a feasible option, whereas the working-class interviewees were a little less likely than those in Blackburn to view female work after marriage as a practical or worthwhile possibility.

as reflected in Appendix C (Jane Lewis, *Women in England 1870–1950* (Brighton: Harvester, 1984), 197).

71 Penny Summerfield, 'Women in Britain since 1945: Companionate Marriage and the Double Burden', in *Understanding Post-war British Society*, eds. James Obelkevich and Peter Catterall (London and New York: Routledge, 1994), 58–72; Dolly Smith Wilson, 'A New Look at the Affluent Worker: The Good Working Mother in Post-War Britain', *Twentieth Century British History* 17, no. 2 (2006): 206–29; Selina Todd, 'Affluence, Class and Crown Street: Reinvestigating the Post-War Working Class', *Contemporary British History* 22, no. 4 (2008): 501–18.

72 Meta Zimmeck, 'Jobs for the Girls: The Expansion of Clerical Work for Women, 1850–1914', in John, ed. *Unequal Opportunities*, 153–77, Gregory Anderson, ed. *The White-Blouse Revolution: Female Office Workers since 1870* (Manchester and New York: Manchester University Press; St. Martin's Press, 1988).

73 On interwar trends see F. D. Klingender, *The Condition of Clerical Labour in Britain* (London: M. Lawrence Ltd, 1935). Also see, David Lockwood, *The Blackcoated Worker: A Study in Class Consciousness* (London: Allen & Unwin, 1958), Bernard Waites, *A Class Society at War, England, 1914–1918* (Leamington Spa and New York: Berg; St. Martin's Press, 1987), chs. 1, 7. The rising entry of women into this form of employment was something that had undoubtedly begun some time before the First World War, especially with the rise of typing over copperplate handwriting skills as the defining manual skill. However, in 1911 there were still over three times as many male as female clerical workers in the economy. By 1921 there were only about 20 per cent more male than female clerks. In 1931 there were still slightly more male clerks but by 1951 there were 50 per cent more female workers than males in the sector. At this point one in five employed women was a clerical worker (compared to one in seventeen employed men), rising to one in four by 1961. Meanwhile, this quintessentially lower-middle-class category of employment had more than doubled in relative importance, accounting for about 4.5 per cent of all economically active men and women in 1911, rising to 10.4 per cent by 1951, reaching 12.6 per cent in 1961 (calculations from Halsey, *Change in British Society*, Table 2.1).

When looking at national marriage and fertility trends during this period, it is clear that these middle decades of the twentieth century witnessed two distinct phases. During the first part of this era both the nation's marriage rates and its fertility rates reached a secular low in the 1930s, following half a century's decline in both measures. From 1945 until the 1960s this was reversed as marriage rates increased and fertility rose back above replacement levels.[74] The post-war period has been referred to as a brief era of 'demographic certainty' in which families and family life were relatively stable.[75] With antibiotics and universal vaccination programmes provided by the new NHS, both infants and children were much less likely to suffer severe illness or to die than in the 1920s and 1930s. Spouses were also increasingly likely to reach their seventies together, while divorce rates, though beginning to rise, also remained relatively low, hence just six of the eighty-eight married interviewees had experienced a divorce, four of them middle-class and two of them working-class.[76] Alongside family stability these two post-war decades of government-backed full employment are also known to economic historians as the 'golden age' of steadily rising affluence throughout western Europe, including Britain.[77] As Figures 3 and 4 in Appendix A show, the childbearing characteristics of each of the two groups of interviewees, from Blackburn and Hertfordshire, broadly conform to these national trends. Marriages producing two births were the most common pattern, as would be expected for these marriage cohorts, and there was a slight tendency for those marrying after 1940 and having their children in the post-war decades to have produced a greater number of births per marriage than

[74] Dudley Baines and Robert Woods, 'Population and Regional Development', in *The Cambridge Economic History of Modern Britain*, eds. Roderick Floud and Paul Johnson (Cambridge and New York: Cambridge University Press, 2003), esp. Figure 2.1 (p. 28).

[75] The term 'demographic certainty' for the post-war decades was coined by Mike Anderson (Michael Anderson, 'The Emergence of the Modern Life Cycle in Britain', *Social History* 10, no. 1 (1985): 86–7).

[76] Hilda msf/kf/bl/#50; Gay msf/kf/ht/#13; Judith msf/kf/ht/#33; and the first wife of Reg msf/kf/ht/#36. The two from the working class were: Emily msf/kf/bl/#13 and Rose msf/kf/bl/#21. This relatively low divorce rate among the interviewees (6–7%), by subsequent standards, and the substantial class difference, were more or less in line with the national divorce rate statistics for these marriage cohorts. While there was a temporary post-war rise and then fall in divorce rates, 1945–8, it was not until 1971, with the implementation of the 1969 Divorce Reform Act, that the divorce rate began a sustained rapid rise (Oliver Ross McGregor, *Divorce in England: A Centenary Study* (London: Heinemann, 1957), Elliott, 'Demographic trends', 91, Roderick Phillips, *Untying the Knot: A Short History of Divorce* (Cambridge: Cambridge University Press, 1991), 211–13, on secular trends in divorce rates).

[77] This contrasts with the period after the 1960s, which saw the return of mass unemployment, and marriage and birth rates once again falling to new low levels in the following decade (where they have since remained), while the divorce rate climbed. Single parenthood and living singly both became more widespread patterns of household residence after the 1960s, eventually surpassing in incidence the more prevalent 'nuclear' family household norm of the mid-century decades (Kathleen Kiernan, 'The Family: Formation and Fission', in *The Changing Population of Britain*, ed. Heather Joshi (Oxford: Basil Blackwell, 1989), 27–41).

those marrying before 1940. While first marriage ages were extremely diverse, as Appendix C shows, nevertheless as a group they exhibited a pattern of age at first marriage which appears to be absolutely typical for the nation at this time, with an average male age at first marriage of 26.7 years and an average female age at first marriage of 24.5 years.[78]

While the decades before and after the Second World War both had distinctive demographic features, there were important continuities in the ideals and aspirations which much of the population had for marriage and family life across the whole of this period, from the early 1920s until the 1960s, as Claire Langhamer and Peter Scott have argued.[79] Langhamer points to the fact that most of the population had been reducing its family size for some time, even the famously fertile colliery communities were doing so from the 1920s. In other words in all sections of society husbands and wives were trying to decrease domestic crowding, and create more space, amenity, privacy and comfort in their homes. The main reason that couples had a little more space to themselves – none of the working-class interviewees here recalled having to share a bedroom in their own marriages with others in their family – was their much-reduced birth rate (the housing stock they inhabited did not change that rapidly).[80] The more secure, spacious and comfortable home-centred life, to which interwar working-class couples aspired and which was already enjoyed by the relatively small middle class and advertised as a model in the daily papers of the popular press, was increasingly becoming a possibility for those on manual wages, too.[81] But this was the case only if they restricted their family size to just one or two children and were fortunate enough not to live in one

[78] In his pioneering article presenting measures of the singulate mean age at first marriage John Hajnal gives a figure for 1935 of 27.5 for men and 25.5 for women; and a figure for 1951 of 26.3 for men and 23.4 for women. For the period as a whole the averages of the two sets of figures he gives are therefore 26.9 for men and 24.45 for women, which are extremely close to the averages for our sample of interviewees (26.7 for men and 24.5 for women), most of whom married between 1930 and 1950 (John Hajnal, 'The Marriage Boom', *Population Index* 19, no. 2 (1953): 80–101, Table 6, 91). See also below, Chapter 4, note 105, on the typical pattern of falling marriage ages of respondents born in each successive decade.

[79] Claire Langhamer, 'The Meanings of Home in Postwar Britain', *Journal of Contemporary History* 40, no. 2 (2005). Peter Scott, 'Did Owner-Occupation Lead to Smaller Families for Interwar Working-class Households?', *Economic History Review* 61 (2008): 99–124, for evidence of more aspirational working-class behaviour from the 1920s related to further restrictions on family size.

[80] On parents of large families having to sleep apart in houses with just two bedrooms, see Roberts, *A Woman's Place*, 95–6. On cramped sleeping in the potteries, see Sarsby, *Missuses and Mouldrunners*, 31, 34.

[81] Peter Scott also points out that by the late 1930s a significant minority of 18.9 per cent of non-agricultural working-class households were buying their own homes, approximately doubling the size of the small minority of fewer than 10 per cent doing so at the beginning of the 1930s (Scott, 'Did Owner-Occupation … ?', 103–4). On this see also Judy Giles, *Women, Identity, and Private Life in Britain, 1900–50* (New York: St. Martin's Press 1995), chs. 2–3.

of the several industrial regions, such as Lancashire, repeatedly blighted by the loss of earnings due to unemployment.

After the Second World War, with full employment a more uniform national experience, provided they had prudently small families, more and more working-class couples found that by the 1950s they could participate in the affluent consumerism they had been aspiring to engage in since the 1920s and 1930s.[82] This continuity of home-oriented, consumerist goals and aspirations from the 1920s through to the 1960s is reflected in the oral history testimony presented here from both regions and from both middle- and working-class respondents. For instance, many working-class respondents from both north and south recall growing up in homes without an indoor toilet or bathroom, a consumerist item of fundamental importance to the comfort of the home. The ritual of weekly bath night using a tin bath placed in the kitchen featured in many testimonies, and the moment when their parents or they themselves as married adults acquired the prized amenity of a home with running hot water and its own bathroom was often a significant memory.[83]

The period 1918–63 is rightly considered to be one during which intergenerational relations also experienced significant change. The rise in affluence, for instance, was played out in the increasing consumer power and leisure activities of the younger generation.[84] Most of the respondents experienced this youthful part of their lives, before the responsibilities of marriage, during the period from the late 1920s to the mid-1940s. Middle-class interviewees, when not in boarding schools as teenagers, tended to recall more home- and family-based leisure activities or participation in membership-fee associations

[82] Car ownership before 1939 was restricted to just one in five of the nation's families, and was a rarity beyond the confines of the middle classes and the Home Counties (Sean O'Connell, 'Motoring and Modernity', in *Twentieth-Century Britain*, eds. Francesca Carnevali, Paul Johnson and Julie-Marie Strange (London: Longman, 2007), 113). Similarly, only 27 per cent of homes had vacuum cleaners while just 3–4 per cent had refrigerators or electric washing machines by 1938 (Peter Scott, 'Consumption, Consumer Credit and the Diffusion of Consumer Durables', in *Twentieth-Century Britain*, eds. Francesca Carnevali, Paul Johnson and Julie-Marie Strange (London: Longman, 2007), 169). After the Second World War all these items became nearly universal over the subsequent quarter-century. For the contemporary recognition of the political significance of the increasingly affluent and domestic consumption-oriented post-war working class of the 1950s and 1960s, see Frank Benchoffer et al., *The Affluent Worker in the Class Structure* (Cambridge: Cambridge University Press, 1969), 17.

[83] See below, Chapter 7 'Bodies', for some of these fond memories.

[84] Andrew Davies, *Leisure, Gender, and Poverty: Working-Class Culture in Salford and Manchester, 1900–1939* (Buckingham and Philadelphia, PA: Open University Press, 1992), David Fowler, *The First Teenagers: The Lifestyle of Young Wage-Earners in Interwar Britain* (London: Woburn, 1995), Claire Langhamer, *Women's Leisure in England, 1920–60* (Manchester and New York: Manchester University Press, 2000), Selina Todd, *Young Women, Work, and Family in England, 1918–1950* (Oxford and New York: Oxford University Press, 2005), chs. 2, 4, 7.

like the local tennis club.[85] Among the working class until the First World War cheap or free voluntarily organised activities associated with church, chapel and various paternalistic philanthropic or self-help voluntary institutions, such as the Boys' Brigade or the Girl Guides, catered for teenagers' needs;[86] indeed, participation in these activities was still reported by many of our working-class respondents during their interwar childhoods. However, at the same time a range of new commercial leisure opportunities for the young of all classes was appearing, most obviously the cinema but also dance halls and clubs and various other associations to join, such as bicycle and sports clubs, as well as attendance at municipal swimming pools and lidos.[87] But it seems most likely from the oral history testimony presented here that most of the youthful discretionary expenditure spent by these informants in the decades from the 1920s until the 1940s went on their appearances – principally in keeping up with clothing and hairstyle fashions.[88]

Indeed it has been increasingly argued that there was a new popular body consciousness and perhaps even a more sexualised public aesthetic, especially of the young female body, by the end of the interwar period.[89] As Chapter 7 will show, the interviewees' testimony confirms the careful attention they paid when young to their personal appearance and especially to the meanings of the clothes worn by themselves and by others, although not quite in the ways suggested by some historians. Dress was seen as being as important as what people said and the way they talked, in providing important clues and signs by which to judge the character and moral and physical healthiness of potential partners of the opposite sex. This was felt to be rather more important by the respondents than any of the sexualised characteristics of bodies of the opposite sex or their personal good looks.

In terms of the wider political and historical context, the period 1918–63 witnessed the decline of economic and imperial dominance, an overall decline

[85] On the role of fee-membership sports clubs in socially exclusive middle-class, suburban sociability in the interwar decades, see McKibbin, *Classes and Cultures: England, 1918–1951*, 357–62. Slater and Woodside confirmed that tennis clubs and music and drama events were perceived as middle-class preserves by their mainly working-class informants (Slater and Woodside, *Patterns of Marriage*, 92).

[86] John R. Gillis, *For Better, for Worse: British Marriages, 1600 to the Present* (New York: Oxford University Press, 1985), 272–6.

[87] Robert J. Morris, 'Clubs, Societies and Associations', in *The Cambridge Social History of Britain, 1750–1950*, ed. F. M. L. Thompson (Cambridge and New York: Cambridge University Press, 1990), esp. 418–43, Marcus Collins, *Modern Love: An Intimate History of Men and Women in Twentieth-Century Britain* (London: Atlantic Books, 2003), ch. 3, Janet Smith and Simon Inglis, *Liquid Assets: The Lidos and Open Air Swimming Pools of Britain* (London: English Heritage, 2006).

[88] See below, Chapter 7 'Bodies'.

[89] Ina Zweiniger-Bargielowska, 'The Body and Consumer Culture', in *Women in Twentieth-Century Britain*, ed. Ina Zweiniger-Bargielowska (Harlow: Longman, 2001), 183–97.

in religious sources of social identity and the gradual rise to pre-eminence of a domestic national politics reflecting the social and economic class interests of the new mass electorate created in 1918, resulting, with the votes of all women after 1928, in Britain's reinvention of itself after the Second World War as a social democratic welfare state.[90] It has been influentially argued that the personal losses and blighted lives consequent on the colossal carnage of the First World War, which few could in retrospect see much sense in having fought, caused many to question their religious faith – this was certainly true among the intellectual and literary elite.[91] However, as mentioned, the interviewees continue to report a considerable amount of religiously organised leisure activity in their youth during the interwar decades and church going was still a habit during their adult lives for about half of the women of both classes interviewed in Lancashire, though rather less so for men in both communities and for women interviewed in Hertfordshire. It is noticeable that although religious teaching and language were used by some in their reflections on the morality of different kinds of sexual behaviour, they were more usually muted, vague or absent in most testimony.

As the importance of religious identities paled during the half-century after 1918, class and status differences became more salient and these erupted into major confrontations at times, especially during the economically turbulent interwar decades. Gill (1920), for instance, the middle-class daughter of a bank accountant living in Shropshire at the time, remembered the Jarrow Marchers:

GILL Well, of course, the Crewe works were very badly hit. We had a charlady whose husband worked for the, er, railway and he was made unemployed and, er, it, life was very hard for the people there. It badly affected me. I never ever forgot, er, er, you know, and the Jarrow Marchers, whom you've no doubt heard about, they came through Crewe some of them and they rather frightened me.

Really?

Well, you see they were all men that were living rough and walking and I felt desperately sorry for them but we didn't do anything, you know, 'cept avoid them (laughs).[92]

90 Paul Addison, *The Road to 1945: British Politics and the Second World War* (London and New York: Quartet Books, 1982), George L. Bernstein, *The Myth of Decline: The Rise of Britain since 1945* (London: Pimlico, 2004), ch. 1, Rodney Lowe, *The Welfare State in Britain since 1945*, 3rd edn (Basingstoke: Palgrave Macmillan, 2005).

91 Paul Fussell, *The Great War and Modern Memory* (New York: Oxford University Press, 1975). More generally, see the historiography on 'secularisation': Grace Davie, *Religion in Britain since 1945: Believing without Belonging* (Oxford and Cambridge, MA: Blackwell, 1994), Sarah C. Williams, *Religious Belief and Popular Culture in Southwark, c.1880–1939* (Oxford and New York: Oxford University Press, 1999), John Wolffe, 'Religion and Secularisation', in *Twentieth-Century Britain*, eds. Francesca Carnevali, Paul Johnson and Julie-Marie Strange (London: Longman, 2007), 322–38.

92 Gill msf/kf/bl/#48.

The decline of religious certainty was accompanied by the decline of a sense of imperial and global superiority for the British nation. Although the Empire in fact reached its greatest territorial extent following the Versailles Settlement of 1919, from the 1920s onwards the British economy, its society and culture experienced a marked and inexorable process of withdrawal from the global trading, financial and military pre-eminence enjoyed under the Empress Queen Victoria. After a second World War fought against fascist expansionary regimes, it could no longer be explained to a democratic British electorate why they would want to exert imperial mastery over other peoples wishing to assert their identity as independent nations, such as in the Indian subcontinent. The formal empire was consequently largely disbanded over the following two decades.

At the same time social security, guaranteed by the democratically elected government, provided a new sense of material certainty in people's lives, in place of religious solace or imperial possessions. Having come through a second costly and sacrificial war in which, with aerial bombing and newsreel journalism, the whole nation – both sexes and all generations – felt directly involved together in the battle front itself, the post-war welfare state was the political gift to itself willed by the weary working-class electorate in returning the first majority Labour government in the country's history.[93] It provided an important new range of tax-funded public goods and services democratically underwriting the living standards of all citizens in society, and granting the universal protections as of right against income and health insecurity, which the Jarrow Marchers had campaigned for and which the middle classes, like Gill, by 1945 married to a mill owner in Blackburn, now accepted was their due.

Were you in favour of it in 1945 'cos it was quite a socialist thing?

GILL Well, it was, yes but, er... I think there wasn't adequate coverage for people. I mayn't have been a socialist but I certainly, er, had a tremendous social conscience, you see, always. Especially, from the day that the Jarrow Marchers came through.[94]

The creation between 1945 and 1948 of a tax-funded universalist social security system, a welfare state of free health care, education and social services, along with a government commitment to full employment that was in practice also fulfilled throughout the next twenty-five years, created many of the conditions for the emergence of a transformed society in which all citizens were,

[93] Though, as Sonya Rose has recently demonstrated, the notion of an overwhelming sense of national solidarity, the Blitz spirit, is a much over-simplified myth (Sonya O. Rose, *Which People's War? National Identity and Citizenship in Britain, 1939–1945* (Oxford and New York: Oxford University Press, 2003)).

[94] Gill msf/kf/bl/#48.

in principle, freed from the physically and psychologically debilitating fears of chronic privation. This was an enormous change. Fear of lack of work and of basic hunger was something which had afflicted the poor as recently as the 1930s in the nation's industrial regions, as contemporary local medical studies of under-nutrition (ignored at the time by the government's Chief Medical Officer in Whitehall) had shown;[95] and as recalled in William Woodruff's best-selling memoirs of his childhood in 1930s Blackburn: 'It was a demoralizing blow for father to find himself on the scrapheap ... I could tell from his sighing in bed at night that the lack of work was affecting his sleep. It gnawed at his heart ... There was work and there was no work. If you worked you ate. If there was no work you went hungry.'[96]

This was the class-divided world of haves and have-nots tangibly close to poverty, which the interviewees recalled from the years of their childhood and their youth.[97] But it was also a world which was significantly changing by the time most of them were mature adults bringing up families of their own under the new conditions of full employment and the welfare state.

How historians have understood marriage and intimacy in this period

This book presents an interpretation of new evidence giving intimate details about the experience of heterosexuality among a diverse group of people who lived through most of the twentieth century. Although there is very little comparable evidence of this sort currently available to historians, there have been a number of valuable studies of many aspects of the history of sexualities during the twentieth century. Furthermore there is a well-established, important and rich historiography of the closely related subjects of the history of gender relations, marriage and family life in modern Britain. In this section such literature, and the diverse source of evidence employed, is reviewed, in order to place this book's approach and intended contribution in the context of previous scholars' work.

95 Steven Thompson, *Unemployment, Poverty and Health in Interwar South Wales* (Cardiff: University of Wales Press, 2006).

96 Woodruff, *The Road to Nab End*, 45, 47.

97 A very similar picture of family life in childhood often disrupted by poor health, poverty, accidents and fathers' war injuries emerges from Slater and Woodside's working-class informants, interviewed October 1943–January 1946, just before the provisions of the welfare state began to take effect (Slater and Woodside, *Patterns of Marriage*, 14, 48–50, 63). Whereas, by 1969 in his second survey of family life, Gorer commented on how, after two decades of full employment and the welfare state, respondents to his survey no longer mentioned 'material circumstances' in their answers to questions about what made for happy marriage (Geoffrey Gorer, *Sex & Marriage in England Today: Study of the Views and Experience of the under-45s* (London: Nelson, 1971), 63).

Gender relations and companionate marriage

The current orthodox general interpretation of the history of gender relations as pertaining to marriage and sexuality in modern Britain envisages the period 1918–63 as encompassing the rise of 'companionate marriage'. This supposedly represented a major transformation, replacing the previous patriarchal 'Victorian' ideology of 'separate spheres'.[98] Separate spheres envisaged that nature had endowed all civilised men with an active, initiating procreative sex drive, which demanded its healthy outlet in regular but not excessive sexual intercourse, while women's reciprocal sex instincts were supposedly more moderate and focused more on the joys of emotional nurturing of the young. This polarisation of supposed sexual natures was not necessarily scientifically endorsed by many medical experts, but it was insidiously and consistently implied in the necessarily euphemistic language of most literature throughout the Victorian period, didactic, low- and highbrow.[99] Companionate marriage, by contrast, acknowledged

[98] Separate spheres legitimised patriarchal power of men over women and of income-earning fathers and husbands over wives and children, who were supposed to be economically inactive. However, during the late nineteenth century the Victorian feminist movement began to campaign successfully for the removal of some of the most obvious legal disabilities on their sex, in regard to marriage, property ownership and child custody, and during the first decades of the twentieth century further legal changes were achieved in relation to the voting rights of all women, though access to employment on an equal basis initially remained limited, especially for married women. The classic text on the formation of 'separate spheres' in British history was Leonore Davidoff and Catherine Hall, *Family Fortunes: Men and Women of the English Middle Class, 1780–1850* (London: Hutchinson, 1987). The parallel seminal study of the origins and significance of the proletarian 'male breadwinner' ideology was Anna Clark, *The Struggle for the Breeches: Gender and the Making of the British Working Class* (Berkeley: University of California Press, 1995). Substantial work by Michael Mason and by Dror Wahrman has consolidated the orthodoxy (Michael Mason, *The Making of Victorian Sexuality* (Oxford and New York: Oxford University Press, 1994), Dror Wahrman, *The Making of the Modern Self: Identity and English Culture in the Eighteenth Century* (New Haven: Yale University Press, 2004)). Amanda Vickery, 'Golden Age to Separate Spheres? A Review of the Categories and Chronology of English Women's History', *The Historical Journal* 36, no. 2 (2009): 383–414 has been a much-cited critique (but see Anna Clark's review of Amanda Vickery's book *The Gentleman's Daughter*, available at www.history.ac.uk/reviews/paper/anna.html (accessed 29 April 2010)). On late Victorian and Edwardian feminism, see Barbara Caine, *Victorian Feminists* (Oxford and New York: Oxford University Press, 1992), Ben Griffin, 'Class, Gender and Liberalism in Parliament 1868–1882: The Case of the Married Women's Property Acts', *The Historical Journal* 46, no. 1 (2003): 59–87. On the history of separate spheres and masculinity in the late Victorian period, see John Tosh, *A Man's Place: Masculinity and the Middle-Class Home in Victorian England* (New Haven: Yale University Press, 1999). For a thoughtful review, see Martin Francis, 'The Domestication of the Male? Recent Research on Nineteenth- and Twentieth-Century British Masculinity', *The Historical Journal* 45, no. 3 (2002). Francis argues that a mid-Victorian 'profound attachment' to domesticity, which subsequently gave way to a late-nineteenth-century 'flight from domesticity', was followed by a re-domestication of males in the interwar decades after the shattering of a high imperial, militaristic heroic 'hypermasculinity' in the unromantic industrial slaughter of the trenches.

[99] Peter T. Cominos, 'Innocent Femina Sensualis in Unconscious Conflict', in *Suffer and Be Still: Women in the Victorian Age*, ed. Martha Vicinus (Bloomington and Indianapolis: Indiana

female capacities for sexual pleasure as more equal with men's – a natural and respectable function provided it occurred within marriage.

Marie Stopes' interwar best-seller, *Married Love*, published in 1918 and selling over 800,000 copies worldwide by 1938, was the starting gun in Britain for the spread of this new ideology. It was the most widely read manual of how to practise and achieve companionate marriage.[100] The current orthodoxy envisages that by the 1950s and 1960s the ideology of companionate marriage had, indeed, risen and become culturally and socially dominant such that the capacity of married partners to provide each other with mutual sexual pleasure was coming to be regarded by most doctors and clerics as normative for marital love and one of the crucial criteria of a good marriage.[101]

As several historians who have addressed the notion of companionate marriage have concluded, the concept itself embraces a number of possible meanings, due to its multi-faceted and transatlantic history, having acquired ideologically diverse proponents in the course of its intellectual elaboration over several decades. They have shown there was often an emphasis on notions of equality and mutuality

University Press, 1972), Carol Christ, 'Victorian Masculinity and the Angel in the House', in *A Widening Sphere: Changing Roles of Victorian Women*, ed. Martha Vicinus (Bloomington, IN: Indiana University Press, 1977), 146–62, Jeffrey Weeks, *Sex, Politics, and Society: The Regulation of Sexuality since 1800* (London and New York: Longman, 1989), 188–92. On the complications of the ideology for sexuality and the consequently enhanced extremism of the age-old depictions of women as 'Madonnas' or whores, see the excellent Angus McLaren, *Impotence: A Cultural History* (London: University of Chicago Press, 2007), ch. 5. For the period's most well-known popular novelist, who seriously challenged this representation, though in a manner which did not attract the legal attention which D. H. Lawrence later encountered, see Rosemarie Morgan, *Women and Sexuality in the Novels of Thomas Hardy* (London and New York: Routledge, 1988). For feminist challenges to the separate spheres sexual ideology during the decades prior to 1918, see Lucy Bland, 'Marriage Laid Bare: Middle-class Women and Marital Sex, c.1880–1914', in *Labour and Love*, ed. Jane Lewis (Oxford: Basil Blackwell, 1986), 123–46; Susan Kingsley Kent, *Sex and Suffrage in Britain, 1860–1914* (Princeton: Princeton University Press, 1987), Caine, *Victorian Feminists*.

[100] Ross McKibbin has provided an illuminating introduction for a new edition of Marie Stopes' classic ideological statement of the virtues of companionate marriage, first published in 1918: Marie Carmichael Stopes, *Married Love*, edited by Ross McKibbin (Oxford: Oxford University Press, 2004). For an excellent account of Stopes' sequence of publications and her publishing strategy, see Alexander C. T. Geppert, 'Divine Sex, Happy Marriage, Regenerated Nation: Marie Stopes's Marital Manual *Married Love* and the Making of a Best-Seller, 1918–1955', *Journal of the History of Sexuality* 8, no. 3 (1998): 389–433. See also McLaren, *Impotence*, 165–80, on Stopes' impact, though McLaren (ibid., 171) also points out that before Stopes, in the first two decades of the twentieth century, 'American writers led the way in advancing this new conception of marital sexuality. The concern for the "synchronised orgasm" ... comparing intercourse to a well-coached baseball game.'

[101] Leonore Davidoff, Megan Doolittle, Janet Fink and Katherine Holden, *The Family Story: Blood, Contract, and Intimacy, 1830–1960* (London: Longman, 1999), 190. See also Gillis, *For Better, for Worse*, ch. 11, Janet Finch and Penny Summerfield, 'Social Reconstruction and the Emergence of Companionate Marriage, 1945–59', in *Marriage, Domestic Life and Social Change: Writings for Jacqueline Burgoyne (1944–88)*, ed. David Clark (London: Routledge, 1991), 7–32, Janet Reibstein and Martin Richards, *Sexual Arrangements: Marriage and Affairs* (London: Heinemann, 1992), ch. 1.

across all aspects of married life as being an essential part of the 'companionate' model, in addition to its focus on reciprocal sexual pleasure. Hence, equal roles in childrearing, equal access to resources and leisure, as well as mutual and non-patriarchal decision-making might all be considered elements of companionate marriage by some proponents. In other constructions, notions of an equal but different partnership with gendered roles in work and childrearing were also acknowledged as a possibility, if combined with confiding sexual intimacy. What is certainly true is that, within an agenda set by the concept of 'companionship', marriage roles, gender and sexual relations have been under a continuous and widening public discussion in Britain throughout the period from 1918 onwards. Protagonists in this debate have included not only radical and egalitarian progressives but also, in response, Christian and a range of other socially and morally conservative reformers, such as members of the National Council of Public Morals at the time of the Great War or those who, twenty years later, set up the Marriage Guidance Council.[102] As Jane Lewis has shown, advocacy of the companionate marriage ideal became a central motif on both sides of the Atlantic during the interwar and immediate post-war decades among those, notably including William Beveridge, architect of the British welfare state, seeking to argue that the altruistic institution of marriage had a vitally important socially stabilising future in an increasingly materialist and individualist society and economy.[103]

[102] In fact protagonists of the companionate partnership in marriage can be found from at least the 1880s onwards. Collins attributes the notion of 'mutuality' to the utopian socialist Edward Carpenter and argues that he was a key early champion of the ideal of companionate marriage (Collins, *Modern Love*, 2). Stopes was strongly influenced by a number of figures including Carpenter and the pioneering sexologist Havelock Ellis. There were diverse sources of more egalitarian thinking about marriage and gender relations, such as John Stuart Mill's text, *The Subjection of Women*, Karl Pearson's Men and Women's Club of the 1880s, and many other strands of feminist, socialist, evolutionary and sexological thinking. See, Judith R. Walkowitz, 'Science, Feminism and Romance: The Men and Women's Club 1885–1889', *History Workshop Journal* 21, no. 3 (1986): 37–59, Weeks, *Sex, Politics, and Society*, chs. 8–10, Lesley A. Hall, *Sex, Gender and Social Change in Britain since 1880* (Basingstoke: Macmillan, 2000), chs. 1–7, Angelique Richardson, *Love and Eugenics in the Late Nineteenth Century: Rational Reproduction and the New Woman* (Oxford and New York: Oxford University Press, 2003), Ruth Livesey, *Socialism, Sex, and the Culture of Aestheticism in Britain, 1880–1914* (Oxford and New York: Oxford University Press, 2007). Lesley Hall has researched the texts and lives of a number of the leading intellectual figures of the late nineteenth and early twentieth centuries: see her entries for William Acton, F. W. Stella Browne, Eustace Chesser, Margaret Shurmer Sibthorp, Marie Stopes, Charlotte Carmichael Stopes, Alice Vickery, Helen Wilson and Helena Wright, in *The Oxford Dictionary of National Biography*, Oxford University Press, Sept. 2004, www.oxforddnb.com (accessed 21 July 2010). On more socially conservative and religious contributors to the debate, see Jane Lewis and Kathleen Kiernan, 'The Boundaries between Marriage, Nonmarriage, and Parenthood: Changes in Behavior and Policy in Postwar Britain', *Journal of Family History* 21, no. 3 (1996): 372–87. On those involved in the National Marriage Guidance Council and its work, see Jane Lewis, 'Public Institution and Private Relationship: Marriage and Marriage Guidance, 1920–1968', *Twentieth Century British History* 1, no. 3 (1990), Collins, *Modern Love*, ch. 4.

[103] Jane Lewis, *The End of Marriage?: Individualism and Intimate Relations* (Cheltenham: Edward Elgar, 2001), 46–55. In the USA socially conservative American functionalist sociologists

Progressive elements within the educated middle classes, sexologists and psychologists, pioneering marriage and sex guidance counsellors, birth controllers and, eventually, from the 1930s and 1940s, clerics and members of the medical profession, increasingly attempted to spread the new gospel to the lower classes.[104] Consequently, the presumed desirability of a companionate model has left a pervasive imprint on many of the most accessible and detailed contemporary sources which historians can use to study marriage and the family during this period, such as marriage guidance manuals;[105] and the letters written to Marie Stopes in response to the companionate agenda that she set out have been the subject of several historical publications.[106] Finch and Summerfield have noted that the string of social investigations of marriage and community studies of the family from the late 1940s until the 1960s, which now provide primary sources for historians of this period, repeatedly examined whether or not companionate marriage was flourishing in the new social conditions of the welfare state society, rising material affluence and increasing female independence.[107]

famously proposed that marriage and the family were undergoing an epochal transformation 'from institution to relationship' (Ben B. Lindsey and Wainwright Evans, *The Companionate Marriage* (New York: Boni & Liveright, 1927), Ernest W. Burgess and Harvey J. Locke, *The Family, from Institution to Companionship* (New York: American Book Company, 1945), Robert O. Blood and Donald M. Wolfe, *Husbands & Wives: The Dynamics of Married Living* (New York: Free Press, 1960); and see Lewis, *The End of Marriage?*, 51–2 on Talcott Parsons.

104 Lewis, 'Public Institution and Private Relationship', Stephen Brooke, 'Bodies, Sexuality and the "Modernization" of the British Working Classes, 1920s to 1960s', *International Labor and Working-Class History* 69 no. 1 (2006): 104–22. See also Hall, *Sex, Gender and Social Change* 2, 124–31; and Wendy Webster, *Imagining Home: Gender, Race and National Identity, 1945–64* (London: UCL Press, 1998), on ideals of companionate marriage as racially specific constructions of family life and gender relations.

105 For instance, J. A. Goldsmid, *Companionate Marriage: From the Medical and Social Aspects* (London: William Heinemann, 1934), which also advocated the companionate model. See also Hera Cook, *The Long Sexual Revolution: English Women, Sex, and Contraception 1800–1975* (Oxford: Oxford University Press, 2004). Cook has mounted a systematic examination of most other sex and marriage guidance manuals available in England 1918–72; Marcus Collins has investigated the social pathology case-work files of the National Marriage Guidance Council, 1929–65, dealing with the very poor in London, and has surveyed the published views of post-war marriage guidance counsellors and psychotherapists (Collins, *Modern Love*, ch. 4).

106 Ruth E. Hall, ed. *Dear Dr. Stopes: Sex in the 1920s* (London: Deutsch, 1978), Ellen M. Holtzman, 'The Pursuit of Married Love: Women's Attitudes toward Sexuality and Marriage in Great Britain, 1918–1939', *Journal of Social History* 16, no. 2 (1982): 39–51, Claire Davey, 'Birth Control in Britain During the Interwar Years: Evidence from the Stopes Correspondence', *Journal of Family History* 13, no. 1 (1988): 329–45, Lesley A. Hall, *Hidden Anxieties: Male Sexuality, 1900–1950* (Cambridge: Polity, 1991).

107 Finch and Summerfield, 'Social Reconstruction and the Emergence of Companionate Marriage', 7–32. These studies included: Eustace Chesser, *Love without Fear* (London: Rich & Cowan, 1941), Slater and Woodside, *Patterns of Marriage*, Ferdynand Zweig, *Women's Life and Labour* (London: V. Gollancz, 1952), Geoffrey Gorer, *Exploring English Character* (London: Cresset Press, 1955), Eustace Chesser et al., *The Sexual, Marital and Family Relationships of the English Woman* (London: Hutchinson's Medical Publications,

Furthermore there is the additional highly dynamic body of recent historiography on gender relations which is very relevant to this book's subject matter. Analysis of the development of 'companionate marriage' has to be understood in the wider social context of developing female roles and positions in society and associated gender relations. There have been a number of recent studies by historians which have contributed to building up a picture of a complex chronology and diversity of gender relations, marriage and sexuality during this period. What can we learn from such studies on the crucial issue of how women's relative status and position in society and the possibilities for equality within marriage changed over the course of the early and mid-twentieth century?

Adrian Bingham's recent review of histories of gender and women's roles in interwar Britain has made a number of discerning points about this historiography that are of direct relevance to the interpretation that follows of the new oral history evidence presented here.[108] In particular Bingham has argued that new research is suggesting there is not a single story or trend of advances – or of backlash – in women's position in society during the period 1918–63 but diverse and, indeed, contradictory developments to comprehend: 'It is easy to understand why historians focusing on the arenas of politics and employment painted a gloomy picture of women's progress [while] historians examining other aspects of social activity, especially leisure and sexuality, reached rather different conclusions and characterised the interwar period as a "modern era" of changing expectations and wider opportunities for young women.'[109] Thus,

1956), John M. Mogey, *Family and Neighbourhood: Two Studies in Oxford* (London: Oxford University Press, 1956), Elizabeth Bott, *Family and Social Network: Roles, Norms, and External Relationships in Ordinary Urban Families* (London: Tavistock Publications, 1957), Richard Hoggart, *The Uses of Literacy* (London: Chatto & Windus, 1957), Madeline Kerr, *The People of Ship Street* (London: Routledge, 1958), Josephine Klein, *Samples from English Cultures* (London: Routledge & Kegan Paul, 1965), Margaret Stacey, *Tradition and Change: A Study of Banbury* (Oxford: Oxford University Press, 1960), Colin Rosser and C. C. Harris, *The Family and Social Change: A Study of Family and Kinship in a South Wales Town* (London and New York: Routledge & Kegan Paul; Humanities Press, 1965), Gorer, *Sex and Marriage*, Norman Dennis, Fernando Henriques and Clifford Slaughter, *Coal Is Our Life: An Analysis of a Yorkshire Mining Community* (London and New York: Tavistock Publications, 1969), Michael Young and Peter Willmott, *Family and Kinship in East London* (Glencoe, IL: Free Press, 1957). On Mass Observation's studies in the 1930s and 1940s, see Liz Stanley, *Sex Surveyed, 1949–1994: From Mass-Observation's 'Little Kinsey' to the National Survey and the Hite Reports* (London: Taylor & Francis, 1995).

108 Adrian Bingham, 'An Era of Domesticity? Histories of Women and Gender in Interwar Britain', *Cultural and Social History* 1, no. 2 (2004): 225–33. In arguing for recognition of a more complex chronology, Bingham closes his review by recognising that this has close affinities with the conclusions drawn by Francis in his historiographical review of masculinity during this period (Francis, 'The Domestication of the Male?').

109 Bingham, 'An Era of Domesticity?', 227. The main focus of debate in the historiography of gender relations in England during the period from the Great War until the 1960s has been the question of why it was that women did not achieve equality in the formal economy, in politics

Bingham points out that it is important to bear in mind 'the wretchedness of the poverty, dismal housing and lack of health care which burdened large numbers of women and children in particular' in the interwar decades.[110] Yet he also acknowledges that Claire Langhamer, Selina Todd, Katherine Holden and Ina Zweiniger-Bargielowska have each shown, with different sources and methods, how many single young women were increasingly able to engage in a range of personally empowering leisure activities.[111]

It is not clear, however, that these changing features of some aspects of youth culture and changing public images of the young female figure, for instance, can be reliably interpreted as signifying corresponding and similar changes in the practical or intimate lives of most women, especially once they became wives and mothers, as increasingly large proportions of them did and at younger ages from the 1930s through to the 1960s. In the final chapter of her excellent study of *Women's Leisure in England 1920–60*, Langhamer shows that this modernist consumerism among the young did not necessarily translate into 'modern' aspirations for their maternal adulthood.[112] As Bingham eloquently puts it: 'Langhamer describes in detail how housewives and mothers generally accepted that the pleasures and freedoms of youth would be exchanged with the wedding ring for a life of duty and service to the family.'[113] In other words once we take into account the reality of gender roles over a woman's life cycle and the practicalities of domestic life in the context of an economy offering adequately remunerated jobs mainly only to men, there seems to be a rather more complex history of gender relations to consider than that which can be

and in most institutional positions of power, despite the substantial legislative gains of voting rights granted in 1918 – fully equalised in 1928 – along with the two prolonged periods in both World Wars when women had access to and proved themselves able to take on a wide range of men's jobs. There has been much productive research and debate over both the extent of and ways in which women were mobilised in each of the wars and the forms of their civic participation and also the character of post-war policies and representations of female roles after each of the two World Wars. In particular there has been extensive debate over the character and extent of a putative gender 'backlash' after the Great War – the fuss over the Flappers, for instance – which ensured that, despite gaining the vote and certain apparent legal advances, women continued to be represented ambiguously in the public media and continued to be more or less excluded from most areas of higher-paid and higher-status employment or public position. The original contributions to this debate were: Gail Braybon, *Women Workers in the First World War: The British Experience* (London and Totowa, NJ: Croom Helm; Barnes & Noble, 1981), Margaret R. Higonnet and Jane Jenson, eds. *Behind the Lines: Gender and the Two World Wars* (New Haven: Yale University Press, 1989). See Bingham's review for the subsequent historiography.

110 Bingham, 'An Era of Domesticity?', citing Cheryl Law, *Suffrage and Power: the Women's Movement, 1918–28* (London: I. B. Tauris, 1997), 229.

111 Langhamer, *Women's Leisure*, Todd, *Young Women, Work, and Family*, Katherine Holden, *The Shadow of Marriage: Singleness in England, 1914–60* (Manchester and New York: Manchester University Press; Palgrave, 2007), Zweiniger-Bargielowska, 'The Body and Consumer Culture'.

112 Langhamer, *Women's Leisure*, ch. 5. See also Langhamer, 'The Meanings of Home', 341–62.

113 Bingham, 'An Era of Domesticity?', 231.

addressed by the debate over whether there should be a narrative of progress or of backlash in either the interwar or immediately post-war decades.

Bingham's own first research monograph offers an impressively rich, subtly revisionist account of the impact of the popular national press, an immensely important interwar cultural and political innovation, in influencing perceived gender roles. Earlier gender historians had predominantly viewed these publications of the new 'press barons', Lords Northcliffe, Rothermere and Beaverbrook, as integral parts of the post-Great War patriarchal propaganda 'backlash' to re-establish traditional 'separate spheres' gender roles and the confinement of women to housewifely domesticity.[114] Bingham's systematic research documents a rather more complex set of messages in the popular press, all of them commercially driven and attempting to reflect, in a competitive readership market, both male and female readers' diverse wishes.

In relation to gender and sexuality, Bingham's interpretation confirms Langhamer's insight about the crucial nature of a widespread general acceptance of a profound change of status for each woman, reaffirming traditional roles, which occurred when she entered into marriage and motherhood. Linked to this Bingham finds two distinctive depictions of the feminine in the popular press: the women's sections of the papers were dominated by features and consumerist advertisements about housewifery, while in the rest of the paper 'decorative' photographs of young, non-maternal women were printed for the titillation of male readers.[115] Hence, women's image was represented as either a lithesome young, unmarried female or as a busy mother and aspirational housekeeper. There was one important area of consumerist overlap between these two principal female roles projected in the interwar commercial press: this was the subject of fashion and dress, which featured extensively both in the women's sections and through the clothing that (usually) adorned the young nymphs.

Bingham also sees his findings as being consistent with the earlier work of Alison Light. She argued, from her reading of four highly popular interwar female, middlebrow writers – Ivy Compton-Burnett, Agatha Christie, Daphne du Maurier and Jan Struther (the author of the Mrs Miniver column in *The Times*) – that their writings propagated a new popular, English interwar 'conservative modernity'.[116] This social conservatism was not part of a reactionary

114 Ibid., 232.

115 Bingham, *Gender, Modernity, and the Popular Press*, 172, 78.

116 Alison Light, *Forever England: Femininity, Literature and Conservatism between the Wars* (London: Routledge, 1991). This consistency is notable given Bingham's focus on the popular press. Light, for instance, examined the Mrs Miniver column in *The Times*, whose middle-class readership never rose above 400,000, while the *Express* and the *Mirror* had a mass working-class readership with circulations of 3–5 million (Colin Seymour-Ure, *The British Press and Broadcasting since 1945* (Oxford: Blackwell, 1996), 28–9).

backlash. It did not simply rehearse patriarchal 'separate spheres' and mere domesticity for women. It advocated and projected a new, but conservative imaginary of inward-looking, pacific, shared domesticity and privacy for both wives *and* husbands. The new domesticated ideal was the pursuit of 'the quiet life' by both partners, or the virtues of 'keeping yourself to yourself' as Enid (1909) put it, and as Judy Giles has argued in a subsequent study exploring similar values among the interwar aspirational working class.[117]

In terms of gender relations in marriage this was envisaged as an 'equal but different' relationship, though Light acknowledges that, being socially conservative, 'it clung to certain rather fixed notions of what was feminine and masculine (child-rearing for example was always assumed to be the woman's business)'.[118] While Alison Light at one point describes this as 'a partnership, a careful balancing of the books', in summary she sees this as 'the companionate marriage' and, as such, as something very different from the highly patriarchal 'separate spheres' Victorian ideology of pre-Great War, middle-class Britain. Thus, and despite the continuing assumption that childcare was primarily maternal work, she concludes that: 'In the image of the companionate marriage we have come a long way from the child-wife of the patriarchal Victorian marriage in which the woman remained dependent upon and protected by her father-husband.'[119]

Alison Light goes on to point out that 'conservatism, of the lower case variety, has been ... unaccounted for; as one of the great unexamined assumptions of British cultural life, its history is all but non-existent'.[120] She finds that 'Mrs Miniver's [fictional] marriage is modern in being semi-detached, spacious and companionate: its pleasures are mutual.' As the Mrs Miniver column, which appeared in *The Times* from 1937 to 1939, put it, 'the most important thing about marriage was not a home or children or a remedy against sin, [i.e. sex] but simply there being always an eye to catch'. Furthermore, according to Light, 'no doubt there was much to be said for the introduction of separate beds, a new feature of respectable married life in the period. Usually cited as testimony to the prudishness of the middle-class wife, it perhaps had the advantage of making sexual relations potentially a matter of choice rather than conjugal right': 'Mrs Miniver's idea of partnership may not be exciting, but neither is it brutal or degrading' (three interviewees slept in separate beds).[121]

This rich and complex set of observations from Alison Light raises a range of intriguing issues about the meaning of intimacy, partnership and companionship

[117] Ibid., 8–11, Giles, *Women, Identity, and Private Life*, ch. 3. For Enid msf/kf/bl/#49, see above note 6. Slater and Woodside also found among their London working-class and lower-middle-class respondents that '"[k]eeping ourselves to ourselves" still prevails, and is felt to be righteous' (Slater and Woodside, *Patterns of Marriage*, 91).

[118] Light, *Forever England*, 123. [119] Ibid., 124. [120] Ibid., 14.

[121] Ibid., 124; all three middle-class: Pru msf/kf/ht/#12; Stan msf/srss/ht#28; Humphrey msf/kf/ht#26.

in marriage among the suburban middle classes at the end of the 1930s, and in particular the place of sexuality within such loving marriages. The thesis of the rise of companionate marriage, according to several of its most influential exponents, also comprises a thesis about the changing importance of sexuality, in which physical intimacy and mutual sexual satisfaction moved to the centre of the marriage relationship during the mid-twentieth-century decades.[122] Alison Light, however, was able to present an interpretation of the Mrs Miniver column, which, although she described it as advocating 'companionate marriage', endowed this with a rather different, contemporary understanding of the central role of a moderate, private, undemanding mutual emotional intimacy, which avoids any simple equations of the rise of companionate marriage with the centrality of a physical, eroticised and demanding sexuality.

Similar conclusions have emerged from the distinct methodology of oral history studying other sections of British society both in the decades before and after the Second World War. Natalie Higgins' unpublished thesis compares the attitudes towards marriage of two different working-class cohorts, one married in the 1930s and the other in the 1950s, in two distinctive cities: Hull and Birmingham. She discovered a considerable rise in the extent to which those married in the 1950s saw marriage as best characterised by teamwork, especially in the areas of childrearing, joint leisure, and household management. But she concluded there was much that had not changed: 'most notably men continued to be the main breadwinners and women did all the housework and were the primary carers for children. There had certainly not been an end to demarcated roles, though some boundaries had been blurred.' She concluded by agreeing with Elizabeth Roberts that 'if the criteria of sharing, companionship and equality are strictly applied, it is questionable if any marriages in this survey can be described as companionate'.[123] In presenting her oral history study of women in another distinct working-class region, East Cleveland during the period 1939–60, Margaret Williamson has recently argued that many women adopted the rhetoric of companionate marriage in describing their own marriages. Focusing on leisure patterns, women's testimony viewed marriage as a partnership in which leisure was equally shared. Yet she found that her interviewees also described the ways in which they in fact had far fewer opportunities for independent leisure than their husbands and demonstrated a continued internalisation of and acceptance of messages which legitimated gendered inequalities, male dominance and female subordination.[124]

[122] Collins, *Modern Love*, Davidoff et al., *The Family Story*. See below Chapter 5 notes 2 and 3.

[123] Natalie Higgins, 'The Changing Expectations and Realities of Marriage in the English Working Class, 1920–1960' (Unpublished Ph.D. thesis, Cambridge: Cambridge University, 2003), 269, Roberts, *Women and Families*, 97.

[124] Margaret Williamson, 'Gender, Leisure and Marriage in a Working-Class Community, 1939–1960', *Labour History Review* 74 (2009).

In relation to the primary claim about marital sexuality entailed by the rise of companionate marriage thesis – that of increasing attention to the importance of mutual sexual pleasure – a consensus is emerging that the rhetoric which positioned sexual pleasure (and in particular the requirement that men ensure their wives experience sexual pleasure) as key to a successful marriage, made few inroads into working-class communities before the Second World War but that a slow thaw probably set in from the 1940s.[125] It is argued that despite the popularity of works such as Marie Stopes', factors such as sexual ignorance and inadequate birth control meant that during the interwar decades many women continued to see sex as a frequently unpleasant marital duty, to value husbands for their consideration and sexual restraint, to choose abstinence in the face of birth control options that were either unpalatable, out of their control or perceived to be unreliable.[126] From the 1940s and 1950s, however, it is argued that public discourse on sexual culture in Britain was slowly changing, such that at least one section of the popular press, the *Mirror* and the *Sunday Pictorial*, were increasingly prepared to campaign that sexual ignorance was no longer desirable or acceptable, arguing that 'it was the duty of the active citizen to be sexually informed'.[127] For men and women marrying after the Second World War, the impact of the new emphasis on marital sexual pleasure is seen as having created considerable tensions as many couples continued to find sex difficult, hampered by continued contraceptive problems, sexual reticence, anxiety and poor technique. According to Hera Cook rates of coitus increased as couples were progressively less resigned to managing through sexual abstinence, but as rates of coitus and fertility rose, so too did marital dissatisfaction.[128] In a sophisticated, and discriminating evaluation of a range of contemporary sources, Claire Langhamer carefully distinguishes between liberalising attitudes towards premarital sex alongside a simultaneous hardening of less-forgiving attitudes towards extra-marital sex during the course of both the 1950s and 1960s.[129]

[125] Gillis, *For Better, for Worse*, 297–303.

[126] Cook, *The Long Sexual Revolution*, 155–62, McKibbin, *Classes and Cultures: England, 1918–1951*, Beier, *For Their Own Good*, 258–60.

[127] Adrian Bingham, *Family Newspapers? Sex, Private Life, and the British Popular Press 1918–1978* (Oxford: Oxford University Press, 2009), 12 and see ch. 3.

[128] Cook, *The Long Sexual Revolution*.

[129] Thus, Langhamer argues that in the problem pages of *Woman's Own*, the responses of the resident agony aunt, Mary Grant, changed from the late 1950s such that 'by the mid 1960s the discourse of forgiveness, as well as the tendency to minimize the effect of affairs on married life, was in decline'. Langhamer's overall conclusion is that,

> '[t]he account offered in this article does not fundamentally challenge readings of the post-war period which identify significant social-sexual change as a facet of the late 1960s: the evidence has demonstrated that attitudes towards adultery did shift in this period. It does, however, suggest that this shift was not a simple reflection of attitudes towards premarital sex and cannot be read as unproblematic evidence of increased permissiveness. Whilst a foregrounding of the

This book will attempt to shed further light on the complex range of issues relating to gender, sexuality and marriages in this era – companionate or not. Prior to presenting the oral history evidence, however, we will consider the place of this research and its approach, in relation to other methodologies which have been effectively used to further our understanding of intimate relationships in marriage in this period.

Methodologies and the history of marriage and sexuality

Alison Light's pioneering research offers one approach to gaining insight into the subjective meanings of marriage for contemporaries in the past. She analyses the content of literature deliberately created for a middlebrow, popular audience of women during the interwar decades – mostly drawn from the respectable and conservative middle and lower middle classes – to explore the shared values of this community of readers. Adrian Bingham has significantly extended this approach with his investigation of the changing content, in relation to depictions of gender, family and sexuality, of the lower-brow, popular press read extensively by the working classes.

Oral history is another quite distinct methodology which also offers scope for further exploring contemporaries' own understandings of the relationship between marriage, love, companionship and sexuality. It provides another way to uncover and give voice to the beliefs, values and ways of life of the socially conservative majority who populated the same era of the past studied by Alison Light, Adrian Bingham and other notable contributors, such as Judy Giles and Claire Langhamer

The oral history methodology can investigate both middle- and working-class contexts, questioning those who would not have been the readers of the Mrs Miniver column in *The Times*, for instance, though some of them would have read the more popular 'romances' like E. M. Hull's best-seller of the 1920s, *The Sheik* (1919) or Du Maurier's romances of the 1930s and 1940s. Whilst it is clear from this popular fictional literature that sexuality was part of an early and mid-twentieth-century discourse about marriage, there are two important points to note about its possible relationship to the social history of marriage practices and attitudes, as opposed to its place in the cultural history of representations of marriage and sex.

First, this popular literature always remained (necessarily given the obscenity laws which caught D. H. Lawrence in their net) allusive and

importance of love and sex to marriage may well have contributed to a softening of attitudes towards premarital experimentation [associated with youth culture and the Pill], that very same emphasis encouraged a hardening of attitudes towards extra-marital sex even as it became more common.' Claire Langhamer, 'Adultery in Post-War England', *History Workshop Journal* 62, no. 1 (2006): 105, 110.

indirect where the description of sex itself was concerned. Even the most sensationalist best-sellers by E. M. Hull and her imitators, like Joan Conquest, 'considered appallingly "low" by literary and cultural commentators at the time',[130] remained 'euphemistic in critical scenes'.[131] As Alison Light notes of the romances of Daphne du Maurier, such as *Jamaica Inn* (1936) and *Frenchman's Creek* (1941): 'There remains for du Maurier no language in which the respectable woman can describe her own sexual desire positively. It is always felt to be socially degrading, incurring a loss of "self-respect", because it can only be thought of by imagining oneself as the "wrong" kind of woman.'[132] Second, as will be shown below in Chapter 4, most of the oral history respondents, especially the working-class interviewees, said that they saw this literature, and indeed all portrayals of romance in film and popular culture, as simply the stuff of fantasy. Far from being in some sense a reflection of reality or of their aspirations for their own marriages, this was its antithesis. As later chapters will show, their attitude was predominantly that romance was all very well as escapist stories, but life was just not like that, nor did they want it to be like that.

Despite the development of the history of sexuality as a vibrant research field, considerable challenges face the historian attempting to uncover evidence of the normal, mundane and unremarkable everyday experiences of the silent majority.[133] Thus, in James Hammerton's view, '[h]istorians have invariably

[130] Light, *Forever England*, 175.

[131] Billie Melman, *Women and the Popular Imagination in the Twenties: Flappers and Nymphs* (Basingstoke: Macmillan Press, 1988), 104. Jay Dixon, *The Romance Fiction of Mills & Boon 1909–1990s* (London: UCL Press, 1999), 134, argues that at least some of these romances were 'sexual' before the 1970s, but concedes that, '[i]t is the emotions of sex that the authors concentrate on, not the physical aspects'.

[132] Light, *Forever England*, 177.

[133] Such a history of the mute majority is a very different matter from Stephen Kern's study of the representation of love (including chapters on sex, marriage, gender and the body), in the genre of (retrospectively judged) 'classic' novels and of avant-garde art during the period 1847 to 1934. In introducing his study Kern states somewhat loosely that 'I treat the novels which are my sources primarily as a reflection of what was happening at the time they were being written' (Stephen Kern, *The Culture of Love: Victorians to Moderns* (London: Harvard University Press, 1992), 7). Yet this can hardly mean what he seems to imply – that they reflect what was happening for most people, or even for most educated people, at the time. Several of the novels he illuminatingly discusses were initially subject to critical censure, formal censorship or even banned from the public for several decades (for instance, works by D. H. Lawrence and James Joyce). As Kern explains (ibid., 5–7), his study is a commentary on the historical emergence in these two art-forms of a particular definition of 'modernity' as individual writers' and artists' endeavours to describe a state of consciousness involving continual reflection on the meaning of experiences including sex itself, corresponding to Heidegger's notion of genuine choice and 'authentic' existence. Our intellectual project in this book is in a sense the reciprocal of Kern's, in that it aims to document the history of the meaning of sex and love for the great majority of the populace, who, according to Heidegger's contemporary philosophy (*Being and Time* was published in 1927), were experiencing love and sex 'inauthentically' (meaning inarticulately, unreflexively).

found these issues of sexuality and responsibility for fertility control the most difficult of all questions to resolve'.[134] It has so far proved easier to find interesting sources for the study of the sexuality of marginal groups, or for what were considered socially unacceptable or illegal practices, through consulting medical, judicial, religious and related primary sources.[135] As Matt Houlbrook concludes, accounts of 'sex between ... married couples behind the curtain of the suburban semi are ... absent from [much of] the historical record'.[136] The emergence of the history of sexuality has been influenced by the agenda of the sexological pioneers, such as Krafft-Ebing and Sacher-Masoch, among whom 'heterosexuality itself ... only came into existence as a concept after the classical perversions'; this bias was coupled with the later development of a social history seeking to uncover the hidden voices left out of mainstream history, which has led historians to a primary focus on illicit sexual behaviour and the lives of previously marginalised groups.[137]

More recently though, a significant body of historical research has been produced on the subject of sex and marriage. Between the 1920s and the 1960s sex within marriage was much debated and much of the recent analysis of this period has focused on exploring these public debates, their implications and their effects on everyday experiences. Such studies have explored these themes by making excellent use of the literature of sex reformers and campaigners, marriage manuals and other forms of advice literature and their related correspondence, as well as resourceful use of a wide range of literary and mass media sources. Increased interest in such matters meant that by the 1940s and 1950s contemporary explorations of the effect of changing discourses about sexuality on individuals' attitudes and behaviours spawned a considerable quantity of

[134] A. James Hammerton, 'Pooterism or Partnership? Marriage and Masculine Identity in the Lower Middle Class, 1870–1920', *The Journal of British Studies* 38 (1999): 311. Martin Pugh's recent popular social history of interwar Britain spent twelve pages discussing homosexuality and just one (161–2) on heterosexuality in marriage, with a further nine pages on birth control and abortion: Martin Pugh, *We Danced All Night: A Social History of Britain Between the Wars* (London: The Bodley Head 2008), ch. 8. The pattern of coverage of these topics, by pages, is almost identical in Juliet Gardiner's *The Thirties: An Intimate History* (London: Harper Press, 2010), 560–82.

[135] Weeks, *Sex, Politics, and Society*, Frank Mort, *Dangerous Sexualities: Medico-Moral Politics in England since 1830* (London and New York: Routledge, 2000), Barbara L. Brookes, *Abortion in England, 1900–1967* (London and New York: Croom Helm, 1988), Matt Houlbrook, *Queer London: Perils and Pleasures in the Sexual Metropolis*, 1918–1957 (Chicago: University of Chicago Press, 2005), Lewis and Kiernan, 'The Boundaries between Marriage'.

[136] Matt Houlbrook, 'Sexing the History of Sexuality', *History Workshop Journal* 60, no. 1 (2005): 218.

[137] Chris Waters, 'Sexology', in *Palgrave Advances in the Modern History of Sexuality*, eds. Harry Cocks and Matt Houlbrook (Basingstoke and New York: Palgrave Macmillan, 2006), 50–6. On the later emergence of the concept of heterosexuality, see Robert Nye, 'Introduction' in *Sexuality*, ed. Robert Nye (Oxford: Oxford University Press, 1999), 14, citing the research of George Chauncey, *Gay New York: Gender, Urban Culture and the Making of the Gay Male World, 1890–1940* (New York: Basic Books, 1994), and Jonathan Ned Katz, *The Invention of Heterosexuality* (New York: Dutton Books, 1995).

surveys and sociological investigations which have provided further information for historians, such as the files and reports of Mass Observation.[138]

Prior to our own research a number of oral history studies of marriage and the family have also contributed to this literature, though in most instances the amount of material on sexual relations within marriage remains disappointingly slight, even where the attempt has been to elicit such information, often in relation to contraception.[139] Thus, from Paul Thompson's pioneering oral history of the Edwardians, through Elizabeth Roberts' and Lucinda Beier's work in early and mid-twentieth-century Lancashire, and recent work by Natalie Higgins and Margaret Williamson, we have an increasingly rich insight into the voices of women (and less frequently men) about their sexual lives from the late nineteenth century onwards.[140]

This book contributes to this growing body of historical material on marital sexuality during the earlier and middle decades of the twentieth century. In particular we will use evidence from marriages contracted both before, during and after the Second World War to investigate the subtle changes in sexual cultures during this long period. In doing so, however, we seek to move beyond the standard questions asked about sex within marriage that we consider are driven by the agenda of twentieth-century sex radicals, marriage manual writers and authors of surveys, from whom much of the previously available information originates.

138 Contemporary sources frequently drawn from in such studies include: all the studies listed in note 107 above; extracts from letters written to Marie Stopes reproduced in Marie Carmichael Stopes, *Mother England, a Contemporary History* (London: J. Bale, Sons & Danielsson Ltd, 1929), Hall, ed. *Dear Dr. Stopes*; various reports from birth control clinics such as Norman E. Himes and Vera C. Himes, 'Birth Control for the British Working Classes: A Study of the First Thousand Cases to Visit an English Birth Control Clinic', *Hospital Social Service* 19 (1929): 578–617, Lella Secor Florence, *Birth Control on Trial* (London: George Allen & Unwin Ltd, 1930), Enid Charles, *The Practice of Birth Control: An Analysis of the Birth Control Experiences of Nine Hundred Women* (London: Williams and Norgate, 1932). For historians' use of this material see, for example, Holtzman, 'The Pursuit of Married Love', Gillis, *For Better, for Worse*, Stanley, *Sex Surveyed*, Giles, *Women, Identity, and Private Life*, John R. Gillis, *A World of Their Own Making: Myth, Ritual, and the Quest for Family Values* (New York: Basic Books, 1996), Claire Langhamer, 'Love and Courtship in Mid-Twentieth-Century England', *The Historical Journal* 50, no. 1 (2007), Langhamer, 'Adultery in Post-War England', Collins, *Modern Love*, Cook, *The Long Sexual Revolution*, Hall, *Hidden Anxieties*, McKibbin, *Classes and Cultures: England, 1918–1951*, Angus McLaren, *Twentieth-Century Sexuality: A History* (Oxford: Blackwell, 1999).

139 One high-profile interview-based BBC television series with accompanying book, for instance, depicted various aspects of sexual history in Britain during the period 1900 to 1950, although the sexual relationship in marriage was not addressed as a central subject matter in any of the programmes or the chapters of the book (Humphries, *A Secret World of Sex*). Steve Humphries' work for Testimony Films has continued to use oral interviews to explore these themes. Sex within marriage was not, however, covered in depth in his work on parenthood or masculinity (Steve Humphries and Pamela Gordon, *Labour of Love: Experience of Parenthood in Britain, 1900–50* (London: Sidgwick & Jackson, 1993), Steve Humphries and Pamela Gordon, *A Man's World: From Boyhood to Manhood 1900–1960* (London: BBC Books, 1996)). A three-part investigation of marriage and sex in 2002 did not produce a related publication (Steve Humphries, *Married Love: Sex on Demand* [VHS videocassette] (London: Testimony Films for Channel 4, 2002)).

140 Thompson, *The Edwardians*, Diana Gittins, 'Women's Work and Family Size between the Wars', *Oral History* 5, no. 2 (1977), Gittins, *Fair Sex*, Roberts, *A Woman's Place*, Carl Chinn,

We contend that, as Chris Waters points out, the very framework by which society has come to understand twentieth-century changes in sexuality is intimately connected to the self-justificatory narratives of the sexologists and other campaigners who can be seen as having been originators of the field of the history of sexuality.[141] These are linear narratives which seek to demonstrate emancipation from repressed to open sexuality, and from patriarchal to companionate marriage. Embedded in so many of the available primary sources, historians have quite understandably been led by this narrative and its categories for conceptualising sexuality and changing sexual mores during the twentieth century. We take the view, by contrast, that as we do not know how far these categories were internalised or part of the ways in which other individuals thought about sex within their marriages, we also need to explore the possibility of distinct, 'lay' conceptualisations of sex and desire and find independent sources of evidence with which to do this.

In addition, we are concerned that historians have approached the history of sexuality during the twentieth century too strongly influenced by recent debates and the current agenda about sex, pleasure and gender politics.[142] Hence many of the existing histories of sexuality and marriage remain dominated by an (implicit or explicit) comparison between past and present, in which a modern framework for understanding heterosexual behaviour frames the questions asked.[143] The period between 1900 and 1960 is frequently conceptualised as the time 'in between' the 'Victorians' and the 'revolutionary' 1960s. While from a modern vantage point it is incontrovertible that the twentieth century

They Worked All Their Lives: Women of the Urban Poor in England, 1880–1939 (Manchester: Manchester University Press, 1988), Roberts, *Women and Families*, Margaret Williamson, '"Getting Off at Loftus": Sex and the Working-Class Woman, 1920–1960', *Family and Community History* 3, no. 1 (2000), Beier, *For Their Own Good*, Williamson, 'Gender, Leisure and Marriage'. Although not based on oral history, Ellen Ross, *Love and Toil: Motherhood in Outcast London, 1870–1918* (Oxford: Oxford University Press, 1993) also provides relevant evidence on family and marriage relationships in late-nineteenth-century working-class London.

141 Waters, 'Sexology', 53–4. On the complex relationship in this field between the ideological constructions of the emerging professionals, such as psychological counsellors and social workers, with their vested interests in defining normal and problematic forms of family and marriage, and the processes of social change, see David Morgan, 'Ideologies of Marriage and Family Life', in *Marriage, Domestic Life, and Social Change: Writings for Jacqueline Burgoyne, 1944–88*, ed. David Clark (London: Routledge, 1991).

142 Two of the most influential recent publications framing contemporary debates have been: Anthony Giddens, *The Transformation of Intimacy: Sexuality, Love and Eroticism in Modern Societies* (Cambridge: Polity Press, 1992), Ulrich Beck and Elisabeth Beck-Gernsheim, *The Normal Chaos of Love* (Cambridge, UK and Cambridge, MA: Polity Press; Blackwell, 1995). For empirically based alternatives and critiques of these theories in relation to sex and gender in contemporary partnerships, see Jean Duncombe and Dennis Marsden, 'Love and Intimacy: The Gender Division of Emotion and "Emotion Work": A Neglected Aspect of Sociological Discussion of Heterosexual Relationships', *Sociology* 27, no. 2 (1993): 221–41, Lynn Jamieson, 'Intimacy Transformed? A Critical Look at the "Pure Relationship"', *Sociology* 33, no. 3 (1999): 477–94.

143 Hall, *Sex, Gender and Social Change*, 23.

has seen what Lynne Segal calls a 'transformation of the sexual landscape', this also means that historians' questions are dominated by the desire to chart how this transformation took place and what form it took.[144]

For instance, Jeffrey Weeks starts his recent book by outlining the ways in which 'we are living... in the midst of a long, unfinished but profound revolution that has transformed the possibilities of living our sexual diversity and creating intimate lives'. He provides the following list to sum up the nature of this revolution: 'from welfarism to the Pill, and women's and gay liberation, from globalization, consumerism and individualization to changing patterns of family life and new forms of intimacy'.[145] In this sense, therefore, the perspective of the present and contemporary assumptions about the nature of sexual attitudes, practices and their regulation profoundly informs the ways in which historians conceptualise the whole twentieth century as a period of increasing liberation, democratisation, diversification, individualism, and so on.

In mapping and questioning the enormous changes in attitudes towards sexuality and sexual behaviour during the twentieth century, the pivotal questions asked about the period before 1960 are not only framed by the experiences, beliefs and constructions of the later period, but also historians are themselves often implicitly and sometimes explicitly seeking to contribute to the continued and vibrant debate about modern sexual cultures. Many therefore present an account of the past which assesses the positive or negative impact of these transformations on modern societies. Indeed, Jeffrey Weeks is explicit in his view of the political purpose of histories of sexuality. Determined to reject contemporary 'cultural pessimism or moral conservatism', his work is framed as a 'balance sheet' of the changes in sexual lives since 1945.[146] In response to the charge that his work is a 'whig interpretation of sexual history', which presents a journey from 'the darkness of sexual repression into sexual freedom', he retorts: 'guilty as charged. Who in their right senses would not prefer living today rather than fifty years ago?'[147] Hera Cook is also unashamedly 'whiggish' in seeing the 1960s, the arrival of the Pill and the subsequent 'sexual revolution' as a period of 'immense positive change' and in highlighting the fraught and unhappy 'emotional and sexual life of previous generations'. Through her work she seeks to demonstrate the full extent to which the sexual revolution has 'improved the lives of women in this society'.[148]

[144] Lynne Segal, 'New Battlegrounds: Genetic Maps and Sexual Politics', in *Sexuality Repositioned: Diversity and the Law*, eds. Belinda Brooks-Gordon et al. (Oxford: Hart Publishing, 2004), 68.

[145] Jeffrey Weeks, *The World We Have Won: The Remaking of Erotic and Intimate Life* (London and New York: Routledge, 2007), i.

[146] Ibid. [147] Ibid., 4.

[148] Cook, *The Long Sexual Revolution*, 340.

Important, insightful and well-researched as the work of these historians is, what this book seeks to contribute is an attempt to analyse the experiences of those marrying during the first half of the twentieth century by excavating and understanding the values and beliefs that they held as a means of appreciating their choices and desires, their pleasures, disappointments and anxieties. Drawing upon Joan Scott's call for historians to 'historicise experience' and reject the notion that experience can be inferred from circumstances, we will interrogate individuals' own constructions of their experiences through an investigation of the frameworks and convictions by which they lived their lives, the values which informed their choices and which formed part of the contemporary contested, contradictory and incoherent ways in which sex was described and constructed around them.[149]

Of course, there is a danger that this sort of history, which pays close attention to the ways individuals lived their lives, and charts their own ideals, opinions and self-assessments can either romanticise the past or suggest that 'culture dictated the meanings attributed to sexual behaviour' (when politics, ideologies and economic relations were all, of course, equally important influences).[150] However, outlining, for example, the myriad ways in which individuals responded to experiences of premarital sex or pregnancy, or reacted to wedding nights for which they were unrehearsed, or responded to the uncertainties of contraception does not amount to a legitimation or a restoration of the values held by those interviewed; nor is it to deny the existence of sexual problems, dilemmas and traumas in the past – there is certainly plenty of that in the ensuing testimony.

Presenting evidence through the eyes of those interviewed, therefore, is not to sentimentalise or engage in acts of nostalgia. Our approach is not dissimilar to that of Matt Houlbrook's 2005 book, for instance, which presents many of the (lost) pleasures and joys of 'queer' life in London in the 1930s, despite the attendant secrecy, anxieties, fears of persecution or periods in police cells. Houlbrook has been charged with (and indeed has professed himself guilty of) nostalgia, yet the central strength of Houlbrook's book is his attention to uncovering the experiences of 'queer' men in the 1930s by interrogating and understanding the frameworks and categories through which individuals understood their lives, and to uncovering the historically specific ways in which those values dominated the way lives were experienced and lived.[151]

[149] Joan Scott, 'The Evidence of Experience', *Critical Inquiry* 1, no. 7 (1991): 773–97. By contrast, critical appraisals of the legacies of the 1960s might be used to prompt a range of different research questions and approaches to the history of sexuality. See, Dagmar Herzog, 'Sexuality in the Postwar West', *Journal of Modern History* 78, no.1 (2006), 144–71, esp. 166–170.

[150] Cocks and Houlbrook, eds. *Palgrave Advances in the Modern History of Sexuality*, 6.

[151] Houlbrook, *Queer London*. These issues were discussed by Matt Houlbrook and Jeffrey Weeks on *Thinking Allowed*, BBC Radio 4, 26 October 2005. The interview can be heard at www.bbc.co.uk/radio4/factual/thinkingallowed/thinkingallowed_20051026.shtml (accessed 4 December 2008). For a summary of this encounter and its methodological implications see, Chris Waters, 'Distance and Desire in the New British Queer History', *GLQ-NEW YORK* 14, no. 1 (2008).

In adopting this same approach in this book we do not dismiss the issues of selection, omission, distortion and retrospection identified by critics of the oral history methodology. Indeed, we recognise that the oral histories of sexual experiences within this book do not provide pure or direct empirical facts about the lives, experiences and beliefs of men and women marrying in the first half of the twentieth century.[152] However, the fact that such narratives are imbued with layers of cultural consciousness, framed by myth and archetype, stereotypes and communal conventions, idealisation and nostalgia is central to the analysis. Stories are marked by 'cultural imperatives' through which individuals asserted their conformity to or rejection of codes of identity and respectability.[153] Not only is it important to recognise that the narratives of those interviewed are 'strategic and performative articulations' but also that it is through the interrogation of these narratives that we can uncover the categories through which marriage, love and sex were understood and internalised. The elucidation of these categories will be shown as key to the understanding of past experiences.[154]

In taking this approach to understanding the sex lives of individuals in the past, many of the standard questions usually asked about the first sixty years of the twentieth century are changed. It is usually taken as self-evident that we would want to know details of individuals' sexual practices – when did people have sex, did people have sex before or outside of marriage, how often did people have sex and what sorts of sexual practices were engaged in? These are the sorts of questions which are common to most sexual surveys and answers to these questions are seen as central to understanding sexual experiences, attitudes and emotions.[155]

We argue that these questions are just as much part of the 'liberationist' discourse as terms like 'repression' which, since the work of Foucault and his contemporaries, have been widely claimed to have been an integral category constructed by the nineteenth- and twentieth-century sexological project. Yet

[152] See for example, Matt Houlbrook, who wondered, given that rich and detailed sources on the private nature of twentieth-century marriages tend to be subjective, selective and often retrospective, whether it is simply impossible to know anything 'of the messy, bodily ordinariness of sex in the past' (Houlbrook, 'Sexing the History of Sexuality', 219).

[153] Judy Giles, '"Playing Hard to Get": Working-Class Women, Sexuality and Respectability in Britain, 1918–40', *Women's History Review* 1, no. 2 (1992): 243.

[154] Harry Cocks, 'Review: The Growing Pains of the History of Sexuality', *Journal of Contemporary History* 39, no. 4 (2004): 665. For an excellent introduction to the importance of studying sexual experiences through the interrogation of contemporary concepts and categories and the complex methodological challenges this poses historians see, Cocks and Houlbrook, eds. *Palgrave Advances in the Modern History of Sexuality*.

[155] Kaye Wellings, *Sexual Behaviour in Britain: The National Survey of Sexual Attitudes and Lifestyles* (London and New York: Penguin Books, 1994), Julia A. Ericksen and Sally A. Steffen, *Kiss and Tell: Surveying Sex in the Twentieth Century* (Cambridge, MA: Harvard University Press, 1999).

Stephen Kern has recently and cogently challenged the validity of the use of the notion of 'repression' itself, arguing that since 'repression is an unconscious mental process' it 'is pretty near impossible to document historically'.[156] Despite both this and a longer-standing recognition that it is historically anachronistic to characterise sexual cultures as permissive, liberated or repressive, these ideas continue to dominate debates about changing twentieth-century sexual cultures, in particular through continued assumptions about the types of sexual behaviour characterised as progressive or conducive to pleasure. Implicit within these questions are beliefs about the intrinsic nature of sexual pleasure and the mechanics of desire.

Thus, the modern rhetoric of sex has constructed a model of 'good' sex which is inextricably linked to liberationist values, such as, in Lynne Segal's summary, 'the importance of sexual openness, indeed the importance of sex as pleasure, sex for its own sake alone'. It is on these terms that sexual experiences are often judged or examined.[157] In this sense a sexual culture that was not 'open' or did not value 'sex for its own sake', i.e. the antithesis to the constructed ideal of modern sensuality, is automatically pre-defined as bad sex. Perhaps it was. But it is this very link from behaviour to the emotional realities of experience that all too often remains unexamined.[158]

Instead of charting individuals' behaviour in this way, this research seeks to explore individuals' reactions to, reflections on, internalisations and rejections of the sexual culture in which they lived.[159] While remaining attuned to the problems and displeasures of factors such as conventions of silence, feelings of ignorance, regulatory codes and sanctions against transgressions,

[156] Stephen Kern, 'When Did the Victorian Period End? Relativity, Sexuality, Narrative', *Journal of Victorian Culture* 11, no. 2 (2006): 329. Kern argues that, '[s]tudies of Victorian sexuality typically confuse three ways that sexuality can be constrained – oppression, suppression, and repression'. While sexual oppression is a constraint with an agent and subjects who are being oppressed, and sexual suppression is a conscious process, Kern points out that sexual repression, on the other hand, is supposed to occur at the *un*conscious level. According to Kern, therefore '[i]t is difficult to assess whether Victorians were sexually repressed, using that term in a strict way, because repression is an unconscious mental process that is pretty near impossible to document historically. But one can document levels of sexual oppression and suppression, and in the Victorian period they were high' (Kern, 'When did the Victorian Period End?', 327–8).

[157] Segal, *New Battlegrounds*, 68.

[158] This is in part what Hera Cook calls upon historians to do when she urges the need for histories which 'investigate and question emotions' (Hera Cook, 'Sexuality and Contraception in Modern England: Doing the History of Reproductive Sexuality', *Journal of Social History* 40, no. 4 (2007): 920).

[159] Of course a clear issue here is the ways in which individuals who have lived through the entire twentieth century, during which time they heard and even contributed to changing debates about sex behaviour, and who are subsequently interviewed at the end of the twentieth century, cannot provide pure or unmediated access to their values and experiences in the past, although many do reflect on changing views and ideals. See section 'What's in it for them?' above.

we seek to avoid bringing prior assumptions about sexual practices and their experienced significance into the interpretation. We hope to resist the tendency to look for modern forms of pleasure in the past and find its absence indicative of 'repression' or inhibition. Rather we hope to reconstruct something of the emotional context through which individuals related to each other and the ways in which historically specific conceptions of marital roles, beliefs about gender, notions of normality and what was natural, ideas about health and well-being and expectations of sexual behaviour influenced the varied choices made by individuals and how they felt about them. In particular, reconstructing the importance of privacy to this generation, and the various ways in which marital privacy was understood, will be shown to be crucial in understanding how many individuals approached both the stresses of sex within marriage and how they conceptualised its pleasures.

This book's scope and its limitations

As stated at the outset this is a pioneering study presenting our interpretation of some new oral history evidence about sex in marriage. It is not a definitive study of sex in the twentieth century, nor, certainly, does it attempt to provide a comprehensive approach to all aspects of the history of sex in marriage during the early and mid-twentieth century – a quixotic ambition. Nor, of course, do the subjects addressed in the following chapters by any means exhaust the evidence on marriage, sex and love which the interview transcripts contain. The research for this book was designed as a study of sex in marriage; it is not a study of the unmarried, the separated, the divorced, lesbians or male homosexuals, although a number of the interviewees had experienced separation or divorce.[160] The project was designed to interview both middle-class and working-class persons of both sexes, including a sample of each class among those who lived in the north in a characteristic industrial city and those who lived in the south in a representative affluent community, these being the two most populous and socially contrasting types of place found in interwar and mid-twentieth-century England.[161]

[160] Emily msf/kf/bl/#13; Rose msf/kf/bl/#21 (three times); Hilda msf/kf/bl/#50; Gay msf/kf/ht/#13; Judith msf/kf/ht/#33; Reg msf/kf/ht/#36.

[161] See Appendix A. Of course, rural communities represent a third, contrasting type of place, although only a small fraction of the national population both resided in and drew their livings from genuinely rural environments by the mid-twentieth century. The 1951 census showed 80.7 per cent of the population of England and Wales residing in 965 urban local authorities and 19.3 per cent in 474 rural district councils (David Marsh, *The Changing Social Structure of England and Wales, 1871–1961* (London: Routledge & Kegan Paul, 1965), 107–8, Table 33). However, by 1951 the majority of those living in these rural district councils were not, in fact, separate in their lifestyles and working practices from the urban, industrial and commercial economy. Thus, the proportion of the national workforce of men and women over age 14

This book is something akin to an ethnographic study of the marital sexuality of a group of socially diverse interviewees drawn from a common historical period, who mainly lived in two regionally contrasting contexts. Due to the methodology, a relatively small number of individuals have generated a large, rich and complex body of evidence to present. Demographically they were all members of the last marriage cohorts involved in the nation's secular fertility decline – at the end of a sequence of several marriage cohorts, starting with those born c.1850–60 (marrying c.1870–80), each of which tended to have significantly smaller families than the previous cohort.[162]

Given the limited number of respondents, and the great individual diversity in the accounts, along with the gender and class differences of those interviewed – a deliberate feature of the research design – it does not make sense to try to use this testimony to attempt to mount a systematic study of change over time. When citing the interviewees' evidence we attempt throughout to contextualise their views by giving brief biographical information always including their year of birth. This often tends to demonstrate various ways in which gender, class and regional cultures were associated with differences in recollections of sexual attitudes and practices. However, differences between older and younger informants (of the same social class and region) were often far more indistinct. What was more evident was the extent to which broadly similar values were often articulated by persons, whether they were born in the 1900s or in the 1920s, whether they married in the 1920s or the 1940s. As discussed, there was quite a strong sense, though it was by no means uniform, in which the interviewees tended to sympathise with and identify more with the private and restrained sexual values they ascribed to their parents' generation, rather than with what they believed to be the more liberal, open and permissive practices of their children and, especially, their grandchildren. There was a suggestion in the evidence that a handful of the very youngest interviewees (who were all born after 1926) tended to exhibit a somewhat distinct set of values and experiences, though there were also some of the older interviewees who shared in this.

In her recent study of the much longer chronological range of working-class Lancashire interviews collected by herself and Elizabeth Roberts, which include significant numbers born in every decade from the 1880s to the 1940s, Lucinda Beier has concluded that 'attitudes towards communication about sex

actually employed in agriculture in 1951 was only 5.2 per cent (Marsh, *The Changing Social Structure*, 135–6, Table 35).

[162] Conventionally to facilitate the analysis of changing reproductive patterns, demographers sectionalise populations into cohorts – all those individuals who experienced the same vital event of birth or marriage during the same time period. Cohorts can be defined as individual year-groups but more usually, when referring to large-scale demographic changes, marriage cohorts are referred to by decades.

changed dramatically between the generations born before and after about 1930'.[163] Our study, which includes middle-class respondents as well as working-class Lancashire interviewees, tends to confirm this, in the sense that we have detected little systematic difference between our younger and older interviewees, who were almost all born several years before 1930, in other words before the watershed birth date of 1930, as detected in Beier's work.

Although not included in Beier's list of the main reasons for that watershed, it is a strong implication of some of the findings in our study, rehearsed below in Chapters 2, 3 and 6, that the gradually increasing provision of sex education in secondary schools after 1944 may have been an important and necessary (though probably not sufficient) institutional shift accounting for these changed attitudes towards communication about sex.[164] In fact Beier provides a considerable amount of positive evidence to support this. All the working-class interviewees she cites, who discuss the way in which school sex education assisted them, were born later than the working-class interviewees in our study.[165] As Beier's respondents attest, school sex education began to equip the nation's rising generation with a different set of values and attitudes towards sexual and reproductive knowledge, providing them with the elements of a publicly acknowledged respectable discourse about the sexual functioning of their own bodies, including such key issues, for adolescents, as menstruation and masturbation.

In the absence of such institutionalised provision of sex education, Part I of this book explores how informants in our study said they came to understand and experience sex when young and before marriage. Chapter 2 examines how respondents present the processes of learning about sex in childhood and youth. Its findings challenge any straightforward acceptance of the notion of sexual 'ignorance' among this generation. It is shown how individuals of both sexes in this society contrived actively to construct a much-valued notion of sexual 'innocence' among the young. Working-class young women wanting to preserve their respectability were encouraged to steer clear of any discussion of sex, even in confiding relationships with mothers or friends. Middle-class interviewees by contrast, mostly secondary school–educated, were more comfortable presenting themselves as having acquired some book knowledge of the mechanics of sex before marriage but were careful to maintain that they were innocent of the physical act itself. Men of both classes presented themselves as

[163] Beier, *For Their Own Good*, 210.

[164] Beier lists instead other interesting and no doubt also important factors: 'the medicalization of sex, family limitation, and reproduction' along with 'changes in the composition of and need for respectability in working-class neighbourhoods' (ibid.).

[165] The oldest interviewee recalling his own experience in Beier's study was 'Mr Christy', born in 1928, with most interviewees cited referring to experience in Lancashire secondary schools in the mid-1950s. Ibid., 236–9.

playfully challenging the public discourse of silence and as actively struggling to 'find out' what sex was and curious to see what a woman's body looked like, though remaining 'innocent' of adult sexual activity.

Chapter 3 focuses on the place of sex in courtship. Here there were very significant differences between the classes in their testimony. Contrary to the implications of the kind of contemporary class prejudices which motivated Mass Observation's well-known attempted surveys of working-class premarital sexuality in Blackpool, middle-class respondents reported a wider range of premarital physical sexual behaviour with their future marriage partners than did working-class respondents. However, middle-class couples also consistently presented themselves as jointly being very careful to avoid sexual intercourse itself before marriage. By contrast among the working-class interviewees the policing of a boy's wandering hands was presented as primarily the girl's responsibility and as an explicit test of her 'innocence' and respectability. However, having passed this initial test, consent to sex was then construed as mutual consent to get married and was much more likely to result in full sexual intercourse before marriage than was typical among the middle classes.

Part II examines what informants had to say about the meanings of love in relation to courtship and marriage. Chapter 4 examines interviewees' expectations about marriage, presented in the context of choices of whom, when and why to marry. The theme of the rise of the ideals of romantic love during the twentieth century, associated with its increasing depiction on the silver screen, particularly in films emanating from Hollywood, is addressed here. Respondents' ideas about romance and romantic love are examined, showing that both classes held to primarily pragmatic views about partner choices and marriage decisions. Only among some middle-class male interviewees was there some endorsement for romantic ideals as motivating their choices of marriage partners.

Chapter 5 explores interviewees' understandings of the central relationship in marriage through their answers to questions about what makes for good, loving marriages or for their opposite. Here the thesis of the rise of companionate marriage is the dominant theme in the historiography, as already mentioned. It is argued that notions of 'companionate' intimacy feature much less prominently in the interviewees' views of love in their own marriage and of what makes marriages work. Instead they emphasised ideas about the importance of working at a balance between caring and sharing. There was little difference between middle- and working-class respondents in their views on this. Each partner should be effective in bringing their quite different, strongly gendered contributions to the marriage; but it was also important that there should be genuine emotional sharing of their consumer and status aspirations and mutual support in bearing the burdens and difficulties of bringing up a family. Lest it be imagined that the evidence to be presented here will constitute simply an encomium to the bliss of marriage from a selected set of fortunate survivors looking back from old age with rose-tinted spectacles, it should be pointed out that the evidence of these ideals came through as much in testimony about difficulties and bitter memories of marital unhappiness and failure, as through fond recollections of loved partners.

Part III proceeds, on the basis of the contextualising knowledge established in Parts I and II, to explore testimony about the experience of sex in relation to love in marriage. Chapter 6 presents evidence on the difficulties which marriages could encounter, by focusing on the relationship between sex and birth control and how this affected the sexual relationship within marriages. The oral history testimony shows how all forms of contraception available to married couples in this era – largely before the lubricated latex condom or the female contraceptive pill – necessarily involved various aesthetic compromises and sexual difficulties for one or other or for both partners. It was not the case that either male or female barrier methods were seen by these interviewees as self-evidently superior to 'old-fashioned' coitus interruptus or even as being preferable to simple abstinence, as the prestigious, contemporary official enquiry, the Royal Commission on Population of 1944–9, fallaciously asserted. It is shown that there were quite distinctive gendered, class-related and regional codes of sexual and contraceptive knowledge, beliefs and practice. Middle-class interviewees were much more likely to present an account of having jointly decided on their contraceptive method when they got married. However, they were also much more likely to present accounts of such serious unresolved disagreements over who should be responsible for contraception later in the marriage that sometimes this ended in their separation or divorce. By contrast working-class respondents quite consistently assumed that husbands would provide the contraception. While there were far fewer serious disagreements focused on the method of birth control used, this could and did lead to severe anxiety for wives desperate to avoid another pregnancy, and also to fearfulness or disinclination towards sex, in respect for their wives' worries, among husbands, too.

Chapter 7 explores perceptions of bodies. It finds that the attitudes of respondents of both sexes and both classes were not focused on the aesthetics of the sexual aspects of their partners' bodies or of the bodies of the opposite sex in general. Instead, they were positively and keenly aware of reading bodies as clues to character, status and class. Consequently they were attentive to appearance and dress, rather than to body forms and figures. Physical appearance was important in denoting healthiness, also personal hygiene and cleanliness of bodies was highly valued. The style and cut of the clothes adorning the body were judged of particular significance but the body itself was a 'natural' endowment. The concluding section of the chapter shows how these understandings of the body informed attitudes towards sexual practices in marriage, with healthiness and hygiene as important as aesthetic considerations.

Chapter 8 challenges the academic and popular view in post-1960s histories that the widespread social acceptance of male conjugal rights, sexual ignorance and codes of privacy in this period necessarily resulted in sexual relationships that were limited, erotically inept or unfulfilling. It was certainly the case that *some* from these generations did experience sexual problems as part of a world in which sex was neither openly discussed in public, nor between husband and wife, and in which ignorance and gendered inequalities could lead to tensions and unhappiness within marriage. Yet later critiques of the supposed restricted nature of pre-1960s sexualities have often missed other ways in which sexual relations in this period might have been fulfilling, or meaningful. This is in part because these approaches have overly focused on ideas of individual pleasure (and orgasm) as *the* key indicator of successful sex, and in part because these generations did not have a language of individual pleasure upon which to draw when making sense of their sexual experiences, and thus did not provide later historians and sociologists with an easily recognisable discourse on sexual fulfilment. Couples often reported sex which was satisfying, but many (especially women) refused to articulate their experiences in the celebratory frameworks of individual pleasure which later generations could easily understand. Indeed, narratives of personal satisfaction were avoided; they ran counter to value systems in which the purpose of sex was connected to collective fulfilment in the marriage, reciprocal exchange and the performance of marital duties and responsibilities. This chapter will use testimony to explore how these generations evaluated what was good or bad sex. Above all, respondents revealed a world in which notions of duty, natural desire, spontaneity and privacy were central to their achievement of marital pleasure and fulfilment. The idea that sex was a private matter was for many linked to erotic satisfaction, dynamism and tenderness born of the secret and personal knowledge of each other.

Chapter 9 interrogates the ways in which interviewees have come to terms with the transformation of British sexual culture and behaviour since the 1960s, which has challenged the sexual codes that dominated their early lives. Interviews were full of ambivalent comparisons between past and present which many used to mount a reflective and considered defence of their own past values and behaviours. In doing so, they placed their own values in sharper relief. Turning the concept of liberated sex on its head, many articulated a version of personal sexual fulfilment based on private sexual creativity and mutual self-realisation behind closed doors. Comfortable with their own marital relationships, most, though not all, were unwilling to accept as valid the attacks on their sexual values which had emerged in the latter half of the twentieth century.

Thus, the book has been structured to focus primarily on how respondents see themselves as having learned about sex and their bodies in childhood and during courtship and their sexual relationship during the fertile years of their marriages. Partly this reflects the shared bias of the two authors, who came to this project hoping to learn more about the gradual trend towards declining marital fertility over the previous decades, which culminated in this period. There are also, inevitably, a number of limitations in having chosen to research the subject in this way and to produce the book in this form. It does not, for instance, attempt to present a detailed account of changing sexuality over the whole course of interviewees' marriages including the later stages or the experiences of ageing.[166] Second, the focus in what follows is on the respondents' own experiences in marriage and evaluations of their sexual relationships, not on their wider attitudes towards sexuality, so there is only a very limited amount of material on homosexuality, for instance. Third, this book has not attempted to present individuals' experiences in a structured way relating to the historical events they lived through. There is, therefore, no chapter here on whether or not the respondents see the Second World War as a time of sexual licence and freedom (certainly, they do not generally present it as such, as far as their accounts of their own lives are concerned).[167]

As stated at the outset, the main purpose of this book is to use this rich and nuanced evidence to explore alternative viewpoints from those which have already been well aired and debated in the historical literature. Our approach has been, through listening, to attempt to understand in their own terms the personal experiences of sex in marriage among the diverse group of

[166] For recent studies of this, see Alice S. Rossi, ed. *Sexuality across the Life Course* (Chicago and London: University of Chicago Press, 1994). Note that even well-informed contemporaries of our respondents did not necessarily view sex as an activity to be expected from those beyond childbearing age. The following statement published in 1951 by two leading, psychologically trained researchers of marriage, Eliot Slater and Moya Woodside, strikes a reader today as reflecting quite surprising assumptions: 'We note with astonishment that men and women who have passed their fiftieth year, and have long lost pretensions to physical attraction, can still derive satisfaction and happiness from sexual relations with one another, and remain for each other sexually attractive objects' (Slater and Woodside, *Patterns of Marriage*, 162). Woodside was 44 years old when this was published and Slater was 47.

[167] See the well-balanced account in ch. 3, 'My Faithless English Rose', of Alan Allport's *Demobbed: Coming Home after the Second World War* (Hew Haven: Yale University Press, 2009). Allport argues, after reviewing the press stories and the statistics of illegitimacy, divorce and various other contemporary studies, that 'despite all the infamy attached to wartime sexual adventures, we have virtually no way of knowing how common they actually were' (ibid., 93). Allport concludes that by the Second World War the shift in British general cultural values, including gender relations, towards temperance, restraint and respect for law and order was probably the most significant influence, resulting in temporarily widespread concern and anxiety over faithlessness among partners, rather than widespread actual illicit behaviour and adultery; this view would also be consistent with the interpretation of the post-war era offered by Claire Langhamer, 'Adultery in Post-War England'.

individuals whose generosity of spirit allowed us access to private details of their lives that many said they had not previously spoken about. The several hundreds of hours of testimony drawn upon for this study provide, we believe, a unique insight into the intimate life of a generation whose experiences are now rapidly passing on into history.

Part I

What was sex?

2 The facts of life: learning about sex in childhood and youth

This chapter explores the ways in which young people growing up between the late 1910s and the early 1940s learned about reproduction and sex in the context of a public culture which avoided explicit reference to the subject and where the only official information available related to potential health dangers. In order to preserve the innocence of its young women, British society and popular culture during the first half of the twentieth century was constructed so as to exclude as far as possible all explicit references to sexual intercourse from both public and even private discourse within the family, particularly during the first decades of the twentieth century.[1] Nevertheless, society did not *insist* on male innocence, though it was as important for a young man's honour as for a young woman's not to be held publicly responsible for a pregnancy in the community, unless he was prepared to go through with marriage.[2] Indeed, it was accepted

[1] For a stimulating exposition of the wider historical context in which this development occurred, see the classic study by Elias: *The Civilizing Process*, 136–60. On the way in which in the pre-welfare state era this public silence on sexual matters was closely linked to a 'dread of pre-marital pregnancy' in working-class communities and the harsh sanctions which parents were capable of exacting on daughters who brought the family's respectability into disrepute in this way by expelling them to the workhouse, see Beier's oral history evidence: Beier, *For Their Own Good*, 221–8. See also Sally Alexander, 'The Mysteries and Secrets of Women's Bodies: Sexual Knowledge in the First Half of the Twentieth Century', in *Modern Times: Reflections on a Century of English Modernity*, eds. Mica Nava and Alan O'Shea (London: Routledge, 1996), 164–6, Lucinda McCray Beier, '"We Were Green as Grass": Learning About Sex and Reproduction in Three Working-Class Lancashire Communities, 1900–1970', *Social History of Medicine* 16, no. 3 (2003): 468, Bingham, *Gender, Modernity, and the Popular Press*, 157, 168, Joanna Bourke, *Working Class Cultures in Britain 1890–1960: Gender, Class, and Ethnicity* (London and New York: Routledge, 1994), 33–5, Sutton, *We Didn't Know Aught*, ch. 6. Among the working classes the anxiety over a daughter becoming encumbered with an illegitimate child had grown enormously since the framing of the infamous 'bastardy clauses' of the Poor Law Amendment Act of 1834: Gillis, *For Better, for Worse*, 239–41. This had made a widely used earlier practice of seeking financial support through an affiliation order from the father of an illegitimate child practically impossible, consequently throwing all the burden for supporting the single mother and her child on her and her family, alone, while her own chances of becoming independent through marriage were of course compromised by the increased sense of stigma attaching to her. See Anthony Brundage, *The English Poor Laws, 1700–1930* (Basingstoke and New York: Palgrave, 2002), 68–9, Lynn Hollen Lees, *The Solidarities of Strangers: The English Poor Laws and the People, 1700–1948* (Cambridge and New York: Cambridge University Press, 1998), 141–2.

[2] Bourke, *Working Class Cultures*, 31, Gillis, *For Better, for Worse*, 255–9.

that somehow young men should and would acquire the necessary knowledge prior to marriage. Crucially, therefore, men and women offer very different narratives of how they responded to the culture of ignorance surrounding sex. Where a young woman, determined to be virtuous, knew it was safest to hold to a strategy of preserving her innocence, a respectable young man needed to acquire a degree of knowledge without being morally tainted by it. Through narratives of actively negotiating their ignorance, both women and men in the interviews asserted their respectable social identities and their distinctively gendered responses to the moral frameworks set up around them.

Men's and women's accounts reveal the variety of ways in which sexual knowledge was acquired within the context of a pervasive public culture of ignorance. Many respondents showed that they had in fact built up a degree of knowledge about sexual matters while simultaneously proclaiming themselves to be 'innocent'. Stories of ignorance and narratives of discovery reveal the status and meaning of knowledge; and analysis of these narratives exposes individuals' social identities as much as the complexities of the experiences of this generation. In drawing out this more complex picture we are not simply arguing that the prevalent consensus that there was a culture of ignorance has concealed a range of information that was actually available. Nor is it being argued here that, despite the silence of parents and the education system, there were other satisfactory sources of information readily available. Rather, our evidence demonstrates that it is the very co-existence of narratives which on the one hand revealed the varied ways in which individuals pieced together an account of the mechanics of sex and reproduction, while at the same time asserting the totality of sexual ignorance, that reveals how the process of discovering sexual information was intimately linked to interviewees' gender identities.[3] Thus, instead of viewing sexual knowledge as a simple matter of acquiring basic information or not, the oral history evidence shows how the moral worlds of individuals of both sexes are embedded in their descriptions of how they acquired sexual information.

A culture of sexual ignorance?

The view that sexual ignorance and reticence prevailed among the generations born around the turn of the twentieth century is widely accepted in both popular and academic histories and was certainly the belief of those at

[3] As Sally Alexander has put it, 'Sexual knowledge is fundamental to the formation of the self; it tells us who we are, man or woman, and what that means in a given culture' (Alexander, 'The Mysteries and Secrets of Women's Bodies', 161).

the time who campaigned against it.[4] Most historical studies have concurred, emphasising that the available evidence, such as it is, indicates profound and widespread ignorance over sexual matters among the young of all classes during the late nineteenth and early twentieth centuries. Memoirs, oral histories and personal reminiscence are commonly used to establish the reality and experiences of a culture of carefully policed ignorance throughout this period.[5]

Thus, Elizabeth Roberts' pioneering oral history research, which interviewed 160 women and men mostly born before the Great War between 1880 and 1914 in Barrow, Lancaster and Preston, found that '[d]iscussion or even mention of sexual matters was not only lacking in respectability: it was verging on the immoral'; and that, '[t]he virtually total ban on the discussion of sexual matters applied to both boys and girls; both grew up equally uninformed'.[6] Leap and Hunter similarly found, among informants born between 1884 and 1923, that '[i]f most women knew little about sex, they knew even less about contraception'.[7] On the basis of eighty-five working-class interviews in Birmingham among those born on average slightly later than Roberts' sample, Carl Chinn agreed that '[s]ex was not a matter for public, nor very often intimate discussion, and sex education for the children of the urban poor remained totally inadequate throughout the 1920s and 1930s'.[8] Furthermore, Sally Alexander has argued that even in the 1920s '[i]gnorance was not confined to the poor or ill-educated': while Vera Brittain looked back on herself in 1921 as having had a 'sophisticated knowledge' when compared with the 'romantic

[4] Ibid., 161–75, Cook, *The Long Sexual Revolution*, ch. 7, Richard Davenport-Hines, *Sex, Death and Punishment: Attitudes to Sex and Sexuality in Britain since the Renaissance* (London: Collins, 1990), Humphries, *A Secret World of Sex*, Mort, *Dangerous Sexualities*, esp. Part Four, Simon Szreter, 'Victorian Britain, 1837–1963: Towards a Social History of Sexuality', *Journal of Victorian Culture* 1 (1996): 136–49, Thompson, *The Edwardians*, 57, Weeks, *Sex, Politics, and Society*.

[5] Beier, 'We Were Green as Grass', 461–80, Evelyn Faulkner, '"Powerless to Prevent Him": Attitudes of Married Working-Class Women in the 1920s and the Rise of Sexual Power', *Local Population Studies* 49 (1992): 51–61, Roberts, *A Woman's Place*, Roberts, *Women and Families*, Ross, *Love and Toil*, 98–101, Williamson, 'Getting Off at Loftus', 5–17. Thompson, unusually, has almost nothing on this topic, apart from a couple of passing references to silence from parents (56) and ignorance among young women (301) (Thompson, *The Edwardians*).

[6] Roberts, *A Woman's Place*, 15–16.

[7] Nicky Leap and Billie Hunter, *The Midwife's Tale: An Oral History from Handywoman to Professional Midwife* (London: Scarlet Press, 1993), 83 and see ch. 4, 'Women's Knowledge about the Facts of Life'. Leap and Hunter interviewed thirty-two informants, thirteen of whom had worked as midwives, were all born between 1884 and 1923 and drawn from all over the country.

[8] Chinn, *They Worked All Their Lives*, 143. The informants cited in this book were born between 1892 and 1937 (ibid.,169–172).

ignorance' of the pre-war era, other equally 'advanced' and highly educated young women, such as the Bloomsbury writer Frances Partridge or the young Fabian, Margaret Cole, still recalled their absolute ignorance when entering university in the early 1920s.[9]

The evidence for widespread ignorance is very strongly rooted, not just in today's historiography but also in the contemporary learned and scientific literature of the period, produced by the sexual progressives who challenged it.[10] Part of the justification for the work of the pioneering sexologists from the late nineteenth century onwards was the rationalist denunciation of 'Victorian' codes of silence among the wider public. Their fight to dispel ignorance in the rest of society in order to promote greater sexual understanding in marriage continued to provide a progressive motivating rationale for the authors of marriage and sex guidance and birth control manuals throughout the interwar period and beyond.[11]

In 1922, the marriage guidance writer Leonora Eyles introduced her chapter on 'The Sex Problem' with a reported discussion with the wife of a carpenter in Staffordshire, married with seven daughters, who confessed of her marriage, 'I could put up with anything but the going to bed side of it', a quote which Eyles followed with her witness's statement that 'I had been brought up in profound and beautiful ignorance of sex.'[12] Marie Stopes (1880–1958), who made it her personal crusade to dispel this widespread ignorance with her sexually explicit, easy-to-read guide to *Married Love*, published in 1918, famously claimed that she had had to spend weeks in the British Library before she realised that despite being married she was still a virgin.[13]

[9] Alexander, 'The Mysteries and Secrets of Women's Bodies', 166 and 173. In 1924 Virginia Woolf was still unable to face the embarrassment of publicly purchasing sanitary towels for herself (Harrison, 'The Public and the Private', 343).

[10] McLaren, *Twentieth-Century Sexuality*, 53–4.

[11] On the late nineteenth- and early twentieth-century publications of pioneer sexologists, such as Edward Carpenter, Havelock Ellis and Stella Browne see, for an introduction, Hall, *Sex, Gender and Social Change*, Porter and Hall, *The Facts of Life*, Part II. On Browne, see Sheila Rowbotham, *A New World for Women: Stella Browne, Socialist Feminist* (London: Pluto Press, 1977). After Stopes (see next but one footnote), other leading interwar popularising figures attempting to dispel ignorance with their publications included, for instance, Chesser, *Love without Fear*, Leonora Eyles, *Commonsense About Sex* (London: Victor Gollancz, 1933), Helena Wright, *The Sex Factor in Marriage: A Book for Those Who Are or Are About to Be Married* (London: N. Douglas, 1930). For an important recent study of twentieth-century sex manuals and guides, see Cook, *The Long Sexual Revolution*, Part II.

[12] Leonora Eyles, *The Woman in the Little House* (London: G. Richards Ltd, 1922), 129–30.

[13] Marie Carmichael Stopes, *Contraception (Birth Control) Its Theory, History and Practice; a Manual for the Medical and Legal Professions* (London: J. Bale, Sons & Danielsson, Limited, 1923), Marie Carmichael Stopes, *Married Love or Love in Marriage* (London: Putnam, 1918), Marie Carmichael Stopes, *Wise Parenthood, a Sequel To 'Married Love'; a Book for Married People* (London: A. C. Fifield, 1918). For an excellent introduction to Stopes' sequence of publications and her publishing strategy, see Geppert, 'Divine Sex, Happy Marriage, Regenerated

The available historical evidence suggests that there were probably some in the middle class who were better informed by the 1920s and that perhaps from about this decade onwards there may have been some increased access to knowledge more widely in society but, if so, it was a very gradual process. While Maureen Sutton's interviews in rural Lincolnshire resulted in her concluding that ignorance prevailed throughout the period from the 1920s through to the 1950s, Lucinda Beier's recent re-analysis of Roberts' oral history testimonies from urban Lancashire, along with a further ninety-eight working-class interviews in the same three towns conducted in the late 1980s with a younger generation of respondents, produced some signs of change in this respect in these communities.[14] Beier re-affirmed the reports of a lack of information from parents or schools among those born before 1930 but found that among the sixty-six youngest respondents, born after 1930, there was some sign of more communication at schools and between the generations.[15]

While the dominant theme of ignorance also permeates the leading general historical accounts of sexual culture in this period right through to the 1950s,[16] it is notable that in his analytical survey, with its primary focus on the differences between classes in their cultures, Ross McKibbin has identified a distinction between the working and the middle classes in the way they acquired sexual knowledge, an observation that will be confirmed and further explored in this chapter.[17] Similarly David Vincent portrays a growing class distinction in this respect in interwar Britain and Hera Cook has argued that prior to the First World War profound ignorance was 'common amongst single people of all classes, but during the inter-war decades profound ignorance ceased to exist

Nation'. Her most recent biographer, June Rose, and also Geppert and Ross McKibbin are all sceptical about the literal truth of Stopes' claim (the basis of her successful legal petition for divorce) that she was quite as sexually innocent as she claimed during her first marriage: Stopes, *Married Love*, edited by Ross McKibbin, xii–xiii. See also, June Rose, *Marie Stopes and the Sexual Revolution* (London and Boston: Faber and Faber, 1992), 77–8.

14 Unfortunately, Maureen Sutton does not supply systematic date of birth information for the interviews she conducted, which were mainly with working-class women in the predominantly rural county of Lincolnshire. Her overall conclusion from this evidence was unequivocally that, 'Sexuality was simply not talked about, and the women in this study were brought up in a situation of almost total ignorance as to what sex was and how their own bodies functioned. The most common feature which the material reveals is the sense of isolation with which each woman faced the taboo on sexual knowledge' (Sutton, *We Didn't Know Aught*, 2).

15 Beier, 'We Were Green as Grass', 461–80.

16 Bourke, *Working Class Cultures*, 27–41, Hall, *Sex, Gender and Social Change*, 108. For a particularly sophisticated and nuanced summary see McLaren, *Twentieth-Century Sexuality*, 29. For the most recent endorsement of the view that in 1950s Britain 'a conspiracy of silence meant in turn deep sexual ignorance', see David Kynaston, *Family Britain 1951–57* (London: Bloomsbury, 2009), 552, *et seq.*

17 McKibbin, *Classes and Cultures: England, 1918–1951*, 317–21.

amongst the sexually progressive or people with extensive formal education. Amongst other groups what passed for sexual knowledge was still very limited even in the 1930s.'[18]

The thousands of personal letters, mostly written in the 1920s and 1930s to Marie Stopes, selections of which have been the subject of several previous studies, are, of course, also testimony to the difficulty which married adults were reporting throughout the interwar period in obtaining reliable public information on contraception because of its association with the 'obscene' subject of sex itself.[19] Working-class correspondents most often asked Stopes for basic contraceptive information about what methods of birth control were available and how to obtain them. Many of the middle-class letters, on the other hand, were more directly concerned with the quality of their sexual relationship and sought detailed, but also basic, sex advice, such as reassurances about the possible dangers of masturbation and different positions for intercourse, problems of premature ejaculation or of female arousal.[20]

Nor were alternative public means to acquire such knowledge easily available, certainly at least until the 1930s. Precisely because it was such an obvious medium of public communication, cinemas quickly attracted close scrutiny and control and a formal censorship system, which ensured that 'obscene' material, which included any explicit information about sex and birth control, was not to be screened.[21] In the informal advice columns of the new, mass-market

[18] Cook, *The Long Sexual Revolution*, 169. David Vincent, *The Culture of Secrecy: Britain 1832–1998* (Oxford: Oxford University Press, 1998), 158–66.

[19] Davey, 'Birth Control in Britain', Hall, *Hidden Anxieties*, Holtzman, 'The Pursuit of Married Love', Hall, ed. *Dear Dr. Stopes*, 29–52. For similar sets of letters written to birth control protagonists in other north European societies in the 1920s, see Ida Blom, '"Master of Your Own Body and What Is in It" – Reducing Marital Fertility in Norway, 1890–1930', in *Gendering the Fertility Decline in the Western World*, ed. Angélique Janssens (Bern: Peter Lang, 2007), 59–84, on 54,361 letters written to Katti Anker Moller in the 1920s. See, Sophia Kling, '"I Think I'd Rather Die Than Go through with a Pregnancy Again": Experiences of Childbearing and Birth Control in Sweden in the 1930s', in *Gendering the Fertility Decline in the Western World*, ed. Angélique Janssens (Bern: Peter Lang, 2007), 177–204, on 500 mostly working-class letters written to the Stockholm RFSU, a Swedish sex education organisation.

[20] This pattern has again been confirmed in an independent study for an undergraduate dissertation supervised by Simon Szreter conducted during 2008–9 by Ms Tanwen Berrington. A random sample of 3,700 letters drawn from the Stopes *Married Love* correspondence held at the Wellcome Library Archive were read. All letters in the following eleven numbered boxes were read: 2, 13, 16, 18, 20, 26, 28, 31, 33, 35, 40. Simon Szreter holds a copy of the dissertation report of this study.

[21] Jeffrey Richards, *The Age of the Dream Palace: Cinema and Society in 1930s Britain* (London: I. B. Tauris, 2010). See Part 2 'The Constraints', esp. pp. 92–3 on the basic censorship rules, known as 'O'Connor 43', in place already by 1917; according to Richards 33 of the 43 rules were bans on depictions of sex: 'prostitution, pre-marital and extra-marital sex, sexual perversion, incest, seduction, nudity, venereal disease, orgies, swearing, abortion, brothels, white slavery and so on'. Kuhn notes that this close attention to screen censorship was by no means restricted to Britain at this time (Annette Kuhn, *Cinema, Censorship and Sexuality,*

popular magazines for teenage girls and young women, which flourished during the interwar decades, Penny Tinkler's study concluded that on all matters relating to sexuality, there was an absence of any detail or explicit information offered because such matters were construed as inappropriate for public discussion: 'Despite their "personal" relationship with their readers, girls' magazines were too much a public medium to address such matters overtly.'[22]

There was some increase in the interwar decades in the availability in the media of public depictions of the human body, though the extent of this should not be exaggerated. Adrian Bingham's study of the interwar popular, national daily press, read by an estimated two-thirds of the adult population, shows that from 1918 onwards the combination of increased photography with advertising transformed the appearance of daily papers, with pictures of girls and glamorous fashion advertisements both on the rise.[23] During the 1930s there was a commercially driven deliberate strategy by the *Mirror*, the *Mail*, the *Express* and the *Herald* to follow the lead of the *News of the World* into 'sex and sensationalism'.[24] However, the social conservatism of these papers meant that while they were quite happy with superficially 'exploiting the tastes of a prurient market',[25] so that '[g]lamorous young ladies smiled out of the picture pages, and there were even examples of beauty unadorned',[26] those in charge were simultaneously adamant when questioned by the Royal Commission on the Press 1947–9 that 'our papers should be such that we should never be ashamed of our daughters reading them'.[27] Thus, the innocence of daughters was still throughout this era a touchstone for the conservative values of the mass media. What this meant, according to Bingham, was that while pictures of attractive young female bodies could be justified on the high-minded grounds that 'the human form divine is actually beautiful',[28] these popular interwar papers judged that giving space to detailed – and potentially educational – discussion of such subjects as birth control or venereal disease went beyond the pale (only the *Herald* in the 1920s, when it was owned by the trade-union movement before its takeover by Odhams in 1929, had consistently accepted birth control advertisements).

Indeed, even into the 1940s and 1950s, in the generally socially conservative climate of 'austerity' and national service for the young at this time, restraining

1909–1925 (London: Routledge, 1988)); on the USA see for instance, Nancy J. Rosenbloom, 'Between Reform and Regulation: The Struggle over Film Censorship in Progressive America, 1909–1922', *Film History* 1, no. 4 (1987): 307–25.

22 Penny Tinkler, *Constructing Girlhood: Popular Magazines for Girls Growing up in England, 1920–1950* (London and Bristol, PA: Taylor & Francis, 1995), 163.

23 Bingham, *Gender, Modernity and the Popular Press*, 3.

24 Ibid., 150–1. 25 Ibid., 171.

26 Ibid., 151, citing Hugh Cudlipp, of the *Mirror*.

27 Ibid., 157, citing E. J. Robertson, chairman of Express Newspapers.

28 Ibid., 168, a 1920 *Mail* editorial defending its pictures of 'bathing belles'.

conventions of respectable public discourse of sexual matters were still being promoted, at least in some quarters;[29] Local Watch Committees, originating in the National Vigilance Society of the Victorian social purity movement of the 1880s, were, for instance, still active in the 1950s.[30] One of their activities, for instance, was the policing, banning and seizing of saucy postcards in resort towns.[31]

In his study of representations of sexuality in the popular press throughout the period 1918–78, Bingham argues that significant change, in respect to useful public information on sex, only commenced in the 1940s: 'In 1942 the *Daily Mirror* led a press campaign to highlight the dangers of venereal diseases [which] paved the way for popular newspapers to assume an educational role on issues of sexual welfare.'[32] However, other sections of the popular press took a different line. Throughout the Second World War the *Express* refused to publish the Ministry of Health's adverts against VD on the grounds that it was a 'family newspaper'.[33] Bingham's next example of a significant press feature on issues to do with sex was not until 1947, when the Mirror group's *Sunday Pictorial* published a series on 'How A Baby is Born'. Hence, as Bingham's evidence demonstrates, these educative features on sex, though innovative, were extremely sporadic throughout not only the 1940s but also the 1950s, not amounting to a permanent change on a daily basis in the sexual content of the popular press.

Nevertheless, increased press interest in studies of sex was observable from the late 1940s onwards. Stimulated by the appearance of the first Kinsey Report in America in 1948, two innovative surveys of sex in marriage were funded and publicised by the popular press in 1949 and 1950, the first carried out by Mass Observation for the *Sunday Pictorial* and the other by Geoffrey Gorer for its rival *The People*.[34] Bingham identifies two further

[29] Ina Zweiniger-Bargielowska, *Austerity in Britain: Rationing, Controls, and Consumption, 1939–1955* (Oxford and New York: Oxford University Press, 2000).

[30] Lucy Bland, *Banishing the Beast: English Feminism and Sexual Morality 1885–1914* (London: Penguin, 1995), Edward J. Bristow, *Vice and Vigilance: Purity Movements in Britain since 1700* (Dublin and Totowa, NJ: Gill and Macmillan; Rowman and Littlefield, 1977). The National Vigilance Society, founded in 1885, became the British Vigilance Association in 1953 by amalgamating with the National Committee for the Suppression of Traffic in Women. Meanwhile the separate Association for Moral and Social Hygiene became in 1953 the Josephine Butler Society (she having been the foundress in 1869 of the original Ladies' National Association for the Abolition of State Regulation of Vice, from which the Social Hygiene Association was formed in 1915) (Weeks, *Sex, Politics, and Society*, 94, n.15).

[31] Elfrida Buckland, *The World of Donald Mcgill* (Poole: Javeline Books, 1985), ch. 7, 'The Censor'.

[32] Bingham, *Family Newspapers*, 62.

[33] Bingham, *Gender, Modernity, and the Popular Press*, 156–7.

[34] Bingham, *Family Newspapers*, 104–11.

eruptions of press interest, with reportage across Fleet Street in 1953 of the American findings of Kinsey's second report on *Sexual Behaviour in the Human Female*, and in 1956 when the *Sunday Pictorial* returned to the theme with a serialisation of Dr Eustace Chesser's survey of *The Sexual, Marital and Family Relationships of the English Woman*. Bingham also points out that problem columns increasingly flourished from the late 1940s onwards in all the popular papers.[35]

However, as Bingham has confirmed, with their need for a mass circulation still firmly tied to the 'family newspaper' image, the popular press's approach to portraying sex in the nation's public discourse remained, until the 1960s, constrained by codes of respectability, which were subject to the well-documented religious revival of conservative moral values during the first post-war decade. This emphasised the stability of the family and marriage through promoting the ideal of the companionate model of an equal but different partnership of gendered work and childrearing roles.[36] The educational features, the advice handed out in the columns and the reportage of the findings of surveys were all careful to endorse the ideals of chaste love within marriage as the basis for (exclusively hetero-) sex, and as the model for emotionally healthy individuals and a physically healthy nation; editors observed definite limits on how far their public educative role would go.[37] Consequently, Bingham concludes that this was still some way from the permissive Britain of 'the sixties', concluding, rather, that: 'The popular journalism of the 1950s helped to prepare the way for the much broader sexualization of the media in the 1960s.'[38]

Nevertheless, at least for the middle classes, there is some evidence that sexual ignorance was becoming less engrained by the late 1940s and 1950s, as

[35] Ibid., 75–6.

[36] On the strength of the post-war decade of Christian religious revival, c.1945–55, see Callum G. Brown, *The Death of Christian Britain: Understanding Secularisation, 1800–2000* (London and New York: Routledge, 2009), 170–5, 212–15. On the increased popularity of a socially conservative form of marriage, see Finch and Summerfield, 'Social Reconstruction and the Emergence of Companionate Marriage', and on renewed emphasis on domesticated maternal roles, see Denise Riley, *War in the Nursery: Theories of the Child and Mother* (London: Virago, 1983).

[37] When his study was published in full in book form, Gorer confessed that he had been irked at not being allowed to ask a direct question of his male and female respondents on their experience of orgasm, because 'the editors thought that it might cause unnecessary offence' (Gorer, *Exploring English Character*, 26). At the end of the following decade when he mounted his next enquiry in 1969 public understanding of sex was still too deficient for the word to be used: Gorer's pilot study showed that too few recognised the term to put it in a question, so 'climax' was used instead (Gorer, *Sex and Marriage*, 124).

[38] Bingham, *Family Newspapers*, 266. Similarly the language used in the personal advertisements placed in newspapers remained reticent before the late 1950s and early 1960s (Harry Cocks, *Classified: The Secret History of the Personal Column* (London: Random House, 2009)).

documented in a flurry of post-war enquiries.[39] How, then, did this group learn about sex, if not from public sources? Mass Observation's 'Little Kinsey' survey investigation into the nation's sexual attitudes and practices in 1949 found that the educated middle classes at this time were often equipping themselves with sexual knowledge through private reading.[40] It found among the middle-class 'panel' of regular contributors to Mass Observation, a group described as 'more or less representative of middle-class "progressive" opinion', who were questioned on their own sex habits as well as their attitudes, that over half mentioned medical, sex hygiene and marriage guidance books, notably works by Havelock Ellis and Marie Stopes, as significant sources for their own sex education. By contrast only one in twelve of Mass Observation's predominantly working-class national 'street' sample said that 'reading' had been one of their means for acquiring knowledge of the facts of life; and it was from this sample that the familiar theme of 'ignorance' emerged.[41]

In 1956 Eustace Chesser's *The Sexual, Marital and Family Relationships of the English Woman* also provided a plethora of information, much of it statistically tabulated, on how the study's respondents acquired their sexual knowledge. Chesser's survey was in the main conducted with a set of middle-class English women, both married and unmarried, aged between 20 and 40 in 1954, prepared to answer a probing questionnaire.[42] Unlike other studies,

[39] The well-researched interpretations by Cook, and by Porter and Hall envisage sexual knowledge diffusing socially at this time (Cook, *The Long Sexual Revolution*, Porter and Hall, *The Facts of Life*).

[40] This study, the first attempt at a national sex survey carried out in Britain, was financed and published as five articles in July 1949 under the title 'The Private Life of John Bull' by the *Sunday Pictorial*, who commissioned Tom Harrison and Len England of Mass Observation to conduct it (Bingham, *Family Newspapers*, 104–11). Mass Observation's methodology for this enquiry was composed of four strands: First, Mass Observation's regular 'National Panel' of Voluntary Observers and correspondents. Second, a national 'street' survey sample of 2,052 persons, who were stopped in the street and questioned on their attitudes. Third, there was a postal questionnaire sent to randomly selected members of three key professions – doctors, teachers and clergymen. Fourth, in-depth participant observation of persons and interviewing of local officials in two contrasting towns – Worcester ('Churchtown') and Middlesbrough ('Steeltown').

[41] Stanley, *Sex Surveyed*, 76. Neither with respect to the panel nor the street sample does the Mass Observation text offer any differentiation by gender in these reported patterns.

[42] Chesser obtained his information by asking about 6,000 GPs for their voluntary assistance in distributing the long and intimate questionnaires to patients. About three-quarters refused to assist on seeing the questionnaire. While about half of this selected set of co-operating GPs then claimed to have distributed the questionnaire at random, about one-third stated they only gave it to 'intelligent', 'high social status' or 'broad-minded' patients. The net outcome of all these selection effects was that the 6,034 completed questionnaires returned to Chesser by October 1954 (from a total of over 18,000 originally sent out, a response rate of about 33%) came disproportionately from the middle classes: over 70 per cent were drawn from the higher social classes (including the clerical lower middle class), which was at least double their proportionate share in the population at this time; and only 30 per cent were from the manual working classes. Among the married women, who comprised three-fifths of the sample, a disproportionate number (70%) were relatively young, aged 40 and under (Chesser et al., *The Sexual, Marital*

Chesser did not dwell on the ignorance that needed to be combated, but rather on the diversity of sources of sexual information which his questionnaire respondents reported. About one-fifth of this predominantly middle-class group identified parents and another fifth identified another adult (including for some a schoolteacher) as having been their main source of sex education. He also noted a marked four-fold rise in the proportion citing books or pamphlets as their main source, from just 4 per cent among those born before 1904 to 17 per cent among those born 1924–34.[43] Thus, both this study and the Mass Observation report indicated that 'ignorance' was not evenly spread throughout society during the decade after the Second World War and that many of the rising generation of the most educated middle classes among those born since the Great War were finding ways to educate themselves about sex. But they did so mainly through informal and, above all, private means: by reading, by advice from a close acquaintance or family member or by all these means.

Attitudes towards sex education did begin to change over the period. Mass Observation claimed that among both its (more middle-class) panel members and its (more working-class) street surveys in 1949 a high proportion were in favour of sex education provision in schools while observing that both at local government and central government level recent changes in policy in the 1940s had been dramatic with both the London County Council and the Ministry of Education moving from a position in which sex education was banned in their schools to one in which it was to be actively promoted.[44] Nevertheless, sex education simply did not exist as an officially recognised possibility for the school curriculum before 1943 at the earliest.[45] Although sex education in schools, advocated by progressives since the 1920s, finally became official policy from 1942, historians have clearly documented that both sex education policy in

and Family Relationships of the English Woman, 14–19). Most of Chesser's respondents were thus born between 1914 and 1935, making them on average ten years younger and much more predominantly middle-class than those interviewed in Blackburn and Hertfordshire.

[43] Ibid., Section C, esp. 161. [44] Stanley, *Sex Surveyed*, 86.

[45] Jane Pilcher, 'School Sex Education: Policy and Practice in England 1870 to 2000', *Sex Education* 5, no. 2 (2005): 153–70. Although a few dispersed initiatives to provide sex education were taken by individual schools during the interwar decades, this generally occurred – and even then only haltingly from the mid-1940s onwards – in the nation's secondary schools, which was therefore too late for most of the Blackburn and Hertfordshire interviewees (Lesley A. Hall, 'Birds, Bees and General Embarrassment: Sex Education in Britain, from Social Purity to Section 28', in *Public or Private Education?: Lessons from History*, ed. Richard Aldrich (London: Woburn Press, 2004), 98–115). As Bashford and Strange point out, sex education in schools was provided significantly earlier in many US states, while in both USA and Australia, for instance, radio broadcasting played a substantial role, which the BBC (a legal monopoly until the 1970s) declined to take on (Alison Bashford and Carolyn Strange, 'Public Pedagogy: Sex Education and Mass Communication in the mid-Twentieth Century', *Journal of the History of Sexuality* 13 (2004): 72–3, 93–8. See also, Patricia J. Campbell, *Sex Education Books for Young Adults, 1892–1979* (New York: R. R. Bowker Co., 1979)).

national government and sex education practice in LEAs expanded at a snail's pace throughout the next several decades. It was only given a partial fillip even by the permissive 1960s, partly because of a determined counter-attack within conservative education circles.[46] Not surprisingly, therefore, the very gradual nature of these changes is reflected in our study (see below note 61), where fewer than one in twelve of the older interviewees claimed to have had any kind of exposure to sex education in schools, compared with just under one-third of the younger ones.

The oral testimony to be presented certainly confirms that an institutionalised culture of public silence and euphemism existed where sex was concerned from the 1910s until at least the early 1940s. Neither parents nor schools nor any other formal institutions systematically provided much detailed instruction for these interviewees growing up before the end of the Second World War. The only significant exception to this, mentioned by a few individuals, were the efforts encountered in the armed forces or occasionally through membership of religious organisations to diffuse information, which tended to focus on the public health dangers and personal consequences of venereal diseases – the film *Damaged Goods*, which appeared in 1916, being the most well-known example of this.[47] However, as will be shown, individuals did acquire knowledge of sex in a number of ways as they grew up. Also the interview evidence demonstrates the profound significance of gender and of marked social class differences in access to theoretical knowledge in the processes of learning.

'Parents didn't tell you'

The view that both parents and social institutions kept to a strict code of silence on sex was frequently expressed among both Blackburn and Hertfordshire

[46] James Hampshire and Jane Lewis, '"The Ravages of Permissiveness": Sex Education and the Permissive Society', *Twentieth Century British History* 15, no. 3 (2004): 290–312. A survey of 1,500 16–19 year olds and 300 parents in the early 1970s still found sex education in schools offering little information on birth control, with many of the teenagers complaining they had only been taught about animal reproduction, so that many still said they learned mainly from peers, rather than in school (Christine Farrell, *My Mother Said… The Way Young People Learn About Sex and Birth Control* (London: Routledge & Kegan Paul, 1978), 124).

[47] Kuhn, *Cinema, Censorship and Sexuality*, ch. 4. See also McKibbin, *Classes and Cultures: England, 1918–1951*, 317–19, and Weeks, *Sex, Politics, and Society*, 211, 214–21, on the interwar efforts of the British Social Hygiene Council, the Society for the Prevention of Venereal Diseases, and other self-appointed bodies for the protection of public morality in promoting such films. Angela Davis' ninety-two interviewees, educated in Oxfordshire 1930–70, remembered little school sex education apart from 'slide shows about VD … very, very unpleasant, quite frightening' (Angela Davis, '"Oh No, Nothing, We Didn't Learn Anything": Sex Education and the Preparation of Girls for Motherhood, c.1930–70', *History of Education* 37 (2008): 671). For an account of the work of the 1913–16 Royal Commission on Venereal Diseases and the consequent official policies, see Davenport-Hines, *Sex, Death and Punishment*, chs. 6–7.

respondents: Daphne (1912), whose parents both worked in the cotton mills, 'never mentioned ... sex ... it was a word that were never used ... we were all very naïve in those days ... very ignorant. Your parents didn't tell you anything.'[48] A younger respondent, Maureen (1920), whose father was of a somewhat higher social status and owned an ironmonger's shop in Blackburn, emphasised that such silence was maintained right up until marriage: 'It was kept under the carpet, you know ... you'd to be married to know about it, you know what I mean.'[49]

Men were far less likely to present themselves as having been completely ignorant, yet they confirmed that throughout childhood they were deliberately kept in ignorance by parents and the older generation. Tim (1917), whose father was a skilled turner and keen union man, recalled 'it was a bit taboo amongst parents, never, never never discussed'[50] and according to Colin (1923), who was brought up in a care home from age 8, 'I, er, never got told nowt ... It were tuck away in them days. It was taboo in t'home.'[51] Similarly, middle-class Hubert (1911), whose father was an estate agent with his own business, also described sex as a 'taboo subject'. He 'had no advice or instruction about it, except one brief visit from my father who said, "I suppose you know as much about it as I do" ... I knew absolutely nothing.'[52]

Both among working-class and middle-class interviewees, born across the social and age spectrum covered by the sample, it was widely claimed that parents maintained this inter-generational silence right through until adulthood. Roger (1910), the son of a Royal Navy commander, resentfully remembered this parental exclusion of him from such knowledge continuing into his twenties:

> ROGER You see sex was cloaked in mystery, sex was cloaked in mystery. My, my, uh, mother and father, uh, were wonderful parents ... but I'll never forget, an uncle of mine and an aunt came down from Hatfield ... and drove down to Rochester to see my parents, and they came in and they wanted to say something about a boy and girl that they knew there. Well, it was, I found out afterwards, he put her up the stick, got her pregnant, and she, her father came round, threatened him with guns! ... Now I was asked to go out of the room because they were talking and I was 21. You didn't mention that in front of the children. But he's 21, yeah, but he's still a child.[53]

Women remembered having to leave the room if sexual topics were being, even obliquely, discussed. Marian, born in 1908 into a working-class Blackburn family, grew up with just one sister, three years younger:

> MARIAN You see our mother wouldn't let us listen to and wouldn't tell us anything, and she wouldn't let us listen in to any conversations; she'd just shove us in another

[48] Daphne msf/jm/bl/#38. [49] Maureen msf/kf/bl/#46. [50] Tim msf/srss/bl/#19.
[51] Colin msf/kf/bl/#36. [52] Hubert msf/kf/ht/#32. [53] Roger msf/kf/ht/#10.

> room if we, if she were talking to anybody. Yeah, they were like that in them days y'know.[54]

Her exact contemporary, Eleanor's (1907) family were strict working-class Methodists in Blackburn – she also had one younger (step-)sister and got on well with her step-father:

> ELEANOR you see our parents wouldn't talk about anythin' like that. If they were goin' to talk about anythin' like that, they used to say, 'Go and play out… go and play out.' We 'adn't to listen to anythin' so we were brought up a bit ignorant really, about… you know, sex… I think…[55]

Marilyn (1914) was brought up in an upper-working-class Blackburn family; her father had tenanted a farm for a period between working as an engineer in a factory and running a grocer's shop with her mother. She remembered how her own male peers protected her from corruptive information:

> MARYLIN And, um, there were a family called Jakeses; they had a farm. They'd three lads and I remember them talking about pigs. They had a pig and it'd had pi-, little un, pig, little pig. (coughs) And, um, some'et about they took it to a sow, took sow to a pig to be serviced. But, um, I know what they mean now but didn't then, um. They were talking amongst themselves and they used to say 'You're not to listen; it nowt to do wi' you.' Um, they wouldn't let you listen.[56]

Respondents also confirmed that the school curriculum did not in general fill the knowledge gap. Phyllis (1921) was a Catholic respondent born in Blackburn, whose father was a carter:

> PHYLLIS I don't know if everyone's telling you the same story as me, that they were completely ignorant but I know I was. Eeh you know, it wasn't discussed at school; it wasn't discussed at home. You know it's just a subject you didn't talk about.[57]

While it is true that from around the time of the Great War onwards educationalists had produced specialist texts for sex education in school, with neither the Church nor the medical profession nor central government backing the idea before the 1940s, there is no evidence of any widespread take-up in the teaching profession itself.[58] Writing in 1951 Slater and Woodside believed there

[54] Marian msf/kf/bl/#28. These parents and daughters were thus conforming precisely in their reported behaviour in the interviews to the injunctions which Norbert Elias identified as having emerged among leading pedagogues in mid-nineteenth-century Europe, such as Karl Von Raumer, whose short *The Education of Girls* (1857) prescribed that, 'A mother… ought only once to say seriously: "It would not be good for you to know such a thing, and you should take care not to listen to anything said about it." A truly well-brought-up girl will from then on feel shame at hearing things of this kind spoken of' (Elias, *The Civilizing Process*, 151–2).

[55] Eleanor msf/kf/bl/#11. [56] Marilyn msf/kf/bl/#7. [57] Phyllis msf/kf/bl/#5.

[58] Cyril Bibby, *Sex Education: A Guide for Parents* (London: Macmillan & Co. Ltd, 1944), Walter M. Gallichan, *A Textbook of Sex Education for Parents and Teachers* (London: Laurie, 1919), Arthur Herbert Gray, *Sex Teaching, Every Teacher's Library* (London: The National

was still much work to be done through extending sex education in schools to redress basic ignorance: 'Parents, nowadays at least, are generally well-meaning, but are themselves too ignorant and inhibited to give reliable information to their children. The only satisfactory way is by education in school.'[59] A small minority of the younger male interviewees recalled that they had come into contact with initiatives from individual teachers or carers. Mark (1917) attended a secondary school where the headmaster had been a Moderator in Biology at the University of Cambridge and was an author of biology textbooks. Colin (1923) counted himself as having had some sex education from anti-VD training given in the navy and Jake (1922) from a lecture volunteered by his scoutmaster. Eleanor (1907) was one of the few from among the oldest of the interviewees who recalled such initiatives, reporting that her husband had received some instruction through 'health lectures' at Cunningham's summer camp on the Isle of Man.[60]

There is, therefore, some evidence from the informants to support the notion of a moderate rise in various forms of institutional provision of rudimentary sex education during the first four decades of the twentieth century, although this was still very much a minority experience recalled by no more than one in five of those interviewed.[61] This is not surprising given that official attitudes towards the propriety of school sex education for teenagers did not change until the mid-1940s, too late for most of these respondents. Several interviewees did mention, however, how the subsequent expansion of sex education provision in schools helped them address the subject with their own children in

Sunday School Union, 1930), T.L.Green, 'Sex Education and Social Biology', *Health Education Journal* 3 (1945): 43, Dame Mary Scharlieb and F.A. Sibly, *Youth and Sex* (London and Edinburgh: T.C.& E.C. Jack and T.Nelson and Sons Ltd, 1919 rev. edn), Ira S. Wile, *Sex Education* (London: Andrew Melrose, 1913), E.L. Packer, 'Aspects of Working-Class Marriage', *Pilot Papers: Social Essays and Documents* 2, no. 1 (1947): 92–104. Packer refers on p. 92, to Pamphlet 119, issued in 1943 by the Board of Education, as being 'purely an informatory pamphlet [which] did not make it obligatory for local authorities to introduce sex education', but reported that 'nearly every authority has made provision of some kind'.

59 Slater and Woodside, *Patterns of Marriage*, 176.

60 Mark msf/kf/ht/#22; Colin msf/kf/bl/#36; Jake msf/ssrs/bl/#22; Eleanor msf/kf/bl/#11. On Cunningham's camp, see Jill Drower, *Good Clean Fun: The Story of Britain's First Holiday Camp* (London: Arcadia Books, 1982). See also Lorna msf/kf/bl/#25, below note 77, regarding the sex education for girls offered at Blakey Secondary School in Blackburn by 1940.

61 Only four of the interviewees reported receiving some sex education at school, all of whom were from the younger half of the respondents (defined as those born after 1915, who comprised 49% of the eighty-eight married interviewees). These four were: Lorna (1917) msf/kf/bl/#25; Alistair (1927) msf/kf/bl/#33; Mildred (1924) msf/kf/bl/#41; Mark (1917) msf/kf/ht/#22. Additionally, five interviewees reported civic institutions (mostly the Church) providing sex education, two of whom were among the older half of respondents: Eleanor (1907) msf/kf/bl/#11; Daphne (1912) msf/jm/bl/#38; Felicity (1919) msf/kf/bl/#37; Vera (1917) msf/kf/ht/#34; Dora (1923) msf/srss/ht/#38. Finally, ten recalled institutional instruction as adults, usually in the armed services during the Second World War focused on the dangers of VD – most of whom (seven) were born after 1915: Olive, Terence, Frank, Colin, Jake, Felicity, Bryan, Herbert, George, Hugh. Altogether this comprises only 19 (20%) of those interviewed.

the late 1950s, 1960s and 1970s, which confirms the chronology and findings of the impact of sex education among the working classes of Lucinda Beier's research.[62]

The consequences of this institutionalised ignorance were at their most evident when working-class female respondents presented the memory of the onset of their first menstrual period.[63] As other oral historians have also found,[64] a great many Blackburn and Hertfordshire working-class interviewees had traumatic memories, declaring themselves to have had no forewarning, because '[n]obody told you anything' as Laura (1923), one of the younger Blackburn interviewees, put it. They emphasised they were taken by surprise and often expressed a sense of emotional shock. Clare (born in Berkhamsted 1912), the youngest of twelve siblings, none of whom forewarned her, '[c]ried ... cried, 'cos I thought I'd got something wrong with me'.[65]

Most working-class female informants portrayed themselves as learning the same two lessons from this experience of their first period and the responses of their elders and others around them. Both were related to the importance of preserving their respectability in a culture which strenuously avoided public mention of sex and which cast girls and young women as innocents. The first principle was that periods were a private matter, to be discussed as little as possible, even with one's mother after a daughter had begun to have them. Eleanor (1907), whose mother was a ring spinner in Blackburn, was taken by her to the doctor when her periods failed to appear by age 14. Her mother still sought to shield Eleanor from the doctor's diagnosis. Rather than this being the start of a supportive, shared discourse about periods between daughter and mother, Eleanor's mother tried to protect her innocence by preventing her from hearing what she was discussing:[66]

ELEANOR me mother took me t'doctor's ... and she said 'there's somethin' wrong with 'er; she 'asn't started 'er periods' (whispering) you know; she put 'er 'and up there so [I] couldn't 'ear' ...

Consequently, Eleanor had to learn what to do from her 14-year-old friend at the mill, who had started before her,

62 For Beier's evidence see Chapter 1, note 165.

63 Also discussed in Julie-Marie Strange, 'The Assault on Ignorance: Teaching Menstrual Etiquette in England, c. 1920s to 1960s', *Social History of Medicine* 14, no. 2 (2001): 247–65.

64 See for instance Beier, *For Their Own Good*, 216–21, Roberts, *A Woman's Place*, 16–18 and also Sutton, *We Didn't Know Aught*, ch. 2 for several examples.

65 Laura msf/kf/bl#6; Clare ht/kf/ht/#8.

66 Sociologists find similar difficulties in mother/daughter discussions of menstruation in contemporary society. See, D. Costos, R. Ackerman and L. Paradis, 'Recollections of Menarche: Communication between Mothers and Daughters Regarding Menstruation', *Sex Roles* 46, no. 1 (2002): 49–59. Emily Martin has argued that to 'conceal and control' menstruation is a widely prevalent cultural response found by anthropologists (Emily Martin, *The Woman in the Body* (Milton Keynes: Open University Press, 1993), 192–212).

ELEANOR I said 'what did you do with all them rags that you used?' She said 'I waited one night and I burnt them', she said, and she were doing that for months! Puttin' 'em all on the fire; ... never told 'er mother ... it never were mentioned.[67]

When it came to be her turn, Eleanor did the same,

ELEANOR about six month later, I started. But I never told me mother. She didn't want to know ... we used to burn 'em you know on the fire (laughing).[68]

The second lesson was that the arrival of periods meant that the sex difference between themselves and boys was now newly significant and many girls were told not to play with boys and to regard them with wariness. Many, such as Marian (1908) in the early 1920s, whose mother was a winder in a Blackburn cotton mill, and Marilyn (born 1914), whose mother ran a grocer's shop also in Blackburn, and even the much younger Grace (1922), an adolescent in Goole, Yorkshire, in the late 1930s, recalled in almost identical terms the same general warning to alter their behaviour and avoid physical contact with boys:

MARILYN Oh I were at school; I were only elev-, ten I think. I were very young ... and I went to me mother. 'You mustn't talk to boys', she said. 'You'll be like that every month.' But she didn't say why or anything; she didn't expand on it.[69]

MARIAN Well I were 15 when I, I started my period. 'Keep away from lads', that's all she said. She never said; never tell you nothin'. She didn't tell you anythin'; you didn't know nothin'.[70]

GRACE Oh don't mention that. I mean my mother was a church woman ... And I was I think three days before I could pluck up the courage and go tell my mam ... (tearful) ... 'Summat to tell you mum.' And she said 'Well?' She said, 'So and so and so and so', she said, 'and don't go near lads'. (firmly) 'Don't go near lads!' But she didn't say why not to go near 'em you know.[71]

Most female working-class respondents insisted that they were not given any specific explanation of the facts of life, only the behavioural admonition to keep away from boys. This and the fact that periods were 'private' and not

[67] With the rise of sensitivity to germ theory, the long-standing practice of simply using rags came to be seen as unhygienic, so that during the interwar decades disposable sanitary towels became more popular for those who could afford them. Various more discreet, absorbent sanitary pads, such as 'Kotex' and 'Modess' were increasingly marketed in the USA, as women's consumer demand facilitated the search for something less restrictive on mobility, resulting in the late 1930s in the tampon. These American products became more available in Britain in the post-war period (Sharra L. Vostral, 'Making Menstruation: The Emergence of Menstrual Hygiene Products in the United States', in *Menstruation: A Cultural History*, eds. Andrew Shail and Gillian Howie (Basingstoke and New York: Palgrave Macmillan, 2005), 243–58). A survey in the late 1940s found that girls from low-income families still used home-made rewashable towels (Strange, 'The Assault on Ignorance', 258).

[68] Eleanor msf/kf/bl/#11. On early twentieth-century sanitary products see, Sutton, *We Didn't Know Aught*, 17–22.

[69] Marilyn msf/kf/bl/#7. [70] Marian msf/kf/bl/#28.

[71] Grace msf/srss/ht/#38.

openly talked about in the home were their main clues that their periods were somehow bound up with sex. Maureen (1920), whose mother did not go out to work, was from the Blackburn commercial middle-class and one of the younger interviewees. She passed the Eleven Plus, went to secondary school and then on to technical college in the late 1930s:

MAUREEN I didn't know much about it. And I mean they never, like your mothers didn't tell you about them in those days, and they didn't tell you about it in schools; they were the last people to tell you. So it was a very private thing really.[72]

This, then, was the most common experience for many young working-class women reaching menarche between the 1920s and 1940s. There was an absence of any forewarning and an absence of an explanation in most accounts. Young women were expected to guard their body's privacy from all others and most especially from the opposite sex.

There were, however, a small number of counter-examples among interviewees from working-class backgrounds, where they recalled a more informative domestic relationship. Mildred (1924), the youngest of four, was born in Ferndale, the daughter of a South Wales miner who had to leave the industry because of his health, and so she had grown up in Huddersfield. Her mother had worked in service before marriage:

MILDRED I thought I was bleeding on my legs and so my mother took me to a quiet part and told me all about it... I was frightened, I wouldn't know what to think. She explained.[73]

While Mildred was one of the youngest women interviewed in Blackburn, Elma (1909) was one of the older informants. As it happened she had also grown up in West Yorkshire, in the steel town of Rotherham. Her father had a rather poorly paid job on the railways but her mother was boarding-school educated, and was described as having married beneath herself.[74] Her high level of education was associated by Elma with her mother's willingness to 'discuss anything', including periods:

Can you tell me how you found out about periods?

ELMA Well, of course you find out about that because your mother tells you... Your mother provides you with the necessary, doesn't she?... Oh yes, yes. I, I could

[72] Maureen msf/kf/bl/#46.

[73] Mildred msf/kf/bl#41. Mildred has been classified as lower middle class according to her husband's occupation, since he was a trained draughtsman who became a secondary school teacher in metalwork and woodwork. She herself worked as a burler in the mills in Huddersfield until retirement.

[74] Elma msf/jm/bl/#42. She herself married a policeman who never progressed beyond the rank of constable.

discuss anything with my mother... She was a very well-educated woman. I could discuss anything with her.[75]

Despite Elma's association of her mother's attitudes with her level of education, schools themselves were rarely mentioned by interviewees as providing information about periods or sex education.[76] Of course, partly this was because there was no sex education at all provided in elementary schools and, outside the middle classes, only a small number could qualify for or afford secondary education before the Butler Act made it mandatory and free after 1944. Even in the secondary schools, as has been noted, pre-war provision of sex education was sporadic at best. Only one working-class respondent (also from Blackburn), Lorna (1917), explicitly recalled that she had forewarning of her periods because of school sex education. Lorna was one of the younger Blackburn respondents and had the rare distinction (as a working-class girl who became a weaver upon leaving school) of having attended one of the city's secondary schools, Blakey Moor, which was unusual, already in the early 1940s when she attended, in providing its pupils with sex education. Despite herself benefiting from sex education at school, she nevertheless portrayed a relationship with her mother essentially similar to that recalled by most other working-class respondents:

LORNA Oh well, I'd... the facts well, I were, I went to, um, Blakey Moor Secondary School, er, well I had to pass me Eleven Plus to go there, and, er, we had two teachers, Miss Roberts and Miss Sharratt... and we got the facts of life from them two, from books and, and straight talking, yeah. Got nothing from me mother because I was turned 16 when I started with me periods and... I said to her 'Ooh, I've hurt meself; ooh me nightie's covered...' She just, just said 'Keep away from all lad... Don't wash your hair and don't suck cowathy.' That's all as I got.[77]

Men, on the other hand, were much more inclined to adopt an assertive, questioning stance towards sexual ignorance and the wall of silence and evasion which they met from parents. In one or two cases, male respondents

[75] Elma msf/jm/bl/#42. Her mother's attitude in the early 1920s would have corresponded to the most progressive approaches being advocated at that time by the newly founded Medical Women's Federation, who distributed leaflets specifically to encourage the dialogue between mothers and daughters they saw as lacking (Strange, 'The Assault on Ignorance').

[76] Strange has shown that the Medical Women's Federation's survey in the late 1940s still found at that time a widespread dearth of sanitary resources provided for girls with periods, in the nation's secondary schools, though this was hardly a surprising finding given the long-standing absence in most such schools of attention to sex education in general (ibid., 258). Beier does find evidence of a number of female Lancashire working-class respondents recalling sex education and advice about periods being given in school but these all relate to younger informants born in the 1930s and 1940s and most of her cited evidence in fact relates to school experiences from the mid-1950s and later (Beier, *For Their Own Good*, 233–9).

[77] Lorna msf/kf/bl/#25. We have not been able to establish the meaning of the reference to 'cowathy'.

explicitly voiced strong hostility to this aspect of their upbringing. Terence (1915) charged his mother, a weaver, and his father, who was a railway blacksmith, with selfishness in refusing to talk to him about sex:

> TERENCE In them days you didn't get any advice ... off your parents. [They] left for you to fend for yourself. I thought they were selfish ... not telling you, tutoring you ...[78]

Most male interviewees, however, viewed the culture of silence in a less resentful way than Terence and took it more as a challenge to their curiosity and initiative, providing an appropriate pretext for them to exercise their ingenuity and to share in clandestine pranks and discourse with other boys. Many portrayed themselves as having been curious about the bodily differences between the sexes and as actively inquisitive of the facts of life.[79] For men, boyhood innocence on matters of sexuality and their ignorance of the facts of life were something to be overcome. Innocent boys needed to become knowledgeable men.

This distinct male response to the culture of ignorance reflected an ideal of men as sexual educators. Female virginity, followed by male-initiated sexual awakening was an ideal which made female innocence an enduringly valued characteristic.[80] Adrian Bingham has shown how this view of young female

[78] Terence msf/srss/bl/#15.

[79] In 1988 Steve Humphries published a book drawn from a television series, where one or two of the men interviewed also portrayed the process of learning about sex through innocent tales of prepubescent childhood curiosity about body differences when playing with girls; by contrast, extracts from the female respondents talked of their uncomfortable experiences of their first periods (Humphries, *A Secret World of Sex*, 35–51). However, it was difficult to evaluate how typical Humphries' interviewees were. He deliberately sought out elderly interviewees, who were prepared to come forward in response to national press advertisements asking for persons to talk to camera and appear on television in person specifically to discuss their experiences of sex before marriage (Humphries, *A Secret World of Sex*, 11, 31). Humphries also offers one account of sexually humiliating initiation rites inflicted on a young man in an East End factory in the 1920s by a group of women workers. However, reporting this single incident hardly seems to justify the generalisation, which Humphries then offered, that '[t]he sexual initiation of young boys was traditionally undertaken by older women and it often seems to have given rise to a desire amongst the boys to "get their own back" on girls through sexual conquest, thus reinforcing the sexism of the shop floor'. We have also come across one such account (though not first-hand) from Norman msf/kf/ht/#17 of a sexually humiliating initiation ritual at the Waterlow Press printing works in the late 1920s or early 1930s, but in this case it was an entirely homo-social initiation among male workers. Paul Thompson makes a brief reference to such initiations in Thompson, *The Edwardians*, 67. The historian of labour Alastair Reid has advised (personal communication) that brief references to sexual explicitness (though not necessarily humiliation) can be found in memoirs of workplace initiation rituals in a number of working-class autobiographies (all male in most craft trades, with mixed participants sometimes in textiles).

[80] Even among Chesser's selected set of relatively well-educated and predominantly middle-class women (see above note 42), who returned his sex questionnaires in 1954, over three-quarters of the unmarried respondents under age 31 (a slightly younger group than most of those interviewed for this book) believed preservation of their virginity before marriage was important (Chesser et al., *The Sexual, Marital and Family Relationships*, 377).

physical beauty was commercially deployed in the interwar and post-war popular press.[81] Men as much as women cherished the concept of virginal innocence as a highly attractive female attribute. Thus, Richard Hoggart wrote approvingly in 1957 in his widely cited study of 'changes in working-class culture during the last thirty or forty years' that 'It is wonderful' how so many working-class girls 'retain both an ignorance of the facts of sex and an air of inviolability towards its whole atmosphere that would not have been unbecoming in a mid-nineteenth-century young lady of the middle-classes'.[82]

Thus, most interviewees, whether middle- or working-class, acknowledged that the subject of sex and reproduction had been a general topic from which they were largely excluded when young. However, there was a marked gender difference in the attitudes and approaches which respondents adopted towards the situation in which they found themselves of being deliberately kept in ignorance. Men were much more likely to see the absence of freely available knowledge as a personal challenge for them and their male peers to overcome. Women distanced themselves from 'disreputable' sources of information and presented their respectability as linked to sexual innocence. They were, in general, more likely to insist that they lived for much of their young lives in a state of ignorance and, as we shall see, to carefully describe the 'respectable' process by which they became better informed, with reference to trusted individuals, family members or future husbands.

'I wanted to keep you innocent'

Sally (1908) had a typical working-class mother who sought to protect her daughter from sexual information, but who was a little unusual in explicitly telling her that the point was to preserve her innocence. She sees such innocence as distinct from ignorance because of her active involvement in avoiding knowledge and preserving innocence:

SALLY I was very, very, not ignorant, because I didn't want to know anything, you see, I did. Anyway I was perhaps, I was an oddity, I don't know, but I didn't want to know and me mother said, 'I wanted to keep you innocent' as long as she could.[83]

For Sally, her mother and others, the pose of innocence was connected both to notions of respectability and, in fact, to female attractiveness.[84] As

[81] Bingham, *Gender, Modernity, and the Popular Press*, 170–81.

[82] Hoggart, *The Uses of Literacy*, 84. The general description of the book's purpose cited here comes from the first sentence of the 'Preface', p. 11. See also Lesley Hall on men's letters to Stopes, proud of preserving their own 'purity' before marriage, too (Hall, *Hidden Anxieties*, 100–1).

[83] Sally msf/kf/bl/#31.

[84] See also, Lesley A. Hall, 'Impotent Ghosts from No Man's Land, Flappers' Boyfriends, or Crypto-Patriarchs? Men, Sex and Social Change in 1920s Britain', *Social History* 21, no. 1 (1996): 63.

the playful and teasing exchange below shows, both Hugh (1926) and Angela (1924) continue to find it amusing and significant to celebrate Angela's 'innocence'. Reciprocally, it was part of a man's role, as Hugh exemplified, that he was expected to pose as the knowing one, in sexual matters, with all the connotations for taking the initiative which this implied. This was an established gender distinction common to all classes, indeed this upwardly mobile, lower-middle-class couple both came from skilled working-class families (her father had been an iron moulder and her mother a weaver, whereas his father had been a train driver and his mother also a weaver). They met at a dance during the Second World War, and married soon after.

ANGELA Um, well the facts are I can only say I was very innocent. (all laugh) My husband thinks I still am, is that so?
HUGH Yes dear; she was 21 before she realised they didn't come from under a gooseberry bush.
ANGELA Yes, yes.
So how did you then start finding out about these things?
HUGH I had to tell 'er.[85]

Stories such as these should not be simply taken at face value as indications of the level of sexual ignorance considered appropriate throughout girlhood even until the age of 21.[86] There is more to these accounts. These narratives reveal what respondents knew they were meant to know, how women were supposed to react to sexual information, what made a woman attractive and what dented her respectability, and ultimately how girls negotiated their development into women and the roles they would play as adults. It is in this context that we should interpret the common assertion that young women were shocked, horrified or disbelieving when presented with pieces of information.

So then when you did start your periods, tell me about that.
ANGELA Well it was a shock, you know. I didn't know what had happened to me. And my mother said, um, 'Well this is what happens to all ladies whatever their colour, they're all the same, only you are later than usual', you see. And, er, she said, 'This is the way that when you're married you, that you can have a child', and she sort of explained and I didn't believe her.
So what did she tell you?

[85] Hugh and Angela msf/kf/ht/#18.
[86] As Harry Cocks points out, the claim that 'a conspiracy of silence' surrounded sexual matters has long functioned as a mechanism by which sex educators and campaigners authorised 'their own expertise' through 'disqualifying existing practices and knowledge' (Harry Cocks, 'Review: The Growing Pains of the History of Sexuality', 661). So, too, here claims about sexual ignorance are always more than descriptions and must be viewed as social interventions and commentaries with their own agenda and purpose.

ANGELA Well, she, you know, she more or less told me, er, about sexual intercourse and, er, and I thought that was disgusting and I did not believe her one bit.[87]

Thus, in one sense Angela (1924) was not completely ignorant and did know about intercourse long before marriage (as we would expect for one of the youngest in our sample – by the late 1930s her mother 'more or less' told her about the mechanics of sexual intercourse), but in her husband's view of her, she remained charmingly naïve, ready to repeat childish myths, such as the idea that babies came from under a gooseberry bush. Such claims work to reveal the ways in which innocence was affected in the face of contact with forms of information about sex. Catherine (1912), who grew up in London, left school at 14 in 1926 but trained as a shorthand typist in a continuation school, told a similar story of refusing to believe the information about sex she received in the 1920s:

CATHERINE Well, I suppose I knew what one did. I was quite horrified to start with. And, oh, before I met my husband, you learn these things, of course, from girls at school or something, you know, and I can remember walking up and down our garden in London and thinking, it can't be (laughs) like that, I was absolutely horrified ... Yes, couldn't believe it.[88]

Lyn (1907), a mill worker in Blackburn who left school in 1921, likewise refused to believe the stories she heard:

And when did you find out how babies got into mothers' stomachs and what had to happen?

LYN Oh, only with boys and girls saying, er, saying ... to you, well ... that's what the lad has the willy for and they stick that into you, you see, and you were horrified at beginning, er, er, you just can't imagine it at all. And then that's how you come to have a baby, but you don't believe it; you think it's all fairy tales. You got told different tales and, er, gradually get to know what it is ...[89]

Some women told stories of coming across information accidentally, perhaps by overhearing a conversation they were not meant to be party to, or discovering a hidden book. In these instances the narratives sometimes sought to finesse the transgression that had led to the discovery of sexual information and included a denouement which re-established the narrator's innocence and respectability. Sally's (1908) mother, who had been a winder in Blackburn, scolded her for reading her hidden sex manual in the early 1920s and for showing it to her even younger friend.[90] Sally's narrative reasserted Sally's own innocence; she was too young to grasp its meaning, she did not

[87] Angela msf/kf/ht/#18. [88] Catherine msf/kf/ht/#1. [89] Lyn msf/kf/bl/#1.

[90] As will be explored in Chapter 7, several middle-class female respondents mention books as a helpful source of information somewhat later in life, at the time of marriage.

comprehend or believe its depictions of sexual intercourse and simply found it amusing:

SALLY Me mother had a book by Miss, er, Mr Monk, I think it was… I thought it were marvellous, this book. (laughs) I found it one day in her bedroom drawer. And it showed every aspect of a man making love to a woman. (laughs) Showed it my friend and we had a right giggly night. I made a mistake, I left it downstairs (laughs); mother found it. She said, 'What's this doing down here?' I said, 'I was looking at it.' '[What] yourself?' I said, 'No. Me and Jill' (that was my friend, she lived next door but one). She said, 'Jill?'. She said, 'she's younger than you.' I said, 'Well, she's only eighteen months younger than me.' She said, 'Well, you shouldn't've shown it her; you shouldn't've looked.' 'Cos I was only 12 (laughs), I think.

So what things did it show you?

SALLY Well, it told you when what period of the month you could have it and have a child… it was funny. It was more funny to me because, I mean, I wasn't serious enough to, to realise. It used to show her laid on her back and her legs wide open. And we, we tittered, you know, we had a good laugh; we had a real good laugh. Anyway, back to front, her back to him and it got silly. She said, 'Do you believe it?' I said, 'I don't know, well, it's a print, a book printed on it.' It was about that thick and it had red wrap.[91]

In these narratives respondents acknowledged that the correct response to information about sex was shock, or disbelief and that when faced with information they sought not to investigate further but to maintain their confusion and innocence. Sarah (1906) came from a skilled working-class family: her father was a pattern maker in an engineering firm and her mother a weaver in Preston. Her family's ownership of Aristotle's *Masterpiece* was not untypical of intelligent and well-read working-class families.[92]

SARAH When I was a kid [there was] a dressing table with a mirror in, in my mother's room and another with a wash basin and a jug, that was the style in those days, with a, a tiled top… and I used to ferret around in these drawers and I found a little red book… and do you know what it was? (chuckle) And I very often think about it, and I used to look at it and I used to see these babies curled up in it. It was Aristo-, Aristotle's *Works of Nature*, I think it was, or something. And they had, my mother and dad had that. And it was tucked away amongst the towels (giggle) in this drawer and I used to ferret [unclear phrase]…

So what did you learn from this book?

I didn't learn anything, very small print. And I was only young. I was only young, but, I would be about 9 I think… I used to look at these babies curled up but I

91 Sally msf/kf/bl/#31.

92 Jonathan Rose, *Intellectual Life of the English Working Classes* (New Haven, CT: Yale University Press, 2001), ch. 6, 206–20. On *Aristotle's Masterpiece*, see also Porter and Hall, *The Facts of Life*, 33–68, 128–31.

didn't understand that they were babies in the womb; I didn't (chuckle). I didn't know anything about it... It was something that I, I wasn't supposed to look at, and I, I don't think, my mother wouldn't know that I'd ferreted it out but she never, she never discussed it... There's something always, there's always something always they didn't tell you about babies, but you, you didn't care about it like they do today and nobody encouraged you, so you didn't, you didn't go any further.[93]

Unlike the middle-class female interviewees cited in the next section, working-class women like Sarah presented themselves as believing they were not supposed to read such things and claimed not to have understood them. Moreover unlike working-class boys, considered below, they did not seek to reconcile new information with old – but to remain as they were – confused, and unsure what to believe.

For women of all classes, the preservation of innocence and modesty was a complex cultural accomplishment in which many around them had to play their protective role and with which they had to comply. It was an enduring, positive element of their self-identity, instilled into them by their parents, especially their mothers. Consequently, several working-class women represented themselves as virtuously avoiding sexual knowledge and deliberately evading anyone who had it. Doreen (1922), whose widowed mother made ends meet by taking in sewing, 'never bothered listening to people; I'd walk off'.[94] Similarly, Dora (1923) came into contact with lewd factory talk before marriage in 1945 when working as a machinist in a clothing factory aged 22 and subsequently in Smiths timers factory in Borehamwood.

DORA I would never listen to anything filth. And if I thought it was going to be naughty then I would walk away 'cos my mother taught me that way. (overlapping) You walk away... There was only certain types of people – and you've got to be that type of people – would do it, to stand and listen. I would never stand and listen.[95]

For working-class female interviewees, preserving innocent respectability by isolating oneself from sexual knowledge was important, not only during childhood and adolescence but if possible until marriage. Maria (1917) was one of the interviewees who knew that her life had been lived close to the seedy side and the margins of respectability at times. She was the eldest daughter of an enterprising, if somewhat shady, Blackburnite, who was by turns a builder, a petrol pump owner, a funeral director and a wrestling promoter, whom she idolised. She married her husband, five years her senior, in 1940, because his heavily scarred face appealed to her, indicating he was a 'proper man' and

[93] Sarah msf/kf/bl/#30. [94] Doreen msf/kf/bl/#20. [95] Dora msf/srss/ht/#38.

'tough' like her father. In talking about why she married him she presented herself as a self-conscious 'gangster's moll':

MARIA I felt like I was going out with a gangster because he used to dress up in, um, you know long black jackets and black and white suits and I felt like I was proud to, to know him.[96]

In fact her husband was one of the dancing instructors at 'Tony's', which was seen by some interviewees as the roughest of the several dance clubs in Blackburn in the 1930s. She happily confessed she had crushes on several of the dancing instructors and was also on the lookout for any Blackburn Rovers players before getting married. She was also comfortable relating how she indulged her future husband in sex before marriage at all times of the day, all over his mother's house (who was absent at weekends). After marriage she related how she had to rebuff her father's ex-business partner's adulterous proposal when working with him as a book keeper for a nightclub. Yet for all her worldly-wise self-image, when it came to questions of her own attitudes towards sex, pregnancy and birth control, she indignantly protested her innocence. Childbirth was 'the shock of me life'; contraception: 'I didn't know such things existed ... Oh I didn't find out about them ... your husband produces one when necessary.'[97]

Thus codes for preserving respectability in relation to sex were highly complex (as indeed were working-class codes of respectability in all contexts).[98] 'Innocence' was the core female respectable virtue where matters of sexuality were concerned. However, the ignorance which women sought to maintain, in order to preserve their prized innocence, could also be problematic for their marriages, as the contemporary sex guidance and marriage manuals studied by Hera Cook consistently argued.[99] Certainly the emphasis on female innocence laid a specific burden and delicate task at the door of young husbands, who themselves were also supposed to have no practical experience of intercourse before initiating their brides on the wedding night. As other oral historians have reported, several respondents reported wedding night nerves.[100]

96 Maria msf/kf/bl/#8. 97 Maria msf/kf/bl/#8.

98 See Weeks, *Sex, Politics, and Society*, 72–6. Szreter, *Fertility, Class, and Gender*, 56–7, 460–1. Historians are agreed that 'respectability' was a key concept and term for the Victorians, meaning 'social worthiness', which continued to retain its purchase during the early and mid-twentieth century. See for example, Peter Bailey, '"Will the Real Bill Banks Please Stand Up?" Towards a Role Analysis of Mid-Victorian Working-Class Respectability', *Journal of Social History* 12, no. 3 (1979): 336–53, Ellen Ross, '"Not the Sort That Would Sit on the Doorstep": Respectability in Pre-World War I London', *International Labour and Working-Class History* 27 (1985): 39–59. Also see, Sonya O. Rose, 'Respectable Men, Disorderly Others: The Language of Gender and the Lancashire Weavers' Strike of 1878 in Britain', *Gender and History* 5, no. 3 (1993): 382–97.

99 Cook, *The Long Sexual Revolution*, Part II.

100 For instance, on the variable experiences of wedding nights and honeymoons see, Sutton, *We Didn't Know Aught*, 42–9.

Mildred (1924) remembered they were '[v]ery shy… both of us'. For Grace (1922) it was '[a]gony… I was terribly shy, I really was'. Hugh (1926) could not penetrate until they later found out about Vaseline and Larry (1917) and Doreen (1922) also found she was 'too small'.[101]

According to Slater and Woodside, their research in the late 1940s indicated that 'The public ignorance of sexual physiology is abysmal.'[102] Preserving innocence could make initial sexual relations in marriages fraught. In the early 1950s Geoffrey Gorer found that the majority of his respondents 'think that both sexes should approach marriage with no prior sexual experience', while at the same time he concluded from the number of his respondents confessing to their sexual 'disappointment', 'distress' and 'failures' in their marriages, that 'ignorance, particularly on the part of the men, is a major hazard in English marriages'.[103] The way in which women in particular perceived the problems and emotional costs that could result from these norms and expectations was perhaps also indicated in an intriguing anomalous finding which Gorer reported from the results of his contemporaneous enquiry. He noted that more women than men supported the 'double standard' that men should gain practical sexual experience before marriage but women should not.[104]

In recognition of the problems that went with ignorance several of the respondents were prepared to acknowledge the value in this respect of an improved sex education in schools for their children. But many also regretted the way in which this was associated with a wider public discourse of sexuality in the mass media, which resulted in a loss of innocence for the young, or they regarded the advent of sex education as a mixed blessing.[105] Marian (1908) was typical, although she was also one of the more religiously active Blackburn respondents and one of the older ones.

MARIAN Young uns today knows more than what we knew when we were married and it's not a wise thing (short pause) see. But they, as I say, they're told too much on television and they learn too much out of magazines.[106]

[101] Mildred msf/kf/bl/#41; Grace msf/srss/ht/#38; Hugh msf/kf/ht/#18; Larry and Doreen msf/kf/bl/#20. See also Chapter 7, 'Bodies', 303–5 for more on accounts of wedding night embarrassments and honeymoon difficulties.

[102] Slater and Woodside, *Patterns of Marriage*, 176.

[103] Gorer, *Exploring English Character*, 104–5.

[104] Ibid., 111–14. While men, Gorer noted, were somewhat more in favour of the 'egalitarian' position that both men and women should adhere equally to chastity before marriage. Similarly, while noting the 'attractiveness' of female innocence, Hall found that many of the men who wrote to Marie Stopes condemned the ignorance of wives and called for better and more comprehensive sex instruction (Hall, 'Impotent Ghosts', 63).

[105] Lucinda Beier's analysis revealed similarly ambivalent attitudes with continued support for the preservation of innocence, especially among girls: 'you were brought up innocent on matters. There was no bad-mindedness' (Beier, 'We Were Green as Grass', 465).

[106] Marian msf/kf/bl/#28.

Although middle-class interviewees were more likely to be comfortable with seeing themselves as becoming knowledgeable about the facts of life before marriage without seeing this as compromising their innocence, they too applied a moral code in which nice girls avoided the public articulation of sexual matters. Thus, the fact that Antonia (1928) 'discovered' masturbation by 'accident' suggests a rather different relationship with her own body than many older or less well-educated female interviewees had with theirs. However, despite this she nonetheless echoed the voices of the rest of the sample in reiterating that she did not talk about sex and avoided anyone who did:

> ANTONIA you didn't talk about things like that [masturbation][...]You didn't do things like that. It was all a bit, er, nasty really ... and there, there were always people who did talk about things they shouldn't. One knew about it but one didn't get involved with them; they were rather frowned on.
>
> All kinds of sexual things were frowned upon. [...] You didn't talk about them. We certainly didn't have classes in, in, er, anything to do with that. Nice girls of, of our generation didn't know about those things or if they did, they didn't talk about it.[107]

The paradox of women in interviews who consistently asserted that they were ignorant, while at the same time presenting details of the information they did obtain, overheard or pieced together, is resolved by understanding that it was their innocence that they prized, not their ignorance. Ignorance was, as many women acknowledged, sometimes a nuisance, but many, at the same time, saw a degree of innocence as central to their attractiveness and their respectability. Contemporary, progressive, middle-class campaigners for sex education and birth control saw ignorance only as a problem to be dispelled, an apparently uncontentious rationalist position implicitly also endorsed by most subsequent historians of this movement.[108] But the oral history evidence allows us to examine women's and men's own perceptions of ignorance. This shows that those advocating greater knowledge have been missing the point that ordinary women at the time – mothers and daughters – continued

[107] Antonia msf/kf/ht/#35.

[108] Cook, *The Long Sexual Revolution*, Part II, Peter Fryer, *The Birth Controllers* (London: Secker & Warburg, 1965), Audrey Leathard, *The Fight for Family Planning: The Development of Family Planning Services in Britain, 1921–74* (London: Macmillan, 1980), Porter and Hall, *The Facts of Life*, Part II, Clive Wood and Beryl Suitters, *The Fight for Acceptance: A History of Contraception* (Guildford: Billing & Sons, 1970). Earlier voices, such as that of Mary Scharlieb, saw innocence as desirable, but argued that ignorance was not the same as innocence and suggested outlining 'the mystery of parenthood' through 'the study of vegetable physiology'. In the case of boys she favoured sex education on the grounds that the alternative was to leave boys to 'pick up information from vulgar and unclean minds'; 'whatever objections there may be to giving explicit instruction on sex matters to the young, such instruction is immensely to be preferred to the almost inevitable perversion which follows ignorance' (Scharlieb and Sibly, *Youth and Sex*, 5, 103–4).

consciously to invest in the idea of female ignorance as a deliberate strategy to maintain the moral core of their female attractiveness as respectable 'innocents'. The interviews reveal how self-respecting women of both middle and working classes were not simply passively ignorant. They fought to uphold and maintain their innocence, and they carefully avoided close exposure to some sources of information.[109]

'Oh yes, I knew ... but it was theoretical of course'

A number of middle-class female interviewees spoke of reading published information about human reproduction when adolescent as a form of written information which could be helpful and respectably read by educated young women like themselves.[110] Even here, however, women stressed the limitations of such information – basic, not detailed or explicit, encountered sometimes clandestinely, sometimes with friends. These stories are juxtaposed with continued assertions about taboo and secrecy. The narratives continue to convey the message that women were supposed to have only limited if any forms of knowledge and that material was not easily available. Thus, despite the easier access these middle-class women had had, especially slightly later in their lives as they approached marriage, to written forms of sexual information, stories of puzzling through personal 'ignorance' continued nonetheless to dominate life narratives.

Judith (1931) remembered curiously discussing matters with her peers and looking for written (respectable) advice and answers to their questions:

JUDITH I certainly didn't get it [sex information] directly from my mother. I think I got it from my schoolmates. We used to discuss things and go through the dictionary: 'What is this?', 'Ohhh, is that what that is!', you know, and so on, that sort of

[109] See also, Regenia Gagnier, *Subjectivities: A History of Self-Representation in Britain, 1832–1920* (New York and Oxford: Oxford University Press, 1991), 93.

[110] Perhaps somewhat surprisingly there does not seem to be any strong evidence that reading sex education material was much more likely to have occurred among the younger half of the middle-class interviewees than the elder half, taking into account possible class effects. Twelve middle-class interviewees reported this form of learning about sex, comprising 34 per cent of the thirty-five middle-class interviewees. Of all thirty-five middle-class interviewees, about half (54%) were born before 1920 and the other half (46%) born in 1920 or after. Of the twelve reporting book-learning about sex exactly half (50%) were born before 1920 and half after. Middle-class interviewees reporting book-learning about sex were: Gill (1920) msf/kf/bl/#48; Judith (1931) msf/kf/ht/#33; Pru (1911) msf/kf/ht/#12; June (1914) msf/kf/ht/#27; Antonia (1928) msf/kf/ht/#35; Roger (1910) msf/kf/ht/#10; Reg (1919) msf/kf/ht/#36; Joanna (1915) msf/kf/ht/#22; Betty (1922) msf/kf/ht/#31; Esme (1921) msf/kf/ht/#9; Gerald (1919) msf/kf/ht/#9; Hugh (1926) msf/kf/ht/#18. (For reference, only six working-class interviewees mentioned coming across book knowledge, a mere 11 per cent of the fifty-three working-class interviewees, confirming that not only did they exhibit a significant qualitative difference in the way they presented their understanding of this information but also that they were three times less likely proportionately to recall coming into contact with it at all.)

way … I think that was it mostly … I read a book that my step-father had and I used to wait until they'd gone out of the house and then I'd read it and I learnt quite a lot that way … very, very basic, a little bit more advanced than you'd give to a schoolchild to read but not much more.[111]

Much older than Judith, June (1914) was the daughter of a bank manager in Yorkshire, though she only attended the local elementary school (failing to get into the local grammar school). She learned about birth control from her schoolfriends; thus revealing the ways in which middle-class girls made discoveries together. She found a condom when searching a friend's parents' drawer:

JUNE We never had any, er, lessons or, or, or it was just a taboo thing … But girls … you know 13 or 14 … you talk amongst yourself; you've read things and I told you last, last week about my friend and I going into her parents' drawer and finding this thing ro- … rolled up [a condom].[112]

Gill (1920), whose father was a bank accountant and mother was from a monied Blackburn family who was living during her teenage years in Shropshire, was asked what she thought of Marie Stopes' book, which she read after being given it by her mother, before she was married in 1945:

GILL Well, er, I think at the time and, er, er, she did an … enormous am- … amount of good because it was not a subject that was discussed, er, anywhere. I mean, you, you know the Samaritans?[113]

It was also a notable class contrast that the middle-class interviewees were less likely to talk of shock and surprise at their first period and that virtually none invoked the common working-class theme of being warned off all contact with boys. Esme (1921), whose father was a Managing Director of a large organisation in London, recalled a forewarning from her mother, who did not go out to work. Rather than a tone of shock, she mirrored her mother's deliberately matter-of-fact attitude towards the whole process:

ESME I think she told me about them a short time before they happened … we didn't wear, er, um, bought sanitary napkins … we had ones that were rather like babies'

111 Judith msf/kf/ht/#33. 112 June msf/kf/ht/#27.

113 Gill msf/kf/bl/#48. Gill then went on to mention the story of (Edward) Chad Varah (1911–2007). This contemporary of the interviewees was Vicar of Holy Trinity, Blackburn 1942–9. His life's work had direct relevance to the topic in the interview, as Gill realised in bringing up the subject. Before founding the Samaritans in London in 1953, Varah developed expertise as a marriage guidance counsellor, sex therapist and sex educator at parish youth clubs. Varah claimed that his dedication to such sex education and counselling work dated from 1935, when in his first parish of St Giles in Lincoln he took the funeral in unconsecrated ground of a 13-year-old girl who had committed suicide because she had been unable to confide or get advice when horrified at the appearance of her first menstrual period (*Church Times*, Obituary 16 November 2007. *Independent*, Obituary 10 November 2007).

nappies and, um, I, er, I, I used to sort of put them out and they were, er, washed by the maid... [114]

Overall, then, middle-class testimony was more likely to reflect a belief that a young woman could and should have an understanding of the biological meaning of her periods, that the existence of periods for instance did not need to be concealed in the household. Furthermore, this principle applied more widely to knowledge – albeit theoretical – about reproduction and sex. Consequently there was considerable class difference in language among female interviewees. Many from the secondary-educated middle classes had confidence in using the correct medical terms when discussing sex in the interviews, such as in referring to the penis and the vagina, even though usage of the terms was evidently not a familiar experience:

And why wasn't withdrawal regular, what was your attitude towards it, what did you think about it?

GILL Well, it's a, er, it's an unsatisfactory end, isn't it, to the sex act? I mean part of the thing is that, that you should really have the penis inside, er, after the sex act, shouldn't you? After the ejaculation. Oh, good grief I'm [using] these words, sound like a medical dictionary or something. (laughs)[115]

Esme (1921) was sufficiently at her ease with the language that she could tell an amusing story about this, which incidentally illustrated how she and her husband Gerald (1919) had shared their knowledge when commencing married life:

When did you first hear terms like orgasm to describe... ?

ESME Well, I suppose probably, er, about the time Gerald and I got married or just before, a bit before, you know.

GERALD I'd read and learned the terms.

ESME He'd read and learned about it.

GERALD And I know I, I, er, mispronounced 'vagina' I mean, 'cos I...

ESME D'you (laughs)...

GERALD I called it 'var-guy-nah' didn't I?

ESME Oh yes, the vagina, yes that's right.

GERALD You used the term to the doctor once...

ESME That's right; he was, he was bemused.

GERALD He looked very puzzled, you said, and you felt very put out because it was the wrong...

ESME Well, only, after all it was the Latin pronunciation, so there's nothing wrong with that. He hadn't sort of got his Latin... [116]

Working-class women did not use these medical terms at all in the interviews, and, as we have seen, tended to portray their contact with such formal,

[114] Esme msf/kf/ht/#9. [115] Gill (1920) msf/kf/bl/#48.
[116] Esme and Gerald msf/kf/ht/#9.

book knowledge, as confusing and unhelpful. As Pearl Jephcott observed of the working-class girls she questioned in the 1940s: 'One of the married girls who borrowed a book on sex from her brother-in-law expressed the view that most books of that kind were no good. "The words are too long. They're frightened to say anything. It's dry, you can't finish it".'[117]

Many working-class women maintained to the interviewer that they had been kept in near total ignorance of any and all forms of reproductive knowledge before marriage. Middle-class female respondents, by contrast, did not see that presenting themselves as having this abstract sexual knowledge necessarily compromised their respectability. They tied their claims to respectable innocence more directly to their status as virgins at marriage, seeing no necessary inconsistency between this and their right, as educated members of the middle classes, to have acquired an adequate, but essentially theoretical, knowledge of sex and reproduction sometime before marriage.

So when it came round to actually having sex would you say you were unprepared or were you prepared at that point?

ESME Oh, I was prepared. Oh yes, I knew what was going to happen etcetera, yes. Um, yeah I wasn't, ha ha, ignorant[…]but it was theoretical, of course.[118]

'You've got to love somebody to do that'

Thus, middle- and working-class female interviewees, with their very different educational resources and attitudes, often had distinct narratives to recount about how their shared commitment to the female ideal of innocence, as something desirable and attractive, had influenced the ways in which they had been able to approach a knowledge of sex while preserving their respectability. Middle-class respondents accommodated theoretical knowledge of the basics with the aim of preservation of their virginity before marriage. Working-class respondents relied much more on the strategy of shunning knowledge and embracing 'ignorance'. This meant that their narratives then had to portray in a quite different manner from the middle-class interviewees how they subsequently came to an understanding of sex as something that could, in the appropriate circumstances, play a valid and respectable role in their lives.

There is a strong current in the historiography on working-class women which rightly emphasises the support (and sanctions) that could be expected from other women and that they could draw on through their social networks and through informal neighbourhood gossip both to form their own identities and to attempt to regulate the behaviour of others around them, including their

[117] Agnes Pearl Jephcott, *Rising Twenty: Notes on Some Ordinary Girls* (London: Faber and Faber, 1948), 89.

[118] Esme (1921) msf/kf/ht/#9.

menfolk.[119] Could this have included providing resources for learning about sex and preparing young women for marriage? Although some historians have implied or suggested this, in fact there seems to be remarkably little positive evidence that has been published for concluding that this mutual support amounted to working-class women equipping each other with a pool of useful and detailed knowledge and practical information about sex and birth control; still less that it provided such a function for unmarried working-class girls.[120]

As is made clear by the oral testimony presented here, the public and community codes of working-class respectability, which these informal networks of discourse were engaged in upholding, tied the personal reputations of girls and women to the moral concept of innocence and to the notion of privacy in sexual matters. The open, public discussion of details of sexual practices was by definition a corrupting activity. Wives might attempt to assist each other by condemning certain husbands as 'too demanding', while girls going to dances might warn others that some boys were too 'rough' or 'pushy' (see the next chapter). Married women desperate to avoid another birth might seek discreet advice from other women on how to get 'regular' again or who to see about their problem.[121]

[119] Ross, 'Not the Sort', 39–59, Melanie Tebbutt, *Women's Talk?: A Social History of Gossip in Working-Class Neighbourhoods, 1880–1960* (Aldershot: Scolar Press, 1995). During the interwar and immediate post-war decades, the importance of these street and neighbourhood communication communities as a resource for working-class women may have been gradually attenuating. This happened in a geographically uneven way, for a number of reasons, such as increasingly dispersed suburban settlement patterns in new estates with a higher level of both publicly provided and privately purchased amenities, and improved levels of income, health and social security requiring less reliance on neighbourhood goodwill to get by. See Langhamer, 'The Meanings of Home', esp. 352–3, McKibbin, *Classes and Cultures: England, 1918–1951*, 188–98. The net outcome of this may have been a greater balance of reliance among these classes on the mass media of newsprint, magazines, cinema and radio for valued information on all subjects to do with daily life. As a result there was increased importance in this period of consulting historians' findings on the content and subject matter of these media, for judging the (limited) amount of public information that was in circulation on sexual matters (see above). On the growth of advice columns in the popular press in the 1940s and 1950s, for instance, see Bingham, *Family Newspapers*, 73–82.

[120] See below, notes 123 and 126. The secondary source which is invariably cited to support the thesis of female networks of birth control information is Gittins, *Fair Sex*, 87–94 and ch. 6. It is somewhat startling therefore to find that there is absolutely no evidence from the oral history transcripts cited by Gittins in her book, *Fair Sex*, to support this thesis. In fact the main kind of evidence cited by Gittins about the imparting of birth control information comes from a completely distinct source which Gittins used: interwar birth control clinics, notably the records of 500 cases of married women, who attended the Manchester and Salford Mother's Clinic between 1928 and 1933. However, there is nothing in the clinic evidence which has any bearing on the possibility of information-sharing of any kind among female workers at their workplaces (Gittins, *Fair Sex*, 10, 30–1, 165–80). Unfortunately Gittins has not preserved the transcripts from her oral history interviews (personal communication to Simon Szreter).

[121] On abortions, see Beier, *For Their Own Good*, 245–53, Kate Fisher, *Birth Control, Sex and Marriage in Britain, 1918–1960* (Oxford and New York: Oxford University Press, 2006),

But these community norms of general moral guidance and networks for crisis support did not amount to an effective and informed community discourse about sex, nor a way of providing young working-class girls with a sex education. On the contrary, they provided a range of more indirect forms of mutual assistance and crisis response necessitated precisely because, to retain their respectability and prized innocence, girls were deliberately not equipped by working-class communities with such knowledge before marriage. Nor was it considered respectable for married women to promote a climate of community discussion of these matters or to instruct their daughters. It was believed that preserving ignorance and inculcating a respectful sense of fear for the unnamed consequences of any physical contact with the opposite sex was the only safe strategy, as we have seen with working-class narratives about their first periods (and as Chapter 3 on courtship will also demonstrate in female respondents' memories, for instance, of parental injunctions over kissing):

> CLARE Oh, you never discussed sex with your girlfriend, or your parents; wouldn't think of doing it. I mean you might think that's odd, but you didn't; you didn't discuss sex like they do today. I always say we were very ignorant.[122]

By claiming they were ignorant, working-class women like Clare (1912), one of a large working-class family in Berkhamsted, effectively placed themselves in a respectable category. By asserting their own ignorance and pointing out that those who had information were loose in some way – prostitutes or its equivalent – respondents reasserted this crucial set of relationships between sexual innocence and respectability.[123]

60–5, 113–29, 156–63, Leap and Hunter, *The Midwife's Tale*, ch. 6, Francesca P. L. Moore, 'Beyond the Ideal: Motherhood in Industrial Lancashire, 1860–1937' (Unpublished Ph.D. thesis, Cambridge: University of Cambridge, 2008), ch. 5, '"Good Deeds for Naughty Ladies": Abortion in Lancashire 1861–1937', 165–216, Sutton, *We Didn't Know Aught*, 95–8.

122 Clare (1912) msf/kf/ht/#8.

123 Some studies have suggested that factories could be open sources of information about sex for young women, partly because these were mixed environments with sexualised forms of banter between men and women; and partly because women might find themselves working in locations slightly removed from the careful policing of female behaviour associated with close-knit working-class neighbourhoods (Beier, *For Their Own Good*, 214–15, Jephcott, *Rising Twenty*, 87). However, in some instances, exposure to bawdy banter or freer conversations encouraged young women to monitor and preserve their own innocent respectability even more carefully and take action to distance themselves from the sources of information or the material gleaned, as we have seen emphasised in the oral testimony in this chapter. Jephcott also found that some of her informants told her that 'it is mainly in factories where unsuitable knowledge about sex and low standards are set' (*Rising Twenty*, 89). Beier was in fact only able to produce a couple of quotations (neither of them discussing information deemed detailed or helpful by the informant) among the 239 Lancashire working-class transcripts in her study (Beier, 'We Were Green as Grass', 467). Beier also acknowledged that Elizabeth Roberts, discussing the same evidence, was of the view that '[t]here is little evidence that women discussed sexual topics in the mill' (Beier, *For Their Own Good*, 214–15). Also see, Jutta Schwarzkopf, 'Bringing Babies into Line with Mothers' Jobs: Lancashire Cotton Weavers' Fertility Regime', in *Gendering*

The following extensive extract demonstrates a number of points made by different informants, all gathered together in the testimony of a single respondent reflecting on two significant learning episodes in her own life. Heather (1916), born into a working-class home in Chelsea, was the youngest of six. Her father, wounded in the Great War, was a postman. After leaving school at 14 she had worked in Harrods' sweet factory, Phillips Mills' paper factory, KLG spark plugs assembly line and Chelsea soap factory before marrying in 1938 aged 21. In particular Heather presents herself as actively resisting the information she received in various contexts and preserving her innocence until finally she claims she was able to make moral sense of it all. In the first episode Heather recalls her reactions at about age 10 to a graphic, purportedly first-hand witness description of sexual intercourse from a friend:

HEATHER She said, 'D'you know what they do when they go to bed?' Well, that age you don't know, you know and ... I went to walk. She said 'No, don't walk away.' She said, 'I haven't told you yet' ... she said, 'my dad, got a, a thing there', she said (that's way they used to talk) ... 'Between his legs, he's got a long thing.' And I was, 'What's she talking about?' I mean, I've never seen my father undressed or even my brothers, you know. 'And he sticks it, sticks it in hi- ... in, he sticks it in my mum's fanny.' 'Oh don't tell lies.' I always remember that; oh I said 'I don't believe it, don't believe that; don't do that, babies don't come like that' ... But I couldn't believe her; I just called her a liar, you know. She said, 'oh', she said, 'one of these days', she said, 'you'll realise what I'm telling you'. She said, 'you wanna watch your mum and dad like we do'; she said, 'we went, we, we watch our mum' (laughs). Er, I just couldn't believe it at the time and I said 'no, it's not right.'[124]

When Heather was rather older, she was again exposed to detailed information about sexual relations from workmates at KLG spark plug factory in Fulham in the 1930s. She was no longer struggling to assimilate the truth of the biological facts of life, as when she was aged 10. It was now a question of when and where sex fitted into her life morally – how it related to her own guiding moral principles, which she attributes to her mother's influence:

HEATHER when I got older and, you know, you go to work, you're working with girls that, er, that're older than you are and know what goes on, and they tell you there and then, oh yeah. You know what happens; you know if you go out with a bloke, you know, what they want and what they don't whatsname and ... ' Specially at the KLG; the girls there, coo dear! The times they at it used to be. (laughs) They used to tell you, you know, when we, they'd say, 'Hello Mary, d'you have it last night?' and 'Ooh yeah'.

And were these girls married or not?

the Fertility Decline in the Western World, ed. Angélique Janssens (Bern and New York: Peter Lang, 2007), 326. See also notes 120, 126.

[124] Heather msf/kf/ht/#14.

> Some of them weren't married. Two of them were married but some of them … weren't married.
> *So what did you feel when they were talking about having sex before they were married and describing it and …?*
> Well, I don't know, you know … [I] always remember when she said that … 'One day, you'll realise what, you know, I'm telling you' … She said, 'I know by the look on your face you think I'm pulling a fast one', she said, 'but I'm not' … and then when I first had sex with Fred, she flashed right across my mind … I heard her saying and I thought that's what she, what she was meaning. But I was young at the time and silly and I just, I just wouldn't take it in.
> *And what about when you were at KLG … what were your thoughts then?*
> Well, at KLG we, and I found out a lot of things about, er, sex and that, you know, that I didn't know before.
> *What other things did you … ?*
> My, my mother never told me anything …
> *Like what sorts of things?*
> Yeah about being with a man and sleeping with a man and all this and that. I said, 'No, you can't. You've got to love somebody to do that.' And [they said], 'Oh no, you don't always have to love somebody.' 'Cos I think two of those girls are prostitutes but we never let on. But I think that, the way they used to talk and the way they used to carry on, they gave themselves away. But the other two were married, they, you know [said], 'That is right, love.' She said, 'Yeah, when you get married that's what you do.' She said 'That's what marriage is.' I said, 'Is it?' And … she says 'You're, you're just being silly.' She said, 'You, you're turning your mind against it, anything like that happens. Well, it does. You'll soon know.' 'One day', she said, 'when you meet the right man and you fall in love', she said, 'you'll know what I'm trying to tell you. That's what you'll, you're hoping you're, you're, you know, you might have.' But, um, not before I was married. My mother used to threaten us, 'Don't you ever come home here and tell me you're going to have a baby' she said (laughs).[125]

The argument for extreme caution in embracing this dangerous knowledge could not be more clearly articulated: 'My mother used to threaten us, "Don't you ever come home here and tell me you're going to have a baby."' However, against this, in this story the two married women are presented as speaking in gentle, reassuring, persuasive terms. She puts the argument for practical resignation and acceptance as follows: '"That's what marriage is." I said, "Is it?" And … she says "You're, you're just being silly."' And '"You, you're turning your mind against it … "' Heather's resolution to this conundrum and to all the conflicting information and advice she had received from so many different quarters was encapsulated in the ethical distinction she made between herself and the views of the two married women at work, on the one hand, and those whose views she equated with 'prostitutes', on the other. The crucial points, she emphasises, are 'you've got to love somebody to do that' and it

[125] Heather msf/kf/ht#14.

must happen in the context of marriage, not outside it. And she also relates the moment of epiphany for the code she had worked out for herself when the recapitulation of the whole confusing learning process she had been through 'flashed through her mind', when finally she first had sex with her husband in the morally correct context of married love. She had concluded that this made the 'unbelievable' act morally acceptable for her and also squared it with the conscience instilled by her mother's admonitions.

Thus, Heather's account makes clear that her learning about sex was occurring as part of a larger process of forging a moral identity for herself that allowed a practical space for engaging in real physical contact with men. The choice of whether to listen and believe the eye-opening tales or deliberately to maintain a distance and state of 'innocence' is itself presented as a moral decision. Heather chose to believe information and to expose herself to the advice of trusted, older, married women. This testimony indicates that the valued role played in the historical testimony by sympathetic older married women in providing confiding and helpful one-to-one advice about sexual matters needs to be distinguished from the more indiscriminate, and largely undocumented, notion that groups of young women – age peers in large workplaces, like textile mills – routinely provided supportive networks of reliable and helpful information about sex. While such work relations may have been the source of mutual support among women in a general sense and especially in a crisis, the evidence does not support the notion that such peer groups provided adolescent girls and young women with what was perceived as practical and detailed or valued and helpful advice on sex.[126]

Female respondents in particular saw sexual knowledge and its acquisition as far more than just a matter of whether or not they obtained hidden information. Because sex knowledge was considered inappropriate and improper for public articulation the very act of acquiring it or listening to it in any public context – including with a small set of workmates – could be tantamount, for a young woman, to identifying herself as unrespectable. Thus, the amount and kind of knowledge acquired and believed, and the context in which it was learned, is presented by respondents as indicative of the kind of moral person they were. Heather negotiated her way through the account of this learning

[126] Thus both of the specific examples cited by Selina Todd from her oral history testimony conform to the pattern of one-to-one advice by older, married women, rather than the more generalised notion attributed by Todd, as by others, to have been supposedly documented in the work of Diana Gittins (on which see above n.120) (Todd, *Young Women, Work, and Family*, 155–6). Langhamer's work is the other instance cited by Todd to support this notion, but the main example fully documented by Langhamer, 'Jane', worked in an office, not a factory and reported herself being advised by one *male* colleague in particular, not a group of other women; while one of the other two cases mentioned by Langhamer, 'Alice', talked only of being given the rather non-specific, perhaps humorous, advice that she should 'take soap powder and a rubber sheet on her honeymoon'. Langhamer, *Women's Leisure*, 123. See also notes 120, 123.

process by concluding that the institutions and ideals of love and marriage rendered sexual intercourse sufficiently respectable. Information imparted to her by a sympathetic married woman was safe and moral knowledge, allowing Heather to present herself as becoming knowledgeable about sex while still remaining respectable.

Above all, for the female respondents there was one correct and respectable way for girls and young women to learn about sex and this was in the context of marriage. Given the absence of a respectable, public discourse about sex, 'knowing' about sex was almost synonymous with personal, physical experience of it; and this was only supposed to happen after and in marriage. This was also the 'natural' way to learn. Natural meant 'normal' – in conformity with conventional, religiously sanctioned norms and with parental ideals and admonitions. Maureen (1920), who married in 1943, saw sex as something natural to be learned by two individuals (within marriage):

MAUREEN You find out from one another, one way or another. It's always the young ones that get married and you know it comes as a natural thing. It was just natural, that we were together. So it was alright, but we never, there were no sex before we were married, I can assure you.[127]

Thus the female respondents emphasise that they were socialised and educated into believing that, in their culture, women were expected to be innocent. Despite the disadvantages of ignorance, which many recognised, innocence became a strategy and an identity for them. This was because they grew up in a world in which parental authority and thoughts of what a mother would think of their behaviour were strong, and in which they came to believe that their own respectability and attractiveness were equally linked to innocence. They were educated into being very discreet about their privately acquired knowledge if middle class, or shy, fearful and unable to talk easily about sex if working class.

Here there was a fundamental gender difference. The men and women interviewed presented themselves as reacting and responding to this culture of silence surrounding the facts of life in entirely distinctive ways. Many women embraced ignorance, and presented sexual information as something that they were wary of because they understood that their innocence was a morally desirable and, indeed, sexually attractive state. Rather than be seen to be seeking to obtain knowledge in the face of a culture of silence, women's encounters with sexual information were presented as dangerous and difficult moments, which might threaten their respectability. Most men, by contrast, rejected ignorance and gave accounts which emphasised ways in which they sought to challenge it.

[127] Maureen msf/kf/bl/#46.

'Lads... knew all the rude words'

What, then, do men's stories of ignorance tell us about masculine identity and men's worlds? As we have seen, men, in a similar fashion to women, presented themselves as having been brought up in a culture of silence where sexual information was kept from them or hard to come by. They stressed the difficulties they had in obtaining information and presented their childhoods as periods of innocence. They were not generally provided with information by their parents or in school. Men also presented open discussion of sexual matters as taboo and as something that would only take place in disreputable circles. At the same time, however, in sharp contrast with female testimony, men revealed that from childhood onwards, they were curious to find out about bodily differences and during adolescence eager to acquire information about sex. Just as women's adolescent identities were tied up with maintaining ignorance, so boys as adolescents were concerned to become competent men who were sufficiently sexually knowledgeable to play their allotted role of sexual initiator with their innocent bride.[128]

Men's oral history testimony highlights the importance of seeing themselves as sexual initiators, and their narratives charted the role sexual enlightenment played in the process of becoming a man. Despite the difficulties in finding out about sex, men did not want to present themselves as having entered marriage in ignorance and were a little embarrassed, rather than proud of it, if they thought they had been poorly informed. While women wished to be viewed as innocent upon marriage, men wished to be seen as prepared, competent and knowledgeable. There is, thus, a clear tension in many men's narratives between the presentation of the acquisition of their knowledge, and the assertion that many sources of knowledge were illicit, seedy or disreputable.

Men's stories were thus carefully constructed to establish a mechanism by which they became informed which does not taint their identities with the suggestion that they had access to or engaged in illicit forms of sexual intercourse or discourse. They talked of discursive games they played and the escapades in boyhood and in adolescence necessary to finesse the opaque public culture and to 'work out' the role of the sexual organs and their functioning. Male interviewees used a number of ploys to render 'safe' their accounts of their own direct contact with the disrespectable and clandestine knowledge that related to sex. This confirms that, like the female interviewees, they remained concerned

[128] As others have noted, young men's bluff bravado and euphemistic, ribald assertions of their sexual knowledge or even of personal experience, often hid their own continued confusion about sexual matters (Gillis, *For Better, for Worse*, 268–9, Humphries, *A Secret World of Sex*, 40, 60–2, Paul E. Willis, *Learning to Labour: How Working Class Kids Get Working Class Jobs* (Farnborough: Saxon House, 1977), 108–9).

SWANSEA LIBRARY UNIVERSITY

with distancing themselves from the dubious nature of any form of contact with sex – including sexual knowledge – outside marriage. At the same time, they acknowledged that it was also part of their identity to have challenged the silence surrounding the subject but they were careful to present themselves as having done this in an innocent way.

Men echoed women's testimony in pointing out the absence of parental or educational advice about sexual matters. However, in contrast to the voices from women, men did not distance themselves from the information available, from playground gossip onwards. Patrick, born in 1918 in East Ham, the son of a gas inspector, stayed at school until he was 16.

When did you first find out the facts of life?

PATRICK (pause) School, I think, yes; never from my parents … from the lads who knew all the rude words. No, there was no, sort of, tuition in schools on that, God! … [W]hen you get to secondary school some of them have got girlfriends and they say how nice it is, you know, and you hear all about it.[129]

Some male narratives were similar to those produced by female interviewees. Like many women, Roger (1910) presented himself when younger as having been baffled as to how babies were born, and highlighted the refusal of his upper-middle-class parents (his father was an officer in the Royal Navy) to impart even such basic information. However, his story focused on the ways in which he sought to become informed and the attempts he made to rectify the gaps in his knowledge, the questions he asked of his parents and schoolteachers (he attended King's in Rochester) and the interest he showed in the knowledge that older married men possessed. That the process of becoming a man was tied up with obtaining sexual information in order to be prepared for marriage is clearly evident in this testimony. Age also runs through Roger's testimony and he makes fine distinctions between himself at 16, when information was 'wrapped up' and 'cloudy', and himself at 17, when he was 'making enquiries', and then at 18, getting 'definite ideas', such as the following, at last, from his father:

ROGER I remember as a small boy, standing there in school and they said 'Well, what is the purpose of this bellybutton?' and we had a long chat about it, very seriously about what a bellybutton was for. They said, 'Well, are girls any different with bellybuttons?' … So they came to the conclusion; one fellow there, if I tell you, I was there, about 14, but he was about 16 and a half, he came to the conclusion that when a girl had a baby, that bellybutton mysteriously opened and it popped out. Now that's God's truth, and that was the sort of … and you didn't ask your parents because they said 'Oh, for God's sake, get on to something wholesome.' They didn't want to tell you, and that was, it was a moral climate.

So how did you find out?

[129] Patrick msf/kf/ht/#16.

(Sigh) Well we found out, as someone said to me some time ago, 'If you were living in this cloudy existence, how did you know what happened?' Well, it's quite simple; the fascinating thing to me when I was young was when one of my friends, and several of them did, decided to get married. The friendship as far as I'm concerned, intensified generally, definitely, because I wanted to grab him when he came back and sit him down with a pint of beer in front of him and listen. 'Cos I didn't know, I wanted to listen to him. And I remember asking one man and I must have been, he was about 19... 'What is it?' and he turned round and told me, but that man honestly wasn't quite certain what to do on the wedding night.

[...]

ROGER [Father] told me ultimately... he said, it's ah, he said, 'You know that a man is different to a woman?' La-dah, yes right, well, 'a woman makes herself available to a man and he goes to her' and he went on and explained... [and] I suppose it clarified what I'd dimly thought, that's what it was. Because when you, when you were 16 it was wrapped up a bit, 17, you were making enquiries, and at 18 you started to get definite ideas.[130]

Just as women preserved their innocence by distancing themselves from disreputable sources of information so many men also presented themselves as having come across information almost by accident. Men's narratives frequently recalled incidents which provided them with opportunities to learn about sex, but in which they nonetheless did not play any instigating role. Men, like Norman (1914), who grew up with three siblings in working-class Islington, portrayed themselves as casual observers or accidental witnesses:

NORMAN Because, you know, certain things were considered taboo... the sexual, sex education knowledge was nil. Anybody who discussed it was accused of being dirty and filthy and, you know, crazed, that sort of thing, you know... I lived in this mean street [in interwar Islington]... and the older boys used to, uh, play all kinds of tricks, you know... these games that they developed where they finished up touching, touching each other's, each other's private parts... and I wouldn't muck around with local furtive activity very much; it wasn't really my cup of tea... I was a bit of a weak kid. When they played tin-can-copper and they all used to finish off doing these dirty games behind the bushes I was always, I, I only discovered these things by accident... somebody had an old tin can and somebody threw the tin can away and one person had to race after the tin can and the others had to hide... and all kinds of things – those who were 13 or so, mucking around with sex. I only came upon this by accident but my sex instincts weren't very, on the horizon. I was a very weak character in that respect for a long, long, some years.[131]

130 Roger msf/kf/ht/#10.

131 Norman msf/kf/ht/#17. Several working-class male respondents, such as Terence msf/srss/bl/#15 and Frank msf/srss/bl/#16, could recall boys and girls displaying themselves to each other at an early age, or otherwise engaged in 'playful' activity, if there was a suitably unpatrolled area available to them. This was also, as noted in the introduction to this chapter, a strong feature of the testimony from Steve Humphries' set of interviewees, though he failed to comment on the significance of the fact that all of those he cited giving such information on sex play in childhood were male and that they used the 'distancing' tactics discussed here

Of course, the key distinction between men's and women's narratives here is that rather than claiming to have been unaffected by such occasions many men presented themselves as having learned what they could from them. Thus both male and female interviewees divorced themselves from sexual discourses and presented the subcultures in which sexual information was available as sordid or immoral, but men's need to appear sexually informed by the time they reached the end of adolescence meant that these learning episodes were viewed as convenient and innocent mechanisms for self-enlightenment.

When did you first find out what a woman's body looked like?

NORMAN Well, (sigh)… when I went to work as a boy, I used to listen to some of the older boys talking. This is on the south side of the river, and they used to, they reckoned, one of them used to say, 'If I'm round on a Friday night I used to go round to Mrs So-and-so's 'cos she washed herself down in her bath', and they had this little place they met and she had big breasts and they, she, she washed her breasts and that, and that was their, their weekly treat. So I mean, that gives you an indication …there wasn't many opportunities… on one occasion the gang met, they were, very, very much in love with the, this girl in the baker's shop, and… they used to send me in for a, a, to get two cakes and I was instructed to… say, 'No, not that, that one!', you see, and I had her moving about all over and they were all peering down her blouse, so that was a terrific treat, these were boys of perhaps 16, 17.[132]

Peter (1921), who grew up in Withnell, Chorley (near Blackburn), the son of a plate layer on the railway, was the middle child between two sisters:

PETER one of the first things I really got to know about this, a bit of it, was, a chap 'ad a woman, be about 23, or 24, an', er, they used to, every Sunday afternoon, they'd go a walk up moor, with, and as you went up this hill, to go on t'moor itself, there was like an open crevice in the wall, an' they used to go an' sit on this crevice and we used to creep up and watch (laughing)… His 'ands were like an octopus (laughing)… Aye, and we used to laugh at him aye.[133]

Boys' adventurous curiosity and voyeurism was evident among both working-class and middle-class respondents. For the more privileged class, access to binoculars presented additional opportunities for essentially the same activities as their working-class peers. Again, Hubert (1911) was able to distance himself because it was not he, himself, who was the protagonist of the story he related:

(Humphries, *A Secret World of Sex*, 35–40). Sutton, *We Didn't Know Aught* produces a number of similar quotations, and many of these are from female interviewees, but unfortunately, as she notes at the outset, her lively and informative book was not written as an academic study and consequently she gives no indication of the ages of her informants, the approximate dates of their memoirs or their contexts, though it is clear that a number were living in rural locations.

[132] Norman msf/kf/ht/#17. [133] Peter msf/kf/bl/#26.

HUBERT I had some friends who'd been to co-educational boarding schools. Heard a lot about their antics and climbing on the roof and borrowing binoculars (laughs) and whatnot. But not in a single-sex school.[134]

Male respondents such as Hubert and Peter were often laughing while regaling the interviewer with these stories. These memories were portrayed as humorous antics. For the women who were the objects of their attentions, however, being exposed to such opportunistic voyeurism could be a distasteful memory of something dangerous and threatening to their respectability, as it clearly was for Rebecca (1903). Her father was a tailor and they lived in a tenement block ('three floors and three families') in the Jewish East End:

REBECCA once what happened to me, we had a workman in the house and, er, he was doing the floor or something. So I went in to have a bath so I noticed there was a big gap in the wood and some, down there I could see eyes looking up. It was this workman was there looking through the gap. Then that finished me; I knew all about that you mu- that you mustn't with, with somebody, you gotta be careful. I didn't know why but I know you have to be careful.
So how did you feel when you saw that work- workman?
When I saw, felt it? I felt terrible.[135]

Men's representation of learning about the facts of life in adolescence involved recounting lots of furtive passing of scraps of ribald information round networks and between pairs of individuals. An often-repeated theme was the recollection that 'others' were actually engaging in sexual contact with the opposite sex and then reporting back or bragging about it, but rarely offering more specific information than '[i]t were great!'[136] and 'they'd be saying "Ee, I 'ad her last night, it were grand", things like this'.[137] Again, male respondents presented this information as instructive while at the same time distancing themselves from the immorality of the protagonist. Bryan (1918), the son of a miner, grew up in South Wales, but left in search of work upon finishing school:

BRYAN One or two lads there used to be a little bit on the 'ot side... Some of the lads used to, but it never bothered me, as I say, it never bothered me at all. Course they used to brag about what they'd done and what they didn't do... never took any notice of it. To laugh, laugh about it but that was about all. Used to say 'randy old sod' or something like that (laughs).[138]

Bragging and reportage of their 'experiences' by older boys tended to be valued, not rejected, by listeners. They might, however, retain a sceptical attitude of suspension of disbelief until they were finally confident they had unravelled

[134] Hubert msf/kf/ht/#32. [135] Rebecca msf/kf/ht#6.
[136] Alistair msf/kf/bl/#33. [137] Peter msf/kf/bl/#26.
[138] Bryan msf/kf/ht/#25.

the mystery and were not being duped. As a result respondents typically felt they acquired their knowledge in a gradual, informal and sporadic way. It was '[p]atchy information with gaps in it'.[139] Roger moved in naval circles and his family travelled with his father, a naval officer, between naval towns across Britain. His testimony is rich with the details of the interactions, jokes and banter between boys in English public schools in the 1920s:

ROGER We always had a joke you see. They said '[h]e's been wanking!', and the other one would say '[o]h, I thought that was at home in China!' (laugh) And that's how it went on, you see, it was innocence with a certain amount of humour.... because the amount of ignorance, and I can safely say this, the amount of ignorance expressed by youngsters who seemed to be fascinated by the role of the District Nurse, now that is true; so much so that when I was at school, preparatory, there was a very dirty joke... that one boy would say to another, 'District Nurse!' and that was the top line in filth. And what it meant to that day, I didn't know, and I don't know till this day, because it was just that... she went into the room [where] babies were born, and they didn't know.[140]

Like women, men reported coming across books about sex. Men additionally reported having had occasional access to more graphic material, which might include pictures of naked female bodies, though historians are agreed that such magazine publications deliberately avoided an explicitly pornographic approach until the mid-1960s.[141] Unlike many female respondents men did not see the need to maintain their innocence in the face of the exposure to such material, but they did feel it necessary to present the circumstances of their exposure to the material as innocent.

MARK I lived in a boys' school, you see, and there were pictures going about all over the place... pictures of naked women (laughs). I suppose, I mean, they, they had, they've a, they've books, magazines, uh, and so forth, you see, so... Oh I suppose they'd be soft porn; I think, I'm trying to think of them, was it *Men Only*, um, *Razzle*... they were the sort of thing that had got dirty jokes in them and so forth, I, I mean, they were the sort of thing that nasty little boys did have.[142]

[139] Patrick msf/kf/ht/#16. [140] Roger msf/kf/ht/#10.

[141] On pornographic publications in Britain during the interwar and mid-twentieth-century decades, see Collins, *Modern Love*, ch. 5. On the 'pin-up' see Bingham, *Family Newspapers*, 207–23. Both historians conclude of these two different genres that the deliberate depiction of explicitly sexualised and erotic graphic or textual material did not appear until the mid-1960s and that the previous decades were characterised, rather, by a 'pornography of alibis', to use Collins' phrase (Collins, *Modern Love*, 134). *Men Only* was not published until 1935, the same year in which *Razzle*, first published in 1932, was relaunched in a pocket-size format, mostly with cartoon depictions but including a colour 'centrefold', pin-up photographed 'Dream Girl', www.magforum.com/mens/mensmagazinesatoz10.htm111 (accessed 10 April 2010).

[142] Mark msf/kf/ht#22.

Mark (1917) was at Newport private Quaker boarding school, the only child of middle-class parents who lived in High Wycombe. Hugh (1926) was born in Trowbridge, Wiltshire, into a working-class family and had lived in Preston after the war until 1955 (when he moved to Harpenden).

Um, about sex, what about things like pornography, was there any dirty material around?

HUGH Oh yes, well, when you say dirty, probably not like it is now, no, no, but there was *Health and Beauty*; I mean that was, there's nothing dirty about that really, not in today's terms anyway. Well, I mean, to see nudity in a book, marvellous, great things, yes.

So what was Health and Beauty, what sort of book was it?

Well this was the, um, it's still going, it's um, I mean, I never bought one but these things they came up your way now and again, and you never refused to look at them. Um, it's the nudist, one of the nudist books; I think there are about three of them in this country, yes.[143]

Despite its illicit connotations, many men also presented themselves as having learned about sex in part through the personal practice of masturbating.[144] Some men recalled being warned against masturbating and presented it as a forbidden act that one might guiltily engage in in private. However, this was also ridiculed as an antiquated attitude by others.[145] Many admitted masturbating and some even presented it as a mechanism by which, in conjunction with other bits of information, they worked out the process of reproduction and intercourse with women. It would appear that most men constructed masturbation as a commonplace and universal practice which was natural. These accounts contrast with many of the interwar letters from men to Marie Stopes, the bulk of which were written by married men – some of them long-married – in the 1920s. Masturbation is often pejoratively described by these correspondents, who expressed considerable anxieties in the letters and frequently worried that it might have a wide range of deleterious consequences. The much more

143 Hugh msf/kf/ht#18.

144 A significant number of the women interviewed (seven) claimed not to have known – and in a few cases still not to know – that there is such a thing as female masturbation: Sally (1908) msf/kf/bl/#31; Elma (1909) msf/jm/bl/#42; Daphne (1912) msf/jm/bl/#38; Lorna (1917) msf/kf/bl/#25; Grace (1922) msf/srss/ht/#38; Emma (1906) msf/kf/ht/#37 and Angela (1924) msf/kf/ht/#18. Only two women (both middle-class) were prepared to acknowledge having masturbated: Antonia msf/kf/ht/#35 and Esme msf/kf/ht/#9. By contrast, there were no men who denied knowledge of masturbation and none who explicitly denied that they had practised masturbation at some point in their lives – most stating that this was confined to the period of their lives before marriage.

145 From around the 1920s most writers on masturbation tried 'to tread a fine line between exploding the old scaremongering myths about masturbation and continuing to discourage the practice' (see, Lesley A. Hall, 'Forbidden by God, Despised by Men: Masturbation, Medical Warnings, Moral Panic, and Manhood in Great Britain, 1850–1950', *Journal of the History of Sexuality* 2, no. 3 (1992): 378).

ambivalent attitudes towards masturbation that dominate the interview material for this study reflect perhaps the slightly younger profile of these respondents, who were mostly not beginning married life until the 1930s. Marie Stopes' correspondents were, therefore, on average at least a decade older than our interviewees and had, in Lesley Hall's description, 'grown up with exposure to the traditional Victorian and immediately post-Victorian views on marriage, sex and the roles of the sexes'.[146]

The rejection of negative warnings about the dangers of masturbation and the conclusion that it was natural turn masturbation into an innocent and therefore respectable means of obtaining information about sex. Framing masturbation as a natural response to puberty played a significant role in male narratives as it provided an account of sexual enlightenment which did not suggest that men had come into illicit contact with women, nor disreputable sources of information, such as pornography. Colin (1923) was taken into care at age 8 along with all seven siblings (his father was shell-shocked and violent following a head injury in the war). He was separated from the others and worked as a farm hand, which he described as a socially isolating, prison-like existence – until he got his 'freedom' at age 18 and joined up with the Royal Navy.

When did you first hear about masturbation?

COLIN I didn't know about it at school, on the farm. I think it was a natural thing, this, this thing come natural... So, when you were walking about and for as no reason at all it, it rose, it's what they call, er, they give it handshake. (laughs) That're masturbation, see. But I was, I was 15, 15 yeah, yeah were 15.[147]

Hubert was born in Limbury, near Luton, in 1911, the son of an independent estate agent. His account of erotic wet dreams similarly emphasised the way in which learning about sex could be 'natural' – and therefore 'nobody's fault':

So when you were a boy when did you first learn about what sex was?

HUBERT Well I suppose it was what was in me, within me. Well there was a natural response, natural reaction. Adam and Eve didn't need teaching, did they?... There is a natural release. You can have an ejaculation without anything, usually in your sleep... Nature's method of leading you into knowledge of such things, I suppose. 'Cause it's usually associated with dreams of women... it's nobody's fault was it? That was perfectly natural thing.[148]

This, then, was another important way to resolve the dilemma, central to male identities, of becoming informed about sex by late adolescence in a respectably innocent way – to claim that sexual knowledge had come naturally. The

[146] Ibid., 380–5. It is also of course the case that the Stopes correspondents represent a self-selected group of letter-writers who were sufficiently anxious or concerned about a perceived 'problem' with a sexual aspect of their marriage that they were prepared to write to her.

[147] Colin msf/kf/bl/#36. [148] Hubert msf/kf/ht/#32.

construction of masturbation as natural was thus part of a wider claim on the part of men that they gained the sexual awareness seen as necessary to make the transition from boyhood to manhood without recourse to any external or dubious forms of information. Many men, from a variety of backgrounds, while acknowledging that they acquired knowledge, proved to be extremely unclear and vague on just how and when they learned about sex. Several emphasised that 'you worked it out for yourself'.[149] Other, similar responses included 'don't know how I found out'[150] or 'you grow into it...eventually'[151] or '[g]oodness alone knows'.[152] Male interviewees' testimony expresses their wishes to portray themselves as knowledgeable, rather than ignorant, while presenting their knowledge as having been acquired in an 'innocent', natural and gradual manner. At the same time they wished to be able to claim that they had fulfilled their masculine role by being prepared and competent at the point of marriage. Similarly, Mass Observation found that among those interviewed in 1947, who were at that time in their sixties and seventies, the majority felt that sex instruction should come naturally in a form untainted by immorality.[153]

Tim's (1917) life was dominated by curiosity about how things were put together. His father was a skilled worker at the Crewe railway works and he himself trained as a precision instrument maker with Leyland Motors and subsequently continued to enjoy taking things apart and making instruments as part of his own clock and watch repair business.

> TIM I can remember it dawning on me...I can remember...I was walking t'school and I thought...about 'aving babies and ya 'ear kids talking about, ya know, the, boys do this and girls are like, yeah, yeah, and it suddenly struck me one day, 'cos ya learn about, um, um, ejaculation for want of a better word (sounds amused), and it suddenly struck me, just like a flash of light, that's it, that's what does it. I can remem-, 'cos, I was always a thinker...I was always interested how things worked.[154]

Thus, most male respondents tend to present the confusing business of learning about sex and piecing it all together when young as one of nature's puzzles and life's games – an amusing and potentially rewarding challenge to be 'worked out'. To see it as an essentially humorous game defused the predicament in the interview of recounting how they transgressed when young, in accessing and sharing unrespectable knowledge.[155] As adults they have mastered this mystery and can look back on the innocence of their youth with a

[149] Christopher msf/kf/bl/#34; Frank msf/srss/bl/#16; Colin msf/kf/bl/#36; Terence msf/srss/bl/#15; Tim msf/srss/bl/#19; Gerald msf/kf/ht/#9.

[150] Bryan msf/kf/ht/#25. [151] Bernard msf/jm/bl/#45.

[152] William msf/kf/ht/#24.

[153] Mass Observation, File Report 2495 'The State of Matrimony', June 1947, 8.

[154] Tim msf/srss/bl/#19.

[155] Branigan, Mitchell and Wellings, 'Discomfort, Discord and Discontinuity', 262.

certain fondness. This is very different from the attitudes of female respondents, who mostly tend, even in these interviews conducted many decades later, to present the process of acquiring knowledge about sex as anything but humorous. For most women, especially working-class women, it is presented as a pretty serious and testing process – an entirely different way of distancing themselves from the unrespectability of the subject.

Conclusion

Oral history respondents confirmed that they grew up in a public culture of secrecy about sex, and claimed to have experienced significant degrees of sexual ignorance prior to getting married. Such claims of ignorance, evidence of the silence of parents and other adults on the subject, the difficulties encountered in obtaining information, and the confusing nature of any snippets of knowledge acquired, are found among the entire sample, from those born in the very early twentieth century to those born in the mid-1920s. This is despite considerable changes in the public availability of material about sex between 1900 and 1950 and public debate about the appropriateness of sex education. Respondents reveal that we cannot necessarily chart changing sexual knowledge in society by simply examining the gradually increasing availability of information in the form of publications, or educational initiatives. We need to look more carefully at the messages that accompanied such potential opportunities for learning and individuals' socialised responses when these moments occurred in their young lives. Despite increases in the availability of information about sex, parents continued to see a degree of sexual naïvety as important for their children, and imbued sexual knowledge with a set of dangerous connotations. Young women in particular became aware that to absorb, understand or repeat sexual information was potentially risky and they were encouraged to associate sexual innocence with respectability and even to see the pose of naïvety as charming and attractive.

Many women subsequently recognised that this degree of sexual ignorance left them anxious or fearful upon marriage, and many explicitly or implicitly criticised their parents' evasion and silence. Yet, female respondents did not present themselves as wishing they had resisted or reacted against the culture. The association of innocence with attractive femininity remained strongly ingrained and the structure of testimony often served to assert an individual's virtuous acceptance of moral codes which regarded the disposition of innocence towards sexual knowledge as a desirable characteristic, not merely for girls but more generally for all respectable women.

Responses to this enduring culture of ignorance were, however, differentiated by class and by gender. Middle-class women tended to adopt a different attitude towards their own possession of sexual knowledge and this reflected the personal encouragement and support they had received from trusted family members and close friends to acquire this knowledge before marriage. As members of the educated class in society – meaning that in their class it was typical, though not of course universal, to have attended secondary school – it was more appropriate to their social identity that they should be in possession of this knowledge. But it was seen as private and discreet knowledge, abstract and merely theoretical, not part of a common public discourse. Middle-class interviewees were as ambivalent as working-class respondents on the issue of whether sexual knowledge should be generally encouraged in society, and they valued its mystery. Middle-class women were as mindful of their respectability as working-class interviewees, and female virginal innocence among brides was as prized in this class as among the working class. However, whereas working-class women preserved innocence by maintaining their distance from 'dirty' information, middle-class women believed it was acceptable and not compromising to their innocence to obtain theoretical information and to avoid actual ignorance.[156]

Male interviewees present a quite different disposition from female respondents towards learning about sex in childhood and youth, though there are less obvious class differences among the men. Most men view the public culture of silence as a challenge to their ingenuity and masculinity, which they had a right to subvert and overcome. By contrast with almost all women interviewed, they often present their efforts to learn something about sex as a humorous subject, 'innocent fun'. It is their role as men to become knowledgeable and masterful so that they can guide their virginal brides through the mystery of sex. Yet it is also important to present themselves as 'innocent' when boys and as coming across knowledge by accident or in a natural way. By claiming that sexual awareness came naturally male interviewees asserted

[156] For an excellent discussion of the prior debate in the 1880s and 1890s among the educated elite between 'maternalist', femininst and 'professionalist' views over the appropriate ways to provide the next generation with sex education, see Claudia Nelson, '"Under the Guidance of a Wise Mother": British Sex Education at the Fin de Siecle', in Claudia Nelson and Ann Sumner Holmes, eds. *Maternal Instincts: Visions of Motherhood and Sexuality in Britain, 1875–1925* (London: Macmillan, 1997), 98–121. The oral history evidence presented here seems to confirm that in some upper- and middle-class families female respondents' mothers had followed the precepts of a version of the 'maternalist' or 'feminist' approaches, encapsulated in the didactic publications of Wolstenholme Elmy of the 1890s, *The Human Flower* and *Baby Buds*: 'that sexual knowledge of a purely theoretical sort is tied to chastity; [whereas] the ignorant are more likely to sin' (Nelson, 'Under the Guidance of a Wise Mother', 112). However, interviewees' testimony also indicates that while this practice occurred discreetly on the individual initiative of certain middle-class mothers, for most of the population the 'professionalist' conviction 'that the home was not the place for such discussions' prevailed. Meanwhile the 'professionalist belief' that 'teaching children, or at any rate boys, about sexual matters' should proceed within the school curriculum (ibid., 99) was never officially endorsed before the 1940s, leaving most of the young in the same untutored state in the 1930s, as had been the case in the 1890s.

that they had not experienced sex before it was legitimate to do so and had not been tainted by illicit forms of sexual information.[157] Becoming sexually knowledgeable and potent is an important component of what it is to become a full man, properly prepared for gaining admission to the adult world through entering marriage.

[157] Angus McLaren argues that from 1900 many educators of boys were concerned to promote manliness in contexts that were 'isolated from the dangerous sexuality of the urban world' (McLaren, *Twentieth-Century Sexuality*, 32).

3 Sexual intimacies before marriage

DAPHNE There wasn't the sex in those days; we were innocent ... I mean to me ... the morals have gone out of life nowadays ... they're living together before they're married. They're sleeping together, they're carrying on and I don't approve of it ... I mean we used to go in back row in pictures and (laughs) that kind of thing, you know ... it was all so simple. We're very naïve I think really.[1]

Some historians of twentieth-century sexuality, particularly those looking at American culture, have labelled the interwar era as a period of sexual revolution, and argue that the 1920s saw the emergence of an affluent and rebellious youth culture for whom premarital virginity was no longer a moral imperative.[2] Social historians of Britain, by contrast, particularly those studying working-class communities, have found little evidence for a British version of such a sexual revolution.[3] They, rather, argued that sex before marriage remained taboo despite the changing leisure opportunities, increased youth affluence and independence, and the emergence of new forms of recreational 'dating' in dance

[1] Daphne msf/jm/bl/#38. Daphne was born in 1912 in Harwood, the only child of a weaver and an overlooker in the local cotton mills.

[2] In his general study, for example, Angus McLaren argues that 'rates of premarital sex rose sharply in the 1920s and then plateaued' until the 1960s (McLaren, *Twentieth-Century Sexuality*, 43). This argument is most prominently made, however, by American historians who have linked changing attitudes towards premarital sex with the emergence of new forms of youth culture. See, for example, Lynn Jamieson, *Intimacy: Personal Relationships in Modern Societies* (Cambridge and Malden, MA: Polity Press, 1998), 24–55, Kevin White, *The First Sexual Revolution: Male Heterosexuality in Modern America* (New York and London: New York University Press, 1993).

[3] Hall, *Sex, Gender and Social Change*, 99. Only a few British historians have identified similar trends this side of the Atlantic. Harry Cocks' work is a notable exception, and argues that new dating rituals, forms of petting, the emergence of semi-public settings such as parks and dance halls alongside an expanding obscene print culture eroticised courtship in conflict with codes of sexual innocence (Harry Cocks, 'Saucy Stories: Pornography, Sexology and the Marketing of Sexual Knowledge in Britain, c. 1918–70', *Social History [London]* 29, no. 4 (2004): 469). Lucinda Beier also sees sexual behaviour as having changed dramatically during the interwar period, and claims that by the mid-1940s courtship included 'heavy petting that would have been unheard-of for an earlier generation', 'intense' games of Postman's Knock in the early 1950s and a transformation in the acceptability of premarital sex and illegitimacy (Beier, 'We Were Green as Grass', 477). See also, Humphries, *A Secret World of Sex*.

halls and cinemas that paralleled changes across the Atlantic.[4] These interpretations often focus on women, who are presented as fearful of pregnancy and social stigma, and restricted by sexual ignorance and inhibitions: hence it is argued that they viewed premarital sex as a dangerous, rather than pleasurable, activity which ought to be avoided. Elizabeth Roberts, for example, found 'fear of premarital sex' and 'unanimous condemnation of sex outside marriage' in Lancashire communities before 1940, and in Preston in particular she found 'several examples of the private punishment and public humiliation' of any girl who got pregnant before marriage.[5]

We know very little, however, of the ways in which individuals managed the negotiation of sexual intimacy during courtship. The motivations behind the actions and choices of couples or the contexts and circumstances of such decisions have received little scholarly attention. Moreover, we understand very little of the cultures of courtship, or the range of social meanings ascribed to premarital relations.[6] Some historians have recognised that we should not place all those individuals who had sex before marriage or who gave birth prior to wedlock in a single category.[7] Nevertheless Reay's point that there were a 'variety of illegitimacies', based on a range of context-dependent beliefs that in varying circumstances could either delegitimise or sanction this practice, has not provoked much consideration of the range of experiences and understandings of premarital sex in a twentieth-century context.[8]

[4] On the changing experiences of adolescents, see, Kuhn, *Cinema, Censorship and Sexuality*, ch. 6, 138–67, Davies, *Leisure, Gender, and Poverty*, 81–9, Fowler, *The First Teenagers*, Ross McKibbin, *Classes and Cultures: England, 1918–1951* (Oxford: Oxford University Press, 1998), ch. 10, esp. 394–5, 403–5, Langhamer, *Women's Leisure*, 49–51, Todd, *Young Women, Work, and Family*, ch. 7, 195–224. In the 1930s British cinema attendance was the highest per capita in the world with annual attendance rising from 903 million in 1934 to 1,027 million in 1940. Greatest attendance was among young, working-class women, but the mid-1930s saw the development of 'super-cinemas' for the middle classes in affluent suburbs and city centres (Annette Kuhn, *An Everyday Magic: Cinema and Cultural Memory* (London: I. B. Tauris, 2002), 1–2).

[5] Roberts, *A Woman's Place*, 72–80.

[6] Peter Laslett criticised Edward Shorter's linkage of rising illegitimacy rates in the early nineteenth century with a 'sexual revolution' and in doing so highlighted the need for historians to recognise that changing rates of sex before marriage are not necessarily indicators of changes in sexual morality and the centrality of uncovering the context behind changing illegitimacy rates. See Edward Shorter, 'Illegitimacy, Sexual Revolution, and Social Change in Modern Europe', *Journal of Interdisciplinary History* 2, no. 2 (1971): 237–72, Peter Laslett, 'Introduction: Comparing Illegitimacy over Time and between Cultures' in Peter Laslett, Karla Oosterveen and Richard Michael Smith, eds. *Bastardy and Its Comparative History: Studies in the History of Illegitimacy and Marital Noncomformism in Britain, France, Germany, Sweden, the United States, Jamaica, and Japan* (Cambridge, MA: Harvard University Press, 1980), 1–64.

[7] On the complexity of illegitimacy statistics and the need to look at the diverse 'social scenarios and human relationships' behind quantitative data see, for example, Barry Reay, *Microhistories: Demography, Society and Culture in Rural England, 1800–1930* (Cambridge: Cambridge University Press, 1996), 175–6.

[8] Ibid.

To a certain extent, our oral history research confirms some of the findings of recent historians. Many men and women believed in the virtues of waiting until marriage before having sexual intercourse, and related their attempts to live up to this goal. Not only did many assert a personal commitment to remaining a virgin until marriage: they also expressed pity or even condemnation of those (past and present) who fell pregnant out of wedlock or engaged in sexual indiscretions. Many others revealed the social stigma which they felt would be exerted by family and the wider community if they found themselves premaritally pregnant, with parental disapproval most acutely feared. Although data was unclear or testimony contradictory in a few cases, of the eighty-two of our interviewees who provided a relatively direct response, sixty-one (74%) said they did not have sex before marriage.[9]

However, despite the common expression of censorious values, many developed pragmatic personal codes of morality which determined the behavioural choices they made. Their decisions to have sex or not were framed by a set of gendered and class-dependent codes, which allowed for a number of circumstances in which premarital sexual intercourse was considered logical, acceptable or even sensible. The dynamics of intimacy in courtship need to be studied with due attention paid to the precise relational context and social geographies which framed the choices made at particular intimate moments; the wide repertoire of forms of sexual practices and their meaning for couples; men's and women's different approaches to premarital intimacy; and class differences in the ways men and women communicated and processed moral codes.

The meaning and significance of premarital sex (as a transgression or a legitimate form of behaviour) depended crucially on context. That the stage of a relationship might influence the respectability of decisions to have intercourse has been recognised.[10] Yet this is just one way in which the sorts of

[9] The one unmarried interviewee is not included in this data. The response was ambiguous or unclear in six cases: Alf msf/kf/ht/#14; June msf/kf/ht/#27; Enid msf/kf/bl/#49; Nora msf/jm/bl/#47; Pam msf/kf/ht/#19; Monica msf/kf/ht/#11. In at least one of these cases, that of Alf, there was a strong suggestion that sex had taken place. Alf described how he and his army pals protected themselves from premarital pregnancy or disease, but elsewhere in the interview denied having had sex before marriage. His wife confirmed that they had not had sex together prior to marriage.

[10] Some historians have highlighted the extent to which British communities did not condemn couples who had sex as part of an engagement and who were married before any children were born, arguing that such instances of premarital intercourse 'marked a point in courtship, a staging post en route to marriage and household formation' (Cook, *The Long Sexual Revolution*, 321). Note also the well-established finding among historical demographers that long-term variations in both the prenuptial pregnancy rate and the associated illegitimacy ratio have been the direct corollary of rises and falls in the marriage rate itself throughout the entire period from the 1540s until the 1960s (see Peter Laslett, *Family Life and Illicit Love in Earlier Generations: Essays in Historical Sociology* (Cambridge: Cambridge University Press, 1977), 106–59). In addition Ellen Ross has drawn attention to the patterns of cohabitation and forms of serial monogamy that were slow to die out in certain districts and among certain occupational

intimate behaviours that men and women were prepared to engage in varied significantly and were highly context dependent. Other factors, such as the geographical location a couple found themselves in (e.g. romantic or seedy), might also give meaning to the act and influence individuals' choices. Some circumstances could reinforce the fear associated with sexual transgression and heighten its status as a dangerous and disreputable practice, while other environments might foster a recourse to sexual intercourse as a means of demonstrating appropriate passion, love and care.[11] We will pay close attention to these varied contexts in examining individuals' choices.

In concentrating above all on whether or not a couple had sex before marriage, historians correctly identify the importance of intercourse as a particularly significant act. Too little attention has been paid, however, to other forms of intimate behaviour and the moral codes associated with a range of forms of sexual intimacy.[12] Here, 'petting' is used to describe the variety of physical expressions of desire and intimacy short of intercourse itself.[13] Natalie Higgins mentions that 'extensive foreplay' was common among those of her interviewees who did not have premarital intercourse but she does not explore this issue any further.[14] Hera Cook argues that before the 1950s genital petting was unlikely to have been countenanced by many women but that such petting increased during the 1950s and was frequently discussed and recommended in marriage manuals from the 1940s onwards.[15] By the 1950s and 1960s, influenced in particular by developments in American sexology and sociology, British sociological interest in petting increased.[16] Jephcott described

groups such as costermongers in the late nineteenth and early twentieth centuries (Ross, *Love and Toil*, 63–4). See Chapter 2, note 1 on the treatment of premarital pregnancy.

11 For an excellent summary of the studies of illegitimacy in Britain before the twentieth century and a convincing, powerful plea for a more nuanced analysis of the range of circumstances and meanings ascribed to premarital sexual activity in precise historical contexts see, Reay, *Microhistories*, ch. 7, 179–212.

12 On British focus on premarital intercourse, see, for example, Gillis, *For Better, for Worse*, 282, Roberts, *A Woman's Place*, 73–80, Derek Thompson, 'Courtship and Marriage in Preston between the Wars', *Oral History* 3, no. 2 (1975), Humphries, *A Secret World of Sex*, Roberts, *Women and Families*, 63–6. On the importance of premarital sex as an index of promiscuity see, for example, Cook, *The Long Sexual Revolution*, 105, 212–19, Gorer, *Sex & Marriage in England Today*, 283–4.

13 'Petting' is an American term for non-coital sexual activity that was widely used in the 1920s. By the 1950s the term 'heavy petting' emerged to signify genital sexual activity that did not include sexual intercourse.

14 Higgins, 'The Changing Expectations and Realities of Marriage', 116.

15 Cook, *The Long Sexual Revolution*, 230–1, 59–60, 321.

16 See, for example, Michael Schofield and Central Council for Health Education (Great Britain), *The Sexual Behaviour of Young People* (Boston: Little, 1965). See also, Hall, *Sex, Gender and Social Change*, 156–8. Many studies did not, however. Rowntree's study published in 1951 included a chapter on 'sexual promiscuity' which only investigated full sexual intercourse (B. Seebohm Rowntree and G. R. Lavers, *English Life and Leisure: A Social Study* (London: Longmans, Green, 1951)).

'promiscuous and lengthy petting' as common and 'satisfactory' between the ages of 17 and 25.[17] Eustace Chesser's research on predominantly middle-class women found an increased incidence in the number of women reporting having engaged in non-coital sex before marriage among those born between 1904 and 1914, which rose still further among those born between 1914 and 1924.[18] Yet such investigations of 'petting' tend to equate levels of petting with degrees of permissiveness and see any increase in levels of petting as signifying a weakening of moral codes. We will go beyond charting what sorts of behaviour couples engaged in, to investigating the subjective feelings and associations behind various sex acts which determined the role they played in couples' intimate relationships.[19]

The different attitudes of men and women, the social politics of masculinity and femininity, and the separate and gendered dangers, desires and aspirations at stake during courtship need to be at the forefront of the examination of the dynamics of premarital intimacy. While women's attitudes have been the focus of much recent analysis, men's approaches to their girlfriends have received comparatively little attention.[20] Forms of intimacy were negotiated in complex and gendered interactions, through which men and women expressed desire, demonstrated commitment and tested each other's respectability, ardour or suitability. Particular forms of sexual behaviour were integral to these complex processes of mutual exploration and the attempts by men and women to demonstrate their feelings, commitment, desire and consideration.[21] Such gender dynamics were, of course, also structured by class distinctions and, indeed, significant differences emerged. In particular, divergent ideas about appropriate levels of communication about sexual matters in working- and middle-class communities led middle-class couples more often jointly to commit to avoiding sexual intercourse, while working-class couples were more likely to develop implicit understandings which could be spontaneously revised as circumstances and passions evolved, resulting in more instances where working-class couples had premarital sexual intercourse alongside greater middle-class use of sexual practices short of intercourse itself.

[17] Jephcott, *Rising Twenty*, 90.

[18] This material is discussed in Weeks, *Sex, Politics, and Society*, 209. Yet, surveys such as Chesser's had an unsophisticated definition of petting: 'no particular aspect of petting was defined and the replies do not specify whether petting, if practised, was confined to kissing or included mutual masturbation', and there is no analysis of the context in which it was practised or its significance for couples (Chesser et al., *The Sexual, Marital and Family Relationships of the English Woman* (London: Hutchinson's Medical Publications, 1956), 329). Chesser saw petting relatively positively as meeting women's emotional needs and in 1959 controversially argued in a quickly withdrawn article for a British Medical Association publication that 'chastity was outmoded' (Hall, *Sex, Gender and Social Change*, 157).

[19] Weeks, *Sex, Politics and Society*, 209.

[20] Giles, 'Playing Hard to Get'.

[21] See also, Ross, *Love and Toil*, 67–8.

'I wanted to be a virgin when I got married'

The majority of respondents claimed not to have had sex before marriage. Unlike other similar surveys there was no significant difference between our male and female interviewees in this regard. Woodside and Slater's research found '45% of husbands and 64% of wives' from the control group claimed to be virgins upon marriage which they compared with the Registrar General report for 1938 and 1939, which estimated that nearly 30 per cent of all mothers conceived their first child out of wedlock.[22] Among our interviewees, while there were no gender differences, there were very significant class differences, with only 8 per cent of middle-class interviewees acknowledging having had sexual intercourse before marriage, compared with 33 per cent of working-class interviewees.[23] Moreover, regardless of whether or not an individual had sex before marriage, a general approval of marital virginity was frequently expressed, particularly for women, but also for men.[24] Sally (1908), who worked as a sales assistant in Boots, was an active churchgoer throughout her life and got married in 1934:

[22] Slater and Woodside, *Patterns of Marriage*, 111–12. However, this was in fact an historically very moderate figure – the 1930s were the centre of a sixty-year period of extremely low illegitimacy ratios in modern British history. As Paul Thompson observed, official statistics showed that illegitimacy ratios (their proportion of all births) had been falling throughout the second half of the nineteenth century to a nadir of just over 4 per cent in the Edwardian decade. Apart from the two temporary wartime spikes when rates rose briefly above 6 per cent (First World War) and 9 per cent (Second Word War), the illegitimacy ratio then remained at very low levels (below 5 per cent) throughout the entire period until the early 1960s; it then began to climb steeply, reaching above 8 per cent by the end of the 1960s, partly reflecting the new trend in that decade away from marriage and towards consensual cohabitation, including in the early stages of reproductive partnerships (Thompson, *The Edwardians*, Table 13, and 302–3).

[23] See Appendix B on the social classification of the respondents, whose individual class affiliations are given in Appendix C. Of the 82 respondents, who gave clear information about sex before marriage, 26 were classified as middle class and 56 as working class. Of these, 24 middle-class respondents claimed not to have had sex before marriage, while 37 working-class respondents claimed not to have had sex before marriage, leaving 2 and 19 middle- and working-class respondents, respectively, saying that they had. In addition, none of the middle-class respondents reported a pre-nuptial pregnancy, whereas seven working-class respondents, all from Blackburn, did: Jennie msf/kf/bl/#27, Rose msf/kf/bl/#21, Colin msf/kf/bl/#36, Mavis msf/kf/bl/#29, Maria msf/kf/bl/#8, Tom msf/srss/bl/#15 and Ed msf/srss/bl/#23. On debates about the accuracy of such statistics see, Weldon T. Johnson and John D. Delamater, 'Response Effects in Sex Surveys', *Public Opinion Quarterly* 40, no. 2 (1976): 165–81, Kevin A. Fenton et al., 'Measuring Sexual Behaviour: Methodological Challenges in Survey Research', *British Medical Journal* 77, no. 2 (2001): 84–92. See also note 9 above.

[24] In some cases one or both members of the couple felt strongly that sex before marriage was morally wrong; this was particularly evident among respondents who were active churchgoers for example, Emily msf/kf/bl/#13; Sally msf/kf/bl/#31; Elma msf/jm/bl/#42; Daphne msf/jm/bl/#38; Bernard and Diana msf/jm/bl/#45; Maureen msf/kf/bl/#46; Angela and Hugh msf/kf/ht/#18; Bryan msf/kf/ht/#25; Dougie msf/kf/ht/#5; Vera msf/kf/ht/#34; Edmund msf/kf/ht/#23; Sam msf/srss/ht/#28. For other respondents the idea that marriage was best begun as virgins was less strongly held and deemed to be appropriate, conventional and socially acceptable.

SALLY I wanted to be a virgin when I got married. And I stuck to it … I just said to him, 'I don't want any sex at all … I want to be a virgin when I'm married because I'm being married in white and I want it to be true.'[25]

Sam (1912) was the son of a bank manager from a market town north of Newcastle and his family played an active role in the Methodist chapel: his mother played the organ, his father was treasurer and Sam was a deacon:

SAM I never indulged before I was married … I taught myself that it wasn't the right thing to do … I can't remember anybody telling me 'thou shalt not intercourse before marriage', but that's what I came to believe and that's what happened.[26]

Hugh (1926), who was training to be an electrician in the late 1930s before serving with the Royal Engineers, articulated more ambivalent views, which confirmed his idealisation of avoiding sex before marriage, but acknowledged that as a young man his principles were less strongly held and might have wavered given sufficient 'temptation':

And what were your feelings about sex before marriage?

HUGH Chance never came my way. (laughs)

Are you saying that you would have taken the chance had it come your way?

I don't know, never had the chance so I don't know. Temptation, who knows? But … when I was 18 … I probably didn't have any principles then! Um, no, if you say would I like my children to have entered into sexual relationships before marriage I would have said 'No'.[27]

Only a few interviewees recognised some benefits to premarital sexual experience. Penny (1916), a factory worker whose husband had a range of labourers' jobs throughout their marriage, expressed ambiguous views on the subject.[28] Despite having had sex before marriage themselves she and her husband threatened they would disown their daughters should they fall pregnant before marriage.[29] However, in the event Penny expressed sympathy with her own daughter's decision to have sex before marriage and articulated well-developed arguments in favour of premarital sexual experience:

PENNY they say … you shouldn't have sex before marriage. But as far as I'm concerned I think that if you're thinking of getting married or getting engaged … you should try sex out – because if you've not, if you've never had it, never done anything about it and you get married, and then it all goes wrong … you know you don't suit

25 Sally msf/kf/bl/#31.

26 Sam msf/srss/ht/#28. Note the religious language, suggesting that Sam obtained this sense of the rightness of premarital virginity from the Church.

27 Hugh msf/kf/ht/#18.

28 Also Doreen msf/kf/bl/#20; Jake and Dorris msf/srss/bl/#22.

29 Eustace Chesser reported that 'the majority of those who had pre-marital sexual intercourse, and thereby "broke" with tradition, wanted their sons and daughters to *observe* these traditions' (Chesser et al., *The Sexual, Marital and Family Relationships of the English Woman*, 343).

> each other sex wise … I mean my daughter, she had sex before she was married – mind you, she ended up getting pregnant … but they made a lovely co- … they're a lovely couple and they've got two nice kids and I've always thought that … if you don't try it out before you buy it, it's too late when you've bought it. I never buy grapes until I try them out.[30]

Such ideas echo some of the themes of marriage and sex guidance during the 1930s and 1940s, which discuss the issue of sexual experience before marriage in the context of an emerging debate about the importance of marital sexual adjustment, and popular Freudian understandings of the dangers of repressing sexual instincts and desires.[31] However, no interviewee debated the merits of premarital experience in quite this way or referred to popular psychoanalytic theories or notions of marital sexual adjustment in outlining their views of sex before marriage or in explaining the decisions they made. Most confirmed the marriage guidance literature's endorsement of waiting until marriage before having intercourse. Most such guides argued, like Leslie Tizard, that although it 'won't make for happiness if a volcano is mated to an iceberg … these things can be gauged pretty accurately without actual intercourse'.[32] Leslie Weatherhead's bestselling *The Mastery of Sex*, first published in 1931, written to reconcile Christian religion with psychoanalysis, concurred that sex before marriage was likely to have an enormous 'psychological' impact on young practitioners resulting in feelings of 'regret, fear, repulsion and disgust'. The enjoyment of the act would inevitably be marred by worry, whatever birth control was employed, and any child born would itself be psychologically damaged. Responding to psychoanalytic understandings of sexual instincts he reassured readers that sexual restraint in courtship was not a form of potentially damaging 'repression' but instead was 'suppression or conscious self-control', which required the exercise of the positive virtues of 'grit, pluck and determination', and the 'dynamic' channelling of a person's sexual drive into 'creative energies in which the soul finds self-realization and the community finds benefit'.[33]

[30] Penny msf/srss/ht/#20. Penny additionally recognised the limited authority that she and her husband had in chastising their daughter: 'He started … he didn't rant and rave but he just said "didn't you know any better than that?" And I looked at him and I said: "there for the grace of God go you and I."' A similar view is expressed by some Mass Observation panellists. Claire Langhamer quotes a woman who felt 'it is a good thing to do, especially when two people cannot get married for some years'. She claimed that this view was 'accepted among some of my friends' although there were 'others who would strongly disapprove' (Langhamer, *Women's Leisure*, 125).

[31] Anna Clark, *Desire: A History of European Sexuality* (New York and London: Routledge, 2008), 174–6, Cook, *The Long Sexual Revolution*, 205–24.

[32] Tizard was chair of Birmingham Marriage Guidance Council. Leslie J. Tizard, *Guide to Marriage* (London: Allen & Unwin, 1948), 30.

[33] Leslie D. Weatherhead, *The Mastery of Sex: Through Psychology and Religion*, 17th edn. (London: SCM Press, 1954), 53–7.

At the same time, however, only a few interviewees wholeheartedly condemned those who did have sex before marriage. Bernard (1907) and Diana (1910) presented their middle-class social lives growing up in Oldham in the 1920s as having centred on the church: he was an accomplished choir boy, and she proudly reported that her great, great-grandfather had founded a Baptist church in the nineteenth century and that she had been keen to devote her life to missionary work. Not only did they condemn sex before marriage, but used strong language to express such views. Sex before marriage was categorised as highly immoral and those who gave up 'chastity' were denigrated as unladylike and cheap:

In those days did anybody have sex before marriage?

DIANA Most definitely not.

BERNARD No. No.

DIANA Dear me no. No, most of the girls I knew were all chaste... that was a thing you reserve.

BERNARD Oh you, you lived a much more religious life...

DIANA You don't cheapen yourself... it wasn't even discussed... you know it wasn't ladylike... it was understood that girls didn't do that sort of thing.

BERNARD It's what's wrong today. There's too much talk about the sex.

DIANA It's only a part of life that should be preserved for married people.

BERNARD All this living with a partner business I don't agree with it. It's highly immoral.[34]

Some others, while not condemning outright those who got pregnant before they were married, expressed disapproval through pity or sorrow. Gill (1920) was also an affluent member of the Blackburn middle class, married to a mill owner-manager. A life-long one-nation Tory, she had a strong social conscience, undertook a lot of voluntary work and eventually became a magistrate in the 1970s. During the war she went to Manchester University where she studied for a Certificate in Social Administration, having failed to gain entry to a degree programme:

GILL There was a girl in the university when I was there and they had a shotgun marriage, you know... and I felt sorry for her, you know, because... having an illegitimate child in those days, and this was during the war, was not a thing that was accepted like it is today... and a lot of working-class people knew their father would show them the door more or less you know. And there were homes for girls that became pregnant and their family turned them away... which I thought was very sad. I don't think my family would ever have turned me away... but I can remember telling [my daughter] once... I would really feel very upset indeed if she became pregnant before she was married.[35]

[34] Bernard and Diana msf/jm/bl/#45. Maureen msf/kf/bl/#48 offered similar testimony.

[35] Gill msf/kf/bl/#48.

Agatha (1910), who married a gardener in the country house where she also worked as a domestic in the 1930s, expressed similar pity, though it is important to note that she herself fell pregnant prior to marriage:

AGATHA There was one of the housemaids where I [worked] and she got into trouble and she told me that they'd been, always been very careful but it happened, so … she left and she had the baby, she lived near … so she was alright. She had the baby and I think they got married … but it's always so sad isn't it when things like that 'appen? I was always scared, I think it's only natural, wouldn't you be?[36]

Far more common than direct disapproval was the placing of strong condemnation in the mouths of others. Without themselves fully identifying with such views, many respondents revealed a belief that families and society at large punished those who had sex before marriage, especially unmarried, pregnant women. June's (1914) father was a bank manager in Yorkshire but did not get into the grammar school and left education at 14:

JUNE It was too dangerous … you would end up getting pregnant. And that was a thing you did not want to do in my day. It was a slight, everybody look[ed] down on girls that had to get married in my day. It wasn't the done thing.[37]

Heather (1916) worked in Harrods' sweet factory:

HEATHER if a girl went home and said they was pregnant nine times out of ten they was slung out the house … automatically be slung out, go … get [him] to marry you or, you know … It was a scandal in those day, oh yes … Yeah, you was in trouble too, ooh! Oh dear oh dear … to try it in those days was a sin.[38]

Hubert (1911) was the son of an estate agent who went to boarding school in Luton in the 1920s:

HUBERT such things weren't heard of in those days … she would have been absolutely cast out of society altogether. It's hard for you to realise how things were in those days … There was no contraception, you see, and girls would not lay themselves open to the chance of pregnancy.[39]

Stories of outcast girls, angry fathers and mother and baby homes had a strong impact on individuals' experiences of courtship.[40] Irrespective of the actual likelihood that an individual would find him- or herself ostracised by society or rejected by his or her family, many relationships, particularly among the working classes, were dominated by fear of pregnancy and its

[36] Agatha msf/kf/ht/#7. [37] June msf/kf/ht/#27.
[38] Heather msf/kf/ht/#14. [39] Hubert msf/kf/ht/#32.
[40] The 'plight of illegitimate children' was also a mainstay of Victorian and later fiction: see Ginger Frost, '"The Black Lamb of the Black Sheep": Illegitimacy in the English Working Class, 1850–1939', *Journal of Social History* 37, no. 2 (2003): 293. Penny Tinkler has studied the ways in which pregnant and unmarried girls were treated in magazine fiction aimed at girls in the first half of the twentieth century: see Tinkler, *Constructing Girlhood*, 166–74.

potential ramifications. For many, the desire to be seen as decent and not to embarrass, shame or let one's family down was a strong motivator, while others genuinely feared brutal societal or familial reactions.[41] Pearl (1915), who was training to become a teacher in Burnley, 'couldn't do anything to let my parents down', and Pru (1911), a typist for an insurance firm in Newbury in the 1920s, imagined her mother's reaction from beyond the grave: 'I had great visions of my dear mother with her lovely face... going, "oh, you've done that, you wicked girl".'[42] The 'only reason' Alistair (1927), one of the youngest respondents, and his wife, a ring winder in Blackburn, 'never had sex, until we were married... was the wife said, "No, I don't want to fall pregnant and upset my mother"... her mother was a strict, strict Catholic... and for anybody of that family to become pregnant before marriage was taboo'.[43] Sarah (1906) was justifiably fearful of the potential reaction of her father, a skilled pattern maker in an engineering firm in Preston, who had a tendency to drink to excess and a capacity for violence. She 'didn't dare think about anything' beyond 'kissing and cuddling', as she was 'scared of my Dad... he would have killed me and then he would have killed him... he would have chucked you out'. Nevertheless, a few months before they got married Sarah and her fiancé did begin to have intercourse.[44]

Worries about premarital sex were far more prominent in women's testimony, but men, too, were fearful of the consequences of premarital intercourse, including the reactions of a girlfriend's father. Roger's (1910) fear of VD perhaps reflects his naval background (his father was a naval officer):

> ROGER I suppose looking back there was a certain fear of things going wrong. There was a certain fear of catching VD. There was a certain fear of the woman becoming pregnant, the girl becoming pregnant. There was a certain fear that her father would come after you.[45]

Although it was often recognised that horror stories were used to impart moral messages and warnings and were not indicative of the extent to which harsh treatments were meted out in practice, rumours were sufficiently common to be genuinely alarming:

> ALF In those days the girls... had that fear in their mind; they mustn't get into trouble. I won't say that... everybody kicked 'em out when they got into trouble but... they've been looked upon as they've sinned... you heard about them: 'Did you hear about old whatsname, old Alice over the road? She had a baby – ' and all that sort of thing.[46]

[41] See also, Slater and Woodside, *Patterns of Marriage*, 113, Gillis, *For Better, for Worse*, 265, Langhamer, *Women's Leisure*, 123–4, Weeks, *The World We Have Won*, 28.
[42] Pearl msf/kf/bl/#40; Pru msf/kf/ht/#12. [43] Alistair msf/kf/bl/#33.
[44] Sarah msf/kf/bl/#30. [45] Roger msf/kf/ht/#10. [46] Alf (1915) msf/kf/ht/#14.

This material supports the conclusion drawn by others that despite progressive and radical debate about society's moral codes and illegitimacy during the first half of the twentieth century, for no sector of society was extensive sexual experience prior to marriage seen as 'acceptable to conventional, respectable people before the 1950s'.[47] Indeed, some have argued that such progressive voices were ambiguous and far from straightforwardly permissive.[48] As Nicola Humble argues, middlebrow novels of the 1930s often present bohemian, sexually open, superior and sophisticated protagonists who are at the same time increasingly conservative in their response to illegitimacy. Girls engaging in premarital sex are frequently seen as ridiculous characters whose attempts to be sexually modern are instead revealed as 'paradoxically gauche'. Stories revolve around naïve girls who, in misinterpreting the 'gospel of sexual liberation', found themselves pregnant and abandoned after 'selling themselves cheap' to married men. While in these stories the message is not one of disgrace or ruin, by the 1930s an image emerged of the true bohemian who had rejected conventional morality and was now frightfully bored by the topic of sexual licence, although far too sophisticated and urbane to be condemnatory.[49] Oral history testimony is similarly ambiguous, with few vehemently denigrating those who had sex before marriage but a considerable degree of mild opposition to it and support for the concept of premarital virginity.

'I were always on my guard'

In a context in which most interviewees saw the maintenance of premarital virginity as desirable and in which confusion and ignorance about sexual behaviour were combined with a fear of the consequences of sexual intercourse, many working-class men and women approached sexual relationships with members of the opposite sex in a state of considerable anxiety and fear. Continued uncertainty about the mechanics of intercourse, anxieties about the nature of human desire and the difficulties experienced in communicating those desires led to fraught encounters between men and women, boys and girls, and considerable variety in premarital practice. Moreover, that sex was not openly discussed between friends or couples meant that individuals were largely left to develop their own internalised codes of acceptable intimate behaviour during courtship. Beyond imprecise parental warnings, there was little in the way of socially

[47] Cook, *The Long Sexual Revolution*, 179, see also Weeks, *The World We Have Won*, 36.

[48] Lesley A. Hall, *Outspoken Women: An Anthology of Women's Writing on Sex, 1870–1969* (London and New York: Routledge, 2005), 190–206.

[49] Nicola Humble, *The Feminine Middlebrow Novel, 1920s to 1950s: Class, Domesticity, and Bohemianism* (Oxford and New York: Oxford University Press, 2001), 240–1. See also Faye Hammill's reading of *Cold Comfort Farm*: Faye Hammill, *Women, Celebrity, and Literary Culture Between the Wars* (Austin: University of Texas Press, 2007), 152–78.

agreed boundaries to help individuals negotiate, in the context of intimate relationships, what behaviour to engage in (short of intercourse) and what to resist or avoid.

As revealed in Chapter 2, upon menarche many girls were warned to stay away from boys, and came into contact with a range of warnings about the dangers of courtship practices, such as kissing. By late adolescence working-class women were by and large aware that there was more to conception than kissing, but they remained unclear how or where to draw the line in policing their boyfriends' testing expressions of desire. Eva's (1911) mother, a market gardener in Blackburn whose husband had died in the First World War, told her not to do anything wrong and she recalled being scared and on her guard as she struggled to pick up what precisely she needed to avoid:

EVA 'Your periods have started', she says, 'and… you can have babies, if you do anything wrong… with boys'… I were always on my guard more or less [but] you pick it up as you go along…[50]

Eleanor (1907), the daughter of a ship's riveter, whose mother was a ring spinner in a cotton mill in Blackburn, knew that she could go further than kissing, but was confused about how much more intimacy would be all right, despite gleaning some information from books she read which she felt had included some pointers about sex (a source which few other working-class women mentioned):

ELEANOR I read a lot of books you know… there's sex mentioned in books, but [I was]… a bit frightened of sex… one girl was so ignorant, she said to me, 'you'll never let a boy kiss you, you may 'ave a baby', she were brought up ignorant weren't she?! (chuckling) 'through kissin'?', I said. 'No, there's more to it, more to it than that.' I knew that![51]

Similar confusion about the precise mechanics of intercourse was expressed by other working-class women, and some suggested that they had found it difficult to decide or work out for themselves what level of intimacy to allow and what had to be resisted.[52] Doreen (1922) 'knew you had to have contact' and 'knew to expect him using that [penis]', but 'how and why and which way, I'd no idea'.[53] Marian (1908), a weaver from Blackburn, initially 'used to think if a lad kissed yer you'd be 'avin a baby, you were that ignorant'. Although she gradually 'knew different' she nonetheless 'didn't know how they did it ''cos you never enquired'.[54] She was left in the position of having to police their

[50] Eva msf/kf/bl/#9. [51] Eleanor msf/kf/bl/#11.

[52] Magazines aimed at working girls during the 1930s were also reticent and oblique in responding to letters asking for the details of the link between forms of petting and pregnancy. Tinkler, *Constructing Girlhood*, 166.

[53] Doreen msf/kf/bl/#20. [54] Marian msf/kf/bl/#28.

sexual behaviour during courtship while at the same time trying to figure out what the precise details of intercourse were.

Working-class women's difficulties in determining where to draw the line during courtship were not simply a result of their deliberately preserved confusion about sexual matters. In addition, conceptions of the mechanics of desire and the nature of human sexuality led to a notion that there were forms of behaviour, levels of stimulation or impulses, which would make full consummation inevitable or unavoidable.[55] Although women were aware that there were sexual activities short of intercourse, they were anxious not to lead men on, or get themselves into a state when sex would inevitably result.[56] It was Marilyn's (1914) fear of overpowering male sexuality which prevented her from getting sexually involved:

> MARILYN I never had sex before I were married … as I say I've always had this fear … didn't want to er get too involved … you see men are not satisfied t- … have a bit of … a cuddle … It's got to [be] the whole way or nothing wi' a man. Well it's not always like that with a woman. So … if they got a bit serious then that were it, ah 'cos one of them said he were very disappointed in me … I give 'em the eye like. And then I, I'd touch and then run off. But I never did 'owt to 'em really. I were really in me late teens before I, I really went with anybody.[57]

Maria (1917), who was prepared to have sex with her future husband, nevertheless wanted to do this on her own terms, in the right context and location, but feared her own desire would get the better of her, and be apparent to her boyfriend, a local dance instructor in Blackburn in the 1930s:

> MARIA He never forced anything upon me. But afterwards, when we really got going I used to have the keys to me dad's garage and workshop and … if we wanted to do a bit of cuddling, you see, we used to go in there … [but] not all the way … just a kiss and a cuddle and saying goodnight really … I think they know if you're in the mood for it. I think they would know, it's just something that just creeps up on you, really.[58]

Grace (1922), who grew up in Goole, also expressed her fear that her own feelings might get the better of her. The force of her mother's admonitions to avoid pregnancy were better explained when she found out as an adult that her eldest sister was illegitimate, born to their mother before she married Grace's father (after an earlier boyfriend was killed in the First World War):

[55] Magazines aimed at young girls also supported this notion of uncontainable male sexuality. In 1946 *Girls' Own Paper* warned its readers, 'Little things that mean nothing to you may cause him to lose his self-control altogether' (quoted in Tinkler, *Constructing Girlhood*, 167).

[56] On the fear that petting might lead to a loss of control and subsequent pregnancy see Langhamer, *Women's Leisure*, 123.

[57] Marilyn msf/kf/bl/#7. [58] Maria msf/kf/bl/#8.

GRACE I just didn't. Just shyness again 'cos I knew what it can lead to really I think … I was a woman after all. I'd got feelings you know and … you was brought up er you wasn't told anything, but you knew you couldn't get into trouble. You knew you mustn't have a baby before you got married.[59]

Alf (1915) also expressed the view that male arousal reached a point of no return:

ALF you can't hold blokes, no – there's nothing can stop them, only the girl. That's the only way you can stop 'em. Nothing can stop a bloke once he gets into that state, be hell of a job to do that, I think.[60]

Indeed, the fear and anxiety which made many of the physical aspects of premarital intimacy frequently fraught for working-class individuals were apparent (although to a lesser degree) in male narratives, too. Larry (1917), a bricklayer from Blackburn serving as a bomb disposal expert during the Second World War, avoided getting 'tied up' in intimate behaviour:

LARRY Oh yes, there were times when I'd kiss 'em. I thought I'll have a go anyway. But er, I never got tied up with 'em … No, I didn't want satisfaction that way. Although there was some decent girls.[61]

Men worried that they might be trapped by their own desires into contracting a marriage they did not want or that they might be blamed for a pregnancy that was not their doing. Peter (1921) was fearful of some of the women who invited him to accompany them to the moor:

PETER The women encouraged it; they'd be in groups [of] two or three women and each one'll say, 'Oh come on, we'll go up moor', but yer knew what they were goin' up moor fer, because yer'd 'eard before … [and] yer couldn't get away from 'em, but I were lucky in never getting picked.[62]

Similarly, Penny (1916) recalled a story told by her husband, a labourer on construction sites in Hertfordshire, of his alarm at the unexpected eagerness of one girlfriend:

PENNY He … went out with one girl … she was a maid in service … took her home once … and he said, 'suddenly she tried to undo my trousers' … She started undoing the buttons of his flies … and he said, 'I'm not stopping here; you're not doing anything to me.' And he just run off from her.[63]

Norman's (1914) anxiety was fed by class concerns. He resisted the middle-class girls he was attracted to, who were expensive to take out, and he feared they might reject him as 'rough'. His father was a worker in the tram depot in London, while Norman was ambitious and described himself as a man of

[59] Grace msf/srss/ht/#38. [60] Alf msf/kf/ht/#14.
[61] Larry msf/kf/bl/#20. [62] Peter msf/kf/bl/#26. [63] Penny msf/srss/ht/#20.

'spirit', who 'wanted to get on'. Yet, he was conscious of the gap between his background and the status to which he aspired:

NORMAN I denied myself such things because I was bloody hard up. I had some very nice girlfriends, and my thoughts [were that] if I used to go round to the house the parents would drop dead if you, if they thought their daughter was going to marry somebody like me ... one of them was a little bit middle-classy, you know ... so I was the one that usually withdrew somehow or other ... But it was awful 'cos they were very nice girls, very nice girls ...

But his motivation to better himself and move out of his social circle in working-class Islington meant he also withdrew from relationships with other girls for fear of being trapped into a poverty-stricken marriage. From the late 1930s he started going to summer holiday camps where he had sex. But his anxiety about the dangers of being trapped into a premature marriage put him off developing any serious relationships with young women:

NORMAN When I saw what was going on around me I was a bit scared, uh, and I had other interests ... couples getting into the state they got into ... and all the disgrace ... I tell you, they got courting and ... the girl got pregnant ... they took a couple of rooms and it must have been, not love, but purgatory, you know ... I think the first one I [had sex with], the girl was a bit drunk and I got a bit chuckerred with it; I don't know what happened but I, I think I left her moaning and groaning around. I think she was drunk, and I thought, 'This is no place for me, I'm going!', so off I went ... plus there was a time when my father died and I was with my mother, and I thought, 'God, if anything happened it would be a complete disaster!', so I couldn't go around lashing my, what money I had around really ... [but] many of the people, people who got girls, that was the end of it.[64]

This fear of a slippery slope of physical affection, combined with an absence of clear codes of acceptable and unacceptable forms of intimacy prior to marriage, meant that the details of intimate behaviour before marriage varied considerably between working-class respondents. While some had sexual intercourse, others engaged in a range of forms of sex play, while others restricted themselves to kissing alone. Such variety is not indicative of different codes of sexual behaviour, but rather of independently developed individual responses to notions of morality.[65] Behaviour varied considerably in British working-class

[64] Norman msf/kf/ht/#17.

[65] Some interest in working-class petting emerged as early as the 1930s. In 1937 Mass Observation sent twenty-three observers to collect information on the precise nature of sexual activity in Blackpool, which was decried in the popular press as the 'seaside sex capital' for the northern working classes. Despite focusing on actual copulation, to their surprise they found a considerable range of different forms of petting: 'when we began work in Blackpool we expected to see copulation everywhere'. However, 'What we found was petting, feeling, masturbating

cultures despite a generally accepted code of principles governing the place of sexual intercourse in courtship. In the absence of any language to describe stages of intimacy or any clear discussion about sexual practices between young people, beyond rather vague and imprecise warnings of potential dangers, individuals independently developed their own behavioural boundaries. Marilyn (1914) worked in the bakery section of her mother's grocery shop and went out with a number of boys in Blackburn before marrying her husband in 1940:

MARILYN I suppose sort of putting their hand into your dress and feeling you, and, you know, just feeling you and their arm round your back and, you know, round your bottom and just put their hands up and down you.[66]

Arthur (1918) grew up in South Africa and was a newspaper print machine operative:

ARTHUR Well we did kiss ... we didn't kiss sexually; I did fondle her breasts ... and I may have put my hand up her dress and things like that.[67]

Rebecca (1903) worked as an alteration hand in a West End department store:

REBECCA You weren't intimate as much – they used to want, want to pet me, cuddle me and kiss me and all that sort of thing but that's all. I don't think I would've let them do anything else ... cuddle me and kiss, oh that's plenty, touch my, my bosoms ... no, that's all and I wouldn't let, oh they tried, they tried but I never let them ... mess about with you with their fingers and I never let them. No, something in me said 'No!', yeah, yeah.[68]

Catherine's (1912) father was a carpenter and joiner in London and she worked as a shorthand typist at a music printers in the late 1920s:

CATHERINE In fact, it's a funny thing. I don't know, I didn't think I was brought up that strict, but I probably was. Um, I wouldn't let chaps wander about on my body, as they say, 'waistline only'.[69]

one another. Observer units combed the sands at all hours, crawled around under the piers, pretended to be drunk and fell in heaps on located sand couples to feel what they were doing exactly ... ' After several weeks, only four cases of copulation were recorded, and one of these involved an observer (Humphries, *A Secret World of Sex*, 176). The data were differently analysed. Initial reports used the discovery of petting alongside the absence of evidence of copulation to suggest, provocatively, that contrary to popular image Blackpool was the 'most moral town in England'. When these findings were incorporated into the Little Kinsey Report, the evidence of petting was reformulated, not as indicative of the endurance of moral codes, but rather as part of the exuberant sexuality of working-class holiday makers (see Gary S. Cross, *Worktowners at Blackpool: Mass-Observation and Popular Leisure in the 1930s* (London: Routledge, 1990), 184). The underlying agenda was an attempt to chart 'promiscuity' and no attempt was made to explore the data on 'petting' by investigating the meanings of the acts to the individuals involved, nor the relationships between those involved (see Stanley, *Sex Surveyed*, 23, 186–9).

66 Marilyn msf/kf/bl/#7. 67 Arthur msf/srss/bl/#24.

68 Rebecca msf/kf/ht/#6. 69 Catherine msf/kf/ht/#1.

The wide variety in levels of intimacy and diversity in the range of premarital sexual behaviours engaged in among working-class respondents reflects the absence of any language of petting or commonly understood boundaries of behaviour. Research into the dating cultures of America during the twentieth century by contrast has charted the emergence of a detailed and publicly known language of courtship, which articulated precise stages of intimacy and linked these steps (which from the Second World War onwards often used baseball-inspired terminology of bases) to permitted degrees of physical contact and types of embrace.[70] Indeed, some contemporaries recognised this distinction between the language and practice of courtship in the US and UK at this time.[71] David Riesman's review in the *American Journal of Sociology* of Rowntree and Lavers' *English Life and Leisure* was intrigued by the apparent difference between British and American cultures of petting. Despite criticising the survey as 'hopelessly amateur', the reviewer pointed out the higher levels of 'promiscuity' in Britain and argued that 'Victorian England appears to have nearly vanished in a way that Victorian America has not'. For the reviewer it was the absence of the American 'compromise of necking and petting' which accounted for this difference: 'with sex on an all or none basis, they go for all'.[72] Beth Bailey also argues that within the United States between the 1920s and the 1950s it was not so much the behaviour of young couples that changed, but public recognition and labelling of distinct periods of courtship and the emergence of a common language describing stages of intimacy.[73] Among

[70] David Q. Voigt, 'Sex in Baseball: Reflections of Changing Taboos', *Journal of Popular Culture* XII, no. 3 (1978): 389–403, Deborah Roffman, 'The Power of Language: Baseball as a Sexual Metaphor in American Culture', *SIECUS Report* 19, no. 5 (1991): 1–6. What behaviour is signified by each base has varied across time, yet it is argued that their meanings were clearly understood by American youths, despite these fluctuations.

[71] Meyrick Booth wondered in the 1930s whether, despite the absence of 'petting parties' in the UK, perhaps 'the loosening of parental control, the spreading ... of a knowledge of birth control, and the revolution in habits resulting from motoring and weekending' had encouraged similar 'barbaric licence' among British youth (Meyrick Booth, *Youth and Sex: A Psychological Study* (London: G. Allen & Unwin, 1932), 52). Other commentators warned that those who 'indulge in what the Americans call 'petting'; or in flirting of the kind in which self-respect is sacrificed, are really losing their chances of happiness when marriage comes' (Gray, *Sex Teaching*, 97).

[72] David Riesman, 'Review: *English Life and Leisure: A Social Study* by B. Seebohm Rowntree and G. R. Lavers', *The American Journal of Sociology* 57, no. 6 (1952): 600–2. American scholars developed a way of 'mapping' levels of intimacy, and broke petting down into three classifications along a 'permissive scale': first kissing, second petting and third full sexual relations. Claiming that these were culturally meaningful and understood categories, they analysed petting behaviour as part of the analysis of sexual permissiveness. See, for example, Dorothy Dunbar Bromley and Florence Haxton Britten, *Youth and Sex, a Study of 1300 College Students* (New York and London: Harper & Brothers, 1938), Jerold S. Heiss, 'Variations in Courtship Progress among High School Students', *Marriage and Family Living* 22, no. 2 (1960): 165–70, Ira L. Reiss, 'The Scaling of Premarital Sexual Permissiveness', *Journal of Marriage and the Family* 26, no. 2 (1964): 188–98. For a summary of this material see Ericksen and Steffen, *Kiss and Tell.*

[73] Beth L. Bailey, *From Front Porch to Back Seat: Courtship in Twentieth-Century America* (Baltimore: Johns Hopkins University Press, 1988), 80. See also, Lisa Lindquist Dorr, 'The

the British working class, it was the very absence of this language describing stages of intimacy which is of critical importance in understanding the diverse expression of intimacy in British cultures of courtship, despite consensus on the ethics of sex during courtship.

'She allowed me to go further than I wanted to'

Women's focus on the dangers of courtship and the expression of anxieties about intimacy before marriage, particularly in working-class cultures, was compounded and complicated by the subtly combative gendered codes of courtship, through which men and women demonstrated their own and tested each other's respectability, restraint and ardour. In working-class (and to a lesser extent middle-class) testimony the responsibility for maintaining and policing sexual chastity before marriage was placed in the hands of women.[74] Men also usually wished to marry sexually inexperienced women (and wished any experience to be limited to themselves), and most men saw it as fair and appropriate (if not necessarily imperative) to remain virgins themselves. However, working-class men did not generally see it as their role to determine where to draw the line in expressing physical intimacy during courtship. Indeed, working-class men and women were clear that men might test women's respectability by pushing at the boundaries of acceptable sexual behaviour. Men used sexual intimacy to test the ease with which women gave in to sexual advances, and to investigate their general potential as a spouse.[75] Women who chased men or did not resist sexual advances might be rejected, and also risked being labelled 'loose'.[76]

Alf (1915) 'had to do the chasing'; when he went out with a girl he 'kissed her goodnight and all that sort of thing. And a bit of hanky-panky sometimes but it was very, er very few of 'em becoming pregnant.' Alf was asked how much hanky-panky was allowed and when he might stop. He responded that that was 'left to the girl, if the woman absolutely refused and definitely said no, that's it' but he added, 'some of 'em give in a bit too easy'.[77] Jennie (1908) concurred: 'lads are lads, aren't they? They, they'll try – if they can get it, they'll have it.'[78]

Perils of the Back Seat: Date Rape, Race and Gender in 1950s America', *Gender & History* 20, no. 1 (2008): 27–47.

74 Gillis, *For Better, for Worse*, 282.

75 Ross, *Love and Toil*, 65–7.

76 See also, Gillis, *For Better, for Worse*, 282, Linda Mahood and Barbara Littlewood, 'The "Vicious" Girl and The "Street-Corner" Boy: Sexuality and the Gendered Delinquent in the Scottish Child-Saving Movement, 1850–1940', *Journal of the History of Sexuality* 4, no. 4 (1994): 549–77, Tinkler, *Constructing Girlhood*, 137–40.

77 Alf msf/kf/ht/#14. Alf did not have sex with his future wife prior to marriage, but it was unclear whether or not Alf had prior experience, and he is thus categorised as one of the ambiguous cases, see above, note 9.

78 Jennie msf/kf/bl/#27.

Men's attempts at 'hanky-panky' had a specific purpose. Men presented themselves as having made distinctions between 'fast women' and respectable ones, and experiments on dates were a crucial way of judging partners. Even some of those men who felt that premarital sex was wrong nevertheless pushed for sex to test the girl's respectable resistance. Edmund (1910), a devout Anglican respondent who worked as a printer in Harpenden, insisted that sex before marriage was wrong. Despite having been 'brought up to respect' girls and avoid getting them 'in trouble' he clearly felt that it was his future wife's responsibility to stop him when he wanted sex.

Did you have sex at all before you were married?

EDMUND No! I think quite frankly it was wrong ... we were brought up much, much stricter ... I was brought up to respect people and on top of that, er (pause), not to do anything that [got] anybody in trouble ... I mean we knew where we stood, y'know (pause), and I think if I attempted to go too far (pause) I was pushed out of the way, y'know ... when I wanted sex yeah, y'know.[79]

Yet, these notions of appropriate gender roles provided men with difficulties; men also had much to lose through sexual activity. Colin (1923), a plumber from Blackburn, married Martha because she was pregnant. He presented this as a mistake ('a terrible thing'), brought on by her sexual licence in allowing him to go too far. He clearly blamed Martha for the pregnancy and resented having to marry her out of his sense of gentlemanly duty. Although this marriage was generally a happy one, his attitude towards Martha was in sharp contrast to his idealisation of his first girlfriend, Nancy. He lacked respect for his wife because she let him have sex and he idealised Nancy, who refused him and left him to play the gentleman.

COLIN I met Martha ... up the dance hall, like you know. Well, we [did] a bit of kissing and cuddling and one thing another well ... there was sex like, you know, which was a terrible thing in them days, you know supposed to be. Er, and then she came to be expecting and in them days it was a gentleman's duty to marry the girl ... I was a gentleman but ... she made more fuss of loving like you know and that was, that was the difference, like you know. She er, she allowed me, she allowed me to go further than I wanted to, you know what I mean?

[...] Nancy is the first girl I ever went out with ... and had a lovely marvellous time ... we got on well together, she were alright ... see we never that we never got into trouble (laughs) ... None, none at all. None at all. It er, she told me that ... I don't know, I still think it's in her nature ... but she said her father had told her sex is out ... I never had sex with Nancy ... kissing and cuddling and not, but no, no groping, no, no no. I, I was too much ... of a gentleman I think.[80]

[79] Edmund msf/kf/ht/#23.

[80] Colin msf/kf/bl/#36. See below on the marriages contracted as a result of pregnancy, and the ways in which individuals assessed such decisions and reflected upon responses to illegitimacy.

As noted above, men not only used sexual intimacy to test the ease with which women gave in to sexual advances, but also to test their general potential as a spouse. A lack of sexual restraint was perceived as indicative of general recklessness, which might then be reproduced in a host of other contexts. As Judy Giles' shows in her study of women's courtship roles, women saw themselves tested during courtship by their boyfriends and through a strategy she terms 'playing hard to get' they demonstrated their suitability as future spouses.[81] Elizabeth (1923), who was working in a fuse factory during the Second World War, rejected her future husband's advances because she thought, 'well if I let 'im 'ave his own way, he'll think what sort of a person is she, yer know, so that's why I never encouraged him at all'. Working-class women like Elizabeth, whose mother had been a weaver and whose father was a baker, knew it was important to reject male advances, both in order to prevent pregnancy and to preserve their reputation as reliable, trustworthy, decent, prudent and responsible.

> ELIZABETH I mean I would, I mean if a lad tried it on wi' me, that would be it, that'd be end. I know I once went t'pictures with one lad at Blackpool, me and our Lilian and we went, it were air force lad, and I went out with one air force lad and our Lilian went with another one, yer know, and we went t'pictures and he kept touching me bottom, yer know, behind me like and I kept jumping and our Lilian kept saying to me 'Will yer keep still?' Well I couldn't-just imagine somebody keep touching yer bottom in the pictures. I kept jumping out. She said 'For goodness sake keep still', but I couldn't tell 'er what were 'appening yer know, and then he wanted me to go and I said 'No way', and they wanted us to meet, but that were it, no, no. 'Owt like that, just put me off, no, because we were brought up so respectable love, yer know.[82]

Thus, although men did some self-monitoring, and many would themselves resist sex if they found themselves unexpectedly meeting little resistance, this was a culture in which men used sexual advances to test women. Yet, sexual activity during courtship to test the suitability of a potential spouse was used by women too: they evaluated men according to expressions of desire and the physical experiences during courtship. In pushing at the boundaries of acceptable sexual behaviour during courtship, men were also fulfilling their roles as thrusting and dynamic sexual initiators and demonstrating appropriate ardour, tenderness, passion and desire. Women were flattered by, and appreciative of, these forms of attention. At the same time, women had criteria of appropriate behaviour and men were also prone to be negatively labelled if they were perceived to have pushed too hard at the boundaries of physical intimacy.

In Blackburn, a vibrant female gossip network, fostered by factory work, meant that pushing one's ardour too far placed men in danger of being labelled

[81] Giles, 'Playing Hard to Get'. [82] Elizabeth msf/kf/bl/#26.

disrespectful and to be avoided. Sarah (1906), a weaver in Preston in the 1920s, remembered: 'The girls used to talk to one another and "don't go with him! Ooh, don't, ooh, don't go with him!", uh, and that's how you got to know about certain boys.'[83] Female respondents told tales of breaking up with boys precisely because they did not 'respect' them enough. Eva (1911) was a weaver in Blackburn and one of the main wage earners in her family responsible for supplementing her mother's army pension, as her father had died in 1917 when Eva was 5:

EVA They used to cuddle ya and kiss ya and that were it. That were it, you know. If they tried anything else on ya, ya didn't go wi' 'im any more, no … I used to give 'em words, proper, you know, and I'd say, 'If you don't behave yourself I'll scream and somebody'll come' you know.[84]

Eva's future husband, Albert, however, behaved differently:

EVA Eh, no, not really, never tried it on, Albert no. That, that's why I really took to 'im more than any, any of 'em. He didn't try anything on, you know. I thought well he respects me, you know and that were it.[85]

Heather (1916), who grew up in London, similarly 'finished there and then' with the 'big headed sorta chap' who would 'get you closer than you normally would wiv 'em and you don't have that … I would never go out with 'em again'.[86]

Yet while men knew they were expected to evaluate carefully the level of ardour that their girlfriends might deem appropriate, they also knew that they risked rejection if they were too circumspect: Doreen 'never went out again' with one boyfriend because she only got a peck: 'I thought well, you are a waste of time, you are a cissy.'[87] At the same time, men were also tested by women and had much to lose, as well as gain, if their sexual advances, which sought to test a girl's suitability and respectability, overstepped the mark.

'You played the field, and weighed them up'

On the one hand, then, physical intimacy and sexual desire were arenas where relationships between young working-class men and women were frequently fraught. Both were fearful of the consequences of expressing physical desire, left unsure where to draw the line, while simultaneously instrumentalising intimacy in a gendered test of each other's desire, love, respectability, prudence and reliability.

[83] Sarah msf/kf/bl/#30. [84] Eva msf/kf/bl/#9. [85] Eva msf/kf/bl/#9.
[86] Heather msf/kf/ht/#14. [87] Doreen (1922) msf/kf/bl/#20.

However, on the other hand, we should not lose sight of the fact that at this time working-class cultures were frequently ribald and suggestive.[88] As Mass Observation found in comparing the public courting activities in Worcester (Churchtown) and Middlesbrough (Steeltown), 'In Churchtown the pattern of overt sexual behaviour is restrained, conventional and unsophisticated – in Steeltown, public behaviour in pubs, dancehalls or parks is much more openly provocative and very much less restrained.'[89] Despite the sexual fears and the anxieties which dogged working-class courtships, this was not a 'repressed' world of inhibited behaviour where 'decent' girls lived in constant worry about the preservation of their respectability. Despite the acceptance of strictures against premarital sexual intercourse and fears of the consequences of pregnancy, despite the difficulties that young men and women had in communicating and policing their sexual desires during courtship, and despite the fact that most young men and women tried to (frequently successfully) remain virgins until the point of marriage, the public exchanges between men and women were full of ribald banter, flirtation and sexualised play.

In other words, maintaining a strict code of respectability, in which sexual topics, jokes or innuendo were taboo, was only necessary in the context of serious exchanges between young men and women. It was only close and relatively committed boyfriends and girlfriends who tested sexual availability and demonstrated respectability, when they were spending time in each other's exclusive company. More casual relationships, and especially exchanges between boys and girls conducted in gangs or small groups, presented considerable scope for men and women to enjoy and participate in exuberant demonstrations of banter and flirtatious play while in the relative safety of numbers and the public arena.[90]

88 Gillis, *For Better, for Worse*, 270, Peter Gurney, 'Intersex and Dirty Girls: Mass-Observation and Working Class Sexuality in England in the 1930s', *Journal of the History of Sexuality* 8, no. 2 (1997): 256–90, Schwarzkopf, 'Bringing Babies into Line', 326.

89 Mass Observation, File Report 3110, 'General Attitudes to Sex', April 1949, 'Article Five, The Position Today', 9. Begun in March 1949, Mass Observation originally sought to focus its 'penetrative work on sex survey' on a comparison of 'Steeltown' and 'Churchtown'; however, by April 1949 it had morphed into a national project comprising a number of different research strategies. See above, Chapter 2, note 40 and Stanley, *Sex Surveyed*, 21–3, Paul Atkinson, *Handbook of Ethnography* (London: Sage, 2001), 102–3.

90 Peter Bailey calls this playful presentation of a sexual demeanour which is understood to bear no relation to behaviour, 'parasexuality' (Peter Bailey, 'Glamour and Parasexuality: The Victorian Barmaid as Cultural Prototype', *Gender & History* 2 (1990): 148–72). Steve Humphries, for example, highlights the 'sexual atmosphere' of factories full of 'teasing, crudity and sexism' (Humphries, *A Secret World of Sex*, 62); Peter Gurney reveals the 'nonchalant attitude to picking-up' the opposite sex which was regarded as a 'bit of fun' by working-class mill girls in Bolton (Gurney, 'Intersex and Dirty Girls', 271–2).

This is evidenced by many working-class interviewees, particularly women, who described their early relationships in quite different terms to the relationships which were more serious or might lead to marriage.[91] As Judy Giles recognises, 'the conventions governing' working-class femininity by the 1940s encouraged flirtatious heterosexual relationships so long as they remained 'just a giggle' and were not taken too seriously and girls could ensure they protected their reputations.[92] Respondents presented themselves as casually flirting and flitting between lots of different boys.

Some women fondly remembered kissing games and midnight parties. Daphne (1912) was apprenticed in a bakery in Harwood in the early 1930s and Maria (1917) was extremely social; while working in a confectioner's, later in the 1930s, she helped her father sell bets at the dog track in Blackburn, and travelled to Manchester to ensure she had the most fashionable clothes.

DAPHNE Consequences, Spinning the Bottle, we used to have a game going up the stairs: you moved and kiss the boy on the next one, then you moved up another and kissed the boy on the next one. Spinning the Bottle: you put the bottle on the table and spun it and the one that spun it, if it pointed to one of the boys you had to kiss them you see. (laughs) It was just all innocent daft fun really.[93]

MARIA There'd be a lot of you, all joining together in a clique of boys and girls and we'd go to these midnight parties ... you'd play games ... Postman's Knock and somebody be in a room and one would knock and they'd shout you in and there'd be a quick kiss and then back out again, you know. And then afterwards you'd like all pair off, if you wanted to and things like that.[94]

In the north of England middle-class girls might tell similar stories. June (1914) came from a middle-class family; unable to go into nursing she began training as a hairdresser:

JUNE You'd do a little bit of flirting but it wouldn't last long. You'd pop onto somebody else and go out with them for a bit and see what you thought about what they thought about you. And in a gang of girls ... you'd meet these different ones ... take you to the pictures ... go to a little dance ... that was the way the courting was done in our days you see. And you played the, what I called played the field ... and weighed them up.[95]

[91] For example, Agatha msf/kf/ht/#7; Daphne msf/jm/bl/#38; Sarah msf/kf/bl/#30; Eleanor msf/kf/bl/#11; Iris msf/kf/bl/#2; Maria msf/kf/bl/#8.

[92] Judy Giles, *The Parlour and the Suburb: Domestic Identities, Class, Femininity and Modernity* (Oxford: Berg, 2004), 56. See also Tinkler, *Constructing Girlhood*, 140–1.

[93] Daphne msf/jm/bl/#38.

[94] Maria msf/kf/bl/#8. Lucinda Beier argues that in Lancashire by the end of the 1940s 'petting parties' like these remembered by Maria were common and indicate a significant change in the degree of sexual knowledge and experimentation permitted among young people (Beier, 'We Were Green as Grass', 477). Maria's experiences date from the mid-1930s.

[95] June msf/kf/ht/#27.

The simplistic divide between loose and respectable women belies a reality in which what determined women's behaviour was not who they were but where they were. It was the context for women's behaviour which was critical: 'respectable' women might join in with lewd chat in certain contexts. When Peter (1921), a stripper and grinder in a cotton mill in Blackburn, encountered a group of girls in the late 1930s who confronted him with deliberately indecent suggestions, he misinterpreted their behaviour and assumed they were 'loose' women. Far from being 'free and easy' this gang of girls had sufficient strength in numbers to use bawdy sexualised language in pursuit of a good time.[96] Through deliberate vulgarity they enjoyed themselves by goading Peter and mocking his masculinity by providing him with offers they knew he would have to refuse. This was not, in this context, unrespectable behaviour, nor did it mark these women out as loose women (except in Peter's eyes), but was the innocent, ribald fun of a group of working-class girls.[97]

> PETER Yer got a few at loose women, 'appen bump into one o' two of 'em and they say 'Oh, I'll take yer 'ome', and somebody else says 'Oh I'll take yer home', and then when you meet again … they start to tell you all these tales … they made out that they were free an' easy kind of thing; well that's one thing that I used to think well what the hell does it mean, free and easy … I thought they were a disgrace to themselves.[98]

The 'monkey parade', a ritualised parade of young people in their 'Sunday best', along a particular street, was the archetypal working-class demonstration of this kind of 'vulgar' public play, where open flirtation and sexual high spirits were legitimised.[99] Particularly associated with British northern industrial towns, in fact they were a common feature of many industrial towns and cities across Britain from the mid-nineteenth century and had rural and suburban versions, too, across the rest of the country, though these were often seasonal walks or associated with festival days.[100] Declining during the twentieth century (London's Fleet Street parade moved to Highbury Fields where it became

[96] On young women's participation in street cliques in Manchester and Salford see Davies, *Leisure, Gender, and Poverty*, 97.

[97] Many historians have examined the popular charges of delinquency or promiscuity which were occasioned by the rise of the independent young working-class woman after the First World War. See, for example, Langhamer, *Women's Leisure*, 53–4, Todd, *Young Women, Work and Family*, 214–16.

[98] Peter msf/kf/bl/#26.

[99] See Davies, *Leisure, Gender, and Poverty*, 104–5, for more examples of the openly flirtatious and inviting language used by women when remembering their involvement in Manchester's monkey parades. The parades declined during the Second World War and had largely died out by the 1950s.

[100] Ibid., Jenny Birchall, '"The Carnival Revels of Manchester's Vagabonds": Young Working Class Women and Monkey Parades in the 1870s', *Women's History Review* 15, no. 2 (2006): 229–52, Langhamer, *Women's Leisure*, 118–19.

a less rowdy affair with less public jostling or obscene catcalling), many died out during the Second World War and references to them in literature from the 1950s are comparatively rare.[101] Frank (1919), who washed floors in a Blackburn laundry in the 1930s, remembered 'whistling to all t'lasses' as he went 'parading up and down Preston New Road and … up Corporation Park' with his 'hair plastered down with Vaseline'.[102] Lyn (1907), a winder in a Blackburn mill, flirted with a whole host of different boys: 'you'd fetch some boys, and you'd pick them up and walk back down with them, got up again, you'd met somebody else and come down with them'.[103]

Just as Peter misinterpreted the high-spirited mock 'come-ons' of the girls he met, so, too, middle-class observers frequently misinterpreted the innocent sex games of the monkey parades as examples of working-class promiscuity or prostitution, as Jenny Birchall has argued regarding the middle-class anxiety at the public display of flirting from the mid-nineteenth century onwards when monkey parades developed in the town centres of predominantly northern industrial towns across England.[104] Such horror at the practice of monkey parading was far less common by the interwar decades; however, middle-class distaste at the custom remained.[105] Peter Gurney, for example, has deconstructed Mass Observation's surveys of working-class girls, particularly the observation of the sexual activities of working-class women on holiday in Blackpool in the late 1930s, as indicative of such middle-class distaste for the ironic pretences of sexual availability and public bawdiness which they mistook for promiscuity, prostitution or sexual looseness.[106] June (1914), the daughter of a bank manager in Barnsley, also connected the working-class pick-ups along the 'bunny run' in the centre of Barnsley with prostitution:

JUNE We knew about prostitutes. (laughs) Ooh, we thought they were disgusting … when a certain street in the town … and do you know what we used to call

[101] Mike Fitzgerald, Gregor McLennan and Jennie Pawson, eds. *Crime and Society: Readings in History and Theory* (London: Routledge & Kegan Paul, 1981), 11–13, Gillis, *For Better, for Worse*, 272, Catriona M. Parratt, *More Than Mere Amusement: Working-Class Women's Leisure in England, 1750–1914* (Boston: Northeastern University Press, 2001), Louise A. Jackson, '"The Coffee Club Menace": Policing Youth, Leisure and Sexuality in Post-War Manchester', *Cultural and Social History* 5, no. 3 (2008): 289–308.

[102] Frank msf/srss/bl/#16. [103] Lyn msf/kf/bl/#1.

[104] Birchall, 'Carnival Revels'. Steve Humphries also presents monkey parades as places of serious sexual encounters, rather than arenas for more 'innocent' sexual merry-making, flirtation and banter, see Humphries, *A Secret World of Sex*, 38–9. On the other hand, John Gillis claims that prostitutes or 'harpies' 'often hung about the margins of the monkey ranks' (Gillis, *For Better, for Worse*, 275).

[105] In Blackburn, for example, the monkey parade was held along Preston New Road, a smart area dominated by large Victorian villas leading out of town ending at Corporation Park.

[106] Gurney, 'Intersex and Dirty Girls'. See also Judy Giles on middle-class fears that dancing provided emotional excitement for working-class girls which dangerously overstimulated their sex instincts (Giles, *The Parlour and the Suburb*, 57–8).

that? The Bunny Run ... that's where they used go to pick [up] and it was right in the centre of the town. (laughs) ... Yes, oh ... I don't know whether they were all prostitutes but we knew that's where they went to pick up.[107]

Similarly, Sally saw the lewd jests of her working-class friends as typical of the vulgarity of working-class life from which she was anxious to escape. She refused to participate in Preston's version of the monkey parade, preferring instead to go on country walks with her rambling friends.[108]

Concern at the apparently overt sexuality of the working classes was not limited to activities such as the monkey parade. Again, rather than seeing the flirtation and innuendoes of such parades as existing despite, or, indeed, perhaps because of the codes of respectability, which continued to structure the close relationships between young men and women, Sally (1908) mistakenly saw the sexual banter and subsequent behavioural boasts as sincere and as indicative of the laxness of working-class morals:

SALLY they went mad for boys. Used to go on Preston [New Road] – they used to call it 'walking the road' on Sunday afternoon. All your best clothes on and walk up and down the road till you caught somebody's eye. Well, I would never go ... would go for a walk in the country ... That one at the school used to say 'He, ooh, he was nice, ooh and his hands were warm.' And I looked [and] I said 'You're disgusting.'[109]

Similarly, Jutta Schwarzkopf has uncovered the 'highly ritualised contexts' in which women might play a 'pro-active role in relationships with men' in Lancashire cotton-weaving factories. Here women were expected to try to 'kiss male colleagues unawares', which, if successful, obligated the man to contribute funds to Christmas and birthday kitties, and young women on the verge of marriage were routinely embarrassed by the ribald jokes of older women. She concludes that occasionally, in factories, 'open displays of sexual behaviour would be observed'.[110] However, participation of young men and women in working-class cultures of public innuendo was not at odds with the existence of strict constraints on the progress of relationships between young men and women, which were conducted according to rules about respectability and

[107] June msf/kf/ht/#27. Compare quote above, where June presented herself as having 'played the field'. See also the memories quoted by Mary Blewett, such as the Yorkshire mill worker who recalled, 'Of course I had my fun with the lads in my time. But I were smart enough to know when to keep the gate shut' (Mary H. Blewett, 'Yorkshire Lasses and Their Lads: Sexuality, Sexual Customs, and Gender Antagonisms in Anglo-American Working-Class Culture', *Journal of Social History* 40, no. 2 (2006): 318–19).

[108] On the emergence of 'rambling' as an organised activity for better-off sections of the working classes in the north of England see, Langhamer, *Women's Leisure*, 77–8.

[109] Sally msf/kf/bl/#31.

[110] Schwarzkopf, 'Bringing Babies into Line', 326. See also, Jan Lambertz, 'Sexual Harassment in the Nineteenth Century English Cotton Industry', *History Workshop Journal* 19, no. 1 (1985), 29–61, Blewett, 'Yorkshire Lasses and their Lads'.

restraint.[111] As Selina Todd has recognised, the 'assertive collective identity' of factory girls, and their boisterousness, both within the workplace and outside it, (displayed during shared leisure activities) created a widespread and misplaced reputation that they were 'rough'.[112] Rather, some limited forms of public innuendo and ironic sexual banter between groups of boys and girls belied intimate relationships prior to marriage which were dominated by fears of illegitimacy and codes of respectability.

'We came close to doing it but we didn't'

Middle-class negotiations of sexual intimacy during courtship were typically quite different from those of the working classes. Such differences betrayed middle-class women's greater confidence and knowledge of sexual matters. As shown in Chapter 2, middle-class women had an equally strong association of femininity and sexual innocence but did not link their sexual inexperience so strongly to sexual ignorance. As a result, many middle-class women found themselves able to discuss the importance of premarital virginity directly with their partners and to come to a mutual agreement that sex would be avoided before marriage. This meant the policing of desire and intimacy became much more of a joint project.

In some respects, Hubert's (1911) testimony was similar to that of working-class respondents; like working-class women, his future wife, a nurse, was also concerned to limit the degree of intimacy during their courtship in the mid-1930s for fear that such behaviour might escalate beyond a point of no return. However, in contrast to working-class narratives, in which men often pushed at the boundaries of acceptable intimacy, seeing it as their girlfriends' role to determine the point at which they should be restrained, he acknowledged that, despite his desires, it was his job to demonstrate his own consideration of her by restraining himself:

111 On working-class traditions of comic vulgarity see, for example, Gurney, 'Intersex and Dirty Girls', 269, Cross, *Worktowners at Blackpool*, 175–7. On the peculiarly British brand of sexual humour typified by comic postcards and popular song see, John K. Walton, 'Blackpool and the Varieties of Britishness', in *Relocating Britishness*, eds. Stephen Caunce, Ewa Mazierska, Susan Sydney-Smith and John K. Walton (Manchester: Manchester University Press, 2004), 61. Ellen Ross noted similar vigour among London's young 'cheeky factory girls' and swearing schoolgirls, earlier in the twentieth century. However, she argues that they must have grown up 'into no-nonsense wives and mothers who would fight and curse when angry and who could laugh at a husband's pretensions' (Ross, *Love and Toil*, 59). It is not clear that such boisterousness translated into different contexts, or that being a rude lass or bawdy young wife was viewed by young women as within the repertoire of permissible identities.

112 Todd, *Young Women, Work and Family*, 215. On the optimistic portrayals of 'mills girls' as sensible yet fun-loving young women who deserved a good time, see also ibid., 216, and Langhamer, *Women's Leisure*, 53–4.

HUBERT Never even kissed me or anything. I was a bit shaken by that, when we, sort of, had agreed [to get married], but I thought, 'Well, she's a bit modest anyway, but er, she's probably afraid that one thing might lead to another'. So ... I restrained myself ... girls in those days were cautious. They didn't allow any liberties at all ... I knew I'd get a thick ear if I did. It was tantamount to saying that, er, you try that with a girl, that, that, you considered she was of no account.[113]

Middle-class male testimony also revealed similar anxieties to those expressed by working-class male respondents that they might be trapped into marriage, and they, too, were put off by women who appeared too eager. William (1902) was working as a clerk for Lever Brothers, while Roger (1910) was articled to a chartered surveyor in Chatham:

WILLIAM we were lying on the grass, sitting there, and she said, 'it's expectant to give a, the lady to give the gentleman her hand', she said, 'just put it inside me', and I wouldn't do it. I, I didn't seem to want to touch a lady, a lady's bosom in those days ... that may have been why, why my first affair fizzled out because I was a bit too (pause) ... I'm almost certain that she wanted a bit more ... she wanted me to touch her between her chest and that, and I did, I shied away from doing it.[114]

ROGER She let her hand wander, dear ... and use such expressions as, uh, 'It would be better in than out!', and she was quite ready and willing ... she used to grab and undo you here, take it out, pull up her skirt and it was all such an eager-beaver business that it frightened me ... and I felt sorry for myself, because I thought you were missing a wonderful opportunity because she invited me round to the house one afternoon, and she disappeared, and when she came down she had what was practically a see-through negligee on her. And I can tell you this, she was a beautiful-built girl ... and I suppose in a quiet sort of way, I regretted that I didn't.[115]

Such stories illustrate some of the shared ways in which both working-class and middle-class young men approached young women and highlight the common fears and expectations:

ROGER I thought to myself, 'I don't know, I don't know, I don't know. She's so forward, what does it mean? ... Has she been with someone and is already pregnant?' You see there were no blood tests in those days, you know? And that was the thing that stopped me dead.[116]

However, Roger's response to these fears was to discuss the matter with his girlfriend. Such forms of communication about sexual behaviour were almost entirely absent from working-class testimony:

ROGER After a while I talked to her and I said, to her, I said, 'You're not a virgin, are you?', and she said, 'No', she said, 'I'm not', she said, 'I lost my virginity', she

[113] Hubert msf/kf/ht/#32. In a similar vein one woman interviewed by Claire Langhamer said of women's understanding of the sexual behaviour of young men: 'we didn't think anybody loved you if all they wanted was sex' (Langhamer, *Women's Leisure*, 125).

[114] William msf/kf/ht/#24. [115] Roger msf/kf/ht/#10. [116] Roger msf/kf/ht/#10.

said, 'at 16'. She was quite open about it and she was then about 19 and she said that, uh, it had been with a boy that she'd known and I think it was that, I remember this, she said that it was a boy that she'd known for a week. And she lost her virginity, and I thought, 'Well, that's a bit quick'. At that time. And I know that that was one of the things that I thought, 'you want to be careful' you see?[117]

Very few working-class respondents talked openly to each other about sexual activity before marriage. Alastair (1927), a cotton mill baler, was extremely unusual in having discussed in detail with his wife, a ring winder in the same factory, whether or not to have sex before marriage, and as a result how to enjoy themselves during courtship. As one of the youngest interviewees, this testimony might also be indicative of later trends and the emergence, during the post-war period, of a new discussion of forms of petting.[118] In 1939, for example, Rennie Macandrew's *Friendship, Love Affairs and Marriage* saw 'no harm' in 'two unmarried lovers going the length of mutual digital masturbation, or for the man to caress or kiss the woman's breasts'.[119] Alastair married in 1952 after a ten-year courtship, and was the son of an unqualified Catholic midwife who was herself illegitimate.

ALISTAIR It was on the borderline, telling the truth. I mean, often I felt like it [intercourse] and often she felt like it, but we made this arrangement, right from day one of courtship, which I said to her, two years after I'd met her, that we wouldn't have sex until she was married, uh, we were open, we were open about this, we spoke about this, she felt like it and I felt like it, but [...]

You'd go out at night-time, she'd sit on me knee and I'd perhaps [be] stroking left, right and ... and all, sometimes she'd had, what you call it, she'd actually had a, a ful-fillment. But uh, she weren't undressed really, just like, stroking ... I touched her shoulder blades, it turned her on left, right and centre ... back of the neck, now. But uh, we'd agreed not to have sex till we were married.[120]

Far more middle- than working-class narratives included similar stories of having had some discussion of the question of sex before marriage, such that each would then enjoy a range of intimate pleasures in the confident awareness

[117] Roger msf/kf/ht/#10.

[118] American pamphlets discussed the dangers of 'petting' during the 1920s (see McLaren, *Twentieth-Century Sexuality*, 40). Joseph E. Scott and Jack L. Franklin, 'The Changing Nature of Sex References in Mass Circulation Magazines', *The Public Opinion Quarterly* 36, no. 1 (1972): 85, argue that in American mass media the 1950s saw a peak in public discussion of 'non-coital sex relations', although much of this was condemnatory. Others argue that by the 1950s there emerged a new emphasis on 'petting' as a strategy in marriage and relationship manuals as an antidote to full intercourse; see, for example, Weeks, *Sex, Politics and Society*, 238, Weeks, *The World We Have Won*, 43, Hall, *Sex, Gender and Social Change*, 156–7.

[119] Rennie MacAndrew (pseud.), *Friendship, Love Affairs and Marriage. Explanation of Men to Women and Women to Men, Etc* (London: Wales Publishing Co., 1939). Quoted in Cook, *The Long Sexual Revolution*, 230.

[120] Alistair msf/kf/bl/#33. Alistair was also one of the very few working-class respondents who received some formal sex education, which again reflects his comparative youth. On sex education provision during this period, see above, Chapter 2, 76–7, note 61.

that both parties were committed to remaining virgins. This is not to argue that middle-class men and women found communication about sexual matters easy or that they engaged in lengthy and in-depth discussions. However, unlike working-class couples, middle-class women were able to articulate their desire not to have sex before marriage and subsequently to rely on their boyfriends to conduct themselves accordingly. Thus, although they shared with working-class women a fear that physical intimacy was dangerous, that self-policing was necessary and difficult, and the worry that one might find oneself getting carried away, such that one would fail to avoid having sex, middle-class women's greater awareness of sexual matters, and less strong feelings of ignorance or confusion about sex and reproduction meant that they, like Yorkshire bank manager's daughter June (1914), tended to be much clearer in their own minds on the precise forms of behaviour which defined where their own personal boundaries between acceptable and unacceptable lay:

JUNE We never went the whole hog; we were too afraid... we never went any further than... what you call heavy petting. You know what I mean, by heavy petting? In the pictures, maybe on the back row as I say. But not much, not much of that sort of thing. No, it was too risky, it was too dangerous... It was dangerous that you would be, you'd you'd get so far and not be able to withdraw further back and then you would end up getting pregnant. And that was a thing you did not want to get, do in my day... but if he, if I thought he was going to go perhaps too far I would terminate it you see... a young girl knows how far you can go and what you do er when your feelings begin to be aroused. You, you, you know how far you can, the kissing can go, the feeling can go.[121]

There were significant class differences in the experiences of petting and levels of intimacy. Crucially, it is only through understanding the cultural associations and meanings ascribed to intimate acts that these differences can be understood. Despite the fact that middle-class individuals tended to be less likely to have had intercourse before marriage, it was not the case that they had different codes of morality, that they valued innocence more highly, were better at self-policing or were less likely to find themselves in circumstances in which having sex brought certain advantages. Indeed, a striking aspect of middle-class testimony was the tendency to characterise petting as having been close to sex, and to suggest that they had in fact nearly had sex before marriage.[122] Reg (1919) and his future (first) wife, a hairdresser, courted during the Second World War while he served as a cameraman in the navy's film unit.

REG As time went on... passions rose... but I was never getting as much as I wanted to; I never made love to her until I was married. I got very near a couple of times,

[121] June msf/kf/ht/#27.

[122] Compare here similar statements made in some American college students' responses to a survey in the 1930s: Bromley and Britten, *Youth and Sex*, 65.

> because they had a brick shelter and during one of the raids we're in there … and the brick shelter had two bunks; her mother went on one and we went in the other and that was as near as I got. It was almost but not, but from there after I, I made rapid progress because I knew all the short cuts.
> *What do you mean you knew the short cuts?*
> Well, I knew all the exciting areas that, um, you could feel them … led to sex but it just didn't … I didn't go any further … I mean I wouldn't say I didn't want to do it, but I, I felt I shouldn't do it.[123]

Such narratives are indicative of the ways many middle-class men and women enjoyed significant and prolonged petting sessions while courting, having come to a shared understanding that both were committed to restraining themselves at the last minute, despite the frustrations and anxieties this caused.[124] Rather than making a significant contrast between those who did, and those who did not have sex, such narratives draw attention to the importance of looking behind crude statistics about intercourse prior to marriage in order to examine the meanings ascribed to different kinds of sexual behaviour before marriage.

Middle-class women in particular revealed an awareness, absent from working-class testimony, that their future husbands would ensure that sexual intercourse itself would not take place:

> FELICITY When you're getting nearer to getting married you get a bit frisky … in the heat of the moment we came close to doing it but we didn't … some inhibition inside me and inside him as well … it was mutual.[125]

Indeed a few middle-class women recalled that in the heat of the moment they were probably prepared to consent, but they did not tell their boyfriends this, who continued to assume that they did not want to have sex despite their manifestations of desire and passion. There was no tacit or spontaneous renegotiation or assumption of consent. Gill (1920) 'very nearly would have' had sex with her husband, who was serving as a major in the army during the Second World War, but didn't because their courtship was very short ('it wasn't long to wait'), and because she didn't make it clear to him that she was willing: 'he would've perhaps if I'd said, "Come on, why don't we do it?", you know, but I didn't, so er, he would never of er, er I, I, he wasn't the sort that would've raped me ever. I can assure you.'[126]

123 Reg msf/kf/ht/#36; another example of such restraint was William msf/kf/ht/#24.

124 Hera Cook argues that central to what she identifies as the post-war emergence of 'acceptable physical sexual activity', both prior to and within marriage were 'substantial changes in women's and men's attitudes to the genitals' (Cook, *The Long Sexual Revolution*, 206).

125 Felicity (1919) msf/kf/bl/#37. Felicity married a claims assessor for British Rail in 1954 at the comparatively late age of 34. She came from a lower-middle-class background – her father had been a grocer who managed a shop and her mother a weaver. She went to grammar school, however, and worked in a British Rail accounts office. Felicity and her husband were relatively devout, although she was a Methodist who converted to Catholicism after meeting her future husband.

126 Gill msf/kf/bl/#48. Also Roger msf/kf/ht/#10; Phyllis msf/kf/bl/#5.

The confidence on the part of middle-class women that their boyfriends were committed, as they were, to preserving premarital virginity meant they were prepared to engage in a wider variety of non-coital pleasures prior to marriage than many of their working-class counterparts.[127] Gay (1928), who was working in a London advertising agency, was anxious, but reassured by her boyfriend, a handsome air force rear gunner, that what they were about to enjoy would not risk pregnancy:

GAY I remember one night... he said, 'let's go in the park and it's dark' (pause) so we go in the park and he'd got a groundsheet and I can remember him saying, 'don't worry, um, you'd never' (pause) because I wasn't going to go, he wanted to go that far and I, I said, 'No!' ... well I know he had his hands in my knickers but um and I know I remember thinking it was rather nice, but no no no, (laughs) so obviously he, he touched the right spot.[128]

Moreover, middle-class women's own knowledge of sexual matters gave them greater confidence and language to express the boundaries between acceptable and unacceptable forms of sexual behaviour.[129] Pru (1911), who socialised with the boys at the tennis clubs she frequented as well as in country house parties in the early 1930s, was prepared to 'make love' in what she termed a 'decent way'. Her full understanding of male physiology meant she was prepared to let her boyfriends 'put their arms around you and squeeze you and press up against you' until he had to 'rush off' because he had 'had satisfaction'.[130] Similarly, Reg (1919) described his girlfriend, a hairdresser from Portsmouth, as having directly indicated what she wanted him to do:

REG Well, we were just fondling, um, like she never took her knickers away and things like that, you know, but we fondle through them and that, and um, and then what would happen was that she'd, she'd move the elastic or whatever away and then she'd, as I say, she'd put my fingers in the spot she wanted them to go, and then you didn't need any telling then that they, they had a spot there that they must know about, you know, and enjoy it.[131]

[127] This is not to conclude that working-class respondents did not engage in these activities. Although many working-class interviewees did indicate the boundaries between acceptable and unacceptable forms of love-making during courtship, many others presented highly ambiguous and euphemistic accounts which make it impossible to determine precisely what was practised, beyond the assertion that it did not involve penetrative intercourse. Of course, such ambiguities are themselves indicative of the lack of communication and the absence of clear vocabulary through which working-class couples could have discussed or formulated sexual boundaries during courtship, and should not be seen as methodologically or empirically problematic.

[128] Gay msf/kf/ht/#13.

[129] Chesser's limited analysis of 'petting' argued that those who had read books on sex were more likely to engage in petting behaviour which did not lead to sexual intercourse than those without any sex education (Chesser et al., *The Sexual, Marital and Family Relationships of the English Woman*, 333–4).

[130] Pru msf/kf/ht/#12. [131] Reg msf/kf/ht/#36.

Antonia (1928), who married in 1949 upon leaving Chelsea Art College, was fully versed in the terminology of mutual masturbation indicating, perhaps, the extent to which debates about 'petting' that emerged in the 1940s and 1950s informed individuals' understanding and interpretation of their behaviour, although her husband, a chartered accountant, came from an earlier generation, having been born in 1914:[132]

ANTONIA A lot of fairly heavy petting ... which I must say I did enjoy. It was only the thought of going any further than that that frightened the life out of me because I mean then if, if, if, if you got pregnant then before you were married it was hell to pay and I don't know what my parents would have said. My father would have been absolutely furious. Erm so that there was never any question of going any further. Erm but as far as it went er I enjoyed it.
What did heavy petting involve? How far did it go?
Well it went quite far. It went to erm sort of mutual masturbation.[133]

Indeed, a few middle-class respondents presented premarital sexual intimacy as sufficiently fulfilling that they were perfectly happy to reserve sexual intercourse until after marriage. Patrick (1918) was a book keeper and clerk in a chartered surveying firm in the late 1930s, while Roger (1910) was apprenticed to be a chartered surveyor slightly earlier in the late 1920s and early 1930s.

PATRICK [We went] all the way except insertion ... you need protection for safe insertion, that was the first thing, that was the binding thing, I think, and, um, if I was going to get an orgasm very pleasantly anyway, why bother to do anything else?[134]

ROGER I mean I'd get, with foreplay and that, get that and she would cuddle me tremendously and to be perfectly frank with you, she'd lift her skirt and put me between her legs, and that would ejaculate then. That was a form of relief, and in point of fact, we did that very often, it satisfied me and she said it satisfied her because she felt she was doing it for me. So there we are but it was, uh, I often, I often said to her, it was a pity we never just rammed it up.[135]

In contrast to middle-class interviewees, working-class couples did not formulate a joint plan to avoid intercourse. Although greater numbers of working-class couples had sex before marriage, it is clear that this was not the result of greater promiscuity or different moral codes.[136] Both classes held an ideal of

[132] See also Beier, 'We Were Green as Grass', 477. She argues that heavy petting became increasingly acceptable during the 1940s and 1950s. Compare, however, the testimony of June above, who also uses this language, despite having been born fourteen years earlier in 1914 and having married in 1936.

[133] Antonia msf/kf/ht/#35. [134] Patrick msf/kf/ht/#16.

[135] Roger msf/kf/ht/#10. Roger met his wife when she was 14 and they married in 1938 when she was 21 and he was 27.

[136] Angus McLaren asks, on the basis of data on the extent of premarital sex, 'Was there a great split between the rough and respectable concerning sex?' He argues that because among all classes there was a shared assumption that sex before marriage was to be avoided, we can

premarital virginity, with probably equal strength. The difference between the two classes' experiences lay in their different responses to the experience of sexual intimacy while courting. The middle classes, and in particular middle-class women, had a much greater sense of exactly what they wished to avoid, what range of pleasures could be enjoyed without having sexual intercourse, and a much greater confidence that their boyfriends would share responsibility for preserving premarital virginity. In the heat of the moment, middle-class couples were less likely to have penetrative sex, because they had a stronger belief that the other did not want to have intercourse, and they interpreted intense and passionate forms of sexual behaviour, short of penetration, as activities which helped them avoid having intercourse.

Thus, when middle-class couples found themselves getting carried away they tended to avoid having sex, even when the reality was that both were actually prepared and ready to have sex. Roger's wife suggested that they abandoned their pledge to wait until marriage before having sex. However, he worried that she did not really want to lose her virginity and ignored her suggestion, thinking she could not really mean it:

> ROGER We did say it's only seven months to marriage, and we did say that we weren't going to until we got married, it's, and I know you want it, because she really did! You see she, women in those days, it was a sacrament to them on the marriage bed, absolutely true. And therefore I was very, very careful and … I thought, 'she doesn't really want it', but when I look back, she's often told me, she's said, 'I did!', she said, 'I'd have done it', but she said, 'Quite frankly, I thought you didn't want it!'. 'Well', I said, 'it was because of you', she said, 'Yes', she said, 'and it was that damn silly time we were in', she said, 'We should have talked it through more.'[137]

Working-class couples' responses to intimate behaviour were different. For these couples confusion about the precise details of sexual matters (particularly on the part of women) and an absence of open communication between couples meant that sex often 'just happened'. Without a clearly articulated joint plan to save intercourse for marriage many working-class individuals found themselves silently consenting to have sex in the heat of the moment. The expression of passion was much more likely to be seen as silent indication that avoidance of sex was no longer considered imperative. Moreover, forms of sexual pleasure seen by the middle classes as alternatives to intercourse might be interpreted among the working class as steps along the road to intercourse, consent to which might be deemed as a tacit agreement to go even

then see differential premarital practices as indicative of distinct class differences (McLaren, *Twentieth-Century Sexuality*, 43). It is here argued that the distinct class differences uncovered are indicative of the different communication strategies rather than moral frameworks or boundaries.

[137] Roger msf/kf/ht/#10.

further. Once certain intimacies had been granted, some working-class couples assumed that they were in a situation in which sex was likely to result and from which it was difficult to go back. In such passionate moments, women concluded that in granting certain liberties, their boyfriends would expect them to go 'all the way'.

In taking such a view of their partners' expectations, women interpreted their own behaviour as tantamount to consenting to sex, and in internalising their own behaviour in this way, they gave the green light for sex to take place. For their part, when working-class men, accustomed to having sexual behaviour policed by their girlfriends, found themselves encouraged to go further than they had before, they too concluded that silent consent to sex was indeed being provided. Eileen (1913), whose parents ran a boarding house in Blackburn, was typical of working-class women who, having been warned that kissing resulted in pregnancy, saw themselves as uninformed and unable to negotiate the pleasures of courtship. She loved being kissed, and realised that this did not put her in danger of pregnancy. Yet she did not have the confidence, language or resources to negotiate a form of intimacy which did not involve intercourse. She was able to articulate to her boyfriend that she did not want to get pregnant, but once she found herself consenting to more than kissing, deemed herself in such a situation that she found sex just happening:

> EILEEN Mum told me if 'e kiss me I'd 'ave a baby, and that's the way I was brought up all me life ... when Robin kissed me yeah, I liked it.
>
> *And did you think you'd have a baby?*
>
> No, did I heck, no! That 'ad gone out of me mind then, I was, something else I was thinking about then (chuckling) ... well I was 'appy when 'e kissed me 'cos I thought it was wonderful, thought it was yer know really good. I like being kissed by fella ... I think I was frightened, at first ... Oh, what was gonna 'appen, I don't know ... I said, 'yer not getting me in trouble, I'm not doing anything like that! oh no, I'm not!' ... it just, it just 'appened an' that was it.[138]

The investigation of individuals' own perceptions of the meaning of sexual intimacies has revealed an absence of cultural categories to describe or chart levels of petting among working- and middle-class interviewees, beyond a shared distinction between forms of petting and full intercourse. By paying attention to individuals' descriptions of the expression of intimacy during courtship we highlight the danger of inferring values from behaviour. While more working-class individuals had sex before marriage, this finding does not support a conclusion that moral frameworks are differentiated by class. The oral history evidence we have collected suggests we should not make too great a distinction between those who had sex and those who did not; instead we can better understand the moral codes and sexual negotiations during courtship by

[138] Eileen msf/kf/bl/#12.

paying attention to the complex circumstances leading some couples to have sex, and others not to.

'If you will play with fire you get burnt'

Within working-class cultures especially, then, fear of pregnancy, inability to communicate or delineate precise codes of intimate behaviour short of penetrative intercourse, combined with strong feelings of love, desire and affection resulted, more frequently than for middle-class respondents, in unintended acts of sexual intercourse.[139] However, for some members of both middle-class and working-class communities, sex before marriage was not avoided, despite the existence of a moral code asserting the importance of avoiding it, because there were circumstances in which sex before marriage brought advantages and benefits. Even for those who regarded sex before marriage as a mistake or a transgression, often personal, familial and communal moral codes proved flexible and pragmatic.[140] Some deliberately rebelled against moral strictures, some preserved their respectability despite such transgressions, and others made use of malleable ethical codes to excuse or legitimise their behaviour.

Women and men not only consented to having sex with each other by accident in the heat of the moment: while sex often 'just happened', it was also frequently a rational and purposeful step in their courtship.[141] Although working-class women often rejected the physical advances made by their boyfriends, judging such moves to be tests of their respectability, for some sex became a way of cementing a relationship and was frequently interpreted as a promise of marriage.[142] Indeed, even the possibility of pregnancy might be welcomed as a means of forcing a man's hand, or ensuring a marriage would take place. Such examples show us the ways in which working-class women were able to engineer their own outcomes in gender relations and use sexuality to realise their desires.[143] Grace (1922) slept with her future husband, who was serving in the army, only four months after meeting him in 1944. She 'knew it

[139] Research in the USA has similarly found that 'premarital intercourse was a more common part of working-class life' yet White argues that 'this group probably lacked the moral and religious inhibitions that generally helped define middle-class men's and women's behaviour, which much more readily stopped at petting' (White, *The First Sexual Revolution*, 85–6).

[140] See also, Beier, 'We Were Green as Grass', 470–1, Stanley, *Sex Surveyed*, 138–42.

[141] Similarly, despite the apparent disadvantages for many modern teenage mothers, pregnancy can equally be a 'rational and meaningful life option'. See Lisa Arai, 'Low Expectations, Sexual Attitudes and Knowledge: Explaining Teenage Pregnancy and Fertility in English Communities. Insights from Qualitative Research', *The Sociological Review* 51, no. 2 (2003): 119–217.

[142] For similar evidence and analysis see also, Higgins, 'The Changing Expectations and Realities of Marriage', 111–13.

[143] This is a common theme in the literature discussing the sexual attitudes of working-class women in the north of England. See, for example, Blewett, 'Yorkshire Lasses and their Lads'.

was gonna happen' but was initially shy, resistant and frightened of pregnancy. However, the advantage, articulated at the time, was that it ensured he would marry her. Grace was determined that Colin would have to marry her and saw sex explicitly as an entrapment strategy:

GRACE It's hard for you to imagine ... you didn't know enough to stop you from having a baby ... If you went with a man how would you not have a baby? And that's one thing even though my mother had died, I would never, ever have done that to her. That's the way she brought me up.

I just said, 'get away', I were frightened ... It was our own front room. We'd been out and gone back in. And I knew it was gonna happen sometime or other. And I knew it, it had got to be Colin and nobody else. But I was just so frightened. So shy. And that was the only time until we got married ... And then I suppose I was guilty after. Worried.[144]

However, the great advantage of a sexual relationship was that it was interpreted as intent to marry.

GRACE It wasn't the risk that he would marry me. I'd make sure he would marry me (determined tone). I wasn't gonna let him go. I wouldn't let him go. And as, as I say, I think I would have killed anybody that had got in my way.

After the event Grace had no worries about whether or not they would get married; being rejected by the man she loved was now, no longer, a risk:

GRACE If that was the only way I was gonna get him, I were gonna get him, you see ... I think I said to him after that 'Now he'll have to marry me!' (chuckles) Yeah.[145]

Penny (1916) found herself in quite a different situation from Grace, yet she, too, illustrated the dilemma many girls found themselves in once they had chosen a boyfriend they wanted to marry. She was engaged to her husband, a labourer on construction sites, for four years before they married in 1938. Early on in their engagement they started having intercourse, using withdrawal for protection. Penny presented sex with her boyfriend as loving and romantic. Sex was not regretted, nor excused; rather, it was natural and 'automatic':

PENNY We had a very very happy courtship ... we would always always go walking, we'd go, there was a lot of fields around us, we'd go walking in fields and he'd pick primroses and bluebells for me and ... you know go in the fields and sort of lay down and, um, have a kiss and a cuddle and I think it just goes on from there ... it just led up to that and then you know it automatically, you, I realise now it automatically came to you that that's something was going to happen ... when it did happen I was, um, quite happy about it ...[146]

144 Grace msf/srss/ht/#38.

145 Grace msf/srss/ht/#38. Ironically, although Grace did not know this at the time, her mother had found herself pregnant by a man she hoped to marry but who was killed during the First World War. She subsequently concealed the illegitimacy of Grace's eldest sister.

146 Penny msf/srss/ht/#20.

Despite professing happiness at this course of events, later in the interview she suggested that she had felt guilty about consenting to intercourse. However, she nevertheless realised that there was a key benefit to this transgression. Despite the use of withdrawal, she started to wish she might fall pregnant, end her protracted engagement, give up her job as a domestic servant and start her married life:

PENNY I felt terrible about it… I mean, I just felt that I was doing something very, very wrong… I always wished that I could've, we, we could've got married earlier. In fact, er, this is going to sound, er, stupid, but a quite a few of the girls um, that, um… were girlfriends of his mates, you know, were getting in trouble and having to get married and I used to think to myself, 'oh, why can't I get in trouble and I'll get married and I can look after him?'[147]

In this context, engagement could become a safe, sensible and rational moment for sex to take place.[148] Through engagement men and women could safely consent to sexual activity without damaging their reputations and cement and establish their commitment to each other. Risking pregnancy both proved and reinforced the seriousness of the attachment. Agatha (1910) courted the gardener at a country house where she was a domestic and they married in 1940 when Agatha was 30. She was anxious to get married as she thought she was rather old and had been told that it was better to have children when young:

When did you first have sex?… Was it before you were married?

AGATHA (pause) yes with my hubby, yeah, but he was the only one… because we was going to get married, and we were getting married yer know what I mean, and um, it was just above board and then it wouldn't 'ave mattered because we was getting married there and then, so it wouldn't have made any difference if I'd a got into trouble.[149]

Christopher (1918), who joined the army in 1937, having previously been a milkman, confused the moment of engagement and the moment of marriage in his memory. The moment of engagement coincided with his loss of virginity. It was this moment, rather than the marriage ceremony which took place in 1947, which has come to symbolise the commencement of the marital relationship in his memory. He said early on in the interview that they did not have sex

147 Penny msf/srss/ht/#20.

148 There is a wealth of evidence to suggest the interwar acceptance of premarital sex during an engagement. See, for example, Jephcott, *Rising Twenty*, 92. Slater and Woodside, *Patterns of Marriage*, 101. ('I had to promise I'd marry her before she'd give way'); Humphries, *A Secret World of Sex*, 67–8, Hall, *Sex, Gender and Social Change*, 122, 39, 59. Gurney, 'Intersex and Dirty Girls', 275 quotes the conclusion of Mass Observation's attempts to confirm Blackpool as a site of sexual promiscuity that, instead, 'to most mill-girls sex is still definitely linked to the idea of marriage and… courtin''.

149 Agatha msf/kf/ht/#7.

before they were married, and that they 'had to get married'. What he meant by this was the point at which they had sex meant that they knew they would get married and it was the loss of virginity which in itself has come to represent the start of the marriage relationship. He talked about 'having to get married', although she was not pregnant, because the very act of having premarital sex indicated that marriage was imminent and necessary.

Did you talk about whether to have sex before you were married at all?
CHRISTOPHER Yes, yes and we decided to wait until we got married … went with her for two years, till we got married, oh, we had a courtship about two years until we got married you see.
Can you remember the first time you did have sex with her?
Yes, yes, yes. Yes … I took her home, we were sitting in the front room on the settee, and, and, we had got engaged you see, we weren't married you see, till we got married you see. (pause) We didn't use any contraception you see. So we'd better get married you see, so we got married … We had to get married. She wasn't pregnant when we got married, no no.[150]

Historians have emphasised the tragic misfortunes which frequently befell those who found themselves pregnant before they were married.[151] Unmarried mothers, pregnant women and their boyfriends might be corralled into hasty marriages. Some were locked away in workhouses, reformatories, mother and baby homes or mental institutions. Others found their babies adopted, or brought up by some other member of the family as their own.[152] Far from premarital pregnancy being a stigma which steadily weakened during the twentieth century, Jeffrey Weeks argues that increased levels of illegitimacy, and the less frequent recourse to 'shot-gun' marriages after the Second World War, meant that the numbers of illegitimate babies, painful adoptions, abortions and loss of reputations increased particularly during the 1950s.[153] Katherine Holden and Janet Fink concur in seeing an increase in negative representations of single mothers in the 1940s and 1950s.[154] Melanie Tebbutt's research into working-class gossip outlines the devastating forms of silent disapproval which demonstrate the impact illegitimacy could have on a woman's status.[155] A few stories

150 Christopher msf/kf/bl/#34.

151 Humphries, *A Secret World of Sex*, 114–17, Mary Abbott, *Family Affairs: A History of the Family in 20th-Century Britain* (London: Routledge, 2002), 17, Cook, *The Long Sexual Revolution*, 2.

152 Frost, 'The Black Lamb of the Black Sheep'. For a summary of the sources in which such horror stories proliferate and a critical analysis of their representativeness and social purpose see, Holden, *The Shadow of Marriage*, 116–18.

153 Weeks, *The World We Have Won*, 44–5, Langhamer, *Women's Leisure*, 124, Cook, *The Long Sexual Revolution*, 185. See also, Pat Thane and Tanya Evans' forthcoming study currently entitled *Unmarried Motherhood in Modern England* (Oxford: Oxford University Press, forthcoming) for a detailed study of this.

154 Janet Fink and Katherine Holden, 'Pictures from the Margins of Marriage: Representations of Spinsters and Single Mothers in the Mid-Victorian Novel, Inter-War Hollywood Melodrama and British Film of the 1950s and 1960s', *Gender & History* 11, no. 2 (1999): 245–51.

155 Tebbutt, *Women's Talk?*, 76–80.

among our respondents were poignant and distressing and indicate the very real dangers that women faced in premartial sexual negotiations.

Rose (1928) found herself in a situation in which having sex before marriage was one way out of abusive family relationships, a course of action which was at the expense of her respectability.[156] Having been removed from a sexually abusive step-father and placed in care, she was required to leave the children's home when she turned 15. In order to avoid staying in her abusive family home to which she had been forced to return, she had sex with, became pregnant by, and got married to a man within twelve weeks of meeting him. This marriage was a disaster and she struggled to maintain her dignity and honour faced with a drunken, unemployed husband. Sex again provided her only escape, again at the expense of propriety. She began an affair with a man (a lorry driver who became her second husband) and was named as the guilty party following her first husband's divorce proceedings. This was a course of events which brought her considerable shame and distress and about which she remained embarrassed. Initially, during the interview she chose to 'skip over that part' before later revealing the details. She sought to reclaim her reputation by pointing out the desperation of her circumstances and the ways in which conducting an affair and encouraging another man to marry her solved considerable financial difficulties. Above all, she revealed that her social standing depended, first and foremost, on economic criteria: she stressed that despite the catalogue of difficulties that beset her life she kept her head above water and managed financially, despite having to bring up a large family:

ROSE Oh, I don't know. I didn't have a very happy childhood ... all I remember about me Dad were th' cat-o'-nine-tails out that door ... So my mother left me Dad when I was 10 ... went living wi' another fellow ... This old man took advantage of me ... and then he got fifteen years, for touchin' me. And I got three. So I was sent away, to Whitley Bay ... And that's when I learned happiness, you know ... Came back 'ere when I were 15 ... And I, started work. George Street, where, an' one of these ladies (coughs) suggested a blind date ... Anyway, I met 'im and within twelve week we were married. Tho' 'e did the right thing [because I was pregnant] and asked me mother for 'er hand in marriage ... [but] he were never workin' (laughs) ... we got married within twelve week ... I wanted to get away from 'ome, move out, I tell ya, I didn't like my stepfather ... I don't think I've ever really been in love, love. P'raps if I had had a good 'usband. You see, me first 'usband were never workin'. If he did a week he'd be off a month

[...] So I've got four children from that [first] marriage ... And then I met round ... this pub just down there. This fellow kept sayin' ''Ello, sweet'art', I mean, I din't know he were married, so, we started goin' out even tho' I were married.

[156] For a further case in which a victim of child-abuse was shamed by her community as being from a 'dirty' and 'unrespectable' family, from whom other children were warned to stay away, see Beier, 'We Were Green as Grass', 472.

> You see, I had all these children to support, and, to me, somebody askin' me to marry 'im, it were a good thing ... That's why I said, if you give me all your money, I'll marry ya, you know ... But anyway, I didn't get put out for not payin' rent. I've always been able to keep me 'ead up. (pause)[157]

Horace (1915), who became a teacher despite initial training to be a clergyman, found himself engaged to marry a woman he had met while serving as an ASDIC operator (anti-submarine detection) in the navy during the Second World War, who, he later discovered, was already pregnant. He told the story as one of a lucky escape, but it is also indicative of the desperate circumstances faced by women who were pregnant and saw marriage as the only way to restore their reputations. Horace subsequently described the girl in highly derogatory terms, assuming she was a good-time girl or amateur prostitute, yet since it is clear that he had been ready to consider marrying her, the narrative also indicates the ease with which respectable women could find themselves stigmatised, humiliated and dishonoured.[158] Horace did not know what happened to Peggy subsequently, but the suspicion must be that the outcome of the story was far less happy for her than for Horace:

> HORACE Peggy! We were silly really. She was in the Wrens. She knew all the answers. I just wasn't interested in her ... she just wanted a good time ... like so many sailors they were set up because the girls wanted to get a hold of a husband in those days. They were desperate.[159]

His wife Betty (1922) filled in the details of the story:

> BETTY She went with another fellow ... and she was pregnant. And she tried to make out it was his ... he took her to the doctor's not knowing what was wrong with her, and, um, the doctor comes out to him and says 'if you will play with fire you get burnt'. He said, 'what do you mean?' Well he just turned around and told her that she could get on and find the person that she did it with, not – he wasn't going to take the responsibility of another fellow's child.[160]

In Mavis' (1908) case, the fears that an angry father might treat a pregnant daughter harshly were realised. The testimony revealed a lingering sense of shame and distress. Mavis' defensive narrative revealed the strength and continuation of a desire to rescue her respectability. She emphasised the speed

[157] Rose msf/kf/bl/#21. As Melanie Tebbutt recognises, those living at 'the social and economic margins' found themselves more frequently the brunt of social humiliation and without resources to counteract such talk or restore their reputation (Tebbutt, *Women's Talk?*, 92).

[158] See also, ibid., 76–80. The lives of illegitimate children might also be affected, especially from the late nineteenth century onwards when a variety of both state-sponsored and charitable organisations were able to remove children from their families and into various forms of institutional care (Frost, 'The Black Lamb of the Black Sheep').

[159] Horace and Betty msf/kf/srss/ht/#31.

[160] Horace and Betty msf/kf/srss/ht/#31.

with which they got married, their happiness and minimised the scale of the transgression ('we only 'ad it once'):

MAVIS I got married right away, soon as I, y'know found out, yeah, yeah... we said we'd better get married y'know right away, and we did... I wasn't worried because we're happy together kinda thing, y'know it we [were] a good couple together kinda thing y'know... Yeah, but we were unlucky, we only 'ad it once and I was expecting.

In continuing her story Mavis recalled the brutal reaction of her father, a rag-and-bone man in Blackburn, the shame of which was only diluted years later, when Mavis' father admitted that she had made a good choice of husband:

MAVIS And when me Dad got me! Ohh he thought I was one of the worst women in the world. Because I were expecting. Phew oh yeah... And before he died he thought he were one of the best husbands in the world (laughs). Ohh he went mad. He went mad he did, oh yeah; it were terrible for 'im with that. And we 'ad to get married.[161]

As in Mavis' case, a frequent consequence of an unexpected pregnancy was a hastily arranged marriage. She married in 1929 aged 21. In many cases, this was merely an acceleration of an already anticipated event, but some marriages were less happily accepted by the parties concerned. Colin (1923), a plumber, spent much of his interview asserting that he was a gentleman. He contrasted the behaviour of some fellow soldiers with his own respect for women and stories of resisting temptations were used to further establish his gentlemanliness:

COLIN [In the navy] you'd to have sex and if you didn't have sex you were a wally. (laughs) But I never bothered... I told [them] I'd had sex you see. I weren't gonna stand there and say I'd been out with somebody and had nothing you know. So they left me alone. (laughs)... But I've always respected women, I've always admired women, you know. Er, whereas a lot of men used to cheat on women, you know, we've had sex and we done this and been, you know, and... it were, it were all degrading to me like, you know, degrading[...]Oh I nearly [had] sex with a Wren... because she really fancied me [but] I hadn't the guts, I hadn't the knowledge... [and] she might've come to have a child and she'd 'a been thrown out in disgrace... I think I we're coming back from Crewe and, you're broad-minded, aren't you? And... I think I ejaculated in me pants, you know... had a bit of a kiss and a cuddle and I could've had it there but I backed out. I... been a gentleman or never wanted to get women into trouble.

When he and his future wife had sex during their courtship the event was packaged differently as a 'grand' and romantic occasion which was not seedy.

[161] Mavis msf/kf/bl/#29.

He stressed the spontaneity of the act, the privacy of the location and the pastoral nature of the urban setting in Blackburn's Corporation Park:

COLIN We thought it was grand. (laughs)... even then you thought you'd done some'et wrong you know. (laughs)... There used to be a little squirrel cage wi' red squirrels in near duck pond, we got up back of there... We were talking and talking and talking and all of a sudden it happened... near where the duck pond is and we just got up back out of people's way and er, we're talking and and it happened – broad daylight. (laughs) Yeah.

His future wife, Martha, who worked in the local valve-testing factory, became pregnant and they quickly got married. Despite the fact that this was a successful and loving marriage, Colin regretted the haste with which they married and wondered whether, if circumstances had been different, he would have married her at all:

COLIN ... there weren't a lot of time to enjoy meself or anything like that before Martha come to me in family way and I got married. But otherwise she were alright, she were great and everything we did together were lovely like you know... and then she said she was expecting like you know. So, now, whether we'd 've got married, I don't know... but the child come along and it was, in them days, it was done thing to marry the girl... I accepted it and I accepted the fact that I loved the girl and I accepted the fact that we'd made love but it, it was too quick... I'd no intentions of er, getting married to her... but of course I'd played with fire and I had to take the consequences.[162]

Although for some sex before marriage and premarital pregnancy did bring unfortunate or regrettable outcomes, for many others pragmatic and flexible moral codes were brought into play in place of the severe injunctions against sex before marriage.[163] Transgressions were not always harshly punished, yet such responses are less often documented in the historical records. As Ginger Frost has noted, historical evidence is skewed towards 'negative experiences', based for example on court decisions, the archives of social services, the records of charitable bodies and institutions, and so on. We simply do not know much about the diverse experiences of most of those who became premaritally pregnant or became unmarried parents.[164] Indeed some respondents saw having sex before marriage as a thrilling and meaningful way to challenge society's

[162] Colin msf/kf/bl/#36.

[163] Melanie Tebbutt also recognises that in private women 'could express considerable sympathy for the plight of the pregnant unmarried woman' in contrast to public condemnation and outlines the ways in which families sought to preserve a woman's reputation (Tebbutt, *Women's Talk?*, 79–80). Ginger Frost's analysis of Elizabeth Roberts' interviews concluded that the majority of illegitimate children were cared for by the maternal family, usually with some community and neighbourhood support (Frost, 'The Black Lamb of the Black Sheep', 295–6).

[164] Frost, 'The Black Lamb of the Black Sheep', 294. See also the forthcoming work of Thane and Evans, *Unmarried Motherhood*.

rules, subvert public expectations or assert their independence. Tim (1917) met his wife when they were both working at Leyland Motors, she as a typist and he as an apprentice precision instrument maker:

TIM We did 'ave sex before marriage, towards the later times of our engagement ... I think you feel at the time you're a little bit daring ya know, and that adds to the excitement of it all a bit, ya know.[165]

Gay (1928) met her future husband, a salesman, at a dance at the end of the Second World War. She accepted the desirability of saving sex until marriage and feared getting pregnant:

GAY It was all very nice (laughs) but I always knew, um, you know that you, you mustn't go too far ... I can remember him saying, um, 'don't worry um you'd never' (pause) because I wasn't going to go, he wanted to go that far and I, I said, 'No!' because I, I said, 'I certainly don't want to be landed with a baby', so he said, 'Oh, c'mon' ... I thought 'Oh God, no way!' (laughs) um, so I didn't.

However, her family did not approve of her fiancé. He had previously had a casual relationship with her older sister, and her parents had objected to a letter he had written to Gay's sister outlining his drunken wartime escapades, and tried to break up the match. She left home and continued her forbidden liaison:

GAY If they had been um you know they'd been very casual about it, I'm sure that I would've broken up with him, you know, and, but as it was I was determined.

In this context her mother's disapproval of premarital sex had less force; indeed, for a defiant and angry Gay having sex was an ideal way to punish her parents and establish her independence and determination:

GAY It was three couples sitting there and, and Terry said, 'how do you fancy a night out?', you know ... I think I thought it was quite awful, quite dreadful to even think about it, but everybody seemed to agree so we did, you know ... He wanted to and we did ... we went to a hotel in St Albans.[166]

In many other situations where sex took place before marriage, and especially in cases where pregnancy resulted, both the couple involved and the wider family and community found a way to resolve matters between themselves: some forgave each other and some legitimised or excused the transgression.[167] Many justified their sexual encounters before marriage by presenting them as one-offs or spontaneous accidents, which did not affect their general decency or

165 Tim msf/srss/bl/#19. 166 Gay msf/kf/ht/#13.

167 A convenient forgetting of a transgression was more difficult if marriage did not ensue but a birth did. The presence of illegitimate children often fostered 'family secrets and shames' which 'implicated many generations' and might lead to 'enormous stresses' especially for the children involved. Frost, 'The Black Lamb of the Black Sheep', 309.

respectability, such as Jennie (1908), a Catholic spinner who in 1930 found she had to get married to a man a year older, a sawmill worker:

JENNIE He knew how to behave hisself and so did I, so we behaved ourselves ... till we got married. Just made that slip that once and that was enough, so we got married ... He were a decent, er, decent chap. He, he, we got married as soon as we could.[168]

Others had a less 'decent' story to tell. Terence (1915), who was employed as a decorator in Blackburn in the late 1930s, described the circumstances in which his girlfriend became pregnant as highly dishonourable; his behaviour was far from gentlemanly or respectful and he was out for what he could get. The sex was seedy, a 'kneetrembler' in the back yard of a local chip shop. However, communal disapproval was avoided: on discovering the pregnancy he was prepared to get married, 'it was about time' and the respectability of himself and his wife was restored:

TERENCE It's still there er er a chip shop, one er, a little back there we used to go, nip in back kiss goodnight round there ...
You knew your wife had got pregnant ... how had that happened?
Well, it, what I did, lads usually do, lads. Played around ... Let's just say it was an accident ... it were just one them things happened ... you have what you could get.[169]

Moreover, in a cultural context in which Marie Stopes (in *Enduring Love* first published in 1922) presented celibate women as 'unbalanced and sex-starved', some attitudes towards the single women who 'gave into their sexual instincts' softened. Certainly, such tensions might be noticed: one of Marie Stopes' correspondents puzzled in 1928: 'girls are only human, they feel the longing for a mate ... Can it be very wrong thus to satisfy it even if there is no possible chance of marriage?'[170] Such material highlights the ways in which attitudes towards sexual activity and illegitimacy were context dependent. Penny Tinkler has argued that messages of both shame and sympathy existed in 1930s magazine fiction aimed at young girls. While in some stories girls who became pregnant were harshly treated, other stories drew upon the 'semi-tragic appeal of the virtuous unmarried mother' and provided happy endings for girls who had been badly treated or who consented to sex before marriage out of a 'maternal' rather than 'sexual' impulse.[171]

Norman (1914) distinguished the sordid forms of premarital sex, which he associated with the working-class back streets of Islington, from the 'decent',

[168] Jennie msf/kf/bl/#27, Christopher ms/kf/bl/#34 and Mavis msf/kf/bl/#29 had similar stories.

[169] Terence msf/srss/bl/#15.

[170] Quoted in Katherine Holden, '"Nature Takes No Notice of Morality": Singleness and Married Love in Interwar Britain', *Women's History Review* 11, no. 3 (2002): 481–2. Jephcott noted similarly tolerant views which saw little problem in premarital sexual behaviour provided that marriage ensued in cases of pregnancy (Jephcott, *Rising Twenty*, 92–3).

[171] Tinkler, *Constructing Girlhood*, 169–70. Pamela Haag's investigation into American dating etiquette books also identifies sympathy towards 'slight romantic lapses', which are contrasted

respectable and comfortable premarital love-making he engaged in, in his fiancée's home after the family had gone to bed. His future wife was a shorthand typist for a London insurance firm, while he did odd jobs in a London distillery, which he hated:

NORMAN The first sign of sex in the street, I told you, was when we played tin-can-copper and I didn't know what they were getting into… the sex was sordid, it was in doorways… you'd finish up in some dirty wall, some bloody archway of a house and uh, the girl's parents were about to come along the road any time and that kind of thing, you know, but as I say, sex was a bit of a stranger to me.
So when did you first have sex with your wife?
Uh… (pause) well, I think it was in her house and I think that all the others had gone to bed.

Norman's sexual experiences clearly highlighted the distinctions drawn between types of premarital sex – the 'sordid' sorts and the comfortable and respectable types:

NORMAN Uh, there was no lack of sex; there was plenty of sex but it was sordid sex… well, I've always hesitated unless, uh, when in later years things came along, it had to be comfortable and reasonable.[172]

Similarly, Maria (1917) made a clear distinction between the sordid sexual advances, such as the rough attempts made by her future husband to seduce her at the unsuitable location of a railway station, and the romantic context in which she consented to sex.[173] In part his roughness contributed to his appeal. A scar down his face made him look like a gangster; he was a dancing instructor at one of the Blackburn clubs regarded by some other interviewees as disreputable and he was experienced with a 'few girlfriends' in his past. Nevertheless she held on to codes of respectability and innocence in determining the sexual progress of their relationship:

MARIA He'd taken me to Accrington one night and we'd been to the dance hall there, we always went dancing. And waiting for the train to come home to Blackburn he got hold of me and started fiddling about and I said, 'I don't like being mauled about'.[174]

When she did have intercourse with him she presented it in a very particular fashion: as a respectable and loving development in their courtship, as spontaneous, natural and as clinching commitment to their relationship. It did not take

with 'promiscuity (that is petting for petting's sake)' (Pamela S. Haag, 'In Search Of "The Real Thing": Ideologies of Love, Modern Romance, and Women's Sexual Subjectivity in the United States, 1920–40', *Journal of the History of Sexuality* 2, no. 4 (1992): 574).

172 Norman msf/kf/ht/#17.

173 Similar evidence was used by Mass Observation's Little Kinsey survey to suggest that the British had variable moral codes, with different moral choices adopted on different occasions (Stanley, *Sex Surveyed*, 133–42).

174 Maria msf/kf/bl/#8.

place in a seedy, public place, but rather in his parents' house, and he asked, rather than simply trying his luck:

MARIA I'd gone in and seen him all dressed in brown with this white tie on. And that's when I found out like that he was the one for me and it just happened... he didn't have to persuade me, not that time. But he asked, you see, he didn't do any forcing or anything... And funnily enough, afterwards when we went out, it was before we'd gone out and we were going up Tony's and I felt, how can I put it, as if we belonged, you know.[175]

Others, for whom sex before marriage was not an accident, found alternative ways to legitimise their behaviour. Lucy (1907) did not have sex as a prelude to marriage, nor was it associated with engagement. She remembered being scared and anxious and excused her behaviour by pointing out that she did not get pregnant, by stressing the naturalness of their desire ('just what happens in't it'), and her age at the time:

LUCY I first had sex with Frank... before we were married... because I think we were a little bit scared... my mum and dad they used to go out at weekend... well it were (chuckles) just what happens in't it yeah but, I didn't 'ave to be married... but we didn't 'ave sex at the very beginning, we'd bin going along and then we started and then that were it, but as I said we were always very careful... we did 'ave it yeah but and then it got naturally like as ya get courting and well I were 24 and Frank were 22 so... well, you go a little bit further and a little bit further, at beginning, you're, well I were a bit scared, but anyway you just get that used to it.[176]

In many instances then, despite a strong rhetoric in support of premarital virginity, and despite parental and communal assertions that punishment for transgression would be harsh, in practice many individuals found themselves breaking the rules. In these circumstances frequently parental threats proved hollow and respectability a little more malleable than the rhetoric suggested, even if familial solutions often involved forms of concealment. In her interview Lyn (1907) initially repeated the clichéd story that illegitimacy brought shame and disgrace to families and ruin to pregnant girls. However, a few seconds later she modified her narrative in acknowledging the variety of familial responses to the realities of illegitimacy:

LYN in my days they absolutely went through hell... and the family suffered as well as them with the shame and the disgrace... quite a good few never got anyone to

[175] Maria msf/kf/bl/#8. Historians have begun to realise that physical locations and spatial structures give meaning to the sexual experiences that took place within them. Fascinating examples of the study of the social geographies of sexual behaviour can be found in Hirsch, *A Courtship after Marriage*, Matt Houlbrook, '"Lady Austin's Camp Boys": Constituting the Queer Subject in 1930s London', *Gender & History* 14, no. 1 (2002): 31–61.

[176] Lucy msf/kf/bl/#10. Lucy was a strong Anglican with a working-class background. Her mother was a weaver and her father a tenter and fitter. Her future husband had a small grocer's shop, in which she helped, before returning to weaving.

marry them because of this disgrace … they either had to stay at home, or, in lots of cases, the family themselves turned them out and they had to get somewhere to live or … it was the workhouse. […]

probably they eventually did meet someone. I suppose the majority would get married … and then on the other hand a lot of families rallied round and said it could happen to anybody and they'd bring this child up sometimes as their own.[177]

Penny Tinkler's analysis of the letters written to the problem pages of magazines aimed at girls during this period suggests that advice was increasingly sympathetic towards a pregnant girl. Girls were given advice on how to retain their respectability and ensure their continued marriageability.[178] Moreover, Joanne Klein's research suggests that during the interwar period working-class communities and indeed the local police forces were remarkably unconcerned by a wide range of 'irregular' sexual unions, concluding that the 'working class continued to accept forms of matrimony that could adapt to individual circumstances rather than insist that married life conform to rigid patterns'.[179]

Catherine (1912), who grew up in London where her father was a carpenter and joiner, was determined not to have sex before she was married, thinking it was 'the wrong thing to do … you were brought up that you just didn't do that'. However, as a young woman she conducted a four-year, serious affair with a married man, while working as a shorthand typist at a ham-boiling factory where he was a clerk. Catherine felt guilty about this behaviour and presented it as a form of transgression:

CATHERINE I went t'is flat once, when she was away, and … we sort of crept in and crept up the stairs, feeling terribly guilty, and trying to be ever so quiet … but we didn't get up to anything! No, you didn't have sex. No, not at all. Funny, isn't it?[180]

Rather than facing anger and disapproval from her parents Catherine found her family were understanding. Despite the apparently rigid morality of her upbringing, in practice these parents felt their daughter needed support and hoped that the affair would blow over.

CATHERINE But one could see there was no future in it, really, and in the end, we split up … but it was a funny thing, I could always tell my mother about these things; and … they must have been concerned about me, but never stopped me …… On one occasion I was going with this chap, we were going down to Brighton, … and Father came and met me, at the station, y'know, I s'pose to see if I was alright … yes, Mum was so understandin', she was wonderful, because, um, well I suppose if you stop people from doing things, then they're gonna do it anyway.[181]

[177] Lyn msf/kf/bl/#1. [178] Tinkler, *Constructing Girlhood*, 165.

[179] Joanne Klein, 'Irregular Marriages: Unorthodox Working-Class Domestic Life in Liverpool, Birmingham, and Manchester, 1900–1939', *Journal of Family History* 30, no. 2 (2005): 210–29. See also, Packer, 'Aspects of Working-Class Marriage', 94, Ross, *Love and Toil*, 63–4.

[180] Catherine msf/kf/ht/#1.

[181] Catherine msf/kf/ht/#1.

Conclusion

With the majority of interviewees avoiding sex before marriage, it would be tempting to portray the generations who got married between the 1920s and the 1950s as bound by 'traditional' codes of virginity. Although many were fearful, often with justification, of becoming pregnant, those who had premarital sex did not necessarily see themselves as having transgressed. There were a range of circumstances in which men and women saw sex during courtship as acceptable or desirable, as a means of securing the future of a relationship or for demonstrating commitment.

The class differences in premarital sexual practices are equally easy to misinterpret. Although we found that more working-class respondents had intercourse before marriage, this was not indicative of its greater acceptability. Certainly some contemporaneous middle-class voices used the seeming obscenity of working-class culture to infer that codes of chastity were casually disregarded by many. Despite the rowdiness of the factory floor or the flirtatious fun of the monkey run, privately working-class men expected women to be attractively shy and sought to protect them from street corner smut. Working-class women were often unclear what forms intimate behaviour might take, and maintained their innocent respectability by avoiding discussion. Working-class men were left silently to interpret the caresses their girlfriends would consent to. Thus there was considerable variation in the intimate acts drawn upon by working-class couples to express love prior to marriage, as each couple stumbled towards understandings that remained unarticulated and therefore ill-defined. Some were cautious and restricted the expression of sexual desire, while, for others, the absence of a shared commitment to observing mutually agreed behavioural boundaries meant they were more likely than their middle-class counterparts to consent to sexual intercourse in the heat of the moment.

Middle-class courtship codes were less adaptable to circumstance. Some recounted moments in which they questioned their earlier resolve to avoid sexual intercourse, for example after engagement, or when desire was strong. However, in such scenarios an earlier promise to save sexual intercourse until after marriage was almost always honoured. Many more middle-class respondents discussed the place of sexual intimacy in courtship early in their relationship, without seeing such conversations as a contravention of ideals of innocent femininity. More confident in their sexual knowledge, these couples were able to articulate an agreed repertoire of sexual practices, and a resolve to preserve virginity was rarely abondoned in the heat of the moment, but rather required more explicit renegotiation of the 'rules of engagement'. Thus gendered and class-based codes surrounding sexual knowledge and communication shaped different communities' premarital intimate behaviours.

Part II

What was love?

4 Romance and love: finding a partner

In generalised and cross-regional histories of Western culture and in sociological analyses it is assumed that young people approaching marriage in the first half of the twentieth century did so armed with a new set of ideas about love, sex and intimacy.[1] New forms of consumer culture created a new emphasis on 'expressivity, romantic attachment and erotic adventure'.[2] In the first half of the twentieth century, it is argued, 'sexual love, in advertising and film emerged as a utopia, wherein marriage could also be exciting, romantic, fun'.[3] The rituals of courtship and the decisions to get married were transformed as 'the emotional attachment between sexual partners, formed through "falling in love" [has become] understood as the *basis* of the relationship'.[4] Distinctive in this vision was first the focus of marriage (as opposed to courtship) as the site for love and passion and second the centrality of sexual fulfilment to the ideal.

Numerous works, either drawing on literary studies or the techniques of social history, have explored these debates in a British context. Some of those historians who have drawn on cultural or literary sources have highlighted the prevalence of romantic narratives in contemporary fiction, marriage manuals, popular magazines and the cinema, which preached the ideal of falling in love with and marrying one's perfect 'other half'. Karen Chow argues that films

[1] Gillis, *A World of Their Own Making*, Stephanie Coontz, *Marriage, a History: From Obedience to Intimacy, or How Love Conquered Marriage* (New York: Viking, 2005), Christina Simmons, *Making Marriage Modern: Women's Sexuality from the Progressive Era to World War Two* (Oxford and New York: Oxford University Press, 2009), 129–31. And for a collection studying the modulations of this ideology more recently elsewhere, see Jennifer S. Hirsch and Holly Wardlow, eds. *Modern Loves: The Anthropology of Romantic Courtship and Companionate Marriage* (Ann Arbor: University of Michigan Press, 2006).

[2] David R. Shumway, *Modern Love: Romance, Intimacy, and the Marriage Crisis* (New York: New York University Press, 2003). Shumway argues that what was distinctive about ideas of romance during the twentieth century was the focus on marriage (as opposed to courtship) as the site for passion and romantic love.

[3] Jacqueline L. Scott, Judith Treas and Martin Richards, eds. *The Blackwell Companion to the Sociology of Families* (Malden, MA: Blackwell Publishers, 2004), 297.

[4] Wendy Langford, *Revolutions of the Heart: Gender, Power, and the Delusions of Love* (London and New York: Routledge, 1999), 3.

such as *The Sheik*, alongside the marriage manuals of Marie Stopes, offered women a new vision of female sexuality and male–female romantic interaction. She sees it as inevitable that women's vicarious participation in these tales of passion will have directly affected their attitudes towards their own lives.[5] Judy Giles draws attention to narratives of finding 'Mr Right' in British women's magazines.[6] Annette Kuhn's interviewees, for example, revealed respondents who drew specific links between the romances depicted in the cinema and 'their own adolescent dreams, desires and courtship behaviour'.[7] Adrian Bingham argues that Birgitte Søland's description of Denmark is equally appropriate to the UK: 'from sources such as films, fashion magazines and advertisements ... young women culled many of their ideas of female modernity, cross-gender camaraderie and romantic love'.[8] Some contemporary voices expressed similar ideas. Pearl Jephcott, for example, as a result of her study of young women in the 1940s, worried about the extent to which young women were encouraged to hold on to unrealistic dreams by contemporary romantic literature.[9]

Yet, other literary historians have also detected different trends in British popular culture. Alison Light highlights the prominence of 'middle-brow anti-romanticism', labelling the imagery from the film and novel *Brief Encounter* as the 'romantic climax of anti-romanticism which signified Englishness between the wars'. In such literature conformity to respectability, and the suppression of sexual desire (at the cost of sexual fulfilment and romantic passion) are heroic values.[10] In British 'conservative' middlebrow literature, she claims heroines were 'thoughtful, diffident and conventional' and even cynical about the possibilities of romantic love or passions borne of 'foolish idealisms'.[11] Ross McKibbin has also argued that early twentieth-century Mills and

[5] Karen Chow, 'Popular Sexual Knowledges and Women's Agency in 1920s England: Marie Stopes's *Married Love* and E. M. Hull's *The Sheik*', *Feminist Review* 63, no. 1 (1999): 64–87.

[6] Although she additionally notes the practical adjunct to such narratives which suggested that if 'Mr Right' did not turn up, women might, through love, self-sacrifice and encouragement, mould him into 'Mr Right' (Giles, 'Playing Hard to Get', 244).

[7] Kuhn, *An Everyday Magic*, 150. Although not directly comparable to British material, the diary of an American woman during the 1920s is interesting in revealing the complex ways in which an individual responded to the various, conflicting discourses about marriage, love and romance from literature, screen and pulpit and how these shaped her personal emotional experiences, dilemmas and choices. See, John C. Spurlock and Cynthia A. Magistro, '"Dreams Never to Be Realized": Emotional Culture and the Phenomenology of Emotion', *Journal of Social History* 28, no. 2 (1994): 295–310.

[8] Bingham, 'An Era of Domesticity?', 230.

[9] Jephcott, *Rising Twenty*, 93. [10] Light, *Forever England*, 158–82, 208–10.

[11] She sees this as an especially middle-class positioning. These narratives appealed in particular to readers who 'imagined they were above' the tawdry pleasures of popular romance literature and instead identified themselves as 'conservative, ordinary and decent', in opposition not only to the foolish romantic dreams of the working-class readers of Mills and Boon, but also the independent, bohemian sexuality of the 'decadent' upper classes. Ibid., 164.

Boon 'romances' offered a restrained and realistic, even humdrum, version of romance. The heroes (who were doctors or bank managers rather than aristocrats or Balkan princes) offered 'love, honesty and a companionate marriage', not passion.[12]

Social historians, by contrast, have addressed this debate in different terms, concentrating on the extent to which these ideas influenced the approaches, feelings and choices of individuals themselves. These studies have focused almost exclusively on working-class communities and have presented a very different view of youth cultures, courtship regimes and ideas about marriage, love and romance before the 1960s.[13] Here the 'unromantic' and practical motivations for marriage within British working-class communities, particularly in the north of England, are stressed. Judy Giles, for example, argues that working-class women wanted stability and respectability, not the possibility of sexual fulfilment or emotional excitement. She claims that while many girls had exhilarating and romantic encounters during their youth, they rarely married the objects of their passion; rather they chose marriages of material security at the cost of their own sexual desires, which were 'suppressed'.[14] Marcus Collins highlights the failure of British versions of 'companionate marriage' to alter the marital expectations or hopes of working-class attendees at Family Welfare Clinics before the late 1950s, who were motivated to marry in order to escape the shackles of family life or simply to avoid being left on the shelf. British, working-class marriages were in Collins' phrase, 'born of bleak necessity'. Individuals had low expectations of the relationship and minimal criteria of suitability: men wanted an efficient housekeeper while women sought a secure breadwinner who was not violent, a gambler or alcoholic.[15] Middle-class courtship cultures have not been studied in any depth by social historians; however, the focus of literary and cultural scholars on middle-class and middlebrow literature means that there is an implicit assumption that it was in middle-class courtship cultures, rather than working-class ones, that the 'sexual element' was increasingly essential in the choice of partner.[16]

[12] McKibbin, *Classes and Cultures: England, 1918–1951*, 488–92.

[13] Reflecting the traditions of social history since the 1960s as 'history from below'.

[14] Giles, *The Parlour and the Suburb*, 58. See also, Sarsby, *Missuses and Mouldrunners*, 73. Judy Giles, '"You Meet 'Em and That's It": Working Class Women's Refusal of Romance between the Wars in Britain', in *Romance Revisited*, eds. Lynne Pearce and Jackie Stacey (London: Lawrence & Wishart, 1995), 279–92.

[15] Collins, *Modern Love*, 10–12.

[16] Jeffrey Weeks further notes that the 'strains of such an emphasis were not to become fully apparent' until the 1950s and 1960s, despite their clear presence in the 1920s and 1930s (Weeks, *Sex, Politics, and Society*, 210). However, British historians' analysis of class and regional differences in love, courtship and marriage is undeveloped, as is the study of change over time during the twentieth century.

Oral history material from both working- and middle-class individuals provides an ideal opportunity to explore the interrelationship between cultural scripts and individual identities and the ways these framed personal choices, values, expectations and hopes. This chapter explores the narrative frameworks developed by individuals to make sense of their own courtships and choices. What personal identities, in dialogue with the narrative frameworks circulating in popular culture, did individuals develop and how did these structure men's and women's memories of deciding to get married? Romantic stories were widely used by individuals to frame and make sense of their own personal courtship stories and were directly drawn upon in representations of the process by which they decided to get married and to whom, what they say they valued in a potential spouse, what dreams or expectations they remember having had during courtship, and what they wanted from a marriage. Yet, narratives of romance, passion and sexual attraction were often part of respondents' stories only to be rejected, not because couples did not find themselves falling in love, or subsequently enjoying erotically satisfying marriage, but because they identified with a culture which denigrated such values as escapist and unrealistic.

Although some narratives, particularly those of some middle-class men, drew directly upon a romantic and sexualised script, many individuals, both men and women, and from middle- and working-class backgrounds, mocked sentimental or unrealistic romantic rhetoric and presented ways in which their own approach to love was tied up together with, and not in opposition to, practical considerations, social pressures or external influence. For interviewees community rituals, parental authority and the rejection of romantic motives were seen as appropriate. They represented themselves as having rejected dangerous or unstable forms of romantic attachment (such as cross-class attachments) born of flighty, naïve and unrealistic dreams, and as having looked to contract marriages which were affectionate, yet prudent, in which lasting love was developed through devotion and duty. The values that will be shown in the next chapter to have been key to individuals' ideas of appropriate behaviour within marriage are here read back into narratives of initial attraction and falling in love, which were nonetheless also pragmatic, sensible and ordinary.

'Don't get mixed up too serious'

Rather than seeing adolescent flirtations as the gateway to marriages similarly full of passion, many saw premarital relationships as part of a distinct time in their lives in which frivolity could be enjoyed prior to a future of hard work and domestic struggle.[17] For young women the period before marriage was one

[17] For example, Agatha msf/kf/ht/#7; Vera msf/kf/ht/#34; June msf/kf/ht/#27; Catherine msf/kf/ht/#1; Pru msf/kf/ht/#12; Sarah msf/kf/bl/#30; Eleanor msf/kf/bl/#11; Daphne msf/jm/bl/#38; Iris msf/kf/bl/#2; Lyn msf/kf/bl/#1; Maria msf/kf/bl/#8.

of relative affluence, a situation which many realised would change upon marriage, when domestic responsibility would diminish both the time and money they had available for leisure pursuits. For young men, courtship itself brought additional costs and constraints.

In the late 1940s, as one of Rowntree and Lavers' young respondents (aged 21) revealed, romantic marriage was not seen as a happy ending to youthful flirtations; rather, some women had a more mundane vision of marriage in which the freedoms of youth and the joys of adolescent leisure pursuits were abandoned in favour of a life of hardship and poverty: 'Marry and have kids you don't want, and live in a poky house, and not have any nice clothes? Not me! Marrying would be all right if it was the way they do it in the pictures, but real life isn't like that.'[18] Interviewees presented the period before marriage as a special time of freedom and independence – some emphasised the length of time they were courting, some remembered wondering whether or not to get married, others claimed they had had little interest in courting seriously. Iris (1914) was a winder in a textile mill who contrasted married life with the enjoyment of being an unmarried young girl in Blackburn in the 1930s – she got married aged 24 in 1938:

IRIS Yer liked going out – good time. Why once you're married you're finished, aren't yer, kind of thing? I think every girl should go and have a good time and enjoy yerself.[19]

Sally (1908), a sales assistant in Boots in Blackburn who got married in 1934, was typical in recognising the freedoms of adolescence that would be absent upon marriage:

SALLY Well, I thought I was a bit odd because me mother used to say 'you want to be getting a boyfriend'. I said 'I don't want a boyfriend.' And I was 20 before I went out with my husband.

She initially decided not to get married at all and was unconvinced by an old school friend's descriptions of the (sexual) joys of married life ('you don't know what you're missing'), asserting instead a determination to maintain her girlish innocence of sexual matters ('I don't want to know'):

SALLY But that one at the school used to say 'He, ooh, he was nice, ooh and his hands were warm.' And I looked, I said, 'You're disgusting.' And funnily enough ... what did she say [years later] – 'Oh, being married's lovely.' I said, 'I suppose it is.' She said, 'D'you never want to get married?' I said, 'No.' I said, 'I just want to go on life as it is.' She said, 'Well, you don't know what you're missing.' I said, 'Well, I don't want to know; don't talk about it.' So we never, never discussed it.

[18] Rowntree and Lavers, *English Life and Leisure*, 249.
[19] Iris msf/kf/bl/#2.

For Sally, marriage signalled the end of her independence and freedom. She finally consented to marriage because her future husband wanted to marry her and warned her that she might become an old maid.

SALLY I didn't want to get married; I wanted to, to be free. Not exactly free but I didn't want… it was funny, me mother couldn't understand it; she said, 'I think you should be a spinster, I don't think you should be married.' I said, 'I don't.'
So why did you get married?
Because he wanted to. Um… he said, 'You don't want to be an old maid. What about when I'm gone? What will you do then?' I said, 'Eeh, I don't know.' So we decided we'd get married.

Sally's recognition that being single provided independence co-existed at the time with the hope that marriage might provide sexual excitement. Indeed, she remembered when she was very young that she had dreams of being carried away by love:

Before you got married what did you think sex would be like?
SALLY I really used to think when I were about 15, be lovely if you had a boy all to yourself and do what you want… And it wasn't like that at all (laughs)… I expected to be carried away with love and… you know I was never overwhelmed with sex, never, never… I'm not one for sex at all. I don't like sex pictures or, I don't like them at all. I often think me mother was right: I should've been a spinster.[20]

Although Sally thought she was odd for not wanting a boyfriend, she was not unusual. Both working- and middle-class women recognised that young adulthood provided them with opportunities for adventure, excitement and independence that would be lost upon marriage.[21] Pearl (1915), whose mother was a weaver, and whose father ended up as the manager of a travel agents in Burnley, who herself became a headmistress, did not get married. She perceived the desire to leave home and set up an independent household as the fundamental reason for most people to choose marriage, an ambition she successfully engineered without getting married.

PEARL Er, well I saw the people who were married and when I got back home I thought I'd have to get back home and thought there's worse things than living on your own.[22]

[20] Sally msf/kf/bl/#31, married 1934.

[21] Indeed courting seriously but remaining unmarried might have been particularly enjoyable. Claire Langhamer points to evidence suggesting that when courting seriously, young women's leisure time increased and parents relieved their daughters of many chores and family demands (Langhamer, *Women's Leisure*, 113). Andrew Davies also describes young unmarried women as 'privileged consumers of leisure' who enjoyed relatively high levels of 'freedom and financial independence' (Davies, *Leisure, Gender, and Poverty*, 81). On the poverty of some working-class single women, however, see, Todd, *Young Women, Work, and Family*, 218.

[22] Pearl msf/kf/bl/#40. This was the only unmarried respondent, who was (partly inadvertently) interviewed. By design the interviewees were intended to be all married persons.

Life for a middle-class single girl doing clerical work, like Pru (1911), was absorbing and independent. She was courted by lots of men and loved her independence, as she dashed from tennis party to amateur operatic society to country house party. The prospect of a little home was horrifying at the time:

PRU There was always somebody behind the scenes you, er, you know you could sort of sit on their lap and have a little chat with and a few cuddles… but immediately they got serious – 'ugh' – I don't know why but that was it: 'No fear! I don't want to get tied up yet.' I don't know what it was, some, something inside that revolted and I, I think I had visions of, oh, a nice little home and nice little man – 'oh pooh to that'.[23]

After the Second World War such perceptions persisted: Mass Observation found in 1947 the central grumble expressed by wives about marriage was the 'loss of freedom of movement'.[24] A subsequent study of teenage girls in London (predominantly employed in clerical work) similarly found a reluctance to rush into marriage until 'after they had had some time in an interesting job and seen a bit of the world'.[25] However, it was the single life of the *young* woman that was particularly enjoyable. Long-term singleness into one's thirties or forties, by contrast, was not a socially attractive option, nor such a financially advantageous one.[26] As Katherine Holden points out there were few positive images of spinsters for women to follow and indeed the status of being single problematised women's relationships with both women and men.[27]

Alison Oram has argued that during the period after the First World War the popularisation of psychological and sexological ideas about the female sexual instinct fed not only into material on the place of sex within marriage, such as Marie Stopes' *Married Love* and other works, but also fostered a negative image of the spinster as sexually repressed, frustrated and neurotic.[28] As a result single women faced very real problems in society and marriage was in

23 Pru msf/kf/ht/#12, married 1935.

24 Mass Observation, File Report 2495, 'The State of Matrimony', June 1947, 17.

25 Mass Observation, File Report 3150, 'Teenage Girls', 12.

26 Judy Giles highlights the material advantages of marriage to working-class women in the inter-war period who could look forward to domestic affluence far in advance of that of their mothers (Giles, 'Playing Hard to Get', 240–1). See also, Holden, *The Shadow of Marriage*, 80–111. Natalie Higgins also highlights the fact that not getting married was not a practical option for most women before the 1960s or 1970s (Higgins, 'The Changing Expectations and Realities of Marriage').

27 Holden, *The Shadow of Marriage*, ch. 2.

28 Alison Oram, 'Repressed and Thwarted, or Bearer of the New World? The Spinster in Inter-War Feminist Discourses', *Women's History Review* 1, no. 3 (1992): 413–33. Yet she argues such a pathologisation of spinsters as sexually frustrated was vigorously challenged by many feminist psychologists: Fink and Holden, 'Pictures from the Margins of Marriage', Holden, *The Shadow of Marriage*. See also, Giles, 'You Meet 'Em and That's It', 282.

reality 'a social and psychological necessity for women'.[29] Despite the determination or desire on the part of some respondents to remain single, it would appear that social forces subtly persuaded most of them to wed.

Men's attitudes to love, sex and romance have been particularly poorly researched.[30] Almost all our knowledge of attitudes towards marriage, expectations of marriage and ideas about love come from studies of women's literature, women's magazines and women's experiences. Yet, some male interviewees told similar tales of resisting serious romances, which promised marriage and an end to youthful freedoms and pleasures.[31] Like Pru, Larry (1917), a builder in Blackburn, who courted during the Second World War, 'back-pedalled' the moment any girlfriends showed signs of getting serious:

LARRY Er, don't get mixed up too serious, that was one of the topics of the day … you didn't want it because you hadn't the money nor the time … so I back-pedalled, in two or three cases, oh aye … I said, 'I'm not bothered about courting or knocking about with women … '[32]

Indeed a few interviewees claimed to have avoided adolescent romances altogether. In working-class communities, especially at times of economic strain, girls were expensive to take out and the pleasures of homosocial groups and activities were more attractive leisure pursuits. Bryan (1918) moved from South Wales to Surrey aged 12, then to Hertfordshire, where he became a gardener in a country house, having left school at 13:

BRYAN I didn't like girls to be honest. I didn't. I never had much to do with girls at all … in those days I was [into] football and boxing and I never had time for girls at all, not really … I mean did know one or two but … if I did take 'em out it was only once and I thought ooh I can't be bothered (laughs). I wasn't very keen … though my friends used to be, you know, lost a couple of friends that I was very friendly with, they started going out with girls.[33]

Having a boyfriend increased a young girl's leisure opportunities by providing her with both an escort and financial sponsorship, whereas for a young man, a girlfriend was not always seen as a worthwhile drain on resources.[34] For ambitious men, like Norman (1914), who was desperate to escape his

[29] Oram, 'Repressed and Thwarted', 415.

[30] Natalie Higgins' work is an exception and is discussed in more detail below (Higgins, 'The Changing Expectations and Realities of Marriage').

[31] See, for example, Bryan msf/kf/ht/#25; Norman msf/kf/ht/#17; Frank msf/srss/bl/#16; Larry msf/kf/bl/#20; Peter msf/kf/bl#26; Terence msf/srss/bl/#15; Tim msf/srss/bl/#19.

[32] Larry msf/kf/bl/#20, married 1946.

[33] Bryan msf/kf/ht/#25, married 1947.

[34] Todd, *Young Women, Work and Family*, 218–23. Todd additionally comments that young women began to look for boyfriends who were well paid or showed financial ambition; such expectations placed additional pressure upon young men and provided them with further reason to delay getting involved with girls.

working-class life in 1930s Islington, girls and marriage had little appeal. He contrasted his own life, in which he refused to get involved with girls, and concentrated instead on both intellectual and physical pursuits to improve himself, with those of his friends whose marriages thwarted any social or geographical mobility:

NORMAN Well, my first romance ... I did come over to her place for tea once and, oh, I did take her over to a dirt-track race ... and she had lovely blonde hair and ... she was ever such a nice character and I went to her place once or twice and I thought, 'I can't get mixed up with this, I've got no money, I've got no prospects!', and I, I sort of hasted off and that was it ... so I think my going with a girl was delayed, which was rather good because many of the people who got girls ... They stayed and got married, and that was the end of their lives in many ways, it was an awful existence.[35]

'Automatically floated into marriage'

Love was central to interviewees' decisions to get married, yet narratives of courtship, of marriage choices and marriage ideas did not emphasise romantic passion.[36] Although the stories of adolescence and courtship were remembered as moments of fun, adventure and playful flirtation between the sexes, such encounters were not generally presented as part of a transition to married life. Rather adolescent romances were often compartmentalised as occupying a separate stage of youthful pleasures. In this context, the finding of a marriage partner and the decision to get married were presented as serious and practical processes in which rationality and social responsibility were emphasised.

Among both working- and middle-class interviewees' narratives – and apparent in both men's as well as women's stories – were descriptions of the pragmatic concerns which determined the decision to get married and the timing of the wedding.[37] Practical, frequently financial and housing considerations were important factors in individuals' memories of why they got married and when, particularly among those interviewees who courted and married during the interwar years.[38] Marian (1908), a weaver in Blackburn, was not planning

[35] Norman msf/kf/ht/#17, married 1944.

[36] Geoffrey Gorer reported in 1955 that nearly 90 per cent of married English men and women considered they have 'really been in love'. Of course, as he acknowledged, what 'being in love' meant was highly variable and this chapter seeks to chart the sorts of versions of love deemed appropriate, ideal or desirable when deciding to get married and in framing a marital relationship (Gorer, *Exploring English Character*, 83).

[37] For example, Emma msf/kf/ht/#37; Humphrey msf/kf/ht/#26; Hubert msf/kf/ht/#32; June msf/kf/ht/#27; Norman msf/kf/ht/#17; Catherine msf/kf/ht/#1; Mark and Joanna msf/kf/ht/#22; Penny msf/srss/ht/#20; Roger msf/kf/ht/#10; Eva msf/kf/bl/#9; Alistair msf/kf/bl/#33; Frank msf/srss/bl/#16; Eileen msf/kf/bl/#12; Doreen and Larry msf/kf/bl/#20; Elma msf/jm/bl/#42; Lyn msf/kf/bl/#1; Marilyn msf/kf/bl/#7; Terence msf/srss/bl/#15.

[38] It is suggested that some women resisted getting engaged as they were subsequently expected to save their money to help fund the setting up of a home. For men, in consequence, the period

to marry, although she was already 30, but a house came up for rent which accelerated the process:

MARIAN We weren't thinkin' of getting married for a bit 'cos we, we hadn't so much money and we were only just startin' saving up… 'Oh', I said, 'there's a house in Mindon Street coming empty'; I said, 'it's an old couple's in hospital', and he said, 'well see if you can get it'. Any road we got it… it were all lovely and clean but… there were no electric in it… and then by time it were decorated he said to me, 'now when are we gonna get wed?', he said, 'when are we getting wed?' So we decided then to get married and… we only had ten pound to get married with and had to get a wedding ring outta that.[39]

Similarly, Lyn (1907), who also worked in the Blackburn textile mills, waited four years, until her fiancé was due for promotion to 'reacher' in the mill before getting married in 1931. Such financial considerations were equally part of many middle-class interviewees' deliberations like June's below. In waiting until her fiancé had himself secured a managerial position before getting married, June (1914), whose father was a bank manager, revealed her concern over whether her husband had a promising future. The son of a miner, he had a 'sharp' mother who set up a small greengrocer's business and determined that her sons would not follow their father into the pit and would better themselves:

JUNE He was promoted and given a shop [to manage] in Halifax, which decided us to get married. So we had to look for a house in Halifax. My husband took over the shop before we were, we were married. Er, and we looked for a house in Halifax and found one and settled down and it was his first shop which he opened in Halifax and he would be about 25.[40]

For some respondents, the desire or opportunity to leave home was pivotal in deciding to get married: this was particularly apparent in the testimony of those who married during the interwar period.[41] Maud (1912) got married when her father, an engineer in a steel works in 1934, remarried and her new stepmother refused to let her live with them. Other women, by contrast, remembered

of courtship was comparatively expensive, and they were perhaps keener to accelerate the process of getting engaged or married. See Langhamer, *Women's Leisure*, 126–7. By the 1940s women increasingly contributed financially to the costs of leisure activities, which may have lessened male reluctance to enjoy the company of young women (Todd, *Young Women, Work and Family*, 282).

39 Marian msf/kf/bl/#28, married 1939. 40 June msf/kf/ht/#27, married 1936.

41 Natalie Higgins' oral histories with men and women married during the 1930s and the 1950s highlight similar narratives of marriage prompted by a desire or need to leave home (Higgins, 'The Changing Expectations and Realities of Marriage', 91–4). Pearl msf/kf/bl/#40, our unmarried respondent, differentiated herself from her peers by pointing out that as a teacher she did not need to get married in order to set up an independent home.

delaying marriage because they were needed at home. Rebecca (1903), who worked in the East End of London as an alteration hand, did not get married until she was 40 years old because 'I couldn't leave my mother'.[42] Monica (1902), whose father's firm had become bankrupt shortly before his death in 1914, did not want to get married at all because she thought her mother needed her at home:

MONICA But I didn't want to leave mother. She was, she, she'd gone through all this sorrow and it seemed a shame, but I did and everything turned out all right.[43]

Others emphasised the involvement of parents, friends and family in the decisions made to get married.[44] In doing so, such narratives (retrospectively at least) conceptualised their marriages as events which family and community had considerable stake in and influence over even while they might mock the tendency of friends and family to take the initiative in sealing the match. Frank (1919), the son of a riveter and a weaver in Blackburn, came home on leave from the navy in 1941 to find, to his surprise, that his fiancée's mother had arranged everything and he was to get married that afternoon (his future wife worked in a local greeting card factory):

FRANK I remember that long weekend. I came home early Saturday morning and on midday on the Friday, that was at Devonport, and, er, I got to Blackburn at – early hours of Saturday morning and when I arrived home her mother says to me: 'You're getting married at dinner time' – Oh this afternoon – that were it. And I said: 'You what?'[45]

In these narratives, the idea of marriage and engagement as an individualised and intimate decision made by two people is challenged. Although the involvement or interference of other parties in individuals' relationships is seen as amusing and in conflict with romantic assumptions, at the same time, the idea of marriage as a social duty is related in a matter-of-fact way and not denigrated or regretted. Some presented themselves as having been bound by circumstances and other people's expectations into getting married. In her interview Dora (1923) was one of the most effusively affectionate in remembering her marriage. However, she did not present this strong love for her husband or her recognition of his qualities as having been particularly present during their courtship. Indeed, she had something of a crush on her future husband's brother, Ted. Dora said she had had 'no love' for her boyfriend and

[42] Rebecca msf/kf/ht/#6, married 1943. [43] Monica msf/kf/ht/#11, married 1933.

[44] Such 'peer group and adult scrutiny' of working-class courtship has been identified as prevalent among working-class communities earlier, as Andrew Davies' study of the late nineteenth and early twentieth centuries shows (Andrew Davies, 'Youth, Violence, and Courtship in Late-Victorian Birmingham: The Case of James Harper and Emily Pimm', *The History of the Family* 11, no. 2 (2006): 113).

[45] Frank msf/srss/bl/#16, married 1941.

future husband, Joe, but agreed to write to him while he served in the army during the war. Despite a subsequent romance with another man, Leslie, whose engagement ring she considered accepting, Dora reluctantly felt unable to reject Joe, who had demonstrated such devotion to her for so long while dutifully fighting in Africa:

DORA Ted said to Joe 'I'll take her out.' (laughing) Joe said 'You won't.' So I just had the two of 'em … And Joe used to say 'You leave her alone.' And we used to have such a laugh. But Ted did look lovely. I mean my heart did used to go bang, bang! …

He [Joe] didn't expect anything, me to wait or anything … but would I write to him … There was no love there. Not, not that I felt[…]I had a date with Leslie and … he said 'What I would like to do is to get married.' And I said, 'No, I'm too young to get married. I don't want to get married.' I liked him. But I didn't want to get mar-. But always at the back I thought what, what am I going to say to Joe? What will I write to Joe? … After being out all them years.[46]

Elma (1909), a factory cook, had an extremely loving and affectionate marriage and her testimony stressed the everyday romance of their life together. However, their relationship barely existed before they got married. Their wedding was prompted by her pity for him, following his abandonment by his fiancée of seven years after the banns had been called, and it was set in motion in order to secure tenancy of a police flat:

ELMA The police had told him he had to get out of the flat within a certain time unless he was married … so he had to either marry somebody and go in the flat or give the flat up and start again. Which wasn't fair. So … Aunt Agatha said 'ask Elma, she'll marry you' (laughs). So he was on the phone, on a Thursday, I can remember the day, 'I've a proposition for you, Elma, will you marry me?' I said, 'what are you talking about?' He said, 'will you marry me?' So I said, 'what's happened, what's wrong?' And he told me that she'd just been and told him that she was pregnant with the baker. I said, 'Oh, my God!' (laughs) I said, 'never mind lad', I said, 'you've not, you've not missed nothing'. So we made it up, 'alright then I'll get married' … What could I do? I couldn't say no, could I? … I couldn't say no, not after, after he'd been courting seven years, and she let him down a fortnight before he should've been married. No, I couldn't do it … It wasn't his fault; he'd done nothing wrong … when he rang me up what could I say? Very little. I was brokenhearted for him. And he'd got a flat there all ready.[47]

Similarly, Olive (1915), a nurse, decided to marry a recently jilted man out of pity. She did not get married until 1951 when she was 36:

OLIVE Well, I felt sorry for him I'll tell you the truth, because he'd been let down by this other girl … and he was so kind to his father. And I thought that if he has the disposition of his father, well he was a kind man. But that's how I … just because

[46] Dora msf/srss/ht/#38, married 1945. [47] Elma msf/jm/bl/#42, married 1933.

> I was so sorry for him ... And we got on very well together ... after we'd got married, yes, we got more attached.[48]

In some representations marriage was portrayed as an event which followed inexorably from certain circumstances which were not perceived to have been fully within the individual's control. Marriage was entered into as the result of a series of accidents or incidents and contracted as a result of social expectations and norms rather than individually determined or based on clear-cut decisions. After a period of time courting together, marriage became a default position, something that was easier to do than not to do.

Nora (1920) revealed the role of community expectations in determining when a couple were thought to be ready for marriage. Born in Blackburn where her father was a motor engineer, she was working in a bank while her boyfriend served in the RAF. Nora first started thinking about marriage when her boyfriend came back from the war and 'everybody's feelings were, yes, we've got to settle down and get a home, you see we were 25 then'.[49] Similarly, Iris (1914), a winder from Blackburn, whose mother ran a second-hand shop, as her father had been injured falling off a scaffold, agreed to marry her husband, a railway porter, after a two-year courtship, because they had been together long enough. His proposal was precipitated by her mother, who found them somewhere to live:

> IRIS Well it were him what wanted to get married. Because we got this house, me mother gave us the house, you know.
> *So what made you agree when he wanted you to marry him?*
> I don't know it was because we're having been with him two year, I suppose.[50]

Others presented themselves as drifting into marriage. Laura (1923), a weaver in Blackburn, 'thought might as well get married and we got married' in 1942 aged 19,[51] and also middle-class, university-educated Emma (1906) 'automatically floated into marriage' aged 30 in 1936.[52] Common also was the claim that marriage was only contracted because others were doing the same. Some respondents felt left out if they were not courting or getting married and became lonely as all their friends got married. Thus, in a range of ways interviewees presented the decision to get married as an expected response to growing up. Monica (1902), who was reluctant to get married following her mother's bereavement, thought her boyfriend was 'nothing much' but thought she 'might as well' get married when he 'used to come down and see me in Tenby'. She explained:

> MONICA I thought oh we might as well. I was getting on then ... my girl friend had already got married, you see, so I was missing her terribly and no, it all came off.[53]

[48] Olive msf/jm/bl/#44, married 1951.
[49] Nora msf/jm/bl/#47, married 1945.
[50] Iris msf/kf/bl/#2, married 1938.
[51] Laura msf/kf/bl/#6, married 1942.
[52] Emma msf/kf/ht/#37, married 1936.
[53] Monica msf/kf/ht/#11, married 1933.

Felicity (1919) did not, like some, deny the importance of 'love' in her choice of partner but nevertheless placed more emphasis on social circumstances, her desire not to be left on the shelf and the feeling of being left out if you did not have a boyfriend and later a husband. She married relatively late, aged 34, having gone to grammar school, been a Wren during the Second World War and worked in a railway accounts office in Accrington. Her future husband was also a clerk for the railways.

FELICITY I didn't want to be left on shelf. No, I, I that's, er, that's nature to want to have a partner, isn't it? And, er, you couldn't have a family unless you had a partner. You couldn't go to a lot of places. And then there was that little word called love that came into it. If everybody was with a man you used to feel out of it.[54]

'There was nothing special'

Alongside narratives of love and courtship which emphasised the practical forces driving couples to get married and which presented decisions to get married as part of an acceptance of communal expectations and a willingness to embrace domestic responsibility, there was an awareness that such portrayals challenged notions of romantic courtship and marriage. These were narratives which self-consciously downplayed the place of romance and love in the decisions to get married. Aware that their representations defied the familiar romantic story, some joked about the trivial reasons which prompted a wedding. Eileen (1913) offered to look after the children of a young widower she met when they were both working at a fuse factory in Blackburn during the Second World War. He responded with a proposal: 'well we'd better get married then 'adn't we?' Sarcastically, she commented on her assent: 'very passionate you know!'[55] Marilyn (1914) made fun of her hairdresser husband's mercenary and unemotional reasons for getting married in 1940:

MARILYN 'I only went wi' me husband six month and er, he said, 'two can, two can live as cheaply as one'; that's what he said.[56]

Some respondents appeared to lament the gulf between their own experiences of love and the fictional romances they encountered. Although Agatha (1910) eloquently remembered falling in love in the late 1930s with a gardener who worked at the stately home where she was in service, she nevertheless felt let down by the unrealistic expectations that had been spawned by the love stories she read, and disappointed that the thrill of their courtship 'couldn't 'ave lasted':

[54] Felicity msf/kf/bl/#37, married 1954.
[55] Eileen msf/kf/bl/#12, married 1943.
[56] Marilyn msf/kf/bl/#7, married 1940.

AGATHA I think, I got to like him … because he used to come in the kitchen with the vegetables … and we started, started walking out with one another and then we decided to get married … when you like them you kind of feel different altogether inside don't you – (laughing) a nice feeling – but yer see that feeling couldn't 'ave lasted (laughing): I'd 'ave been walking on air now! …

I like love stories [but] … you never seemed to get the love that they got; that's the trouble with love stories, it puts you off a bit … I mean they make them so … you think oh dear if only my hubby had been like that, sort of thing … Did everything for them an' shared everything and did everything to make them 'appy … I mean, they did everything to make them 'appy, in their sex life, sort of thing.[57]

More typical than such expressions of regret or disappointment, however, was a scorn for the unrealistic and soppy fictional depictions of love and romance and a defence of the contrast with their own more pragmatic approach to love in the past. Quakers Mark (1917) and Joanna (1915) met through Joanna's father, who had got to know Mark at a pacifist social club in the 1930s. They described their attachment as born of 'mutual interests' and laughed at the ridiculous extremes of romance in films:

JOANNA It wasn't love at first sight or anything like that (laughs) … We're not really a terribly romantic lot, are we?
MARK No, I mean we, she talks about romance doesn't she, and it's silly isn't it?
JOANNA Not being like the films, you know … [They are a] bit too much. (laughs)
MARK A bit too much.
JOANNA Doesn't ring true.[58]

Far from glamorising love and marriage, the representations of love and romance in cinema provided a stark contrast with life at home and were dismissed as unrealistic fantasies, even, in Andrew Davies' phrase, breeding a 'scepticism to temper romance'.[59] Eleanor (1907), who had a happy marriage to a mechanic – 'a steady fella' – from Blackburn in 1934, rejected the idea that there had been anything romantic in her relationship, and explicitly contrasted her courtship with the passions she felt for film stars. Her real-life liaisons were presented as having had much more to do with social norms and the desire to conform than to a heady attachment to her fiancé:

ELEANOR You know, like the girls of today, eh, who was it I used to like? There were silent pictures then. I used to love them; ee I liked the pictures: Mary Pickford and Douglas Fairbanks and, eh, Eddie Polo … but there weren't a lot of romance in them days … all the other girls 'ad boyfriends, and you wanted to be just like

[57] Agatha msf/kf/ht/#7, married 1940. [58] Mark and Joanna msf/kf/ht/#22, married 1947.
[59] Davies, *Leisure, Gender and Poverty*, 96. Similarly, Annette Kuhn points out the picture palaces of the 1930s occupied a 'heterotopica' far away from the everyday world, 'located at some distance from home; their architecture and interiors are exotic or avant-garde; and they provide amenities of unaccustomed splendour – wall-to-wall carpeting, heating, plush seats' (Kuhn, *An Everyday Magic*, 146).

them you see … but if 'e'd a stopped coming I wouldn't 'ave bothered, but he did, 'e keep, 'e kept coming and me mother liked 'im 'cos he were Methodist, but eh, 'e made a good husband.

She here reveals the various social pressures that respondents remembered as having had a direct influence on the decisions to get married.

ELEANOR My mother said to me, 'it's time you were getting married you know, you're getting on' … I think I wanted to get married because everybody else were getting married.

Eleanor was ambivalent in debating whether or not she loved her husband and concluded that she simply wanted to be like everyone else.[60] Crucially she identified a rejection of sentimentalised romanticism as core to her personal character and identity. This unromantic match was not an unhappy one, nor was the absence of passion or romance regretted. Rather it was exactly what Eleanor wanted. She presented herself as down to earth, not someone who wanted to be 'fussed over':

You were in love with him?

ELEANOR I don't know, I, I don't really … I don't know what love is really, you know. You love your children when they're born; there's different kinds of love isn't there? No, I think I wanted to get married because everybody else were getting married (laughing). I don't think I were very romantic. I must 'ave 'ad a bit of love in me somewhere, but we weren't brought up to be fussed over, you know, that's what it is.[61]

A northern middle-class version of this narrative, albeit from a later period, which takes a similar pride in a no-nonsense approach to love and is disdainful of 'soppy' forms of romance, is evident in Sheila Rowbotham's personal memories of growing up in 1950s Yorkshire. Recalling a 'kissing session' with an Italian beau she wondered: 'did he like doing all this … ? He certainly seemed very intent on it all. My brain wandered off, surveying the amorous absurdity of it. Yorkshire me snorted inwardly, all this soppy stuff to look sophisticated … at this point Yorkshire won out. Such a display of emotion was horrifying … All those gushy words.'[62]

Such 'unromantic' presentations of the decision to get married were *not*, then, affected by the retrospective analysis of the success of the marriage itself, although the extent to which they reflect feelings articulated at the time is

[60] For similar stories see also, Higgins, 'The Changing Expectations and Realities of Marriage', 98.
[61] Eleanor msf/kf/bl/#11, married 1934.
[62] Sheila Rowbotham, 'Revolt in Roundhay', in *Truth, Dare or Promise: Girls Growing up in the 1950s*, ed. Liz Heron (London: Virago, 1985), 205.

difficult to determine.[63] Yet, it was a representation that was common to many, irrespective of whether they subsequently found marriage happy or not. The central issue here was not whether one loved one's spouse; indeed, many characterised themselves as having been 'in love' at the point of getting married. At the same time, however, many worked to reject the notion that their chosen partner was particularly special, different or 'right'.[64] Maud (1912) had a very loving marriage to a warehouse man who rose to become a despatch foreman in Blackburn. She had known him for many years, described him as a 'lovely person' who was 'very, very popular', adding that 'everybody wanted him'. Nonetheless her narrative downplayed the particular attraction between them:

MAUD There was nothing special I don't think really; I don't know, just sort of happened.[65]

The quotes above predominantly reflect the memories of female interviewees; however, the denial of romance was also present in male narratives. Horace (1915) affectionately joked throughout the interview that finance rather than love or sexual attraction brought them together. Horace had grown up in London where his father worked for London Transport. Horace left school at 14 in 1929 but had ambitions. He thought about becoming a clergyman, but was accepted into teacher training college when he finished his service in the navy. Many of his stories involved money. However, when pushed further to provide less mercenary reasons for choosing his wife, Horace focused on more functional, convenient and prosaic factors. He did not idealise Betty, but she was safe and familiar:

HORACE Well, you see when I met Bet I thought I was on to a good thing ... she was saving up for a motor car. (laughs) She had 90 pounds in the bank, she ...
BETTY Oh go on with you.
HORACE No, no. No, er ... I suppose when we discovered that we were both Cockneys. And that we lived fairly near in London.
That made you feel ...
HORACE Safe (laughs).[66]

Norman (1914) explicitly denied that he experienced any kind of 'explosion', despite loving his wife. As quoted above, he avoided romantic attachments and worried that getting married might hold back his career ambitions. He pointed out that there was no 'spark' as implied by the interviewer, but rather that marriage occurred in order to gain independence from the family

[63] Mass Observation, File Report 2495, 'The State of Matrimony', June 1947: 16 commented that it was those who had been married longest among those they surveyed in 1947 who were less 'inclined to say they married for love'.
[64] See also, Giles, *The Parlour and the Suburb*, 55. [65] Maud msf/kf/bl/#18, married 1934.
[66] Betty and Horace msf/kf/ht/#31, married 1948.

and because everyone else was also getting married and Norman did not want to be left out. In addition his wife's status as a clerical worker appealed to ambitious Norman, who became a teacher:

So did you fall in love with her?

NORMAN (pause) I think, I don't, I suppose, yeah, I suppose I did, but, it's very difficult for me to say that it was an explosion or something like that…I think in those times…lots of marriages just took place. [It] seems rather silly but most of the people I knew were married, and you kind of drift into it. I heard again and again from other people…he said, 'Jack got married, Bill got married', he said, 'I was the only one not married, that wasn't married!'…so all this spark and stuff you're referring to wasn't really present.[67]

However, some male interviewees saw a romantic ideal as having had a strong influence on their decisions during young adulthood and did remember having looked for a heady romantic attachment to their spouse. Alf (1915) had a variety of low-paid jobs in London, including unloading delivery vans at Harrods. He avoided romantic attachments, preferring the company of his mates, until he met his future wife, Heather, at which point the attractions of playing snooker diminished:

ALF I might be, might be, might seem strange to you but Heather was the only, only serious girl I ever went with. I've had girlfriends, yeah…one or two. I got on very well with them, actually…but…[for] some unknown reason I always finished up with me mates again. 'Cos they used to egg each other on – 'no, you don't want to go out with her, you want to come out with us' – and all that sort of thing… 'come with us, we'll…go an' have a game of snooker'. 'No, no I don't want to do that.' And then sometimes I might, I might do what they say and might not see her. But all the time I was thinking of her: 'what am I doing standing here – I could be over there having a little cuddle somewhere'. (laughs)[68]

Reg (1919), who joined up as a marine upon leaving boarding school in the late 1930s, was serving in the Royal Navy's film unit during the Second World War when he met his future wife, a hairdresser, about whom he was 'completely crazy. I was totally besotted…she was beautiful…she was a cracker'. This was a marriage which lasted fifteen years, while Reg spent much of his time abroad with the navy where he had several affairs, as did the wife he left behind.[69] Gerald (1919) gushed about his feelings for his wife during courtship and held her hand during the interview. He served in the army as a signalman, while she was with the WVS. Addressing his replies to her, rather than to the interviewer, he said:

[67] Norman msf/kf/ht/#17, married 1944. [68] Alf msf/kf/ht/#14, married 1938.
[69] Reg msf/kf/ht/#36, married 1942.

GERALD I was very *deeply* in love with you ... and to illustrate the sort of thing, I can remember going up the east coast in Cyprus (this was during the war) and I had a vision of you in the sky.

His narrative contrasted with that of his wife. They met just before the war and were engaged while he was serving in Africa. They wrote regularly and got married just four days after he came back. Gerald presented a highly romanticised account of his never-wavering love, his confidence in their attachment and his idealisation of her. Esme on the other hand presented her own emotions as much more circumspect. Although she loved Gerald she did not idealise him and expressed doubts regarding whether or not to go through with the wedding.

ESME I wasn't sort of struck all of a heap like he was, partly because I had several boyfriends, you see, and I had more ... to compare, shall we say? Um, but I was impressed ... he had nice curly hair and uniform; the officer's uniform was very attractive ... but I think that I was certainly a bit more nervous about it and it worked out alright ... We'd got all the marriage arranged and everything and it would've been very difficult to un-arrange it.[70]

In this instance it is striking that Esme was happy to articulate the difference in the level of passion felt between the two of them during their courtship and to admit to her own anxieties about whether or not to marry Gerald. Theirs was evidently an extremely loving and happy relationship, in which the stresses and difficulties of marriage were openly articulated (at least to some significant degree) during the interview.

To a certain extent such a divide indicates the gendered dynamics of courtship norms and rituals, whereby men were expected to make a more overt choice, picking out a woman and seeking to marry her, whereas women were expected to play a more subtle game, in responding to the attentions various men paid to them. It was the memory of such deliberations which encouraged the incorporation of social and prudential factors into the decision-making process in the minds of women and fostered idealised memories of active choices among men. Indeed, what was atypical about some of the women who told unusually idealised love stories about their courtship was that they saw themselves as having chosen a particular man and successfully engineered a match.

Grace's (1922) narrative was unusually romantic, as was her self-presentation as having deliberately snared her husband and ensured that he married her and no one else.[71] She met her husband in 1944, while he was stationed

[70] Gerald and Esme msf/kf/ht/#9, married 1945.

[71] Few women told stories of their courtships in these terms, but other romanticised narratives can be found, for example, in Clare msf/kf/ht/#8; Heather msf/kf/ht/#14; Dora msf/srss/ht/#38; Rebecca msf/kf/ht/#6; Betty msf/kf/ht/#31; Emily msf/kf/bl/#13; Olive msf/jm/bl/#44; Lorna

in Yorkshire, where she lived. They married soon after and went to live in his home county of Hertfordshire:

> GRACE I mean when I met my husband it was, well, I mean, it was like being hit by, erm, I don't know what. I mean I knew he was the one and (clap) that was it… honestly, I think I would have (chuckle) killed anybody that got in my way with him… [he] was everything I wanted. He'd got blue eyes and a big cleft in his chin and very strong arms… I mean young and romantic.[72]

'She was on the same wavelength'

Yet, most other respondents were not disparaging or regretful in rejecting a model of highly romantic and passionate love as the basis for marriage, and in presenting narratives which emphasised the ways in which the decision to get married and the choice of partner were influenced by material concerns, social trends, acceptance of social responsibility, and community expectations. Such marriages were not bleak contracts born of financial or social necessity. Pragmatic concerns were themselves capable of spawning deep emotional and romantic bonds, while forms of romantic love which were deemed unstable or unworkable were avoided or broken off. Indeed, as Claire Langhamer realises, despite the existence of narratives of spousal selection and ideas about the place of love and romance in marriage which emphasised pragmatism and were suspicious of forms of romantic attachment, this 'was not necessarily a counterpoint to romantic love… rather pragmatism could itself inform narratives of "falling in love"'.[73]

Respondents did not, in rejecting the idea of romance, seek to emphasise the rationality of their decision-making but mainly sought to demonstrate their commitment to a workable version of love, in contrast with heady passion or fleeting infatuation. The desire for a marriage based on a relationship to a partner which promised material security, domestic harmony and family acceptance was in itself conducive to romantic love and tenderness. This was fuelled by a vision of married love which emphasised the need for a marital bond that was sustainable in the long term. Far from being regretful or wistful, narratives which highlighted an absence of passion or romance in their courtships were retrospectively informed championings of a particular sort of married love.

Dora (1923) linked her realisation that she loved her future husband with recall of his skill in looking after children and her parents' regard for him. Dora was a particularly family-focused interviewee, who described her parents

msf/kf/bl/#25; Mildred msf/kf/bl/#41; Maud msf/kf/bl/#18; Phyllis msf/kf/bl/#5; Enid msf/kf/bl/#49; Gill msf/kf/bl/#48.

[72] Grace msf/srss/ht/#38, married 1944.

[73] Langhamer, 'Love and Courtship', 190.

as her closest friends; and her husband arranged for them to move into the house next door to them in Radlett in the early 1950s. Her perspective is given particular poignancy in the light of her husband's family history. Dora's future husband's father had been disowned by his family – the wealthy owners of a major engineering firm – as they did not approve of his choice of bride. He went to Yorkshire and became a miner, and Dora's husband was subsequently born and bred in Yorkshire without contact with his wealthy relatives.

DORA I thought to myself, yeah that's, that's the bloke I want to marry. Because he was so, so nice. He was nice. He was lovely with the children[...]He just said to me, 'I've got something to tell you.' I said, 'What's that?' He said, 'I'd like to get married. What about it?' So I said (pause), I said, 'Well I'll have to ask my mum and dad.' And my mum and dad were thrilled because they did like him.[74]

Other respondents similarly associated the emergence of their own feelings of love for a future spouse with the realisation that their parents were equally happy with the prospect of the match. Heather (1916) sought her mother's help in working out whether or not she was experiencing feelings of love, and chose a partner that both her mother and sister held in high regard. Alf (1915) unloaded goods at Harrods' receiving bay, but his father was unemployed having been sacked by Harrods for his involvement in an illegal betting ring:

HEATHER I had another bloke and ... he wanted to get engaged and ... my mother ... said 'Well', she said 'how d'you feel?' She said, 'you, you must know.' ... She said, 'do you love him?' I said, 'Well, dunno mum', I said, 'really not truthfully I, I can't really say that I do.' 'Cos you know I liked being with him but that's it. [But with Alf] I went with him and clicked like that ... not the first day sort of thing but after that ... I felt as though it can't be ... this word they keep calling love ... and it just hit me like that. And I told mum; she said, 'oh well ... that's quite right you are in love.' ... I just wanted to be with him ... when he kissed me it just, you know, I knew; I knew I was right. I was in love with him. And my mother and my sister thought the world of him.[75]

Such respect for parental authority was evident even among those marrying late into their twenties and early thirties. This is not to suggest that marriages could not take place in the face of parental opposition, but many individuals integrated parental approval of a marriage into their narratives of romance and love. Indeed, some of those who got married in defiance of parental opinion tried to reintegrate respect for their parents' authority into their narratives. Eva (1911) found that her family thought she was too young to marry at 21, especially given that her future husband was ten years her senior. Clearly dismayed by this disapproval, her account served to restore intergenerational harmony

[74] Dora msf/srss/ht/#38, married 1945. [75] Heather msf/kf/ht/#14, married 1938.

by claiming that her family had come to accept the proof of the suitability of the match:

EVA When we were getting married me mother said you know it won't last… he's too quiet for you… and his mother said, she's too flighty for you! (chuckles)… she's too flighty; it'll not last George, it'll not last, but we proved them wrong… although everybody were putting me off (laughing) wi' 'im being older… They said he were too old for me, eh, they said he were too set in his ways and that.[76]

Regardless of whether an individual was led by parental advice in deciding to get married, for those who found their parents in favour of their choice, such support was presented as an integral part of the loving emotions associated with the period of getting married. In 1943 Maureen (1920), who was highly religious, married a sales representative for a local building firm whom she met at church in Blackburn. She did not want to get married, but he was keen as 'all people around him were married'. She noted that, as well as the two of them getting on well together, she took to his family and he got on very well with her parents:

What made Sid different?

MAUREEN Well, I don't know, he was perhaps older and, er, I think he was a bit more… he wanted to start courting and he wanted to settle down… you know me parents liked him and he got on with my parents and I got on with his family… My parents seemed to accept him, you know… I mean sometimes I'd… been out somewhere… he was sat in the chair chatting to me Mum and Dad. Ahh![77]

Finding that a potential partner was solid and reliable and had attributes that would make them a good long-term spouse often sparked strong feelings of desire, love, affection, excitement and enthusiasm. Many respondents described themselves as falling deeply in love precisely because a future spouse got on well with their family, had shared interests and came from a similar background. The sort of love deemed an ideal basis for marriage was distinguished from a blind, reckless romantic passion, but was presented as no less powerful. That the discovery that a potential spouse came from a similar background and shared similar interests could fuel a mutual attraction was shown by the shared narrative of Joanna (1915) and Mark (1917):

JOANNA I knew I got on very well with him, and, as I say, we seemed to agree about so many things. (pause) And, as I say, we have the same kind of background… I mean, your father was a Quaker, and my parents were and we sort of, I suppose, had that connection all the while.

[76] Eva msf/kf/bl/#9, married 1932.

[77] Maureen msf/kf/bl/#46, married 1943, and see Chapter 7, note 102, where she describes them as getting on well together and him as 'a smart lad', 'the jelly in the pot'.

MARK Well, I think that was, that uh, the main thing was that she was similar cast of mind, that was uh, the main thing. That she was on the same wavelength. That seemed to be important.[78]

Emma (1906) fell in love with someone with whom she could share intellectual interests. They met at university in Leeds, while he was studying for a Ph.D., although they did not marry until 1936 when she was 30 and he 38. 'I knew he was quite clever; we could talk. Because we'd both done science and we both liked music.'[79] Humphrey (1914) worried that he, a civil engineer and building surveyor, and his wife, who was training to be a secretary and was the daughter of an accountant, were not sufficiently intellectually matched when they met in 1933:

HUMPHREY My wife was a very cheerful person. We fell for each other when we were around 19 or 20; she was a year older than me actually, she was 20 and I was 19, but it was a genuine love at first sight and we both fell for each other. Although I was head boy at school and that sort of thing, um, this didn't affect our relationship. She was not intellectual; she was very musical (pause) – the whole family belonged to the Finchley Operatic Society.[80]

In response to questions about what individuals found attractive in a boyfriend or girlfriend, most working-class respondents surveyed here identified attributes which related to the sort of domestic role the potential match was likely to play.[81] Mutual attractions were described in terms which emphasised stability, respectability and social acceptability, rather than glamour, love or sexual attraction. Similarly, when Mass Observation conducted a survey of London teenage girls in the 1940s, predominantly white-collar workers, the qualities most praised in boyfriends were their 'good temper and pleasant company'. Men were sought who had 'good manners' and were 'polite'. A copy-typist, for example, said, 'he's very nice mannered and he doesn't swear and he's always smart and very decent'.[82] This survey also found that 'many of those to whom marriage was so important seemed to be looking forward, not so much to romance, but to domesticity'.[83] Alistair, born in 1927, spent his early youth going out with a group of lads and a group of girls in Blackburn. His wife, a ring winder in a textile mill, was different and worth marrying because she had a different attitude: 'she used to dress well, compared to the others ... and she

[78] Mark and Joanna msf/kf/ht/#22, married 1947.

[79] Emma msf/kf/ht/#37, married 1936. [80] Humphrey msf/kf/ht/#26, married 1938.

[81] See also Giles, 'You Meet 'Em and That's It', 283.

[82] Mass Observation, File Report 3150, 'Teenage Girls', 10–11.

[83] Mass Observation, File Report 3150, 'Teenage Girls', 15. See also Mass Observation, File Report 2495, 'The State of Matrimony', June 1947, 14, which found men who wanted wives to be 'home-loving and a good housekeeper' and single women who wanted men who were 'considerate, thoughtful and loving' and able to provide 'comfort and security'.

made all her own dresses'.[84] For Alistair, a girl who made her own dresses was particularly attractive as she had demonstrated a suitable frugality, practicality and prudence.

Working-class respondents valued attributes which revealed the owner to be sensible and thrifty.[85] Bryan (1918) chose his wife, a shop assistant in Hertfordshire, because 'she was always neat and tidy in her clothes and that'. Lorna (1917) liked her husband, who worked as a valve tester in a Blackburn factory, because 'he was smart, he was clean and he was, er, was a right nice bloke'.[86] Elizabeth 'loved' her husband because he 'was a quite smart fella' who had 'decent parents'.[87] She met him while she was working in a fuse factory during the Second World War when he was working in a local loom factory.[88]

Judy Giles sees such anti-romantic portrayals of courtship as ambivalent memories, in which working-class women both regretted the absence of passion or sexual excitement in their past lives while simultaneously proudly upholding and defending their choices and values. On the one hand, Giles identifies the rejection of 'romance' as a key way in which women took control of their lives and rejected a passive model of femininity that was responsive to the romantic interventions of the men around them. She argues that women's decisions revealed the extent to which they moulded identities for themselves as sharp and shrewd, clever and thrifty, sensible and detached, rejecting an alternative vision of womanhood as flighty and romantic, gullible or silly.[89] However, in doing so, Giles argues that women were forced to adopt a non-sexual identity, to 'repress' their sexual feelings and desires, and give up on a search for love.[90]

Many of our respondents also contrasted passionate relationships they had known with the prudential marriages they had chosen, but unlike Giles' interpretation these were not regretful stories of loss or alienation.[91] Instead, too

84 Alistair msf/kf/bl/#33, married 1952.

85 See below, 285–303; also, Giles, 'Playing Hard to Get'.

86 Bryan msf/kf/ht/#25, married 1947; Lorna msf/kf/bl/#25, married 1939.

87 Elizabeth msf/kf/bl/#26, married 1947.

88 Ellen Ross found similar ways in which earlier in the twentieth century working-class women 'tested' suitors' suitability for marriage, although the deliberations she uncovered were dominated by a fear of future domestic violence, which was not nearly so dominant among our interviewees whose courtships took place between the 1920s and 1940s (Ross, *Love and Toil*, 67).

89 Giles, 'Playing Hard to Get'.

90 Giles, 'You Meet 'Em and That's It', 281, 287.

91 Moreover, among Judy Giles' representation of stories of loss and alienation following repressed romances, were narratives in which heady romances are regretted or disparaged as 'impossible' or unwise. One of her respondents contrasted her own 'impossible' and 'unspoken' love for a gynaecologist with the unexciting man she married (Giles, *The Parlour and the Suburb*, 56–7). Another respondent portrayed her own whirlwind romance with a 'marvellous dancer', whom she married to her parents' horror, as a 'cautionary tale' with an 'unhappy ending': a troubled marriage to an unreliable provider (Giles, 'You Meet 'Em and That's It', 287–90).

strong a romance was (in retrospect at least) seen as dangerous and short-lived. When Antonia (1928) was in her early forties, in the late 1960s, she fell 'madly in love' with her next door neighbour, a younger man who was a priest. Her marriage was failing as her husband's faltering chartered accountancy business drove him to alcoholism, and he blocked her ambition to go to work. Despite recognising that she would have had an affair if he had reciprocated, she was ultimately grateful that nothing came of this passion and that her marriage and family remained together. Again the suppression of the sexual desire she had for this man, even in these circumstances, and in much-changed social times, was deemed not only the right thing to have done, but also for the best. She presented her sexual desire as unrealistic, fleeting and misplaced, despite also expressing pity (alongside relief) that nothing had come of it. She wondered whether the object of her affection was a dangerously charismatic man who did not share her sexual feelings and who had similar relationships with other women:

ANTONIA I met a very charming man who…was the first person I ever really met who made me feel I was worthwhile because he chose to come and see me and he chose to talk to me and he obviously enjoyed my company and I thought gosh…I mean if he had said 'Come on let's dash off somewhere', I'd have gone like a flash. I was just ready for it, but fortunately it didn't come to that…I would have been sorry to lose all that I had. My children especially. And, erm (pause), you know it would have been just a sort of fleeting thing really because he was perfectly lovely, dazzlingly charming, quite (pause) inconstant. I mean he had that effect on every woman he met, and I just fell for him with a crash. I didn't realise I could feel like that. It was quite a shock to me actually…honestly I could have done anything given a bit of encouragement. And luck- I say luckily – I didn't get it. And I think he made a bit of a, bit of a career of, er (pause), turning moths into butterflies as it were. Because I heard of a lot of, of women afterwards…where this had happened…because he was making us realise our potential which – [it] had never occurred to me before that I had any potential…oh, he was so gorgeous. My goodness me. I could have eaten him really. But I've never felt so overwhelmingly, such overwhelming desire for anybody. Erm (pause), but I didn't do anything about it because I didn't dare. I was, I think I was afraid, well I'm sure I was afraid that he'd be revolted and push me off and say get away from me and all that sort of stuff. So I never risked it. Pity really.[92]

Catherine (1912) compared her future husband with the married man with whom she had a secret and exciting affair. A number of times she described herself as having been 'completely fascinated' by her married lover, who was more educated than her and earned a higher wage as a clerk in a big provisions firm where she was a shorthand typist:

CATHERINE It's funny thing how you get so fascinated by a person. I mean, he wasn't a bit good looking – bit like a prize fighter, or a boxer, you know. It's

[92] Antonia msf/kf/ht/#35, married 1949.

> amazing, but 'e was, better education, educated, than I was … I s'pose he seemed more of a, man of the world, you know … I's so fascinated by him, you see, I thought it would be wonderful, if he could g-, if we could get married (laughs), yes.

She portrayed her relationship with her husband, a watchmaker, quite differently. He was presented as serious, cautious with the little money he had and lacking in excitement. Hence, far from being fascinated by him, she claimed she did not like him at all:

> *So what attracted you to your husband?*
>
> CATHERINE Well, I don't know, nothing much, I don't think. He was so very serious, you know, (laughing) used to frighten the life out of me, really. I suppose prob'ly, as time went on, he was very generous man, and you appreciate that sort of thing, you know. And … I told 'im more about this chap, you know, and … 'e said, 'well, there's no future with a fellow like that you see, we'll have, you know, more future with me'. He's then said, 'well, we'll never be rich, but you won't have to (laughing) go out charring', sort of thing. Y'know, and, as I say, we married in, in 1941.

Crucially, however, rejecting romance was often not at the expense of love; rather, the discovery that a potential partner was a sensible match played an important role in the process of falling in love. Despite presenting her future husband as almost disappointingly sensible, and emphasising his reliability, diligence and gentleness, Catherine nonetheless used the language of being 'hooked' and 'falling in love' to describe the relationship that developed between her and her future husband:

> CATHERINE It took me quite a long time before I really fell in love with my husband … gradually I got fond of him … I don't know really what it was, I suppose just being together we got hooked … because he was a generous sort of man, and gentle man, you know, and hardworking and all this, you know. He was interested in his job.[93]

Lyn's (1907) presentations of her first and second loves were very different. The first, with the mill owner's son, was narrated as a dramatic story of forbidden, thwarted passion. The second, with the man who became her husband, was not told as a high romance but presented as a prudent and sensible match, where the date of the marriage was determined by her future spouse's promotion. This contrast was reinforced by claims that she had not even liked her future husband, Walter, at first. However, although this was a tale in which Lyn prudently rejected a potential love-match in favour of a solid and reliable breadwinner, whose status was appropriate to her own, it was nonetheless a story with a happy ending:

[93] Catherine msf/kf/ht/#1, married 1941.

LYN It was Christmas time, well there were kissing under the mistletoe and that, and, um, he suddenly went and got hold of some mistletoe and came, and naturally he would get hold of me, the youngest, most near his age in all the mill. And he held me quite a long time, so of course all the winders were all: 'Ooooh' – you know – and all that sort of thing – and I remember this terrible blushing especially [him] being the mill owner's son ... And, um, in fact, we really got a little bit friendly ... and eventually his father heard about it, and had a do with my father – he had two mills ... and Richard was put in another mill ... that were the first time, really, and it was a pretty high one. It just came about like that, but nothing came of it, you see. There wasn't much chance ... it was, er, difference in class; they wouldn't've allowed ... so that was really, first, very romantic love, as they say – your first love, you know ... I started saying to the friends, 'well I'm going a walk with Walter tonight, you see', and they said, 'well, I thought you wasn't struck on him', and I said, 'Well, I'm not really, but anyway', and, er, that's, that was kind of, I would say, how it started. I wouldn't say love at first sight; oh definitely not ...
Did you say your husband was romantic?

LYN ... well it certainly wouldn't have been romantic for quite a lot of people and definitely not in this day and age. But, um, if you're happy in each other's company and, er, and that.[94]

This was not a story of regret. It was not a pessimistic lament that she had not had an exciting life. Choosing the unromantic local lad with the same background, similar occupation and the same interests was presented as the best, if banal, choice. Moreover, the story was laden with social pride in and identification with Lancashire working-class communities. Her self-presentation is not dissimilar to that of the typical Lancashire heroine who appeared in the mill-girl romances found in weekly papers aimed at girls between 1890 and the 1940s, who had a 'sensible attitude towards life and love', who did not seek social mobility through marriage but rather remained true to her own people and to working-class values.[95] These romantic stories often involved a competition between a southern 'toff' and an honest industrious working-class Lancastrian for the heart of a mill girl. Invariably, she chose the honest mill-hand.[96] In Lyn's story, too, a Lancastrian rejection of cross-class passions was also present.[97] Stories of love transcending class lines were rejected as unrealistic day-dreams of future riches.[98]

Having met her suitor in Harpenden, Penny's (1916) family thought her husband too poor for her, while his family thought her too posh for him. Penny's

[94] Lyn msf/kf/bl/#1, married 1931.

[95] Indeed, it shared many of the characteristics of these romances, set in Lancashire mills, which proliferated in girls' magazines during the interwar period. So central were these stories to these magazines that they became known as 'mill-girls' papers'. See, Melman, *Women and the Popular Imagination in the Twenties*, ch. 8, 121–33.

[96] Ibid., 128. [97] See also, Langhamer, 'Love and Courtship', 186.

[98] On the idea that 'rags to riches' stories were unworkable fantasies among British working-class girls see also, Higgins, 'The Changing Expectations and Realities of Marriage', 96.

father was an NCO in the army, while her future husband's father was a farm labourer:

PENNY: [My mother] didn't like the look of him actually; he was a country boy right through ... she didn't think much of him ... his accent wasn't quite ... I think we were a little bit posher than some of the others ... And they weren't very keen on me because they thought I was posh.[99]

William (1902) was far from poor: his father owned and managed a major company producing acetylene gas cylinders. Nevertheless, he presented it as inevitable that his relationship with a rich girl with an inheritance did not have a long-term future.[100]

WILLIAM I fell in love with another young girl ... who was educated in College ... and I fell in love with her and for about a couple of years or so we went about together and we got along famously ... I would, I would've liked to have married her but of course then I was not earning very much and unfortunately ... she had an inheritance ... about twenty pounds a week ... [101]

Behind these various stories was a fundamental critique and persistent attack on the notion that a passionate romance could be sustained in marriage. Respondents did not see themselves as having abandoned passionate relationships or sexual happiness, in favour of stability and respectability; rather, the presentation of loved spouses as sensible rather than as exciting, passionate or exhilarating served to establish the success of the marriage and to highlight the dangers, instability and ultimate unhappiness of a choice based on sex or passion.

Conclusion

Gracie Fields' popular ballad *Walter, Walter, Lead Me to the Altar* (1928) mocks highly sentimentalised popular ideals of love and marriage.[102] In a deliberate contrast with standard, highly romanticised popular songs, in her hammiest Lancashire accent, Gracie Fields outlined a long list of the prosaic and practical reasons why Walter should marry her: it was about time ('we've

[99] Penny msf/srss/ht/#20, married 1938.

[100] See also, the comment of one Mass Observation observer: she 'was staff and middle class; I was a factory worker and working class. It was hopeless' (Mass Observation, 'Courting and dating', men no. B1989, born 1927, quoted in Langhamer, 'Love and Courtship', 187).

[101] William msf/kf/ht/#24, married 1931. In the 1920s he was a clerk for Lever Brothers which he subsequently left to set up his own, successful, plastics factory. For other narratives which revealed a belief in the unworkablity of cross-class relationships see, Doreen msf/kf/bl/#20, married 1946.

[102] On the ways in which Gracie Fields consistently subverted conventions of romantic heterosexuality on stage and screen see, Bruce Babington, *British Stars and Stardom: From Alma Taylor to Sean Connery* (Manchester and New York: Manchester University Press, 2001), 56–7.

been courtin' for years'); financial circumstances were favourable ('my bottom drawer's all packed and ready', 'I don't cost much to keep in food'); her family expected it ('mother says you oughta'); and she has no better life opportunities ('I don't want to die an old maid', 'It's either the workhouse or you').[103] The target of this parody – the syrupy emotion of popular song – was hit directly by the line in which she urged Walter to 'make all me nightmares come true'.[104]

In oral history testimony, too, a similar light-hearted anti-romanticism was evident. Moreover such narratives were not confined to the northern working-class respondents, but found a parallel, albeit slightly different, version in southern and middle-class narratives. Although the circumstances and contexts in which marriages were contracted differed between working-class and middle-class interviewees, versions of courtship narratives which downplayed the significance of passion or romance, and highlighted the ways in which social circumstance, family pressure and pragmatism drew them towards marriage to a particular individual were common in middle-class as well as working-class narratives. Moreover, while the processes of courting and getting married occurred in varying circumstances between the 1920s and 1940s, the 'anti-romantic' rhetoric remained consistent in these retrospective stories.[105]

[103] Gracie Fields became the embodiment of Lancashire women and maintained national appeal while at the same time asserting regional identity: see, Patrick Joyce, *Visions of the People: Industrial England and the Question of Class, 1848–1914* (Cambridge and New York: Cambridge University Press, 1991), 320–5, Jeffrey Richards, 'Cinemagoing in Worktown: Regional Film Audiences in 1930s Britain', *Historical Journal of Film, Radio and Television* 14, no. 2 (1994): 147–66, James J. Nott, *Music for the People: Popular Music and Dance in Interwar Britain* (Oxford: Oxford University Press, 2002), 233, Simon Featherstone, 'The Mill Girl and the Cheeky Chappie: British Popular Comedy and Mass Culture in the Thirties', *Critical Survey* 15, no. 2 (2003): 3–24. On the position of the north of England as both 'frighteningly other' while at the same time 'indispensable to older Englishnesses and Britishnesses' see Jeffrey Richards, *Films and British National Identity: From Dickens to Dad's Army* (Manchester and New York: Manchester University Press, 1997), ch. 9, 'Lancashire', 252–79.

[104] Will E. Haines, Jimmy Harper and Noel Forrester (1928). Performed by Gracie Fields. On the relationship between Lancashire working-class cultures and Gracie Fields, the comments of J. B. Priestley in his *English Journey* are clearly exaggerated but nonetheless significant: 'Listen to her for a quarter of an hour and you will learn more about Lancashire women and Lancashire than you would from a dozen books on the subject. All the qualities are there, shrewdness, homely simplicity, irony, fierce independence, an impish delight in mocking whatever is thought to be affected and pretentious' (quoted in Jeffrey Richards, 'Fields, Dame Gracie (1898–1979)', *Oxford Dictionary of National Biography*, Oxford University Press, Sept. 2004 www.oxforddnb.com, accessed 30 July 2008). Her working-class audiences identified with much of the sentiment of her work; while others saw her as an authentic representative of Lancashire culture.

[105] As Claire Langhamer notes, marriage became more 'popular' after the 1930s with marriage ages falling and the proportion of people getting married increasing until the 1960s (Langhamer, 'Love and Courtship', 178). See also, Cook, *The Long Sexual Revolution*, 263–4. Average age at first marriage was marginally lower among the youngest of our respondents, particularly among men. Among women interviewees, the average age at first marriage for those born between 1900 and 1909 was 27, which dropped to 25 for those born between 1910 and 1919

Anti-romantic, self-deprecating or pragmatic accounts, which emphasised the social and economic drivers towards marriage, were regularly provided by interviewees despite considerable changes in the context of courtship and marriage. For those getting married in the interwar period, youthful freedom and relative affluence were weighed up against the constraints of married life. For these interviewees awareness of the difficulties of managing a domestic household and the need to select a good breadwinner or accomplished and prudent housekeeper were at the forefront of many minds and practical considerations dominated the recollections of deliberations about whether to get married.[106] For those courting during the Second World War different practical considerations were added to the mix in the construction of courtship narratives. Here many courtships were fractured, even rushed romances. Such interviewees presented themselves as having married before they were sure they wanted to, because others expected or wanted them to, or because life was somewhat confusing. Despite these changing circumstances, respect for parental and social opinion, practical considerations, and concern for the future continued to dominate respondents' memories of courtship throughout the period under study.

Yet, it would be a mistake to see the anti-romanticism of British courtship stories as passionless. They were not, as in Marcus Collins' view, 'borne of bleak necessity'; nor did they require, as Judy Giles has suggested, women to suppress sexual feelings or desires. Indeed, in much the same way as the lyrics of *Walter, Walter* simultaneously undercut this image of marriage as a practical arrangement, by slipping in hints of the attractions of working-class marriage, so, too, did oral history narratives champion the form of love that dominated their choice of spouse. Gracie Fields jokes that she needs to marry Walter to avoid the workhouse, but at the same time alludes to the joys of building 'a love nest for two', creating a happy family life together and the private pleasures of intimacy ('I'll show you where I'm tattooed').[107] In thinking about love, romance and marriage we should not simply depict opposed criteria: pragmatic choices in opposition to passionate ones; the individuals' desires opposed to

and to 23 for those born between 1920 and 1929. Among male interviewees, the average age at first marriage for those born between 1900 and 1909 was 28, 27 for those born between 1910 and 1919, and 25 for those born between 1920 and 1929.

106 For this set of interviewees, marriage age was also relatively high and weddings frequently delayed for economic reasons.

107 There is, in addition, perhaps a regional and class element to the rhetoric of romance in Gracie Fields' *Walter, Walter*. Much of Gracie Fields' oeuvre, while appealing to a national audience, nevertheless implicitly contrasted northern values, with southern. On the contrast between Lancashire and the south in Gracie Fields, useful comments are found in Richards, *Films and British National Identity*, ch. 9, 'Lancashire', 252–79. However, as Ellen Ross has pointed out, a sceptical view of courtship and marriage had long been core to the music-hall canon throughout British society (Ross, *Love and Toil*, 65).

those of parents, family or community. In talking of their decisions to get married interviewees constructed a balance between romance and realism, which robustly deprecated anything too sentimental or soppy, while still reserving a space for acknowledging the importance of love and intimacy, albeit within the practical context of the kind of hard-working partnership that would be necessary for a successful marriage.

5 Married love: caring and sharing

The most recently published historical interpretations of the history of love, sex and marriage in twentieth-century Britain have reaffirmed the long-standing orthodoxy that the era from 1918 to 1963 witnessed the rise of the companionate marriage as an ideal and a practice.[1] Marcus Collins, for instance, sees this model of mutualist companionship rising to the point of enjoying social ubiquity and dominance in the 1960s and 1970s before subsequently coming under challenge. For Collins '[t]he keywords of companionship were intimacy and equality'.[2]

In their recent interpretative textbook, Davidoff et al. agree with Collins that the companionate model became ideologically dominant in mid-twentieth-century Britain. However, they also emphasise tensions between the ideal and practical realities: 'based upon the idea of an exclusive emotionally and sexually intimate relationship... It was a powerful ideal, which stressed the importance of romantic love, sexual attraction and mutual interests, while disguising realities of gendered inequalities of power and access to resources.'[3] As Langhamer has argued, the experience of love is 'rooted in material and cultural as well as emotional, considerations'.[4]

[1] See Chapter 1, section 'Gender Relations and Companionate Marriage' for a general historiographical introduction to this popular orthodoxy.

[2] Collins, *Modern Love*, 93. Similarly Richards and Elliott see intimacy and companionship as its two key characteristics: Richards and Elliott, 'Sex and Marriage in the 1960s and 1970s', 33–4. Collins prefers to use the term 'mutualism' throughout his book, but this is clearly functioning as a close synonym for 'companionate marriage'. He argues that since achieving its apogee in the 1960s and 1970s, this model of 'mutualism' in marriage has been in decline, subject to both feminist critique and exposure of the tensions it contains – the unreachably high expectations of finding a perfect partner. According to Collins the interdependence of companionate mutualism has been in process of being superseded since the 1970s by a new emphasis on individual autonomy. For a recent usage of the notion of companionate marriage in relation to a marriage in the Victorian era, see Jennifer M. Lloyd, 'Conflicting Expectations in Nineteenth Century British Matrimony: The Failed Companionate Marriage of Effie Gray and John Ruskin', *Journal of Women's History* 11, no. 2 (1999): 86–109.

[3] Davidoff et al., *The Family Story*, 190.

[4] Langhamer, 'Love and Courtship', 190.

These judicious formulations suggest the need to explore tensions and contradictions and the desirability of a more complex depiction of gender and sexual relations in marriage during the early and mid-twentieth-century decades than one which confines itself to conformity with a linear narrative of the rise of the ideology of companionate marriage. In his pioneering oral history study of *The Edwardians*, published in 1975 at the height of the vogue among contemporary sociologists for advocating the notion that the companionate marriage and the accompanying 'symmetrical family' had arrived in British society, Paul Thompson was deeply sceptical that this provided a satisfactory contemporary description of marriage in the 1970s or an adequate account of historical change in the twentieth century.[5] Thompson pointed out that historians have found evidence that marriages based on a companionate model of equal sharing were widely prevalent even in early modern English society in the sixteenth and seventeenth centuries and that home-centred husbands could be found among the working classes right at the beginning of the twentieth century, too, especially in regions like Lancashire, West Yorkshire and the Staffordshire Potteries where both partners were often in employment in the local industries there.[6] In other words companionate marriage, in the sense of 'a rough and ready' equality of resources and roles between the partners, and also marriages of mutual affection, were not such an historically novel development of the early and mid-twentieth century led by the educated middle classes, as they were claimed to be, but might relate to longer-term continuities and demotic practices in British society as well.[7]

To what extent did our respondents see love in marriage and love in their own marriages as conforming to an idealistic commitment to companionate intimacy and equality? As Peter Stearns has recognised, albeit using American sources, early twentieth-century discourses about marriage championed a version of 'love' which involved 'practical accommodations … [to] allow a couple

[5] Thompson, *The Edwardians* (London: Weidenfeld & Nicolson, 1975), 304–5. This section in the first edition was a direct response to the arrival of the symmetrical family that had been proclaimed two years earlier by two of Britain's most influential sociologists: Michael Young and Peter Willmott, *The Symmetrical Family* (London: Routledge & Kegan Paul, 1973).

[6] Thompson, *The Edwardians*, 77–81.

[7] On evidence for a rough-and-ready equality of marriage partners and their mutual affections from at least the sixteenth and seventeenth centuries onwards, see Keith Wrightson, *English Society, 1580–1680* (London: Hutchinson, 1982), ch. 4, Linda Pollock, *A Lasting Relationship: Parents and Children over Three Centuries* (London: Fourth Estate Ltd, 1987). See also the editors of the most recent collection of studies of the subject, who see companionate marriage as a 'slippery and capacious concept that offers little purchase for historians trying to map change over time': Ben Griffin, Lucy Delap and Abigail Wills, 'Introduction: The Politics of Domestic Authority in Britain Since 1800', in *The Politics of Domestic Authority in Britain since 1800*, eds. Lucy Delap, Ben Griffin and Abigail Wills (Basingstoke: Palgrave Macmillan, 2009), 13.

to live together harmoniously, sharing various interests including sexuality; soaring ideals and moral regeneration were absent'.[8]

The interviewees were of course influenced by the enduring public discourse promoting the values of companionate marriage which had accompanied their lives during the twentieth century. However, their testimony was also remarkably independent of it. The term itself, for instance, was almost entirely absent from their language. In discussing their expectations and disappointments and their understandings and experiences of love in marriage, they emphasised most strongly the importance – but also the attendant difficulties – of successfully combining a precarious balance of caring for each other and for their families with a sense of emotional sharing. The touchstones of the companionate marriage ideal – romantic love, expressive sensual intimacy and egalitarian sharing of marital responsibilities – were much less apparent as the leading characteristics of respondents' testimonies.

'A real, good, loving, working marriage'

In presenting their experiences of love, outlining their ideals of love and their marital expectations of love, respondents frequently championed a version of love in opposition to a certain model of romance. The kind of love which many sought to achieve in marriage (and which strongly informed their decisions and desires during courtship as we have seen in Chapter 4) was a version of love deemed to be ordinary and workaday yet highly satisfactory, loving, even passionate and, above all, enduring.

When asked about love within marriage interviewees stressed a workable version of love focused on a successful and loving accommodation to domestic trials, hard work and household management. For Rebecca (1903) love was not an overwhelming emotion, like that experienced when disliking someone, but a powerful yet subtle desire to do things for the other person and a feeling of calm security and well-being. She did not get married until she was 40 in 1943, despite having had many previous suitors. She was an alteration hand in a London store while her future husband was an ambulance driver:

REBECCA we just grew together, you know ... I was so comfortable with him ... there's nothing I disliked about my husband. I knew he loved me; I know that because the little things ... that he used to do ... we were so comfortable together that, er, I mean, people talk about love – ooh – I think they don't really think ... when you don't like somebody you know it. But when you love somebody you take it for granted, know what I mean? Yes, I think that's the only sensible way ... you like them to be with you; you have to do things for them and they do things for you. That is love.[9]

[8] Peter N. Stearns and Mark Knapp, 'Men and Romantic Love: Pinpointing a 20th-Century Change', *Journal of Social History* 26, no. 4 (1993): 781.

[9] Rebecca msf/kf/ht/#6.

One reason why many were suspicious of romantic love during courtship was because it was seen as existing in opposition to a workable form of marital love. One woman wrote to *Woman's Own* in 1945, worried that her feelings of love were signs of a doomed marriage: 'I heard talk on the wireless lately saying that if you marry simply because you are violently in love, your marriage may fail. My boyfriend and I are passionately in love, and now I feel worried in case we are making a mistake.'[10] Indeed, in Gay's (1928) case the fact that her marriage failed was interpreted as having been because the romantic passion she felt blinded her to the pragmatic realities. A very glamorous and fashionable respondent, she fell madly in love with a number of dashing young men when courting during the Second World War. Her relationship with her future husband was disapproved of by her family, which added an extra layer of romantic frisson.

GAY I think I was besotted with him [her future husband, subsequently divorced] ... when I think back, I mean, I'm really, you know, 'Why did I?' [marry him] but there you are, I did![11]

In contrast, many others saw the success of their marriages as being part of their commitment to the development of a particular 'unromantic' version of love. For several respondents, romance or excitement was 'another thing' from love in marriage. Bryan (1918) worked as foreman in a rubber factory in Hertfordshire after service in the war; and was married in 1947 to a Harpenden-born woman who did not go out to work, with whom he had two children; Elma (1909) worked as a cook throughout her life and married a policeman in 1933, with whom she had one child:

Did you have a romantic marriage?

ELMA Me? No, I couldn't say it was very romantic, not really. No, romance – romance is another thing. But I loved him; I loved him very much ... And I could do with him now. I could do with him now. I could.[12]

BRYAN we never really had what you call an exciting life really. It was just a nice ordinary (pause) – and we were so contented with our lot, put it that way, that we didn't worry about anything else or anybody else apart from the children.[13]

There was also a pervasive consensus among both working-class and middle-class respondents of both sexes that what was central to a happy and successful marriage was something quite distinct from what they termed 'romantic' love – instead they valued an enduring, loving relationship dedicated to helping each other. Colin (1923), a qualified plumber in Blackburn, married twice.

10 *Woman's Own*, 20 April 1945, 18, quoted in Langhamer, 'Love and Courtship', 188.
11 Gay msf/kf/ht/#13, married 1947.
12 Elma msf/jm/bl#42.
13 Bryan msf/kf/ht/#25.

His first marriage in 1947 was happy and yet the love that sustained it was not ideal. Colin saw himself as having been carried away by his romantic feelings into having sex with a girlfriend who subsequently became pregnant. He saw himself as having been forced into a marriage he had not anticipated, sought or particularly welcomed. He described his love for this first wife as 'exciting', yet it was not as valuable as the love he enjoyed with the woman he married in 1978, following his first wife's premature death. This love was the perfect form of unromantic, practical marital love sought, he felt, by all:

COLIN I think it were kind of love that, er… most people are looking for all their life. Just a nice kind, mild love – not the excitement of [the] first wife, you know.[14]

Dennis (1915) was a skilled worker in the printing trade in Dunstable who had married in 1940:

So what would you say is important in a good marriage? What's the most important thing?

DENNIS Well, loving trust – to trust each other and do all that you can to help each other.[15]

This was what powered a 'real, good, loving, working marriage', as Lorna (1917) put it, a weaver from Blackburn who remained in work throughout her life, marrying a local, working-class man in 1939, with whom she had two children. It was a more prosaic but also more profound, more constant and committed love than the exciting or possessive states of romance or 'being in love':

LORNA It might not've ever been [an] exciting marriage but it was a loving one and in our way [a] happy one… You've to trust one another, work together, give and take – no use always taking – you've got to give and take; and, er, well, we discussed everything – any money matters – as I say, we, everything were discussed… Yeah, we had a real, a real, a real good loving, working marriage… I'd do it all over again with the same man.[16]

Hubert (1911), the director of an agricultural engineering firm in Leighton Buzzard, concurred that a practical resilience in coping with the difficulties of family life was the chief ingredient for a happy marriage (even though he did not think that his own marriage, contracted in 1936, had been a particularly happy one):

What do you think the most important thing is to have a happy marriage?

HUBERT Well to work together and to agree to work together. Naturally there's, inevitably there is a – the physical side of it – an attraction which nobody's been able to explain yet but certainly exists – very powerful too. (pause) But it is, as

[14] Colin msf/kf/bl/#36. [15] Dennis msf/kf/ht/15. [16] Lorna msf/kf/bl/#25.

I've said before, working together as a team. The more difficulties almost the better.[17]

Bernard (1907) and Diana (1910) were interviewed together. They had married in 1936 and had one child in 1939. They moved to Blackburn two years after marriage where he took up a job as a managing director while she had not worked since marriage. They were both born into the middle class and they also saw love in marriage in this way and the test of its value in its capacity to overcome difficulties:

BERNARD You meet all the problems in life together and you overcome them together. And if your love is worth anything, then this is where it comes in and where it comes out.[18]

Dora's (1923) memories of her husband and herself coming to terms with both a hysterectomy and then a breast operation exemplified this kind of loving relationship exactly. They had married in 1945 and lived in Radlett. He was a car mechanic while she was also employed throughout their marriage, even when their children were small, in a variety of jobs including doing clothing alterations from home, being a nanny, or shop work. They had an extremely happy marriage.

DORA He was wonderful. He was. I cried; we, I – honestly speaking – we cried together ... and I did think that Joe would leave me because I couldn't have a baby any more and then, this happened to my breast ... Yeah, he said to me, 'Doll, I love you more than ever'. He said,'with all what you've been through'. He said, 'and I do really love you' ... And to have a man like it – I loved him all the more.[19]

With a cross-class consensus, then, male and female respondents spoke of the importance of a 'working' love, based on trust, which was specific to a good and lasting marriage and was different from the other forms of love they recognised. This could only come from the time-tested experience of being in a practical relationship together and making a go of it during the ups and the downs; and the value of such a real, good, loving, working marriage was appreciated as much by those who believed their marriages had exemplified it as by those who did not.

'I'm not going out to work and coming home, making my own tea!'

When addressing the issue of the balance of roles within marriages, respondents talked a lot about the desirability of sharing, and many, like Elizabeth

[17] Hubert msf/kf/ht#32. [18] Bernard and Diana msf/jm/bl/#45.
[19] Dora msf/srss/ht/#38.

(1923), who had been married to her first husband in working-class Blackburn from 1947 until his death in 1991, valued doing things together.

And what do you think is the most important thing in a good marriage?
ELIZABETH ... sharing everything, an' working together. If yer both work at it, there [is] nothing [to] go wrong ...[20]

Nevertheless all those interviewed also recognised that it was of overwhelming and primary importance that each spouse satisfactorily provided for the family in the gender-specific way which was conventional and normative at this time.[21] Respondents of both sexes and all ages recognised that a husband had to be dependable in bringing in the family's income, fulfilling his primary role as the family's breadwinner: Rebecca (1903), Catherine (1912) and Colin (1923) were spread across the age range of those interviewed:

So what's important in a good husband?
REBECCA Well, he looked after me – saw that I had everything I needed.[22]
COLIN my money went on table and I always thought that the money belonged to you both, whether one [of you] earned it, or not.[23]
CATHERINE My husband, I don't think he did much. He might have changed the odd nappy but he wasn't the most domesticated of men, you know (laughs). He kept working and bringing in enough money to feed us; that's right.[24]

Wives, correspondingly, were deemed to exhibit their vital caring contribution primarily as good home-makers, looking after the family home and nurturing the children. This is of course precisely what all girls were officially taught in the nation's schools and in the popular literature they read until at least the late 1950s.[25] Clare (1912), from Berkhamsted, was married twice to working-

20 Elizabeth (1923) msf/kf/bl/#26.

21 As Ann Sumner Holmes intriguingly demonstrates by examining changes in statute and case law regarding child custody, between 1885 and 1926 growing emphasis on the importance and exclusivity of women's nurturing, maternal role meant that from the 1920s even a wife found guilty of adultery might nevertheless be awarded custody of the children, with the father compelled to pay maintenance. Correspondingly, legal acknowledgement of the inappropriateness of expecting a woman to take on a breadwinning role meant that from 1925 an adulterous wife would no longer necessarily be denied maintenance from an ex-husband if the adultery 'was conduced to by the failure of the husband to make such payments'. These new legal arrangements thus reflect the extent to which British society institutionalised a normative view of polarised gender roles with men as family breadwinners and women as childrearers and home-makers (Ann Sumner Holmes, '"Fallen Mothers": Maternal Adultery and Child Custody in England, 1886–1925', ch. 3 in *Maternal Instincts: Visions of Motherhood and Sexuality in Britain, 1875–192*, 5, eds. Claudia Nelson and Ann Sumner Holmes (London: Macmillan, 1997), 53).

22 Rebecca msf/kf/ht#6, married 1943.

23 Colin msf/kf/bl/#36, married 1947.

24 Catherine msf/kf/ht/#1, married 1941.

25 Not until the 1956 revised edition of the Ministry of Education's handbook, *Health Education*, was a chapter on 'Mothercraft and Infant Care' replaced with a chapter on 'School and the Future Parent', while the term 'parentcraft' was adopted in the text (Jane Pilcher, 'Body

class husbands in 1936 and 1947 and brought up two children; Ed (1913), a carpenter, lived both in London and Blackburn after his marriage in 1937 and had two children; Maud (1912) had lived throughout her life in Blackburn, her first marriage lasted from 1934 until her husband's death in 1977 and she had remarried in 1979:

And what do you think is important in a good mother?

CLARE Looking after the children and cooking for 'em and washing fer 'em.[26]

What do you think makes for a good wife?

ED She's got to be a good housekeeper, hasn't she? Good cook, understand you – I don't know what else I could say ... Oh aye, yeah ... love of children I should say.[27]

And what's the most important thing to make you a good wife?

MAUD I don't know. I suppose looking after them and eh, ya know – all the work and keep the house clean and tidy and the cooking an' all that – looking after them really.[28]

A good wife was defined first by her home-making skills, especially her role as preparer and provider of the family's food. As middle-class Phyllis (1921) from Blackburn, who married in 1943 and had two children, saw it, a good wife provided all meals whenever they were required and would certainly not leave her husband to fend for himself:

And were you a good wife?

PHYLLIS I think so. I always had a meal ready for them when they came in. He used to start work very early in the morning when he was a salesman. So I used to get up early with him to cook his breakfast about 5 o'clock in the morning.[29]

As Catherine (1912), born in West Ham, who had lived most of her married life in Berkhamsted bringing up one child, saw it, if she compromised this role by going out to work, this meant that her son risked less adequate nutrition.

CATHERINE I was at home till Johnny was 13, and then we had somebody in the shop, and he wasn't all that satisfactory and my husband said, 'Well, I think you'll have to come down.' And Johnny thought that was the end: Mum going out to work, mmm. But, uh, and I used to think the school dinners weren't nutritious enough – they didn't have a choice.[30]

Work: Childhood, Gender and School Health Education in England, 1870–1977', *Childhood* 14, no. 2 (2007): 224); on girls' popular reading, see Stephanie Spencer, '"Be Yourself": *Girl* and the Business of Growing up in Late 1950s England', ch. 7 in *Women and Work Culture in Britain c.1850–1950*, eds. Krista Cowman and Louise A. Jackson (Aldershot: Ashgate Press, 2005), 141–58.

26 Clare msf/kf/ht#8.

27 Ed msf/srss/bl/#23.

28 Maud msf/kf/bl/#18.

29 Phyllis msf/kf/bl/#5. Her husband was briefly a salesman between more extended periods of work in the grocery trade both before and after the war.

30 Catherine msf/kf/ht/#1, married 1941.

As it was of fundamental importance to most respondents that a loving marriage partner should satisfactorily perform their primary role of 'looking after' their spouse's needs and their family in the manner that was appropriate to their gender, respondents, like Sarah (1906) married in 1928, told disapproving stories of fathers or fathers-in-law who imperilled the family's finances with their drinking problems.

SARAH He [her own husband] was, well, he was – he was a decent chap. He was, uh, (pause) well, he was everything me dad wasn't. He didn't drink; he didn't smoke (pause) – he was everything me dad wasn't. His dad was like my dad – his dad used to drink, and his mother had quite a bit to put up with in her life but, uh – he was like me – I didn't drink and I wouldn't have warmed with a chap who drank either… [31]

Contrary to the class stereotypes, the theme of alcohol indulgence imperilling the marriage was, if anything, more common among middle-class than working-class respondents. Pru (1911), for instance, was unfortunate enough to encounter it both with her father and the husband she married in 1935.[32]

The worst partners were considered to be those who fell down on their primary gendered responsibility and role, like working-class Pam's (1907), a local Hertfordshire man she had married in 1932, who had a series of low-paying jobs:

PAM Oh well, he used to give me my money and – I can't remember – don't ask me how much he had because he never did tell me, I don't know. And I don't know what he give me – but course he used to spend his money on drink, and then come to me and got to borrow. He'd say, 'Will you lend me so and so?' Yeah, I'd lend him it but I didn't get it back… he knew I tried to save a bit – I did try to save a bit, but he knew I'd got some money and he'd say, 'Oh well, I'll ask somebody else then, to lend me some'. And I said, 'No.' I wouldn't – I didn't want him to do that, so I just had to give him mine.[33]

[31] Sarah msf/kf/bl#30. Other examples of fathers or fathers-in-law who had a drink problem were mentioned by: Marian msf/kf/bl/#28; Terence msf/srss/bl/#15; Frank msf/srss/bl/#16; Ed msf/srss/bl/#23; Peter msf/kf/bl/#26; Reg msf/kf/ht/#36. Brian Harrison's classic study of the Temperance movement concluded that it 'ceased to be a live political issue after the first world war' (Brian Harrison, *Drink and the Victorians: The Temperance Question in England, 1815–1872* (Keele: Keele University Press, 1994), 367). While this may be true, the transcripts show that it remained a live social issue throughout the interwar period. Choosing a Methodist as a husband could still be considered a safe bet for this reason in the 1930s (e.g. Eleanor msf/kf/bl/#11).

[32] Pru msf/kf/ht/#12 – see below notes 74 and 78. Antonia's husband degenerated into alcoholism later in her marriage: Antonia msf/kf/ht/#35; and Phyllis' husband was a benign alcoholic throughout much of the marriage (having been in the bomb disposal unit throughout the war and having lost many of his friends): Phyllis msf/kf/bl/#5. Judith msf/kf/ht/#33 and Hilda msf/kf/bl/#50 also reported husbands who had degenerated into alcoholism later in their lives. Reg's msf/kf/ht/#36 second wife became alcoholic towards the end of her life, though in her case this was partly because she was suffering from an incurable condition.

[33] Pam msf/kf/ht/#19.

How to combine the highly distinctive, gendered roles of caring for the family, in such a way as to contribute to a sense of emotional sharing of their lives together, constituted a central, unstable dynamic and focus of contention in the meaning of love in the respondents' marriages. Neither male nor female informants were comfortable with the subversion of their conventional role as prime provider of specifically gendered services or with conceding control over it to the other partner.

Husbands, like Sarah's (1906), a well-paid upholsterer four years her senior, could be very sensitive about their wives expressing an interest in going out to work, as a possible affront to their pride and manhood, putting them, for instance, in the improper position of having to make their own tea after a day's work:

SARAH this was my husband's idea – if his mother didn't work, I shouldn't work, see? (chuckle) That was my husband's idea.
[...]
So did you ever have arguments about your work?
Oh yes. He didn't like me working; oh, he didn't like me working: ... 'I'm not going out to work and coming home, making my own tea!' – that sort of a thing – 'My mother never went out!'[34]

Larry (1917), a bricklayer who was also several years older than his wife, was another husband for whom the suggestion by his wife, Doreen (1922), that she wanted to go out to earn could be perceived as hurtful and as diminishing his own status and contribution to the marriage:

DOREEN He didn't want me to go out to work, did you? And I was bored stiff at home all day.
LARRY No, no.
Why didn't you want her to go out to work?
LARRY Well, I felt as though I could keep her. And I did.
DOREEN Yeah, but it was tight. But I'd got me – I'd got through for domestic science and I had eleven subjects and I could – I wanted to go teaching you see; I were capable. And he objected to that. I think it was because he thought it would be a higher thing than being a builder.
Tell me about that.
DOREEN Well, I can't in front of him but, er – caused a lot of friction. You wanted to be proud and keep me, you see?
And how did you feel?
DOREEN Frustrated. I'm still frustrated about it.[35]

Antonia (1928), married at 21 to a chartered accountant, also echoed this problem:

You said you had bad patches with your husband. Tell me about the good times and the bad times.

[34] Sarah msf/kf/bl/#30, married 1928. [35] Doreen and Larry msf/kf/bl/#20, married 1946.

ANTONIA I think a lot of the trouble we had was because when we first got married I thought he probably knew most things. I mean I was 21, he was 35. And consequently I expected him to be the leader and to do the – make the decisions and do everything. And as time went on and I grew up a bit I found I wasn't quite happy to accept things like that. I wanted a bit more of an equal partnership and this wasn't his idea at all. So we did come – I wouldn't say we'd come to blows – but we did disagree quite strongly about that because I wanted to, erm, I would have liked to get a job when the children all went to school and he was absolutely against it because to him men's wives – if your wife worked that was a signal of failure – that you were not doing well. And so, erm, it was pretty – made pretty clear to me not, not to work. Which considering that (pause) my oldest four children all went to boarding school – I mean I easily could have done. But, er, with a bit of encouragement I would have done, but I didn't get any encouragement so I didn't.[36]

Equally, however, female respondents could be very protective of their own area of jurisdiction. Managing the children in the household on a daily basis was usually acknowledged to be one of the mother's principal areas of responsibility, which a sensible husband respected, if for no other reason than that a hard-working husband was out of the house for many hours of the day, no matter how much he was considered a loving father. Dora (1923), married to a motor mechanic, and Dennis (1915), a qualified printer working in Dunstable, both presented themselves as having very contented, well-adjusted marriages, in which fathers played with children and participated fully in family life; nevertheless they were equally clear on where the authority and responsibility for the children's upbringing lay:

DORA Joe left it to me. Joe said, 'I'll leave it to you because I'm not here.'[37]

Did you ever have differences of opinion on how to bring the children up?

DENNIS No! No! There again we were one – two as one – I mean I acknowledged that Eve was the, er, most essential because I mean she was the home …[38]

Real, full involvement and emotional sharing of all aspects of children's upbringing by the husband required a significant concession from the wife in an area of her recognised control. Women, such as Maria (1917), married in 1940, did not necessarily want such 'interference':

What about bringing up your daughter: what was his role in that?

MARIA Oh, he never interfered a lot, not with bringing Jane up. No, he wasn't a kind of a strict man.[39]

Penny (1916), for instance, very happily married since 1938 to a factory shift worker in Hatfield, was very careful to manage her partner's contribution to the childcare:

[36] Antonia msf/kf/ht/#35, married 1949. [37] Dora msf/srss/ht/#38, married 1945.
[38] Dennis msf/kf/ht/15, married 1940. [39] Maria msf/kf/bl#8.

You were the disciplinarian?

PENNY Yes... Day in and day out. I was – they, they were my – that was my job.

[...]

Why didn't you want him disciplining them?

Because I thought he would be heav- too heavy-handed – if he hit them or something. Um, when we started having – when we were having the children, we [made] an agreement, you know – when they were old enough to be smacked, I said to him, um, how I want it to happen.[40]

For Penny, as for many mothers, as regards the children, 'I was the boss'; and she saw it as one of the most important things in her marriage that 'as far as the children were concerned, he agreed with ... how I wanted to bring them up'.[41]

Some respondents, such as Angela (1924), married to Hugh in 1947, and Daphne (1912), married a decade earlier in 1937, did talk in general terms of sharing the childrearing equally:

Tell me more about bringing up your children.

ANGELA Um, oh, we've always done things together ... [42]

Who did more with the children?

DAPHNE Well, neither of us – we brought them up together. Er, I mean I used to wash the clothes and do that sort of thing but ... we shared everything really.[43]

Interestingly, in both these cases these two women probably did share a more equal work role with their husbands than in many other marriages. They each had had fairly continuous working lives throughout their marriages but mainly of a flexible form in terms of their command over their own time, enabling them to combine earning with continuing childcaring.[44] Each had had just two well-spaced-out births (Daphne's were eight years apart and Angela's five years apart). In Daphne's case her husband had joined her in running a confectioner's shop in Blackburn after his butcher's business folded. In Angela's case she had had a series of convenient local clerical jobs, including working at home typing for a barrister for seven years starting when her elder child was 10 and the younger 5 years old.

Most women, though, did not want others caring for their loved ones, just as most men did not want anybody helping them to earn the family's income.[45] Judith (1931), a trained midwife, unusually portrayed her middle-class husband

[40] Penny msf/srss/ht/#20. [41] Penny msf/srss/ht/#20.

[42] Angela and Hugh msf/kf/ht/#18. [43] Daphne msf/jm/bl/#38.

[44] On the long-standing importance of the domestic economy of time as well as of income-earning employment in relation to childbearing and childrearing practices among different occupational communication communities and especially among shopkeepers, see Szreter, *Fertility, Class, and Gender*, 495–501.

[45] See Tim Fisher's account of the tensions along these gendered lines besetting an unusual inter-war initiative: Tim Fisher, 'Fatherhood and the British Fathercraft Movement 1919–39', *Gender and History* 17, no. 2 (2005): 441–62.

(whom she subsequently divorced) as positively wanting her to go out to work when the children were young. But she would not:

JUDITH No because I became pregnant fairly quickly – this was just something that always annoyed Graham: 'You never earned any money; never worked for me.' I said, 'I'm working. I'm bringing up your children, keeping the house.' But he wanted me to work – but, well, I didn't want a nanny. I wanted to bring up my own children, so that was a bone of contention; I'd forgotten about that – quite right that was a bone of contention, still.[46]

And, as implied by Judith ('I didn't want a nanny'), women could be intensely competitive in this respect towards other women, such as Penny (1916):

PENNY I just wanted to get married to look after him… I thought I could have looked after him better than, you know, than his mother – his mother was looking after him. I mean that's what you always hope. I could cook – his mother couldn't cook. I mean if she boiled water she'd let it burn.[47]

The gendered caring role which mothers and wives performed was seen as carrying great responsibilities for the welfare of their families – but with that went great status and domestic authority. It was one of the male interviewees who expressed, in a most telling way, the kind of high status and authority that he considered to be due to a good wife and mother because of the emotional importance of the daily caring work she carried out which was acknowledged as the primary female role in marriage. Alf (1915) and Heather (1916) were both born into the working class in West London, had married in their early twenties in 1938 and brought up two children in London:

ALF This is how it should be I think. After all, I've always said the main thing about any family in my opinion is not so much the bloke, who's supposed to be the breadwinner. It's not; it's the mum; it's the mother. She's the figurehead of that family. I don't care what anybody says… no matter how good the bloke is and how clever he might be bringing the money in. A kingpin is – if the kids get hurt at school they come running, you know? They don't go running for their dad. In the army with blokes that were grovelling on the ground – they're being shelled – they don't ask for their dad, they're calling out for their mum. Always, it's always the same… That's why I think that's what it all bases down to… And if you get a relationship like that – it's nothing better – I don't think; it's marvellous.[48]

This fulsome praise of a wife's role as 'the figurehead' of the family and the general deference shown by respondents to women's primacy in matters of child-rearing was an agreed division of labour, which saved such marriages from much of the conflict depicted by Hammerton in his studies of the immediately

[46] Judith msf/kf/ht/#33, married 1958. [47] Penny msf/srss/ht/20, married 1938.
[48] Alf and Heather msf/kf/ht/#14.

preceding generation, such as lower-middle-class John Goffin (1879–1964), whose 'obsession to correct early childhood "faults and weaknesses"' sowed seeds of long-standing tension, as his wife 'refused to confirm his reprovals and deeply resented his censure and correction'.[49] Consequently, female interviewees, such as Elma (1909), married to a policeman, did not necessarily want a 'domesticated' man for a husband (even though she herself was not a stereotyped house-bound wife and had in fact worked throughout most of her marriage, having just one child in 1934):

Did you ever want your husband to do more work in the house?
ELMA No, no. That's something I never asked. No, I don't believe in a man being a slave in the house, no.[50]

Women such as Sarah (1906), one of the older Blackburn interviewees, or Grace (1922), one of the younger respondents interviewed in Hertfordshire, each of whom had suffered the loss of a child in infancy and had consequently brought up a single child, might even be proud of the fact that their men were 'not like the dads today' and quite accepted that they were expected to demonstrate that they were not domesticated 'Mary-Annes', who were under the thumbs of their wives:

And what about your husband: was he a good father?
SARAH Oh yes, yes; he, he didn't (chuckle) – he's not like the dads today, you know? The dads today change nappies and God knows what. He wasn't like that – he wasn't domesticated, but he was a good father. Oh yes. No, he didn't take much interest till she started taking notice (chuckle) and all dads were like that then – all dads! And if there was any young fella that mucked about changing the nappies and one thing and another, they'd say, 'He's a Mary-Anne, isn't he?' (giggle) Nowadays it's quite different.[51]
GRACE Colin wasn't a bit domesticated. Not a bit... Colin would dry the dishes and he used to say 'Look sharp if our Chris knocks at door.' He said, 'I don't want him watch- catching me drying the dishes.' And his brother were making bread and doing everything, but Colin wasn't a bit domesticated.
Did you mind that?
Me? No. No. I preferred, erm, no.[52]

[49] Hammerton, 'Pooterism or Partnership?', 319. Hammerton argues that his diverse evidence shows an increasing commitment to privacy and partnership in both the satirical depiction and the autobiographically recorded experience of lower-middle-class suburban marriages, 1870–1920, which subsequently became 'the more universal model for twentieth-century family life' (ibid., 321). However, the patriarchal language used by Goffin, Hammerton's principal autobiographical source, is quite distinct from that of our interviewees in articulating their conception of working together: Goffin describes, as his 'ideal arrangement', 'that there must be a master and a mistress and each should accept responsibility for the work and duties consequent thereon' (ibid., 318). See also A. James Hammerton, *Cruelty and Companionship: Conflict in Nineteenth-Century Married Life* (London: Routledge, 1992).

[50] Elma msf/jm/bl/#42, married 1933.

[51] Sarah msf/kf/bl/#30, married 1928.

[52] Grace msf/srss/ht/#38, married 1944.

When women said they would have appreciated more help around the house or commented negatively on how little their husbands did, they did not want husbands to do this in place of their primary role as breadwinners. Nor did they want husbands who would encroach on their wives' domestic authority. They wanted some handy assistance, on their own terms. Lorna (1917), who worked throughout her marriage (in 1939) as a weaver while bringing up two children born in 1942 and 1945, and was married to a factory supervisory worker six years older, described approvingly how careful her partner was to defer to her greater talents in the household, when giving her some assistance:

LORNA I did all the housework – he never. He would when he was on shift work and I was working. He'd – especially when it was 2 till 10 – he tried to do – he'd do the housework, and he said to me, 'Do you know, you know, cock, it neither looks like it's been done like you do it when I do it'. But he'd done it, and I were pleased he'd done it. And he had to mention it, you know – well, 'It'll have to do ... [until] you've done it – it'll have to do till next time round.' But he did try; we, we did actually pull together, which you must do.[53]

Taking care of the garden and doing DIY and the work of decorating (though most women wished to retain control over choices of colours, etc.) were three commonly 'sub-let', self-contained areas of domestic work, where men's input was typically allowed, expected and appreciated, relieving his partner of a set of responsibilities in these demarcated areas of physical work.[54] They were not seen as encroaching on a wife's authority and control over the rest of the home and over the children. Penny, who was quoted above as keen to outdo her mother-in-law as her husband's carer, did not seem to count the garden, DIY or decorating as 'the housework', which was her own responsibility, and she was grateful that it was done for her by her husband:

PENNY I never expected him to do housework ... I mean if I said to him 'I wish I could have a shelf up there', I would have a shelf up there. He did all the decorating

[53] Lorna msf/kf/bl/#25.

[54] Julie-Marie Strange notes a somewhat earlier expansion in the market for popular self-help publications on gardening, relative to DIY, with the launch of the magazine *Popular Gardening* in 1920. Of course, those living in rented accommodation, the vast majority of the working class until well after the Second World War, did not need to be home-owners to benefit from either growing vegetables in the gardens of their rented homes or the recreational use of the gardens so, unlike DIY, the rise in popularity of this domestic activity did not have to wait on the expansion in working-class home-ownership. In addition to their urban gardens working families had a long-established practice of subsidising family incomes and diets with the produce from allotments, regulated by a series of Smallholdings and Allotments Acts, 1908, 1919, 1922 and 1925 (Julie-Marie Strange, 'Leisure', in *Twentieth Century Britain: Economic, Cultural and Social Change*, eds. Francesca Carnevali, Paul Johnson and Julie-Marie Strange (London: Longman, 2007), 197–213). On DIY and trends in home ownership, see below, note 62.

without any trouble. He loved doing decorating 'cos that [was] what he used to do when he was on the buildings a little while. And he'd keep the garden all tidy and clean.[55]

Thus, wives like Penny did not begrudge husbands with long working days who did not share childcare and housework when they themselves were not at work:

PENNY When we had the children I would never – if they cried or anything at night – I would never expect him to get up and see to the children, because, um, I'm – in my theory, he'd got to get up and get to work by half past 6. I hadn't got to go to work – I could've gone to sleep during the daytime while the children were asleep or something like that.[56]

However, when a wife was at work, herself, then she looked for some sharing of the load at home and this was equally true of the several middle-class wives who worked after marriage, once their children were older, such as Pru (1911), married in 1935 to a banker:

So did he have any duties in the house?
PRU Oh, he would wash up and occasionally do that sort of thing.
And did you ever want him to do more?
Well, yes, I think I wished in a way he'd be a bit more co-operative ... just when I was working.[57]

'Mind you, we always helped one another to do anything'

Thus, given the strong commitment to fulfilling their respective, polarised gendered roles in caring for their families, the aspiration that many respondents also articulated to 'work together' practically and emotionally to share their married lives together was not at all easy to achieve in practice. When interviewees discussed in detail the meaning of a good, loving, working marriage, both working-class and middle-class informants talked of the importance and difficulties of combining 'caring' with 'sharing' in their marriages. Most informants, regardless of class, saw this as of central importance to a lasting relationship of love in marriage, but it was also something as likely to cause upset as harmony.

Elizabeth (1923) and Peter (1921) were both widowed working-class Blackburnites who had recently remarried in the late 1990s. As the following extract from their joint interview exemplifies, they both talk about the reciprocal contributions each partner makes by performing work in the marriage – the caring work of providing. They also talk about expressing their love and

[55] Penny msf/srss/ht/#20, married 1938.
[56] Penny msf/srss/ht/#20. [57] Pru msf/kf/ht/#12.

esteem for each other – showing they emotionally care about each other, as well as physically caring for each other:

So why is he a good husband?

ELIZABETH Because he's caring, yeah, and he always wants t'buy me something, you know, and I feel like I'm takin' 'is money and he'll say, 'No, yer worth it, love', yer know. Everything he does, he'll say 'Yer worth it', yer know, oh no.

PETER Well, she does a lot fer me, love; oh, aye. It's a matter of making meals fer me, and, as she said – I've bin asleep on settee there and I've woke up and she says 'I'll 'ave t'make yer a drink of tea' – things like that and – but I finish up washing up (both laughing). I'm chief washer-up.

ELIZABETH He's great; he's really, yeah.[58]

For Bryan (1918), who married in 1947 and brought up two children with his Harpenden-born wife (who had died in 1993), sharing was most meaningfully demonstrated in actions and behaviour agreed and carried out together:

BRYAN As I say, we done everything together. We used to do the shopping together, and whatever we done in the house we done together. And we always used to help one another whenever we could in different ways.[59]

Working-class husbands, who routinely handed over their wage packet to their wives – typically receiving something back for their own leisure – were seen as good providers but this form of economic caring for the family did not necessarily amount to a true sense of emotional sharing with their partners. For Lorna (1917) that also required a husband to give his full time and attention to the marriage, as well as his income, actively sharing together in choosing how to spend the money for the family and the home:

LORNA he'd give me his last ha'penny. We worked together – we put our wages together – paid our way before we did anything and then we saved a bit. He had a bit – he used to hang back before he got any spending money you see, but that were all together and we used to go – when we'd saved up enough and wanted something – we'd go off and, and enjoy that – shopping, you know… [60]

Sharing choices together over discretionary spending was the point of intersection, where the female role of 'caring' for the household and the family members met with the male role of providing for it economically. Choosing together how to make domestic improvements combined these two roles. Working-class respondents in particular, like Lyn (1907) from Blackburn, married in 1931 to a mill worker with whom she had one child, could express an intense pride and joy in the detailed memory of shared

[58] Peter and Elizabeth msf/kf/bl/#26. [59] Bryan msf/kf/ht/#25.

[60] Lorna msf/kf/bl/25, married 1939. For more information on Lorna's marriage see text above preceding notes 16 and 53.

activities with their partner in this respect to achieve a loving outcome for their family home and children, even where the focus of the whole story was 'just a carpet square'.

LYN It was very hard – very hard at the beginning because we had so little, you see ... I remember, I had a frying pan ... and everything we cooked had to be done in this frying pan, and then at weekend when Walter got his money – 'cos I wasn't working, this slump had come in, I had no work – we bought a pan, and then the weekend after you'd buy another pan, or something else, and you'd gradually – a pair of pillow cases – one thing a week, or sometimes one thing a month! ... And we got a three-piece, leatherette suite, brown. I can see it now, yet: brown velvet cushions, two-piece settee, two easy chairs and there were like a pattern in the leather; it wasn't really leather ... And, um, you treasured, them ... when we'd paid for that then we did the same with a carpet – a carpet square. And lino on the outside ... We were frightened of walking on it – it was lovely. And we put trimmings up, paper trimming as I'd made, and a little Christmas tree, and when I brought this baby down expecting – he was about 2 – with the Christmas tree and trimmings all he did was, 'Aaaah nice, nice' – he were thrilled to bits with the carpet! ... And it were nice and soft for him, crawling on there, you see? Yes, it was beautiful – just a carpet square.[61]

Similarly, Dora (1923) recalled with great warmth a story of her joint DIY feats with her late husband in their first family home.[62]

DORA When we had our cottage in Radlett, we was sitting there one morning and he said, 'You love this, don't you?' And I said, 'Oh yeah, I've always loved the cottage.' And he said, 'You wanted some beams, didn't you, doll?' And I said, 'Oh yeah, they'd look lovely.' So he said, 'Come on, get your coat' ... He didn't want to put cheap beams up. He wanted them to look like good beams with the, erm, steel holding them up, you know ... When we got them home he said, 'Help me to clear away', he said. Mind you, we always helped one another to do anything. Even we done a little bit of painting, I was always with him and he used to call me his mate really (laughs) and, er, erm – we, he put these up and it was about

[61] Lyn msf/kf/bl/#1.

[62] Oddly, the growth of DIY among the home-owning population is barely mentioned in the historiography of the rise of a consumer culture. It is absent, for instance, from Matthew Hilton's *Consumerism in Twentieth-Century Britain: The Search for a Historical Movement* (Cambridge: Cambridge University Press, 2003) and John Benson's *Rise of Affluent Society in Britain 1880–1980* (London: Longman, 1994). Julie-Marie Strange helpfully mentions that the Odhams Press popular manual *The Handyman and Home Mechanic* was first published in 1936 and thereafter went through several editions by 1959 (Strange, 'Leisure', 208). Before the First World War, home-ownership was probably restricted to about 10 per cent of families. Though increasing through the interwar decades, it remained mainly a middle-class phenomenon until the 1930s. It was the period from the 1930s to the 1960s (with a wartime interruption) when home-ownership increased significantly among the lower middle and upper working classes with 27 per cent of all homes owner-occupied by 1939, rising to 47 per cent by 1966 (John Burnett, *A Social History of Housing, 1815–1985* (London and New York: Methuen, 1986), 252, 282; Scott, 'Consumption, Consumer Credit', 177).

1 o'clock when we was finished and he sat in the dining area and he said, 'What do you think of it?' I said, 'Oh Joe, it's lovely.' And he said, 'Yeah, I think it's lovely.'[63]

Eileen (1913), married in 1943 to a factory worker, illustrated the same point, but inversely. She did not set any store by her husband's protestations of love because they only happened in bed; whereas he did not consult with her over saving and spending on important consumer items. Words meant little if deeds did not match, and she resented it that he bought himself a motor bike and then a car, forcing her to go out charring to make some pocket money to be able to afford the things she wanted for the house:

Did you ever tell your husband you loved him?

EILEEN Yes! Any time! 'E said 'e loved me. I didn't believe though but 'e said so.

Why didn't you believe him?

In bed 'e used to tell me; I don't know. I don't know (pause)...

Did you have a happy marriage?

(Eileen paused)

What makes you wave your hand, unsurely?

Yes and no. Yes and no, ya know? We never fell out or anything – 'e'd only about £7 a week, yer know, when we married. There was five of us and of course as time went on we 'ad more, and course when 'e went to Thew's [an employer] it got more... I didn't get 'is wage then, so I went on home help, 'cos I'd no money and I kept me wage to meself – so I used to buy little ornaments and things for the 'ouse and all sorts of things... yeah, 'e bought a car... he had a motor bike at first.[64]

Thus, while many individuals valued sharing as an important aspect of love in marriage, this could equally be the cause of much resentment, or even conflict. Respondents did not necessarily get from their partners the kind of sharing that they wanted or thought fair.

Fair sharing of money was the most common point of tension, especially for working-class couples. As men themselves, like Colin (1923), recognised, anything but a full and equal sharing of a man's weekly wage could be viewed as unfair and as failing to fulfil the role of 'looking after' a wife:

COLIN if you tucked anything in your back pocket you were robbing the family, you see, you know? But I were more or less, I think, a home loving – if I got a woman I kept her, like, you know – I looked after her.[65]

Elizabeth's (1923) first husband, whom she had married in 1947, had a succession of low-paid jobs in Blackburn at the mill, as a milkman and then as car mechanic. She recounted the way in which sharing money was a highly

[63] Dora msf/srss/ht/#38, married 1945. [64] Eileen msf/kf/bl/#12.

[65] Colin msf/kf/bl/#36, married 1947.

sensitive issue and a real focus of their relationship with hard-pressed budgets:

So what did you argue about with your first husband?

ELIZABETH Um, well, we didn't exactly argue, love, but money were very tight; money were very tight, and 'cos I couldn't go t'work proper, yer see – and then it were, it were sort o' taking all money we 'ad to keep car on the road, yer know? We didn't exactly argue but there were times when I thought – 'e 'ad some money and I 'ad nothing and I used t'say to him, 'Oh, you've got some money in yer wallet.' He say, 'Yes, love, but I can't give it yer because if anything goes wrong wi' car while we're out, I've got t'find that money to make, yer know, 'ave car repaired' ... and then as time went on, as I said t'John – he used to say to me, when we'd a little bit more money coming in, he say, 'You 'ave £10 a week spending money ... Now, yer do what yer want wi' that; yer either put it away an' save it fer 'oliday, or if yer see anything you go and buy it', yer know? But, no, we weren't selfish with one another, love. No, we shared; we always shared yeah.[66]

A closely related area of negotiation was leisure activities. Ed (1913), who was born in Blackburn but worked in the south and in London during the 1930s in the early years of his marriage before returning to his home town, drew a distinction in these terms between himself and men who had not adjusted to marriage and were still trying to live the life of a single man:

Do you know any men who you think were not good husbands or not good fathers? And why would you say they were not good?

ED They were fond of their beer too much, neglected their homes ... Well, they'd spend their money on beer and the rest on theirselves. And didn't give it to their home. Wanted to live a life of a single man; then they couldn't do it – you can't do it if you're married, can you?[67]

This was a view echoed by Pam (1907), a working-class wife from Harpenden:

PAM I went once to the pub, opened the door, and see him sitting surrounded with other fellas and they're singing their heads off, and I just come out and shut the door – I didn't think much to that.

[...]

And I thought that's the life he likes – he liked that life best; yeah he did. He never got married; not really. (pause)[68]

For both middle- and working-class respondents, a related issue was the extent to which free time was shared or spent apart. For instance, Marilyn (1914) was dissatisfied with her husband's absenteeism from the home – he spent most of his time at work or at male clubs. But for her, there was some compensation

[66] Elizabeth msf/kf/bl/#26. [67] Ed msf/srss/bl/#23, married 1937.
[68] Pam msf/kf/ht/#19, married 1932. For more on Pam's husband, see text at note 33.

in that, with his own hairdressing business, he was at least a very good income provider who gave her and her relatively large family of three children a good standard of living.[69] It was where there was no such compensation, as in Pam's case, that women could be very resentful of having been left alone too much of the time by husbands going off to the pub in the evening:

PAM Well that was the worst thing I, it was – he went to the pub so much.[70]

The equivalent problem experienced by some middle-class wives was husbands 'staying at work':

PRU I was soon disillusioned because he could be led astray – not with women, oh no, but drink. And, er, that sort of thing … he used to tell me lies.
What sort of lies?
Well, he'd say he'd been working late at the office … [71]

Thus, if combining caring with sharing was the core of what working at love in the context of marriage meant for this generation, it was something that they represent as having been subject to much negotiation, adaptation and conflict, too, along the way. As many got the balance wrong as got it right at different points in their marriages. Furthermore, there is no sign among the interviewees that in general the middle-class partners managed this conflict and negotiation better or more effectively than the working-class respondents. While some working-class respondents, particularly females, wished that their partners had been more sympathetic, communicative and sharing, others believed that their own marriages had been characterised in the main by the kind of mutually supportive, empathetic relationship to which they aspired. This was also the case among about one-third of the middle-class interviewees.[72] However, about a third of the middle-class respondents portrayed their marriages as falling into an extreme version of the dysfunctional opposite. Four husbands were depicted (one by the husband himself) as virtual absentees from the marriage – two of whom were workaholics,[73] and two of whom were alcoholics.[74] Two other middle-class men portrayed themselves as having sought refuge from emotionally cold wives through devotion to their careers

[69] Marilyn msf/kf/bl/#7, married 1940. [70] Pam msf/kf/ht/#19.

[71] Pru msf/kf/ht/#12, married 1935.

[72] This applied to three of the ten Blackburn middle-class marriages: Felicity msf/kf/bl/#37; Mildred msf/kf/bl/#41; and Hilda msf/kf/bl/#50 (referring only to her second marriage of 1947 – to the man who had been best-man at her first wedding in 1935, which ended in divorce ten years later); and to eight out of the eighteen Hertfordshire middle-class marriages: Emma msf/kf/ht/#37; Roger msf/kf/ht/#10; Sam msf/srss/ht/#28; Patrick msf/kf/ht/#16; Reg msf/kf/ht/#36; Mark and Joanna msf/kf/ht/#22; Betty and Horace msf/kf/ht/#31; Esme and Gerald msf/kf/ht/#9.

[73] Humphrey msf/kf/ht/#26; Antonia msf/kf/ht/#35.

[74] Pru msf/kf/ht/#12; Phyllis msf/kf/bl/#5 (Antonia's, Judith's and Hilda's husbands were also reported as having degenerated into alcoholism, see above, note 32).

and their personal interests (of course, we cannot know how their wives perceived their husbands' behaviour in these cases);[75] while three marriages were represented as being subject to a lack of emotional commitment of a different kind, in the form of adultery, associated in each case with the curtailment of the marriage.[76] Thus, an absence of shared interests or co-operation between spouses was as likely to occur among middle-class as among working-class respondents.

Gill (1920), for instance, from a comfortable professional home and married in 1945 into a wealthy mill-owning family, claimed to have happily adapted to a life that was lived really quite separately from her consort, whom she said she 'admired'. Theirs was not a relationship founded on shared interests and close co-operation, but rather a marriage with a well-demarcated division of labour and a segregation of their social lives, which extended even to the regular practice of taking separate holidays.[77]

GILL Oh well. He was terribly a man's man and he was not a sociable man … He loved the … rugger club and he was captain of [the] rugger club at one time and, you know, Saturdays were rugger and a night out with the boys. Er, so … I think it took me quite a long time to adjust to it[…]
What do you think were the best things about your marriage, the things that made it a good marriage?
Trust and unselfishness.
So in what ways was your husband unselfish?
Well, he wasn't very – in the first you know early – you see, with being an only child I think they are on the whole more selfish[…]I suppose he always had this need of having male friends, but, you see, we did work it out because he used to go off to the Lakes at Easter when he had a short break – not such a long break – and I would go for a week and stay first with my mother, and then go to Edith's … and, er, I had a wonderful holiday …

Thus, in this impeccably middle-class marriage, portrayed as perfectly successful and satisfying by the respondent, there was little emphasis on a confiding or sharing or emotionally mutually supportive relationship. This even included a period when her husband was encountering difficulties in his business life.

And what could you do to help when your husband was so depressed when the business was having difficulties?
GILL Just, er, keeping the housework going smoothly, I suppose, you know.
And did he talk to you about the problems?

[75] William msf/kf/ht/#24; Hubert msf/kf/ht/#32.
[76] Judith msf/kf/ht/#33; Hilda's msf/kf/bl/#50 first husband; also Reg msf/kf/ht/#36 and his first wife were both adulterous.
[77] A practice which Sam msf/srss/ht/#28 also referred to, but in relation to his middle-class parents, not his own marriage.

No, not much. He'd talk to his father really about it, 'cos his father was still alive then and went into the office every morning.[78]

Gill was proud to report how she forged her own, parallel social life by learning to drive, doing voluntary social work and latterly by serving for a number of years on the bench as a magistrate.

Some middle-class women, such as Gill, accepted and adapted to leading rather separate lives from their spouses. Others, such as Jane (1925), from the lower middle class of Blackburn, complained at a perceived lack of 'understanding' from her partner. Yet, she and her husband, Dick (1920), whom she had married in 1953 (they had two children), had more genuine shared interests than Gill and her rugger-playing husband. For instance, they enjoyed tennis and local opera-going together – through which they had originally met. However, despite these shared activities, Jane claimed she found Dick taciturn, believing that some men were capable of more 'understanding' and regretting that her husband had not been one of these:

JANE Um, he doesn't tell me these things. I did hear from his cousin, Jan, who went to visit him when he was in the Fountains Home at, er – 'he couldn't've managed without me and I'd been wonderful', so – but he doesn't tell me things like that. (laughs)[...]As far as Dick's concerned, if he was well fed and his house was looked after – well you were quite content, weren't you?

DICK Yeah.

And what do you think's the most important thing in a good husband?

JANE (pause) Well, (pause) understanding – which isn't always there – understanding how you feel, understanding – understanding how you feel when you have your bad days particularly[...]I don't think – men don't always understand why or bother to find out – I think some men are very much more understanding about that sort of thing than others.[79]

By contrast, there were two middle-class respondents who each presented their marriages as having been quite dominated by an equal and shared mutual interest with their partner, in apparent conformity with the 'companionate' ideal. In one case, opera was the focus of the couple's shared passion;[80] and in the other case, it was their sexual relationship with each other.[81] However, equally, there was also a small minority of two working-class respondents who each

[78] Gill msf/kf/bl/#48.

[79] Jane and Dick msf/kf/bl/#32.

[80] Emma msf/kf/ht#37, married 1936. Jane msf/kf/bl/#32 also mentioned that she and her husband, Dick, had shared interests in the local amateur operatic society, but the commitment of Emma and her husband to 'our mutual love of opera' was altogether more obsessive. It extended to spending so much of their joint professional incomes attending Covent Garden on a regular basis that they continued to rent a cramped, two-bedroom flat in Harpenden for 16 years while bringing up three children. Emma was prepared to acknowledge that some 'people thought it was disgraceful'.

[81] Roger msf/kf/ht#10, married 1938.

articulated the view that an ideal married life meant social exclusiveness for the couple concerned:

And what do you think tends to wreck a marriage?

ELIZABETH Well, I think a lot is, a man going out on 'is own, yer know, love? And a woman going out on their – I don't like that; I don't see any point in that, no … I think, if yer married yer should go out together, love, yeah – that's my idea of a married life … [82]

Marian (1908), married in 1939 to a low-paid working-class Blackburnite, with whom she had two children (one of whom died at 12 months), was proud of this ideal of exclusivity of the companionship she had had with her partner in marriage, which she contrasted with the pattern of a wider friendship circle before marriage, but also with the different pattern of her sister in her marriage.

So what was really good about your marriage?

MARIAN We … both talked things over together and we both – we never went out without – he wouldn't go out – we never had no mates; we always went out together and the only time he went out when he went to [the] library – he liked reading; he were a good reader and he liked – he used to go [to the] library for books, but he weren't ever so long before he come back … and if, if he fancied a drink he'd have one in [the] house – he wouldn't go for a drink with hisself in [the] pub …
When you were younger – when you went out with girls … them were your mates. Well, when you got married your husband were your mate. He were both your mate and your partner, but you see … a lot of folk had to have couples to go out with. They couldn't go out on their own two selves (long pause); so it's a – it's a funny way to live is that – to me when you – just you and your husband can't go out together; has to be with somebody else before you can enjoy yourself (long pause). No – and me sister were like that … [83]

But this testimony was unusual among informants of both classes.[84] What most middle-class and working-class respondents said they wanted in relation to their partner and their leisure activities was not exclusiveness but a balance of enjoying some interests and pursuits together – especially those related closely to children and family life – along with some personal freedom and independence:

So what do you think is the most important thing in a happy marriage?

HUGH Give and take …

[…]

[82] Peter and Elizabeth msf/kf/bl/#26. On Elizabeth (1923) and Peter (1921) see text at notes 20, 58 and 66.

[83] Marian msf/kf/bl/#28.

[84] Slater and Woodside found shared interests outside the home were 'considered less important' to the happiness of the marriage by their married informants than 'give and take' and 'pulling together' inside the marriage (Slater and Woodside, *Patterns of Marriage*, 142).

ANGELA We don't like to be apart[...]But I belong to different things and he does, you know. We're not, sort of, not doing anything – we have a good variety of friends and family, of course, yes[...]Having lots of friends, having different interests, not being selfish ... [85]

LYN Mostly we went out together but, um, when he was in different concert parties, he was in some that I wasn't in; he'd go to them. He, er, he would join the choir; that was right, at the church – well, I wasn't in the choir so he'd have one night out a week at the choir practice, you see? There were things like that ... [86]

Indeed, the importance of some balancing individual autonomy and freedom within the marriage relationship was expressed whimsically by Emily (1917), who had married in 1938 and had two children with a man who had then left her for another woman in 1947:

What is it you miss about married life?

EMILY Oh, the companionship.

And what are the advantages of not being married?

Well you can please yourself, huh; yeah (pause) ya haven't to ask.[87]

One of the complaints from a number of female respondents was that they had to do more than 'ask' – they felt their husbands had spoiled their experience of 'sharing' because of a claustrophobic possessiveness, which had been too insistent on exclusive 'togetherness':

MARILYN Well when we went away on holiday I hadn't to speak or be friendly wi' anybody else that were in hotel – he used to say 'Come on' – like he wouldn't bother with anybody else; like he were – he were such a jealous somehow.[88]

It was in relation to sexual jealousy that violence was mentioned by some of the respondents. Alistair reported that when helping out at his wife's corner grocery shop, on three occasions there were women customers 'who've actually tried it on: "can't pay the bill this week; can you have it another way?"' and that when told about this his wife would 'go berserk; she'd lose her rag'. For his part, he had to go to court and was fined for putting the man 'known as the, uh, romantic boy on the street' through his own glass front door after he made a pass at Alistair's wife.[89]

[85] Hugh and Angela msf/kf/ht#18.

[86] Lyn msf/kf/bl/#1, married 1931.

[87] Emily msf/kf/bl/#13.

[88] Marilyn msf/kf/bl#7, married 1940. On Marilyn see text accompanying note 69. Other examples of female respondents complaining of their husbands' excessive jealousy were: Eileen msf/kf/bl/#12; Gill msf/kf/bl/#48; Angela msf/kf/ht/#18; Penny msf/srss/ht/#20. Women were also quite capable of manifesting jealousy at times: for instance Sam's msf/srss/ht/#28 wife; Hubert's msf/kf/ht/#32 wife; and Grace (confessing it of herself) msf/srss/ht/#38.

[89] Alistair msf/kf/bl/#33. However, in only two cases did interviewees recall violence against themselves from partners (Rose's msf/kf/bl/#21 second husband and Hilda's msf/kf/bl/#50 husband, whom she divorced). The theme of domestic violence was much more likely to be recalled by respondents in relation to their parents: Elma msf/jm/bl/#42; Iris msf/kf/bl/#2;

Thus, while respondents talked of aspiring to a sharing relationship with their partner, for several interviewees – both middle- and working-class – this was not necessarily seen as the reality of their married lives. Most women and men in both middle and working classes talked of marriage as ideally something in which the two partners pulled together as a team, but they recognised that this was not easy to achieve and some had not necessarily seen eye to eye with their spouse over how to do this with the practical allocation of their fundamental resources of time and money. The aspiration of sharing was the source of dynamic tension and of difficulties and misunderstandings in marriages, which required skills to manage and diffuse.

The difference in living standards between working-class and middle-class marriages did not mean that the fundamental issues were any different, but the details were. The fact that fewer middle-class female respondents raised the issue of domestic help from their husbands as a concern does not necessarily mean husbands participated more equally but, quite the opposite, that it was an even more unquestioned assumption that husbands did not do such work. Middle-class wives had the financial resources to afford home helps and to have at their disposal the full range of new, domestic household appliances. High-earning middle-class husbands were less likely to see their role as participating in housework since their higher incomes provided their spouses with this supposedly labour-saving equipment.[90] Even within the male sphere of domestic work middle-class men probably did even less round the home because they could afford to pay to have the work, such as decorating and handiwork, done by tradesmen (or they did not have the skills or inclination to do it themselves or saw such manual work as beneath them). For the working classes, therefore, testimonies focus more on the home and enhancing its material comforts, as the locus for spouses' shared activities and interests, while for the middle classes the focus was more on shared leisure pursuits and exclusive cultural activities, such as the tennis club, theatre or opera.

In this generation most women of the middle classes were as dependent financially on their husbands during the childbearing and childrearing years of

Lorna msf/kf/bl/#25; Rose msf/kf/bl/#21; Colin msf/kf/bl/#36; Hilda msf/kf/bl/#50. Unhappy childhoods were also often associated with the memory of unpleasant, sometimes vicious step-parents: Olive msf/jm/bl/#44; Enid msf/kf/bl/#49; Diana msf/jm/bl/#45; Pam msf/kf/ht/#19; Hubert msf/kf/ht/#32; Hugh msf/kf/ht/#18. For a fine study of such domestic problems in the preceding period, see Hammerton, *Cruelty and Companionship*; and for violence against women during this period, see Shani D'Cruze, *Crimes of Outrage: Sex, Violence and Working Women in Victorian and Edwardian England* (London: UCL Press, 1998); and Shani D'Cruze, ed. *Everyday Violence in Britain 1850–1950: Gender and Class* (Harlow: Longman, 2000).

90 Scott, 'Consumption, Consumer Credit', 169–75. On the time-using as well as time-saving aspects of household appliances, see Avner Offer, *The Challenge of Affluence: Self-Control and Well-Being in the United States and Britain since 1950* (Oxford and New York: Oxford University Press, 2006), ch. 8; Ruth Schwartz Cowan, *More Work for Mother* (New York: Basic Books, 1983).

their marriages as were most women of the working classes. However, there was a class difference in opportunities after childrearing. Middle-class women with their secondary educations, especially those interviewed in Hertfordshire with access to the Home Counties service-oriented economy, seem to have had more possibilities to go back to work after their children were grown – and to earn a decent income from respectable, office-based work. Consequently, if confronted with an entirely unsatisfactory spouse, they were more likely to divorce them.[91] Working-class women, like Sarah (1906), on the other hand, were much less likely to consider this a realistic option, since, despite there being opportunities in mill towns such as Blackburn to work after marriage, the factory rates of pay for women were too low to maintain a family household and alternatives were limited:

> *And during that difficult time when you were so short of money and you had all these rows, did you ever consider leaving him?*
>
> SARAH Oh yes, many times! (giggle)Yes, oh yes, yes, (chuckle) many times. Yes. But you didn't (chuckle). You didn't because you'd nowhere to run! You simply couldn't! I couldn't go back to my dad, could I?... No. You just had to grin and bear it. (chuckle)... [Y]ou never thought of divorce; that was only for the upper crusts (chuckle); that wasn't for us... they could afford it; we couldn't...[92]

It was because the health of a loving marriage was perceived to be intimately related to the balanced ecology of reciprocal roles, combining a husband's primary earning contribution and a wife's practical household and child management, that periods of male unemployment (such as the periods of short-time working experienced in Blackburn in the 1920s and 1930s) could be recalled as especially disruptive, not simply of the family's standard of living, but – very revealingly – of the loving relationship itself:

> SARAH we were on three days a week for years; we were on three days a week. I did all my own sewing; all (chuckle) my own everything, and I learned how to manage my money, the hard way, I really did and love nearly went out of the window, because (chuckle) money is really, it's the centre of everything, if you haven't got it...[93]

This was the same respondent (above note 28), whose 'husband's idea [was] if his mother didn't work, I shouldn't work'. The husband's short-time was

[91] Four respondents reported middle-class wives divorcing husbands: Hilda msf/kf/bl/#50 in 1945; Gay msf/kf/ht/#13 in 1966; Judith msf/kf/ht/#33 in 1975; and the first wife of Reg msf/kf/ht/#36 in 1956.

[92] Sarah msf/kf/bl#30. Eileen msf/kf/bl/#12 recalled leaving her husband for her mother's house (her father had died long before) but returning the next day when her husband asked her to come back. Only two working-class respondents did divorce partners: Emily msf/kf/bl/#13 in 1947 and Rose msf/kf/bl/#21 (who was involved as plaintiff or defendant in four divorces in 1958, 1968, 1975 and 1982).

[93] Sarah msf/kf/bl#30, married 1928.

perceived as generating such serious problems, not just in the family's finances, but in the loving relationship. This was because the normal balance of mutual caring and power broke down, with the husband's identity and principal caring role challenged by his inability to provide an adequate flow of money, while the wife continued to struggle with all her caring duties, though with far less money to manage on.

> *Now you say there was a stage at which love went out the window: tell me about that.*
>
> SARAH Well, you know, you never had any money. You never had any money; you never did – you couldn't do anything, and … I had my two children … your money was spoken for before you got it … on three days a week, oh (sigh). And there was no (chuckle), no social … couldn't go there for that, and if you didn't have it in your purse, you didn't have it and you did without. (pause) Yeah. What can I say about it? You had rows – you had rows [over] something and nothing, because you were tensed up all the time … [94]

It would have taken exceptional resources of sympathy and communication between the spouses to cope with this relentless pressure on their living standards and the disruption to their normal roles and identities. Wives like Sarah found that, even with husbands who they felt, overall, were good partners and with whom they could be amicable in their later lives, they were both too tensed up to talk over and share the burdens when they were under such chronic strains:

> SARAH my housekeeping money didn't stretch to what it should – what I wanted it – uh; I just had to do without. And it's awful doing without, you know? When you've not got two ha'pennies to rub together, it really is [awful] … I was irritable, very short-tempered, just a short fuse. And, uh, I couldn't tell him as I hadn't any money. I couldn't, you know? I couldn't have. It was just something – I couldn't approach him about money. (pause) But he was (pause) basically a good man. (pause) (sigh) And a clever chap who should have been better off than he was.
>
> […]
>
> *And why did you think that leaving would help?*
>
> It didn't help; I knew, I knew jolly well it wouldn't help. I had (chuckle) enough sense for that (giggle). I knew it wouldn't help. No, it, uh, (chuckle) it was just – (pause) lack of understanding, lack of communication.
>
> *So you felt that he didn't understand?*
>
> (pause) He didn't – never wanted to talk. He never wanted to talk … and I suppose I didn't help either. But we were quite amicable, in our later years, you know; we, we sort of settled down and, uh, uh, forgot about all those – all the rows that we used (giggle) to have.[95]

For the middle classes, inadequacy of the husband in performing his primary role as income earner could also be a major issue in the marital relationship, as

[94] Sarah msf/kf/bl#30. [95] Sarah msf/kf/bl#30.

it was for Gay (1928), married in 1947 to a highly paid but also highly erratic salesman, with whom she had two children:

GAY there were a lot of rows about money, um. Well I suppose not rows – me complaining about, um …

So what would happen in these rows?

(sighs) He'd borrow from his father (pause) and his father kept a little book – he used to put down all the money he lent him. God … Oh! It was terrible (pause) … Oh dear, it was dreadful, but anyway, I stuck it for eighteen, no seventeen years, and, um, oh dear, he had – if I tell you that he had twenty-three jobs in the eighteen years we were together, um! I never knew from one minute to the next, y'know, if he'd be out of a job or not.[96]

Where a middle-class husband fell down on this primary caring role of income provision, it was equally likely to be interpreted as a failure in the loving relationship by both sides, not simply as a financial inconvenience:

PRU Um, I regretted – now this I shouldn't really be saying I suppose – but I regretted marrying my husband almost before we were on our honeymoon because I found he'd been borrowing money from my relations.[97]

Pru's (1911) husband's lack of probity with money ultimately resulted in suspension from his employment as a bank official. His public fall from grace and loss of social identity as a male breadwinner produced a form of emasculation. A marriage, in which sexual expression had already been a problem for some time, now became a marriage with little or no love because of his complete withdrawal.

And how did the relationship with your husband, as it got worse, how did that affect your sex life with your husband?

PRU No, it completely stopped. We didn't have [it] any more … after all this business – he'd been embezzling his mother's money.

So, was it your decision to stop, or was it his, or was it mutual?

I don't know. I didn't have the chance. He was a person that used to – if he was in trouble he'd go to bed. He was a bit odd like that.

And what about many years after this scandal with his mother's money? Did your sex life resume again or did it stop then forever?

Stopped all together … I tried, I tried to be pleasant and that but he didn't give me the chance – he was just as – because don't forget, you see he was in an awkward position; he was suspended from the bank.

And what about years after that, when the children had left home and things like that, did things change?

Um, no, I don't think there was any change.[98]

96 Gay msf/kf/ht/#13, married 1947. 97 Pru msf/kf/ht/#12, married 1935.

98 Pru msf/kf/ht/#12. See below, p. 317, on Pru's distaste for sex earlier in the marriage due to his drinking, but which she continued with out of duty.

In both working-class Sarah's and middle-class Pru's marriages it was the sense that they and their husbands had failed to share the burden of their predicament which was an upsetting aspect of the memory of the difficulties in the relationship. In one case, 'he wouldn't talk' and 'left it to me' and in the other, 'he just went to bed'.

Conclusion

Thus, the oral testimony shows how absorbingly difficult middle-class as well as working-class respondents found it to achieve their aspirations for a loving marriage as one of emotional sharing while combining to work effectively together as a partnership with strongly gendered caring roles. As Stephen Brooke has shown, middle-class proponents of the companionate marriage model and investigators of working-class marriages often patronisingly portrayed working-class marriages and associated sexual relationships as deficient in this respect during the interwar decades and as modernising and improving with the arrival of affluence in the 1950s.[99] The oral history evidence indicates that the companionate model was never such a clear class discriminator of behaviour, nor were its ideals clearly endorsed by any of the respondents of either class. Genuinely egalitarian sharing was not in fact an explicit aim of any of the individuals interviewed. All accepted that husbands and wives performed quite distinct roles and neither side found it easy to concede ground and to have their own gendered area of authority and control diminished. Nevertheless many respondents, of both classes, portrayed marriages in which emotionally fulfilling sharing took place, effectively negotiated on the basis of expectations of strongly polarised caring roles, according to gender.

Caring for each other quite definitely carried two meanings simultaneously. Individuals cared for their partners and families with their breadwinning and their home-making but it was also important in a loving marriage that these gendered activities were interpreted as signifying their caring for each other in the emotional sense. When husbands just brought in the weekly wage and promptly disappeared down the pub or just left their wives to it in times of difficulty, this was not caring in that second, emotional sense. Respondents principally used the term 'sharing' to talk about the importance of this second aspect of caring and of love in marriage. It was important to most interviewees that caring for each other in reciprocal and complementary ways was combined with a sense of sharing, while carefully respecting the other partner's domain of authority. With such an understanding maintained, trust in each other and a capacity for generosity, give and take could all grow. These were the widely

[99] Brooke, 'Bodies, Sexuality and the "Modernization" of the British Working Classes'.

desired characteristics of love in marriage which respondents valued. Good, loving, working marriages involved maintaining a delicate balance in combining caring with sharing. As has been seen, perceived disruption to this balance could upset the sexual relationship. As the following chapter will show, the practical problems of effective use of birth control could be a particularly delicate matter in this respect and were central to the way in which 'love' – that balance of caring and sharing – was experienced by many informants in their sexual relationship.

Part III

Exploring sex and love in marriage

6 Birth control, sex and abstinence

The dramatic reduction in average family size from the late nineteenth century through to the mid-twentieth century has dominated historical and demographic study of marital relationships during this period.[1] At this time, not only did family sizes fall and the small family norm embed itself (permanently) in British culture, but so, too, did public discussion of contraception: birth control clinics were set up, the birth rate was discussed, sex and marriage manuals provided information about methods, technology changed (condoms altered, a range of female caps and diaphragms were produced), and general availability improved significantly.[2] Nevertheless among social and demographic historians recent research has increasingly emphasised the continuation of 'traditional' methods of contraception alongside the newer appliances during the course of the fertility decline.[3] Despite the increased use of 'appliance' or barrier methods, such as condoms and a range of female devices during the first half of the twentieth century, many also continued to turn to withdrawal, abortion and forms of abstinence from sexual intercourse. In previous publications we have examined the oral history evidence paying particular attention

[1] Banks, *Prosperity and Parenthood*, Gittins, *Fair Sex*, Roberts, *A Woman's Place*, David Levine, *Reproducing Families: The Political Economy of English Population History* (Cambridge: Cambridge University Press, 1987), Wally Seccombe, *Weathering the Storm: Working-Class Families from the Industrial Revolution to the Fertility Decline* (London: Verso, 1995), Roberts, *Women and Families*, Davidoff et al., *The Family Story*.

[2] Fryer, *The Birth Controllers*, Wood and Suitters, *The Fight for Acceptance*, Leathard, *The Fight for Family Planning*, Davey, 'Birth Control in Britain', Jane Lewis, 'The Ideology and Politics of Birth Control in Inter-War England', *Women's Studies International Quarterly* 2, no. 1 (1979): 33–48, Angus McLaren, *A History of Contraception: From Antiquity to the Present Day* (Oxford and Cambridge, MA: B. Blackwell, 1990), Porter and Hall, *The Facts of Life*, Part II, Lesley Hoggart, 'The Campaign for Birth Control in Britain in the 1920s', in *Gender, Health and Welfare*, eds. Anne Digby and John Stewart (London and New York: Routledge, 1998), 143–66, Cook, *The Long Sexual Revolution*, Part II, Hera Cook, 'The English Sexual Revolution: Technology and Social Change', *History Workshop Journal* 59, no. 1 (2005): 109–28.

[3] Roberts, *A Woman's Place*, 93–100, Brookes, *Abortion in England*, Gigi Santow, 'Coitus Interruptus in the Twentieth Century', *Population and Development Review* 19, no. 4 (1993): 767–92, Szreter, *Fertility, Class, and Gender*, ch. 8, Cook, *The Long Sexual Revolution*, Fisher, *Birth Control, Sex and Marriage*.

to withdrawal and to abortion.[4] This chapter makes use of this unique set of personal accounts of marital intimacy to explore the relationship between birth control practices and abstinence.[5] This involves considering the differences in attitudes among the interviewees to various methods of birth control and how contraceptive use was negotiated between couples in relation to ideas of love and their sexual relationship. In particular, we will explore reported variability in contraceptive practices and coital frequency and the links drawn by respondents of all classes between levels of sexual activity and periods of stress, marital conflict or contraceptive anxiety in their marital relationship.

Respondents give accounts of diverse contexts during their marriages in which they described various forms of sexual abstinence related to birth control. While forms of partial, temporary and sometimes permanent abstinence were reported by both working-class and middle-class interviewees there were also marked class differences in the reported reasons for such abstinent behaviour. As was shown in Chapter 2 many middle-class female respondents had rather different attitudes from working-class women towards the propriety of acquiring reproductive and sexual knowledge before marriage. This was shown in Chapter 3 to result in distinct patterns of sexual behaviour in courtship. It also resulted in different assumptions about the gendered control of contraception among young couples when they commenced marriage. Among the working-class informants there was a virtual unanimity that birth control was something which husbands provided for their wives throughout the marriage and was not a matter which they wanted to discuss between them. On the other hand, many middle-class respondents of both sexes said that when they got married they saw birth control methods more as a matter of choice and deliberation between the two partners.

There were, of course, a range of both male and female possible methods of contraception which could be used during this period. Although the oral contraceptive pill was not relevant for most of the women interviewed, as all but a few of the youngest informants were past childbearing by the early 1960s, female methods of varying degrees of efficacy were available, ranging from the cap and

[4] Kate Fisher, 'Women's Experiences of Abortion before the 1967 Act', in *Abortion Law and Politics Today*, ed. Ellie Lee (Basingstoke: Macmillan Press, 1998), 27–42, Kate Fisher, '"Didn't Stop to Think I Just Didn't Want Another One": The Culture of Abortion in Interwar South Wales', in *Sexual Cultures in Europe: Themes in Sexuality*, eds. Franz Eder, Lesley A. Hall and Gert Hekma (Manchester: Manchester University Press, 1999), 213–32, Kate Fisher and Simon Szreter, '"They Prefer Withdrawal": The Choice of Birth Control in Britain, 1918–1950', *Journal of Interdisciplinary History* 34, no. 2 (2003): 263–91, Fisher, *Birth Control, Sex and Marriage*.

[5] For an important recent study of a wide range of late Victorian, early and mid-twentieth-century medical, literary and psychological texts, which examines ideologies of male self-restraint, abstinence and continence in relation to changing ideas of masculine sexual adequacy, see McLaren, *Impotence*, chs. 5–7.

diaphragm to spermicidal pessaries, sponges and douching. There was also the possibility of various forms of self-induced abortifacient practices and drugs or procured procedures; and there was abstinence. The main male methods were either withdrawal or wearing condoms ('French Letters').[6] Condoms were a very variable product during the decades from the 1920s until the early 1960s, ranging from thick, reusables through to thin, latex throwaways, first available in the 1930s (but not in pre-lubricated form until the 1950s).[7] Abstinence was also the other ever-present alternative contraceptive possibility for men, as for women. As this chapter will show, class differences in assumptions about gendered control over contraception resulted not only in different patterns of contraceptive practice but also distinct forms of abstinence associated with these differing forms of birth control. Interviewees' understandings of sex as part of expressing love in their marriages, through combining caring with sharing, is also shown to have influenced their attitudes towards abstinence in varying contexts.

Almost all interviewees used some form of birth control to regulate their family size. Overall 58 per cent used withdrawal and 58 per cent used condoms, 10 per cent used female pessaries, 17 per cent female caps or diaphragms and 16 per cent tried to abort. Additionally about half (46%) mentioned periods of abstinence. That these percentages add to over 200 per cent reflects the fact that very many individuals recalled use of more than one method at different points in their marriages (or, indeed, at the same time): partly dissatisfaction with one method led to swapping and switching; partly changing motivation to avoid pregnancy led individuals to adopt methods seen as more reliable; while a number continued to use various methods as the mood took them.

As well as variation within each marriage, there were also systematic differences in methods typically used during the course of a marriage in Hertfordshire and in Blackburn and also between social classes as depicted graphically in Figures 5 and 6 of Appendix A. Withdrawal was clearly the predominant method used by Blackburn's working-class respondents; but among the Hertfordshire working-class interviewees, it was the other male

[6] Respondents occasionally mentioned manual stimulation but not as a systematic, mutual contraceptive practice. It was only usually mentioned in association with coitus interruptus and in relation to male sexual needs – see, for instance, Doreen msf/kf/bl/#20, referring to giving her husband 'help' – note 60 below. Not surprisingly, given many respondents' views about the importance of cleanliness in relation to sex (see next chapter, especially the discussion in the final section on attitudes to oral sex), anal sex was rarely mentioned and never presented as a regular or a contraceptive practice. Only Gay msf/kf/ht/#13 acknowledged having permitted it (just once with a lover in the 1960s, not with her by-then-divorced husband), while Rose msf/kf/bl/#21 reported it as something unwanted done to her when drunk by her abusive second husband. There is no support in the oral history evidence we collected for the claim by Eustace Chesser that as many as 15 per cent of married couples among his patients in the interwar period practised anal sex, not for pleasure but as a form of contraception (Eustace Chesser, *Sexual Behaviour, Normal and Abnormal* (London: Medical Publications Ltd, 1949), 183).

[7] Cook, *The Long Sexual Revolution* 137–9.

method – condoms – which played the more major role.[8] Among the middle-class informants in Hertfordshire there was very considerable use of female methods, rather less among the northern middle-class interviewees and less still among the working-class respondents in either north or south. Reportage of preparedness to countenance abortion was also most likely among southern middle-class interviewees. Finally, in both Hertfordshire and Blackburn, among both the middle classes and the working classes forms of abstinence were generally important, though for very different reasons as will be examined in the course of this chapter, which will address these systematic class and regional differences in contraceptive methods through the novel perspective of a focus on abstinence. Abstinence has often been considered an alternative to or antithesis of the use of contraception but the oral history evidence demonstrates how pervasive and diverse was the experience of abstinence and the practices of reduced coital frequency and how integral this was for many respondents both to their birth control needs and practices and to the experience of sex and love in marriage.

If abstinence is defined rigidly, as by the Royal Commission on Population of 1944–9, as complete avoidance of sexual intercourse on a permanent basis and lasting for a period of at least six months,[9] the number of respondents in Blackburn and Harpenden definitely recalling such abstinence in the fertile period of their marriages would be somewhat under one in ten.[10] But much more important than these cases of absolute abstinence is the evidence, which will be discussed in detail in this chapter, that many respondents gave of various forms of partial and more temporary abstinence or reduced coital frequency. This occurred in testimony relating to almost half (46%) of the marriages.[11]

[8] For an earlier interpretation of the reasons for the popularity of withdrawal among the Blackburn working-class respondents, only, see Fisher and Szreter, 'They Prefer Withdrawal'; and for an extended analysis, including the birth control practices of working-class respondents interviewed by Kate Fisher in South Wales and Oxford, which also found a predominance of withdrawal in these two communities, see Fisher, *Birth Control, Sex and Marriage*.

[9] On the shortcomings of this investigation's methodology and its questioning procedure in relation to partial abstinence, see C. M. Langford, 'Birth Control Practice in Great Britain: A Review of the Evidence from Cross-Sectional Surveys', in Mike Murphy and John Hobcraft, eds. *Population Research in Britain*, Special Supplement to *Population Studies* 45, no. 1 (1991): 49–68, Szreter, *Fertility, Class, and Gender*, 398–405, Fisher, *Birth Control, Sex and Marriage*, 111–13.

[10] Terence msf/srss/bl/#15; Hubert msf/kf/ht/#32; Bernard and Diana msf/jm/bl/#45; Penny msf/srss/ht/#20 (temporarily after birth of third daughter); Eva msf/kf/bl/#9; Eleanor msf/kf/bl/#11. That is six marriages out of a total of seventy-one for which detailed birth control information was given (see next footnote).

[11] There are a total of seventy-one marriages represented in the transcripts, where the respondents talked in detail about their birth control practices. In as many as thirty-three of these seventy-one marriages (46%), they mention one of the forms of abstinence discussed here. The oral history interviews with eighty-eight married individuals relate to a total of eighty-three different marriages (because some individuals were interviewed as couples representing the same marriage): forty-eight from Blackburn and thirty-five from Harpenden. Only seventy-one of these

Additionally, in a number of other marriages coital frequency was reported to have reduced significantly after menopause but these cases are not counted here among the 46 per cent relating to birth control, though they do attest to the wider general prevalence and variety of forms of perceived abstinence in marriage at this time. Nor of course was regular abstention during the menstrual period counted here as birth control-related 'abstinence', although it is clear that some women certainly feigned menstruation in order to excuse themselves from sex, as Doreen, cited below, owned up to doing.[12] Abstinence was presented as occurring for a range of reasons relating in one way or another to the desire not to risk a pregnancy and, interestingly, there was no pronounced class difference in the general prevalence of the overall incidence of reported partial and temporary abstinence.[13] Not uncommonly respondents mentioned a reduced frequency combined with the use of some other contraceptive method, such as withdrawal.

Defining, counting or assessing abstinence is conceptually fraught. As Harry Cocks explores in his review of Hera Cook's book – which argues that for many men and women during the first half of the twentieth century, 'abstinence' was a positive response to the range of available birth control methods which chimed with women's attitudes towards sex and pregnancy – it is problematic to make 'a priori decisions about "normal" rates of coitus based on present notions of what that is. The past appears "repressed" to us perhaps, but for those in the past, how much sex was enough, or too much? Would this question even make sense … ?'[14] Moreover, we do not really know what 'normal' sexual

eighty-three marriages are counted in here because in twelve cases the respondents gave no detailed information on the kinds of birth control used. In four cases this was because the known sub-fertility of the marriage precluded the respondent making any relevant statements: Alistair msf/kf/bl/#33; Phyllis msf/kf/bl/#5; Mildred msf/kf/bl/#41; Dennis msf/kf/ht/#15. The other eight cases of absent information, several simply because of reticence or professed ignorance, were: Hilda msf/kf/bl/#50 (second marriage); Rebecca msf/kf/ht/#6; Clare msf/kf/ht/#8 (two marriages); Monica msf/kf/ht/#11; Maud msf/kf/bl/#18; Rose msf/kf/bl/#21; Enid msf/kf/bl/#49.

12 'I put sanitary pads on to tell him I was, I was like that when I wasn't', Doreen msf/kf/bl/#20 (note 60). For similar examples see, Sutton, *We Didn't Know Aught*, 27–8.

13 Among the Blackburn working class: Lyn msf/kf/bl/#1; Olive msf/jm/bl/#44; Colin msf/kf/bl/#36; Terence msf/srss/bl/#15; Sarah msf/kf/bl/#30; Lorna msf/kf/bl/#25; Eleanor msf/kf/bl/#11; Frank msf/srss/bl/#16; Glynnis msf/kf/bl/#4; Marilyn msf/kf/bl/#7; Arthur msf/srss/bl/#24; Doreen and Larry msf/kf/bl/#20; Jake and Dorris msf/srss/bl/#22; Peter msf/kf/bl/#26 (second marriage); Sally msf/kf/bl/#31; Eva msf/kf/bl/#9; Molly msf/srss/bl/#17; Christopher msf/kf/bl/#34; Daphne msf/jm/bl/#38; among the Blackburn middle class: Bernard and Diana msf/jm/bl/#45; Hilda msf/kf/bl/#50 (first marriage); Felicity msf/kf/bl/#37; among the Hertfordshire working class: Penny msf/srss/ht/#20; Edmund msf/kf/ht/#23; Bryan msf/kf/ht/#25; Vera msf/kf/ht/#34; and finally among the Hertfordshire middle class: Gerald and Esme msf/kf/ht/#9; Pru msf/kf/ht/#12; Antonia msf/kf/ht/#35; Hubert msf/kf/ht/#32; Sam msf/srss/ht/28; Humphrey msf/kf/ht/#26; William msf/kf/ht/#24.

14 Harry G. Cocks, Review of Hera Cook, *The Long Sexual Revolution: English Women, Sex and Contraception, 1800–1975* (December 2005), available from www.h-net.org/reviews/showrev.cgi?path=164411141759612 (accessed 15 April 2010).

frequency was for any period during the twentieth or twenty-first century, and have no potential benchmark against which to assess coital frequency or patterns of 'abstinence'.[15]

Asking respondents whether or not sex was avoided in order to reduce the chance of pregnancy produced a range of oblique and indeterminate answers; in general the majority did not claim to have deliberately and systematically avoided sex in order to reduce the chance of pregnancy. However, on the other hand, a considerable number of interviewees pointed out that they thought their sexual frequency was relatively low and some linked periods during which their ardour waned with fertility issues (the effect of contraception on sexual pleasure; anxiety about the burdens of a large family; health worries about pregnancy, and so on). The oral history testimony uncovers many of these kinds of complex versions of abstinence, where narratives of low sexual frequency and modified sexual desire combined with discussion of the pressure to use birth control and ambiguous responses to methods of contraception.

Lorna (1917) was typical of this: her version of abstinence linked low sexual frequency to the pressures of working hard while bringing up children. Her husband was a valve tester at Mullards factory in Blackburn, whose childhood rheumatic fever excused him from military service. They had married in 1939 and she worked as a busy weaver throughout the period they brought up her two children, born in 1942 and 1945. In this extract Lorna distinguishes between the importance of sex in a loving marriage when young, and how other things take its place later – looking after children together, working and bringing in money – and a notion that a different form of sexual love emerges: one focused on spontaneity and which is sensitive to tiredness and other burdens. She emphasises how her marriage was a loving one because sex *was not* performed regularly, to order, as part of a husband's 'conjugal rights'. She sees her marriage as a loving relationship in which sex was spontaneous but flexible and took account of her and of the other pressures she was under, her need to sleep after work and look after children. This is a testimony about the role of sex in the caring and sharing balance required in a loving marriage, and the way in which a considerate and moderate form of male sexuality was appreciated as expressing that love in 'caring for' a wife, not only in the act of sharing sex together but also in the circumstances in which sex occurred:

LORNA Well, when you were younger it's [sex] part of a loving life but as I say – two children, we're both working, plenty housework, go out to work all day, come home manage children and meals so ... you get – you were tired at night. And then you see when the war came it was shift work ... as I said I had six looms and coming home, running a home – I were tired. So really it just were one of them things

[15] Vaughn Call, Susan Sprecher and Pepper Schwartz, 'The Incidence and Frequency of Marital Sex in a National Sample', *Journal of Marriage and the Family* 57, no. 3 (1995): 639–52.

that wasn't essential ... It wasn't a thing as either of us were in, in, indulged in, you know? As I said it was spontaneous ...

During that time how many times a week or a month would you be having sex?

Well, it wasn't every day, every night, you know; um, if it were once a week it would probably be a picnic, you know? But, um, it wasn't ... Maybe when we were first married, you know, but when Terence were born ... He never bothered all that much and then after Carol – as I said as Dr Howarth said, 'no more babies'. So that were when he were extra special careful and it was less.

So did you reduce the amount of sex in order to reduce the chance of pregnancy?

Well, we really weren't interested in it all that much. We had ... he was five years older than I was but – as I said men are stimulated more than women even till we're about 90 – but, um, no he respected me really and he knew my fears so he controlled his – and he was a controlled man.[16]

After motivation to avoid pregnancy increased, following a doctor's warning, a version of 'abstinence' was described, in which the practice of withdrawal (for which the common term was 'being careful') and abstinence were intimately linked. Even before the doctor's health warning, with their busy, hard-working lives Lorna's husband 'never bothered all that much' and after the second, difficult birth, 'we really weren't interested in it all that much' because although she is clear that her husband, like all men, still had his sex drive, he respected her fears and was a controlled man, so that when sex did occasionally occur, he was 'extra special careful'. 'Abstinence' was thus conceptualised and presented by interviewees as a natural, spontaneous and temporally specific response to the pressure and challenges of their busy lives, not something that was deliberate, explicit or worked out. It was a response that was indicative of the strength of the loving relationship, in which both partners were sensitive to each other's feelings and desires.

In a little under one-half (thirteen) of the thirty-three cases in which some form of abstinence was recounted, the degree of abstinence practised was represented, as here, as being by mutual agreement of the two partners.[17] In almost exactly one-half of cases (sixteen) it was portrayed as something primarily imposed or proposed unilaterally by the wife.[18] In the remaining four cases it was the husband who was presented as the principal instigator.[19]

16 Lorna msf/kf/bl/#25, married 1939.

17 Lyn msf/kf/bl/#1; Olive msf/jm/bl/#44; Colin msf/kf/bl/#36; Terence msf/srss/bl/#15; Sarah msf/kf/bl#30; Lorna msf/kf/bl/#25; Eleanor msf/kf/bl/#11; Frank msf/srss/bl/#16; Bernard and Diana msf/jm/bl/#45; Penny msf/srss/ht/#20; Edmund msf/kf/ht/#23; Esme and Gerald msf/kf/ht/#9; Daphne msf/jm/bl/#38.

18 Glynnis msf/kf/bl/#4; Marilyn msf/kf/bl/#7; Sally msf/kf/bl/#31; Eva msf/kf/bl/#9; Arthur msf/srss/bl/#24; Larry and Doreen msf/kf/bl/#20; Jake and Dorris msf/srss/bl/#22; Peter msf/kf/bl/#26 (second marriage); Hilda msf/kf/bl/#50; Pru msf/kf/ht/#12; Antonia msf/kf/ht/#35; Hubert msf/kf/ht/#32; Sam msf/srss/ht/28; Humphrey msf/kf/ht/#26; Vera msf/kf/ht/#34; William msf/kf/ht/#24.

19 Molly msf/srss/bl/#17; Christopher msf/kf/bl/#34; Bryan msf/kf/ht/#25; Felicity msf/kf/bl/#37.

Several interviewees, like Lorna, stated that abstinence was adopted following a difficult confinement, often accompanied by medical advice that a further pregnancy would be unadvisable. Indeed, this was a consideration in about one-fifth of the marriages where it was reported that abstinence was adopted – abstinence was typically part of the response of couples in those cases to an urgent medical warning.[20] In four cases abstinence was practised according to the rhythm method because at least one of the partners was a strict Catholic. These have been counted as marriages characterised by abstinence because its practitioners understood that this is what the method required. Daphne (1912) and her husband were both raised as Catholics and ran a confectioner's bakery together. They had two children, the first born in 1939 two years after they were married, and another in 1947.

DAPHNE I don't think either of us wanted another child after Anne was born ... There was certain times ... when you don't conceive ... just before you start your first – your next period ... so many days before hand. I couldn't really say definitely now 'cos he used to work it out and ... we'd both read the book and agreed on what it said ... during that period you didn't have sex you just abstained ... That was the only way that you could make sure of not getting pregnant.[21]

'You made sure you didn't have the full intercourse'

Contraceptive cultures varied significantly between each of the four social groups: northern and southern, middle and working class. Either of the two male methods of withdrawal or condoms were reported as their initial choice

[20] This was reported in just over 10 per cent (8) of marriages: Lyn msf/kf/61/#1 (see below note 52); Lorna msf/kf/bl/#25 (see above); Eleanor msf/kf/bl/#11; Molly msf/srss/bl/#17 between her first and second birth; Frank msf/srss/bl/#16 (see below); Penny msf/srss/ht/#20 (see below note 63); Gerald and Esme msf/kf/ht/#9 (see below); and Humphrey's wife msf/kf/ht/#26 (see below). (In addition Iris msf/kf/bl/#2 was sterilised after a third birth by caesarean at age 35 on medical advice because of the dangers to her of a further pregnancy; as was Molly msf/srss/bl/#17 after her second birth; Heather msf/kf/ht/#14 probably also had an operation to prevent conception.) While it might be argued that these cases of 'medical necessity' should not be counted as birth controlling abstinence, it should be pointed out that others, faced with the same threat of a medical need to avoid a further conception, chose, instead of abstinence, a more secure method of contraception, for instance 'doubling up' and using two methods together: Hugh and Angela msf/kf/ht/#18 used cap and condom together; Ed msf/srss/bl/#23 switched to the cap after a third child. There was, therefore, a possible contraceptive alternative in these circumstances of 'medical necessity', which those electing for abstinence could have taken but did not.

[21] Daphne msf/jm/bl/#38; also William msf/kf/ht/#24, who presented the rhythm method as having been imposed on him by his Catholic wife (he was an Anglican). Vera msf/kf/ht/#34 was a Catholic born in Ireland who married relatively late at 32 years old. She said she was against using condoms and so she and her husband attempted to use the rhythm method. However, she had a 'slip up' with it rather quickly after having twins and thereafter they practised withdrawal as well as rhythm; the fourth was Felicity msf/kf/bl/#37, married to a Catholic.

by most working-class respondents. However, in many marriages several methods, as well as abstinence, were used interchangeably or sequentially for a variety of changing reasons.

Among the working-class respondents, particularly those interviewed in Blackburn, all forms of barrier methods were less frequently used than among the middle-class respondents. In part, this was because of the relative absence of formal sexual knowledge among the working classes, but it also reflected the difficulties husband and wife had in discussing sexual matters, which extended to deliberation over birth control strategies. A further contributory factor, as we have shown elsewhere, was that withdrawal, though not without its own risks and difficulties, was perceived to be more 'natural' and spontaneous, so that many of those who experimented with condoms or caps either rejected them outright in favour of withdrawal or only used them from time to time alongside withdrawal.[22] A considerable number of Blackburn working-class interviewees (five) claimed to have used condoms at least once, but only for a very short period, having then rejected them in favour of the practice of withdrawal.[23] Additionally, seven others started to use condoms but said they also continued to practise withdrawal at times, as well.[24] Although there were rather fewer reports of outright rejection of condoms after trying them from Hertfordshire working-class respondents, this was the case among some, such as Agatha (1910), married to a gardener in a stately home, and Grace (1922), married to a part-owner of a small motor car business:

And you said sometimes you used French Letters?

AGATHA Yes.

And sometimes he withdrew?

AGATHA Yes.[25]

When you said that you were practising contraception with condoms, a[nd got] pregnant twice in fact... did that mean that you then changed method? What did you change to?

GRACE Withdrawal.

And, so how many years were you practising with condoms and then withdrawal?

GRACE Not very many [years] because it wasn't satisfactory for Colin.

What, which wasn't?

GRACE The condoms.

They weren't satisfactory?

GRACE Well neither – neither was really.[26]

22 See Fisher and Szreter, 'They Prefer Withdrawal', Fisher, *Birth Control, Sex and Marriage*.

23 Once only: Merlin msf/kf/bl/#35; Lucy msf/kf/bl/#10; Doreen and Larry msf/kf/bl/#20; for a short period: Eleanor msf/kf/bl/#11; Frank msf/srss/bl/#16.

24 Sarah msf/kf/bl/#30; Iris msf/kf/bl/#2; Marilyn msf/kf/bl/#7; Emily msf/kf/bl/#13; Ed msf/srss/bl/#23; Terence msf/srss/bl/#15; Christopher msf/kf/bl/#34.

25 Agatha msf/kf/ht/#7, married 1940.

26 Grace msf/srss/ht/#38, married 1944.

As detailed in a previous publication, working-class respondents invariably presented birth control as something women usually relied on men to provide, and the evidence for working-class men from Blackburn shows that they generally chose withdrawal.[27] A working-class husband, such as Eileen's (both were born in Blackburn in 1913, they married in 1943, and had one child in 1944), who worked in a factory, was expected to 'provide' this form of contraception for his 'innocent' wife:

And you said you were careful. What does that mean?

EILEEN Well I don't know – you're, we were really too scared to have any more really; we didn't want any more.

So how did you make sure you didn't have any more?

Well you don't go all the way; that's what they say in't it; so I don't know really.

And how did you find out about that?

Well I suppose he knew all that, knew more than me 'cos he were older than me, you know. I'm a, er, bit innocent on that part.[28]

Jennie (1908), a life-long Blackburnite, worked in a spinning mill before she married a sawmill factory worker a year older than herself in 1930, the same year her one child was born.

JENNIE We didn't use, er, what they use today; we didn't use them. You just had to rely on them being, er, being good ... he would be careful ... the men knew what to do, didn't need telling.[29]

Sally (1908), daughter of an engineering fitter, was also a working-class Blackburnite and married to a man a year older. Her testimony demonstrates how this convention of relying on the husband and his typical choice of withdrawal extended across the spectrum of working-class cultures in Blackburn. Her husband was from the upper working classes, having taken over his father's small business (a painting and decorating firm) several years before their marriage in 1934. Their one child was born in 1945 after an initial miscarriage. Sally portrayed herself as very much involved in decisions to delay having a baby at the beginning of the marriage:

SALLY I didn't want to be married and have a baby. And then we couldn't have one for five years – we'd been married five years and we'd decided to go in for a child and we didn't get one for another five years.

But when it came to birth control methods, she was entirely in her husband's hands. Indeed his care for her in practising withdrawal was something she much appreciated:

[27] Kate Fisher, '"She Was Quite Satisfied with the Arrangements I Made": Gender and Birth Control in Britain, 1920–1950', *Past & Present* 169, no. 1 (2001): 161–93, Fisher and Szreter, 'They Prefer Withdrawal', Fisher, *Birth Control, Sex and Marriage*.

[28] Eileen msf/kf/bl/#12, married 1943.

[29] Jennie msf/kf/bl/#27, married 1930.

So did he sometimes not manage to get off at Mill Hill?
SALLY No. No, he was very careful. He was very good; he was very patient.
So would you say that every time you had sex he would get off at Mill Hill?
Um, always.[30]

Mill Hill was the last suburban stop before the central station on the railway line into Blackburn. The metaphor of getting off at the penultimate stop on the line was a widely used local working-class idiom to refer to the practice of withdrawal, as other researchers have found.[31]

By contrast, working-class respondents interviewed in Hertfordshire were much more likely to recall the use of condoms by husbands. But, while their methods were more varied, they certainly shared in common with working-class interviewees in Blackburn their portrayal of wives as too innocent and shy to be taking the initiative where contraception was concerned. Dora (1923) and Joe married in 1945 and had two children. He was a car mechanic. She was religiously active and had attended a mission throughout her youth in Bethnal Green.

Did you use contraception at any point? Did you need to use birth control?
DORA (overlapping) I think Joe did because I didn't want to (pause) …[32]

Our evidence suggests that part of the explanation for the finding that both middle-class and working-class men in Hertfordshire were much more likely to try to use condoms and rely less upon withdrawal than men in Blackburn may be due to variation in the availability of various types of condoms between the metropolitan south and the rest of the country from the 1930s through to the 1950s. Hera Cook notes that thin, latex condoms were first manufactured in the USA from 1929 but available in Britain only as American imports from the beginning of the 1930s.[33] The oral testimony suggests that the imported condoms may have been more accessible earlier to those living in London and the Home Counties, perhaps until their army issue in the Second World War made them more widely familiar (though not necessarily any more acceptable for use

[30] Sally msf/kf/bl#31, married 1934.
[31] See, for instance, Williamson, 'Getting Off at Loftus'. Indeed, among the Blackburn interviewees discussion of withdrawal encompassed the further refinement of making a distinction between 'Mill Hill' and the next station further out from the centre, 'Cherry Tree'. Peter and Elizabeth in a joint interview laughingly explained how, according to local lore, 'if he climaxes at Cherry Tree [instead of waiting till Mill Hill] he's a long way off' and 'he's jumping the gun too soon'. It's significant that the terms of this extended metaphor were familiar to both interviewees, since they would not have practised withdrawal together as a couple because they had only got married in 1998. Elsewhere in the interview both independently discussed using withdrawal in their respective earlier marriages. Peter's first wife died in 1946, leaving him with one child. He remarried in 1948 and had two further children in 1948 and 1951 with his second wife, who died in 1996. Elizabeth had been married to her first husband from 1947 until he died in 1991 and they had had one child in 1948.
[32] Dora (1923) msf/srss/ht/#38. [33] Cook, *The Long Sexual Revolution*, 137.

within marriage given this context of their dissemination in the armed services from 1942, principally as protection against venereal diseases, the dangers of which were also advertised on posters in public toilets put up at this time throughout Britain).[34] In fact, it was not until the marketing of pre-lubricated latex condoms from the late 1950s that their usage rapidly increased nationally, though still not capturing half of the market until 1963, according to a *Which* Report of that year.[35] This was just at the point when all but the youngest of the interviewees were completing their childbearing years.

The Nottingham-based network of chemists, founded by the Methodist Jesse Boot, whose branches were particularly dominant in the north and midlands, prohibited the sale of condoms (they would only sell contraceptive pessaries) until the 1960s. Anderson and Berridge's oral history research has shown that '[m]any independent pharmacists followed Boots' example ... Those chemists which did supply them [condoms] did so very discreetly ... much of this business was lost to the local barber shops'; furthermore, where they were sold in chemists, they were kept out of sight of the junior staff, just as they were secretly kept in parents' drawers at home.[36] Frank (1919) claimed that condoms were not generally on sale in Blackburn, but only discreetly available in men's barber's shops.[37]

FRANK Well, you see condoms, aye, but they weren't on sale like they are here. Now you know ... the favourite place to get 'em funnily enough was the barber's shop ... you go round to barber's – you know smart like, for, for going out at Saturday. And

[34] Hall, *Sex, Gender and Social Change*, 133–5.

[35] Cook, *The Long Sexual Revolution*, 139. Thus, nowhere near enough condoms were sold in the era before the Second World War to account for more than a minority usage within the population. Peel found that the single largest domestic manufacturer of latex sheaths, the London Rubber Company, was only producing 2 million per annum during the mid-1930s. Even if we multiply this ten-fold, as a maximum possible estimate of the total number available on the market in Britain each year in the late 1930s, it still falls far, far short of the over 100 million sold each year in Britain required to meet national demand in the early 1960s, the point at which the widespread general usage of the new, pre-lubricated condoms represented about half the market for contraceptives. See John Peel, 'The Manufacture and Retailing of Contraceptives in England', *Population Studies* (1963): 113–25, esp. 22.

[36] Stuart Anderson and Virginia Berridge, 'The Role of the Community Pharmacist in Health and Welfare, 1911–1986', ch. 2, in *Oral History, Health and Welfare*, eds. Joanna Bornat, Robert Perks, Paul Thompson and Jan Walmsley (London: Routledge, 2000), 66: an interviewee working as an apprentice chemist in Portsmouth in 1939 recalled of condoms, 'Only the pharmacists sold them ... In fact I wasn't shown where the Durex was kept. They were in a drawer ... but I discovered those on my own. That was rather like the whole conception of birth and everything between parents and their children.' Compare with the recollections of June msf/kf/ht/#27, Chapter 2, note 112.

[37] Similarly, Maureen Sutton reported a Lincoln chemist recalling that 'The sheath or French Letter was sold in the 1930s and 1940s with discretion. We weren't allowed to advertise or display them.' Sutton also argues that the thicker reusable sheaths served the function of reducing male embarrassment in having to make repeated requests to purchase the disposable ones (Sutton, *We Didn't Know Aught*, 88–9).

when he'd cut your hair he'd just bend down like and he'd say, er, 'Anything for the weekend, sir?' You know? Er, but that were as far as it went – you didn't see 'owt, but he had 'em there in t'drawer. Not like they are now – you can buy 'em, you know, over counter, kind of thing.[38]

By contrast, in London Humphrey (1914), a civil engineer and building surveyor who married in 1938, recalled the ease with which he bought condoms from the chemist. Moreover, he was presented with a variety of different types to choose from, between the more robust reusable and the thin disposable type – which he preferred.

HUMPHREY There was a shop, shops in London where I often used to go and also publications which had adverts – there was no problem as far as that was concerned ... I used to get them from the chemist I think ... the throwaway type ... they seemed to be a – it wasn't obviously so heavy and thick and seemed to be the most sensible.[39]

The familiarity of those in the London area with condoms, including in working-class communication communities, was illustrated by Dora, who revealed that her brother-in-law had thought it (just about) acceptable and amusing to present his brother's new wife with a packet of condoms as they departed on their honeymoon in October 1945.

DORA And Joe's brother said to me, 'Here you are, there's a present for you.' And Joe said, 'What's he given to you?' ... And he said, he said to Guy, (fiercely) 'Don't ever do that to her again.' He said, 'Come on.' He said, 'you go home', and we had to get on the train! And I said to Joe, 'What you got?' And my cousin's husband turned round and said (laughing), 'You'll soon find out.' (laughs)

And what had he given you?

He'd got contraceptives; he'd got a little packet ... they were saying to me, you know, 'We've given Joe something so don't ... ', and I'm saying to Joe, 'Well, what is it?' And he said, 'Oh don't worry about it. I'll tell you when we get to the hotel.' (laughing)[40]

There is no such story, illustrating popular familiarity with condoms, from any of the Blackburn respondents. Indeed, there is positive testimony of quite the opposite set of attitudes. Tim (1917), a watchmaker and one of the few Blackburn interviewees who regularly used condoms during his marriage, ordered them by mail-order on the advice of a highly educated acquaintance (a university lecturer). He still did not want the subject brought up in front of his wife even at the time of the interview.

Was that important for you that you were getting contraceptive supplies without having to go to a chemist or a barber's or would you have gone anyway?

[38] Frank msf/srss/bl/#16, married 1941. [39] Humphrey msf/kf/ht/#26.
[40] Dora msf/srss/ht/#38.

TIM Well, I might 'ave, I don't know. I'd never thought about it … I should imagine, I should imagine it was … I know, eh – if me wife comes in, by the way, you won't, eh – you won't discuss … ?

No I won't.

Be careful what you say … she wouldn't be annoyed – so much – she might be a bit embarrassed, ya see?[41]

Not only were condoms much more familiar to the respondents interviewed in Hertfordshire, but it would appear that some of those in Blackburn only knew about the thick reusable sheaths, which they complained about. Terence (1915), a self-employed decorator in Blackburn who married in 1939, bemoaned the fact that 'they irritated'.[42] One Blackburn sheath-user had spent time in the south of England, where latex condoms were more readily available. Eleanor (1907), and her husband, a mechanic born in the same year, moved to Kingston upon Thames in search of work in 1934 soon after they got married. They returned to Blackburn during the war and started using sheaths after their third and final child was born in 1949. They obtained them from a surgical chemist but rejected them because they were 'so thick'. She contrasted them with the better, thinner latex condoms, although it is not directly indicated whether she had come into contact with them in the south during her time there in the 1930s:

ELEANOR He got one of them sheaths – what they call a sheath, but for some reason (laughing) 'e couldn't use it, I don't know … they were thick rubber in them days … now when you see them hangin' about all over they're thin aren't they? … This was a very thick rubber one … it was 'ard to get on! … [I]t were yella and about that thick – I bet a lot didn't use them … no – so what you did – ya didn't do it properly … you you, you come off before you'd finished; that's what you 'ad to do.[43]

As already pointed out, there were fewer reports of outright rejection of condoms after trying them from Hertfordshire respondents.[44] Thus, while a number of respondents from Blackburn discussed the embarrassments and difficulties they had in obtaining satisfactory condoms, among interviewees in Hertfordshire they were sufficiently part of the repertoire of common knowledge to be the focus of jokes and pranks, analogous to the way in which the Blackburn communication community playfully demonstrated their common familiarity with the practice of withdrawal through their references to 'Mill Hill' and 'Cherry Tree'.[45] It is likely, therefore, that the significantly greater availability of and familiarity with latex condoms among both middle- and working-class respondents from London and the Home Counties may be part of the explanation for their more persistent use reported by these interviewees.

[41] Tim msf/srss/bl/#19, married 1947. [42] Terence msf/srss/bl/15, married 1939.
[43] Eleanor msf/kf/bl/#11. [44] See notes 23 and 24. [45] See above, note 31.

Among working-class respondents, caps and pessaries were also generally disliked and rejected. The strong assumption that it was an inappropriate role in marriage for attractively 'innocent' wives to be responsible for the contraceptive method meant that few women were interested in using female methods of contraception.[46] Dorris (1921) had been a nursemaid before she married Jake (1922), a foreman at a Blackburn engineering firm, in 1945. Catherine (1912) was a shorthand typist before marriage, and her husband was a watchmaker in London. They married in 1941 and moved to Hertfordshire where her husband bought a watch repair shop after the Second World War.

DORRIS But I didn't like using it [her cap]. I don't – I don't, I think it spoils, I think it spoils the, um …

JAKE (overlapping) Enjoy …

DORRIS … of sex.

[…]

JAKE It's a lot – it's messy, you know.

DORRIS Well, he didn't like [it] really, ya know, but you 'ad it to do, you 'ad it to do anyway because – we used to use both didn't we?[47]

CATHERINE We knew about pessaries … but … in those days they used to leave it to the men; um, the women probably, you know, thought it was a bit embarrassing to, (giggle) be thinking about that sort of – even thinking about having the sex (giggle) in a way.[48]

'I suppose there were times … I'd rather … forget it'

Alongside these birth control practices which focused on male provision as part of their caring role in the marriage, both men and women were motivated to reduce the amount they had sex at particular times during a marriage and said that either consciously or unconsciously they found themselves disinclined to have sex at those times. Such periods could include immediately after marriage as a couple struggled to set up house together or during the final fertile decades when the desired family size had been reached. For both men and women, fear of pregnancy was a powerful disincentive. Many respondents linked lulls in sexual frequency with particular periods of their marriages when a pregnancy was deemed risky, dangerous, financially unsustainable or emotionally impossible.

During self-employed decorator Terence's wife's somewhat early and prolonged menopause, which began at age 41, the fear of a further pregnancy resulted in more or less total abstinence:

TERENCE Well, just laid off, just laid off … you didn't bother because, as I say, the fear, fear of making her pregnant again stopped you. The fear, it stopped you.[49]

[46] Fisher, *Birth Control, Sex and Marriage*, 175–9, 209–21. See also Fisher and Szreter, 'They Prefer Withdrawal'.

[47] Jake and Dorris msf/srss/bl/#22.

[48] Catherine msf/kf/ht/#1.

[49] Terence msf/srss/bl/#15, married 1939.

While others in similar situations continued to have sex, this was frequently combined with a partial form of abstinence. Eleanor (1907) and her husband were 'very careful' when warned not to have another child after an operation, following her very late third child, which she had aged 42:

> ELEANOR Oh I didn't want no more than three, oh no. I didn't want no more than three ... but when I've 'ad that operation they told me never to 'ave another baby ... so you see after that we were very careful ...

This version of being 'very careful' involved a reduction in coital frequency:

> ELEANOR He didn't want another and I 'ad – I didn't want another ... so, eh, like, we didn't, didn't bother doin' that much.[50]

Thus both male and female respondents recognised that a fear of another conception could make sex a less enjoyable prospect and that, rather than continuing regularly to take risks with contraceptive methods they knew not to be entirely trustworthy, in these circumstances they often 'didn't bother' so much with sex.[51]

For Lyn (1907), married in 1931 to a reacher in a mill, the fear of pregnancy, combined with the frustration of using withdrawal, made sex a less pleasurable experience that was consequently practised less often. She had a very happy marriage and they only had one child, born in 1932, although they subsequently discovered that contraception was unnecessary, as she was unable to conceive again:

> LYN I had a very difficult confinement and something went wrong; in fact, I nearly lost my life and the baby's, you see ... but we were so afraid afterwards [of] another baby coming ... and we didn't know nothing about contraceptives, so ... we just had to practise self-control, you know. You made sure you didn't have the full intercourse ... the man would have to withdraw before he reached a climax. As you've got older you realise the frustration ... it would probably cause in your married life, really. You're not even aware of it then ... but later on you realise that it wasn't a help to having a real happy intimate relationship, you see? So, that was what you had to do ... [or] deliberately trying to avoid having intercourse, which I think you very often did, you see? Especially I think more on behalf – my part, than, er, my husband's, you know? Tired, or deliberately not doing [it] because that fear was utmost in your mind.[52]

Furthermore, the likelihood that partial abstinence would occur when motivation to avoid pregnancy was particularly high was increased by the finding

[50] Eleanor msf/kf/bl/#11, married 1934.
[51] Cook, *The Long Sexual Revolution*, Cook, 'Sexuality and Contraception in Modern England'.
[52] Lyn msf/kf/bl/#1.

that some respondents still articulated the ancient, popular 'orgasm-generation' belief, despite the fact that historians of medical texts have identified this as falling out of currency by the twentieth century.[53] Orgasm-generation was the belief that female orgasm as well as male had to occur for conception to take place. While no middle-class respondents mentioned the idea, four Blackburn and two Hertfordshire working-class interviewees brought it up in the context of discussions of female sexual pleasure in intercourse.[54] While such respondents tended to be aware that it was possible to get pregnant without the woman experiencing orgasm, the notion that conception was positively linked to orgasm was strongly enough held to encourage some women to resist enjoying sex in order to minimise their chances of getting pregnant. Such women also found themselves with further incentives to avoid having sex at all.

Agatha (1910) initially denied that she and her husband, six years older than her, whom she had married in 1940, employed abstinence and declared that they would have sex 'quite often … once a night perhaps'. However, she found her anxiety to avoid pregnancy severely affected her ability to enjoy sex. After the birth of her first (and only) child they both continued to work, as a gardener and domestic, respectively, in a country house in Hertfordshire and did not want another child. In addition her belief in the relationship between conception and orgasm meant she frequently held herself back.

AGATHA Making love (laughing) – I was always too scared to tell you the truth. I'd never kind of relaxed like other people would …

Which did you prefer or which did he prefer? Withdrawing or using a French letter?

I don't think it made any difference, not really, because, yer see, if you're scared at all … yer not kind of happy …

I was always scared and I could never [let] myself go – like they used to say let yerself go and have some – I was always squeezed up.

So did you ever have an orgasm?

Now what's that?

Um, well that's like a climax in sex.

You mean, a thrill? Oh, yes, yes, but very rare, very rare. I mean to put it quite bluntly, I could have done without sex altogether for what it did for me.

So what in sex made you have the thrill and what didn't?

To tell you the truth I don't know. I don't know how that come about, but I must have had a thrill when I 'ad Edward, mustn't I, my son.

Why?

Must 'ave done to 'ave joined up, mustn't you? [You] must join up together when you're making love, otherwise there wouldn't be a baby would there?

[53] Mason, *The Making of Victorian Sexuality*, 201–3. Also see, Santow, 'Coitus Interruptus', 17. Santow comments on sporadic evidence of the belief's survival into the twentieth century.

[54] Eva (1911) msf/kf/bl/#9; Marilyn (1914) msf/kf/bl#7; Peter (1921) msf/kf/bl/#26 and Elizabeth (1923) msf/kf/bl/#26; Agatha (1910) msf/kf/ht/#7; and Catherine (1912) msf/kf/ht/#1.

But if you didn't have the thrill did you then know that you couldn't get pregnant?
Oh, yes, yes.
So is that why you tried to avoid having the thrill?
Yeah, probably it was.
Because you thought… ?
Yes, I think… the thought that I was going to be like mother, yer see – mother 'ad a lot of children; there was six younger than myself, and there was quite a lot that 'ad died and I mean it frightened me that much that, oh dear, yer know.[55]

Most working-class respondents did not recall overt conflict between partners concerning contraceptive practice. This is not, however, to suggest that, unlike some of the middle-class interviewees discussed in the next section, approaches to family building were entirely consensual or harmonious. The imperative to keep discussion of sexual matters to a minimum, combined with a generally accepted gender division of responsibilities towards birth control, meant that working-class relationships were full of implicit tensions and silent consensus. Women did not necessarily passively accept male contraceptive decision-making and there were of course times when working-class men's and women's contraceptive aims differed.[56] In such instances sexual frequency was often reduced at the instigation of one partner or the other. Despite the fact that most women accepted the notion that a husband had a right to regular intercourse, in times of contraceptive conflict periods of abstinence might be engineered. For Doreen (1922), married in 1946 to a man five years older, sex was frequently painful and difficult. She developed a range of non-confrontational strategies to avoid having sex too often:

Did you talk about when to have sex?
DOREEN No, just if the mood came over him. If it came over two nights together I was late to bed the night after! (laughs) Because I've always been sore, you see… you try to go to bed a bit later than them and hope they're asleep. There's no arguments; there's no debates and if they waken up, well, it doesn't last long then. Or, use loads of cream inside, that's all. But he's never been a demanding person.[57]

The avoidance of sex (without open conflict or argument) increased at times when the marriage was under considerable strain. Larry, a foreman bricklayer,

[55] Agatha msf/kf/ht/#7.
[56] Fisher, *Birth Control, Sex and Marriage*, 221–7. Ellen Ross has contrasted the 'peaceful and co-operative marital arrangements' in working-class communities in areas of the UK, such as the textile districts of Lancashire, with the more openly confrontational strategies employed by Cockney women in the late nineteenth and early twentieth centuries (Ross, *Love and Toil*, 58).
[57] Doreen and Larry msf/kf/bl/#20, married 1946.

was adamant that Doreen should not go out to work after the children started school, which she resented. She had a poor upbringing, but middle-class relatives, and was independent, intelligent and ambitious. Larry apparently feared that she thought herself superior to him and wanted to be recognised as a sole breadwinner able to support his wife alone. Whereas for her employment was an expression of her talents, for Larry a wife who worked signified his financial failure.[58] Although she initially rejected the idea that her frustrations affected their sex life, and stressed the ways in which she silently put up with her situation, it was clear that avoiding sex was one of the weapons she used to demonstrate her annoyance. In particular, she found his willingness to apologise in bed and to make up through sex, before the cycle started over again, particularly infuriating. She began to see sex less as an expression of his care or love for her and rather as a new element of his selfishness. If sex was merely something he desired for his own pleasure, then she was less inclined to provide sexual access:

And how did the arguments between you and Larry affect your sex life?

DOREEN Er, erm, well, I don't know that it did really in a way. It was a case of, er – we still slept together ... He'd go all sorry ... and then, er, he would start again the day after. So, what I used to [do] then was stay up late and [to] save any arguments ... I put sanitary pads on to tell him I was like that when I wasn't.[59] (laughs) It was the only way. I made him go hungry ... got to shake hands with it himself. (laughs) I've been a bit mischievous. Do you not think so?[...]

We didn't have a lot of rows ... I'd go quiet ... I gave over bothering [which] was easier than arguments because he can argue for a long time.

And finally, Doreen related her efforts to impose partial abstinence to her recalled memories of her own sexually unsatisfactory experiences of withdrawal:

DOREEN I've forgotten now because we got used to it. He didn't, he didn't finish ... he could have help. It's the woman that can't have help ... accept what you get – half measures. Half a cup of tea instead of a full'un.[60]

Men's attitudes towards sexual frequency were formed in a silent dialogue with their wives' views. Many men were concerned to ensure that their wives enjoyed sex. They were thus determined to choose a method of birth control which suited their spouses. Merlin (1908), a bus and tram driver, had married the daughter of a Labour councillor in 1940. He had had seven siblings himself and left school at the minimum age. His only child was born in 1949. He used withdrawal, despite the fact that he thought

[58] For more on this aspect of their marriage, see Chapter 5 note 35.
[59] For similar examples see Sutton, *We Didn't Know Aught*, 27–8.
[60] Doreen and Larry msf/kf/bl/#20.

withdrawal interfered more with his own personal pleasure, because his wife hated French Letters:

What about things like French Letters? Did you know about them?
MERLIN Of course, I knew about them, yeah; they've been going donkey's years, girl!
And did you ever use them?
Once, and she didn't like them: 'Don't use those again, Merlin, it's horrible!'
Did she tell you why she didn't like it?
No, if she says she didn't like it, she didn't like it.
So we never used them again.
And how did you feel about using them? Did you prefer them to withdrawal?
Well, it was more satisfaction to me, weren't it?
With a French Letter, it was more satisfaction?
Yeah, of course.
So did you mind that she didn't like it?
No.
Was that a disappointment?
If she didn't want it, she didn't want it, that was it.[61]

Similarly, Lucy (1907), a weaver married in 1931, and her husband, a grocer in Blackburn, who had one child in 1937, used withdrawal because they did not enjoy sex using 'rubber things'.

LUCY Well, what the man puts on. I never tried anything but there's things for women today isn't there? No, no, we didn't like these rubber things – we never, no – didn't like 'em – tried 'em once or twice, didn't like 'em.
Why didn't you like them?
I don't know ... we didn't seem to enjoy ... We never used anything. We were just very careful ... when 'e [was] at the ending up – sort of thing – well 'e must have come out.[62]

However, men who recognised the effect that fear of pregnancy had on their wives might, in addition to regularly and conscientiously employing a method of birth control preferred by their partner, simply approach her less often, especially if she made clear that she preferred this. The values of showing caring consideration in a loving marriage meant that rather than objecting when their wives resisted their sexual advances, some men sought to match their expressions of desire with those of their wives, such as Gerald (see p. 262), Colin (p. 338) or Bryan (p. 345). Abstinence, or moderation of frequency of intercourse, can, therefore, be understood as part of a caring and loving husband's consideration for his wife's feelings and pleasure, and not only as part of his birth control technique (reducing frequency of sex to minimise the chance of an unwanted conception). A lot of women said they enjoyed sex, but many also

[61] Merlin msf/kf/bl/#35. [62] Lucy msf/kf/bl/#10.

observed that they had not wanted it quite as often as their partners had seemed to, such as Penny (1916), interviewed in Harpenden, who had had a long and enjoyable sexual relationship with her husband, and Agatha (married in 1940):

PENNY I was nowhere near as sexy as he was. I mean I enjoyed sex but…I didn't have it every time it was offered. I would say 'no, sorry I can't be bothered' but he wasn't over- I don't mean he was oversexed – he didn't want it every night or every day or anything like that.[63]

AGATHA I think I was terrible to him really… saying 'oh I', yer know, 'I'm tired' (laughing). I was never one for sex really to tell you the truth… 'I didn't feel very well', that was the best one.

And how often would you make these excuses?

Oh, every now and again, not too often, but I bet you it was night after night many times (laughing). He was very, very kind and very thoughtful. I was very lucky there, very lucky – couldn't have wished for anyone nicer really, thoughtful, yer know what I mean?[64]

Acceptance of a reduction in frequency of intercourse by husbands among the working class could be both to reduce the risk of unwanted conception as we have seen in cases of medical warnings, and because considerate and caring husbands reacted to signals from their wives and the experience of being refused at times, so as to suit their wives better by initiating sex less frequently. Thus, there is an explanation here for the findings in the mid-1940s, which Slater and Woodside professed themselves unable to explain, which showed that while sexual adequacy ('orgasm capacity') on the part of wives was associated with reports of happiness in their marriages, couples reporting relatively frequent intercourse correlated with reports of less happy marriages.[65] The oral history testimony would indicate that, given the acknowledged tendency of wives to prefer a lower frequency of sex to husbands, which Slater and Woodside fully recognised,[66] a lower frequency of sex was part and parcel of considerate husbands' attentiveness to female pleasure. Perhaps these marriages of lower sexual frequency were those that were mutually considerate and therefore more likely to be reported as loving and happy ones.

Finally, many working-class men also had their own reasons for avoiding sex; many found problems of dissatisfaction with birth control had a negative effect on their own sexual desires. Frank (1919), who was married in 1941 to a local factory worker a year younger, had a range of jobs in Blackburn,

[63] Penny msf/srss/ht/#20, married 1938. Early on in their marriage Penny feared that she might be unable to have children, as her husband had lost a testicle as a baby. After ten years of marriage, however, she fell pregnant and they had three children in three years in 1947, 1949 and 1950. Warned not to get pregnant again, the period of the early 1950s was additionally a fraught time in their marriage when Penny felt isolated and exhausted.

[64] Agatha msf/kf/ht/#7.

[65] Slater and Woodside, *Patterns of Marriage*, 148–89 and Appendix E.

[66] Ibid., 166–71.

spending his longest periods as an ambulance driver attendant. He disliked condoms, and chose to use withdrawal most of the time:

Sheaths... did you use them occasionally?

FRANK At the beginning, you know how it were – yes – but very occasionally and then, as I say, you got more experienced [and] they just went by the board.

Right. So you were using them at the start because you weren't sure about being able to control yourself?

Exactly, yeah, I should put it [like] that, yeah... but not – I wouldn't say on a regular basis... but, er, we, I did use them.

And did you find them satisfactory?

Er, well – if I can go back that far but, er, let's say it dulled the sensation. Er, I don't know whether you've ever used them or what, but, er, that's as far as I can go – yes it achieved the main object but it's – it doesn't, er – there's nothing like nature.[67]

Although withdrawal was the preferred option among both men and women of the Blackburn working class, many interviewees, like Frank, did not perceive it to be unproblematic. Contraception was a high priority for Frank, as following two miscarriages in the early 1940s, his wife had been told that pregnancy was dangerous for her health (and their marriage remained childless), but he still preferred withdrawal to condoms.

So you practised withdrawal?

FRANK Oh yes, oh aye. Well, you had to do, yes... naturally it was a problem but, er, you just had to be careful, that's all, you know... You didn't, er, get the fuller – the full satisfaction, you know what I mean? You'd to, er, cut it kind of thing.

Frank explained that to be practised properly and 'carefully', withdrawal required a 'performance' from the husband:

FRANK It got really – er, you'd to really perform and get it, you know, get it exact. But to be on the safe side you had to withdraw before anything like that happened. Because at back of your mind you knew that, er, you didn't want, you didn't want her to be expecting.

This meant that, given the perceived limitations as to the sexual satisfactions it offered, even a man like Frank, proud of his mastery of the technique, would 'forget it' and 'rather have a drink' at times:

So afterwards when you had to be careful, when you had to withdraw and you didn't want to get your wife... could you say how often you would have sex?

FRANK Very, very, no very, very irregular[...]certainly, er, more than what? Twice a month?[...]But, er, this rate you see, as I say, it were never, it were never an important thing[...]I suppose there were times when, er, as I say, I'd rather have a drink or, or go to bed and you know forget it. It were never uppermost in me mind.[68]

[67] Frank msf/srss/bl#/16. [68] Frank msf/srss/bl#/16.

Slater and Woodside concluded from their interviews, conducted in London in 1942–6 with a set of working-class husbands and their wives (interviewed separately) who were born in the same decades as our interviewees, that '[n]early all methods of contraception were felt to have their disadvantages'.[69] They also found withdrawal and condoms to have been the main methods used, that there was great individual variation in frequency of intercourse,[70] and also that '[q]uite frequently we were given reports that both partners had but little desire, and when this was the case, it was accepted by both with thankfulness: "we're lucky, we're not terribly passionate", "we enjoy intimacy, if you want to know, but neither of us is sexual", "I'm not highly sexed, and my wife is the same"'.[71] These two trained psychologists also observed that '[f]ear of pregnancy is a potent inhibition, and shows that anxiety may cause female as well as male "impotence". It spoils the relationship for both partners and is often openly mentioned by husbands. Some women deliberately "hold back" in the belief that thereby they will prevent conception.'[72]

Thus, many working-class respondents talked of partial or total abstinence featuring in their marriages at various points, some of it by mutual agreement, some unilaterally imposed and some of it closely associated with the general ethos that good, loving husbands should be considerate and patient, careful and not greedy, sharing by caring. Many working-class men and women found the two main methods of birth control available to them – withdrawal and condoms – had disadvantages. Consequently, often without explicitly discussing the matter, some women discouraged husbands from sex. Sometimes this was resented or ignored by husbands but many men also respected their wives' wishes; and this was one of several reasons expressed for moderating sexual activity as part of loving and caring for each other.

'She said, "I'll see what I can do. I'll call in at that Marie Stopes Clinic"'

By contrast with working-class interviewees, many middle-class respondents claimed that wives, as well as husbands, had had knowledge of birth control methods around the time they got married. Mostly secondary school-educated, as Chapter 2 has shown they had a different approach to book-based

[69] Slater and Woodside, *Patterns of Marriage*, 276. The sample was a somewhat unusual one, though the methodology was rigorous by the standards of the period. Eliot Slater was a Physician in Psychological Medicine and Moya Woodside was a Research Psychiatric Social Worker. They selected a sample of 100 men invalided out of the army during the war for psychological reasons and an equal number of 'controls' invalided for physical injuries. Almost exactly half of couples approached refused to be interviewed, leaving a total of 102 husbands and wives, from which the careful study was constructed.

[70] Ibid., 166, 292. [71] Ibid., 171. [72] Ibid., 170.

knowledge and were far more likely to approach printed information about sex and birth control, for example in the growing marital advice genre, as respectable and appropriate reading, provided it was done discreetly and in private. With this greater degree of co-ordinated discussion, middle-class respondents were only about half as likely to have had a birth within the first two years of their marriages (35%) as working-class respondents (65%), although after three years of marriage there was no difference (three-quarters of both groups).[73]

That it was acceptable for young middle-class women to have some knowledge of birth control was revealed by the cases of parents or close relatives, as well as friends, actively providing information and support.[74] In 1942 Gill (1920), who was studying for a Certificate in Social Administration at Manchester University and was engaged to a young army major, reported reading a marriage guidance manual given to her by her mother:

> GILL Oh my mother gave me a book before I was married: Ma- Mary Stops, think it was; Stops was she called, Stops, Stopes? … I read that.[75]

By contrast, no working-class women reported receiving such a gift from a family member at this stage in their lives, despite the well-documented efforts of the nascent birth control movement and the intention that the information in marriage guidance manuals be propagated among the working classes.[76] Nor did they recall consulting such books to assess birth control options at the outset of their marriages, as we will see was commonly the case among middle-class interviewees.[77]

[73] These statistics relate only to the seventy-one first marriages which produced at least one birth.

[74] In addition to Gill, Antonia (1928) msf/kf/ht/#35 also reported being given Stopes' books by her mother, while Betty's (1922) msf/kf/ht/#31 sister (who was actually a couple of years younger than her) gave her a marriage guidance manual before she married in 1948 aged 26.

[75] Gill msf/kf/bl/#48, married 1945.

[76] It is, however, noticeable that one or two working-class informants recall coming across such literature, which their parents owned but did not share with them. In addition to *Aristotle's Masterpiece* (mentioned by Sarah msf/kf/bl/#30 in Chapter 2, note 92), Sian Pooley has remarked on the range of explicit and practical birth controlling information plainly expressed in Henry Allbutt's, *The Wife's Handbook* (Sian Pooley, 'Parenthood and Child-rearing in England, c.1860–1910' (Unpublished Ph.D. thesis; Cambridge: University of Cambridge, 2009), ch. 5, esp. 225–9). Priced for the working-class market (6d), this handy booklet sold 4,300,000 copies, 1886–1913. It may be that helpful, cheap and accessible written information of this kind actually became somewhat less available to our working-class interviewees, brought up in the interwar years, than had been the case for their parents. Although marriage and birth control manuals proliferated during the interwar decades, they became more self-consciously scientific and elaborate in their language, thereby failing to provide adequately for working people, as even Marie Stopes explicitly acknowledged, in writing her more down-to-earth *John Bull* articles (see Chapter 7, notes 10, 11).

[77] On the interwar birth control movement and its clinics, see Fryer, *The Birth Controllers*, Wood and Suitters, *The Fight for Acceptance*, Leathard, *The Fight for Family Planning*, Lewis, 'The Ideology and Politics of Birth Control', 33–48, Davey, 'Birth Control in Britain', 329–45, McLaren, *A History of Contraception*, Porter and Hall, *The Facts of Life*, Part II, Hoggart, 'The

As Chapters 2 and 3 have shown this considerable class difference in attitudes to reproductive knowledge meant that there were also marked differences in courtship. Many middle-class women permitted their partners various sexual intimacies, short of intercourse itself, because their knowledge made them more confident that they knew what intimacies would and would not risk a pregnancy. Similarly, middle-class respondents were much more likely than working-class women to have had some awareness of the options for preventing pregnancy before marriage and many were eager to find out more upon marriage. Unlike their working-class counterparts they did not assume they would rely solely upon their husbands to provide contraception. The male culture of contraception was thus subtly different in middle-class marriages. Although some husbands assumed control of birth control matters, and were expected to do so by their wives, many sought to share their knowledge with their wives and come to a joint decision about what to do. Among some middle-class couples, in complete contrast with all working-class testimony, women took the initiative and sorted out birth control practices from very early in the marriage. While most preferred male methods of contraception, and most tended not to discuss the matter subsequently during their marriages, many middle-class women were much more involved in the initial process of deciding what birth control to use than in working-class partnerships.

Some middle-class women chose to avoid taking any responsibility, despite having their own independent knowledge of methods. Betty (1922), a teacher in Brighton who married in 1948 just before her twenty-sixth birthday, read *The Woman's Medical Guide*, which her husband, Horace, who was also a teacher and seven years her senior, joked meant she had 'taught him' about birth control. She challenged this interpretation and claimed they used condoms because she 'left it to my husband to decide'.[78] When Hilda (1914) got married in 1947 to her second husband, owner of several cotton mills, they were fearful that a baby might inherit a mental deficiency suffered by her sister. This discussion did not extend to deliberation about what method to use; rather she saw herself as typical in leaving contraceptive matters up to her husband:

> HILDA I presume he, you see, it was years before the pill, and it was just usual for the man to take precautions ... You see things are very different in the '40s ... Everything was left to the men.[79]

In other marriages, however, middle-class women were more prepared to be directly involved in contraception and as a result family limitation was initially approached as a joint problem to be solved by couples in discussion with each

Campaign for Birth Control in Britain in the 1920s', Cook, 'The English Sexual Revolution', Cook, *The Long Sexual Revolution*, Part II.

[78] Betty and Horace msf/kf/ht/#31, married 1948. [79] Hilda msf/kf/bl/#50.

other. Mark (1917) and Joanna (1915), both Quakers brought up in Hampstead, who married in their early thirties, discussed birth control before they got married in 1947 and Joanna decided to go, with a female friend, to get advice from a lady doctor in Finchley (Dr Augusta Landman). The doctor 'told me what he [her husband] should do'.[80] As a result they used condoms, which Mark bought by mail-order.

A number of middle-class men sought their wives' co-operation in birth control matters. Men assumed (usually accurately) that their wives were less well informed than they were. Many thus undertook to inform them, so that they might take part more equally in the decision-making. Angela (1924) and Hugh (1926) both came from working-class backgrounds, were highly intelligent and socially mobile. He became an electrician and established his own electrical contracting business soon after the war ended while Angela was employed in various clerical jobs. They married in their early twenties in Preston soon after the Second World War ended. She had carefully preserved her innocence, and she was aware that as a Catholic her mother disapproved of birth control.

HUGH She didn't know anything about it when she got married; [if] I didn't know about birth control, she wouldn't have known anything. We'd have finished up with a big family again ... I had the book Marie Stopes ... I bought that. It's maybe still up in the loft; I don't know. (both laugh)

ANGELA Well, I think it probably taught me because I was very innocent.[81]

Similarly, Roger (1910), whose naval background and experience of public school provided him with plenty of exposure to sexual banter, initiated a discussion about contraception with his wife (whose father was also a naval officer), before they got married in 1938. He suggested condoms, but his wife decided she'd rather 'call in' at a Marie Stopes clinic for a female method. No working-class respondents talked of a visit to a birth control clinic in such a casual manner, nor were they at all comfortable with the female methods offered there.[82]

ROGER When we were married, when we were engaged we had frank things. I said 'Well, what about babies?' She said, 'Well, I don't want them immediately'; so I said, 'Well then', I said, 'We've got to' – I used to refer to it as a raincoat (chuckle) – I said 'buy raincoats then', and she said, 'Yes, I don't much like that', you see? Now that was, that was it, you see? And she said, 'I'll see what I can do. I'll call in at that Marie Stopes Clinic.' And she went up ... to be prepared and then she was told that, as she was a virgin – I'll be quite frank with you – they couldn't

[80] Joanna and Mark msf/kf/ht#22. Dr Augusta U. Landman (died 1966) was later (from 1958) a member of the North West London Family Planning Clinic and a member of the Marriage Guidance Council. In 1949 she had joined the Eugenics Society.

[81] Hugh and Angela msf/kf/ht/#18.

[82] Fisher, *Birth Control, Sex and Marriage*, ch. 4.

do very much for her. So she'd have to wait until things had happened. So, we had to be very careful on our honeymoon and then she shot off back.[83]

Gerald (1919) and Esme (1921) were both from middle-class homes and had both attended grammar schools. He knew more about contraception than Esme did and saw it as part of his role to gather sufficient information before they got married in 1945. Esme was grateful to him for informing her, but she revealed her commitment to a joint approach to the subject, adding that, if necessary, she would have asked her doctor:

GERALD I did a lot of reading and I managed to get hold of quite a library of books on the subject ... And I knew far more about the mechanics than you did I think.
ESME Oh indeed, yes certainly.
GERALD And so I was educated in regard to the basic physical situation ...
ESME I don't think I particularly knew about Marie Stopes, er, you know? Until – I mean her philosophy, etcetera – not when we were particularly young. I think it's something I simply learned about – you know in the course of, of ...
GERALD You may have learned about it from me because I found a book in my father's bookcase.
ESME Oh, did you?
GERALD Yes, and it was just entitled 'Marie Stopes'.
So my eyes went as round as saucers and I sort of read all about her pessaries, all this kind of thing and, um, so ...
ESME So it may've been you!
GERALD I knew about it.
And I had read enough of this to be equipped sufficiently for us to meet up and get married and for you not to have babies year after year after year.
ESME Well, I mean, had you not done something about it and we did discuss it after all, before we'd married – I would've had to have gone to, er, the doctor I suppose and – there weren't any family planning clinics in those days.[84]

There were also a few accounts in which it was portrayed that the wives were expected to take responsibility for contraception from the very beginning, often with assistance from female friends, or even a mother: London-born Antonia (1928) was one of the youngest interviewees. She had one sister and was boarding school educated. Her father was a solicitor and her mother worked as a secretary in the voluntary sector.

ANTONIA When I first got married my mother sent me along to the doctor and said, 'Get him to fit you up with something' ... She had got both Marie Stopes books which she gave me to read.

Her mother's action may have been prompted by the fact that Antonia had left Chelsea Art College in 1949, aged 21, to marry a well-off chartered accountant,

[83] Roger msf/kf/ht/#10. [84] Gerald and Esme msf/kf/ht/#9.

fourteen years older than her. However, she and her new husband did not share her mother's wishes ('always wanted to have a large family; we both agreed on that'). Nor was the doctor at all helpful:

> ANTONIA I mean the doctor just sort of bunged it in and said 'there you are' and 'go home and try it' sort of thing. Which didn't help. Didn't help at all because I didn't really want to use it.

However, after her second child was born in 1952 (the first was in November 1950), Antonia did take control of her contraception, using a cap to regulate her fertility (though she also went on to have six children, the last born in 1965).

> ANTONIA After my second daughter was born I went along to the Marie Stopes clinic in Tottenham Court Road, and, er, they fitted me up properly. I mean it was the same thing except that they took the trouble to show me how to use it – how to put it in. [They] made me practise and all together the whole thing was much more sensible.[85]

Emma was one of the older interviewees, born in 1906. She married in 1936 and was the sole woman among the interviewees who had taken a university degree. She had taken a biology degree at a northern red-brick university, where she had met her husband, who worked throughout their marriage as a biological research scientist. Despite his disciplinary training, she portrayed her partner as too cerebral and other-worldly to have been able to manage the physical details of contraception. At the time of her marriage, with the assistance of a female friend, she adopted a female method:

> EMMA I went to somebody who advised about the anti-, you know, anti- whatever you call them. I had a friend and we went together I remember because she was getting married as well.[86]

Middle-class women's generally greater knowledge of contraceptive matters and their desire to be involved in birth control discussions, combined with many men's determination to seek out their wives' opinion on the matter, meant that a much greater range of contraceptive methods were used or experimented with, including far greater use of female methods such as pessaries, caps and diaphragms, than in working-class relationships. Female methods of contraception were used at some point in as many as half of Hertfordshire middle-class respondents' marriages and were in fact the sole method used in one-third of them.

However, resulting choices not infrequently remained fraught and problematic. Female methods were rarely positively embraced. A few respondents were happy using a cap, but the majority found them difficult to use and at odds with their expectation that they should play a relatively passive role in

[85] Antonia msf/kf/ht/#35. [86] Emma msf/kf/ht/#37.

sex. The following respondents were all relatively well-educated middle-class interviewees:

So where did you get hold of the pessaries that you tried?

REG Um, at Boots. The first lot we got was at Boots in The Strand because The Strand Palace Hotel was where we stayed [on his honeymoon with his first wife] ... We hopped across and ... she got these and we used them, but she didn't like them.[87]

ROGER Well in the end, my dear Stella, she said to me 'I'm damn fed up', she said, 'pushing this thing [in] every time'; she said, 'We'll go at it without' ... So ... for, we had it then for, years and years and years, for nearly forty years we never took any contraception at all.[88]

HILDA I knew about them [caps], yes, but I didn't want anything like that ... I don't like being rummaged up, down there.[89]

ESME We decided that that [condoms] was the most effective, and least traumatic method to use – for us ... the fact is you put a sheath on when you need it. If you have to put a pessary in you have to put a pessary in whether or not ... Anyway jellies and things like that, that were supposed to, er, you know, kill most of the tadpoles but then you only need one to get through you see?[90]

Although some middle-class women were portrayed as positively preferring to take control of the couple's contraception themselves by using female methods,[91] more frequently found was testimony from middle-class women asserting that they personally preferred to opt for male methods, conforming to the more general pattern found almost universally among working-class respondents of both sexes in the north and the south, who assumed that birth control was primarily a husband's responsibility.

Withdrawal posed similar challenges for middle-class as it did for working-class respondents. More middle-class informants preferred condoms, but nevertheless a significant number chose withdrawal as their preferred method and others combined the use of withdrawal with condoms or other appliances:

JUNE It was withdrawal all our married life.

What about French Letters? Did you use those at all?

Occasionally. Yes, occasionally. But we still, er, I think we used more of the withdrawal method than – we did try – we did use, er, the French Letter.

Why was that? Why did you choose withdrawal more often than French Letters?

I think it – I don't know, I can't tell you that. I don't know. We weren't, er, the type of couple that, er, wanted intimacy every night, you know?[92]

87 Reg (1919) msf/kf/ht/#36, married 1942.

88 Roger (1910) msf/kf/ht/#10, married 1938.

89 Hilda (1914) msf/kf/bl/#50, married 1935.

90 Esme (1921) msf/kf/ht/#9, married 1945.

91 In fact in only three cases did women portray themselves in this way: Emma msf/kf/ht/#37, Angela msf/kf/ht/#18 and Gill msf/kf/bl/#48 (see note 95 below). In the other cases this portrayal might have been convenient, wishful thinking on the part of the surviving husband: Roger msf/kf/ht/#10, Reg msf/kf/ht/#36, Patrick msf/kf/ht/#16.

92 June (1914) msf/kf/ht/#27, married 1936.

June (1914) was one of the handful of middle-class Hertfordshire interviewees who had in fact lived in the north for most of her life. She had a very happy marriage contracted in 1936 to a Lipton's-trained grocery manager, born 1912, who owned his own business in Brighouse, West Yorkshire; they had had two children born in 1937 and 1947 (and one miscarriage). Note also the hint in this last sentiment that withdrawal was appropriate for a couple with a moderate attitude towards sex and that only those who 'wanted intimacy every night' would need to use condoms, implying an association for June of condoms with lack of restraint and decorum.

While middle-class respondents were far more willing to use condoms than were working-class informants, and had greater access to disposable, latex versions, nevertheless complaints about them remained from both male and female respondents.[93] Hubert (1911), married in 1936, was a director of the agricultural engineering firm established by his wife's family. They had a fraught marriage: his wife did not want to have many, if any, children (they in fact had three in 1940, 1942 and 1945). His views on French Letters also reflect his anger at her resistance to embrace family life and love with him:

HUBERT Very unsatisfactory. Like eating sweets with the paper on. (chuckle)... And she felt that that was something foreign introduced that was even more unpleasant. (pause) Strange isn't it?... Something that you put on to have sex, which didn't seem right... Not natural. It certainly wasn't satisfactory.[94]

Gill (1920) and her husband, who came from a family of mill owners, first used French Letters on honeymoon in 1945, though she did not know where he got them, and assumed it was a chemists (although he had served throughout the war as a major in the army and perhaps had acquired them in military service).

GILL [French Letters] are a menace, aren't they? (laughs) Well, you've got to stop and fiddle about, you see? No, they're not... I mean he would use them [condoms] yes but, um... not because he thought it was especially, er – it doesn't make it more enjoyable.

Did it make it much less enjoyable?

Well, it's the paraphernalia, isn't it? I think that's really the thing, you know? You've got the – you're not totally relaxed [if you've] got the thing on I suppose, I don't know.[95]

[93] See above notes 30–8 on the greater availability of the latest condoms in chemists in the metropolis and the Home Counties, which was, of course, where the country's 'white-collar' middle classes worked and resided in disproportionate numbers (Garrret et al., *Changing Family Size*, Table 6.2.1). They also tended to have more access to the manuals and associated published information on all appliance methods and where to buy them.

[94] Hubert msf/kf/ht #32, married 1936. For more on Hubert, see below note 109.

[95] Gill msf/kf/bl/#48, married 1945. She claimed that this was a unilateral decision on her own part – 'he more or less left it to me'. As we have seen in Gill's case, her mother had given her a

Humphrey (1914), a civil engineer, and his wife, born a year earlier, started using sheaths in the late 1930s which he obtained from a variety of chemists across London, having seen them advertised.

How did you feel about using the sheath that you used?

HUMPHREY Well, I didn't give it an awful lot of thought. I realise that it could be better, particularly when we decide – tried for a child, er, without using one. But um, (pause) we'd, er – wasn't particularly obsessed by it, you see?
And I – and certainly Violet wasn't (pause) – neither of us were oversexed. In fact if you like we were undersexed.[96]

Thus, compared with working-class marriages, middle-class respondents reported the employment of a much wider range of birth control methods, embracing the male method of condoms and withdrawal but also all the available female methods, too. Often both partners in a middle-class couple are presented as being directly involved in a choice among several options, although this could also have its drawbacks, leading to disagreement and tension.

'Well, then she really, sort of, drew up the drawbridge'

The issue of the choice of birth control method at the beginning of their marriages, although presented by many respondents as an aspect of their sharing love, was equally capable of resulting in marital disharmony, even acrimony. In fact choice of contraceptive method was much more likely to be a source of anxiety and tension, even dispute or resentment, in middle-class relationships, in which, unlike among the working classes, there was not a universal, silent agreement that it was the husband's responsibility to select and provide the method of birth control to be used. Although many middle-class couples might approach marriage both with a degree of shared knowledge about contraceptives and a determination to canvas each other's views and preferences, this did not amount to a commitment to a shared responsibility for birth control throughout their marriage. The negotiation that occurred at the commencement of the marriage over which contraceptive method to adopt was not necessarily the prelude to a continuing and harmonious discussion of sexual matters and birth control choices throughout the ensuing marriage. Contraception remained a difficult topic of conversation and few middle-class couples regularly discussed birth control questions or problems of family planning during the course of their marriages.

Despite the fact that both men and women in the middle classes had much greater access to books providing advice and information about birth control,

copy of Stopes before she got married and this helped resolve this dissatisfaction with condoms, as she then had herself fitted with a cap. She had three children in 1947, 1949 and 1950.

96 Humphrey msf/kf/ht/#26, married 1938.

this continuing difficulty with discussing the subject was partly because suspicion remained that such information was not entirely respectable. For many, Marie Stopes continued to have a morally dubious status, and even a salacious public reputation. Sam (1912) was training to be an articled clerk in the 1930s, Reg (1919) was a navy cameraman who had been involved in the filming of anti-VD films during the Second World War, and Roger (1910) was a chartered surveyor.

SAM There was, um – yes there was one or two books went the rounds of the fellas. What we used to call 'dirty books' ... Stopes, Marie Stopes ... I don't know where it turned up from. But, um, that was very naughty.[97]

REG I mean, don't forget Marie Stopes was ... frowned on by everybody. She was a fallen woman doing all that and making a lot of money out of it.[98]

ROGER Everyone in those days, if they were sensible they got hold of Dr Marie Stopes' book on married love, that was it, I remember that name *Married Love* ... Yes, Dr Marie Stopes. A woman who had never been married but who knew all about it and it was referred to by one or two people I knew as a really filthy book (laugh).[99]

In this climate of opinion, although there was greater female awareness of birth control methods and many couples were able jointly to work out what contraception to use upon marriage, talking about sexual matters remained difficult for most. Gill, quoted above, who was given Stopes' book before marriage by her mother and thought Stopes did much good dispelling ignorance, nevertheless would not have discussed her knowledge of Stopes' work with anybody at the time:

What did other people think of Marie Stopes around that time? What did you hear being said about her?

GILL Nothing. (laughs)

Nothing?

Well, I didn't discuss it with anybody.[100]

In spite (or perhaps because) of the knowledge of a range of birth control methods, many remained unsatisfied with the methods adopted, knowing there might be better alternatives. Such dissatisfaction meant that contraception frequently became an issue of tension and friction between husband and wife, and this could be difficult to resolve because of the problems many had in discussing the matter. Consequently, sexual frequency might wane, for those unsatisfied with their contraceptive choices but who could not openly debate the matter with their spouse. Norman (1914), born in working-class Islington and married in 1944, subsequently trained as a teacher in the post-war Emergency

[97] Sam msf/srss/ht/#28, married 1941. [98] Reg msf/kf/ht/#36, married 1942.

[99] Roger msf/kf/ht/#10, married 1938.

[100] Gill msf/kf/bl/#48, married 1945. See Chapter 2, section 'I wanted to keep you innocent'.

Training Scheme and taught in a junior and then a secondary modern school in Tottenham.[101]

NORMAN We didn't have many conversations about it, no. (pause)... I mean, if she had spoken out about it and said so-and-so-and-so I would have acted up.

So how did you feel about using French Letters?

Oh, a bit of a pain... When a man is eagerly entering into sex, he doesn't want any obstacles does he, really? I'm speaking generally now; when you're cool and calm you can do all these things, but, uh –there's an awful lot of sex without condoms of course.

And how about you and your wife, did you always use condoms?

Some of the time; not always, um... If you didn't have any French Letters left etceteras and, uh... (pause) It's another item of shopping which wasn't always easy; uh, they got pushed aside. That's all I can remember. (pause)

That never induced you then to have discussions whether to do something else – if you weren't completely happy with the method you were using?

I can't recall any long discussions on it, no. She left it to me... And I think she was pleased to leave it to me.

Although she enjoyed her sex. (pause)

So... you'd still have sex if you'd run out of condoms, for example?

Well, I don't know, it's probably a mixture of both. Sometimes you took a chance, and sometimes you left her before you finished. A great deal of sexual dissatisfaction at times... if it was interrupted, uh – she could perhaps finish me off easily enough; I couldn't easily always finish her off... A good large family would have ruined me, would have frustrated me and stopped me and everything else, so, I expect things like that had a halting effect.[102]

The absence of effective discussion between married couples can thus be closely associated with descriptions of various forms of abstinence in their marriages. Sometimes this could be presented merely as considerate behaviour on a husband's part, rather as has been shown in some working-class marriages. Gerald, for instance, whose wife described, above, a joint decision to use condoms as 'the least traumatic' option, talked of 'becoming diplomats with one another', while also describing how effective his wife could be in 'chilling' his ardour. This very happy, solidly middle-class marriage, contracted in 1945 when both partners were in their mid-twenties, produced three children, after which Gerald and Esme were warned not to risk another pregnancy. It was at this period – when Esme felt additionally resentful at her husband's inability to fully appreciate how difficult it was to look after three children – that he found his overtures less frequently welcomed. Moreover, three years

[101] Norman was a socially mobile individual. He had thoroughgoing working-class origins and a working-class employment history until he entered the Emergency Teacher Training programme in his thirties. He is nominally classified in Appendix C as 'working class' but could just as plausibly have been allocated as (lower) middle class.

[102] Norman msf/kf/ht/#17.

after the birth of her third child Esme fell pregnant again. She successfully induced an abortion, but in these circumstances Gerald's consideration of his wife and the need to avoid pregnancy might have further affected their coital frequency.

GERALD Well, I think we became diplomats with one another sufficiently to give indications that one's overtures were not wanted and believe me if one isn't wanted the message you get is so chilling.[103]

However, some other middle-class respondents recalled difficulties with their birth control methods generating unresolved sexual dissatisfactions and resentful memories. William, one of the oldest respondents, born in West London in 1902, a successful businessman, in 1931 had married a Catholic five years older than him. They had no children:

So, how did you avoid pregnancy?
WILLIAM I don't know. I've forgotten now what we did. (silence) Oh dear. Oh dear. (pause) No, it's something I don't want to talk about.
Okay.
Ssso bad mem- so unhappy memories (pause)[…]
Well first tell me about the difficulties because she was Catholic.
Well that side of it is, um (pause). No I'd rather not talk about that side of it. I think you can guess what I'm – the problems …
Well the problem is briefly as a Catholic she was not – there was – contraception was completely out.
You, you can gather that the problems that, er …
Did that upset you?
Well it did really; yes it did. Things, things were not quite normal in those, in that way. Still, we had a very happy life really[…]
And um, and – and we did, I'll, I'll be, I'll be (pause) – I'll confess really that once or twice I used a contraceptive but she confessed it – my wife confessed it to the priest and it made her so unhappy that we had to cut – cut it out.
That must have been very difficult.
Yeah, it was difficult, yes. So now I've told you.[104]

Both men and women had painful memories about the unsatisfactory contraceptive methods they felt they had been compelled by their partner to adopt. Three of the youngest women interviewed (two born in 1928 and one in 1931) were each extremely resentful that, in their view, their husbands had selfishly and unilaterally imposed the use of a female method upon them in full knowledge of their own dislike of the method. They were all middle-class respondents interviewed in Hertfordshire. The men in these three marriages were each in the position that their considerable wealth and income meant

[103] Gerald msf/kf/ht/#9. [104] William msf/kf/ht/#24.

that if their attitude led to an unusually large family (which it did in two of the three cases – marriages which produced five and six children), this would not be financially crippling. These two wives were quite happy to go along with a large family up to a point but eventually they wanted no more, yet they found that their husbands' uncooperative attitudes towards contraception did not change.

JUDITH Oh he didn't care less as long as I did something. He wasn't there to do it; I had to do it.

How did you feel about that?

I wasn't too pleased at all, but, erm – so he was very pleased when I took the pill and he still didn't have to do anything and I had to do less – it was easier to remember to take the pill.

So did you ever have arguments about contraception?

Erm (pause), yes I suppose we did but, erm (pause), not, er, not enormous arguments – discussions perhaps would have been a better way …

And what would be said in these discussions?

Oh god, I can't remember (pause), just sort of: 'Have you got a cap? Have you done it? Have you got it?' 'Yes.' 'Well put it in.' 'I have.' 'Alright but, erm, you should go and get more or get another one.' And then there was something called the coil and I'd heard that hadn't worked for some people so I was very much against that and I didn't have it. I think one of my friends had it, and she still became pregnant and I didn't like the idea because that was metal and I thought – with my nursing training – I don't think this is a good idea; you could get cancer of the cervix and, er – I was thinking on those lines, so I never took the coil.

Did your husband want you to take the coil?

No, no, he, he – well he didn't really know what it was, and he didn't think it was a good idea so no. (laughs)

Did you ever want your husband to do anything?

Yes, I said, 'I think it's time you took some responsibility.' (mocking) 'Oh don't be so silly; there's nothing I can do.' And I – well vasectomies hadn't been invented, or at least I suppose they had for medical reasons, but not for contraceptive reasons so that never came up at all.

What about things like French Letters?

Yes, we – he couldn't be bothered with that. He didn't like that – the feeling of that. He tried them and he didn't get on with them.[105]

Each of the three women felt they had been forced to use female methods because their husbands had abdicated any responsibility for birth control, making it clear that they did not see why they should compromise their personal enjoyment of sex by taking any contraceptive action. Antonia disliked the method she adopted after marriage, when 'the doctor fitted a cap for me, which

[105] Judith (1931) msf/kf/ht/#33, married 1958.

I found very unpleasant and I hated using'. But she found her husband would not try any alternatives:

And why was it your responsibility to deal with contraception?

ANTONIA Oh, because condoms were most – not only uncomfortable, but lessened your pleasure and were much more of a nuisance, erm, which is probably still what people say nowadays. Erm, and he simply wouldn't have used them because he thought they were too…

(overlapping) Did you talk about them?

Er, yes we did because I think he knew I hated what I had and so we did talk about it, but he always refused to use anything himself.

Did you try them [condoms]?

No.

What about withdrawal? Did you hear about that?

We knew about that but we didn't do it. I mean as far as he was concerned that wasn't a proper result.[106]

These three middle-class husbands were, in effect, adopting completely the opposite attitude to that of the ubiquitous working-class norm, abdicating all male responsibility for birth control in the marriage and assuming that this was something which their wives should take care of.[107] Clearly, however, their wives did not share this viewpoint, punishing them with avoidance if possible:

And did you ever avoid sex in order to avoid pregnancy?

ANTONIA (pause) I don't think so. (pause) Except that I did avoid sex when I could manage it. I mean I was very disinclined to have it except when I really couldn't avoid it.

How would you manage to avoid it?

Well (pause) by saying 'no' to a certain extent. But it used to make him very cross. Erm, or by (pause) you know trying to go along with him and really not managing to. Fighting him off at the last minute, which he used to get even crosser about, which is hardly surprising really. And I just thought I simply can't cope with this. (pause) No, it was not a good thing. And he used to go stumping off somewhere to sort things out for himself.[108]

Thus, several middle-class respondents portrayed episodes of abstinence in their marriages where the partners had fallen out over their use of contraception. Hubert (1911), for instance, a director of an engineering firm, whose wife had been a trained nurse, but who he insisted should not work after their marriage in 1936, was unable to shift his wife's absolute opposition to sexual relations after she felt she had been let down by the failure of the contraception he provided (withdrawal). He had known in advance that she definitely did not

106 Antonia (1928) msf/kf/ht/#35, married 1949.

107 The third was the husband of Gay (1928) msf/kf/ht/#13, whom she married in 1947 and divorced in 1966. See Chapter 5 note 86 and note 91.

108 Antonia msf/kf/ht/#35.

want the resulting third birth (and she had asked him to approach a doctor for an abortion), whereas he said that he would have been happy to have had even more children.

You say that sex was very important to your life and to your marriage?
HUBERT It was, but I got – (pause) the fires got damped down rather. I had to just put up with it.
So how would she damp down your fires?
By not responding in any way – not encouraging me, in fact, the opposite.
How would she show that she wasn't interested?
(pause) Well, just being like a log, not approaching, not giving me anything like a passionate kiss of any kind. A peck occasionally, for show, and that was it[…]
And after your third child was born, did you decide that was enough for children?
Yes. Yes. Well, then she really, sort of, drew up the drawbridge and we were very hard put to it to get on, anyway.
Did your sex life end completely then?
Completely.[109]

Hubert (1911) and his wife (born 1912), like William (1902), represented the older respondents. As his testimony exemplifies, it was not only younger middle-class female respondents who talked of wives withholding sexual access from husbands for what was perceived to be sexually selfish behaviour on their part, related to disagreements over their birth control practices.

Conclusion

Thus, although birth rates in marriage had become tightly controlled by the 1930s and 1940s, this did not necessarily indicate an easy mastery and widespread use of the most efficient and modern techniques of contraception throughout the population. Long after the end of the secular fertility decline, traditional contraceptive methods of moderation, periods of abstinence and of withdrawal were as likely to have featured in many of these marriages in the 1940s and 1950s, including those which the respondents viewed as successful and loving, as the modern female and male barrier methods.

Though it was mainly the latter methods which were advocated in contemporary marriage guidance and birth control manuals of the period as the key to a sexually and rewarding loving relationship, this was not reflected in the evidence. Interviewees did not view the use of any method in particular as conducive to the establishment of a loving partnership, which rested instead on a perceived balance of caring and sharing between the two spouses which extended to include the manner in which birth control was provided so that

[109] Hubert msf/kf/ht/#32, married 1936.

sex could be experienced as an expression of love, not lust or selfishness on either part. Nor, therefore, was it the case among those interviewed here that couples abandoned traditional methods as they became more experienced or more knowledgeable about modern techniques. There were many cases where condoms were abandoned in preference for withdrawal or where condoms and withdrawal were used interchangeably during the marriage.

Thus, 'modern' and 'traditional' methods, also often incorporating varying degrees of abstinence, were used in combination and in varied ways in the course of marriages. Experience and expertise or medical advice could lead to the adoption of 'modern' male or female barrier methods, but just as frequently informants reported having discarded a barrier method, either for the more 'natural' method of withdrawal or because abstinence was viewed as preferable by one or both partners. Indeed, partially abstinent moderation was seen by several respondents as part of a caring, loving relationship of emotional sharing, rather than an emphasis in their account on equating companionship or love in marriage in this period with the greater quantity of sexual activity supposedly made possible by modern, reliable contraceptives.

The picture that has often been drawn of a general trend towards gradually increasing sexual freedom of expression, alongside the emergence of the companionate marriage and increased technical control over conception, supposedly signified and indexed in the secular trend of fertility decline, c.1880–1940, therefore needs reassessing. Rather than seeing the increasing adoption of methods of contraception during the early and mid-twentieth century as reducing the need for a couple to avoid sex, or the likelihood that they would, if wanting to avoid pregnancy, this enquiry has confirmed that withdrawal, abstinence and other methods of birth control co-existed throughout this period as parts of a mixed repertoire of responses to varying circumstances, motivations and desires.[110]

The oral history testimony also points to the importance of a shift during the course of the twentieth century from the assumption of male responsibility to the presumption of female responsibility for contraception between partners. This chapter confirms the conclusions reported previously by Kate Fisher that male responsibility for contraception had been the social norm before the 1960s and fleshes out the suggestion that a gender reversal in this respect was occurring within the educated middle classes, where the testimony of our youngest respondents suggests that as female contraceptive methods became better known, a number of men, particularly those wealthier middle-class men for

[110] Szreter, *Fertility, Class, and Gender*, ch. 8, Cook, 'The English Sexual Revolution'. Also see David and Sanderson for a theoretical calculation of the considerable fertility-reducing effect of combining withdrawal with reduced coital frequency (Paul A. David and Warren C. Sanderson, 'Rudimentary Contraceptive Methods and the American Transition to Marital Fertility Control, 1855–1915', in *Long Term Factors in American Economic Growth*, eds. Stanley L. Engerman and Robert E. Gallmen (Chicago: University of Chicago Press, 1986), 307–79).

whom extra mouths to feed did not represent a significant financial burden, were disinclined to see the restriction of their own personal sexual pleasure, through use of male methods of contraception, as a worthwhile activity.[111] However, this then placed the onus on their wives.

The importance of mutuality in sexual relations was something which marriage and sex guidance manuals were increasingly insistent on from 1918 onwards and is, of course, the essence of the 'rise of companionate marriage' thesis. However, the oral history testimony indicates that there may still have been some men among the middle classes who were deaf to this message of joint responsibility in the intimacy of their marriages in the 1940s, 1950s and even 1960s.[112] Whereas abstinence was reported by many working-class respondents as something tacitly imposed on husbands or which they voluntarily accepted, either when there was a perceived need to be extra careful or because they understood moderation as part of a more loving and caring approach to sex in their marriages, among middle-class interviewees abstinence was more likely to be recalled in relation to open, articulated conflicts between the two partners, often related to unresolved disagreements over who should take responsibility for contraception in the marriage, given the range of options that they both knew were available for either partner to employ.

Indeed, as Judith, above, intimated, and as is well known, part of the subsequent mass appeal of the oral contraceptive pill in the 1960s was that some men saw it as releasing them from taking responsibility for contraception, a condition of freedom for men which licensed the aggressively libertine and hedonistic 'permissive' stance, promoted in the new brand of popular male pornographic magazines published from the mid-1960s onwards.[113] This ethos was integral to those aspects of the new sexual culture which many of the interviewees found objectionable and antithetical to their own values, as Chapters 8 and 9 will demonstrate in detail.

[111] See also Fisher, *Birth Control, Sex and Marriage*, 219–20.

[112] The contemporary survey findings of Slater and Woodside, Chesser and Gorer also all found that there was plenty of sexual discontent in British marriages in the 1950s owing to male ineptitude. The findings here suggest this was compounded by both the relative ignorance of some men and their disinterest in their wives' sexual pleasure.

[113] Collins, *Modern Love*, 135–49.

7 Bodies

The experience of sex is closely linked to people's physical bodies. As historians have fully demonstrated, both scientific and popular understandings of the physical body have greatly varied in the course of history, including during the last two centuries.[1] This chapter therefore presents testimony concerning what our informants thought about their own bodies and about other people's bodies. The chapter concludes by examining some of the ways in which their understandings of the body informed sexual practices in marriage.

The oral history evidence provides an alternative perspective to that of other historians' researches on changing experiences and attitudes towards the body during the twentieth century. There is a long-standing history of the increasing interest of the state in the healthy bodies of its citizens, particularly of infants, children, mothers and young men of fighting age in the century of mass conscript armies.[2] Recent historiography has argued that this was

[1] The seminal historical studies have been: Michel Foucault, *The History of Sexuality, Volume III, The Care of the Self*, Part Four 'The Body'. Transl. by Robert Hurley (Harmondsworth: Penguin, 1990; first published in French 1976, 1984); Catherine Gallagher and Thomas Laqueur, eds. *The Making of the Modern Body: Sexuality and Society in the Nineteenth Century* (Berkeley: University of California Press, 1987), Peter Brown, *The Body and Society: Men, Women, and Sexual Renunciation in Early Christianity* (New York: Columbia University Press, 1988), Thomas Laqueur, *Making Sex: Body and Gender from the Greeks to Freud* (Cambridge, MA: Harvard University Press, 1990). See also the remarkable classic of historical sociology: Elias, *The Civilizing Process*, Part Two; and for an anthology of early studies in the social and biological sciences, see Ted Polhemus, ed. *Social Aspects of the Human Body* (Harmondsworth: Penguin, 1978).

[2] On the Edwardian period see, Carol Dyhouse, 'Working-Class Mothers and Infant Mortality in England, 1895–1914', *Journal of Social History* 12, no. 2 (1978): 248–67, Jane Lewis, *The Politics of Motherhood: Child and Maternal Welfare in England, 1900–1939* (London and Montreal: Croom Helm; McGill-Queen's University Press, 1980), Ina Zweiniger-Bargielowska, '"Raising a Nation of Good Animals": The New Health Society and Health Education Campaigns in Interwar Britain', *Social History of Medicine* 20, no. 1 (2007): 73–89. On the interwar era, see Bernard Harris, *The Health of the Schoolchild: A History of the School Medical Service in England and Wales, 1908–74* (Buckingham and Philadelphia: Open University Press, 1995), John Welshman, 'Physical Education and the School Medical Service in England and Wales, 1907–1939', *Social History of Medicine* 9, no. 1 (1996): 31–48, John Welshman, '"Bringing Beauty and Brightness to the Back Streets": Health Education and Public Health in England and Wales, 1890–1940', *Health Education Journal* 56, no. 2 (1997): 199–209.

also accompanied by a marked rise from the interwar decades onwards of a sexualised body consciousness. A leading historian of changing attitudes towards the body during the twentieth century, Ina Zweiniger-Bargielowska, sees the history of popular attitudes towards the body as fairly directly aligned with trends of rising consumerism and with the associated history of clothing fashions.

From the 1920s onwards a majority of young women have spent substantial amounts of money, energy and time in order to manipulate their bodies and change their looks to copy the ideal beauty of a particular era. The emphasis on perfect bodies and particularly on self-improvement through the purchase of consumer goods is a central feature of twentieth-century consumer culture.[3]

In this interpretation the fashion industry in its broadest sense – including not only clothing and cosmetics, but also the marketing of lifestyles including such quintessentially 'modern' preoccupations as dieting and exercise regimes – provided a mediating link between the rise of mass consumerist affluence and a rise to cultural prominence of the aesthetics and individual management of the increasingly sexualised body.[4] Zweiniger-Bargielowska's interpretation is aligned with Jill Julius Matthews' pioneering research on early twentieth-century texts relating beauty to physical fitness and on the interwar Women's League of Health and Beauty. Matthews, in turn, sees her work as confirming the interpretation of the pre-eminent historian of the fashion industry, Valerie Steele, in arguing that '[i]t was in the interwar years that the modern feminine body became popular. Desire became flesh.'[5]

Without detailed first-hand accounts from ordinary middle-class and working-class people of their attitudes towards bodies, however, this interpretation has been based on studies of the activities and discourses of those individuals and associations actively involved in the promotion of bodily awareness, physical fitness, clothing and fashion. This history of advertising, government propaganda and physical fitness and dieting clubs does not offer evidence of the more widely held common attitudes towards the body of the ordinary people, whom these innovators and their institutions were trying to influence.[6] These

[3] Zweiniger-Bargielowska, 'The Body and Consumer Culture', 184.

[4] See also Ina Zweiniger-Bargielowska, 'The Culture of the Abdomen: Obesity and Reducing in Britain, Circa 1900–1939', *Journal of British Studies* 44, no. 2 (2005): 239–73.

[5] Jill Julius Matthews, 'Building the Body Beautiful', *Australian Feminist Studies* 5, no. 1 (1987): 17–34, 19, Valerie Steele, *Fashion and Eroticism: Ideals of Feminine Beauty from the Victorian Era to the Jazz Age* (New York: Oxford University Press, 1985), esp. ch. 11. There is a paucity of research on male fashion and clothing in Britain for the entire transwar period, c.1914–50. For an earlier period see Christopher Heward, *The Hidden Consumer. Masculinities, Fashion and City Life 1860–1914* (Manchester: Manchester University Press, 1996); and for something on the later period of the 1950s and 1960s, see Part 2 of Frank Mort, *Cultures of Consumption: Commerce, Masculinities and Social Space in Late Twentieth-Century Britain* (London: Routledge, 1996).

[6] Sometimes multiple editions of publications or the statistical findings of early official or consumer behaviour surveys can be cited to back up inferences about such wider attitudes and

valuable histories of the various agencies promoting and debating physical fitness and body consciousness therefore need to be placed alongside historical research on the attitudes of members of the rest of society towards the body.

In addition to these various institutions promoting body consciousness, the interwar decades also saw the publication of a number of new marriage guidance manuals.[7] Many of these contained advice, some very detailed, advocating ways in which marriage partners should pay close attention to each other's bodies in their love-making. Marie Stopes' *Married Love* published in 1918, which sold more copies than any other such manual (715,000 by 1931), famously provided an accessible range of encouragements in this direction. Several subsequent publications, including, for instance, the second best-selling manual of the period, Van de Velde's *Ideal Marriage*, translated in 1928, offered much more specific detail.[8] Van de Velde gave a comprehensive, scientific guide to the different stages of arousal in each sex and detailed advice on the erogenous zones and on a diversity of practices for mutual stimulation.[9] Thus, in the marriage guidance and sex manual literature of the interwar decades, the sexualisation of the body and the appreciation of the sensual and sexual potential of one's partner's body was also strongly to the fore.

behaviour, but, in the absence of first-hand testimony, there must always remain a strong element of interpretation in these claims. For instance, Zweiniger-Bargielowska has cited a finding of the Wartime Social Survey that two-thirds of women were using some form of cosmetics in 1942–3 (Zweiniger-Bargielowska, *Austerity in Britain*, 91, Zweiniger-Bargielowska, 'The Body and Consumer Culture', 187). Zweiniger-Bargielowska points out that Jorgen Peter Muller's best-selling physical culture exercise manual, *My System for Ladies*, went through twenty editions between 1911 and 1957, and that Mary Bagot Stack's Women's League of Health and Beauty had 166,000 members by the end of the 1930s, though she does not appear to have been able to discover any circulation or readership estimates for the several journals, such as *Health and Strength* or *New Health*, discussed in this important article (Zweiniger-Bargielowska, 'The Culture of the Abdomen', 255, n.101). On the Women's League, see in particular Jill Julius Matthews, '"They Had Such a Lot of Fun": The Women's League of Health and Beauty between the Wars', *History Workshop Journal* 30, no. 1 (1990): 22–54. It should be noted that a membership of 166,000 women, while certainly substantial, still only equates to between 1 per cent and 1.5 per cent of the 12 million or more women aged 20–50 years in the UK in the late 1930s. This would be quite consistent with the possibility that it remained almost entirely unknown to the working and lower middle classes and still only a minority interest even among women of the upper and the middle classes. None of the interviewees in our study mentioned it. In a related activity, members of British nudist clubs remained an almost invisibly small group in this period with just 4,000 members in 1953 (and still only 12,000 even in 1975) (Harrison, 'The Public and the Private', 339).

[7] For a discussion and annotated bibliography of these, see Cook, *The Long Sexual Revolution*, Appendices A and B, 341–54.

[8] *Ideal Marriage* had sold 700,000 copies in Britain by 1970 (and 1 million in the USA). Stopes' *Married Love* had sold 715,000 copies in Great Britain by 1931; and by 1955 had sold 1,032,000 worldwide. For sales figures see: Geppert, 'Divine Sex, Happy Marriage, Regenerated Nation', 397, n.19, Cook, *The Long Sexual Revolution*, Appendix B.

[9] On the ways in which marriage manuals also discussed details of bodies in relation to genital hygiene, see Cook, *The Long Sexual Revolution*, 146.

Again, this does not mean, however, that we can necessarily conclude that the ideology and practices advocated in these innovative publications accurately represent the generality of the behaviour and values of those who married in the 1930s and 1940s, even though increasing numbers were evidently buying and at least partly reading these texts. With sales in the hundreds of thousands, not the millions, this strongly suggests a readership constrained to a section of the upper and middle classes, rather than the whole of British society at this time. In *Married Love*, Stopes herself claimed she was speaking 'primarily of our educated classes' and, as Ross McKibbin has pointed out, 'this remained true of all of what we might call her "marriage guidance books"'.[10] When Stopes wished to reach out to the wider mass of society, she wrote a series of articles in the popular magazine, *John Bull*, not extolling companionate marriage and bodily sensuality but focusing instead on the practical issue of birth control.[11] Thus, even Stopes herself did not necessarily see her message about sensual love in marriage and the sexualised body as something which could appeal generally throughout interwar British society.

The oral history testimony presented in this book provides an opportunity to examine the attitudes towards the body of a number of middle- and working-class individuals in England who were sexually active during the interwar and post-war decades and who were 'ordinary', in the sense that they were not interviewed because of their special interest in the fashion industry or in physical fitness. Nor did we know, before they were interviewed, whether or not they had any familiarity with the marriage guidance and sex manual literature of the period (some did, most did not).

'You dare expose your body to your mother'

The great majority of respondents emphasised that they had not been accustomed to seeing unclothed or partially clothed bodies in any context when growing up. There were also few opportunities for casual observation of the human body outside the household. Respondents presented themselves as immersed in a culture which encouraged them to think of their own and of others' bodies as, above all, private and personal. Parental training taught that bodies were to be kept to themselves and not foisted upon others or displayed in any way, starting with careful regulations in the home.[12] This meant that Elma's (1909) situation, as the second of six children in a working-class household (her father was a low-paid rail worker in Rotherham), was not unusual:

[10] See McKibbin, 'Introduction' to Stopes and McKibbin, *Married Love*, xxxvi.

[11] For an analysis of these, see Davey, 'Birth Control in Britain', 329–45.

[12] Other oral historians have discovered similar rules and rituals. See, for example, Thompson, *The Edwardians*, 328, Davey, 'Birth Control in Britain', Roberts, *A Woman's Place*, 15–16.

ELMA I knew what babies looked like. (laughs) … No, I never saw a man's body. I never saw me father without clothes on. Never saw me father stripped. I never saw any of the boys bare, the three boys. I never saw any of them.[13]

Several respondents recalled their own childhood training in domestic bodily privacy through the routine of the clearly signposted and carefully choreographed ritual of bath night in homes without bathrooms, such as Bryan (1918), who spent his first twelve years in Caerphilly, and was the son of a miner:

BRYAN I had a sister but, er, I was kept well out the way (laughs) whenever she had a bath or things like that. We were a pretty strict family in that respect.[14]

In Bryan's case he could recall the extent to which he wished to preserve his own bodily privacy even when it did not suit his mother during her confinement:

BRYAN When my mother … had, my youngest brother, Mrs Ransome used to come and look after us kids, you know. Mum was in bed, and she used to bath us you see. And I wouldn't undress; I wouldn't strip off. 'Come on', she said. 'I got boys of me own', she said, 'Come on'. (laughs) And my mother used to say, 'Don't be so silly, Bryan'. I said 'No, I'm not going to undress in front of her.'[15]

There is certainly some evidence that attitudes in at least some middle-class circles could be a little more relaxed over sex segregation at children's bath-times, though proprieties might still be preserved. Hubert (1911) was an only child, the son of an estate agent, whose own mother had died when he was 2:

HUBERT I was put to bath with the cousin I was talking about. Both together, but she had a big sponge strategically placed. So I said, 'What does she want that for?' They said, 'Well boys and girls are different', which I found hard to believe. I've forgotten what happened. I know the sponge was not removed anyway.[16]

However, as with working-class Bryan, Gerald (1919), born in Sutton Coldfield, Birmingham's affluent commuter suburb, the son of a professional electrical engineer, presented himself in childhood as somewhat indignant that his mother might be prepared to relax sex segregation at bath-time when he wanted 'privacy', while his wife, Esme (1921), confirmed that this would not have occurred in her middle-class home in North London, either.

GERALD I remember on one embarrassing occasion I was standing up in the bath – probably washing myself or something – and my younger sister was sitting on her mother's knee right by the bath. She was probably getting ready to come in for her turn, too, and ha! She grabbed hold of my dangling thing and pulled it … Well, I was absolutely appalled by this and I took jolly good care never to be in the

[13] Elma msf/jm/bl/#42.
[14] Bryan msf/kf/ht/#25. See below note 121 on absence of bath rooms.
[15] Bryan msf/kf/ht/#25.
[16] Hubert msf/kf/ht/#32.

same room again, you see. But, and I do remember that and it was funny really. (laughs)…

ESME Well, we never had any communal baths when I was a child; I must admit. Perhaps because we were rather separated in age.

GERALD There would be that, too, yes, and, I mean, I don't know why this happened; I didn't want it or welcome it at all. I wanted privacy of course.[17]

Betty (1922), born into a lower-middle-class London home, recalled a less strict regime in early childhood, but one which changed once she reached adolescence:

BETTY Let's put it this way: I knew what my brother looked like. Because Friday night was bath night. And, um, once I got to puberty, I was not allowed in the bathroom with the other two.[18]

Furthermore, once children reached adolescence, parents not only ensured their more definite segregation but were prepared to reinforce the lesson of covering up in the home quite strictly, if they felt their children had not learned the code of privacy and non-exposure of the body properly. Horace (1915) recounted an incident from 1931–2 in his Bermondsey home, where his disciplinarian father had been a long-serving Company Sergeant-Major in both the Boer and Great Wars.

HORACE I shall always remember… when I was 16 or 17 I came downstairs with me trousers on. Just me vest, vest and trousers. And he [father] gave me such a hell of a clout. He knocked me from one side of the room to the other: 'You dare expose your body to your mother.'[19]

Indeed this story is all the more significant as testimony to the lasting effect of such childhood training into adulthood because of the context in which it appeared in the interview: the episode was related by Horace as an explanation when recalling his embarrassment and coyness about undressing on his wedding night in 1948.[20]

In fact some interviewees commented that it was only after the experience of sharing their body with an infant through childbirth and breastfeeding that they believed they became more relaxed about the exposure of their bodies in front of their partners. Dora (1923) was an East-ender who got married in 1945 to a

[17] Esme and Gerald msf/kf/ht/#9. [18] Betty msf/kf/ht/#31.

[19] Betty and Horace msf/kf/ht/#31.

[20] In view of such childhood training, contemporary popular marriage guidance manuals sympathetically advised their readers that, '[o]ur ideas of nakedness and exposure of the body are changing, and, whilst it is no longer considered indelicate for a couple to see each other undressed, it is not to be supposed that such a state of affairs can be attained all at once' (Edward F. Griffith, *Modern Marriage and Birth Control* (London: Victor Gollancz, 1942, first published, 1935), 126).

motor mechanic who had maintained correspondence with her throughout his military service in the war.

DORA I'd shut the door, the lock on the bathroom door when I first got married and he used to say, (indignantly) 'What do you – open it. Let me in.' I'd say, 'No, no! You're not coming in', because I was very, very shy.

However, she then related how she became used to sharing her bathroom with other, small male bodies:

DORA but when the children came along I mean it was different altogether because, you know, (pause) things was altering in life and my mum said to me one [day], 'Well get them in the water', and they came in the bath with me ...[21]

Dora does not present her changed attitude as related to the influence of wider society or to public discourse and culture, but as due to practical changes in her own private family life and, crucially, as something which she was encouraged to do by her mother. She had also enjoyed breastfeeding both of her children and so loosening her shyness and sense of bodily privacy.[22] Consequently Dora presented herself as much more relaxed about nakedness with her husband – but only later in her marriage, not from the start.[23]

DORA I mean when you get in a bath. If I'd forgotten something he'd walk in and say, 'here darling; here it is'. Splash me a little bit, kiss me, walk out. (laughing) And that's how it should be. What's the good of hiding up your figure if you love one another?

Were you able to do that from the very start [of your marriage]?

No. No, (laughing) I wouldn't take my nightie off ... No, he came – Joe took everything gentle.[24]

By contrast, in the case of Mark (1917) and Joanna (1915), a middle-class couple who had married in 1947 and lived during their marriage in High Wycombe, Mark remarked on the continuing shyness of his wife, whose body he had still never seen naked after over fifty years' marriage; her physical fastidiousness meant that she also 'didn't care for kissing'.[25] Joanna had never had the experiences which Dora emphasised as she had remained childless.

21 Dora msf/srss/ht/#38.

22 Although many health professionals in the interwar and post-war periods recognised the benefits of breastfeeding, many shared women's concerns that breastfed babies did not gain sufficient weight and as a result considerable numbers of British babies were bottle-fed during this period. See, Beier, *For Their Own Good*, 31–48. Furthermore, in addition to the prevalence of bottle rather than breastfeeding, it is also the case that very few husbands witnessed their wives giving birth. Dora, though, was proud that she had breastfed both of her children and said it had been 'lovely'.

23 Grace msf/srss/ht/#38 was another example of this: 'I would think it would be after I had Donald [her first child] that things lightened up a little bit.'

24 Dora msf/srss/ht/#38.

25 Mark and Joanna msf/kf/ht/#22.

It certainly was not only wives who could be intent on protecting their modesty and bodily privacy in marriage. There were also a number of descriptions of husbands who wished to avoid the exposure of their naked bodies in front of their wives. Eileen and her husband were both born in Blackburn in 1913 and married in 1943. He had been previously married and had two boys to care for and they had one child of their own in 1944:

> EILEEN I never see me husband undressed, never in me life... no, no; well, [I was] very old fashioned, [as I] told you I were[...]I used to go to bed first, get ready, get in bed and then e'd come up... always like that. Never saw him undress, never, never... I [was] supposed to wash 'im before 'e went away [due to illness]. I washed 'is – up to 'ere (points to waist) and I was gonna take 'is trousers: 'Don't take those off! Don't take those off!' (shouting). I 'ad to go out while 'e washed himself; 'e wouldn't let me wash 'im, no.[26]

Thus, patterns of behaviour and norms about covering up the body established in childhood continued to influence many throughout their lives. Consequently, nakedness and the nude, visible body, was not something that was central to ideas about sex or practices of making love for many in this generation. Having been thoroughly trained in privacy, discretion and covering up in childhood, many felt more comfortable, normal and 'natural' if continuing to be at least partially clothed even in the bedroom.[27]

Many historians and contemporaries have tended to assume that social norms which encouraged the covering up of bodies inculcated a sexual shyness in young people which was productive of inhibitions, and difficult and unsatisfying sexual relationships.[28] For Thompson's Edwardians, in an earlier era, the taboo on nakedness was directly linked to sexual inhibitions, and quotes

[26] Eileen msf/kf/bl/#12; other very similar accounts about their partners were provided by Daphne msf/jm/bl/#38 and Sally msf/kf/bl/#31.

[27] A practical point of some significance here about conventions of dress within the home is that until comparatively recently it was just too cold in most houses to be comfortable without outer clothes on in all rooms throughout most of the year. Working-class homes tended only to keep a fire on continuously in one living room, not in bedrooms. It was only during the 1970s that central heating became a widespread amenity in homes. As recently as 1971 still only one-third of households had central heating, a proportion which had doubled to two-thirds by 1983 (Burnett, *A Social History of Housing*, 283). It has been one of the consequences of the rise of central heating and lower relative energy prices that homes are now kept at an average of 18° centigrade, a rise of fully 5 degrees since 1970. (Paul Warde, 'Facing the Challenge of Climate Change: Energy Efficiency and Energy Consumption', available from www.historyandpolicy.org/archive/policy-paper-65.html, accessed 15 April 2010.) Of course preferences, technology and norms evolve in a complex interrelationship. It is arguable that if English culture in the 1930s and 1940s had happened already to value nudity or light clothing in the home they might have spent much more on domestic fuel to facilitate this long before the technology of central heating, or there would at least have been a more rapid take-up in the conversion of homes to central heating.

[28] On taboos on nakedness, and notions that all nakedness is 'rude', see McKibbin, *Classes and Cultures: England, 1918–1951*, 314.

from the factory talk remembered in Robert Roberts' memories of Edwardian Salford similarly illustrated the diminishment of sexual pleasure experienced by men whose wives would not let them have sex while naked: one husband was reported as complaining that, since his wife 'insists on full clothing – it's about as exciting as posting a letter'.[29] Such associations between nakedness, sexual inhibition and sexual dissatisfactions were equally evident in middle-class observations of working-class cultures in the interwar period. Mass Observation saw the street antics of unmarried youths in Blackpool as necessarily impoverished by the need to remain dressed: 'So much depends on clothes. For wherever you have your love, unless it be in a safe bedroom, there will be clothes separating bodies, and thus a frustration from full knowledge.'[30]

However, Phyllis (1921), who married in 1943 and lived in Reading, where she and her husband had a small grocery business, recognised that modern audiences would find their bodily shyness 'silly', yet they were a loving and playful couple, who 'thought the world of each other', and who, despite having had a very successful and mutually satisfying sex life, nonetheless found it impossible to undress in front of each other:

PHYLLIS He wouldn't undress in front of any one. (laughs) Stupid, isn't it? Married all those years and, er, I don't [think] either of us would. I mean we'd never get in bed naked or get undressed, you know, in front of people. (coughs)[31]

For others, however, a distaste for nakedness was directly linked to sexual inhibitions, shyness and in turn to embarrassed and difficult sexual relationships. Sally (1908), a sales assistant in Boots in Blackburn who married in 1934, was an intensely private interviewee, and regular church attender, who described herself as 'prim' and unable to be 'forthcoming about sex or anything'. A refusal to be seen naked was part of her general sexual embarrassment and inability to fully enjoy the experience:

If you and your husband never saw each other naked, does that mean you kept your clothes on during sex?

SALLY Vest, my vest, always. Yes he never saw me in the nude. In the nuddie, as they say, no ... And yet we were very, very happy. So you don't need sex to be happy.[32]

Similar attitudes were expressed by Daphne (1912), a practising Catholic (who owned a sweet shop near Blackburn):

DAPHNE There was no stripping off like there is these days and we did cover our bodies (laughs); we covered our bodies up to begin with ... I'm a square ... I mean it just happened at night and weren't one of them that were jumping into bed during the daytime and that sort of thing.[33]

[29] Quoted in Thompson, *The Edwardians*, 34–5.

[30] Cross, *Worktowners at Blackpool*, 176.

[31] Phyllis msf/kf/bl/#5.

[32] Sally msf/kf/bl/#31.

[33] Daphne msf/jm/bl/#38.

Yet it would be a mistake to see shyness around the sexual body as inevitably inhibitory or problematic for this culture. Such attitudes towards nudity did not always correlate with an absence of sexual playfulness, or sensuality. Penny (1916), who married in 1938, four years later than Sally, also emphasised the absence of nudity at the commencement of her sexual relationship with her partner – when courting:

> PENNY once we started having sex ... you know the funny part about it ... you'd, er – because you didn't undress ... I didn't ever undress and have sex; it was sort of pull your knickers down and ... you know you'd have it up against a wall or something like that ...

But she also talked about how this was merely an initial constraint which could be overcome after marriage when: 'you learnt' and 'loved the feeling and the closeness of it all' and her husband learned to 'caress different parts and, and that which would excite me'. Overall she concluded of their sexual relationship, 'I'm sorry it was just, um, ordinary dull sex. It would be dull sex to people now but, um, it wasn't to me.'[34] Although Penny saw their approach to sex as perhaps 'dull' to people now, at the forefront of her description was the fulfilling closeness and sensuality of sex and the fact that initial constraints on nakedness were in no way determinate of their attitudes to their bodies and to the patterns of sexual pleasure and behaviour subsequently enjoyed in her marriage.

'I've seen male figures like in museums and things'

Not only were the interviewees brought up to keep their own bodies covered and private when in the home, but also when outside in public, as was everybody else in society according to their testimony. This meant that opportunities to observe, reflect on and compare other bodies were somewhat rare and by definition unusual. Apart from the exciting, voyeuristic escapades that some boys reported when they sought to catch glimpses of female bodies, mentioned in Chapter 2, there were really only two occasions mentioned by respondents when partially clad bodies of the opposite sex might be available for casual view: visits to the local swimming baths and holiday trips to the seaside. However, the latter were still far from a regular event for many interwar families and furthermore many kept their clothes on for much of the time at the beach.[35] Thus the seaside seems almost to have fallen into the same category

[34] Penny msf/srss/ht/#20.

[35] John K. Walton, *The British Seaside: Holidays and Resorts in the Twentieth Century* (Manchester: Manchester University Press, 2000). Walton confirms that only in the 1950s and 1960s did annual seaside holidays become a regular feature of working-class life. On clothing worn at the beach see, for instance, Juliet Gardiner, *The Thirties: An Intimate History*

as the voyeuristic in the memories of the small number of male respondents who told stories about holidays and the opportunity this could provide to see rather more of the female body, such as Norman's (1914) recollection of his respite from working-class Islington when visiting a Butlin's camp in the early 1930s:

NORMAN I can remember a bloke giving us a lift and about four of us going to a camp ... it was completely different ... you lived in a nasty little street ... and you're suddenly in sun, a place with sunshine and girls walking round in costumes.[36]

There were also several respondents who mentioned the swimming baths as providing them with a rudimentary introduction to the shape and form of the body of the opposite sex, such as Eva (1911):

EVA I used to go swimming a lot when I were younger and we had mixed baths in those days [and] during the summer holidays ... I used to see them then in their shorts, you know.[37]

However, even visits to the swimming baths were by no means a guaranteed experience of childhood, especially it seems for working-class girls in Blackburn.[38] Several went out of their way to recount that they could not swim, while pointedly noting that their husbands could swim.[39] Male respondents did not mention this as an issue. In addition to the wish of parents to protect their teenage daughters from public exposure – both of their own bodies and

(London: Harper Press, 2010), photograph preceding p. 577 entitled 'A family enjoying a day on the beach at Blackpool on 1 July 1939'. Catherine Horwood concludes that throughout the period until at least the 1940s 'all classes, especially older women and those with children ... did not bother to change into a costume on the beach ... many men and women were content to enjoy the sun without ... the inconvenience of changing in and out of wet costumes' (Catherine Horwood, '"Girls who Arouse Dangerous Passions": Women and Bathing 1900–1939', *Women's History Review* 9, no. 4 (2000): 653–72, 666.

36 Norman msf/kf/ht/#17.

37 Eva msf/kf/bl/#9. Marilyn (1914) msf/kf/bl/#7 provided similar testimony.

38 After several decades of building public baths, a 1915 national survey for the Carnegie Trust still concluded that only about one-third of the local populations regularly used them (Virginia Smith, *Clean: A History of Personal Hygiene and Purity* (Oxford and New York: Oxford University Press, 2007), 312). Furthermore, as Catherine Horwood explains, throughout the period until the Great War 'female swimmers were largely excluded from public bathing places ... there was reluctance by councils to provide facilities in public baths for women'. In the interwar years there was expansion of facilities for women, though often still segregated as in 1930s Bolton; and there was also provision in the new form of open-air lidos, where the new phenomenon of 'mixed bathing' drew periodic comment in the press (Horwood, 'Girls who Arouse Dangerous Passions', 656, 659–64). However, Blackburn was not one of the many towns in Britain which built itself a lido during the interwar decades. On the history of lidos, see Smith and Inglis, *Liquid Assets*. See also, Langhamer, *Women's Leisure*, 79–80. Pearl Jephcott also noted the rarity with which the 103 young women in her sample, born 1925–9 in working-class London, a northern industrial town and a County Durham colliery, regularly went swimming after the age of 14 (Jephcott, *Rising Twenty*, 55–6).

39 Eleanor msf/kf/bl/#11; Marian msf/kf/bl/#28; Eileen msf/kf/bl/#12; Lucy msf/kf/bl/#10.

the sight of male bodies – it may well also be that fewer women had learned to swim in childhood because working-class parents were more likely to see it as an unaffordable luxury for daughters to acquire such physical skills, given gender stereotypes about sport and physical activity. Laura (1923), one of the younger Blackburn working-class interviewees, claimed that her capacity to swim was only courtesy of her aunt's financial patronage:

LAURA I were always at swimming baths because me auntie paid for me to learn swimming ... so I used to go swimming once or twice a week, you know, and we didn't get out much otherwise, you know. She were really good with me, were me Auntie Nelly, you know what I mean.[40]

Lucy (1907), born in Blackburn much earlier, recalled that the gender stereotyping was institutionalised at her school:

LUCY I can't [swim]. When I went to school, boys went swimming, but girls – they didn't allow us girls to go to learn swimming, so I never learnt swimming.[41]

Some, like Eleanor (1907), talked about museums or statues when asked about their knowledge of the body of the opposite sex:

ELEANOR When I got married I'd never seen a man before ... but I've seen male figures like in museums and things, you know, and if you go abroad they're all over the place aren't they (laughing)? I mean in Rome and them places, you know ... but ... I know they're different than us.[42]

Thus, as also shown in the previous section, many respondents, from those born in the 1900s to those born in the 1920s, claimed to have seen little of the body of the opposite sex before entering marriage.

Dancing and going to dances was very popular among our respondents, recalling their adolescent and young adult years. It has been suggested by some historians that this was all part of a general thawing of attitudes towards bodies and their physicality during the interwar decades – part and parcel of the thesis of a gradualist consumer-driven transformation of popular attitudes towards the body. Thus, Ross McKibbin has written:

After the First World War, except for debutantes ... dancing ... was an activity beyond parental control. This was important for both sexes but doubly so for girls. A dance was one of the few social occasions where convention permitted them to take the sexual initiative. During the so-called 'excuse me' or 'buzz off' dances ... For many girls, dancing was to some degree creative and expressive, particularly if a girl were lucky enough to have a good partner.[43]

40 Laura msf/kf/bl/#6. Much older than Laura, Sally (1908) msf/kf/bl/#31 was another Blackburnite who reported having to cajole her father to pay for the swimming lessons she wanted.

41 Lucy msf/kf/bl/#10. 42 Eleanor msf/kf/bl#11.

43 McKibbin, *Classes and Cultures: England 1918–1951*, 395.

That dances provided an opportunity to 'take the sexual initiative', in the sense of searching for a possible marriage partner, was confirmed by our respondents, many of whom met each other through dances as Chapter 3 showed. This was the main interpretation which the contemporary observer, Pearl Jephcott, put on the popularity of dances among the 152 teenagers she quizzed in the early 1940s. Jephcott found in 1941–2 among these 14–18-year-olds, born 1923–8, who were all working girls at the time they filled out her questionnaire and who had received elementary education only, that '[d]ancing itself is extraordinarily popular among adolescents', matched in popularity only by the regularity of visits to the cinema.[44] In her subsequent study of a slightly older group, she concluded that, 'Sixteen to 17 [*sic*] was the age at which the girls spent the largest proportion of their money dancing' and that the main object was to meet and find a suitable partner: 'To say that you are going dancing implies that you are going man-hunting, in a perfectly reputable sort of way.'[45] She also found that going dancing often tailed-off in their late teens and early twenties once a partner had been found, again confirming that this was the main purpose of attending the dances.

A good number of the female respondents in our study confirmed that dancing and attending dances was an important and enjoyable activity. For many working-class girls the opportunity of getting away from their chores in the claustrophobic family home and socialising with girl-friends in the presence of the opposite sex was very welcome. However, the physicality of some dances, such as the notorious Charleston, or the Black Bottom, was not necessarily presented as an enjoyable or positive aspect.

> SALLY I didn't like silly dances. I could do them all but I didn't like [them]... there were such a lot of twirling round and twisting round and trying to get your legs under their legs, you know, and I would never do it... I didn't like the way they held you or pulled you round, shouted: they all shouted when they were doing it, you know, 'Oooh'... They weren't dancers they were just show-offs. There was no proper steps to them; you used to run and skip and twist round and, no, there were no proper[...]Then they brought one out – 'Black Bottom' they called it – and you used to do three steps and turn round and bang bottoms and I thought that were disgusting. (laughs) I didn't, I didn't take to that at, at all... For me to go and dance with a stranger and turn round and bang his bottom against mine – I'll not have it.[46]

44 Agnes Pearl Jephcott, *Girls Growing Up* (London: Faber and Faber, 1942), 121.

45 Jephcott, *Rising Twenty*, 68.

46 Sally msf/kf/bl/#31. Sally's (1908) attitudes reflect those of contemporary arbiters of 'good taste', who preferred ballroom dancing to 'jazz music and dubious steps [which] ... originated in low Negro haunts and had *au fond* a prurient significance' (McKibbin, *Classes and Cultures*, 404–6). See also Robert Graves and Alan Hodge, *The Long Weekend: A Social History of Great Britain 1918–1939* (London: Macdonald & Co. 1991; first published 1940), 38–43, 48–9.

Marilyn (1914), another keen attender of dances, six years younger than Sally, reminisced about appropriate attire to cover, not expose, the body when going to a dance:

MARILYN And them days you, if you went dancing [on] a Saturday night, you always had a long dress on and gloves, but they don't today.[47]

There is an important sense, illustrated in these quotations, in which respondents do express a strong 'body consciousness' through their stories and attitudes, but this is far from a sexualised body awareness. It is a consciousness of their body's integrity, and an enjoyment of its independence and autonomy from the control of others. This was a significant element of the exhilaration of going out dancing for teenagers – getting out of the working-class home and the workplace. This was also identified by Pearl Jephcott in youngsters in the 1940s, who were the same age as the very youngest of our oral history interviewees: 'A great many boys and girls at work lead severely controlled lives ... the bodies of these growing adolescents are either kept immobile all day or are worn out with too much standing of which so many shop girls complain ... The dance hall offers the company of young people, an opportunity for rhythmical movement, a very considerable measure of emotional excitement.'[48]

Historians should therefore beware of imputing to the popularity of dancing evidence for the beginnings of a rising general appreciation from the 1920s onwards of the sexualised body familiar to popular culture by the later twentieth century. Young women enjoyed dancing because of the physical freedom and independence it offered, lacking such plentiful opportunity for organised sport – and even for swimming – as boys enjoyed. They were not, therefore, looking for physical contact with boys' bodies at the dances; nor did they necessarily see dances as an opportunity to display their bodies in a sexual sense. As Chapter 3 has shown, this norm applied in general, not only on the dance floor but also to the rules of physical contact when being walked home afterwards: only those young women considering themselves as being seriously courted could respectably permit some physical contact. As Jennie (1908) and Phyllis (1921), born over a decade apart in Blackburn, agreed, 'pushy' boys or, worse still, those who attempted to 'maul', were not what they were looking for as young women in either the 1920s or the late 1930s:

So what was different about your husband? Why did you like him?

JENNIE Well, he, he was, he wasn't, you know, like lads maul you about; he wasn't that sort, wasn't that sort.[49]

Why was it shy boys that you liked?

PHYLLIS Er, I didn't like them rowdy and noisy and pushy, you know.[50]

[47] Marilyn msf/kf/bl/#7.
[48] Jephcott, *Girls Growing Up*, 124.
[49] Jennie msf/kf/bl/#27.
[50] Phyllis msf/kf/bl/#5 and see above, 133–4.

'It's what you're born with; can't do much about it'

Brought up to view respectable bodies as both private and unseen, respondents were often notably diffident or reticent in response to direct questions about the possible attractiveness of their own bodies when they were younger. They did not themselves tend to volunteer opinions about their bodies and even a leading question, such as to Angela (1924), one of the younger Hertfordshire interviewees, still produced little response.

Did you have any opinion about what sort of figure you had?
ANGELA Well I didn't really think about it much, no.
So if you were in the bath and looked at, looked at your body, what did you think?
I don't – I don't think I did, um, think of my body that way; in fact, I still don't.[51]

Daphne (1912), born twelve years earlier than Angela, similarly presented her personal looks as a matter almost of indifference:

When you were younger did you think you were attractive?
DAPHNE: Did I think I was? No, I'd never any big opinions of meself as being good-looking or, er ... I was just ordinary.[52]

Most men, such as Bryan, born in Mid Glamorgan in 1918, also saw this as a matter of no consequence:

BRYAN Did I think I was handsome? No, I didn't. I didn't think I was handsome at all. Didn't think I was very good-looking really but there you are. Didn't make much difference ...[53]

Marian (1908), a Blackburnite, recalled being discouraged by her mother, a winder in the mills, from indulging in any form of vanity about her looks:

If you looked at yourself in the mirror what did you think?
MARIAN Me mother used to say, 'Devil will come to yer' (laughs) if you kept lookin' at yourself in mirror; me mother used to say, 'come away from there; you'll have devil comin' to yer'.[54]

Elma (1909), born in working-class Rotherham, was one interviewee who, in a series of contradictory statements, did acknowledge thinking about her appearance when younger. However, when it came to questions linking this with her views of her body, she was perfectly concise, referring only to its state of cleanliness.

Did you think you were attractive when you were younger?
ELMA: Well, I wasn't bad looking.
[...]

[51] Angela msf/kf/ht/#18. [52] Daphne msf/jm/bl/#38.
[53] Bryan msf/kf/ht/#25. [54] Marian msf/kf/bl/#28.

When you were young did you worry about the way you looked?
No, not particularly, not particularly, love. I used to look in the mirror. And I used to say things like 'Oh, you are ugly'. (laughs)… 'Ugly devil'. (laughs) I used to often say that. I didn't think I was pretty or anything. I'd no ideas about meself. I'm satisfied with me as I am and that's it. Nothing else matters. Nobody likes me, don't matter. It doesn't matter…
Was there anything you didn't like about your body?
No, I've got a nice clean body.[55]

Grace (1922), thirteen years younger than Elma and also brought up in South Yorkshire (Goole), gave a very similar response about the meaning of her body:

GRACE Because your figure, your body it was just something to keep clean. Yeah. It was to keep clean.[56]

As discussed above, recent historiography has argued for the rise of a new, more sexualised body consciousness during the interwar period and much of this research has indicated that young women were the focus of most of the attention among those attempting to foster this consciousness. However, contemporary surveys do not necessarily corroborate this. In reporting on his random questionnaire survey, based on 11,000 responses from all classes published in 1955, Gorer was impressed that in response to the question 'What do you think are the three most important qualities a wife (or husband) should have?', '[n]either sex pays any appreciable heed to the aesthetic qualities of their spouse: beauty or strength, good looks or good figure are very seldom mentioned'.[57]

Our questions tended to produce uniformly self-distancing responses from female interviewees, regardless of whether they were teenagers in the 1920s, the 1930s or the 1940s. They were diffident or neutral, self-deprecating or making a joke out of it. These are all different ways of indicating that respondents felt that thinking about their own physical *bodies* in relation to issues of attractiveness to other persons was inappropriate or pointless. Their own bodies were unlikely to be on view and while appearance could be manipulated through paying attention to clothing, in relation to the body itself, you 'can't do much about it' was the pre-eminent attitude, as Daphne (1912), born in Harwood, put it:

Did you like anything about your appearance?
DAPHNE Well, I was always nicely dressed and, er, good clothes, you know; we were particular about our appearance in those days.

[55] Elma msf/jm/bl/#42. [56] Grace msf/srss/ht/#38.
[57] Gorer, *Exploring English Character*, 125; Slater and Woodside, *Patterns of Marriage*, 104–5, reported very similar conclusions from their enquiry conducted in the mid-1940s.

> *Was there anything you didn't like about your appearance?*
> Can't say there was really. I were quite happy as I was. I didn't give it much thought. (pause)
> *Were you happy with your body?*
> Yeah, was all, yeah well it, (laughs) it's what you're born with; can't do much about it.[58]

This diffidence was consistent with an assumption that the body itself was not something it was appropriate to display or look at. It was better covered up: 'I think that clothes are there to wear and you should wear them.'[59]

However, going along with this absence of discrimination towards the physical form and appearance of their own bodies, many informants valued highly and explicitly the independence of their bodies from others and their personal and physical autonomy and this is as true of female as male respondents. For most men interviewed this is simply an assumed condition of their social existence, which goes with their gender and is implicit in many of the stories they tell about childhood and street play, DIY and gardening pursuits, and, of course, in the many and varied organised and informal sporting activities in which they participated, both in school and as a voluntary adult leisure activity for many of them.

But for many female respondents, personal bodily independence is presented as something they could not simply assume. It was more conditional and constrained and so, if anything, was more of an achievement to be fought for in their lives. The need to negotiate with parents, especially fathers, over permissions to go dancing was of course important, as already mentioned (Chapter 3), as was the fact that a number of women pointedly commented on never having learned to swim.[60] Just as some girls found themselves resisted by fathers over the cost and need for learning to swim, driving could be an aspect of female bodily independence and autonomy which became an issue of contention with their husbands. Eva (1911) expressed strong resentment that she had been denied this freedom:

> EVA I know one thing that really peeved me during our married life, and I never got over it: I didn't get to learn to drive a car, and Albert did. He said, 'You're always too busy and you'll never get hold of t'wheel', he says, 'with children and your work', and I never got to learn. Well, I didn't like that; that did go against [the] grain proper. I was peeved (chuckle), and I've brooded ever since. It's always in the back of my mind, you know.[61]

[58] Daphne msf/jm/bl/#38. [59] Sally msf/kf/bl/#31.
[60] See previous section, notes 37–41.
[61] Eva msf/kf/bl/#9. Despite her victory over her father over swimming, Sally (1908) was another who expressed regret at not having prevailed over her husband in her wish to learn to drive: Sally msf/kf/bl/#31.

Other types of bodily independence provide an important positive memory, for instance cycling for some of the more comfortably off respondents, such as Antonia (1928), one of the very youngest interviewees, the daughter of a London solicitor:

ANTONIA We had total freedom because we had our bicycles and my sister used to go to the nearest stables, which was three miles away and spend the entire time there … and I used to take my drawing things and go out and scour the countryside and it was, it was lovely because there were lots of butterflies and birds; it was totally peaceful. You could, you could ride round the lanes in perfect safety and one's mother was perfectly happy that you should do that. She said, 'Be home in time for supper', kind of thing. It seems extraordinary now because I don't think anyone would dare let their teenage daughter do that nowadays because of the possible consequences. And it was unspoilt countryside too, Norfolk … and we used to go to the beach sometimes … It was a nice beach; we used to go and bathe, erm, take our tea down to the beach sometimes.[62]

Thus personal independence and autonomy of their bodies was expressed as a widely held value among the respondents of both sexes, though the possibility of its regular and routine enjoyment was perceived as strongly gendered. Women, both of middle- and working-class origins, discussed at length the importance to them of achieving a sense of personal mobility, bodily freedom and independence. In fact most frequently this was expressed by the working-class informants through fond memories of walking at weekends in the countryside, which was probably the most popular single courtship activity, partly of course because it was costless; among the more prosperous upper working and middle classes, it was often in recalling the freedom afforded by bicycles or (for men) their sporting activities.[63]

'People said she could have been a mannequin'

When it came to asking respondents about those physical aspects of the bodies of the opposite sex or of their partners which they found attractive or appealing, they offered a relatively restricted range of comments. When men talked of the attractive physical attributes of women's bodies, they emphasised, like Gerald (1919), a retired senior manager talking about first meeting his future

[62] Antonia msf/kf/ht/#35. Several other female respondents of all ages, especially from Blackburn, also had happy memories of cycling when young, either independently or by joining local associations, such as Sarah (1906) msf/kf/bl#30, who met the man she married (in 1928) through joining a local cycling association. Others were: Doreen (1922) msf/kf/bl/#20; Nora (1920) msf/jm/bl/#47; Mildred (1924) msf/kf/bl/#41; and Pru msf/kf/ht/#12.

[63] Cycling was one of two physical recreational activities which Jephcott found to be very popular among Antonia's exact working-class contemporaries, whom she questioned in their late teens in 1945 in three localities (the other being ice-skating, though obviously this was by no means as ubiquitously available as cycling, as Jephcott noted) (Jephcott, *Rising Twenty*, 56).

wife in 1941, that complexion and the 'natural' was what was important and attractive.

GERALD Oh, I absolutely fell, you see. I had already got a preconceived idea of the look of the girl I wanted to marry. Esme had all those appearances. Her hair was just right; it's like a sort of French bun, which I liked the look of. She had a lovely complexion and she was so natural and I hadn't had any girlfriends as such, ever before and she was so easy to get to know.[64]

Indeed the specific attribute which was most frequently mentioned by men was skin complexion: a fresh, natural, rosy-cheeked complexion and good skin, as emphasised by Peter (1921), a cotton-mill worker:

PETER I was taught this, oh years ago: if you want a woman, like, just look at her complexion, and her dress … and I think that's the first thing you look for in anyone is the complexion … [65]

Skin and complexion were also valued by women and were one of the few things that even 'prim' Sally (1908) was prepared to compliment herself on, emphasising that this was a boon of nature, not a cosmetic contrivance.

Did you think you were attractive?
SALLY Me? No I never bothered. I wasn't vain at all.
But were you attractive anyway?
Yes, I think so.
So if you looked at yourself in the mirror what did you think?
I used to think 'you're not so bad', you know … I liked the fact that I'd no wrinkles and I have very few wrinkles for me age. And I've never used a lot of make-up or cream or anything, just used Palmolive toilet soap right from being a girl.[66]

In addition to its association with healthiness, the high evaluation placed on a fresh and natural complexion does seem to be related to its obvious connection with the more general, dominant value of female 'innocence', which was so prized by both sexes through their socialisation, as we have seen in Chapter 2. Virginia Smith notes that the emphasis on the natural beauty of the female skin and an abhorrence of 'paint' for virtuous women was something especially emphasised in Victorian culture and in the arts from the mid-nineteenth century onwards, in reaction to previous fashions and habits of the eighteenth century.[67] Alisa Webb's fascinating content analysis of the short-lived *Girls'*

[64] Esme and Gerald msf/kf/ht/#9. [65] Peter and Elizabeth msf/kf/bl/#26.
[66] Sally msf/kf/bl/#31.
[67] Smith, *Clean*, 289–91. Though there were also clearly historic continuities from before the Enlightenment also being expressed in this demotic valuation of the complexion as expressing an individual's true 'nature': see Valentin Groebner, '*Complexio*/Complexion: Categorizing Individual Natures 1250–1600', ch. 14 in *The Moral Authority of Nature*, eds. Lorraine Daston and Fernando Vidal (London: University of Chicago Press, 2004), 361–83.

Best Friend, a half-penny weekly aimed at mill girls in the closing years of the nineteenth century, finds many of the same themes as those voiced by our informants: beauty defined above all as healthiness; a healthful appearance denoted in a natural, rosy-cheeked complexion; along with a rejection of 'painting' as deceitful artifice, masking the natural.[68] These values were straightforwardly endorsed in praising his wife by Alistair (1927), a factory worker and the youngest male interviewee:

> ALISTAIR Well, she never used lipstick and she always did her own hair. She used to dress well, compared to the others... dolled up with powder and stuff like that, now then. Like looking at a clown, are you with me? And you knew then it wasn't right. But the wife she never had any of this, and that's how I knew, the difference between her and them.[69]

The implication that being too 'dolled up' and especially that the use of lipstick was morally dubious was bluntly spelled out by Felicity (1919), one of the (lower-) middle-class interviewees from Blackburn:

> *And what do you mean by 'a bit of a tart'? What sort of girls were ... ?*
> FELICITY Well all lipsticked up ...[70]

However, some female interviewees also adopted a more flexible and pragmatic approach to the use of make-up. There could be a legitimate use for a little powder for honest, homely factory girls, needing to restore their 'natural' colour to pallid cheeks. But this was to be carefully distinguished from its meretricious use for immoral purposes by non-innocent prostitutes in the big city, preying on unsuspecting young men. Eleanor (1907), whose mother had worked in the mills as she had also done – and in various other jobs – before her first child arrived at the age of 30 in 1937, recognised that both the factory girls and the prostitutes were attempting to put across the same 'natural', youthful look, but drew an important moral distinction between, in one case, using make-up to restore an appearance reflecting their 'genuine' character, and, in the other case, creating a sham effect for morally dubious, commercial purposes:

> ELEANOR I've seen them in London. Minnie and Walter came down once, and we'd been to a pictures place – Odeon in Piccadilly ... And when we come out – Walter were very ignorant of prostitutes; 'e knew nothin' about them, bein' on a farm – anyway all these girls were passin', all with rouged faces and eyes made up and,

[68] Alisa Webb, 'Constructing the Gendered Body: Girls, Health, Beauty, Advice, and the *Girls' Best Friend*, 1898–99', *Women's History Review* 15, no. 2 (2006): 253–75. Penny Tinkler also identifies an interwar tension in magazines aimed at girls in which there were many adverts for cosmetics alongside articles championing a 'natural' look (Tinkler, *Constructing Girlhood*, 156–7).

[69] Alistair msf/kf/bl/#33.

[70] Felicity msf/kf/bl/#37.

and Walter said to me, 'aren't there some beautiful women round 'ere?' (sounds amazed) I said 'yes of a kind'. He said 'what d'you mean?' ... I said to Minnie 'does 'e not know?' She said, 'no!' I said, 'they're prostitutes' (speaking sharply)... 'ee', he said, 'I thought they were just ordinary women'. (chuckling) Well they did look different under t'lights 'n all; they all 'ad pink cheeks, you know. Well in them days we were all pale wi' working in the mill... that's workin' in them makes you like a ghost, you know: you 'ave no colour... so that's why they started putting pink, pink on their chee-, and then they'd pinch they cheeks like this, and colour would come in, you know (chuckling), yeah... nay, Walter we finished 'is education up![71]

When female interviewees talked of attractiveness in men, if they mentioned any specific part of the body at all, it would invariably be a comment on their hair. Middle-class Esme (1921) liked Gerald's 'nice curly hair and uniform' when she first saw him.[72] Similarly, working-class Dorris, also born in 1921, commented:

JAKE Women now, they say, oh, he has a nice bum.
DORRIS We never looked at 'em like that; they had to have nice hair...[73]

Interviewees were happy to discuss hair in the context of questions about attractiveness, whether their own, their partners', their children's, other women's or other family members'. Hair – its colour, form and style – seems to have been the one physical and natural feature of the body, in addition to a natural complexion, which respondents saw as almost on a par with clothing, cleanliness and manners as making a meaningful statement about a person's attractiveness.[74] Even when talking about a schoolfriend of hers who had been considered exceptionally beautiful and attractive to the opposite sex and who had ended up marrying a professional footballer at a top team, June, a middle-class woman born in 1914 who had lived most of her life in West Yorkshire, dwelled first on her hair before talking about her figure:

JUNE She was beautiful, she was. She'd beautiful jet black hair which was natural, blue like. And she'd a glass-hour [*sic*] figure, you know – a beautiful figure, and she knew she was attractive, you see to, er, to the opposite sex.[75]

[71] Eleanor msf/kf/bl/#11. [72] Esme msf/kf/ht/#9.
[73] Jake and Dorris msf/srss/bl/#22, married since 1945.
[74] Slater and Woodside noted that among particular physical features of the body which their respondents identified as physical attractions, clearly hair ranked first (Slater and Woodside, *Patterns of Marriage*, 105). On young girls' attention to their hair in the 1940s see Jephcott, *Rising Twenty*, 61–2. Gorer also, in his inimitable manner, acknowledged the attractive power of hair for his informants: 'For some reasons, which I confess to finding obscure, a permanent wave is considered particularly efficacious in bringing a straying husband back to the fold' (Gorer, *Exploring English Character*, 149).
[75] June msf/kf/ht/#27.

Hair was the one aspect of the body that was recognised to be controllable and manageable even with the constrained budgets and circumstances of the working classes. As Pearl Jephcott put it, of the '[g]ay coats and shining hair' of her young working-class informants in the mid-1940s, '[s]ome have achieved this result against the odds of dirty work, a squalid home, no long mirrors, seldom a bathroom, and little time for clothes washing, drying, ironing and mending. They have wisely concentrated on their hair.'[76]

It is notable that, by contrast with the topics of complexion and hair, interviewees talked very little about any of their partners' other natural facial characteristics, including their eyes, their teeth or their smile, even when asked direct questions about how they first became attracted to each other.[77] In their answers to such questions, apart from hair, interviewees were much more likely to focus instead on personality characteristics, such as their future partner's friendliness, cheerfulness, gentleness or cleanliness. Facial features, smiles and gesturing were certainly both implied in such answers and clearly this would have been important to the emotional exchange in such circumstances, but the more individualised features of bodies and faces, though important for face-to-face communication, do not seem to feature in respondents' testimonies about the beauty and attractiveness of individuals of either sex. Lyn (1907) was a working-class Blackburnite who in 1931 had married a factory worker two years her junior:

LYN He were a very nice-looking boy. He had red hair and it was curly – lovely wavy and curly. He was considered very good-looking and was always nicely dressed and always spotlessly clean. And I think … that, you know, attracts your attention. And then he were very considerate and understanding and we seemed to like the same things and all that sort of thing, you know.[78]

Neither bodies nor the sexually specific aspects of bodies were voluntarily mentioned or evaluated in any detail by the great majority of respondents in their answers to questions about attractiveness. A couple of male and several female interviewees each independently mentioned that it was acceptable when they were younger for men to express their admiration for women's legs with phrases such as 'nice pair of legs' (or 'pins'), and one of the men, Christopher (1918), born in working-class Barrow, claimed that for him this had been a

[76] Jephcott, *Rising Twenty*, 61.

[77] Stephen Kern concludes that '[a]side from the face and hair, the only other unclothed and visible area of the body in nineteenth-century literature was the hands' (Kern, *The Culture of Love*, 70). He then traces how much this subsequently changed in 'classic' modernist novels during the first four decades of the twentieth century. However, the oral testimony suggests that this would be a poor guide to the chronology of change in wider British social norms and practices, as also does the analysis of Alison Light and others of interwar middle-brow and low-brow literature (Chapter 1, note 116).

[78] Lyn msf/kf/bl/#1.

principal source of attraction to his wife, ten years his junior, whom he married in 1947.[79] Comments on girls' ankles seem to have been a related, distinctly middle-class variant on this. Felicity (1919) liked '[m]e legs. I always had a slim ankle … I was told'.[80] What Gill (1920) 'didn't like was my fat legs. And especially after my father'd remarked, "Gosh that girl has got fat ankles, hasn't she?" (laughs)'.[81]

Only three women, all working class, referred to their own 'figure' or their 'bust' or 'bosom', in discussing their own appearance.[82] Eva (born 1911), the oldest, was in fact the most forthcoming of these three on the subject, and the only interviewee to respond to a question about her appearance with some discussion of her own body's appearance, rather than her clothes, though complexion and hair were, as usual, the first to be considered:

> *If you looked at yourself in the mirror, what did you like best about what you looked like?*
>
> EVA Well, I had good hair, for a start, I'd nice hair. And, uh, (pause) as I say, I'd rosy cheeks in those days.
>
> […]
>
> *And if you were lying in the bath, did you like the way you looked?*
>
> Oh yeah, yeah, nowt bad at all; in fact, young fe[llows] … lads used to call me the Pocket Venus! I had the right things in the right places, you know. I always got the Pocket Venus 'cos I was small but yet I've everything they would have (laugh). And they called me the Pocket Venus, I got that for years; in fact, my cousin only mentioned it last week. You know … I'd a small bosom and everything and I were shapely made. In fact when I were married at first I were six stone, thirteen pound, so, I were only (laugh) small, weren't I? But I were shapely with it, hhm.[83]

When asked, just two working-class women, one an older respondent from Blackburn and one a younger one from Hertfordshire, made approving comments on the look of their partners' bodies: 'We've had lovely holidays together. (pause) And he always looked good in his trunks and lovely broad shoulders and he always went a lovely tan.'[84]

One middle-class male respondent, Roger (1910), did talk admiringly of his wife's 'beautiful breasts' and also used precisely the same admiring term, in describing his wife as a 'pocket Venus', as his exact contemporary Eva had used of herself, though she lived a social world away in working-class Blackburn.[85] Apart from Roger, only three other male respondents – all middle-class – mentioned

[79] Christopher msf/kf/bl#34. [80] Felicity (1919) msf/kf/bl/#37.
[81] Gill (1920) msf/kf/bl/#48.
[82] Eva (1911) msf/kf/bl/#9; the other two were: Maria (1917) msf/kf/bl/#8 and Grace (1922) msf/srss/ht/#38.
[83] Eva msf/kf/bl/#9.
[84] Dora (1923) msf/srss/ht/#38. See below, note 111, for Elma's (1909) msf/jm/bl/#42 comment.
[85] Roger msf/kf/ht/#10.

the female 'figure' at all.[86] One of them did comment (after first making a reference to hair) on the sexual dimension of the feminine 'backside', though tempering this by stating that as far as he was concerned it was less attractive than a woman's capacity to play tennis!

SAM I think sometimes the way they did their hair and if they wobbled their backside about a bit. But, you see, a woman was more attractive to us if she was a good tennis player.

Sam (1912), the son of a bank manager in a Northumberland town, was also one of the few men to reminisce about the bodily attractions of dancing, but carefully qualifying his appreciation of an attractive female dancer as one who was not moving her body in a suggestive fashion.

SAM And if she could dance nicely not ssssuggestively [*sic*], not rubbing herself up against, if she could do an old-fashioned waltz or a military two-step well ... that's what I was interested in.[87]

These few references from female and male respondents were the limit of the explicitly public language reported in any of the interviews as terms to describe the sexual features of the bodies of either sex. As one of the younger interviewees, Grace (1922), put it:

GRACE You weren't aware of it. In the war girls didn't talk about their figures so much as they do now. Their eyes, yes. Their hair, yes. The legs, yes. But figures. I didn't know what a pair of bras was till I got – was having Donald [her first child].[88]

The sexually distinctive physical features of bodies were not, then, seen as integral to most informants' understandings of physical attractiveness in the opposite sex.

When interviewees were asked about their own personal attractiveness, in what at first sight appears to be almost a non sequitur, most, like the

86 Sam msf/srss/ht/#28; the other two were Patrick (1918) msf/kf/ht/#16 and Hubert (1911) msf/kf/ht/#32, who could be said to have given testimony to the passing of general comments of this sort by acknowledging that his wife's unflattering nickname before they married was 'Nurse lamppost' and that 'there was no attraction in her figure'.

87 Sam msf/srss/ht/#28.

88 Grace msf/srss/ht/#38. Penny msf/srss/ht/#20 also mentions pregnancy as the first time when 'they told me to get a bra'; and similarly Angela msf/kf/ht/#18 speaking of herself before pregnancy: 'I didn't even wear a bra. I hadn't anything to put in it.' There appears to be little research on the history of bra wearing in twentieth-century Britain. There is no equivalent to Jill Fields' excellent cultural and social history of women's undergarments and lingerie in USA, which, in Chapter 3 (and to some extent chs. 5 and 6) has provided a history of the development of the bra and its production and marketing in USA during the interwar and postwar decades (Jill Fields, *An Intimate Affair: Women, Lingerie, and Sexuality* (Berkeley: University of California Press, 2007)). However, Field presents little direct statistical evidence on the proportionate size of the market or extent of take-up among girls and women of different ages and social groups. Alisa Webb has argued that in the late nineteenth century in Britain corset wearing was socially widespread because it was deemed a 'hallmark of virtue' (Webb, 'Constructing the Gendered Body', 260–1). During and after the Great War, Fields finds that in the USA corset wearing declined, partly superseded by the girdle (Fields, *An Intimate Affair*, ch. 2).

Blackburnites, Iris and Marilyn (both born in 1914), automatically interpreted this as a question about dress and apparel.

And did you think you were attractive?

IRIS Yes I did. I used to have smart clothes; yeah always had, er, smart clothes. I spent a lot of money on clothes.[89]

And when you were young did you think you were attractive?

MARILYN Oh yeah, well we were; we had loads of lovely clothes. Me mother were a good sewer. I had some lovely clothes, I had. I [never] went to a dance wi'out I come home with somebody. I were, were attractive when I were younger.[90]

While these statements confirm that respondents saw themselves as fashion conscious, they do not support the notion that there was a strong link between this and body consciousness – attention to the shape and form of their bodies. As mentioned above, skin complexion was the only female physical characteristic voluntarily discussed:

LYN Well, I've been very lucky – I've had a lovely skin … and all my life people have commented about my skin … [91]

Interestingly, immediately following this observation about other people's comments on her own bodily appearance (her skin), Lyn (1907) was asked 'what did you like best about the way you looked?' Yet even in this context, she still interpreted this question, like most other respondents, as a cue to discuss her clothes (and her cleanliness):

LYN Well, er, I don't know really. I couldn't really say because I was always dressed nice and neatly, spotlessly clean that's, um, at 16, and 17 I looked at myself in the mirror, I would probably be wishing I had some nicer clothes than what I had … [92]

Bryan's (1918) description of his Harpenden-born wife, a shop assistant five years his junior, whom he married in 1947 when he was a trainee tailor (still at that time recovering from a war injury to his arm), was exceptional precisely because it dwelled principally on her body form in explaining what he meant by 'smart'. However, the choice of the word 'mannequin' is very interesting, suggesting that to a would-be tailor what he believed people thought admirable about her figure was its capacity to show off clothes!

BRYAN She was always very smart my wife; she was tall and slim. Many people said she could have been a mannequin if she wanted to or a model but she wasn't; but

[89] Iris msf/kf/bl/#2.

[90] Marilyn msf/kf/bl/#7. In response to a question about what she looked like, Marilyn did in fact – unusually – at least mention that she had 'nice legs' and was 'plump' but not 'fat'; but these were brief statements within a whole long paragraph of testimony devoted to hair, hats, clothing and shopping.

[91] Lyn (1907) msf/kf/bl/#1. [92] Lyn msf/kf/bl/#1.

she, she always looked very smart. And I tried to look smart along with her but I don't know whether I succeeded or not. (laughs)[93]

Alistair (1927), the youngest male interviewee, who married his 24-year-old wife in 1952, offered a similar description of his wife's 'smart' appearance, focusing on her dress sense, as so many of the female interviewees also did when asked about themselves:

And what did your wife look like?

ALISTAIR Well... always well-dressed; always smart and... she was keen on the sewing machine and she took knitting up, and eventually I bought her a knitting machine but she didn't think it was the same thing as hand knitting, you know what I mean, so. Aye.[94]

The respondents' answers, including even Bryan's, reflected an assumption, articulated by members of both classes, that bodies and physical features were essentially a given of nature:

FELICITY But you don't think what you like about your appearance. You've got it and what do you do? You've got to get on with it.[95]

Interviewees therefore saw questions about attractiveness less as a matter of people's physique and more as about signs in their outward appearance that could reflect virtues in their personality or other desirable social attributes. Clothing and cleanliness were indicative of 'attractiveness' because these were well within individuals' spheres of influence, whereas the physical features of their bodies were not. Since dress-making was a home-acquired skill of which many women were extremely proud, how they or their mothers clothed themselves when younger could carry positive connotations of their female home-making prowess. This was not least because it could also have significant financial implications for the family budget, and was fully appreciated by many working-class husbands, who went out of their way, like Alistair in the extract above, to point out that they supported their wife's interest in such activities, by buying household sewing or knitting machines. Thus, while many remained diffident about their own bodies as something immutable that one was just 'born with', dress offered great scope for the exercise of personal taste and ingenuity and really 'said something' about oneself, embracing a number of dimensions of one's personality and status.[96]

The interviewees exhibit a relatively rich language of discernment about the attributes and characteristics they wanted to project in their own clothed bodies and what they wanted to see in the clothed bodies of persons of the opposite

93 Bryan msf/kf/ht/#25. 94 Alistair msf/kf/bl/#33.
95 Felicity (1919) msf/kf/bl/#37.
96 Hence, Selina Todd argues that the affluence of young working-class working girls was often expressed through dress (Todd, *Young Women, Work and Family*, 199).

sex. They are quite comfortable and familiar talking about clothed bodies and what these signify to them. However, like attitudes towards lipstick, for most interviewees, such as middle-class Esme (1921), clothes which revealed rather than covered the body could only have one, disreputable purpose.

ESME In the 20s, when I was a little girl I can remember being told that bus conductors would refuse to allow women on buses if their skirts were above the knee … So, er, I mean, that was tarty, you see? … I mean in general anything very low cut in front would've been a bit tarty.[97]

What, therefore, did the respondents positively value in their own clothed bodies and those of others, including members of the opposite sex? How did the interviewees 'read' these covered bodies?

'Very smart and very, very tidy and very clean'

In discussing appearance, it was commonly mentioned that 'smartness' or neatness or cleanness was all-important. Both women and men looked for 'smartly dressed' members of the opposite sex and saw this as physically attractive in their partners. As Elizabeth (1923), born in Blackburn, said of a serious boyfriend she had had, whom she did not in the end marry:

And what did you love about him?

ELIZABETH Well, there was certain things about 'im yer know: 'e were a quite smart young fella really, yer know, always nicely dressed, yer know, and e'd decent parents, yer know, yeah. 'E were alright, love, yeah.[98]

So what did the key term, 'smart', mean when applied to physical appearance? It was clearly primarily a term applying to a person's dress, and only more indirectly to their bodies. Our informants were certainly using a term with strong contemporary currency in the 1940s, reflected in surveys of the period.[99] Cultural historians of the body and of fashion have also identified the term 'smart' as a salient one at this time in British culture, though they have focused on a single, restricted meaning. Following Valerie Steele's account of the high-fashion industry in the first three decades of the twentieth century, Jill Julius Matthews has claimed that a 'cult of smartness' was the most crucial element in the popular 'commercialisation of beauty' in the interwar years and that this related to idealisation of 'the slender figure', a phrase which ingeniously combines reference both to a body type and to dress style.[100] There is considerable

97 Esme msf/kf/ht/#9. 98 Elizabeth msf/kf/bl/#26.

99 Slater and Woodside, *Patterns of Marriage*, 104–5, Gorer, *Exploring English Character*, 125.

100 Matthews, 'Building the Body Beautiful', 19, Steele, *Fashion and Eroticism*, 224–42. Note that in discussing similar trends in post-war bourgeois Denmark, Søland observes that in adopting the new slim look for women, with much-reduced female underwear and dispensing with laced corsets, 'modern dresses carried the advantage of allowing a woman to dress herself

confirmation for this here, in that although 'slender' was never used by any of the interviewees, the word 'slim' was frequently used by respondents to denote their own youthful attractiveness or that of others.[101]

If we focus on informants' use of the word 'smart', there were, however, two far more salient dimensions of meaning expressed in its usage, beyond that of slimness. For the respondents a 'smart' appearance signified, first, a respectful, lady-like or gentlemanly person. This was, of course, as much a comment about imputed behaviour and implied social status associations as about physical appearance. A smart appearance was considered to signal a person with high standards of politeness and a respectful demeanour, which were also conventionally deemed typical of the more refined sections of society. Second, the term 'smart' was often used in close association with the word 'clean'. While cleanliness also undoubtedly had important social status and behavioural connotations, it additionally invoked notions of healthiness and fitness, a vitally important bodily attribute at this time.

First of all, then, respondents saw a well-dressed, neat and tidily presented appearance as indicating a respectful and well-mannered person. Women valued an appearance which indicated a man who gave attention to detail and was self-disciplined and dependable – an observer of the rules. They presented this as signifying somebody who had been well brought up (''e'd decent parents, yer know', as Elizabeth, above, put it), and would respect them and would be 'gentlemanly':

MAUREEN He was particular; he was particular about himself; he liked himself to be nice, you know. He was the jelly in the pot. Even before he went in the army, he was a smart lad really. He was a smart man, and I just got to know him really ...[102]

And being smart about himself and his appearance, Maureen (1920), a lower-middle-class daughter of a small-business proprietor, felt she could expect that to mean her future husband, five years her senior with a job as a sales representative in the building trade, would also want to ensure she herself was kept decently:

MAUREEN He were always smart himself so he probably wanted me to be – er, he'd want me to look decent anyhow, wouldn't he?[103]

without assistance' (Birgitte Søland, *Becoming Modern: Young Women and the Reconstruction of Womanhood in the 1920s* (Princeton: Princeton University Press, 2000), 26). During the first quarter of the twentieth century the number of live-in domestic servants available to dress their mistresses at the beginning and end of the day was falling (though it rallied in the late 1920s and 1930s before rapidly falling again in the 1940s and 1950s as bourgeois housewives made do with daily helpers and cleaners) (Selina Todd, 'Domestic Service and Class Relations in Britain 1900–1950', *Past and Present* 203 (2009): 183–8).

[101] For instance, Bryan msf/kf/ht/#25, above: 'She was always very smart my wife, she was tall and slim.'

[102] Maureen msf/kf/bl/#46. [103] Maureen msf/kf/bl/#46.

The reciprocal appeal to men of a woman who was able to keep her appearance smart in this sense indicated a good housekeeper capable of getting the most out of a budget and keeping up appearances. A woman's capacity to dress well could be considered to speak volumes about this key aspect of her 'attractiveness' – her capacity to manage on a limited budget, as Peter (1921) enthused regarding what he had liked about his future first wife (whom he married in 1940 but who died of tuberculosis in 1946), both of them mill workers:

PETER How she dressed; and she was smart, like. She 'adn't a lot of money because ... they don't get paid all that [much], about 15 shilling a week then ... and, she'd save up an' buy.[104]

And women like Sally (1908) were themselves proud of their prowess and skill in this respect:

SALLY [I was] always fashionable ... I used to make a lot of my own dresses, used to design them and make them and trim them myself.[105]

A husband could be as 'smart' and well mannered as a gentleman in his partner's eyes, regardless of the formal status of the type of work he did for a living, even where a respondent might acknowledge that it was undesirable, 'dirty' work (Marian's husband, whom she married in 1939 when she was 30 and he 28, was a Corporation dustbin man from 1952 until his retirement):

MARIAN Oh I liked him all time ... he were proper; he were gentlemanly in a lot of ways ... when you were out and you see anybody you knew – 'hello' – he always raised his hat and that, you know, a right gentleman he were and he weren't, er, he weren't a rough sort of a young fella. He were very smart, very smart and very, very tidy and very clean; that's why he didn't like bins: it were a, a dirty job; he didn't like dirty jobs ... [106]

Also the frequently mentioned attraction of women to 'a man in uniform' seems to be picking up on this meaning of smartness in appearance linked to impeccable manners and being personally well disciplined; this was equally appealing to both working-class Elma (1909), and middle-class Esme (1921), the latter addressing her husband, in their joint interview:

ESME The officers' uniform was very attractive, that was nice. And ... your manners were excellent, as indeed they still are.[107]

Elma, married in 1933 to a policeman in Manchester, where they lived through most of their marriage, was quite transported by the memory of his

[104] Peter and Elizabeth msf/kf/bl/#26. [105] Sally msf/kf/bl/#31.
[106] Marian msf/kf/bl/#28. [107] Esme msf/kf/ht/#9.

uniformed appearance, which symbolised for her his gentlemanly, restrained character:

ELMA He was a gentleman, right to his fingertips; he never lost his temper. (coughs) He never lost his temper; he was typical police constable. And all the children used to worship him. They used to fall out [over] who was going to hold his hand across and all that sort of thing… He used to direct traffic at Belle View… It's got a pedestal in the middle of the crossroads, about four roads… And he used to stand in there in his uniform in his white gloves. (laughs)[108]

Uniform did not necessarily work in quite the same way on the female body.[109] Male respondents did not mention it with similar approbation. On the rather more rare occasions (apart from during the war, of course) when women wore uniform, its effect was presented in a somewhat ambivalent way. Penny (1916) recalled the whistles she would attract in her servant's outfit as a teenager in 1930s Harpenden – flattering, but hardly a gentlemanly response:

PENNY You usually had tradesmen and they would whistle and if you went outside the door and they'd go past on their bikes, you know, they'd all whistle because it was afternoon. I mean the uniform was very nice really.[110]

The second, extremely important meaning of a 'smart' appearance for the interviewees was that it denoted somebody who was healthy and sound in body. Elma (1909), one of the few women who was comfortable commenting (approvingly) about her husband's body (he had died in 1972, aged 65), explicitly combined both meanings of gentlemanly behaviour:

ELMA He'd got a very fine body for a man, for an elderly… well, a middle-aged man; he was very well muscled. And he was smart and everything. Yes, he was; he was a grand lad. He was everything. To me he was everything a man should be. And he was polite and a gentleman.[111]

[108] Elma msf/jm/bl/#42.

[109] In his outstanding global conspectus, *The Birth of the Modern World 1780–1914* (Oxford: Blackwell, 2004), Chris Bayly explains that while there was a global move towards adopting uniformity of dress codes such as men's suits expressing bourgeois virtues of responsibility and self-discipline (ibid., 13) – a trend that was less evident, less affordable and therefore all the more desired among the working class (ibid., 15) – such dress codes of uniformity, because they were associated with 'modernity', were 'thought to be more appropriate for men than for women … [who] were expected to inhabit a domestic space … itself a product of public uniformity'. Thus, it was normative for women's attire to remain more 'ornamental and impractical' (ibid., 15). See also Rita Felski, *The Gender of Modernity* (Cambridge, MA: Harvard University Press, 1995) for a stimulating exposition of the cultural and intellectual history of the associations of modernity with masculinity.

[110] Penny msf/srss/ht/#20.

[111] Elma msf/jm/bl/#42. See also note 138, below.

Health was, of course, valued by all respondents for obvious reasons.[112] Personal health and freedom from disability or life-threatening disease was not something which any individual growing up in the 1910s, 1920s or even 1930s could take for granted. Although nationally mortality was falling substantially throughout this period, this was mainly because of reductions in infant, hygiene-related diarrhoea and in childhood infectious diseases. Medical science remained an expensive and uncertain remedy for many serious illnesses in this era before antibiotics and a universal, free health care system. The transcripts of the eighty-nine respondents are laden with many stories of serious childhood illnesses and their lifelong consequences, family tragedies and individual disabilities, particularly after childbirth for women and industrial accidents and war-related injuries for men. Peter (1921), for instance, who was so enthused about the memory of his smart and frugal first wife, was justifiably still anguished that he had returned after Commando service at the Normandy beachhead and 11 months as a POW to find her, a young mother aged 24, on her deathbed from tuberculosis, which he believed was due to her grief because he had been erroneously posted missing presumed dead.[113]

Thus, although respondents presented themselves as quite diffident about their own bodies' physical appearance when younger, they were highly conscious of the importance of their bodies' health, fitness and vigour. Some male interviewees were at pains to point out the significance of impairments they believed they had suffered to their personal bodily fitness, and the implications they felt this had for their prospects in life. For instance, Tim (1917), an apprenticed tool-maker at the Leyland motor works, had chronic chest problems. He did not marry until shortly before he was 30, the year after he had established himself in independent business in Accrington in 1946 as a watchmaker and repairer, because he was worried that a man of unreliable health was of no use as a potential marriage partner.

TIM I met a distant cousin, or cousin by marriage, some years ago and 'e said… 'I never expected to see ya around, ya know', and I said, 'Why?' He said, 'Well when we were young, ya know, they used to say he's bloody bad this Tim; he'll do well to reach 20, odd.' (chuckle)… I went out with one girl, I was courting one girl, till I was taken ill, when would that be? I was in 'ospital twice – it was just as the war started in 1940 and… I was courting a girl in Leyland for three or four months but after this illness I said it's no – I said, 'There's no point in us carrying on'; I said, 'I don't know how I'm goin' to be for, for 'ealth reason. I think you'd be better off without me', sort of thing, ya know (chuckling). 'Ow ya feel when you're young

112 In general on working-class attitudes and experiences of health throughout this period, see the excellent recent study of oral history testimony by Beier, *For Their Own Good*, and other studies referenced in note 117 below.

113 Peter msf/kf/bl/#26.

and ya not really fit and ya think I'll be a burden on someone (chuckle), ya know, and I didn't wanna do that.[114]

Female interviewees also dwelled on the importance of health problems they had experienced. A large number had anatomical and reproductive tract problems, which affected their married lives, such as Betty (1922), born in Peckham, South London – eldest of three children of a London Transport pay clerk – who was left almost lame from a medically mishandled childhood accident. Before she was able to marry him in 1948, she had felt she had to inform her partner, Horace, whom she met when they taught together at a secondary school in Brighton, that she had been told by medical experts that she could never have children.[115]

The importance of health was also closely related to the idea of cleanliness. This was simultaneously an observable property of bodies and a sign of personal character and the standards of home life. Respondents said they valued cleanliness highly and this was part of 'smartness' and tidiness of appearance. A person who kept themselves clean and their clothing spotlessly clean was attractively smart:

ELMA I mean, he was nice; he was clean. And that was the main thing with me: they've got to be clean. Always if he – if he wasn't – a man wasn't clean, I couldn't do with him. And he was spotlessly clean, my husband. He used to shave and keep himself nice. Polish his buttons; polish his shoes. Yeah, he was always very clean and I liked him. I mean, that was it. And he asked me [to marry him]; he asked me. And I said, 'yes, all right then'.[116]

As can be seen in this extract, cleanliness of the body was intimately linked in respondents' minds with cleanliness of their attire. After over two generations of increasingly intense public health propaganda by both local and central government agencies emphasising the importance of personal and domestic hygiene in the nation's battle against germs and disease, strong health implications were commonly understood to flow from attention to all-round cleanliness.[117] Virginia

114 Tim msf/srss/bl/#19.

115 Betty and Horace msf/kf/ht/#31. Though, following two miscarriages and a therapeutic abortion she went on to have two live births.

116 Elma (1909) msf/jm/bl/#42.

117 Lucinda Beier has provided the fullest recent account, using the oral history material which she and Elizabeth Roberts collected. Beier argues that the interwar decades saw 'a transformation of working-class health culture' induced by a mass media of popular press and radio (Charles Hill was the BBC's first Radio Doctor from 1933), including a consensus in working-class neighbourhoods that germs were responsible for many diseases (Beier, *For Their Own Good*, 149, 335, n.83). See also Smith, *Clean*, 297–306, 7–17, Anne Wilkinson (now Hardy), 'The Beginnings of Disease Control in London: The Work of the Medical Officers of Health in Three Parishes, 1865–1900' (Unpublished Ph.D.; Oxford: University of Oxford, 1980), Anne Hardy, *The Epidemic Streets: Infectious Disease and the Rise of Preventive Medicine, 1856–1900* (Oxford: Oxford University Press, 1993), Michael Worboys, *Spreading Germs: Diseases,*

Smith concludes that during the period 1900–39, '[p]ersonal hygiene had now reached the stage of a general consensus'.[118]

However, the achievement of cleanliness required a continual struggle, in the face of the elementary features of the soot-filled urban environment in which most grew up. Clean clothes were highly valued as the outward sign of clean bodies and of status and respectability. They signified not only the orderliness of the home from which the wearer came but also the adequacy of their household's income. As Pearl Jephcott observed of some of her working-class informants' homes that she visited in the mid-1940s: 'Certain of the girls' houses make mere cleanliness a feat, while others are shockingly unsuitable places in which to recover from any illness.'[119] However, for those battling successfully with the environment, she gave her approval: 'Very many of the girls' homes, despite their cramped nature, are spotless, cared-for places that are a tribute to the energy and skill of the people who have made them.'[120] With no Clean Air Act until 1952, however, smoke remained ubiquitous in towns a decade after Jephcott's observations; and the lack of basic hygienic facilities, such as bathrooms in working-class housing, was only gradually redressed over the course of the 1950s and 1960s, so that all interviewees, whether born in the 1900s or the 1920s, shared in these memories and the class differences they signified.[121]

The typical regime, therefore, for many working-class families still into the early decades of the twentieth century was that small children were given a weekly 'good wash' in a tin tub brought in and placed on the floor, usually of the kitchen. This was supplemented when they were adolescents, for those who could afford it, with weekly or fortnightly swimming or washing visits to the public baths – the late nineteenth-century municipal response to the rising public demand for cleanliness at an affordable price in the city.[122] Adults similarly had regular tub washes and some would visit 'slipper baths' or 'private baths' (with individual cubicles) once a week.[123]

Theories, and Medical Practice in Britain, 1865–1900 (Cambridge: Cambridge University Press, 2000). On a slightly earlier, similar development in the USA see, Suellen M. Hoy, *Chasing Dirt: The American Pursuit of Cleanliness* (New York: Oxford University Press, 1995), Nancy Tomes, *The Gospel of Germs: Men, Women, and the Microbe in American Life* (Cambridge, MA: Harvard University Press, 1999).

118 Smith, *Clean*, 308. 119 Jephcott, *Rising Twenty*, 52. 120 Ibid., 38.

121 While the Housing Act of 1923 had deemed it mandatory that all new homes should be built with a fixed bath to be placed in a separate 'bathroom', many in the working class continued to live in older and unconverted homes without baths for many decades after the 1923 Act. Beier cites a Preston respondent, who brought up her five children in the 1950s and 1960s, recalling that most houses in her neighbourhood did not have bathrooms (Beier, *For Their Own Good*, 256). Nearly fifty years after the Act in 1971 almost one in eight households in Britain, living in unmodified pre-1923 housing, still did not have sole use of a fixed bath or shower (Burnett, *A Social History of Housing*, 232, 83). On the 1952 Clean Air Act, see John Sheail, *An Environmental History of Twentieth-Century Britain* (Basingstoke: Palgrave Macmillan, 2002), 247–9.

122 Sally Sheard, 'Profit Is a Dirty Word: The Development of Public Baths and Wash-Houses in Britain 1847–1915', *Social History of Medicine* 13, no. 1 (2000): 63–85.

123 For example, Lucy msf/kf/bl/#10 (note 130, below); Jennie msf/kf/bl/#27 (note 147, below).

The unattainability of the ideal of cleanliness and the great efforts required for avoidance of dirt and germs were therefore fundamental to all interviewees' experience of the body, and to their social status evaluation of themselves and other persons, as Jephcott's value judgements exemplified.[124] Patrick (1918) was an only child born into a lower-middle-class family in East Ham, who worked in a series of local government and clerical jobs (having been a conscientious objector during the war).

PATRICK I looked alright. Um, not that I looked at any – looked attractive to her [his future wife], but that wasn't my point. The point was that I was clean and tidy…Any girl who was friendly and bright, attracted me. Um, didn't have to be, well they were only young, but still that age you gets ideas about who's beautiful and who isn't. They didn't have to be beautiful – that didn't matter – but if they, if their faces were clean and well scrubbed, you know; no seriously, if they, they looked friendly and, and, um, speakable to, I would talk to them.[125]

Norman (1914) was brought up in a very poor family in working-class Islington between the wars (he eventually became a secondary school teacher in Tottenham). After Norman almost died of diphtheria as a child, his father had later put him in touch with one of the East End university settlement houses, which provided him with four years of disciplined, mainly sporting activities, contact with university students and with a life-transforming sense of socially superior cleanliness.

NORMAN So that sort of changed my life plus, as I told you, there were shower-baths, and, uh, uh, (pause) and, and I was cleaner than I'd ever been before. Which in a way probably made me feel a little bit superior.[126]

Interviewees almost unanimously valued cleanliness in persons and their clothing, and were repelled by its opposite.

Why was being clean so important?

DORA Think, well (pause) I've, I've never wanted to, erm – you get near some people and I mean you can smell them can't you?

Raised in the heart of Bethnal Green, Dora (1923) could recall the intense envy which her own, pristine appearance elicited in another pupil at her school in the 1930s:[127]

DORA And my mum was always for cleanliness. And my grandmother was always for cleanliness. I used to have to clean all my clothes before I went to school…and I used to – I always wore a little gym slip…and they had to be pressed of an evening and she showed me how I had to stitch my pleats down and hung up by the door and a white blouse. And a girl, er, Thelma, Thelma somebody her name was. She

[124] See also, Cook, *The Long Sexual Revolution*, 144–5.

[125] Patrick msf/kf/ht/#16. [126] Norman msf/kf/ht/#17.

[127] On the ways in which keeping children looking clean at school was essential to a working-class family's reputation see, Beier, *For Their Own Good*, 300–3.

didn't like me at all. And, er, I know a lot of it was jealousy because we'd, we had a lot of poor kids in the school … and my mother did keep us nice and we had a lovely little clean blouse. I had about two blouses: one you had to wash out and then the other one was ready for the other week. And do you know, honestly, she came up one night she said, 'Oh you', she said, (funny voice) 'Oh she always has to have a white blouse on.' (laughs) She threw a lump of mud at me.[128]

Keeping bodies clean was no easier than keeping clothes spotless for the working classes. Very few working-class respondents, even those counting themselves a cut above the ordinary, recall having indoor toilets or bathrooms with running hot water in their homes when young. Felicity (1919) recalled that when her father, who ran a grocer's shop in a working-class district, installed a bath in their home it was the first in the street and he charged neighbours to use it.[129] More typical in this respect was Lucy's (1907) childhood home in Blackburn, where she was one of four children of a skilled railway worker:

LUCY Where my mother lived, there was a big parlour, a big living room and a very big kitchen. It was a grand family house and upstairs there were three large bedrooms but there was no bathroom in them houses, not in them days, and, you know, me and my two sisters, we used to go to Freckleton Street slipper bath every Friday night, to 'ave a proper bath, yeah; we used to go. Because you hadn't baths in your 'ouses in 'em days.[130]

For most working-class interviewees it was not until they themselves were married adults that they could purchase a more modern house in a better district, built under the newer by-laws with an indoor toilet and – even more memorably – a bathroom.

Most respondents born into middle-class homes, by contrast, tended, like Gill (1920), to casually take for granted the facility of a bathroom: 'Oh yeah. I've always had a bath every day.'[131] Others from the middle classes recalled their family's acquisition of this amenity in their own childhood.[132] For Betty (1922), whose lower-middle-class family moved from Peckham to more salubrious Eltham when she was 7 years old, her parents had achieved this form of domestic comfort by converting a room in an older house, which she recalled with glee.

BETTY It had been a bedroom and it was made into a bathroom and toilet. Which was smashing.[133]

[128] Dora msf/srss/ht/#38. [129] Felicity msf/kf/bl/#37.

[130] Lucy msf/kf/bl/#10; Felicity msf/kf/bl/#37 similarly recalled her parents charging neighbours for occasional use of their bathroom.

[131] Gill msf/kf/bl/#48.

[132] For examples: Felicity msf/kf/bl/#37; Maureen msf/kf/bl/#46.

[133] Betty and Horace msf/kf/ht/#31.

However, shortly before this in the interview she had been on her mettle, affecting to be affronted when the interviewer suggested her parents had only had a tin tub:

BETTY So, my mother's sister, who was twelve years older than me, used to come over on a Friday evening and help Mum with the bathing and the hair washing.
Right. Yeah. Was it a tub? ...
No, we ... how dare you! (laughs)
Well, a lot of people were using tubs at this time.
I know they were.
Yeah, yeah, yeah. No, so you had a bathroom?
We had a – we had a bathroom.

Thus, cleanliness and the domestic facilities to achieve it were highly class-sensitive issues for the interviewees. When respondents repeatedly said how much they valued a 'smart' appearance this was an integral part of what that signified. This key term combined together notions of respectfulness of character and comportment with connotations of healthiness and of the kind of prosperous home and social status that made personal cleanliness achievable.

'If you planned to love each other ... you had to be very hygienic'

As has been shown, respondents valued both for their own bodies and those of their partners a sense of autonomy, a natural unadorned beauty, and cleanliness. These were also the values which informed our interviewees' discussions of bodies in relation to sexual activity in marriage.

The strong positive valuation of their own body's independence and privacy, combined with an unfamiliarity with the sight and shape of other bodies, let alone those of the opposite sex, allied to the notion that bodies were 'natural' givens, could result in considerable awkwardness about their bodies at the beginning of marriages. On the wedding night the two young persons found themselves alone, with their own body, whose physicality they were not accustomed to thinking about carefully, in close proximity to somebody else's. That this experience was challenging was attested to by many respondents.[134] For at least one middle-class respondent, Antonia (1928), married at age 21 in 1949 to a chartered accountant fourteen years her elder, it was the inauspicious beginning of longer-term sexual difficulties.

[134] See also Chapter 2, notes 100–1 and reference there to Maureen Sutton's similar evidence. Of course, the contemporary investigations by Slater and Woodside, *Patterns of Marriage*, 173, and Gorer, *Exploring English Character*, 105, both emphasised the sexual and bodily problems that married couples faced at the beginning of their marriages, which they primarily attributed to their 'ignorance'.

So tell me about the first time you had sex.

ANTONIA It was the first night we got married surprisingly enough and I was absolutely terrified and we went to this hotel and my husband said 'I'll just get you a drink'; 'cos you know that he knew I was nervous. Erm, so he got me a drink and, er, he kept on saying relax, relax. And I couldn't. I was far too terrified of the whole thing. I didn't want to do it; I didn't want to be there; I wanted to, you know, go away and think about something else for a bit. And I've since, since thought if he had been more, erm, mature he wouldn't have forced me into it.

[...]

But I remember afterwards we were having a discussion at art school about first-night nerves and things and this other student who I always thought was a bit insensitive and, and, er, tough and he'd got married quite recently and he was rather sort of showing off about the way he treated his wife and how he never forced her into anything and how he hadn't – he knew she didn't want to so they took their time and it was some time before they achieved it, and I remember thinking I wish Richard understood that. But to him, he wanted to, you know – it's what he'd been waiting for; he wanted to get on with it and he didn't understand my reluctance. He thought, you know, sort of never mind; you'll be alright.

And had he had sex before?

I think he had a couple of times. Erm, when he was in the army with a, with a prostitute. Because I did ask him. And he said it wasn't very satisfactory. So he, he was (pause) it was totally foreign to him, the idea that you know this was something you enjoyed and you did 'cos you wanted to. Erm, I think from his point of view it was his prerogative because he was married and, and it was up to me to sort of sit back and then settle back and enjoy it.

Did he enjoy it?

Well I suppose so. He got what he wanted anyway. Erm, so I always imagined he did. But it was never – I never found it satisfactory because it was all too rushed.

[...]

And did that change during your marriage?

No, it didn't. He was always much too, in much too much of a rush and it never seemed to occur to him that he could delay things.[135]

In negotiating a young wife's maidenly reticence, husbands, though expected to take the initiative, were apprehensive and could be 'damn clumsy', as illustrated by the following extract from a joint interview with Doreen (1922) and Larry (1917), working-class Blackburnities who married at 24 and 29 years old, respectively, in 1946, having known each other for ten months. Their account focuses on matters of clothing and observing correct proprieties in their behaviour, while their physical bodies are presented as almost alien presences ('thick as two planks'):

[135] Antonia msf/kf/ht/#35. Note that these problems in their physical relationship from the start of the marriage were not attributable to Antonia's ignorance or shyness over her own body's sexual capacities – she was one of the few female respondents who freely acknowledged practising masturbation as a teenager (see Chapter 2, note 107).

DOREEN And (laughs) when we, when we went to bed on our honeymoon, he went in the toilet to get changed, didn't you? And you put your pyjamas on… you did. So I went and did the same; I thought he wanted me to do it. (laughs)

LARRY I don't remember that.

DOREEN Ay? I never forgot that, 'cos I thought 'who gets undressed first?' And I were fiddling about with me things in [the] room – I thought 'who gets undressed first? Is it me or him? What do I do?' And I didn't know what he was thinking and I think he was like that with me. So he picked his pyjamas up and went in [the] bathroom [to the] toilet, so I thought 'Oh I'll do t'same.' See. And when we got in bed we both laid… one at each side. I can remember that like that – thick as two planks! *And then what happened?*

DOREEN Well, eventually we got together but he were damn clumsy. Grabbed me with his one hand [by] me back and oh I was, didn't know what to expect.

LARRY Surprising how nature takes over, in't it?[136]

There were many variations on this theme in accounts related by those respondents who claimed they were unfamiliar with their partner's body at marriage. Bryan (1918), married in 1947, also five years older than his 23-year-old Harpenden bride, remembered some sense of apprehension:

BRYAN We were a little bit apprehensive beforehand, wondering how we'd go on and that, but that was about all. [We] just used to wonder how we would feel if we saw one another naked and that, and a little bit apprehensive about that… [137]

Accounts ranged from those resentful of the experience, like Antonia, to the many who bumbled through it, like Larry and Doreen, to a few who recalled no significant problem with the novelty of their partner's body, such as Elma (1909), one of the older respondents who married in 1933 at age 24 to a Manchester policeman two years her senior.

ELMA (laughs) The first time I saw George [was] when he got in the bath. When we were just married. Just after we were married… he'd, he'd got a fine body.[138]

Just as, for many, the norms for keeping bodies covered up and the positive values of bodily autonomy affected ways in which respondents reported their memories of the initial negotiations of the at least partial uncovering required for sexual activity in marriage, so, too, the importance of maintaining healthiness and cleanliness influenced interviewees' understandings of appealing forms of sexual behaviour with each other in their marriages. Intimate contact between bodies in marriage brought respondents face to face with the practical issues in these new circumstances of maintaining health and cleanliness, something on which they placed an especially high valuation. In relation to sexual behaviour and the body in marriage, the linked health values

[136] Doreen and Larry msf/kf/bl/#20. [137] Bryan msf/kf/ht/#25.
[138] Elma msf/jm/bl/#42.

of keeping bodies clean, fit and healthy and valuing personal bodily privacy and autonomy all came together. These values were all under challenge when engaging in the sexual act. One respondent, Eileen (1913), declared outright that sex itself was plain dirty: 'In fact sex is dirty; me mother used to say, sex is dirty, yeah.'[139] The majority of informants, though less categorical than this, were certainly wary of the fact that the physical intimacy of bodies during sex was generally associated with the risk of diseases. Such wariness might be expressed in quite vague and ill-informed terms, as by Maureen (1920), a Blackburn lower-middle-class interviewee married at 22 in 1943 to a sales rep five years her senior:

MAUREEN Well, I wouldn't've wanted to go near anybody if I had a period like that. Would you? No fear. No, that's when men get these diseases and things like that. They should leave women alone if, er – when you're unwell and just keep that private.[140]

However, for most this did not of course mean they saw sex in general as dirty or bodily closeness with their partner as undesirable in itself. It did mean that for many it was important for cleanliness and germ consciousness to be kept in mind, so that certain forms of bodily contact and sexual activity did not seem at all appealing or wise to most respondents. Keeping free from diseases and dirt came together in respondents' frequently expressed strong rejection of open mouth or French kissing as a practice, as expressed by Doreen (1922), born in Preston:

And what sorts of kisses would you have?

DOREEN Not sloppy ones; you wouldn't get to put the tongue in my mouth. Don't believe in that . . . I wouldn't tolerate that; I wouldn't tolerate it . . . well, if you've got any complaints it's the easiest way to pass it on, in't it? – In your mouth – the infection. No, I wouldn't do it. Um, I've had plenty of kisses but they've had to be proper ones; oh no, none of that business. I'd bite him if he did it. (laughs) I would. No, no, he wouldn't do it anyway; he's not like that.[141]

Several respondents understood a question about oral sex to be one about open-mouth kissing, to which they objected:

When did you first hear about oral sex?

SALLY I don't believe in it. I don't think it's healthy at all. I don't believe in it at all. I would never let my husband kiss me with his mouth open and waggle his tongue about, no way. That goes against the grain completely. It does.[142]

So how do you feel about things like oral sex when you read about them in these books?

139 Eileen msf/kf/bl/#12.

140 Maureen msf/kf/bl/#46.

141 Doreen and Larry msf/kf/bl/#20; and for similar negative views on 'French kissing': Felicity msf/kf/bl/#37.

142 Sally (1908) msf/kf/bl/#31.

EILEEN I think it's, eh, I think it's dirty… I do… putting their tongue in their mouth; my husband wouldn't do that, wouldn't do that, no, no. I've read all those, in those books – no, 'e wouldn't do anything like that Robin no. [I] tell yer, we were very, very old fashioned the pair of us, very old fashioned – must 'ave bin.[143]

Not surprisingly for such respondents as Eileen (1913), contact between the mouth and the private parts of the body was viewed as quite unwise, if not downright dirty.

And what about kissing each other's private parts: have you ever heard – did you hear about that?

EILEEN No, I've read that, I've read that in books an' all, in those books, yes!… It's dirty; I don't like it![144]

Respondents believed that such behaviour was not only unwise in health terms but also debased, i.e. both literally and metaphorically dirty.

Would you've, er, engaged in – [do] you know what oral sex is?

ED Yeah. Oh I know. We'd've, no, we'd never. I still get disgusted with that. I know what oral sex is; I – blimey!… I never practised it… No. No, we didn't go in for that, er, well, I used to call it 'the rubbish'.[145]

Terence (1915), a self-employed decorator who married aged 24 in 1939, thought that sexual behaviour could put people at risk of terrible diseases, such as cancer, when they did not keep to commonsense healthy practices.

TERENCE This is why [there is] so much cancerous growth in a woman's breasts today through that: the kissing, sucking, biting 'em. I think there's more cancers in that than something. I think so.[146]

Jennie (1908), a working-class Blackburnite seven years older than Terence, who married at 22 in 1930, clearly articulated the link she saw between cleanliness of the body, moderation in sexual behaviour and disease avoidance, incidentally implying that for her and her husband sex was a once-weekly activity associated with a visit to the local baths.

JENNIE But they do these days, these young people. Out of bed with one and into bed with another. No wonder there, there's heart trouble and cancer and all this and the other: 'cos they don't look after theirselves. And we'd no baths. The only bath – we used to have to go to the baths. Every Friday night – once a week, er, during the week you had a bath tub and, er, when they'd all gone to bed you used to get in

143 Eileen (1913) msf/kf/bl/#12.

144 Eileen msf/kf/bl/#12; for similar sentiments when asked about oral sex: Marilyn msf/kf/bl/#7; Lorna msf/kf/bl/#25; Christopher msf/kf/bl/#34; Frank msf/srss/bl/#16; Colin msf/kf/bl/#36; Alistair msf/kf/bl/#33.

145 Ed (1913) msf/srss/bl/#23. Others who used exactly the same term, 'disgusting', included Felicity msf/kf/bl/#37, Grace msf/srss/ht/#38, Dora msf/srss/ht/#38, Angela msf/kf/ht/#18.

146 Terence msf/srss/bl/#15.

there and have a good wash but Friday night … I used to go to the baths, 'cos we had no baths. It wasn't easy but, er, as I say it was no bother.[147]

Without a bath and attention to cleanliness, sex, even with one's marriage partner, was always a potential health risk in Terence's view.

So, did you always have a bath available in your house when you were married?
TERENCE Yeah, yeah. [Or] [y]ou risked what you got.
So, do you think you could actually get ill if you had sex and you weren't clean?
Yeah, yeah. That all happened.[148]

Such attitudes reflected a general germ consciousness, no doubt enhanced by the widely propagandised and understood health dangers of venereal diseases (see Chapter 2, notes 32, 47). Particularly where commercial sex was involved, therefore, the likely lack of control over the hygienic circumstances surrounding sex outside marriage would have exacerbated the conventional perception of its dangerous and risky nature and in turn compounded its moral unrespectability.

Despite the extent to which they had been accustomed since childhood to a bathroom and bodily cleanliness, most middle-class respondents were hardly any more positive about French kissing or oral sex, though their responses to these questions were less uniformly negative than those of working-class respondents. In the Hertfordshire sample there were several middle-class respondents, of both sexes, and one working-class female interviewee, who acknowledged having 'tried' oral sex, although only three of these were in any way positive about it as part of their sexual repertoire.[149] The majority were either unenthusiastic if they had tried it, or, like most of the working-class respondents who were asked, either ignorant of it or positively repulsed:

And when did you first hear about things like oral sex?
GILL Well, I still don't know what people get up to with oral sex. Sounds revolting to me, it really does. We certainly never did that … when they get round to the ejaculation and what happens to that? Because if it happens orally that just, er, would switch me off completely. They'd be thrown out (laughs), never mind anything else. I don't know … I would feel disgusted, er, er … [150]
So when did you first hear about sexual practices like oral sex?
ESME Oh, well, really not that long ago, really. I mean, it, it's the sort of, er, er, er, thing that I find almost impossible to contemplate now …
GERALD Oh yes, disgusting … And very dangerous … the mind boggles … It was referred to as unnatural practices. And, er, very good reason – they are too.[151]

Another lower-middle-class respondent who raised the dirtiness of bodies as a reason to avoid too intimate contact during sex, Mildred (1924), was one of the

[147] Jennie msf/kf/bl/#27. [148] Terence msf/srss/bl/#15.
[149] Catherine (1912) msf/kf/ht/#1; Reg (1919) msf/kf/ht/#36; Gay (1928) msf/kf/ht/#13.
[150] Gill (1920) msf/kf/bl/#48. [151] Esme (1921) and Gerald (1919) msf/kf/ht/#9.

younger women to be interviewed in Lancashire. She had commenced her married life in 1947, aged 22, with another self-confessed 'very shy' virgin, aged 20, in a home lacking both an indoor toilet and a bathroom. This formative period of their sex life together as a newly married couple had thus, unusually for middle-class respondents, been spent under the conditions of inadequate domestic sanitary facilities more commonly encountered by working-class couples:

> *Did you ever hear of things that other people did that you didn't want to do, in sex?*
>
> MILDRED Yes, er, touching er, your penis and touching my vagina ... it isn't very nice, is it? ... We thought it was dirty, at, at that time ... I didn't like it.[152]

Thus, personal hygiene and bodily cleanliness were vitally important and sometimes a practically quite problematic issue for many informants in relation to sex. Some respondents, when they did have the opportunity to keep themselves clean, with a higher standard of living in later life than they had had in childhood, did so with great application. Hugh (1926), who had, like Mildred, also married in 1947, had grown up in working-class Preston but had moved south and was interviewed with his surviving partner, Angela (1924), in Harpenden. They discussed their own scrupulous ablutions both before and after having sex. Hugh explained his appreciation of his wife's cleanliness throughout their marriage by evoking distasteful youthful memories:

> ANGELA if you planned to love each other, you see ... you had to be very hygienic, which we both are – and respect, you know, our bodies ...
>
> HUGH Oh yes; going back on [the] hygiene side, you see, I used to, when I first went to Preston, I used to travel by bus in the morning to, to work. [I] used to have a penny workman's fare. You see, if you travelled before 8 o'clock you went half fare. On those buses were girls who work – mill girls. All they had on was a pair of knicks and their overall. But they hadn't washed for a month. I couldn't stand that in a woman and I never have with her; she's always sweet and clean.[153]

Of course, not washing 'for a month' was a class-inflected reference to the regular hygiene difficulties which many working-class girls and women in the earlier part of this era had experienced in poor households with such limited washing possibilities.

Given the importance of cleanliness in imposing constraints on opportunities for sex, acquiring a bathroom could be much valued in enabling partners to engage in sex more spontaneously, as the feeling took them, than under the regime dictated by the regular weekly paying visit to the public baths. Furthermore, this could be attractive to a wife enabling her to exercise new powers of discretion in the sexual relationship, extending her established role

[152] Mildred msf/kf/bl/#41. [153] Hugh and Angela msf/kf/ht/#18.

as the household's domestic authority where all matters of cleanliness were concerned:

ALISTAIR Now then many [a] time I could tell when the wife were ready for sex, like, when, 'Go and have a bath tonight' and that was the signal for me right away (chuckle). So she'd have her bath; I'd have a bath; once we got to bed then, lights went out, (chuckle)... we were both brought up... very conscious about cleanliness. She was the same, as I said – she'd wash your shirt today, she'd wash it again tomorrow, sideboard she'd dust it... No, she was the perfect woman to me.[154]

The ownership of a bathroom was certainly a great convenience, which allowed respondents to maintain bodily hygiene in relation to the ambivalent – from the point of view of both health and salubrity – activity of sex.[155] It meant a lot in particular to women, both in relation to cleanliness in sex and because one of their prime roles was to maintain cleanliness throughout the home and for all its members. A husband who provided a bathroom for the home was proving his 'caring' love with a highly valued gift, while at the same time female respondents could appreciate how it empowered them, including sexually, in the relationship.

DORA What I loved about him... he was never dirty (laughs); he wasn't. I mean he'd come home, get in the bath and then my son would get in the bath and I'd go to have a look and it used to be all steamed up, you know, and... he built me a gorgeous bathroom. It was as big as that... And, er, erm, it took two years to (laugh) build. He was a devil really, honestly.[156]

Thus, there was a widespread perception among the interviewees of both sexes that the health of the body, one's elementary human capital, was a precious possession. It was also a precarious asset, whose preservation was of paramount importance to their own and their family's long-term life chances and to the quality of life they had been able to experience and enjoy. Sexual activity was potentially threatening in this respect and so, ideally, needed to be approached with some care, to try to ensure that bodies remained clean and healthy. This added dimensions of mutually reinforcing, practical health considerations to other perhaps more diffuse religious notions of the moral importance of preserving one's 'purity' and bodily integrity when it came to the risky activity of sex.

For many of our informants, then, the meaning of bodies in relation to sex in marriage was wrapped up in a set of powerful, interrelated moral and behavioural ideas about the importance for one's self-respect and social status of preserving the health and vitality of this natural endowment, its integrity and purity, its cleanliness, and its propriety and privacy. The natural body was also

[154] Alistair (1927) msf/kf/bl/#33.
[155] Cook, *The Long Sexual Revolution*, 146–7.
[156] Dora (1923) msf/srss/ht/#38.

the truthful body, innocent of deceit: morally clean. These were respondents' main positive understandings of the meaning of bodies. By contrast there was comparatively little attention in the testimony given to the body's physical appearance, the importance of its sex-specific features in ideas of relative attractiveness, or, indeed, to the possibility of manipulating by artifice its 'natural' shape or form in any way so as to render it more desirable.

Conclusion

When interviewees were asked explicit questions about what they considered to be attractive both in themselves and in the opposite sex when younger, they talked principally of modes of dress and behaviour. The body, defined as specific shapes and forms of flesh, was not what they admired in either sex. People's physical appearances were presented as having been 'read' primarily from their style of dress as valuable clues to a range of important personality characteristics and social status signifiers. The physical body is not presented as being interesting or 'readable' in the same way, with the sole exception of the hair. Variations in bodies – some men's are tall, some strong; some women's are hour-glass shaped and some have beautiful complexions – were seen to reflect the lottery of nature: the body was natural, not mouldable. The body's shape and sexual characteristics were not seen as reflecting much that is culturally or aesthetically significant or that provided an opportunity for an individual to manipulate their 'attractiveness'.

Respondents did, nevertheless, exhibit a strong 'body consciousness'. For most this manifested itself in a desire for bodily independence, autonomy and privacy along with a pervasive interest in maintaining and preserving the healthiness and the cleanliness of the body. Many portrayed this form of body consciousness about health, and its corollary in the avoidance of dirt and disease, as extending to what they considered appropriate sexual behaviour in general and in particular with their partner's body in marriage.

In her important recent studies of the cultural history of body management in the twentieth century, Zweiniger-Bargielowska quite correctly points out that '[t]here is no natural way to look' and that 'the visual representation of the body is a site for the construction of identity'.[157] Most of the interviewees believed that their bodies were unmediated gifts of nature, over whose shape and form they had little meaningful control. Of course, Zweiniger-Bargielowska's point is that this belief is itself an historically produced and culturally mediated ideology. It is clearly the case that respondents went to some lengths to attempt to maintain their bodies in a natural, clean and healthy state. However, given

[157] Zweiniger-Bargielowska, 'The Body and Consumer Culture', 185.

these beliefs about their bodies, the interwar fashion and advertising industries may have had something of an uphill battle on their hands to change the attitudes of the majority towards a more commercialised body consciousness. By contrast, government interest in promoting physical fitness and health may have been pushing on a more open door in this respect.

The oral history evidence suggests, therefore, that the history, ably documented by Zweiniger-Bargielowska, Matthews, Steele and others, of changing fashion and clothing styles, and of gradually growing interwar interests in dieting and exercise as beauty regimens, should not necessarily be seen as reflecting the rapid take-up of a new set of attitudes towards the body among the populace at large. This was no doubt the commercial intention of many of those involved in the emerging fashion, magazine and cosmetic industries and in promoting related physical fitness and slimming activities as they sought to expand their markets. However, for the socially conservative majority of the population the widespread social change in popular attitudes towards a more reflexive body consciousness and a more sexualised focus on the body's aesthetic form and shape may not in fact have really occurred until rather later, probably not until the 1960s on a society-wide scale.[158] Marcus Collins' recent examination of the textual content and the depictions of women's naked bodies in the commercial pornographic trade would also support this chronology. He finds that 1964 was the year of 'the first recognizably modern pornography' with new publications such as *Penthouse* and *Mayfair*, founded during the next two years, publishing much more explicitly erotic, sensual and sexualised images of women's bodies than the previous 'pornography of alibis' found in the 1950s market leaders, *Men Only* and *Lilliput*, both originating in the late 1930s.[159] The mid-1960s also saw these magazines championing an assertive

[158] There is evidence for increased popular and voluntary uptake of activities designed to keep the body in shape during the late 1950s, notably with the inauguration of the Keep Fit Association in 1956 and, more significantly, with the popularity of Eileen Fowler's innovative 'Keep Fit' classes on BBC Radio from that year, which were estimated to have attracted half a million, mainly female, followers. However, it is doubtful whether this truly represents popular interest beyond the upper and middle classes. Suzanne Newcombe's recent study of the social reception of yoga in post-war Britain finds that it was an exclusively middle-class and strongly female minority interest during the 1950s and 1960s. Furthermore its associations with body beauty, in addition to health and relaxation, did not become part of its public image until 1971, when ITV launched a popular TV series featuring a glamorous actress, Lyn Marshall, as the model demonstrating Yoga asanas (postures). The series ran successfully for three years (the only previous attempt to put yoga on TV by the BBC, in 1948, having been judged a complete failure in terms of surveyed audience response at that time) (Suzanne Newcombe, 'A Social History of Yoga and Ayurveda in Britain, 1950–1995' (Unpublished Ph.D. thesis; Cambridge: University of Cambridge, 2007), chs. 5, 7).

[159] Collins, *Modern Love*, ch. 5, 134, 35–9. The naturists' magazine, *Health and Beauty* (which depicted bodies with genitalia and pubic hair airbrushed out), was mentioned by one or two of the male respondents, such as Hugh msf/kf/ht#18, cited in Chapter 2 above (at note 143), as examples of opportunistic occasions when they saw images of the female body. This, along

new philosophy of libertarian sexual permissiveness, not seen in their predecessors. Meanwhile, sales of the new titles tripled over the decade 1966–76, reflecting a rapid expansion in the market for these new, sexualised depictions of the female body.[160]

The oral history evidence indicates that the positive reasons for resistance to changed body consciousness in the populace at large before the 1960s most likely lay in the salience of ideas about the body as something natural, allied with the ethos of privacy in relation to the body, strongly inculcated from childhood onwards. Respondents did have an intensely individualistic body consciousness but it was focused on privacy and autonomy of their bodies, values which would strongly militate against public display and exposure of their bodies. A change from this disposition towards markedly greater acceptance of the publicly displayed naked body as a suitable object for a public discourse, and as the subject for a sexual aesthetics, could only have happened as a cultural revolution, rather than a gradual, accumulative process. An extremely powerful conjunction of forces was required to overturn the opposite set of integrated mutually supporting values about bodies and sex, as espoused by the interviewees.[161] Indeed, these respondents, interviewed in the later 1990s, remained disconcerted by this revolution in values, which they acknowledged

with 'amateur photography' journals, was a paradigmatic example of what Collins terms a 'pornography of alibis'. See Bingham, *Family Newspapers*, 205–27 for a similar analysis of the depictions of pin-ups from the 1920s to the 1970s. Sonya Rose also discusses pin-ups and images of girls in swimming costumes during the war, continuing the pre-war trend identified by Bingham. Hers is principally a study of government policy and the media, noting that during wartime 'sexualized femininity' was 'riddled with contradictions'. These tensions reflected the problems facing official efforts in attempting both to buoy up the morale of the female workforce with notions of the glamour of earning and the discretionary spending this made possible, while also emphasising demands for their selflessness and stoicism in caring for family members, which included paying attention to their family members' bodies and to their own fitness and physical efficiency (Rose, *Which People's War?*, 128–36, quotes on 135). See also, Andy Saunders, *Jane: A Pin-up at War* (London: Leo Cooper Ltd, 2004). The frequently scantily clad wartime Jane was, of course, a cartoon depiction.

160 See Collins, *Modern Love*, ch. 5 (esp. 134–6); and Table 1 (p. 41).

161 As Mary Douglas' celebrated anthropological work has emphasised, systems of belief and thought related to concepts of moral purity and danger, cleanliness and dirt, are pervasively rooted in cultures and their discourses, so it should not come as a surprise that society-wide cultural change would take on the form of a rapid tipping point, rather than a process of gradual modification (Mary Douglas, *Purity and Danger; an Analysis of Concepts of Pollution and Taboo* (New York: Praeger, 1966)). On tipping points, see Thomas Schelling, *Micromotives and Macrobehavior* (New York: Norton, 1978). See also Callum Brown's emphasis on the rapidity of cultural change in religious discourses during the 1960s, which, he argues, was closely related to rapid popular changes in gender ideologies and sexual practices (Brown, *The Death of Christian Britain*, 175–80, 220–78). For Brown, 'discourses … are to do with injunctions on conduct formed, circulated and hybridised in culture as a whole' (ibid., 204) – in other words moral codes. Therefore, if widespread, a discourse can only end relatively abruptly: 'Discourse is about a *dominance*, and that dominance is not negated by the shifting patterns of its circulation – only by its end' (ibid., 210; emphasis in original).

as having happened during their lifetimes but which they did not themselves, on the whole, endorse (as shown here in Chapters 1 and 9). They were disapproving of its consequences for public life and discourse and for the sexual behaviour of the younger generations which they persisted in seeing as unwise, risky in health terms and immoral.

When and exactly how this widespread social revolution in public and popular attitudes towards the body occurred in British society, and the extent of both its impact and its limitations, therefore constitutes an important subject for future research and something that has not been explained by previous historians' accounts documenting the gradually growing activities from the 1920s onwards of those individuals and associations promoting such a sexualised body consciousness. It seems most likely that the decades of the 1960s and 1970s encompass the period of this cultural revolution in British society and that the key concepts of 'privacy' and 'nature' must have undergone transformations in their popular meanings and usages among both the young and in demotic culture at this time, particularly in relation to the body and sexuality, but exactly how this happened remains a fruitful topic for future research.[162]

Consequently, most of the discussion in this chapter has found similarities in attitudes and beliefs about the body, attractiveness, health and hygiene articulated by both the younger and the older respondents interviewed. There were only patchy and quite ephemeral signs of changing attitudes towards body consciousness and display of the body found in the interviewees' evidence. An example of this was a quite distinct understanding of the use of cosmetics in the testimony of four of the younger female middle-class

[162] It may not be coincidental that Raymond Williams' classic text, *Keywords: A Vocabulary of Culture and Society*, was first published in 1976 following this period of rapid cultural transformation. Born in 1921 in the Welsh border village of Pandy, Williams was an exact contemporary of the interviewees for this study, though unlike all but a few of them he had gone to university. Both the words 'private' and 'nature' (and also 'sex') were among the 110 keywords, whose conceptual history was presented in *Keywords* (twenty-one more were added in the second edition of 1983). Of all the words studied Williams concluded that '[n]ature is perhaps the most complex word in the language'. He distinguished three main 'areas of meaning' which he demonstrated were often effortlessly elided and conflated together in usage: nature as the essential character and quality of an object (such as a person's body); nature as the inherent force which directs the world and humans to be as they are; nature as the material world itself (including human beings' physical bodies). He also noted that 'one of the most powerful uses of nature, since the late eighteenth century, has been in ... [the] sense of goodness and innocence'. Certainly his contemporaries – our respondents – were clearly using all of these meanings of nature in the conflated manner identified by Williams, with the notion of innocence also strongly salient, as Williams noted (Raymond Williams, *Keywords: A Vocabulary of Culture and Society* (New York: Oxford University Press, 1983)). For an extraordinarily wide-ranging historical and geographical exploration of the term's usages and meanings, see the collection of essays in Lorraine Daston and Fernando Vidal, eds. *The Moral Authority of Nature* (London: University of Chicago Press, 2004). On 'privacy' in modern British history, see also the stimulating essay by Harrison, 'The Public and the Private'.

respondents interviewed for this study.[163] They mentioned the use of lipstick and nail varnish as glamour accessories, rather than as means to achieve a natural look.

GAY When I was retiring, we had a big do and several people made speeches and one of the fellas said, 'when I started here it was, er, seven weeks before I ever saw Gay in the same thing twice and never ever saw her with anything but red nails, and they were never chipped' and you know, um, so yes, I was known as glamorous.[164]

Gay (born in 1928) did not start working in the town hall accounting department, from which she retired and where she acquired her reputation for glamour, until after her divorce in 1966. It was notable that these four younger informants all referred to the era of the Second World War or later when talking of their use of cosmetics in this way:

And did you wear make-up at all?

ANGELA Um, I don't think I did till my sister went in uniform NAAFI and she gave me a lipstick.[165]

This pattern of testimony would be consistent with the thesis put forward by Zweiniger-Bargielowska of a significant increase in the use of cosmetics during and after the Second World War.[166] It would also confirm that, to the extent that this produced a permanent sea-change in wider attitudes towards cosmetics, it was something which may only initially have affected the younger, rising generation during the mid-1940s, rather than 'converting' the attitudes among older women at that time; hence it is only reflected in the attitudes of some

[163] Gay (1928) msf/kf/ht/#13; Gill (1920) msf/kf/bl/#48; Angela (1924) msf/kf/ht/#18; Jane (1925) msf/kf/bl/#32.

[164] Gay msf/kf/ht/#13. [165] Angela (1924) msf/kf/ht/#18.

[166] It has been plausibly suggested by Zweiniger-Bargielowska that wartime austerity limitations on most items of dress resulted in something of a re-evaluation of the capacity of relatively cheap and available cosmetics to provide an alternative focus for attention to personal appearance (Zweiniger-Bargielowska, *Austerity in Britain*, 91–2). However, it should also be noted that after the war the 1949 official survey of consumer expenditure still found extremely low levels of monthly average spending on cosmetics and toiletries and that this was associated with low average frequencies of hair-washing by women (only once every ten days) (Smith, *Clean*, 388). Jones' recent comparative study found British spending on 'beauty products' only one-tenth that of the USA in 1950 (i.e. about three times less per head of population) and also slightly lagging behind the similarly sized populations of France and Germany (Geoffrey Jones, 'Blonde and Blue-Eyed? Globalizing Beauty, c. 1945–c. 1980', *Economic History Review* 61, no. 1 (2008): 125–54; Table 1, 31). Thus the oral testimony reported here and Jones' statistics seem to show that throughout the first half of the twentieth century British society was quite different in its values from the USA in relation to cosmetics. In the USA Peiss has argued that 'by the early 1900s', 'the infrastructure for beauty culture ... reached into every level of the social scale ... urban immigrants, African-Americans, and rural women' (Kathy Peiss, 'Making Up, Making Over: Cosmetics, Consumer Culture, and Women's Identity', in *The Sex of Things: Gender and Consumption in Historical Perspective*, eds. Victoria Grazia with Ellen Furlough (London: University of California Press, 1996), 322).

of the youngest women we interviewed.[167] Indeed the word 'glamour' (or its derivatives) was only used on a handful of occasions in all the hundreds of hours of interviews (by just two of the female and two of the male respondents).[168] As Carol Dyhouse explains: 'Glamour has almost always been linked with artifice... and often sexual-allure.'[169] This conflicted with the interviewees' core values in relation to the naturalness of their bodies and of sex.

In summary, the evidence presented in this chapter reveals that most interviewees enjoyed a sexual relationship during their marriages without sexualising or eroticising particular physical aspects of their bodies. Many sought to maintain important standards of health and cleanliness where possible and to avoid impinging upon each other's sense of bodily privacy. However, as subsequent chapters will show, this was also part of a positive aspiration for beautiful and respectable marital sex, as something natural and spontaneous. Bodies were viewed as natural – 'givens' – and sex was also best when experienced as a natural and spontaneous experience. By contrast, eroticised bodies or the use of artifice or cosmetics to positively enhance women's appearance was viewed with suspicion by all but a few of the younger middle-class interviewees, as something linked to illicit or disreputable sex of a contrived, non-natural form.

[167] Thus, the Wartime Social Survey cited by Zweiniger-Bargielowska, which found that two-thirds of women were using some form of cosmetics in 1942–3, also found that this related to as many as 90 per cent of 'the under-30s', but only 37 per cent of those over 45 years of age (Zweiniger-Bargielowska, *Austerity in Britain*, 91; 'The Body and Consumer Culture', 187). Such an uneven pattern by age would help explain the low averages of cosmetic use and domestic ablutions found by Jones, cited in the previous note.

[168] Grace msf/srss/ht/#38; Gay msf/kf/ht/#13; Norman msf/kf/ht/#17; Reg msf/kf/ht/#36.

[169] Carol Dyhouse, *Glamour: Women, History, Feminism* (London: Zed Books, 2010), 1. Consistent with our oral history findings, Dyhouse's book argues that 'glamour', as a popular concept and fashion style, did not flourish in British society until as recently as the 1980s and 1990s, when it became so rapidly 'democratised' that by 'the first decade of the twenty-first century the word "glamour"... came to dominate the discourse of magazines aimed at women' (ibid., 5).

8 Sex, love, duty, pleasure?

Following the First World War, an emphasis on mutual sexual pleasure emerged in public discourse about marriage. For the ever more numerous writers of the marriage manual a central cause of marital unhappiness was sexual maladjustment: they sought to educate couples in erotic technique and in particular to teach men how to awaken women's sexual feelings and elicit pleasurable responses.[1] Many historians stress the limited effect such messages had on the experiences of married couples. Indeed, arguably, the proliferation of sexual guidance literature and its popularity support the claim that couples struggled to enjoy mutually satisfying sexual lives during the early decades of the twentieth century. Lesley Hall has argued that despite Marie Stopes' championing of 'ecstatic marital sex', the letters written to her by thousands of women in the interwar period attest to a 'picture ... of English marital sexuality during the nineteenth century and the early part of the twentieth' that is 'grim and depressing'.[2] Writing about the interwar period, Hera Cook linked women's descriptions of sexual unhappiness with the continued acceptance of male conjugal rights: 'Mutual pleasure and tenderness was absent from these women's constructions of marital sexuality. They had disengaged from mutual sexual activity; what they accepted was a duty.'[3] According to this critique, for many

[1] See, Margaret Jackson, *The Real Facts of Life: Feminism and the Politics of Sexuality, 1850–1940* (London and Bristol, PA: Taylor & Francis, 1994), 160–1. On the rising rhetoric of marital sexual pleasure, see, for example, Holtzman, 'The Pursuit of Married Love', Lewis, 'Public Institution and Private Relationship', McKibbin, *Classes and Cultures: England, 1918–1951*, 297–301, McLaren, *Twentieth-Century Sexuality*, 46–63, Brooke, 'Gender and Working Class Identity in Britain'.

[2] Lesley A. Hall, 'Review of Hera Cook, *The Long Sexual Revolution: English Women, Sex, and Contraception 1800–1975*', *Continuity and Change* 19, no. 2 (2004): 331. See also, Weeks, *The World We Have Won*, 37–8.

[3] Hera Cook argues that marriage manuals from the 1920s stopped talking about sex as conjugal rights but that many continued to describe the provision of sex as a marital duty. In developing psychological and physiological theories of male and female sexual needs this literature required men to ensure their wives obtained orgasms, while women were obliged to be available and sexually responsive partners. Particularly during the 1950s and 1960s, she argues that a new version of women's sexual responsibilities and obligations emerged and outlined a range of sexual services which women had to perform (with enthusiasm) (Cook, *The Long Sexual Revolution*, 236–8). Margaret Jackson argues that the concept of 'conjugal rights', which nineteenth-century

women before the transformations of the 1960s, sexual experiences remained stymied by widespread sexual ignorance, the use of primitive methods of birth control, taboos against sexual experimentation, the acceptance of female passivity and the absence of open discussion of sexual issues.[4]

To a certain extent, the descriptions of marital sexual relationships in oral history testimony support the claim that sexual intercourse between married couples was infrequent and unsatisfactory. Many working-class women in particular found little to enjoy, especially where contraception was seen to be unreliable or not used at all: a state of affairs that left them fearful of pregnancy.[5] Few couples were able to talk about sexual matters; for some, this meant they were unable to communicate their desires, or work at improving their sex lives. Such 'inhibitions' equally meant few sought assistance for, or information about, their sex lives from marriage manuals or advice books. Beliefs about germs and dirt also fostered a reluctance to experiment with positions or practices such as oral sex.

At the same time, however, for many it was precisely those conventions which later generations vilified as having produced unsatisfactory sex lives which were fundamental, for some respondents, to sustaining meaningful sexual experiences.[6] Cultures of silence and strict moral codes were not necessarily antithetical to the enjoyment of sexual intercourse.[7] This chapter seeks to go beyond a simple focus on what couples did in bed – such as the range of erotic techniques or the question of female orgasm – and instead looks to investigate individuals' complex constructions of sexual desire.[8] In particular, it will focus on the very different criteria which pre-1960s generations used to assess their sexual relationships, examining the role that ideas about duty, hygiene,

feminists had attacked as one of the most pernicious elements of women's sexual slavery within marriage, still had a profound influence on early twentieth-century relationships (Jackson, *The Real Facts of Life*, 10).

4 Sally Alexander, 'The Mysteries and Secrets of Women's Bodies', Cook, *The Long Sexual Revolution*, 182–6, Roberts, *A Woman's Place*, 83–8.

5 Cook, 'Sexuality and Contraception in Modern England'.

6 On the ways in which social contexts produce 'multiple narratives of sexual life' see Jeffrey Weeks, 'History, Desire, and Identities', in *Conceiving Sexuality: Approaches to Sex Research in a Postmodern World*, eds. Richard G. Parker and John H. Gagnon (New York and London: Routledge, 1995), 33.

7 These findings demonstrate, as sociologists have long understood, the ways in which the meanings attributed to sex and the experiences of it are socio-culturally produced. See, Richard G. Parker and John H. Gagnon, eds. *Conceiving Sexuality: Approaches to Sex Research in a Postmodern World* (New York and London: Routledge, 1995), Leonore Tiefer, *Sex Is Not a Natural Act and Other Essays* (Boulder, CO and Oxford: Westview Press, 2004). See also, Weeks, 'History, Desire, and Identities', 34.

8 See also Nicola Gavey, Kathryn McPhillips and Virginia Braun, 'Interruptus Coitus: Heterosexuals Accounting for Intercourse', *Sexualities* 2, no. 1 (1999): 35–68. These researchers 'mapped the meanings of sex' expressed by heterosexual 'Pakeha' (New Zealand Europeans), interviewed in the mid-1990s, finding that 'pleasure is seldom mentioned as a reason for having intercourse'.

naturalness, spontaneity and privacy all played in their evaluations of what constituted successful sex. For these generations, sex was viewed as fulfilling when part of a private relationship in which it was not discussed, when natural, spontaneous and free from cultural interference, when it represented the coming together of pure and clean bodies, and when couples used it to demonstrate the giving, rather than the receiving, of pleasure. Discussions of sexual pleasure were thus intimately connected to codes of respectability, female sexual innocence, caring and sharing, duty and privacy.

'It's an expression of love'

The study of sexual pleasure – historical, sociological and sexological – has frequently focused on the attainment of orgasm, particularly in women. Throughout the twentieth century sexologists and marriage guidance literature identified the wife's climax as the key to marital sexual satisfaction, and in turn to the harmony of the marriage itself.[9] Early marriage manuals urged men to awaken in their wives a capacity for sexual awareness and fulfilment, through sensitive and chivalrous love-making.[10] Specific techniques and instructions on precise forms of stimulation began to be outlined in some manuals.[11] By the 1930s, claims that women had a right to sexual pleasure were evident in popular women's magazines.[12] Sociological surveys investigated sexual pleasure in narrowly defined terms, and as a result much of the material available for analysis ties historians into reproducing these frameworks.[13]

9 Jessamyn Neuhaus, 'The Importance of Being Orgasmic: Sexuality, Gender, and Marital Sex Manuals in the United States, 1920–1963', *Journal of the History of Sexuality* 9, no. 4 (2000): 447–73.

10 Ibid.

11 Notable here is Van de Velde's description of the 'genital kiss' and his acknowledgement that female orgasm might be roused by digital stimulation of the clitoris, if 'genital friction' [i.e. coitus] was not enough; and Helena Wright's insistence that husbands were best advised to initiate their young wives into coital pleasures by first inducing orgasms through digital stimulation (Wright, *The Sex Factor in Marriage*, 31–2, 70–2, 95–6, Theodoor H. Van de Velde, *Ideal Marriage: Its Physiology and Technique* (London: William Heinemann, 1947, first published 1928), 148–9). See also, Hall, *Outspoken Women*, 180–2, Simmons, *Making Marriage Modern*, esp. ch. 5, 178–217. Chesser also discussed the genital kiss in 1941, though he felt it would shock an inexperienced young wife or bride (see Cook, *The Long Sexual Revolution*, 230–1). In such literature we see a particular focus on the achievement of the female orgasm as the goal of and proof of sexual pleasure, the emergence of debates about women's physiology, and an attempt to explain female orgasm by locating it within specific parts of the female body – cervix, vagina and clitoris (Cook, *The Long Sexual Revolution*, 245–51). In the post-war period the sexological literature on female orgasm was increasingly ambivalent, with women, rather than male technique, blamed for its elusiveness and some manuals by the 1950s and 1960s suggesting that women might try to find happiness in sex without orgasm (Neuhaus, 'The Importance of Being Orgasmic', 461–8).

12 See, Lewis, 'Public Institution and Private Relationship', 237.

13 Stanley, *Sex Surveyed*, 58–64.

Increasingly, however, the complex conceptual problems facing the study of sex and pleasure, and the inadequacy of frameworks which focus on orgasm as a means of thinking about desire and fulfilment, have been highlighted by sociologists, feminists and contemporary sex therapists.[14] Lynne Segal has criticised the ways in which the biological focus of sexuality studies on the physiology of orgasm has blinded scholars to the complex cultural and social experiences of pleasure and desire.[15] Stephen Garton has charted and criticised the way in which, since the Kinsey Report, 'objective' ways of measuring pleasure have been sought. The pervasive theoretical problem with the study of sexuality, he claims, has been the way it has tended to reduce 'a larger world of sensuality to a mechanistic search for orgasm'.[16] However, historians have, as yet, paid little attention to investigating women's more oblique descriptions of sexual satisfaction (or, indeed, its absence) and have continued to see documentation of orgasm as central to any evaluation of female sexual pleasure.[17]

Yet, among oral history respondents pleasure derived through orgasm was seldom at the forefront of women's depictions of the joys of marital sex. This was not because women were blind to their own physical, bodily capacity for pleasure; indeed, many spoke about the successes and failures of the erotic techniques they employed. Nor was it because pleasure and orgasm were rarely experienced by women in the sample, although a good many did not have very satisfactory sex lives. Instead, many women found it difficult to frame the discussion of their sexual experiences in terms of orgasm. In part, of course, this reflects the embarrassment women felt in describing their sexual experiences in an interview. Yet, it is also indicative of the ways in which many interviewees emphasised the giving of love as the primary purpose of sex. Indeed, the desire for orgasm was sometimes presented as a destabilising force in marital relations, as it evidenced a need for individually experienced exhilaration that was at odds with sex's central function in this culture: of indicating love by caring for one's partner. Implicit in testimony is an objection to the idea of

[14] Peggy J. Kleinplatz, *New Directions in Sex Therapy: Innovations and Alternatives* (Philadelphia, PA and Hove: Brunner-Routledge; Accelerated Development, 2001).

[15] Lynne Segal, *Straight Sex: The Politics of Pleasure* (London: Virago, 1994).

[16] Stephen Garton, *Histories of Sexuality* (New York: Routledge, 2004), 203–9.

[17] There has been considerable debate on this matter with regard to Celia Mosher's survey between 1892 and 1913 of American women's sexual experiences. While some see her survey as indicating the extensiveness of women's sexual pleasure in this period, others see the absence of clear accounts of orgasm as indicative of the limits on the sexual pleasure documented and instead see her survey as evidence of women's sexual repression (Carol Z. Stearns and Peter N. Stearns, 'Victorian Sexuality: Can Historians Do It Better?', *Journal of Social History* 18, no. 4 (1985): 625–34, Carl N. Degler, 'What Ought to Be and What Was: Women's Sexuality in the Nineteenth Century', *The American Historical Review* (1974)). For a careful evaluation and use of the Mosher survey see, David and Sanderson, 'Rudimentary Contraceptive Methods'.

celebrating individual sexual pleasure. Discussions of marriage, sex and its pleasures frequently hedged around the issue of orgasm, as individuals sought to demonstrate above all their commitment to appropriate spousal obligations and responsibilities.

Pleasure, through orgasm, or sexual technique, was not at the forefront of many women's depictions of the 'pleasures' of marital sex. Even where sex did bring intense pleasure, many women placed greater emphasis on the ways in which, through having sex, they provided their partner with a thrilling experience, a sense of being cared for and confirmation that they were loved. Gill (1920) admitted it was 'essential to enjoy it' but emphasised that this was so that sex could fulfil its function of providing an 'understanding between you'.[18] For some women, discussing their own orgasms was dangerously selfish, and suggested a lack of commitment to ideas that sex was above all a way for women to demonstrate love for the male partner: an individual woman's own personal enjoyment of the act was often presented as secondary in importance to the attempt to give or provide love, care and pleasure. Penny (1916) saw sex as a key means by which she could love and look after her husband, a farm labourer she married in 1938:

PENNY I loved him and wanted to look after him ... the thought of having sex, um, was a help ... I enjoyed it when, you know, I used to sort of have it once a week ... you indulge in it and when you, when you, when you sort of felt like it.[19]

Phyllis (1921) reluctantly and ineffusively admitted her personal enjoyment of sex only after having first demonstrated that she saw it as a means of showing love to her husband (a salesman):

PHYLLIS It's a, to me it was just a way of saying 'I love you', you, er, showing your (coughs), showing your affection for each other really.
And did you enjoy it?
Yes I suppose so, yes.[20]

Also (lower-)middle-class Felicity (1919), a convert to Catholicism who married quite late (in 1954 aged 34) and had done clerical accounting for one of the railway companies, enjoyed sex, but valued it above all as a way of telling her husband (who was a railway company claims assessor) that she loved him:

And what did you like about it?
FELICITY What did I like about it? I don't know; it's an expression of love, in't it? ...[21]

[18] Gill msf/kf/bl/#48, married in 1945.
[19] Penny msf/srss/ht/#20.
[20] Phyllis msf/kf/bl/#5, married in 1943.
[21] Felicity msf/kf/bl/#37, married in 1954.

For all these women their own personal enjoyment of sex was downplayed; they emphasised instead the role that sex played in the provision of care for their husband. Eleanor (1907), who had a 'very happy', 'ordinary' marriage from 1934 to a 'steady man', who was a car mechanic from Blackburn, discussed her own pleasure in terms of her husband's desires. Having sex was the least important of the list of things she provided for her husband, including cooking meals and organising the house:

> ELEANOR Some women are worse than men – nymphomaniacs – they're worse than men aren't they? They go after men ... well I were never one of them ... no I were never one of them ... you know, I'd be a willin' partner, but it never worried me otherwise.
>
> *(overlapping) So did you enjoy sex?*
>
> Yes I did, after, yes I did, yes ... he were a good partner.
>
> *What did you enjoy about it?*
>
> Well, the actual thing, you know (pause) yeah the actual thing ... it's nice, for a woman to enjoy sex because a man likes you to enjoy it doesn't 'e? ... Oh yes I think it's part of your marriage and, if it's going well and, it, eh, it's going well in bed everythin's going well because your 'usband keeps by your side, doesn't 'e? Yes, oh yes
>
> [...]
>
> *And how important was sex to your marriage?*
>
> It's not that, it wasn't that important ... other things were more important to me.
>
> *What was more important?*
>
> Eh, makin' a dinner and things like that, and seein' people enjoy a meal, yeah, domestic work, you know, I used to like that ... no it weren't that important; the house and, eh, 'olidays and things like that were more important.[22]

For women who conceptualised sex as a way they cared for and provided for their husbands, too great a focus on their own personal pleasures was considered insensitive and selfish, and denigrated as self-seeking, unreciprocal and thus destabilising to marital harmony. Moreover, women also held to these views about personal pleasure in their evaluations of what constituted appropriate expressions of male desire: they sometimes criticised their husbands when they felt that a spouse had not sought sex in order to express care, but instead was seeking solely to fulfil his own needs.[23] Thus, despite the fact that women thought men had a certain biological need for sex, they did not want to be given the impression that his own desire for personal satisfaction was at the forefront of his mind. Hilda's (1914) sex life with her first husband was 'terrible' because he was 'insatiable' and she 'just felt like a stud'.[24] Doreen's (1922) sexual relationship was fraught and unsatisfactory, in part because of gynaecological

[22] Eleanor msf/kf/bl/#11.

[23] Similar sentiments can be found in the Dennis et al.'s *Coal is our Life* study of the 1950s, quoted in Brooke, 'Gender and Working Class Identity', 785.

[24] Hilda msf/kf/bl/#50, born in 1914 in Cheshire, her first marriage was to a pharmaceuticals sales director in 1935, one child.

problems which frequently made sex painful, but mostly because she did not see her husband's approach to sex as one which was focused on love and reciprocation. She criticised his technique as self-serving:

DOREEN There's times through life that it's not a pleasant – you're not ready for it and it's not pleasant and it's forced on you. I don't think, I don't think that's necessary ... in fact I've done it when I can't enjoy it to please him, you see ... if you played with it for him – he was as happy – he went back to sleep as long as he got what he wanted. He didn't give a damn if I got it or not, as long as he got it ... I don't think he stopped to ... there were other ways of doing it, to make it pleasing [to] you.

She even found his attempts to be caring disingenuous. At times when he sought to mend an argument by showing sexual affection, she was annoyed that he looked to placate her in a way that would simply give him so much individual pleasure:

DOREEN The only way he'd want to make up was with that [sex]. I said 'that doesn't make it up with me; it makes me more mad – bad-tempered. Makes me wild does that. You're only thinking about making yourself happy, not me.'[25]

The oblique ways in which women discussed their own experiences of sexual climax did not simply reflect its absence or women's embarrassment and unease at discussing the subject; rather, such testimony highlighted the alternative functions of sex in many women's conceptions of their marital responsibilities and relationships. Their understanding of appropriate marital sex as selfless and concerned with the provision of care and love meant that many rejected an approach to sex that was simply concerned with personal pleasure. Thus, when women did relate the pleasures of sex, or testify to orgasm, they were careful to diffuse its association with individualistic 'selfish' enjoyment, and rather presented it as a happy by-product of a loving and caring act.

'It was more vital for men'

Key to women's construction of sex as a mechanism for caring for their husband was a set of beliefs about male sexual make-up.[26] Men were, in general, thought to have stronger sexual desires than most women, though variation between individuals was also regularly commented upon.[27] Many women,

[25] Doreen msf/kf/bl/#20, born in 1922 in Blackburn, she married a foreman bricklayer in 1946, two children.

[26] It is argued that 'a male sexual drive discourse' continues to dominate Western conceptions of heterosexual sex, see, Virginia Braun, Nicola Gavey and Kathryn McPhillips, 'The "Fair Deal"? Unpacking Accounts of Reciprocity in Heterosex', *Sexualities* 6, no. 2 (2003): 238. See also, Gavey, McPhillips and Braun, 'Interruptus Coitus'.

[27] Margaret Jackson has studied the dominance of this theme of different male and female patterns of sexual desire in Marie Stopes' *Married Love*. See, Jackson, *The Real Facts of Life*, 132–7. On

like June (1914), thus saw the provision of sex as important in satisfying their husbands' basic needs.

JUNE 'Cos we always had that idea that men, men were into, more into sex than what we women were. They needed sex; it was more vital to men to have se- . . . to get relief. Well, that's what we used to think anyway.[28]

Many who did not like sex were happy to report that their husbands were not especially sexual themselves, and saw themselves as lucky if they did not have to provide sex too often. Gill (1920) and her husband, a Blackburn mill owner, had a very successful sex life and a happy marriage, although they did not spend much time together as he was a 'man's man'. Nevertheless she noted that her husband wanted more sex than she did, and was grateful for his patience and consideration of her desires in not approaching her too often:

GILL I would try to relax a bit more and be more relaxed for him if I didn't feel particularly like having sex . . . but he wasn't keen on doing it if he thought I wasn't feeling like that . . . If I didn't feel particularly like having sex . . . he would have stopped . . . it's natural for men to have more, a lively sex life, isn't it? You know I think they, on the whole, they need more.[29]

In fact, even those women who got little personal enjoyment from sex were anxious if the sexual relationship became too infrequent. As Gill, above, indicated, many men faced with a less than enthusiastic wife themselves lost interest in showing their love or care for their wife in this way. This was rarely welcomed; the idea that men needed sex led many to worry that their husbands might find an alternative outlet. Moreover, even if women did not enjoy intercourse, they nevertheless wanted to experience it with a regular frequency, in part because they needed to know that their husbands still cared for them, and they saw this demonstrated through sex. Thus, even a husband who was aware that his wife did not enjoy sex was expected still to approach her for it. Agatha (1910) and her husband both worked in the same country house and married in 1940:

Did you have sex when you didn't want to have sex?

AGATHA Oh I suppose so really 'cos I wasn't really interested in it tell you the truth . . . I don't think I ever refused. I don't think I was that stupid . . . I should think that would be silly in a way . . . because he was a fella that considered you . . . and he waited until you was ready yerself sort of thing; he was very good like that . . . so he was very kind, very careful and very good, he was thoughtful, couldn't have wished for anyone better . . . I think if you do that [refuse sex] too often they

the impact of Freudian and other contemporary psychological categories for understanding sexuality see Gillian Rose, *Love's Work: A Reckoning with Life* (London: Chatto & Windus, 1995), 63, Melissa Tyler, 'Managing between the Sheets: Lifestyle Magazines and the Management of Sexuality in Everyday Life', *Sexualities* 7, no. 1 (2004): 100.

[28] June msf/kf/ht/#27, married in 1936. [29] Gill msf/kf/bl/#48, married in 1945.

think you don't care for them don't they? That's my feeling anyway. I thought now if you keep telling 'im you don't want [it] he'll think there's something wrong – he'll be goin' somewhere else ... and you couldn't blame 'im ... no he was a very thoughtful fella ... I mean to say we seemed to be quite happy, must have been.
But what sort of role do you think sex played in making you happy?
Well, to think that he cared, knowing that he didn't go off with anyone else, he was always at home, yer know what I mean (laughing)?[30]

Male respondents also confirmed this form of behaviour. Hubert (1911), who had been a journalist before he became a director of his wife's family's agricultural engineering firm, and his wife, who had been a nurse, had a very unhappy marriage, in which sex was rarely enjoyable for either party. Yet both sought to keep the sexual side of their relationship alive:[31]

HUBERT As I said, she got very upset if I didn't offer. (pause) Although she responded not at all. And then there were accusations that I, I'd relieved myself elsewhere which I certainly hadn't.[32]

Similarly, Glynnis (1901), the oldest female interviewee, who was unusually adamant in the extent to which she professed to have disliked almost all aspects of sex, neverthless thought it was both her marital duty to provide pleasure for her husband and was worried that he might no longer request it if she rejected him too often. Fearful that he might seek love elsewhere the provision of sex was seen as a necessary act, in order to keep a husband feeling happy, loved and provided for. Refusing sex outright was not an option:

GLYNNIS I didn't like it ... I thought it was overrated and that sort of thing. I thought it was something we could do without.
And what did your husband think?
I don't know what he thought. He used to have it but I don't think he were, I don't know, not very thrilled I don't think, I don't know.
Did you tell him you didn't like it?
Er no. No I didn't tell him, no. Might've put him off forever then ... I thought, you never know. I knew my husband was alright but I've heard of other folks refusing and they've gone somewhere else, see, and I thought well, I don't want that.[33]

Rejecting a husband's sexual advances was thus seen as an abnegation of the wifely role to provide and care for her husband. Many wives found themselves disinclined to have sex, particularly when feeling tired and worn out by domestic life. Yet, in such instances most nevertheless thought it important

30 Agatha msf/kf/ht/#7.

31 This was despite his wife's additional desire to avoid pregnancy and their conflictual contraceptive practices (see Chapter 6, notes 94, 109).

32 Hubert msf/kf/ht/#32, married in 1936.

33 Glynnis msf/kf/bl/#4, married to a plumber in 1924.

not to reject their husband too often.[34] In a few cases, wives were presented by their widowers as having always been sexually responsive. Roger (1910) was a chartered surveyor; his wife had been a hairdresser. They married in 1938 and after the war they lived in comparative affluence. His wife did not work. In these circumstances, Roger revealed, a devoted husband certainly appreciated the constant 'availability' of his wife:

ROGER I had a very, very, very happy sex life. And it didn't matter, quite frankly, when – it sounds very manlike but if I wanted to, she was always ready – and never refused. And it's one of the most beautiful – and I mean it – beautiful passages of my life that I've ever had, that I could come in the door, and say 'Come here!' And she did.[35]

When women avoided a sexual relationship or started regularly refusing intercourse they presented it as a sign that they were no longer prepared to care for their husbands or provide for them. The refusal of sex might be a deliberate and conscious rejection of the caring role and indicative of a major rift in the couple's relationship. Pru (1911), who married in 1935, avoided sex when her husband began to drink. However, her commitment to her duties as a wife meant that this withdrawal was not total (although later in the marriage after her husband suffered the humiliation of losing his privileged post in a bank, he withdrew completely from their sexual relationship):

PRU What I did like, did dislike – after a certain time he used to drink but he pretended he didn't and that did put a big rift between us and I really never got back to it [sex] except as a, a duty, you know and I was very conscious of my duty. But there you are, things happen.[36]

'You could call it a duty to be performed'

In drawing the connection between their responsibilities to love and care for their spouses and the experience of sexual pleasure, many respondents presented sex as a marital duty. Many women accepted that the provision of sex was both a husband's right and a wifely responsibility from which they could not completely disengage. Yet in many cases they did not link women's sexual duties in marriage and sexual misery, despite the dominant association of these categories in both contemporary literature and later historical works. For them,

[34] Modern sociologists have analysed the ways in which, in Gillian Rose's phrase, 'love-making is never simply pleasure'. As Melissa Tyler points out, the emotional experience of eroticism and sexual intercourse is refracted through the 'cluster of rules and role expectations' which structure people's understandings of sexual behaviour (Rose, *Love's Work*, 63, Tyler, 'Managing between the Sheets', 100).

[35] Roger msf/kf/ht/#10. [36] Pru msf/kf/ht/#12, See Chapter 5, note 98.

dutiful sex could also be pleasurable. It did not necessarily denote an absence of sexual gratification, and indeed was more commonly related to a feeling of emotional satisfaction connected to their identities as caring wives and mothers. Whereas many from this generation would have found themselves ill at ease in celebrating sex for reasons of personal adventure or satisfaction, the idea of duty allowed them a sexual identity with which they were comfortable, in which intercourse was regarded as an expression of marital love towards their husbands.

The conviction that a wife had an obligation to provide regular sexual access for her husband was relatively uncontested among the majority of interviewees. Although most women argued that sex should be a consensual act and that men should not press sex upon wives who were not in the mood, at the same time most women supported the notion that it was their duty to be sexually available some of the time, and recognised that this entailed consenting at moments when they did not want it for themselves. For some interviewees, then, sex was an unpleasant obligation. Maria's (1917) marriage to a Corporation painter and decorator from Blackburn was generally happy, but she rarely enjoyed sex. Nevertheless, she regarded it as her duty to submit to her husband's desires, whenever they arose, regardless of her own inclinations:

> MARIA You could call it a duty to be performed ... I never was in the mood, but with men it's a kind of an experience that can happen any time, because I remember that there'd be many a night I'd be woken up during the middle of the night; I'd be fast asleep so it must just come upon them ... even though I wasn't really thrilled I never refused ... I put up with it, you know.[37]

Such descriptions have supported a common elision between dutiful sex and unpleasurable sex. From the 1930s onwards, some British sex radicals, sexologists and marriage counsellors challenged the idea that women had this 'duty' and established a connection between poor-quality marital sex and women's attitudes towards sexual availability. Radical voices began increasingly to see dutiful sex as antithetical to pleasure. Bertrand Russell's controversial condemnation of conventional sexual attitudes, *Marriage and Morals*, claimed that society's sexual anxieties meant that for many women sex was a distasteful and painful duty:

> Very few men or women who have had a conventional upbringing have learnt to feel decently about sex and marriage. Their education has taught them that deceitfulness and lying are considered virtues by parents and teachers; that sexual relations, even within marriage, are more or less disgusting, and that in propagating the species men are yielding to their animal nature while women are submitting to a painful duty. This attitude

[37] Maria msf/kf/bl/#8, born in 1917 in Blackburn, married a Corporation painter and decorator in 1940, one child.

has made marriage unsatisfying both to men and to women, and the lack of instinctive satisfaction has turned to cruelty masquerading as morality.[38]

Similarly, socialist journalist, novelist and agony aunt Leonora Eyles' popular *The Woman in the Little House*, also attacked the notion of marital sexual duty for having undermined mutual sexual enjoyment:

The prevalent idea among men … is that … he 'is entitled' to his pound of flesh. The very idea of being 'entitled to' something that should be mutual puts the wrong construction upon it at once; the very moment that people begin to mention their 'rights' over each other, all the mutual joy of loving and giving vanishes automatically.[39]

The idea that sexual pleasure was in direct opposition to marital sexual duty gained considerable force after the Second World War, and remains a core axiom in modern twenty-first-century sexual advice and relationship therapy. Engaging in sex as a form of marital obligation has become almost by definition an unpleasurable experience and evidence of a relationship in crisis. James E. De Burger's book, *Marriage Today*, is typical in suggesting that the moment at which either partner starts to view sex as a marital duty, it 'immediately begins to go down hill'.[40] In academic histories, too, the notion that women viewed sex as a marital duty has become shorthand for asserting that they did not experience any sexual pleasure. As Ross McKibbin concluded, for many women in the early decades of the twentieth century, 'sex for most was a duty, and there were no great expectations of pleasure'.[41]

For interviewees, however, dutiful sex was not necessarily connected to sexual dissatisfactions or male selfishness. As discussed above, many women embraced the notion that sex was a marital duty, as it reinforced their identities as selfless providers of love and care. Their descriptions of sex often downplayed ideas of individual pleasure; this was not necessarily the result of unsatisfactory sex, but rather because they wished to emphasise the role sex played in the provision of care for their husbands.[42] Lucy (1907) recognised that she did not always want sex but saw her accommodation to her husband's desires as a positive aspect of their relationship, commenting that it 'were good', that she 'liked that' and 'loved Frank'.

[38] Bertrand Russell, *Marriage and Morals* (London: George Allen & Unwin Ltd, 1930), 98.

[39] Eyles, *The Woman in the Little House*, 140.

[40] James E. De Burger, *Marriage Today: Problems, Issues, and Alternatives* (Cambridge and New York: Schenkman Pub. Co.; J. Wiley, 1977), 406.

[41] McKibbin, *Classes and Cultures: England, 1918–1951*, 297.

[42] As E. L. Packer commented, when women who do not have high expectations of sexual enjoyment in marriage find themselves disgusted by or indifferent to sexual activity many did not see this as a 'matter for special comment'. To a certain extent, then, women's acceptance and apparently contented reaction to sexual relations which they framed as primarily providing pleasure to the husband are indicative of the degree to which women were not expected to enjoy sex (Packer, 'Aspects of Working-Class Marriage', 98). However, this realisation should not prevent us from also appreciating the importance for the women interviewed in constructing sex as a

LUCY Sometimes well, yeah, I didn't want, but I didn't say 'Oh no Frank I don't want', no, but I would help him; I would do it, yeah – fair's fair – I would do it even though I didn't enjoy it, but if Frank wanted it I would let him 'ave it – oh yes, oh yes – because I mean it were a good, I like that, I loved Frank.[43]

Moreover, pleasure and duty were not mutually exclusive sexual categories. Women's descriptions of their marital duties revealed the ways in which the very construction of sex as a duty was itself linked to satisfaction and fulfilment. Angela (1924) talked proudly about her desire to carry out her duty to 'love' her husband even when exhausted, and connected such self-sacrifice to the general success of her marriage:

ANGELA Well, I had to go to work when Gail was six months old because of, er, of, er, Hugh's job, um, and Gail was in a day nursery, so I was tired but I still considered it my duty to love my husband and, er, I still wanted to, so you have to put into marriage what you hope to get out of it.[44]

Grace (1922) acknowledged that sex might not be pleasant when done out of duty, but nonetheless connected the times when she had sex though she did not want it with the expression of mutual love, her desire to help her husband, and added that sex was mostly enjoyable:

GRACE When I went out to work ... and he knew I didn't want it ... it was your duty in a way. Yeah. So it wasn't very pleasant[...]But I think if two people do love one another it is quite important. I wouldn't say it's the be-all and end-all of everything. But I think it is important[...]but yeah we enjoyed sex. And I think sometimes I did it for him 'cos I think it helped.[45]

Such pride in fulfilling marital responsibilities perhaps reflects the social influence of the concept of doing one's duty in nineteenth- and twentieth-century Britain.[46] Jane Lewis, for example, has charted the ideas of duty central to Christian socialist motivations for philanthropic work. In opposition to the Utilitarians' championing of an ethic of self-interest, the Christian Socialists stressed the duty of citizens to act selflessly. Lewis concludes, 'the idea of

mechanism through which they cared for their husbands and the different forms of satisfaction and pride they took in the performance of this role.

43 Lucy msf/kf/bl/#10, married in 1931. There are similar examples in the testimony; for example June msf/kf/ht#27.

44 Angela msf/kf/ht/#18, born in Preston in 1924, married an electrical engineer in 1947, two children.

45 Grace msf/srss/ht/#38, born in Goole in 1922, married a motor engineer in 1944, two children.

46 We might think here of the centrality of doing one's duty to the framing of the appropriate performance of a wide variety of male and female roles (mothers, fathers, soldiers, etc.) during the early twentieth century. See Stefan Collini, 'The Idea of "Character" in Victorian Political Thought', *Transactions of the Royal Historical Society* 35 (1985): 29–50, and Frank K. Prochaska, *Women and Philanthropy in Nineteenth-Century England* (Oxford and New York: Clarendon Press; Oxford University Press, 1980), on philanthropy and missionary work, a particularly female duty.

the importance of self-giving as a manifestation of Christian obligation was central to many Victorian women social reformers. While it often involved a measure of self-sacrifice, it was not about self-denial, for only through giving to others would joy and happiness be achieved.'[47] The idea that women would gain joy through self-sacrifice endured in twentieth-century depictions of marriage. Mary Scharlieb, for example, portrayed a wife's duties as bringing great joy; she pitied the bachelor woman who missed out on becoming the woman 'whose joy and duty it is to provide dressing gown and slippers, a cheering fire and an easy chair'.[48]

Some interwar debates about marriage, sex and pleasure drew on this particular value of doing one's duty, too. Marcus Collins examined the forms of mutual sexual adjustment advocated by some post-war sex reformers which did not denigrate concepts of duty as antithetical to sexual happiness in marriage. John Macmurray, for example, called for the sex act to become a 'means of communion' created through an 'essentially mutual' self-giving.[49] Unlike the radical and feminist voices of this period, the conservative sex and marriage reformers, whom Collins labelled 'Christian mutualists', developed an understanding of sex equality and mutual sexual pleasure in which a notion of marital duty (on the part of both men and women) was still fundamental. For them, wedlock was not to be patriarchal, but rather based on 'the mutuality or reciprocity of duty and respect... between husband and wife'. For Christian mutualists, sex was potentially 'electric' and able to 'bring couples together in light and warmth', yet could not be sought for 'selfish gratification'.[50]

This was a culture whose highly valued notions of duty and responsibility even invaded the bedroom. With sex conceptualised, above all, as a mechanism for giving, women lacked an appropriate framework for describing the personal physical pleasures it was capable of delivering. Women framed sex as something they dutifully provided and their own pleasure was only reluctantly and obliquely discussed. Women were not provided with a language of sexual pleasure to describe their intimate marital experiences, even when those experiences were clearly very pleasurable indeed. This tension is revealed in the difficulty the interviewers faced when asking women about their experience of pleasure during sex. When women talked about the subject, it was usually after significant interviewer probing. Moreover, pleasure was rarely described as something they sought in sex, but rather as something their husbands gave them as a demonstration of their commitment to caring for them. Thus, women

[47] Jane Lewis, 'Women and Late-Nineteenth Century Social Work', in *Regulating Womanhood: Historical Essays on Marriage, Motherhood, and Sexuality*, ed. Carol Smart (London and New York: Routledge, 1992), 82.

[48] Of course, by the interwar period Mary Scharlieb's views were becoming increasingly old-fashioned. Quoted in Holden, *The Shadow of Marriage*, 37.

[49] Collins, *Modern Love*. [50] Ibid., 45–6.

with highly satisfactory sex lives, who personally enjoyed a great deal of pleasure from the act, also placed considerable emphasis on sex as a marital duty. Only through dogged questioning did Clare (1912) address the question of her own personal pleasure, and go on to reveal that she regularly had orgasms (though more frequently with her first husband than her second). However, she sidelined the discussion of female orgasm because she saw the purpose and benefit of sex as primarily connected to being a dutiful wife:

So describe to me the first time that you had sex.

CLARE Oh, God, no I can't. [It] comes natural dunn't, when yer married? ... You can't really explain that. They called it love then – when I was first married, they called it love, yeah ... With my first husband I thought it was wonderful ... I can't say what I liked about it, but I think it was because we become one another, you know, we were one sort of thing ...

How important was sex love as a part of your true love?

Well, it was what they used t'call then, it was a duty, they used t'call it a duty, but with my first husband it was, oh, he was lovely, he was really lovely ... Well, they used to say it was a wife's duty to satisfy the man and that's how you were brought up ... I don't think there was anything as lovely.

Yes. So what did you enjoy about sex love?

Oh, don't know. I always think we felt it was a duty and that was that ... it was your duty as a wife ... you took it as a duty and it was, that was that.

So when did you first hear about orgasms?

Never. There was never such a word. It was never explained to us in that sense, no, it wasn't. Oh, it was different then.

So what did you then think when you first heard about things like that?

What, I don't remember what I thought, I only thought it was yer duty ... because they used t'say it's the woman's duty to satisfy a man, that's how they used to put it.

And would you get a climax yourself in sex love?

Oh, yes you did, yes you did, but it was more difficult with my second husband because he'd never bin married before ... Because it never used to, never used to, um (pause), what would [one] say – never used to climax like it did with yer first husband; it wasn't the same sort of love if you know what I mean.[51]

Many sex surveys in the twentieth century had problems interpreting women's oblique and apparently contradictory descriptions of their sexual experiences.[52] It is the complex relationship between the purposes of sex, the meanings of pleasure and women's identities as providers of love and care that often lies

[51] Clare msf/kf/ht/#8, first married 1936, second marriage 1947.

[52] Eustace Chesser's 1956 study *The Sexual, Marital and Family Relationships of the English Woman*, the analysis of nearly 11,000 replies to a questionnaire sent to women by their GPs. He found women's descriptions of sex and its pleasures extremely opaque and difficult to interpret. He commented that 'many women have difficulty in describing their sexual sensations, in defining the nature of their sexual pleasures and are confused as to the definition of their genital experiences' (Eustace Chesser et al., *The Sexual, Marital and Family Relationships of the English Woman*, 421). See also the analysis of such surveys in Stanley, *Sex Surveyed*.

behind these seemingly confusing and ambivalent narratives. For example, when Eliot Slater and Moya Woodside conducted their survey for *Patterns of Marriage* in 1943–6 they found a variety of intriguing descriptions of female sexual pleasure, often couched in far from effusive terms. One said: 'there's a certain amount of pleasure involved'. Having found a widespread perception that 'sex is a duty' they were puzzled to note that women would often talk about duty 'with pride'.[53] They were confused to find that women who did not 'expect any particular pleasure' in fact embraced sex: these wives, they discovered, never refused their husbands, tried to be accommodating and expressed contentment in providing 'satisfaction for him'. Such surveys have failed to look behind women's silences and evasions or to appreciate the implications of their reluctance to effusively or enthusiastically admit to sexual pleasure. Many analyses too readily see such circumlocutions as evidence for women's limited sexual enjoyment. However, in many cases, such descriptions reflect less an absence of sexual pleasure than the absence of a language of pleasure through which women could interpret positive sexual experiences.

The language of duty, by contrast, provided an acceptable framework for discussing sex: a strategic vernacular which allowed women to demonstrate their understanding of the central purpose of sex in marriage and their ideas of what being a good wife was about. For many women, talking about doing their duty in having sex with their husbands was not necessarily about attacking his sexual technique, or establishing the absence of sexual pleasure (though in some cases pleasure was absent). Rather, the claim that sex was performed out of duty was a means by which women ensured they appeared respectably caring, and allowed them to frame sex as a sharing mutual act.[54] Such assertions helped women deflect attention away from the embarrassing or potentially selfish implication that they were seeking personal gratification alone and provided them with a framework through which sexual pleasure could be legitimately enjoyed.[55]

'Give her the impression that it's not just sex'

The importance of sex as a means of providing love and showing care and consideration was equally central to many men's attitudes towards sex. Many

[53] Slater and Woodside, *Patterns of Marriage*, 166–9.

[54] This is not to argue that the rhetoric of sharing means that we should see these relationships as having been 'genuinely' reciprocal. A discourse of reciprocity, in modern as well as in past relationships, has been critically examined as part of continued gender hierarchy and inequality. However, it is clear that such a discourse framed individuals' approaches to sex and their personal evaluations of whether or not their marriages were sexually successful. See, Braun, Gavey, and McPhillips, 'The "Fair Deal"?'

[55] Of course, in so doing, women were demonstrating the existence of what feminists (and others) have rightly identified as a form of sexual inequality (oppression), but here we are interested in outlining how individuals personally conceptualised and incorporated these values into their lives.

considered the means by which they could ensure their wife's pleasure, while some wives praised (and others criticised) their husbands' sexual skills. Roger (1910), for example, would put his 'finger carefully across' a spot 'just inside the vagina, up on the right' to give his wife 'a hell of a… ' – a technique he learned while serving in Africa during the Second World War: 'I know that, because that was told me by an Arab! In fact he told me several things.'[56] While Merlin (1908), a bus and tram driver from Blackburn, thought 'foreplay was the most important thing', which gave his wife 'an organism [*sic*] and if she didn't and you did, it's not fair'.[57] Men had easier access than their wives to a language of the giving (and receiving) of pleasure. Ed (1913) reformulated builders' banter about keeping wives 'well oiled' into a positive appreciation of his wife in which he charted his determination to love her every night:

ED We enjoyed our life together… I really loved her and she loved me… you know every, every, every night for years. Them on buildings used to say 'Keep 'em well oiled.' (laughs)… I loved her every day. She were marvellous woman. Felt like cutting my throat when she went.[58]

Despite men's more easily vocalised appreciation of sexual pleasure, their descriptions of sex were equally focused on the idea that it should not be a selfish act, but rather one focused on the demonstration of love. Men like working-class Ed (1913) or middle-class Reg (1919) saw sex as a means of indicating the extent to which they cared for their wives, and criticised men who were lustful or animal in their approach:

REG I suppose if you put something beautiful around a thing it's, it's nice but if, if you look at it, you know, gruffly in a sort of animal way if you like, it's not really the same.[59]

Some men were concerned that their sexual advances were regarded as caring and loving, and often contrasted their love-making with less considerate forms. A 68-year-old labourer from Exeter told Mass Observation in 1949 that those 'who cannot be happy without sex are more beasts than men', in explaining how he and his wife maintained their happiness during the eighteen months after the birth of a baby when she was ill.[60] Colin (1923), a plumber from Blackburn who married his first wife in 1947 (after she died he married again in 1979), criticised selfish men who only considered their own pleasure. He made sure that each of his two wives had known that he was caring for them during sex:

COLIN I tell you what I learned and I think it's the biggest thing in a woman's life. That after you've had sex for God's sake, don't roll over and go to sleep. Get hold of the woman, squeeze her, give her a kiss, that's me.

[56] Roger msf/kf/ht/#10, married in 1938.
[57] Merlin msf/kf/bl/#35, married in 1940.
[58] Ed msf/srss//bl/#23, married in 1937.
[59] Reg msf/kf/ht/#36, married in 1942.
[60] Mass Observation, File Report 3110, 'General Attitudes to Sex', April 1949, 'Article One: Sex Attitudes', 10.

And why do you think that's the most important thing?
Well, anybody can have sex, there's not a lot of people can have love, you know. And sex wi'out love is nowt. What's wrong wi' giving 'em a kiss or a squeeze, you know? There's nowt wrong; you're there, she's worked all day, you know. And it, it'll give her the impression that it's not just sex, it's something a little bit more like, you know. You, that, you learn things like that you know. I've heard of these come home, he's had a few pints and he's got leg over and then next thing errrg (makes snoring noise), there we are frustrated like, you know.[61]

Thus, whatever men's perception of their own sexual urges or needs, most only wanted to engage in sex as part of a caring relationship. Gerald (1919), who was a manager of a large government service, was fully aware that he wanted sex far more often than his wife, Esme (1921). He gratefully accepted her accommodations as indications of her love for him, and sought himself to continue to show his affection through sex. For him, intercourse was crucial to the way in which he expressed his love for her, despite knowing that on occasion she engaged in sex in order to please him:

ESME Well, on the whole I think sex was pretty okay for us, wasn't it? I have to say that Gerald needed it more often than I did – um, but generally speaking I accommodated him. (coughs)

GERALD Every time, yes.

ESME Um, partly of course I was too tired, because when we had children ... by the time I got to bed I just literally was too tired to stay awake for sex and – I did stay awake – I mean, I didn't want to ... I just sort of, er, accommodated him because I'd always learned ... that it was so essential that you should have sex that in fact, if you didn't have it, you know, you would be, um, sort of upset and all the rest of it and so I'm, just sort of went along with it. And I think I was probably typical of my generation, I don't know.

[...]

GERALD you very soon learnt to recognise the signs but you see in the case of Esme specifically she was so kind and good and willing that I never sensed this as a massive drawback, you know; it just did really exist but it was going on all the time, wasn't it? I just thought she was wonderful ... You were really rather good at co-operating.

ESME I think I was too. (laughs)

So how important would you say sex was in your marriage?

ESME Oh yes, very important ...

GERALD Well, I still tell Esme (sometimes many times a day) how much I love her – that's a different thing ... But sex in marriage is a sort of communion which keeps that going.

So what, how would you show Esme that you loved her?

GERALD Hold her hand, kiss her, tell her.

ESME He's very good, much better than I am.

[61] Colin msf/kf/bl/#36.

And how do you show him that you love him?

ESME Well, of course, I kiss him and I, I hug him and so on but not as much as he does me. Now it doesn't mean I love him any the less but it's just that I'm not as demonstrative – I never have been.

[...]

So what would you say that you liked best about sex?

GERALD Well, when it's mutually enjoyable and... afterwards you'll both say 'oh, I did enjoy that' and 'you are a darling'.

ESME Um.

GERALD And loving hugs and caresses and everything else.

ESME Yes, that's fair comment, um, yes.

GERALD As I said it's a communion between husband and wife.[62]

That many men saw caring for their wife through sex as central to their marriages is apparent from the testimony of men who experienced impotence or low libido. In such instances the men professed themselves far more concerned about the impact the absence of sex had on their wives than on themselves. When Alistair (1927), a supervisor in a paper mill in Blackburn, experienced impotence, he did not comment on the effect it had on him, but rather expressed his anxieties about not being able to satisfy her:

ALISTAIR On occasion, now then, she'd feel like sex and I didn't. And, but we tried to satisfy one another. But sometimes I couldn't perform and that's... disappointing... And we actually started off, now then, and I wasn't giving as much attention as I should have done, so, we actually sat down and talked about it... She said, 'have you another woman stacked away?' I said, 'no!' But when I started to explain to her how tired I was – I mean, twelve hours in the paper mill, red hot, noisy; I was knackered – she more or less accepted this... I could feel she wanted sex – I tried to perform but I couldn't do – I was too dog-tired, you know what I mean?

When I had my accident... our sex lives changed... I mean, I were having all sorts of pills, left, right and bloody centre and... she were disappointed 'cos I were giving her – I couldn't give her a full sex life at that time, because of all these tablets, and when I eventually went off the tablets, I discussed it with her – I said, 'well, it were the tablets', now we're leaving the tablets alone... And when I went off them, me sexual urges came back, so thankfully after a long trail of medication I chucked the lot of them and that were it... So, that was a disappointment to me, more disappointment to the wife, so I tried to be – relieve her in other methods, you know [what] I mean, which sometimes it worked, sometimes it didn't, so. She quite understood, I had no erection and that was it, so.[63]

Although many husbands (like most wives) assumed that men's sexual needs and desires were greater than women's, they did not simply see sex

[62] Gerald and Esme msf/kf/ht/#9. See also Chapter 6 note 103 on Gerald and Esme being 'diplomats' with each other over sex.

[63] Alistair msf/kf/bl/#33. Alistair was one of the youngest respondents and he and his wife were married in 1952. Alistair suffered fissure burns when his hand was trapped in a roller at the paper mill where he worked. He was subsequently prescribed pain killers and valium.

as something women dutifully provided to them. Many were concerned to ensure that their wife enjoyed sex and were dismayed if they felt unable to provide her with pleasure. Indeed men were much more interested than women in the encouragement of the female orgasm, and marriage manuals throughout the twentieth century saw male technique as key to women's sexual satisfaction.[64] In sharp contrast to much women's testimony, in which female pleasure through orgasm was welcomed but not directly sought out or actively investigated, some men were disappointed if they felt that their wife did not enjoy sex and others took steps to try to ensure they were satisfied. As Eleanor (1907), who married in 1934, commented: 'It's nice, for a woman to enjoy sex because a man likes you to enjoy it doesn't 'e?'[65] Reg (1919) believed he had initially been misinformed, but had 'quickly learnt' through his own practical experiences (with a number of women) of the female capacity for sexual pleasure:

REG Well, to tell you the truth, to start off with … I really didn't think that they enjoyed it. This was my first information about it. I thought that the women were providing the facility but, of course, that easily went because … once I started getting into close encounters with them then, of course, obviously I quickly learnt that the excitement is, um, is mutual, you know.[66]

The desire on the part of some men to improve the experience of sex specifically for their wives, rather than themselves, is revealed in the letters some wrote to Marie Stopes. Lesley Hall has drawn attention to the requests from men for advice on how to give 'my wife the satisfaction to which she has a right'. Without a mutual experience of pleasure, Marie Stopes' male correspondents felt 'selfish and mean' or 'like a cad'.[67] Similarly, Hubert (1911) recalled the ways in which his sexual pleasure was constrained without erotic response from his wife. Hubert saw sex as an important way to express love for his wife, but was dismayed to find that she did not welcome this form of love:

HUBERT She was virtually frigid, which was not my style at all …[68] She said, 'You think I'm gonna behave like a loose woman, I'm not.' She said, 'If you must, you must', but of course it was hopeless. So I took refuge in work, and my pets and

[64] See, for example, Jackson, *The Real Facts of Life*, 160–7, Cook, *The Long Sexual Revolution*, 202.

[65] Eleanor msf/kf/bl/#11. [66] Reg (1919) msf/kf/ht/#36.

[67] Hall, 'Impotent Ghosts', 63. Hall notes that few of these men saw themselves at fault, and asked for means by which their wives could be helped. Jessamyn Neuhaus' study of predominantly American marriage manuals argues that during the 1920s and 1930s sex manual authors predominantly saw men as at fault for lack of orgasmic response on the part of their wives, but by the 1950s the notion of the 'frigid' woman who needed to address her coldness, inhibitions and neuroses emerged (Neuhaus, 'The Importance of Being Orgasmic', 464–6). See also, Hall, *Hidden Anxieties*, 82.

[68] For an analysis of frigidity in sexological texts and sex manuals see Jackson, *The Real Facts of Life*, 116–18, 75–9. For Freud's use of the term see Dean Rapp, 'The Early Discovery of

my garden … She shied away from it as much as possible. (pause) And you can only insist so far … Casual sex is something I just couldn't do at all. Mind you, I'm pretty highly motivated internally; I mean I'm fairly highly sexed, but I just could not contemplate casual. It's got to be all or nothing … had to be totally devoted to somebody or I couldn't contemplate it.

Hubert was desperate to find some kind of response from her that would justify his continued attempt at a sexual relationship (she expected him to continue to require sex and wanted to provide it as part of her side of the marital bargain):

HUBERT I used to kiss her and cuddle her. (pause) As I said, I rarely got any response. Well sometimes she was less stiff than at others (pause) and allowed such things to happen … Somewhere I learned, I read the necessary methods … to rouse her in the first place by the hand, and to continue with the penis. (pause) I learned that there was a sort of erection and the nipples are too, of course. But she seemed to restrain herself terribly.
How could you tell whether she had an orgasm?
Well, it's a sort of electric shock goes through the body. Don't know how else to describe it. Very similar to that.
And did she enjoy that?
Must have done, I think. She never let on though (pause). I learned by hard experience mostly.[69]

Men's interest in pleasuring their wives was equally apparent from women's testimony. Catherine (1912) recalled how concerned her husband was to ensure that she was getting pleasure, too:

CATHERINE I suppose you'd, you'd get that [an orgasm] by the foreplay, or whatever you like to call it, um. With – you know – before the man had an orgasm. My husband'd say – you know what he used to say? 'Have you been a bad girl?' sort of thing, you see. He, would really wanted to know that I was getting pleasure out of it, you see. Okay, you felt that you had – you'd reached some sort of – had a bit of a thrill out of it, uh, yes.[70]

Many women, recognising that their husbands were looking to use sex as a means of caring for them, realised that they needed to provide some kind of response, in order that his consideration could not be interpreted as selfish or self-serving, and that physical encounters could also become an experience of sharing.[71] Phyllis (1921) and her husband had an extremely affectionate and

Freud by the British General Educated Public, 1912–1919', *Social History of Medicine* 3, no. 2 (1990): 217–43, Oram, 'Repressed and Thwarted'.

69 Hubert msf/kf/ht/#32. 70 Catherine msf/kf/ht/#1, married in 1941.

71 Such interactions might be seen to support feminist critiques which have identified men's increasing interest in women's sexual pleasure during the twentieth century as the 'eroticisation of women's subordination'; however, our purpose here is to understand what these beliefs meant for individuals' own assessments of their experiences. See, Stevi Jackson and Sue Scott, 'Gut Reactions to Matters of the Heart: Reflections on Rationality and Sexuality', *The Sociological Review* 45, no. 4 (1997): 560.

loving marriage. She described him as 'courteous, well-mannered' and as having 'spoilt me to death'. She remained sympathetic rather than resentful of his alcoholism and saw sex as a key means by which they expressed love and togetherness:

PHYLLIS My husband was very, very patient though. If I hadn't [had an orgasm] he would – you know – hold back until I had, and there're some times I'd even have to, er, pretend I had them – you know – otherwise I'd think 'crikey, going to go on all night here' and I couldn't. I used to pretend.[72]

Agatha (1910) and her husband had a happy marriage, contracted in 1940, though she was particularly fearful of pregnancy and rarely enjoyed sex. She described her husband as a quiet and kind man, but difficult to get talking. It is clear that Agatha's sexual resentments or difficulties were actively covered up by her:

So did you tell your husband that you didn't enjoy it?

AGATHA No, oh, no, I wasn't going to spoil his pleasure … probably I said to him 'oh that was nice', 'oh it's nice' or something; some silly little thing like that yer know, to kind of make him think maybe it was on top of the world, when it wasn't.[73]

Indeed, for some men, the idea that their wives would have sex with them because they saw it as their duty was abhorrent. Colin (1923) did not want to have sex with either of his wives when they were doing it to please him, but, aware that they would 'never say no', he found himself having to try and interpret their secret desires and wishes:

COLIN I mean, just because a woman's married doesn't mean to say she should have it every time like – you know – a fella. She might've had a busy day wi' kids – anything, you know – something gone wrong wi' t'bills, or something gone wrong wi' washing machines or anything, you know … You see in them days Martha and Amy thought it was a woman's job to give a man sex. They would never say no – you know what I mean? So, I'd to say no for them. I knew when they … so I say no for them. But they always thought that if a man wanted sex, regardless of whether they enjoy it or not, they'd give the man sex and, thank God, it's changing like you know.[74]

In evaluating the role played by sex in marital relationships, both male and female respondents considered the ways in which it allowed them to care, provide for each other and communicate love. Personal pleasure had to be carefully negotiated. While welcomed by both parties it had to be managed in order that neither felt that they were engaging in sex for selfish reasons. Men

[72] Phyllis msf/kf/bl/#5. [73] Agatha msf/kf/ht/#7. [74] Colin msf/kf/bl/#36.

had a much more fluent language of pleasure and gratification to draw upon when remembering their sex lives, but were often concerned to demonstrate the absence of sexual selfishness in their accounts. Men's narratives, too, were framed by the desire to demonstrate that they had used sex as a mechanism for indicating their love and consideration for their wives.

'I'd cuddle up to him, if he'd had a bath'

Respectable and appropriate forms of sex were not just determined by ideas about duty and reciprocity. A complex set of ideas about dirt, cleanliness and hygiene also determined notions of what constituted appropriate and fulfilling, or morally dubious or unpalatable, sex. Intercourse was perceived as both potentially beautiful in its purity, and dangerously dirty, in a sense of being both morally and physically sordid (see above pp. 305–10). These beliefs affected in particular ideas concerning the right or appropriate contexts for love-making.

Many saw it as fundamentally important that they were clean and freshly washed before and after having sex. As one of the younger respondents, Alistair (1927), who married in 1952, benefited from post-war developments in interior plumbing in working-class homes, which he contrasted with his childhood in which all washing took place in a small tub in the kitchen:

> ALISTAIR We were both, brought up – [I] mean many time I had two or three baths a day, me. Plus working in the paper mill, I used to sweat like a pig. I'd go and have a shower before I'd come home and then when I got home I'd go for a bath, but I'm very conscious about cleanliness; she was the same ... One thing the wife was adamant about – after we had sex she went to have a bath, and I followed her ... I mean, sometimes while she was in the bath ... she'd say, 'Come on, get in the bath!' That was it. She was so clean and I remember it.[75]

Few would countenance having sex while a woman was menstruating, seeing this as unhygienic:[76]

> BRYAN Regards the periods well we knew that was a messy – anyway if you tried to have sex during a period so that, that would disgust me more than anything else so, so we didn't [do] that; we always waited – always used to wait 'til it was clear.[77]

[75] Alistair msf/kf/bl/#33.

[76] In the USA where disposable sanitary towels which did not need washing were used far earlier than in Britain, it is argued that periods became seen as a moment of 'hygienic crisis'. See, J. Jacobs Brumberg, '"Something Happens to Girls": Menarche and the Emergence of the Modern American Hygienic Imperative', *Journal of the History of Sexuality* 4, no. 1 (1993): 99–127.

[77] Bryan (1918) msf/kf/ht/#25.

Notions of dirt also informed the range of sexual practices deemed to be enjoyable or appealing. Many rejected forms of kissing which were thought to spread germs:

SALLY We only had dry kisses, never wet ones. I thought that was awful . . . I mean, you should – you're swapping spit, germs and I couldn't've done [that]. That's me faddiness again.[78]

The clearest example of the impact of ideas about hygiene and attitudes towards sexual practices was in the case of oral sex, which was engaged in by only a tiny proportion of interviewees.[79] Emily (1917) moved to Wood Green from Blackburn when she married in 1938 when her husband became a telephone engineer:

EMILY Oh, I don't believe in that. Oh no! Oh, I wouldn't like 'aving – in my mouth – oh (anguished), I think it's horrible . . . but I certainly wouldn't like a penis in me mouth – Ooh, I think it's 'orrible . . . Ooh! . . . I mean you can catch all sorts from that serum [*sic*] that they let go.[80]

Gill (1920) moved to Blackburn in 1945 when she married her husband, a mill owner:

GILL Well, I still don't know what people get up to with oral sex; sounds revolting to me, it really does. We certainly never did that![81]

Norman (1914) married in 1944 and was a teacher in Tottenham after military service in the war:

NORMAN Oral sex – I don't know anything about that now . . . it panders to the people who have got peculiar wishes. I mean, before I had oral sex with somebody I would most likely go and give my winkle a good scrub.[82]

We might have expected that such resistance to engage in forms of sexual expression deemed unhygienic might be less pronounced in younger respondents, particularly among the middle classes who were exposed, later in their marriages, to changing attitudes, particularly during the 1960s.[83] Indeed, an

[78] Sally (1908) msf/kf/bl/#31. On attitudes towards deep kissing see, McLaren, *Twentieth-Century Sexuality*, 53.

[79] See also, Cook, 'Sexuality and Contraception in Modern England', 917–18.

[80] Emily msf/kf/bl/#13. [81] Gill msf/kf/bl/#48.

[82] Norman msf/kf/ht/#17.

[83] On the association between genitals and dirt and the encouragement of genital cleaning in sex manuals see Cook, *The Long Sexual Revolution*, 146–7. Cook argues that (ironically) for many the idea of washing one's genitals was rejected as a dirty procedure in itself. Using predominantly American sex manuals, Jessamyn Neuhaus has also identified increased emphasis on the importance of sexual hygiene after the Second World War. She argues that during the 1950s women were chastised for inadequate genital cleaning, which had the capacity to destroy a marriage (Neuhaus, 'The Importance of Being Orgasmic', 463–5).

awareness of oral sex was far greater among these individuals.[84] Gay (1928) was a particularly interesting case; she did not engage in fellatio with her husband, a salesman whom she married in 1947, but enjoyed receiving oral sex in a later adulterous relationship which took place in the 1960s. However, her beliefs about hygiene, which dominated her approach to sex with both partners, meant that despite the pleasures of oral sex she continued to feel anxious about cleanliness and had to fight retching:

> *So what did Gareth tell you about oral sex and what did you think?*
>
> GAY Well I was a bit apprehensive at first, um, but then you see I loved him so much that I – you know, I would've tried anything with Gareth – and did – but it was special – but I couldn't imagine doing anything like that with Roderick, that would have been absolutely abhorrent… but as I say with Gareth he, he was very clean which Roderick never was – but even so, I wasn't madly keen about it. I had my reservations about it – um, but you know I did… I did it because he wanted it, but… it almost made me retch…
>
> *And what about him doing it to you?*
>
> Well that was alright, that was fine, that was lovely – yes thank you! – yes (laughs), but I, then again I always used to worry about me being clean enough (pause). But I knew I always was – but, um, that did used to worry me.[85]

Despite the importance of hygiene within sexual practice for these respondents, we should be wary of interpreting their associations between dirt, morality and sex as necessarily negative, or of viewing such beliefs straightforwardly as a form of inhibition or handicap to sexual pleasure.[86] Certainly, there was a strong connection between notions of moral cleanliness and dirt-free hygiene. However, we must also recognise that beliefs about cleanliness were integral to the ways in which people such as Reg (1919) enjoyed sex:

> *So describe to me the first time that you did make love to your [first] wife.*
>
> REG Oh, it was indescribable, you know. Um, I suppose because I'd waited so long that the subconscious was – it was beautiful, it was clean, it was something wonderful, you know? I felt that I'd done something that was, you know, really, really something very special.[87]

Elma (1909) found her policeman husband's cleanliness highly appealing. They married in 1933 and had one child. For Elma, and others, a clean body

[84] Bruce Curtis and Alan Hunt, 'A Genealogy of the Genital Kiss: Oral Sex in the Twentieth Century', *Canadian Journal of Human Sexuality* 15, no. 2 (2006): 69–84.

[85] Gay msf/kf/ht/#13.

[86] Cf. Hera Cook, who sees early twentieth-century beliefs about hygiene, alongside the absence of sex education, as contributing to a long association between sex and guilt which meant young girls 'confused the pleasurable mess of sex with the dirt of excreta' (Cook, *The Long Sexual Revolution*, 145). Edward Shorter discusses hygiene as part of the 'hindrances' preventing earlier generations from enjoying 'total body sex' (Edward Shorter, *Written in the Flesh: A History of Desire* (Toronto and Buffalo: University of Toronto Press, 2005), *passim*).

[87] Reg msf/kf/ht/#36.

was itself highly attractive and an enticingly pure 'turn on'. Here she implies that it was her husband's cleanliness which contributed to her own desire to reciprocate:

ELMA If, if he wanted something [sex] he'd tell me, in a nice kind of a way [with] two arms round me instead of one. (laughs) No, I had a good life with him. I can't complain at all about anything and he never, never once upset me... He never did. He was very, very clean and very nice, nice man.[88]

Our interviewees have revealed particular connections between ideas about sex, health and cleanliness.[89] Respondents were concerned that some sexual activities were unhygienic; but more strikingly they idolised, indeed eroticised, cleanliness, such that sexual experiences were intensified when conceptualised as the coming together of clean and pure bodies.

'Just when the mood took us'

Respondents' assessment of sexual fulfilment or dysfunction was linked to particular constructions of the connections between innate nature and sexual need. For many, sexual desire was an inbuilt, unalterable force that was most appropriately expressed spontaneously in natural, private settings. Thus, many from these generations rejected the idea that sexual relationships between couples should be consciously or artificially worked at. Nor was it seen as appropriate to turn to external sources for tips and techniques in a search for more pleasurable sex. Thus their criteria for assessing the quality of sex were quite different from those of later generations, who valued the possibility of self-improvement frequently based on the interventions of outside 'sexual authorities' in the development of marital relations. Rejected, too, was the idea that conscious attempts to modify sexual behaviour – by changing sexual frequency or experimenting with different practices or techniques, for instance – would be likely to have a positive impact on sexual desire or pleasure. Respondents saw such conscious modifications of sexual practices as unnatural, and forced, and championed an instinctual approach in which sexual relationships developed, changed and improved 'naturally' within the home. Indeed, Mass Observation concluded that the idea that sex was natural was 'the keynote to popular sex

[88] Elma msf/jm/bl/#42.

[89] During this period the relationship between sex and health was much discussed. Some sexual practices were deemed, by some, to be unhealthy, particularly masturbation; while from the post-war period the idea that sex itself contributed to an individual's well-being began to take hold. On masturbation and health see, Jackson and Scott, 'Gut Reactions to Matters of the Heart', 558, Alan Hunt, 'The Great Masturbation Panic and the Discourses of Moral Regulation in Nineteenth- and Early Twentieth-Century Britain', *Journal of the History of Sexuality* 8, no. 4 (1998): 575–615, Cook, *The Long Sexual Revolution*, 146–50, Robert Darby, 'The Masturbation Taboo and the Rise of Routine Male Circumcision: A Review of the Historiography', *Journal of Social History* 36, no. 3 (2003): 727–57.

attitudes'.[90] Daphne (1912), a practising Catholic who married in 1937, was typical in emphasising the importance of sex as natural and an expression of organic and spontaneous desire:

DAPHNE It was a natural thing. I mean you just came together... you came together and it happened.[91]

Whereas contemporary marital advice urged couples to work at their sexual relationships by learning new techniques and educating themselves in sexual matters, many rejected such interventions as inappropriate and artificial, and instead asserted the importance of following one's natural instincts. Many respondents were consequently reluctant deliberately to change their sexual practices, to discuss sexual technique or to experiment with new ideas.[92] Catherine (1912) and her husband lived in a small town in Hertfordshire where he ran a watch repair shop.

CATHERINE You didn't say, 'right, we'll try it this way', you (chuckle) – probably just do it, sort of more naturally, yes; you wouldn't plan it all (chuckle) beforehand, no... I think really, you know, [you] decide to do things [without] even thinking about it... But um, no – as I said... it wasn't so important in a way, no – I mean, some people must find sex so exciting, yes. They probably want to try all (chuckle) sorts of things. I think we were so ordinary (giggle).[93]

This rejection of sexual self-improvement was partially the result of seeing desire as an innate but 'unalterable' personality trait, a view particularly observable in working-class respondents. Successful sexual relationships were not generally seen as ones in which couples had developed effective erotic techniques together (although many acknowledged that sex improved as they learned each other's preferences). Rather, respondents saw successful sex as dependent on the compatibility of each individual's own, personal, inbuilt, natural sexual inclinations. Respondents hoped to marry someone to whom they were naturally sexually suited and often attributed sexual problems to an unfortunate mismatch of unalterable sexual personalities. Eva's (1911) husband was a cobbler in Blackburn and they married in 1932:

EVA Some of them, well, they're highly sexed and the other partner isn't; there's going to be sparks flying, isn't there, really? And I think maybe that's a break of some of the marriages.[94]

[90] Mass Observation, File Report 3110, 'General Attitudes to Sex', April 1949, 'Article One, Attitudes to Sex', 12.

[91] Daphne msf/jm/bl/#38.

[92] Indeed, as Stevi Jackson and Sue Scott have revealed, there is something of a tension within 'modern discourses around heterosexuality' between the notion that sexuality is 'special' and spontaneous and the imperative to pursue sexual pleasure by subjecting the self to rational management, control and knowledge (Jackson and Scott, 'Gut Reactions to Matters of the Heart').

[93] Catherine msf/kf/ht/#1. [94] Eva msf/kf/bl/#9/.

Catherine (1912), who married her watchmaker husband in 1941:

CATHERINE Some people were more highly sexed than others ... well, that wouldn't have happened with my husband, (laughing) ... But in our own quiet way, you know ... we suited each other. I can remember him saying, 'well, don't forget we're married!', when I didn't seem interested. (laughs)[95]

Lyn (1907) and her husband both worked in a mill in Blackburn (she as a winder and he as a reacher) and they married in 1931:

LYN I don't think Walter and I was, what you would call terribly oversexed, you know ... I do think that in so many cases people are far more sexual than others, you see – and no demanding in any way on Walter's part at all, like, which I did know happened with friends of mine, you know – 'I didn't want to bother but ooh'. They give way to shut the man up kind of a style. In fact, I mean ... in the old days I dare say quite a lot of married women were actually raped: they were forced to do it against what they really wanted to do because of their husband's sexual demands, you see? But, fortunately my husband was not like that ... I'm not saying [we] didn't enjoy the sexual side at all. But, um, er, you know, we wasn't oversexed.[96]

The sincerely held belief in natural sexual compatibility was powerfully revealed in those cases in which wives expressed gratitude that their husbands did not approach them for sex too often. Historians have tended to interpret such comments as evidence of (especially working-class) women's hostility or indifference to sex.[97] Eliot Slater and Moya Woodside's conclusion that 'good' husbands were those who made relatively few sexual demands upon their wives is often employed as evidence for this.[98] Yet in both working- and middle-class testimony such expressions were in fact more often indicative of women's relief that they were sexually compatible with their husbands. These women believed that both their own and their husbands' individual sexual responses were fixed; hence the realisation that one's chosen spouse had an equal disposition to sex was embraced as a fortunate prelude to a satisfied, and not overly burdensome, marital sex life. June (1914) married the owner of a small grocery firm in Halifax in 1936:

JUNE Just when we were in the mood ... 'Cos we were very compatible.[99]

Felicity (1919) married a Catholic claims assessor from Bolton in 1954 when she was 34:

95 Catherine msf/kf/ht/#1. 96 Lyn msf/kf/bl/#1.

97 See, for example, McKibbin, *Classes and Cultures: England, 1918–1951*, 297–8.

98 Slater and Woodside, *Patterns of Marriage*, 168.

99 June msf/kf/ht/#27.

FELICITY I think we were both averagely sexed … it was, must [be] awful if one's very highly sexed and one's the other. I think we were about the same. Yeah. Oh we were, very lucky.[100]

Some of those who found that their husband approached them too frequently for sex saw themselves as unfortunate. However, this was not because they viewed their husbands as excessively demanding, but because their own sexual desires did not match his. Doreen (1922) complained about her husband's (a bricklayer from Blackburn) poor erotic technique, castigated him for his selfish attitude to sex, and remembered a marriage fraught with other tensions, particularly those caused by his refusal to take her desire to take on paid employment seriously. Yet, Doreen additionally put their sexual difficulties down to a basic, natural and unfortunate physical and emotional sexual incompatibility:

DOREEN Every time he went inside me – I was so small … so really in a way we weren't compatible, were we? He was too big for me … but I was so tiny … He wanted it too often – 'cos I was soon sore. I weren't really good enough for him, I think, down there. (laughs) I think he could've done with somebody more active … it's no pleasure when they start messing about … it causes friction and it caused a lot of pain you see. It's not his fault, it's me – he married the wrong person really probably, for that, for sex.[101]

Seeing desire as an innate force, and regarding sex as best when allowed to be the spontaneous expression of that unalterable drive, meant that many respondents were suspicious of both a modern rhetoric of sexual variety and adventure, and the notion that sexual frequency was an indicator of sexual quality. Sex was at its finest when it was at its most spontaneous, and did not require a certain frequency to be considered normal or fulfilling:

JUNE You just had intercourse when you felt like it … It was just a matter of being close and that sort of thing … I wasn't sex mad or anything like that. We just did it when we felt we needed to – when we were in the mood sort of thing. We'd no set times or anything, you know. But I never like it in the mornings; I always wanted it in the evening, put it like that. (laughs)[102]

Bryan (1918) and his wife lived in Hertfordshire, where he was a foreman in a rubber factory. They had two children and four miscarriages in the ten years between their two successful pregnancies:

BRYAN Just used to come natural with us. I sometimes felt like it and she didn't and that was it. And sometimes she would and I didn't and – well we'd just get over it that way … That just come naturally; I mean I s'pose it was how we felt but we felt like it two or three times in the week and then gradually went about a couple of

[100] Felicity msf/kf/bl/#37. Eva msf/kf/bl/#9 expressed very similar views.
[101] Doreen msf/kf/bl/#20. [102] June (1914) msf/kf/ht/#27.

times a week and then once a week or once a fortnight – just how the mood took us … just depends how things work out.[103]

Regularity of sexual intercourse was not deemed an important factor in assessing the status of their sexual relationships. Few were alarmed by a changing ebb and flow of coital frequency, which they saw as entirely natural. Patrick (1918) was a book keeper and clerk who became a salesman in his early forties. Married in 1941 in East Ham, he was a conscientious objector in the war. His Christian beliefs also drew him towards volunteering at the marriage guidance bureau in the late 1960s in the hope that because 'we were happily married … we could say … why don't you try to be?'

PATRICK No special time allocated to it. No, I'm not joking, but some people do, oh, tonight's the night, sort of thing, you know, and I don't think that's very helpful. (pause) It puts it on a level with what time do we have tea, or do we have a roast on Sunday?[104]

Mark (1917) and Joanna (1915) were committed Quakers, who married in 1947. He worked in the civil service as a clerk in the statistical office.

JOANNA We didn't have any rules like that, did we?
MARK No, no rules like that (chuckle) …
JOANNA (unclear phrase) when I feel it's right.
MARK It was just, just spontaneous at the time, I think, that was how it was …
JOANNA I don't see there were any special times, were there?[105]

Maureen (1920) was an extremely religious respondent in whose social life the Church played a dominant role. She was the daughter of a Blackburn weaver and attended the grammar school, and then learned typing and shorthand at the local technical college. She married a sales representative in 1943 who had a lowlier upbringing: his father had been a wagon driver for a builder's merchants.

MAUREEN So I mean we weren't sex mad … we just enjoyed life together; we had all the sex we needed, I think, you know … But I didn't believe in saying oh, it's Saturday night, it's sex night … that doesn't happen. It has to come naturally; you got to … be in the mood and very often wasn't in the mood. (laughs)
And what sort of things would put you in the mood?
I don't know. No, any time, I don't know it's just being close together really. I don't know, it just happened, I think.[106]

Reg (1919) married his second wife in 1957. She was an extremely lively woman who had worked as a crane driver before becoming a stage manager at Granada Television. She was also a big band singer.

103 Bryan msf/kf/ht/#25. 104 Patrick msf/kf/ht/#16.
105 Mark and Joanna msf/kf/ht/#22. 106 Maureen msf/kf/bl/#46.

REG You couldn't set the number of times a day or a week or anything else, they were spontaneous. We'd be out, maybe we were out, um, at some pub or somewhere, you know, and, um, that was it, we'd suddenly fuse and then we'd fly back home or whatever we'd do but, um, her life was really based on being spontaneous, you know. One was like it, the other one may not be but because the other one was like it in no time at all you got excited yourself and, you know, and, er. But the magic of that was that we learnt the, the magic spots of each other so if one was cold the other one would quickly warm you up, you know.[107]

Consequently respondents were often baffled by questions asking them to quantify the frequency with which they had intercourse. Alongside being difficult to answer with any accuracy, it was also a question which jarred with their approach to sex. Bernard (1907) and his wife Diana (1910) were intelligent, well-educated and widely read informants. As a journalist he was presumably aware of the debate surrounding the publication of Kinsey's research findings in the 1940s and 1950s, and his response to a question about frequency revealed his critique of sexual surveying as an abnormal fascination with quantifying sex and evaluating it along statistical lines:

BERNARD We didn't say, 'oh, we'll have sex tomorrow' – like you were asking her how many times a day? That, those never entered our head – those figures and that way of looking at it never entered our heads. You're making it too, too technical, you know, as though – it's as though you should run your lives on that sort of a basis: how many times have you had it a week, how many times have you known it, would you have it at night... if you're living a normal life those things don't enter your head.[108]

Natural and spontaneous forms of sexual activity were frequently drawn upon in descriptions of the satisfactions and joys sex might provide. Patrick (1918) defined intercourse as the most pleasurable sexual act, on the grounds that it was a natural use of the body's organs. His rejection of oral sex and mutual masturbation was not based on moral objections, but rather the notion that neither of these activities was the most direct expression of the body's most 'natural' functions. Hence he considered them 'second-best' forms of sexual activity that a couple would only engage in if they were avoiding intercourse:

PATRICK I think boys at school talked about it [oral sex] and I didn't believe it. I didn't think anyone would do that because there, there are other things to do, you know... we never tried it... because penetration was always available... from the physical aspect it wasn't very much different, but it, it was something which was more natural to do, and something for which the various parts of the body had been made.[109]

[107] Reg msf/kf/ht/#36. [108] Bernard msf/jm/bl/#45. [109] Patrick msf/kf/ht/#16.

The testimony of Roger (1910), a chartered surveyor, was unusual for its frank detail. In his eroticisation of spontaneity, and his association between sublime sex and nature, however, he was typical:

ROGER You're standing there and the next minute you're on the bed ... uh, but, (pause) my wife once, I'll never forget ... suddenly I found her looking at me very, very hard, and I thought, 'Aah, it's the old Stella!'; you could tell that, she wanted to ... And she said ... 'the boy is going to bed early tonight' ... and she went into his cot, and, uh, she, as I've told you, she fidgeted around with him and ... I kissed him goodnight and I went towards the back of her, and she said, 'Ooh, like that?', and I said, 'yes' ... and she immediately bent over, you see ... we were absolutely natural with one another. She knew I wanted it backward and she bent over backwards and I went in. Oh, I think sex is lovely ... Yeah, it's natural.[110]

Christopher (1918), a regularly unemployed builder, also focused on the joys of spontaneous sex and the pleasures of their instinctive and impulsive interpretation of each other's unspoken desires:

CHRISTOPHER We went for a walk; it was going through, going to the local golf ... and he was conceived in the bunker, in the sand ... She was always ready for sex ... I knew; you didn't have to tell me; she didn't have to tell me. I knew ... just spontaneous was that ... yeah, it was. Hhm.[111]

In valuing sex as a natural act, individuals prized spontaneity and did not generally measure their sex life according to frequency (which they saw as fluctuating naturally). Many avoided conscious or calculated modifications of technique and saw the incorporation of ideas about sex gleaned from external sources, such as marital advice books, as unnatural and contrived interventions. Often, successful sex was viewed as the outcome of the lucky pairing of two compatible libidos. Sexual failures were equally seen as a natural, if unfortunate, outcome of a sexually ill-matched union, rather than the fault of ignorant and clumsy technique or the result of inhibitions and anxieties.

'It doesn't concern anybody else'

Privacy was possibly *the* key concept to understanding how these generations conceived of marital sexual relationships. In placing privacy at the centre of their marital relationships, couples saw themselves as a distinct and separate unit from the wider society. A commitment to keeping sex a private matter meant few discussed sex with friends or relatives and communication between spouses was often non-verbal and discreet. This led to a very particular relationship to

[110] Roger msf/kf/ht/#10. Compare also Roger's descriptions of his wife's response to the discussion of premarital sex (see ch. 1, 11–12).
[111] Christopher msf/kf/bl/#34.

sexual knowledge: many individuals sought to isolate themselves from the public discussion of sex, even if such discussion might occur in respectable contexts such as in a religious one. Additionally, they were reluctant to read marriage guidance literature in any depth or with a view to altering their behaviour as a result. Where sexual information was obtained individuals might avoid compromising the privacy of the marriage by refusing to act upon it. Indeed, many respondents knew almost nothing about the sexual practices of others; nor did they care to know. They had only the vaguest understanding of what 'typical' marital relationships were like and had little direct information about 'normal' practices against which to compare themselves. The maintenance of privacy was nonetheless key to respectable and satisfactory sexual relationships in marriage in which the isolation of the marriage was valued. Respondents described learning about sex together in private and revealed the satisfaction they gained from developing an intimate understanding between themselves. In this way, privacy was directly implicated in the pleasures of marital sex.

Many couples saw themselves as a distinct sexual unit and avoided discussing intimate matters with friends, neighbours or relatives. As Sarah (1906), who married an upholsterer in Preston in 1928, and Jennie (1908), who married a sawmill worker from Blackburn in 1930, emphasised:

SARAH Even though I had three women friends and we all had children, we didn't discuss sex; we didn't tell of our bedroom activities, none of us. We were quite discreet; we drew a curtain over that. So I've never been able to talk.[112]

JENNIE You didn't talk about, er, you didn't talk about sex; you, you kept sex like to yourself, private … Sex life is what you keep private.[113]

Bernard (1907) was a well-educated journalist with an extremely wide circle of friends, with whom he and his wife played bridge, golf, badminton and billiards. Both were active in a number of societies: amateur dramatics, the rotary club, the inner wheel, the masons and the Mothers' Union. He stressed that he did not let sex discussion into his public life and saw sex as a private matter concerning him and his wife alone:

Did you enjoy your sex life in your marriage?

BERNARD Well, it, it was pleasurable [but] it didn't enter into your daily life to such an extent. It was [a] private thing between you and your wife. You didn't even talk to your friends about it.[114]

For some, the determination to keep their sexual relationship completely private dictated when and where sex could take place. Many commented on the difficulties they experienced in conducting a sexual relationship in semi-public

[112] Sarah msf/kf/bl/#30. [113] Jennie msf/kf/bl/#27.

[114] Bernard and Diana msf/jm/bl/#45. For similar testimony on the links between not discussing sex and not prying into 'other people's business' see Beier, 'We Were Green as Grass', 465.

spaces – such as hotels or holiday cottages, or at the homes of relatives. Some chose not to have sex when on honeymoon, preferring to consummate their marriage in the privacy of their own home upon their return.[115] Dougie (1919), a gardener from Berkhamsted, remembered the struggle to persuade his wife, a factory worker, to have sex in places which she did not feel were private enough:

DOUGIE She'd never let me have it while we was away on holidays, not when kids were there. I used to have to wait until I got home, (chuckle) 'cos of next door neighbours ... Yeah ... but I persuaded her to, now and again ... on our late honeymoon ... she said 'Shut up!', she said, 'Mr and Mrs Amos will hear us!' I said 'Never mind about them', I said, 'they've had it before, I ain't' (laugh). So we went down there for a fortnight. I had it once the first week and once the second week (chuckle). Yeah. She was always like that though, even on holiday, she wouldn't, I had to persuade her, you know, to get round her.[116]

The value placed on privacy was so great that many individuals isolated themselves from external sources of sexual information. They were reluctant to accept any suggestion from outside the conjugal unit that they transform or modify any of their sexual practices, by, for instance, introducing more variety into love-making, or adopting a new form of contraception. Indeed, such changes were often avoided, unless they emerged as part of a couple's independent, private sexual learning with each other. Incorporating unexpected or unusual sexual techniques might have implied that the privacy of the sexual bond had been broken: it suggested that one partner had spoken about sex with others, or obtained information from some external, even illicit, source. Colin (1923), a plumber from Blackburn, fondly remembered the ways in which he and his first wife's sex life improved as they experimented together. However, he was anxious not to change their repertoire of practices too radically in case she suspected he had obtained new information through experience with another woman:

COLIN Well, we weren't really experienced for a while like, you know, but it got better as it went on [...]

Well, I think Martha were like me: she'd no experience whatsoever and I hadn't like, you know. And, er, it was just a on-the-top job and that were it like, you know. Er, but er, then you found two or three different ways you see. But er, I used to think to meself well, if I try it that way she'll happen [to] think I've been out with another woman like, you know.[117]

[115] Further insight into the centrality of privacy to mid-twentieth-century sexual respectability can be seen through the ways in which those agitating for the legalisation of homosexuality frequently strove to construct an image of the respectable, domesticated homosexual, who had a right to engage in whatever sexual behaviour he liked behind closed doors, and whose acceptance of the importance of sexual privacy also qualified him for respectability and recognition. See, Houlbrook, *Queer London*, esp. ch. 8, 195–218.

[116] Dougie msf/kf/ht/#5. [117] Colin msf/kf/bl/#36.

Indeed, the efforts of 'respectable' sexual authorities to impinge upon a couple's privacy were often resented. Some respondents were horrified to find their local churches providing their parishioners with sexual advice. Felicity (1919), who worked in a railway accounts office in Accrington after the Second World War, was given moral guidance on family planning by Jesuit priests in the early 1950s when she sought to convert in order to marry her husband. She had been insulted by the fact that they had seen it as appropriate to discuss an issue that she felt ought to remain a private matter between a wife and her husband:[118]

FELICITY The flipping Jesuits told me about this. Just imagine. In fact it got on my nerves so much I said, er, to Julian, 'I'm not going to change' …

They told you about the way they thought we should live. And the things we hadn't to do. It was all this not eating meat in those days at certain days, you know; well, it's not like that now. And, er, contraception was a big thing … I mean, honestly, the way they talked, they always used to tell you to withdraw and things like that.

I mean we weren't married and – talking about withdrawal and I didn't know what it were all about properly. Huh … he said, 'We don't believe in contraception except this counting the days … between your periods'. That was it … Oh yes, that priest was very, very explicit. I don't know how he knew all that but he did; 'e told us what to expect. Which I didn't like very much … I thought it was too intimate.[119]

Few respondents discussed directly the relationship between their own sexual attitudes and religious moral codes. This is not to argue that the Church or moral beliefs that stemmed from Christian ideology did not have a profound impact on many individuals' experience of sex within marriage. Yet, perhaps the most important moral principle that they drew from a general Christian approach to sex within marriage was the idea that it should be conducted in private and that each couple should keep sexual issues to themselves.[120] Sally (1908), a sales assistant from Blackburn, who married in 1934, felt that in keeping 'oneself to oneself' she was following Church teaching. Indeed, so strong was the absorption of this message that she refused to listen to any of the more specific moral messages which the Church promulgated:

Is it the Church that tells you not to have sex before marriage or is it something else that tells you that?

[118] Increasingly, of course, many churchmen were interested in constructing a new Christian morality which drew upon the work of contemporary sexologists and psychologists. The development of the Marriage Guidance Council should be seen as an example of this. Lewis, 'Public Institution and Private Relationship'.

[119] Felicity msf/kf/bl/#37.

[120] Indeed Kate Lynch has argued that this was a characteristic of organised Christian religion in many contexts in the late nineteenth and early twentieth centuries. In seeking to place birth control and therefore also sexuality in the public domain, secularist birth control advocates threatened the uneasy peace which the established churches had maintained in this most

SALLY No, it's the Church … [but] we didn't follow it because of the Church, we followed it because we felt it was right that we should keep ourselves to ourselves, and we did …

What about things like birth control and contraception? Do you know what the Church says about that?

No, I don't, I don't.

What about things like abortion? Do you know what the Church says about that?

No, I'm afraid I don't [know] where that comes in. It's just one of those things, I gave it a wide berth. I don't know why but I wasn't interested.[121]

Thus, few sought direct moral instruction on sexual matters from the Church or read about religious views on sexual questions and issues. Churchgoers did not expect to hear about sex when visiting church or from spiritual leaders, as Vera (1917), an Irish Catholic who trained to be a nurse, recalled: 'They don't talk about it [sex and contraception] in church, not to my knowledge, maybe some churches do … but, er, you sort of grow up with it … how, you're not supposed to use contraceptives.'[122]

Few respondents engaged in any depth with the newly emerging sexual advice literature of the period, regarding it as both an unwelcome challenge to a natural and spontaneous approach to love and sex, and as an invasion of their privacy. For many, the importance of maintaining a relationship governed by nature and developed in private, without external influence or intervention, meant more than the advantages of any new technique or improved sexual relations. Despite the exposure that many had to such material, few wished to consciously change or adapt their practices as a result of new information. Rather, the desire to preserve the privacy of the marital bond, with little overt discussion of sexual matters between partners, meant that sex manuals could not have a positive impact on the ways in which individuals tried to enjoy sexual relations. Only in a few cases did the advice of marriage manuals contribute to an individual's approach to sex, or views of marital relations, and in these cases it was generally an exposure to new forms of sexual debates after the 1960s that transformed their attitudes.

Many respondents were aware that the role of sex within marriage had become part of public debate even during their early lives. Marie Stopes' *Married Love* was an immediate best-seller upon publication in 1918; even two of the oldest respondents came into contact with her books.[123] Sexual advice literature

difficult area of human behaviour and morals, by adhering to the convention that sex was, above all, a private matter (Katherine A. Lynch, 'Theoretical and Analytical Approaches to Religious Beliefs, Values, and Identities During the Modern Fertility Transition', in *Religion and the Decline of Fertility in the Western World*, eds. Renzo Derosas and Franz Van Poppel (Dordrecht: Springer, 2006), 21–39, 34–9.

121 Sally msf/kf/bl/#31. 122 Vera msf/kf/ht/#34.

123 Sally msf/kf/bl/#31, born 1908, called it 'codswallap'; and Sarah msf/kf/bl/#30, born 1906, did not read it 'as I should have done'. Although Lesley Hall reminds us that there was no absence

provided specific and detailed technical advice. In Britain the emergence of the Marriage Guidance Council in the 1940s saw members of the medical profession and the clergy involved in the task of 'helping couples to achieve a high degree of sexual satisfaction' in marriage.[124] In his widely read manual, Van de Velde criticised men, whom he asserted do not know 'that there are numberless delicate differentiations and modifications of sexual pleasure, which can banish the mechanical monotony of the too well known from the marriage bed, and give new attractions to conjugal intercourse'. Van de Velde's ensuing chapters provided very detailed instruction on the precise means of kissing, love-biting and caresses to various particular areas of the body.[125] Similar messages are found in the works of Helena Wright and Marie Stopes, although the latter expressed them in much less precise and more oblique ways.[126] In 1947, E. L. Packer commented that women's sexual dissatisfactions 'centred around the fact that husbands did not "pet" enough before intercourse – thus indicating clearly the male's ignorance of sexual technique ... husbands fail to realise that the co-operation of the woman can only be obtained by conscious erotic technique'.[127]

Although many respondents were aware of such texts, they chose to ignore them or reject their advice. The very existence of such works was seen as an unnecessary challenge to a moral world in which the privacy of marriage and sexual relations was sacrosanct. Interviewees' codes of privacy were at odds with a notion that they might improve their sex lives by comparing themselves with others, talking to other people or seeking out new information or new techniques from various authorities. Quakers Mark (1917) and Joanna (1915) were given Dr Helena Wright's *The Sex Factor in Marriage* when they married in 1947. Joanna 'looked at it several times' and recalled that it provided 'extensive' 'information ... how to behave ... with sex'. Mark, a clerical officer, did not read it. Together, they did not choose to be guided by the advice, preferring

of marital advice in earlier periods and that Victorian marriage literature implied that 'sex was an enjoyable and natural activity', it was after the publication of *Married Love* in 1918 that sex advice focused on the techniques necessary for the achievement of mutual pleasure (Hall, *Hidden Anxieties*, 63–6). On *Married Love*, see Chapter 1, note 100.

124 Lewis, 'Public Institution and Private Relationship', 235.

125 Van de Velde, *Ideal Marriage*, chs. 10, 11. However, as Hera Cook has pointed out, even though *Ideal Marriage* went through several editions and in many ways it provided the most detailed and precise instructions, it was also true that its language was obscure and technical and it was regarded by other manual writers as too detailed for lay use (Cook, *The Long Sexual Revolution*, 196).

126 Cook, *The Long Sexual Revolution*, 209–10, Hall, *Sex, Gender and Social Change*, 121.

127 Packer, 'Aspects of Working-Class Marriage', 99. See also, Hall, *Hidden Anxieties*, 80–2. On the place of foreplay in American marriage manuals' discussions of sexual technique see, Peter Laipson, '"Kiss without Shame, for She Desires It": Sexual Foreplay in American Marital Advice Literature, 1900–1925', *Journal of Social History* 29, no. 3 (1996): 507–25.

to let their sexual technique develop 'naturally'.[128] Marian (1908), whose husband worked in a dye works in Blackburn, before becoming a Corporation bin man, was adamant that 'sex teaching' was unnecessary:

MARIAN You learn them things together; that's why I can't understand why they keep saying on these books: 'read about sex'. There's no need to read about sex, it comes to yer natural doesn't it? When you get married it comes to yer natural.[129]

Jane (1925), and her husband Dick (1920), two of the younger Blackburn respondents, who both had clerical jobs, had an ambiguous response to changing ideas about the place of sex in marriage and the advice provided by a marriage manual written by Leslie Weatherhead.[130] Despite carefully reading this text, they did not specifically take any of its advice, and sought instead to develop a relationship by themselves uninformed by outside views, seeing such an approach as conducive to pleasure and satisfaction:[131]

JANE Everything was very, traditional and (laughs) nothing, nothing, nothing out of the ordinary … I mean, you read about, you read about all sorts of sexual enjoyment but just, there was – there was nothing special really, just, er – just straight sex and it was always very good, wasn't it? … It never really entered my head to, um, indulge in anything out of the ordinary. (laughs) …

Like which ones?

Oh well, you hear of so many, er – oral sex and – and all these things that you read about like bondage – and … it just doesn't appeal, no, no … it just doesn't seem right … I think that's the only one [book] really that I've read at length, yeah, um, I never, (laughs) never really felt the need to … read much about it … To me it's better to learn yourselves as you go along than to, um, sort of just follow what somebody else is doing.[132]

In a world which so highly valued privacy, it is not surprising that so few respondents saw such sex manuals as having made a positive impact on their sexual relations. Only in a few exceptional cases did interviewees present sexual advice literature as having had a direct impact on their lives. Reg's (1919) own sex life changed dramatically after the Second World War, following his encounters with new forms of sexually explicit material. He signed up to the navy immediately upon leaving school in 1936 and stayed until after the Korean War, marrying his wife, a hairdresser from Portsmouth, in 1942. Trained as a cameraman he travelled widely. He read Marie Stopes, and, while serving in the Far East, read the Kama Sutra and studied erotic carvings on temples in

[128] Mark and Joanna msf/kf/ht/#22. [129] Marian msf/kf/bl/#28.

[130] Weatherhead, *The Mastery of Sex*. On the impact and content of this text, see Cook, *The Long Sexual Revolution*, 94, 177, 343.

[131] On idiosyncratic readings of marriage manuals and the reluctance to read marriage manuals and other similar texts see, McLaren, *Twentieth-Century Sexuality*, 63.

[132] Jane and Dick msf/kf/bl/#32.

India.[133] He presented his own sexual technique as having been directly influenced as a result:

And how did you learn your sexual technique?

REG By, um, just by going along the way we went, (laughs) I suppose. Marie Stopes was there, I suppose, if you wanted them, but of course, there was a book floating round from India then, which was banned, um, which was, what was it called now? It's still, they've got the update of it ... Kama Sutra, er, which was published in the, in the, I think it came out in 1935 or '36; so we're talking about those. I wish that I'd kept a couple of those ... if you were following the sex the way they said, you know ... you would do this or do that ... with your hands and, you know, the, the mechanics of the thing. But of course, in India ... all round the temples were all the different positions of sex, they were shown in the Kama Sutra ... But of course, it did give me ideas because afterwards after the war and then we went into love-making and, er, and I suppose that I explored every conceivable way of trying to emulate those things that were, (laughs) that were around the temple, you know.[134]

Antonia was one of our youngest interviewees: she was born in 1928 and married young in 1949. Her marriage was not a happy one. Her husband was a domineering, alcoholic chartered accountant who was much older than her. In sex, as in many other aspects of their relationship, Antonia presented him as selfish, inconsiderate and impervious to her views. They agreed on the fact that they both wanted a large family, but rarely found sex a source of mutual enjoyment. She was given a Marie Stopes book by her mother just before she got married, but found it of no use in addressing her sexual problems. It was only in the 1960s, when she defied her husband's long-standing objection to her seeking employment and enrolled on a degree programme and went to a family planning clinic, that she came into contact with a feminist rhetoric of female sexual pleasure and empowerment, at a family planning clinic. It was these experiences in the 1960s which provided her with the language to critique her experiences of sex within marriage; prior to that, she commented, she had not had the facility to grasp the message of earlier sex education material.

ANTONIA I never found it satisfactory because it was all too rushed. He never gave it enough time ... rushing through what he wanted and not really taking any notice of what I wanted. That was very unsatisfactory ... [then] our sex life was – I mean

[133] On the impact of the Kama Sutra in elite circles following its translation and private printing in 1883 by Richard Burton see, James McConnachie, *The Book of Love: The Story of the Kamasutra* (New York: Metropolitan Books, 2008), ch. 6. The fragility of American culture in the 1960s was satirised by John Updike whose possibly impotent character in *Couples*, Freddy Thorne, keeps a copy of the Kama Sutra by his bed.

[134] Reg msf/kf/ht/#36. Of course, Reg's experiences here are exceptional and far from typical of British men in his generation and class, given his extensive sexual experience overseas (see Chapter 4, note 69). The influence of mainstream British texts like Stopes' which many men read, in fact, played a relatively minor role in his account.

it did improve … after my youngest child was born in 1965 and I was feeling free because I'd got proper contraception. I got a loop and I felt safe … but [earlier] my mother … had got both Marie Stopes books, which she gave me to read. Erm, so she had the right idea but it never quite sort of came through to me – that this should be fun. And by the time I got into my head that this should be fun it was far too late, which was a great pity.[135]

Similarly, it was Gay's (1928) exposure to a language of sexual pleasure and female emancipation in the 1960s which framed her analysis of her sexual relationship. She married a salesman eight years older than herself in 1947 and presented his attitude towards sex as old-fashioned, insensitive and incompetent. However, it was her experience of an affair later in life with a younger man in the 1960s, and her engagement with the rhetoric of the sexual revolution in the 1960s, that allowed her to develop a different understanding of sex and pleasure. She now saw the marital life she had endured with her husband as one of 'sexual oppression', came to value intercourse for the indvidual pleasure it could provide, and began to view the salient aspects of a good sex life as variety, adventure and the achievement of female orgasm.

GAY Yes, but I mean (pause) he wanted, he wanted sex (pause) but, er, well you know it was 'wham, bam and thank you ma'am' sort of thing. There was nothing romantic about it … I mean I was never satisfied, put it that way … and I realise now what a lot I missed when I was young (pause) but, er, no, he, he, it was all just, you know, for him and that was it, nothing more … I thought it was going to be wonderful, I thought it was going to be this wonderful experience, and I'm trying to remember whether it ever was at any time. I never from the time we were married, I never looked forward to it or anything like that … but he certainly, he was no, no great shakes as far as sex was concerned with him, oh no […]

I fell in love with, er, someone what twenty-odd years ago … and once we sort of got to know each other, um, God, I, you know, we couldn't wait to get to bed; ohhh that was wonderful, it really was, um, so then I knew what I had missed … and well there was more to it than just the actual, you know, sex. I mean there was all the foreplay and the leading up to it, but, um, makes all the difference … I mean I hadn't known sex before, I really hadn't, I hadn't a clue, I was so naïve: the first time we went to bed I couldn't, I, I was (laughs) absolutely amazed, I really was. I mean in a way I think I was shy and embarrassed because I'd never, never, you know, experienced any of this before … I didn't know there was a clitoris; I didn't know there was anything … I didn't know that, you know, that there was a sensitive spot. I didn't know that […].

So what did you like especially about the good sex that you had?

Well I suppose because I had an orgasm every time … and it was really, oh, it was great, um, which, you know, I thought, God, what have I been missing all these years; it was very sad really.[136]

[135] Antonia msf/kf/ht/#35, born in London in 1928, six children.
[136] Gay msf/kf/ht/#13.

The importance of privacy within each couple's relationship meant that few had anything but the vaguest idea of what an 'ordinary' sex life might be or what other people did. Respondents generally described a normal sex life as one where sexual intercourse did not take place 'too often'; though what this amounted to in a quantitative sense varied significantly.[137] Indeed, when Mass Observation published a summary of the findings of their 'Little Kinsey' sex survey in *Public Opinion Quarterly* in 1950 they concluded that 'a wall of secrecy is built up about sex' and that individuals were so confused that they had no idea what sexual practices were 'normal' or commonplace.[138] Similarly, Slater and Woodside in 1951 concluded that wide variation in coital frequency reflected the total ignorance people had of the behaviour of others. Consequently, they argued, there was a lack of any common understanding of norms of sexual behaviour.[139]

This widespread absence of awareness of others' sexual practices sometimes led to surprising (and often inaccurate) comparisons between respondents' own sex lives and what they imagined others from their generation had been doing. Catherine (1912) was only one of three interviewees who regularly engaged in oral sex;[140] nevertheless, despite initially asserting that she had little knowledge of what other people did behind closed doors, she assumed that it involved a wider repertoire of practices than she had engaged in:

CATHERINE I don't know what people get up to, all sorts of things (laughing), obviously, yes ... I suppose so, I 'spect they did different things to each other. Which would perhaps give them a thrill, get them sort of worked up or something. Yes ... I suppose, playing with each other's private parts, I would think, and perhaps the rest of the body, and, um, prob'ly kissin' each other, and, uh, some people have oral sex, won't they, and that sort of thing? And I think this is prob'ly what happened. Yes, I think prob'ly kissing each other 'round the private parts and all that sort of thing, yes. But, um. Yes, but I don't really know, as I say [...]

I think I wished that I got more out of it ... you'd have the climax and yes, that was quite good, yes. Hhm. After that you just felt you wanted to have a nap, you know (laugh), tired out ... [but] I never felt such tremendous urge that I would absolutely die (chuckle) if ... no, not at all.

137 As Ellen Ross has realised in her study of an earlier period, women's reluctance to discuss sex in anything but rather coded and euphemistic terms with their neighbours and relations meant that in contrast to financial matters the silence surrounding sex meant that women did not 'develop a collective sense of [exactly] where their "rights" or "interests" lay' (Ross, *Love and Toil*, 100).

138 *Puzzled People* was deemed the most appropriate title for this report; however, they had already used this title for a survey of religious beliefs (England, 'Little Kinsey', 598).

139 Slater and Woodside, *Patterns of Marriage*, 166, Hall, *Sex, Gender and Social Change*, 139.

140 Catherine (1912) msf/kf/ht/#1; Reg (1919) msf/kf/ht/#36; Gay (1928) msf/kf/ht/#13.

Indeed, Catherine expressed some anxieties that she was less highly sexed than those around her, because she found it easier to reach orgasm through foreplay, digital stimulation or oral sex than through intercourse:[141]

CATHERINE To get any sort of thrill out of it, you gotta have a certain amount of foreplay … that will get you to the sort of p-, pitch, but the actual intercourse didn't have that, no, didn't do that with me … I s'pose if they were touching your private parts, you know, that sort of thing, yes. Well, but, actual intercourse didn't seem to have an effect on me, no … So … [he said] 'now we'll do something to, a'least, have some sort of orgasm', you see … sort of play with you … after, yes, after. So that he, that I, at least, was satisfied […]

I suppose yes, you would kiss each other's private parts or that would be part of it, uh … the breasts always come into it, as you know, this sort of thing … The other would be sort of, manual, with the hands sort of thing, you know.[142]

And, of all the things that you would do, um, sexually … what did you like best?

Oh, well possibly being kissed in your private parts, yes, that sort of thing, yes, mm [and] if they put their hand into your private parts sort of thing, that would give you, (laughing) yes, that sort of thing.[143]

It is a mark of the impact of the silence surrounding sexual issues and the importance of privacy in her sex life that she did not realise how unusual such practices were among her contemporaries and was able to perceive herself as relatively sexually unadventurous and inhibited.[144]

For the majority of respondents, the importance of privacy meant few compared their own sex lives with those of their contemporaries, and thus few expressed anxieties or fears about their own choices by contrasting them with the supposedly 'normal' experiences of others. The lack of awareness of

[141] This testimony is, of course, related to and reveals the impact of the twentieth-century controversy surrounding vaginal and clitoral orgasms. On Freud's origination of the notion that women can experience two types of orgasms see, McLaren, *Twentieth-Century Sexuality*, 119–20. See also, Cook, *The Long Sexual Revolution*, 45–60, 235–6. For an analysis of the ways in which modern sexual advice is dominated by a managerial discourse which imposes a 'performance imperative' on individuals see Tyler, 'Managing between the Sheets'.

[142] Reference to oral sex as genital kissing is reminiscent of its descriptions in Van de Velde, *Ideal Marriage*. He suggests it as a remedy for inadequate vaginal lubrication which excites acute pleasure and a variety of tactile sensations. He claims that it is a good means of overcoming frigidity and fear in inexperienced women. He cautions its practitioners to ensure sufficient hygienic preparations are made and that steps are taken to ensure the supreme beauty of sex is not affected. While he focuses primarily on men as the providers of the genital kiss he suggests that experienced women can take a more active role in sex by performing the genital kiss upon their husband without losing their 'distinctive dignity and sweetness' (Van de Velde, *Ideal Marriage*, 148–50, McLaren, *Twentieth-Century Sexuality*, 52–3).

[143] Catherine msf/kf/ht/#1.

[144] On the absence of evidence for the practice of oral sex in this period and an argument that it was very rarely employed see, Cook, *The Long Sexual Revolution*, 128–31. See also John H. Gagnon, *An Interpretation of Desire: Essays in the Study of Sexuality* (Chicago and London: University of Chicago Press, 2004), 150–2.

others' choices, combined with the conviction that sexual experiences should be kept private, fostered for most an acceptance of and contentment with their own sexual repertoires. Sarah (1906), a weaver in Preston, who married an upholsterer in 1928, described her marriage as a happy one, in which sex was 'very important':

SARAH Everything's been alright, we've had a good sex life ... well I'd nothing to compare it with. I don't know how anybody else went on but, it was alright for us.[145]

Thus, it is important not to assume that these strict codes of privacy both within and outside marriages cemented inhibitions that necessarily led to unsatisfying experiences. For these individuals, open communication about sexual matters, either with each other or with members of their community, was not the key to a successful sex life. Rather, notions of privacy were central to those aspects of sexual relationships that were particularly valued and enjoyed. Descriptions of pleasure, exhilaration, tenderness and satisfaction were often intricately linked to these codes. First, privacy was seen to foster a meaningful form of gentle intimacy. Second, the process of developing a sexual relationship in private was seen to provide a relationship with its own dynamism and variation. Finally, some respondents eulogised their abilities to develop private forms of communication in which they were able to silently and intuitively respond to their spouses' desires.

For Esme (1921) and Gerald (1919) sex was made pleasurable by the knowledge that they were engaging in a private act; modern sex, by contrast, was for them brutish due to its indelicate and public representation. Indeed, during the interview they were reluctant to discuss aspects of their sexual technique, feeling that to do so would rob their experiences of their delicacy and intimacy. Demonstratively affectionate (they held hands during the interview), they did not want to discuss mutual masturbation. They believed any open and 'public' articulation of such practices, or the use of certain language to describe behaviour, would demean their marital relationship: it threatened to establish associations between their love-making and illicit, crude or dirty practices. Preserving the privacy of their sexual practices was crucial to maintaining their meaning as a way of expressing the love, affection and commitment that reinforced their marital bond:

ESME Before that, er, er, you know, the films sort of showed the loving couple walking into the bedroom and the door shut, you know. Er, nowadays of course huh – you can't avoid seeing the whole shebang, can you really ... ? Well, I think it, it removes, er, the delicacy of it.

GERALD Sanctity.

ESME It makes it so brutish in a way.

[145] Sarah msf/kf/bl/#30.

I suppose it [sex] was moderately adventurous in the, er, in – when we were younger, yes. Yes, but you were the instigator of the adventure, adventurous bits [but] I'm not going into any details, sorry (laughs).

GERALD Because it's a fine line between just masturbation and overall love-making. So don't push us on that.[146]

Many idealised the fact that they had little or no experience of sex prior to marriage, despite the often tense and unsuccessful nature of coitus on wedding nights or in their early married lives. Respondents described with some satisfaction the ways they slowly learned about sex together as their marriages progressed. Male, female, working- and middle-class respondents all focused on the practice of learning about sex together as potentially exciting personal processes of discovery. Dougie (1919) had a range of low-paid jobs, including gardener and postman:

DOUGIE Well, it was very nice. I enjoyed it (chuckle). Yeah. (pause) I had to learn the techniques (giggle)… to make her come on a bit… trying all the time (chuckle)… if you make a fuss of them and moan you're alright.[147]

Daphne (1912) grew up in a Catholic family and both parents were employed in the local cotton mills. Daphne's father bought her a confectionery shop near Blackburn, which she ran with her husband when they married in 1937.

DAPHNE I didn't know anything about it so I was just green… I mean it grows on you… I mean… when you sleep together you're together all the time it, er, it just happens. They're not subjects you talk about … when you're living together it just happens.[148]

Bernard (1907) and Diana (1910) also emphasised the privacy of the relationship, in describing their intimate and dynamic journey to greater mutual sexual understanding:

BERNARD You grow into it.
DIANA It's not forced down your throat… you worked things out for yourself.
BERNARD No, you didn't talk about it, you see.[149]

Roger (1910) rejected the use of pornography seeing it as a lazy and unfulfilling mechanism for stimulating one's sex life and far inferior to the pleasures of privately inspired creative strategies. His father was a naval commander and he was familiar with military banter and the bawdy jokes of English public schools. He was remarkably effusive and enthusiastic when talking about sexual pleasure in a way which set him apart from all other interviewees. However,

[146] Gerald and Esme msf/kf/ht/#9.

[147] Dougie msf/kf/ht/#5. Dougie had a volatile and passionate relationship with his wife. Both of them were unfaithful and throughout their marriage he was suspicious of her and fearful that other men found her as attractive as he did.

[148] Daphne msf/jm/bl/#38.

[149] Bernard and Diana msf/jm/bl/#45.

despite this striking difference the codes of privacy common to many interviewees remained central to his conception of married love and its pleasures:

ROGER I remember when we were in the army, a, a book of, uh, a magazine came round which was, uh, illustrated, you know, men and women and that, a pornographic book. But, uh, I just glanced through a couple of photos. I wasn't interested in it because I was, I, I had a perfectly satisfactory sex life.

Yeah. So do you think people use pornography because they don't have a satisfactory sex life?

I think that, in fact I know that there are men who get a kick out of pornography. I when I was a lot younger I knew one couple who (chuckle), before he could engage his wife, he used to go in the lavatory and look at the pornography book and I always said, it gave him ideas. And he said it brightened him up and he'd carry – which I always thought was horrible, I mean I might be old-fashioned also, but I always thought it was horrible... he'd carry, he carried that man and woman doing that certain thing into the bedroom just before. I couldn't do that!... Because to me, you should be able to generate your own.[150]

Eleanor (1907) also expressed the value placed on private learning about sex without external influence and took pleasure in developing what she and her husband saw as individual and original techniques. Eleanor, who had a very happy marriage with her husband, a mechanic, was proud of the 'position of our own' that she and her husband discovered:

ELEANOR We always seemed to do it on our side, eh, sideways; I find it more comfortable like that, you know, but, eh, the original position is supposed to be on your back! But we didn't do it like that. We did it sideways; it were just as good, more comfortable (laughing) yeah! Well, we seem to 'ave got a position of our own that just, we'd just fit together (chuckling) but I know that, eh, most, most women is on their backs, but I, we never did it that way; so we 'ad our own position. It were comfortable (laughing), very comfortable... [151]

For many, that they did not explicitly discuss sexual issues within their marriages was not considered inhibiting or destructive, even in retrospect. Rather, many took great pleasure in their ability silently and subtly to interpret the other's desires and respond accordingly. That sex was private, and little discussed, contributed to their satisfaction with their partner.[152] Frank (1919), an

[150] Roger msf/kf/ht/#10. [151] Eleanor msf/kf/bl/#11.

[152] This aspect of respondents' testimony challenges historians' assumptions about the effect of sexual ignorance and public silence about sexual matters on individuals' experiences. For example, Stephen Kern, in analysing the impact of modernism, concludes that: 'A conspiracy of silence reduced Victorian sexual intercourse to a mute and mindless routine' whereas 'modern lovers' broke that silence, sometimes with annoying exuberance, but their thinking and talking enabled them to fashion ways of having sex that was [*sic*] more their own.' Kern, *The Culture of Love*, 349. Kern is here consciously drawing upon the notion, originating with Martin Heidegger's founding existentialist text, *Being and Time*, that for experience to be 'authentic' it must be subject to individuals' own reflective choices and deliberations, not simply 'instinctive', 'natural' or the result of 'common sense' (see ch. 1, 45). For Heidegger,

ambulance driver attendant in Blackburn, recalled with considerable pride the ways in which he learned to interpret his wife's desires and 'communicate' without talking:

> FRANK It were never, it were never discussed... you could, er, tell... by her reaction... we had that understanding, you know, you, you didn't need to say anything... We had [it] worked to a fine art, whereby we knew by just looking at one another... just how, how deeply you were involved and, and what really was wanted. So you just did it more or less automatic, as I say, you, you were gradually gaining experience, er, and, er, you always do it in private... [153]

Conclusion

In 1931, in summarising her findings since setting up a 'marriage guidance centre' in 1929, Janet Chance concluded that 'on the whole in England, sexual life is a poor thing. It is not happy; often it is wretched.'[154] Similarly, Leonora Eyles was convinced in 1933 that 'most people go through life without experiencing sexual pleasure worth the name'.[155] Commentary in the post-war period continued in this vein: E. L. Packer concluded that 'sexual maladjustment in marriage seems to permeate the whole relationship'.[156] For women in particular he claimed, 'indifference and dislike of sexual intercourse is the norm'.[157] Helena Wright's *More About the Sex Factor in Marriage* (first published in 1947), similarly claimed that despite the optimism of her and others' attempts during the previous fifteen years to educate men and women, female satisfaction in marriage remained elusive. According to Wright, half of wives had still not recognised that 'physical satisfaction can, and should, be as real and vivid for them as it is for their husbands'.[158]

While these contemporary observers may have correctly identified some of the sexual problems associated with a culture in which husbands and wives rarely discussed sexual matters openly, and in which public debate on the subject was still regularly seen as seedy and disreputable, they nevertheless missed the range of other ways in which individuals in this period regarded their sex lives as satisfactory or fulfilling. In part this was an outcome of a

'inauthentic' experiences were the product of unthinking obedience to social conventions and norms. Indeed, these respondents could be seen as having reversed Heidegger's position in asserting, reflexively, that seeking privacy in order to enjoy spontaneous, natural, untutored sex was their own authentic choice, and as suggesting that modern relationships are inauthentic products of prescriptive cultural pressures and commodification.

153 Frank msf/srss/bl/#16.

154 Janet Chance, *The Cost of English Morals* (London: Douglas, 1931), 15.

155 Eyles, *Commonsense About Sex*, 77.

156 Packer, 'Aspects of Working-Class Marriage', 98. 157 Ibid.

158 Helena Wright, *More About the Sex Factor in Marriage* (London: Williams & Norgate, 1954), 11. See also, Joan Malleson, *Any Wife or Any Husband: A Book for Couples Who Have Met Sexual Difficulties and for Doctors* (Harmondsworth: Penguin, 1962).

tendency – observable among both contemporary sex reformers and later scholars – to focus narrowly on the purely physical aspects of sexual feelings as the key indicator of a fulfilling sex life. In addition, such conclusions were also in part a result of the absence of a legitimate discourse of sexual fulfilment among those who were surveyed. Without a recognisable language of thrills and climaxes, analysts have been deaf to the more oblique descriptions of marital satisfaction which focus on the giving, not the receiving, of pleasure, and which emphasise the relationship between sex and marital duties and responsibilities. Couples often reported sex which was satisfying, but many of the interviewees (especially women) talked obliquely and reluctantly about their own erotic pleasures, not simply out of embarrassment, but because a celebration of the experience of orgasm conflicted with their self-identities as providers of sex, and as wives whose duties were to selflessly care for others. Oral testimony revealed the particular values and beliefs which structured individuals' experiences of sex and framed what they deemed fulfilling, or even pleasurable. First, men and women thought successful sex would contribute positively to the ways in which married partners provided for, and cared for, each other. Second, couples were happy only with expressions of sex which were clean, hygienic and 'wholesome'. Third, couples enjoyed sexual experiences provided they were spontaneous and felt natural, an attitude which led many to resist the external advice of the sort provided by marriage guidance material. Fourth, and most importantly, couples thought their sexual relationship should be conducted and enjoyed in complete privacy.

9 The morning after

ALF I've got to say this, that in my days when I was a youth, well, as a youth, I think there's more respect towards women than there are today . . . I mean . . . we were sort of limited in those days; they've got so much freedom today . . . I blame it all down to . . . when they discovered the Pill. When they discovered that everything went up the wall . . . It was freedom, actually . . . they got actual freedom today, the women . . . They were afraid in the old days . . . young girl was afraid to get into trouble . . . [but] today it is the emancipation of, emancipation of women . . . which I don't know whether a good thing or bad thing 'cos some of these girls – the way I see it – is some of them are not very . . . they're naïve I think, the way they spread theirselves. Why don't they keep keep us at arm's length? I mean, don't start giving into 'em like that.[1]

The shadow of the sexual revolution hangs over all histories of sexuality during the twentieth century. A study of the attitudes towards, and experiences of, sex in Britain between the 1920s and 1960s will inevitably draw upon assumptions about the nature of changes associated with the 1960s and after. Indeed, as the title of this book illustrates, the period under investigation here is popularly thought of as the period 'before' the sexual revolution. Implicit in this project is a comparative question which takes as its starting point the knowledge that modern sexual cultures are very different from those of the first decades of the twentieth century.[2]

This comparative framework was also at the heart of respondents' narratives. Having lived through a period of extraordinary change, many interviewees felt they were now living in a world that shared few of their past sexual values. Respondents found themselves confronted by a culture which denigrated the sexual privacy and silence – that they had valued so highly – as

[1] Alf msf/kf/ht/#14.

[2] On the sexual revolution and its aftermath see, for example, Jeffrey Weeks, *Sexuality and Its Discontents: Meanings, Myths and Modern Sexualities* (London: Routledge & Kegan Paul, 1985), Sheila Jeffreys, *Anticlimax: Feminist Perspective on the Sexual Revolution* (London: Women's Press, 1990), Segal, *Straight Sex*, Cook, *The Long Sexual Revolution*, Marcus Collins, ed. *The Permissive Society and Its Enemies: Sixties British Culture* (London: Rivers Oram, 2007), Weeks, *The World We Have Won*.

having impoverished sexual experiences and inhibited sexual expression.[3] Testimony revealed a sense of alienation from modern sexual norms and distance from the morals, views and expectations of the media and younger family members and friends.

In response, interviewees sought to explain their choices and principles; they defended their past values in the light of the different sexual codes they now perceived to be dominant.[4] They identified key differences between the opportunities, expectations and moral values which had framed their experiences and contrasted these with a range of behaviours and attitudes which they claimed to have observed in contemporary society, in the media and in the behaviour of their younger relatives and friends. However, their defence also often drew upon vague understandings of modern sexual culture which were not necessarily grounded in direct observation or experience. Interviewees constructed a crude version of a dysfunctional and unhappy present using clichéd representations gleaned from socially conservative and often sensationalised mass media reports. However, the validity of such contrasts, or the extent to which respondents' observations of recent mores were grounded in anything more than hearsay or conservative outrage, is not important here. Rather, this chapter interrogates the contrasts drawn between past and present, exploring how individuals who were socialised before the 'sexual revolution' understood the sexual values of the modern world around them, and came to terms with its

[3] Many historians have echoed this critique. Hera Cook reminded readers of the sexual gains that feminism achieved and that the introduction of safe, accessible, easy and reliable contraception allowed. She argued this had transformed sexual experiences from a risky and anxiety-ridden activity into one which could be engaged in freely according to desire (Cook, *The Long Sexual Revolution*, 'Introduction', pp. 1–8). Focusing on the politics of sexuality, Jeffrey Weeks urged historians not to lose sight of the positive transformations that have had a beneficial influence on individuals' experiences of sex (Weeks, *The World We Have Won*, 3). Before the 1960s, he reminded readers, Britain was a culture impoverished by a marital 'ethic', constrained by 'taboos on non-genital sexuality' and marred by 'the stigma against non-marital relations and illegitimacy'(Weeks, *Sexuality and Its Discontents*, 15).

[4] Oral historians have developed the notion of composure, as a methodology for exploring the dialogue between past and present and the ways in which historians can use such comparisons to inform their investigations of individuals' past experiences: the idea that oral history testimony involves the 'composition' of life narratives that provide individuals with 'subjective composure' – a version of themselves which makes sense of their lives in the context of the public narratives about the past that exist around them (Graham Dawson, *Soldier Heroes: British Adventure, Empire and the Imagining of Masculinities* (London and New York: Routledge, 1994), Michael Roper, 'Re-Remembering the Soldier Hero: The Psychic and Social Construction of Memory in Personal Narratives of the Great War', *History Workshop Journal* 50 (2000): 181–204). Penny Summerfield has argued that this process is often better seen as one of 'dis-composure' since life stories often reflect the tensions engendered by the attempt to reconcile competing historical understandings of the past into a coherent narrative (Penny Summerfield, 'Dis/Composing the Subject: Intersubjectivities in Oral History', in *Feminism and Autobiography: Texts, Theories, Methods*, eds. Celia Lury, Tess Cosslett and Penny Summerfield (London and New York: Routledge, 2000), 91–106.

challenge to their earlier-formed moral worlds. Moreover, it will address what such responses tell us about their attitudes to sex both now and in the past.[5]

Central to their comparisons of sexual mores across the twentieth century was a vigorous defence of past values. In the light of a perceived attack on the morals that governed their worlds, respondents sought to defend their choices and in turn denigrate modern sexual mores. First, modern values were attacked on the grounds that any benefits or pleasures gained were outweighed by the negative effects they engendered: a high divorce rate, marital infidelity, illegitimacy, sexually transmitted diseases, the public visibility of pornography, unrealistic expectations of sexual pleasure and the supposed lack of respect between men and women. This defence championed respondents' own sexual worlds as having been stable and content by contrast. Such testimony posits an image of past sexual relationships as limited, restricted, restrained and staid, but ultimately more meaningful, committed and happy. The second defence rejected the modern society's contention that it had constructed an era of new erotic freedoms, denied to previous generations. Here they adapted some of the terminology of sexual pleasure associated with a modern approach to high-quality sex, such as variation, dynamism and experimentation, in order to construct a version of a sexual past which better embodied these values.[6] A modern rhetoric of variety, adventure and spontaneity was reinterpreted and attributed to their own past sexual relationships. Older generations, they claimed, had managed dynamic sex lives without the morally problematic consequences of the 'sexual revolution'.

It should be noted that not all respondents were unequivocally critical of modern sexual mores. Some did seem to offer a more positive engagement with the revolution in sexual values, particularly the benefits of sex education and the liberating potential of reliable contraception. Yet even in these cases, their approval of aspects of modern sexual practice did not in fact reflect an acceptance of a liberationist critique of their own customs. Criticisms of past sexual values and positive contrasts with the present were usually located within a conceptual framework drawn from the period before the sexual transformations of the 1960s. On the one hand, for example, some were broadly supportive of the provision of sex education was provided to the younger generation. On the other, their understanding of this 'positive development' was shaped by the encounter with the much more limited ideas about sex education in their earlier lives: they frequently argued that children today were provided with too much information, too young, and, in an echo of much mid-century

[5] Respondents commented on various aspects of modern sexual culture, such as the increased tolerance of and visibility of homosexuality. These are not discussed here and the analysis is confined to the contrasts drawn by couples relating to the moral codes associated with marriage and sexuality.

[6] The language of freedom or liberation, however, was rarely drawn upon.

opinion, they advocated the provision of basic biological details only. Thus even the criticisms they acknowledged of the sexual worlds they had grown up in, and the degree of support some expressed for current values, were often in fact further evidence of a defence of past values. Central to these interviewees' life stories was an encounter with a monumental shift in sexual attitudes, in the face of which they continued to uphold values that they still held dear.

While little of this testimony directly engaged with the full intellectual sophistication of many of the debates about sex that emerged after the 1960s, or fully recognised the complexity of the 'liberationist' critiques of past sexual attitudes, the limited nature of respondents' defence of their pasts itself demonstrates the force and intensity of their own value systems. Unwilling to fully appreciate the radicalism embedded in the modern attempt to transform sexuality, interviewees responded to the perceived challenge to their own lives on their own terms. Such responses were tied to the core principles that informed their lives, which continue to dominate their worlds, and which now reveal their values to later generations.

'The fantastic buzz has gone out of sex – so goodbye'

In robustly defending their sexual histories against a perceived challenge from 'liberationst' values, many respondents attacked modern sexual culture as morally depraved or vulgar. Many toyed with, and even accepted, the charge that their lives were boring in modern terms, limited in forms of sexual expression, unadventurous and comparatively abstinent. At the same time, however, they claimed that moral values and family stability had been eroded and saw this as the unacceptable cost of a modern quest for sexual excitement. This vindication of the past rested on weighing up the benefits of an unexciting, but stable, traditional marriage, on the one hand, and a sexually vibrant modern world marred by divorce, infidelity and unrealistic expectations of sexual fulfilment, on the other.

Maureen (1920), a typist from Blackburn, held particularly strong views on the vulgarity and moral decay of the modern world. She defended previous generations' approaches to sex on the basis that they were governed, above all, by love. Her views reflected her personal religious standpoint. She decried the absence of knowledge of the scriptures in modern society and the failure of the Church of England to take a stronger line against sex before marriage:

MAUREEN television – it stinks of sex, it stinks. It's horrible, it's vulgar, you know, and really, er, it's, it's ruined, it's ruined everything; it's ruined people's lives … it's not sort of love, it's sex, you know what I mean? … The sooner we get rid of sex and put love first, that'll be something …

And describe to me how sex is different when love is involved. What, what is it, what … ?

It is, well – I think you come naturally together I suppose and when you're together in bed at night and you snuggle up.[7]

For Esme (1921), a shorthand typist who later worked as a school secretary once her children left school, modern relationships were damaged by a desire for sexual pleasure which fostered casual encounters and unrealistic expectations of enduring exhilaration, which in turn precipitated an overly cavalier acceptance of divorce:

ESME I think it's the casual way people have sex without any commitment. Um, and also the fact that sex seems to be the most important thing in life now. Whereas we know that though it's very important it's still only part of life. And if a young couple … they split up … They sort of say, well the sort of fantastic buzz has gone out of sex – so goodbye – you know, we'll find someone else.[8]

Similarly, Esme's husband Gerald (1919) attacked what he saw as the negative consequences of the social acceptability of sex before marriage. He argued that experiences with more than one partner would give a spouse an 'inbuilt' tendency towards unfaithfulness, and foster a readiness to move on to another partner during times of difficulty or disagreement:[9]

GERALD Nowadays, as far as I can judge, people are always hopping into one another's bed all around the place and I say this: if you've been used to that when you weren't married why should your nature fundamentally change to steadfastness afterwards? I don't see how it could … so that unfaithfulness is in marriage – is a built-in factor nowadays; it's not something viewed with a horror and a deep sin … it's something that you've always done – what's the big fuss?[10]

Catherine (1912), a shorthand typist who grew up in London, also linked the promiscuity of the contemporary world with unstable relationships. She was unusual in that she did try to understand the motivations of today's youth, including her son, granddaughter and the interviewer. Yet she remained baffled by the values espoused by these representatives of the modern world and professed herself sceptical of the benefits. She found it particularly difficult to relate to the supposed ability of modern women to rapidly switch their affections between men. In particular, she was robustly critical of codes of sexual play and adventurousness displayed by her son and daughter-in-law. Scornfully linking their 'embarrassing' open sexual games (love-bites and red bras) with their subsequent divorce, she suggested that modern indicators of sexual quality were not signs of real love or lasting affection, but indicative of relationships doomed to fail.

[7] Maureen msf/kf/bl/#46. [8] Esme msf/kf/ht/#9.

[9] On the prominence (and celebration) of the dissolution of relationships in modern relationship manuals see, Rebecca Hazleden, 'The Pathology of Love in Contemporary Relationship Manuals', *The Sociological Review* 52, no. 2 (2004): 211–14.

[10] Gerald msf/kf/ht/#9.

CATHERINE You didn't … go around with all and sundry. And I, nowadays I wonder how the young people can jump into bed so quickly with each other, and have sex, because it's such an intimate thing … But they seem to do it … even my granddaughter … having sex with all sorts of different young men … And I do wonder … I'll probably ask her one of these days, (laugh) how on earth do you manage to get round to having sex with, you know, a fellow that they've only known a few weeks, it's … it just amazes me. As I say, because it seems such an intimate thing, oh dear (giggle); yes life's changed (chuckle). Hhm. Can you approve of all this?

Um, yes I can.

Can you, because you're modern? You can, yes, hhm. And that seems alright, does it?

[…]

Before they were married, he'd [her son] have love-bites, you know, on his neck. Well, they don't realise what an older person sees … and she used to tempt him with different things, and I (giggle), I could see her now in the kitchen over in the old house, behind my back she's holding out a red bra … uh, yes, she was more highly sexed … But, um, he'd, he'd say … well, 'we love each other', you see. So much so that they're now divorced; marvellous isn't it (chuckle)?[11]

In other cases, a defence of past values which charted the negative consequences of the period of the sexual revolution and after was more ambivalent. Many respondents acknowledged the ways in which, to modern eyes, their own sexual experiences were monotonous, staid and perfunctory, marred by embarrassment and inhibition, limited by the fear of pregnancy in the absence of contraception, and often restricted to just one life partner. Daphne (1912) was a practising Catholic who had owned a sweet shop near Blackburn:

DAPHNE There was no stripping off like there is these days and we did cover our bodies (laughs) – we covered our bodies up to begin with … I'm a square … I mean it just happened at night and weren't one of them that were jumping into bed during the daytime and that sort of thing.[12]

Such testimony often mocked the restrictions of past sexual codes, even while robustly criticising the present. Some interviewees joked about their own inhibitions and derided their own lives as boring and mundane. At the same time, they frequently embarrassedly poked fun at contemporary sexual shenanigans and criticised modern culture's obsession with sexual matters. Lyn (1907) mocked today's sex as exhausting, before denigrating it more fundamentally as animalistic and loveless:

LYN I think I'd be absolutely exhausted – way they're talking about wriggling about and all the rest of it … I should think when some of them say they're at it nearly day and night, well … I don't know how they manage it to be truthful, meself. Sexual desires, for me, is when you really love anybody – you really love 'em but you

[11] Catherine msf/kf/ht/#1. [12] Daphne msf/jm/bl/#38.

don't want to be doing that all the time. Even animals are not like that. So, I don't know. But whether I'm right or wrong, I don't know.[13]

Sarah's (1906) complex and ambivalent analysis of contemporary sexual culture attempted to reconcile a defence of her life as fulfilled and happy with a concern that modern audiences might claim her marriage was staid and inhibited. She revealed herself to be retrospectively anxious that she had not been sufficiently adventurous sexually and that, as a result of her own 'shyness', she had been ignorant of, and thus neglected, male sexual needs. Yet ultimately her analysis upheld the values of her past. She weighed up the benefits of a stable and happy marriage against her image of modern sex which was insufficiently private, and had created a whole host of new anxieties, for example surrounding penis sizes.

SARAH Sex dominates everything … Let's put it like this: it wasn't as important, not like it is today; sex, sex, sex all the time today … I mean … nowadays the things that they do in sex, uh, you think, 'Well, I never did that!' And it did really make you think that you sold your husband short … Because I didn't know, because I didn't understand men's wants … I know that men need it more than women now, but I didn't used to think so then, you know … I remember, there's a little incident here that might (chuckle) just … when I was in Bolton [recently] … my friend and me, and we were passing the Odeon and, uh, she says, 'Just look!' … and there was a big poster (chuckle) … it was a, a cabaret dancer, and … it showed her in the position, like this, you know, and I said, 'Well … I never did a fandango in the nuddy for my husband!' … But you might have missed out on something, but have we? Have we? […]

Like today, they'll have a row, they'll have an argument about something and before you can say 'night' there are married couples that are going in for a divorce … I think they talk about sex and what they do and they make it seem as if it's the norm … they talk about it and – as if it's the norm – and they, they go off on one-night stands … No, it, they've sort of brutalised it somehow … no, I don't approve of what they do today … maybe, not brutalised, that's probably the wrong word; they've … that is the wrong word … (pause). Uh, it's not sacred anymore. (pause) And perhaps sacred is the wrong word but, uh (chuckle), you know, it's, it's not, it's not private anymore … things have changed; there wasn't all that anx-, anxiety while we were young, you just, you, you just took yourself, well, 'It's just my bad luck!' (giggle), you know (laugh). No, it's, it's, that anxiety's put there … there's dozens and dozens of magazines come out now for girls. I remember the first time I, I saw anything in, in a magazine – it was my granddaughter, Charlotte, and she, I went in, I went in the lounge (they had an upstairs lounge at Matlock), and she'd be about 14 – she'd be 14 or 15 – and she was looking at something and she put this book away, sharp and I says, 'What's that, Charlotte?' And we, I could talk to Charlotte, I could say, 'What's that Charlotte?' She said, 'Oh, it's just, just a new magazine that's come out' … and it, she showed it me; I couldn't believe it, and I said, 'Oh that blooming rubbish!' I said, I said, 'You

[13] Lyn msf/kf/bl/#1.

> want to read something better than that, Charlotte' (chuckle)... It was, it was, um, 'Do you admire a boy because he has a large penis?'... *Women's Realm*, all, and they started getting more and more and more sex, you know... well, everything's changed – it's, they've [changed] from being nice and a nice romantic story, they're full of sex now. And going to bed and what they did, you know?[14]

At the core of these comparisons between past and present was a defence of the past which championed contentment and stability over sexual excitement, variety or exhilaration. Modern sexual values were seen to have produced erotically fulfilled yet precarious, comparative and sexually competitive relationships, while traditional ones were valued for their apparent tranquillity and relative stability, despite their erotic limitations.

'It's creative and instinctive'

For other respondents, their defence of past sexual cultures meant an explicit rejection of liberationist critiques which framed marriages in the past as erotically limited or restrained by codes of privacy and innocence, from which the sexual revolution had broken free. Instead, these individuals produced a version of erotic adventure and pleasure which turned the language of sexual liberation around: they claimed that in their world, experiences of erotic excitement, dynamism, adventure and variety were intimately connected to codes of chastity and innocence. Moreover, they argued that modern culture's emphasis on knowledge and education robbed sexual experiences of mystery and creativity.

Some recast the present-day emphasis on sexual experimentation and variety as an indication, not of the quality of modern sexual life, but of its dysfunction. Modern couples were pitied for being unable to gain sufficient sexual satisfaction without resorting to new forms of inspiration or sexual stimulation. Others focused on the ways in which learning about sex with one partner in the privacy of a marriage, far from being a boring, staid or limited experience, was one which had its own forms of excitement, dynamism and variety. Such responses attacked modern culture for supposedly needing to turn to external, derivative or artificial forms of sexual stimulation, and championed the private sexual self-sufficiency they saw as having characterised sexual relationships in the past.

Dora (1923) had an extremely loving relationship with her husband, a motor mechanic, whom she married in 1945. She described the delicate beauty of the ways in which her husband cared for her during sex and contrasted this with the 'revolting' images of sex portrayed on television. Dora attacked the contemporary emphasis on the use of various sexual positions, arguing that

[14] Sarah msf/kf/bl/#30.

pure and loving relationships had no need for such artificial forms of additional stimulation. The notion of 'spicing up' one's sex life was rejected as indicative of a relationship that had become sexually dysfunctional and unable to sustain the erotic needs of the couple without external help:

DORA We both loved one another so dearly that it was agony at times ... not like when you see them on here (points to television) trying to eat one another – 'Hello darling mmmmm'. No, he was gentle. He was really gentle. He was lovely ... When you see it and I think it's revolting ... Joe gave a really lovely kiss. A gentle kiss ... Sometimes I couldn't breathe. (laughs) ... I'd have tears in my eyes sometimes because he was so gentle. He was so loving ...

What about variety in making love? Did you, did you try different positions for making love?

(overlapping) Nope. Nope. No. No ... No. I don't think you have to do it if you love one another ... really and truly my married life was, was lovely with him. He really. He was gentle. He was kind. Everything that I wanted in a man ... It was just pure love.[15]

In a similar dismissal of a modern equivalence between sexual variety and good sex, Bryan (1918), foreman at a rubber factory in Hertfordshire, assumed that a search for new sexual positions, or a need to experiment with new ways of having sex, was the resort of couples with sexual problems.[16] His marriage and sex life were happy, though marred by a series of miscarriages in between the births of their two children. He did not link variety and experimentation with enjoyable sex, but rather hinted that only those who were 'worried' or found sex unsatisfactory might feel the need to investigate alternative ways of accomplishing it:

BRYAN I say we led a very close life and anything that we done and that was just between the two of us ... Didn't matter much what positions as long as we had a bit of sex – that's all the matter; didn't have to worry about positions at all.

Did you tend to experiment with positions or did you have one that you liked that you stuck to?

15 Dora msf/srss/ht/#38. This claim was clearly important to Dora. Note, however, that Dora was by no means simply misty-eyed about her husband, whom she said she had not initially fallen in love with during their courtship (see Chapter 4, note 46).

16 The association of sex in the 'missionary' position as staid and perfunctory, on the one hand, and, on the other, the adoption of a variety of positions as indicative of a positive embracing of a new ethos of mutual sexual pleasure in marriage was emerging in some contemporary sex advice. Edward Charles' *The Sexual Impulse*, first published in 1935, was one of the earliest manuals to advocate that sex should take place in a variety of positions (see, Cook, *The Long Sexual Revolution*, 212–18). Kenneth C. Barnes and G. Frances Barnes, *Sex, Friendship and Marriage* (London: G. Allen & Unwin, 1938) also advocated the use of a variety of positions on the grounds that 'variety is the spice of love' (quoted in Collins, *Modern Love*, 252, n.41).

No, well, we just carried a straightforward one. I just got on top of her and that was it.[17]

Bryan also defended past codes of sexual innocence and premarital chastity on the grounds that inexperience turned the early stages of their conjugal relationship into an adventure of discovery. Describing that period as 'magic' he presented the experience of initial marital innocence as joyous and exciting (not inhibited or inexpert) and was convinced that his sexual experiences in marriage were more enjoyable than those of modern couples:

BRYAN Well really I thought it was better. Judging on my own experiences I thought they would probably enjoy it better if they waited until they got married ... because it was a new experience – something that we were looking forward to all the while probably. I thought it was magic.[18]

Like others, he argued that codes of privacy provided the sexual relationship in marriage with its own dynamism, excitement and variation.

In part, Grace (1922) accepted the modern critique that sex in the past had been inhibited. Describing her young life as having taken place in 'nearly Victorian times', she identified herself as prim and old-fashioned and presented her sexual experiences as having been negatively affected by her shyness. Yet, it was the absence of privacy which she ultimately blamed for having impoverished sex in a wretched period of her early married life when, as a result of living in the same house as her parents-in-law, she and her new husband 'couldn't enjoy' each other physically for fear of making too much noise. Sex behind closed doors, by contrast, was eulogised as beautiful. Her sexual shyness and desire for privacy was defended from a liberationist attack and instead idealised as central to the development of a highly meaningful and fulfilling sexual relationship. Here privacy was not something respondents prized above variety and sensuality in marriage: it was part of what made sex fulfilling. Grace saw their love-making as beautiful precisely because it was conducted patiently and in private:

GRACE It was nearly Victorian times ... It was just through understanding and Colin's patience that we finally knew what making love was all about. And it was lovely. It really was ... Because of the times we lived in. Because of the non-privacy ... And I think I said to you last week that to me – and it always has been, and it always

[17] Bryan msf/kf/ht/#25. For example Dennis mfs/kf/ht/#15 expressed similar views. Bryan's analysis is not unlike Van de Velde's: different positions are recommended for people with particular problems or: particular circumstances (e.g. pregnancy, tiredness, when conception is desired, if overweight, if unwell in Van de Velde, *Ideal Marriage*, ch. 11). Betty and Horace msf/kf/ht/#31, for instance, talked about how they spent some time experimenting in the early years of their marriage before they found a comfortable position because she had a bad hip injury from childhood.

[18] Bryan msf/kf/ht/#25.

will be – I think making love between a man and a woman is something very, very private… And I think – I'm very old-fashioned – I think that's where it should stop, in the bedroom, because I think when a man and woman's in love it's summat really lovely, but now I think they're making it dirty. No, we didn't talk about it. We knew we loved one another… I do really think it's something private. And maybe that's what was wrong with me.

But on the other hand did, did you enjoy it at the time?

Yeah. Yeah. Oh yeah (enthusiastic). But I, I think it were more when, when we were on our own, we'd got our own home and it were private, that you knew nobody was gonna be knocking at the door or whatever. Oh, we had fun as well. I mean I always remember one particular night up there: Colin was feeling that way and we was all ready, and I just moved to one side like that and (laughing) and I just said 'Oh you missed me.' And he put his hand up to me mouth like that because his mum and dad was in the next bedroom. You see you couldn't. You couldn't enjoy. No, Simon. Yeah. I, Colin made love beautifully. I mean he's the only man I made love with – ever wanted to make love with. And ever will make love with.

Did you, erm, did you experiment with different positions for making love?

No. I don't think it's very nice. No. Er, I'm a prim. A bit (pause) old-fashioned, if you like… Yeah, I did enjoy it. But it was, it was just this awful shyness. Er, it really was awful. Er, really I don't suppose I should have married really… Yeah. Love-making with Colin in the end, it was really lovely. It was a pleasure. Something that you wished could have gone on forever if you like.[19]

Although June (1914) identified herself as having been inhibited as a result of her sexual shyness, and thought modern couples got 'a lot more pleasure' than she had, she also championed the influence which an earlier culture of innocence and sexual ignorance had had on her married life. Criticising modern couples who 'knew too much', she celebrated the ways in which she and her husband learned about sex and experimented together from a shared position of innocence:

JUNE when we were first married we didn't know much about it. And neither of us had had intercourse, you see, [so] it was a matter of learning with each other what suited each other… It was an experimenting and we didn't know much about it and we didn't read much about it. Er, er, there's too much knowledge now, you see, which we didn't have.[20]

These individuals attacked the forms of variety and experimentation seen as characteristic of contemporary modern individuals' quest for sexual satisfaction and fulfilment, and advocated instead private versions of adventure, discovery and independent learning that some felt had characterised their own

[19] Grace msf/srss/ht/#38.

[20] June msf/kf/ht/#27. June had a 'wonderfully happy' marriage to a grocer in Yorkshire. They had two children, and were moderately active Anglicans who had their two children confirmed.

lives. As Patrick put it: 'it's always adventurous, isn't it? Each act is, yes, from that point of view'.[21]

Only a few men (and some women like June) debated whether their own marriages had suffered from a lack of modern forms of sexual adventurousness. Even in these cases, however, respondents had not wanted to embrace new sexual practices. Colin (1923), a plumber from Blackburn who married in 1947, and Patrick (1918), a salesman who married in 1941, were wary of framing the absence of such practices in their own lives in terms which suggested disappointment or dissatisfaction. They focused instead on the potential dangers of introducing new techniques into their marriages, and highlighted that they had no desire to jeopardise their very successful and happy sex lives by trying anything new:

COLIN Were there 'owt kinky? No... It were just straightforward unadulterated sex. There were no whips, anything. No leather boots or shorts – nothing like that going on. It were just, it were th'only way I knew, th'only way I knew and wife were enjoying it and I were enjoying it so why change a good thing, you know.[22]

PATRICK She once said, 'I'm, er, remember, I'm not an athlete.' She had no reason for saying that but she was, she's been thinking about something. I said, 'that's alright, don't want an athlete, I want a wife' ... But I think she'd got ideas about people sitting up in odd positions, you know, and ladies riding a horse apparently, and, no, she wasn't interested in that... [and] I was very well satisfied with what we did, and, um, I was anxious not to try anything else in case it didn't come off, and then I would have been fed up and she might have been upset... There were one or two things we, we could have done I suppose, um, like with her on top. And, um, she didn't fancy that; I don't think I did really, but it would have been worth trying. And, er, (pause) I think that would have been about all. Because it was all going so nicely, you know. You don't want to rock the boat, if I may use that expression?[23]

Such ideas were central for Reg (1919), a navy cameraman who joined up upon leaving boarding school in the late 1930s, and who eventually owned his own film production company. He saw his youthful naïvety and the challenge of developing a sex life without an extensive understanding of its mechanics as creating a sense of wonder and thrill missing for modern couples, for whom, he suspected, sex had become bawdy and crude:

REG I can't really believe that people nowadays can have the thrill, the wonder and the beauty of what we had then, because it's not something of beauty now; it's something that you – to quote one of the raw, bawdy films of the year, 'He whipped his old bazooka out and that was it' – that was the end of it, you see, and his bazooka

[21] Patrick msf/kf/ht/#16.

[22] Colin msf/kf/bl/#36. Colin was married twice, and it was not entirely clear which wife he was referring to here, but it was probably his first whom he married in 1947 and who died in the mid-1970s.

[23] Patrick msf/kf/ht/#16.

wasn't the thing that used to fire at tanks – um, no, I think the magic, the love and all the things that went with it – in an enduring and, you know, really, really (pause)...[24]

He also highlighted the pleasure and excitement in 'creatively' and 'instinctively' exploring sex with his first wife, a hairdresser from Portsmouth, and developing techniques from a position of innocence:

REG I went into that totally innocent of everything – that's techniques and all the rest of it – but, um... I wouldn't change, because it was gentle, it was exploring and going through together...

The best position was whatever happened when you suddenly had the urge and, um, it's extraordinary if you're laying on your back and turned sideways and you come up behind and try and put her leg behind the back of your shoulder or something like that; in other words, you got – you tried to discover a new way... I think everybody's the same once they finally get started and they're in the safety of their own home with their own person and that [...]

Yes, it's, it's creative and instinctive, you know; whatever you don't know, it happens, it happens, doesn't it?

He explicitly contrasted this process with modern couples who entered marriage informed to such an extent that their resultant experiences were likely to seem boring and mundane.

REG I suppose our minds were more active probably than anybody's today, because, I mean, they've got all this stuff, they can turn on the television, you know... I really feel sorry for the present-day people now because they have all the lurid stuff right down to the absolute bitter, bitter, bitter parts of it, which leaves virtually nothing for their imagination, you know. I mean, it's, it's just like going for a shave.[25]

Reg's testimony here appears perhaps to be in tension with other sections of his life story.[26] His sexual worldview was transformed during his second marriage (in 1957) to a sexually experienced crane driver and nightclub singer, who was very knowledgeable, introducing him to new sexual practices:

I'm going to ask you about oral sex.

REG Yes, yes, um, my second wife, as I said, there was nothing that she didn't know about... [and] she went down on me and I nearly went through the ceiling, you know; then what was good for her I thought was for me and then I went down – boy-o-boy – I found it was, I liked it, I enjoyed it, I must say. And, of course,

[24] Reg msf/kf/ht/#36. [25] Reg msf/kf/ht/#36.

[26] He is also the respondent who himself was inspired into new forms of love-making by Indian sex carvings on temples, who enjoyed an exciting wartime affair in South Africa and a 'totally different' encounter in post-war Siam with some kind of 'palace prostitute' (whom he described as having been attached to the 'chief controller of the royal household' and given the role of 'looking after' him. He describes her as 'very willing' but acknowledges that this was 'the way it was with the Siamese'; she was there 'to do as she was told').

> she pointed me right to the most sensitive part that she liked to be pointed on, you know... so she'd be screaming and she'd be trying to push me away but I wouldn't because I knew I'd got her, you know, and, er, and it was nice, you know, squirming, but she was desperate... I was, went mad, hell for leather (laughs) and really, really enjoyed it and, um. So sex with her was, was something out of this world...[27]

Despite this direct and exhilarating personal experience of modern sexual values with his second wife, Reg continued to champion codes of privacy and innocent sexual exploration when recalling the sexual excitements of his first marriage.[28] He did not dimiss it as less fulfilling than his later experiences, but instead carefully outlined the different enjoyable experiences provided by all his sexual encounters, and the ways in which such different pleasures were part and parcel of different sexual codes and expectations.

'I would've been more adventurous if I was young now'

Not all interviewees mounted such a clear defence of their past sexual practices. Some testimony could in fact be highly critical of the moral codes that had dominated respondents' earlier lives. Not all past values were upheld in the light of recent transformations in sexual culture. Indeed, many respondents linked the stresses or anxieties of their lives to the sexual values that were embedded in pre-1960s Britain. In particular, the absence of sex education and the unreliability of contraception were seen to have caused problems which they assumed modern couples no longer had to face. However, such testimony should not primarily be read as a favourable response to recent changes in sexual culture. Interviewees positively evaluated only those aspects of a modern sexual world and denigrated only those parts of their earlier practices around which critiques had already been established in the 1930s and 1940s. Support for sex education, and criticism of the culture of ignorance that had surrounded them in their youth, did not reflect their support for other aspects of the post-1960s 'sexual revolution', but was rather grounded in the terms already set out by sex reformers in interwar and post-war Britain.[29]

Some respondents identified with a modern critique that linked past cultures' sexual ignorance, the irregular use of unreliable birth control, the fear of

[27] Reg msf/kf/ht/#36.

[28] This is in contrast, for example, to Gay (quoted above) whose later sexual experiences (after her divorce in 1966) she saw as liberating and which helped her recognise the deficiencies of her husband's sexual technique.

[29] On this movement and its literature, see Chapter 2, notes 11 and 58. The ways in which respondents drew upon such debates raise further questions about the transmission of changing ideas about sexuality during the century, and provide further support for the argument that codes of sexual innocence were deliberately maintained by individuals, many of whom in fact had some exposure to emergent public discussions of sexual issues.

pregnancy, and reluctance to discuss sexual matters with prudish inhibitions. June (1914) agreed that, unlike modern women, she was brought up to be prim and embarrassed about sexual matters. She outlined her inability 'to let go' and contrasted this with the adventurous and enjoyable experiences she might have been able to have were she sexually active today.

JUNE I've never been a person that thought a lot about sex ... because I'm [the] sort of person who didn't let go ... So I would have to be in the mood ... and I didn't know what was expected – what I was expected to let him do to get that climax, you see; so it was only through marriage and experience that in the end I got to understand how to get more climax, you see? To let myself go more, to relax more ... and when I look back and I think, well, if I could live now I'd have had a lot more enjoyment out of that, of marriage and life ... I think I would've been more adventurous if I was young now ... I think I missed a bit, you know.[30]

While individuals often acknowledged the validity of 'liberationist' attacks on their past and recognised the strains, tensions or anxieties that had inhibited their sexual experiences, they nevertheless sharply criticised modern values. Lyn (1907) supported the idea that unmarried girls could enjoy sex before marriage and condemned the ways in which women from her generation had been shamed by illegitimacy and victimised by illegal abortions. However, her support for modern freedoms was limited. Her advocacy of a tolerant approach to illegitimacy was a view she espoused earlier in her life and she decried what she saw as the abuse made by young women of the sexual freedom they had been awarded, particularly the careless conception of children outside of marriage:

LYN Well, if you became to have a baby before, um, you was married that was really one of the worst scandals, and ... abortions then, they weren't looked upon like they are now; they were very much backstreet, done on the quiet, quite a lot losing their lives through them ... but then they said, 'well shouldn't have done it' ... it were far worse in lots of ways [...]

But ... today, well in fact they get all the help, too much help in my opinion, the single parents, because a lot of them – what I resent, now, really, is I do resent them bringing unwanted babies in the world, because in this day and age they can avoid it; they've means to avoid it. They can have as much sex ... and enjoy it as much as they want ... if it were like it was in my days ... they absolutely went through hell and ... the family suffered as well as them with the shame and the disgrace ...[31]

Yet this critique was not a response to the new values she experienced, and the single mothers she encountered, later in life. Rather, her views on the treatment of single mothers were formed in the 1930s, when she helped her mother, a progressive trade unionist and active Labour Party member, undertake

[30] June msf/kf/ht/#27. Agatha msf/kf/ht/#7 expressed similar sentiments. [31] Lyn msf/kf/bl/#1.

charity work in a home for unmarried mothers and their babies in Blackburn. Furthermore, Lyn married a man who had himself been born before his parents got married, and, much to his and Lyn's shame and annoyance, had not been given his father's surname.

Similarly, when respondents contrasted modern 'omniscience', with regard to sexual matters, with the sexual fear and anxieties which they had grown up with, this was not necessarily a sign that they had embraced 'modern values'. Here again many respondents were simply drawing on arguments in favour of greater sexual knowledge and education formulated by progressives in the mid-twentieth century prior to the 'sexual revolution'. Indeed, their criticism that modern sex education was excessive echoed the more restricted agendas of sex reformers in the 1930s and 1940s.[32]

Although Sarah (1906) outlined the difficulties she faced as a result of sexual ignorance she nonetheless continued to see some benefits to a culture of innocence. One of the oldest interviewees, she married an upholsterer with his own business in 1928. She had been ambitious but had seen the opportunities open to her as limited; thus she recognised that later generations of working-class women had been provided with many more opportunities than had been given to her. Indeed, as she proudly but regretfully noted, her daughter was able to become a teacher. She had had a very strict upbringing, and lived in fear of her drunken and violent father, who was struggling to look after Sarah and her four brothers following the death of his wife from TB. She resented his restrictions on her behaviour, and felt deprived of any form of female assistance in negotiating the sexual side of growing up. In particular, she regretted the absence of advice over how to deal with periods and boyfriends. However, she also conjured up her father as a positive deterrent to illegitimate pregnancy and found herself conflicted when deciding what to tell her own daughter about sex in the 1950s. Gratefully, she assumed that school had provided sufficient information and she kept her own interventions to a minimum. Just as her father had once instructed her, she warned her daughter not to get too friendly with boys following puberty:

SARAH I don't like children today knowing too much, I don't; I, I really don't. I think they know too much too soon, but you do need to know … I had no sex education at all, none at all, and … I couldn't talk to me dad … I'd nobody, nobody I could talk to. And I'm amazed at how I got through – I'm amazed … I got through through being frightened … Fear … No, I, I think some of these kids that are having, ooh, (pause) no – they wanted my, they wanted my dad behind them; that's what they

[32] Indeed, it was the starkness of the contrast between the ubiquity of sexual imagery and information in the mass media and the apparent omniscience of modern youth, which heightened respondents' retrospective assessments that they had been kept in ignorance despite the increase in the availability of sexual information that occurred during their lives and which differentiated the experiences of some of the younger from the older interviewees (see Chapter 2, note 61).

wanted (laughs)... Oh, I'll tell you, I was afraid of my dad. (pause) No, he, he, what'd happen to me if I'd have got, I'd have got pregnant – oh dear me, I couldn't bear to think (laugh).

[...]

I just thought... she didn't need to know... I used to say 'Now mind what you do when you go out'... and... she was picking it up at school... which I was glad of. But, uh, um, (pause) she didn't ask a lot of devious questions like kids do today; she didn't.[33]

In criticising the absence of sex education during their own upbringings, while at the same time distancing themselves from the practicalities of providing sexual information to their children, many respondents' attitudes towards sexual knowledge reflected trends in contemporary thought during the 1930s and 1940s. While 'innocence' remained an attractive attribute of girls, a degree of formal sex education was increasingly advocated in place of silence. Mass Observation found some support for sex education in schools among those it surveyed in 1947. Many of its cohort decried the absence of such information provided to them, yet simultaneously showed little enthusiasm for the suggestion that 'such instruction was the parents' responsibility'.[34] Eliot Slater and Moya Woodside's investigation into marriage also found that the majority of those they had interviewed between 1943 and 1946 decried the absence of sex education and called for it to be given by schools.[35] Indeed, the testimony of Pearl (1915), who became a teacher, directly reflected the subtle cultural shifts of this period. She too criticised her own upbringing and the ignorance that was deliberately fostered, but in supporting an extremely basic version of sex education, such as the kind that she herself provided to 9 and 10 year olds in the 1950s and 1960s, her views were typical of mid-twentieth-century acceptance of very limited forms of sexual information alongside a continued appreciation of innocence.

PEARL Well, some other girls, a bit older, used to go round backstreet corners talking about things like that in those days. That's where you got your information from... I think that was a bad way... I think, er, I think you should be told. I believe in sort of it all being open and above board... [not in] a really, a dirty smutty way, you know, with all the giggles... I mean some people even got married without knowing the fundamentals [...]

But when I was a teacher I taught it at school... on a very, very simple, um, very simply. It was more like hygiene... I used to give a talk on hygiene just for the girls... and we started off and did the digestive system. 'Cos they're interested in food, you see... then on another day... do the respiratory system... then finally... we'd do the, er, you know, the baby system?... But I believe that now they do too much [sex education]. They do too much of it and, um, the children want to experiment practically... I didn't go into too much detail.[36]

[33] Sarah msf/kf/bl/#30.

[34] Mass Observation, File Report 2495, 'The State of Matrimony', June 1947, 8.

[35] Slater and Woodside, *Patterns of Marriage*, 173, 176.

[36] Pearl msf/kf/bl/#40.

Rather than identifying with or accepting modern liberationist critiques, interviewees' views on sex education, and their criticisms of the past, were identifications with a mid-century view on the appropriateness of sexual ignorance. Respondents distanced themselves from the trends that emerged in the later decades of the twentieth century, which encouraged clearer or more explicit forms of advice and education.[37] Consequently many were highly critical of contemporary society with its culture of widespread sexual information, which they saw as directly implicated in current social problems, such as high teenage pregnancy rates. Thus, most of those interviewed portrayed themselves as, ultimately, remaining committed to the attitudes towards sexual knowledge which they had grown up with.

Doreen (1922) reacted against the ignorance which characterised her own youth and advocated providing sex education to her sons. She had in fact been trained as a domestic science teacher in the early 1940s and found her attitudes towards sex education differed from those of her husband (1917) – a foreman bricklayer. Doreen asked her husband to tell their sons about sex. He refused, on the grounds that he had been able to make all the necessary discoveries by himself, and she subsequently found ingenious ways to talk to her own sons about sex:

> DOREEN I said to them you, you'll know a lot more as you grow older but if you have any intercourse with a girl you'd better beware … I said I'd rather you didn't do it till you were married, but I said if you do and you make a mistake and there's a child born, well then you're responsible for him. And this is how I talked to my boy and I used to say – the eldest boy – I used to say to him, 'if there's any questions you want to ask me about growing up … if you want to ask me any questions about going out with girls and things like that, put a newspaper up in front of your face and ask me any questions you want'. I said, 'if not, go under the stairs and shut the door and ask me from there'. I said, 'and when you come out and I've given you the correct answers I'll go in the kitchen and wash up or something like that' … Larry never talked to them about anything. Never. He said, 'there's no need'. I said, 'do you not think you should talk to them?' I said, 'I got married to you gormless … I didn't know anything … I didn't know enough at all.' He said, 'you don't need to tell them; they learn for themselves. I had to learn for meself'. He said, 'they'll laugh at me'.

Despite being in favour of sex education, and critical of the ignorance which she had experienced, Doreen remained opposed to modern codes of sexual knowledge. Her narrative defended her own views on sex education as effectively discreet and modest and attacked more liberal approaches to the matter. Indeed, in the late 1960s, she was directly confronted with these later values

[37] Hampshire and Lewis, 'The Ravages of Permissiveness', Campbell, *Sex Education Books*, Cook, *The Long Sexual Revolution*, 251–60, 282–95.

when her two children, born in 1949 and 1952, were given explicit forms of information by a local advice centre, and counselled that sexual experience before marriage had advantages. Her response was embedded in the values of the 1930s and 1940s. Although she was in favour of sex before marriage, her arguments drew upon the notions of sexual compatibility, common in the mid-century, and her approval of sex before marriage was limited. She suggested that her own sexual difficulties might have been prevented if she had been able to find out whether or not she and her husband-to-be were sexually suited by experimenting prior to marriage, while at the same time she disapproved of those who had multiple sexual partners or indulged in casual sex:

> DOREEN they said, if you don't, if you don't have sex before you're married and you don't like it, the marriage won't go forward. Well, I quite agreed with it... I mean, I'm narrow-minded on them having sex before they're married but I think if they're certain sure they are going to marry they ought to, er, um, I think it's a good idea. I don't believe in them freelancing like they do now, with anybody.[38]

Here respondents' comparisons of their own attitudes and those of later generations, and their musings on the ways in which attitudes towards sex have changed, reveal the effect of contemporary debates during the century on the development of individuals' views and practices, and provide insight into the relationship between changing discourses about sexuality and individuals' developing attitudes.

Conclusion

The contrast between modern sexual mores and past experiences served as a catalyst for many interviewees to reappraise and reformulate their own memories. Since the 1960s, as Lynne Segal has pointed out, sexologists and other 'expert' voices have 'tended to stress the multiple pleasures of sex, once men and women learned to overcome their "psychological inhibitions" and all acquired the appropriate skills for giving and receiving full orgasmic satisfaction'.[39] Respondents thus recalled their past in a contemporary context in which the popular understanding of sexual quality was equated with the absence of inhibition, open communication, sexual variety, and experimentation, and in which relationships without such practices were viewed as static, staid and perfunctory.[40] For example, Relate's online advice (2007) advised couples in long-term (married) relationships to work at keeping 'sex sexy' and suggested a number of practical tips: 'change the scenery – bathroom, living

[38] Doreen msf/kf/bl/#20. [39] Segal, 'New Battlegrounds', 67.

[40] Jackson and Scott, 'Gut Reactions to Matters of the Heart', 565. See also, Gail Hawkes, 'Liberalizing Sexuality?', in *The Sociology of the Family: A Reader*, ed. Graham A. Allan (Oxford and Malden, MA: Blackwell, 1999), 35.

room, alfresco; watch an erotic movie; experiment with new sexual positions; introduce a new sex toy; change the way you initiate sex; play some role play sex games; learn a new stimulation technique'.[41] The very existence of Relate, as well as the content of the advice provided, were the result of the emergence of a modern belief that open communication about sex between couples was the key to a successful sexual relationship. They acknowledge that 'discussing your sex life may feel impossible', but they assure their audience that they can help them develop the techniques 'to make this delicate subject more approachable'. Communication is seen, then, by Relate as essential to tackling sex problems and marital dissatisfaction.[42]

In response, many individuals felt alienated from such shifts in sexual culture, and a defensive and reactionary tone informed some personal recollections, even where such testimony also acknowledged the conflicts, stresses and strains that affected their sexual relationships. A perception that a rejection of the past was fundamental to modern mores coloured testimony; the memories of past relationships were often articulated as part of an implict defence of old-fashioned values that were seen to be under attack. When comparing (imagined) pasts and presents interviewees highlighted the core values which informed their sexual codes, and which continued to be central to their understanding of the purpose, significance and pleasures of sex within marriage. Some, in acknowledging the validity of aspects of modern critiques of past sexual codes, outlined what they saw as the emotional advantages that outweighed such drawbacks. Others dismissed more robustly the critique of sex in the past as inhibited by codes of privacy. This response presented a vision of contemporary approaches to sexual practices that were instead hampered by modern society's emphasis on sexual knowledge and communication. Respondents implied that the very exposure of individuals today to explicit forms of sex education, to information about a wide range of sexual practices and to various forms of sexual imagery constrained their sexual imaginations. Seeing modern relationships as prosaically derivative, they championed their own approaches as having been natural, spontaneous, individual and creative.

[41] www.relate.org.uk/sexproblems/commonsexualproblems/FAQ_2296.html (accessed 20 July 2007). Relate is the largest provider of UK relationship counselling and sex therapy. It runs a nationwide counselling service and receives local authority and other government funding. The advice provided on its website is not necessarily indicative of the advice that might be provided in a particular counselling session, but does capture the thrust of much contemporary popular belief and guidance about sexual pleasure in various forms of mass media.

[42] By contrast, some modern relationship manuals advise that communication can be a dangerous form of 'amateur therapy' (Hazleden, 'The Pathology of Love').

10 Conclusion: private lives

Throughout the early and mid-twentieth century, various progressive critiques of sex emerged which, despite their differences, denounced silence and secrecy surrounding sex as conducive to ignorance, inhibitions, incompetence, intolerance and sexually unsatisfying marriages. From the beginning of the twentieth century, radical and conservative voices alike increasingly saw sexual satisfaction as a cornerstone of marriage and urged couples, especially men, to educate themselves in improved sexual technique. Sexologists and marriage reformers called for men and women to become sexually literate and able to communicate such knowledge in the quest for sexual ecstasy. This critical viewpoint has informed and stimulated various sexual debates and transformations throughout the twentieth century particularly since the 1960s when the (contested) idea of 'liberation' was heralded as a break from the 'repression' of the past. In all these debates the enemy was the restricted, taboo sexuality of the past, which from the beginning of the twentieth century became labelled 'Victorian' but which was seen as having a lingering impact on individuals' attitudes and practices long into the twentieth century.

In addition this interpretation has framed the ways in which historians have examined the sexual cultures of the past century. They have studied these debates and gone on to question the extent to which individuals' own lives were transformed in response. They have also been influenced by the intellectual and conceptual framework of twentieth-century constructions of sexuality. They proceeded from its assumptions that silence and ignorance, restrictive moral codes, unequal gender relations, a regard for sexual restraint, beliefs about sexual duty, associations between sex and dirt, and suspicions about birth control would have the effect of fuelling difficult, erotically limited and uncommunicative sexual relationships dominated by fear, anxiety and tension, especially for women. This critique has, in particular, identified women as the victims of such a sexual culture, ignorant of the possibilities and mechanics of sexual pleasure, fearful of pregnancy and subject to the clumsy and inexpert attentions of their husbands.

On its own terms, this construction is powerful and significant and moreover is supported by the historical evidence we have unearthed in which for some sex was marred by sexual ignorance, contraceptive anxiety, fear of transgression and unequal gender relations. Yet, this analysis of sex and marriage also has its own limitations: imposing too linear a narrative of changing sexual cultures onto the twentieth century and so providing an incomplete and unsubtle insight into individuals' lived experience. Alongside the evidence which fits this familiar 'liberationist' teleology we have uncovered a world in which the values of duty and innocence were not seen as inhibiting, destructive forces but were rather conceptualised as values informing a loving, dynamic and mutually satisfying partnership.

Our first conclusion, then, is that the deterministic, 'whig' model of sexual liberation encourages a simplistic story of changing sexual attitudes in the twentieth century in which sexual relationships are seen to have 'modernised' in response to sexological ideas, companionate models of marriage, feminist critiques of gender relations, technological advances in birth control and progressive attitudes towards sexual diversity and behaviour. This model divides the nation into, on the one side, couples who were egalitarian companions, who discussed their desires, obtained information about sex, placed satisfactory sex high on their list of marital priorities and turned to modern forms of contraception and, on the other side, traditionalists stuck with patriarchal attitudes, poor sexual techniques and old-fashioned efforts at birth control, resulting in anxious and sexually unfulfilled wives. Historical change over time is envisaged as an ideologically and technologically induced expansion of the former category and a gradual withering away of the obsolete, latter category, with the educated middle classes in the vanguard of the movement.

The oral history evidence explodes these stereotypes and the associated model of historical change. It is true, as this research has shown, that there were transformations in these areas with a rise in the amount of sexual knowledge acquired during adolescence; changes in the general availability of sexual information and the public visibility of sexual material; shifts in beliefs about gendered roles in marriage and the expectations of sexual satisfaction in marriage; and developments in the availability of forms of birth control. However, the relationship between such shifts and lived experience was highly complex and structured in particular by the dominant and constant belief that sex was a private matter. There was no simple trend towards the acceptance of a 'modern' approach to sex in marriage, but rather an ambivalent response mediated above all by the values of privacy.

Thus, increased public discussion of sexual matters did not diminish the extent to which young women were expected to demonstrate sexual innocence. The younger middle-class women in the sample cannot be described as 'ignorant' in the same way as the older working-class women interviewed, but nonetheless all women attested to having grown up in a culture in which feminine respectability was tied to notions of sexual innocence; all men and women used their narratives to demonstrate the ways in which sexual knowledge was tainted and difficult to come by. The increased public emphasis on sexual compatibility and on the erotics of marriage did not override the centrality of the notion of sexual privacy. Some interviewees revised their ideas about sexual relationships in marriage, as a result of coming into contact with new models of sexual behaviour, particularly during the later post-war period, but the importance of marital privacy nonetheless fostered an enduring suspicion of public sexual display or literature. This combined with dissatisfaction with modern technological forms of contraception and a reluctance to incorporate the techniques or messages emanating from marriage manuals or guides into their own marriages in any direct or self-conscious way across the entire sample.

Secondly, the teleological narrative of twentieth-century marriage and sex, which opposes a 'modern' eroticised version of marriage against a 'traditional', 'repressed' version, dominated by ignorance and an absence of communication between partners, posits too crude a contrast between sexual pleasure versus sexual shyness, inhibition and reticence. Consequently it masks the more complex ways in which individuals necessarily accommodated themselves to the cultural values with which they had grown up. The liberationist insight that for many men and, especially, women ignorance had a profoundly negative impact on their understanding of their own bodies and capacities for sexual pleasure, while true in many cases, does not help us understand how men and women brought up to see innocence as an attractive female attribute themselves approached, enjoyed or developed sexually once married. This book puts the exploration of the diverse emotional realities engendered by changing twentieth-century moral codes at the heart of the analysis.

Many individuals entered marriage feeling uninformed about various aspects of sexual intercourse. Naïvety and inexperience were, however, deliberately adopted and endorsed by many informants as key characteristics of marital sexuality, at least at first. Few used sexualised terms to describe their bodies or those of the opposite sex and instead evaluated them in terms of healthiness and status. Contraception was not eagerly embraced as a means of improving sexual relationships; instead mechanical methods of contraception were seen as interfering with the preferred naturalness of sexual relations. About a half of respondents in all classes acknowledged periods of abstinence or restraint, both as part of their approach to birth control and as part of the belief that sex should be an expression of caring love in the marriage, not of sensual individualist self-indulgence.

For all that a culture of silence and strict moral codes created difficulties, stresses and fears, many individuals nonetheless accepted the moral values that underpinned them and incorporated those values into the framework through which they internalised experiences of pleasure and love. On the one hand, then, we have found a significant amount of testimony which some historians might see as part of 'repressed' attitudes towards sexuality: sexual ignorance, concerns over the dirtiness of bodies, divided gender roles in marriage, ideas of duty towards each other, cautious courtships, an emphasis on virginity at marriage, and the portrayal of sex lives which stressed the absence of experimentation, lack of adventurousness and reluctance to see sex as something to work at, to study or to spice up. We have mapped the attendant sexual problems that many experienced as a result. For many the fact that they had had little or no experience of sex prior to marriage made the early stages of their conjugal relationship fraught. For many who were uneducated in sexual technique, reluctant to improve matters by discussing or reading about sex, coitus was unsatisfactory. For many, sexual shyness and in particular the association between sex and dirt (both literal and moral dirt) fostered restricted sexual relationships. For many, fears of pregnancy and suspicions of the efficacy of birth control created considerable marital conflict. And, for many, beliefs that men had a right to demand sexual access on the grounds that it was a wife's duty resulted in relationships dominated by male sexual selfishness and female sexual dissatisfaction.

On the other hand, equally, we have found that informants brought up in a culture of sexual silence, who valued privacy above all, constructed and experienced sexual pleasure on these terms. Sexual ignorance and private relationships were associated by both men and women with a range of sexual pleasures. Interviewees often focused on the experience of initial marital innocence as joyous and exciting; this journey from innocence to greater and greater experience provided the first few years of marriage – and beyond for some – with an inbuilt dynamism. Both male and female testimony focused on the practice of learning about sex together as an exciting personal process of discovery, and individuals placed great significance on and remembered with joy the ways in which they learned about sex without external assistance and developed ways of pleasuring their spouses independently as a couple. In addition, the hygienic imperatives fostered for some an almost aphrodisiac appreciation for the cleanliness of their bodies, symbolising and manifesting the notions of purity and naturalness which they so valued. Even women's acceptance of the provision of sex as a duty was linked to their experience of the pleasures of sex. Women's sexual pleasure, amply and widely evidenced in the testimony, was conceptualised and legitimised by women only as part of a moral framework in which they used sex above all to demonstrate their wifely commitment towards providing for and caring for their husbands. In these important respects, therefore, some of our respondents did not find themselves enjoying sex despite their 'inhibited' and private culture, but, rather, because of it.

Appendix A: The oral history sample: summary of project design and socio-demographic characteristics of the interviewees in Blackburn and north-west Hertfordshire

According to the most recent historical demographic research on England and Wales by Szreter (1996) and by Garrett et al. (2001), reproductive patterns during the fertility decline were extremely locally diverse, not only in terms of social class, but also community and 'place'.[1] Before this project was initiated Kate Fisher had commenced her doctoral oral history study of working-class birth control in the South Wales collieries and in the city of Oxford. Therefore, two complementary contrasting communities were selected for this investigation and also a middle-class sample was included from each of the two new locations.[2] The textiles towns of both Lancashire and the West Riding of Yorkshire are considered to provide the greatest working-class contrast to the country's coal-mining communities, in terms of their reproductive patterns during the fertility decline. Whereas mining families recorded the highest fertility in the 1911 national census, workers in the textiles industries exhibited among the lowest fertility in the working class, as low as some sections of the middle and lower middle classes.[3] Blackburn in Lancashire was selected as a representative mill town. It had a high proportion of women weavers in the workforce and had characteristic low fertility in 1911.[4] For a further dimension of contrast, a thoroughly middle-class community was sought. A district centred on Harpenden, along with a cluster of nearby affluent commuter towns in north-west Hertfordshire, just outside London, was selected as it exhibited some of the highest concentrations in England and Wales of residents in the Registrar-General's Social Classes I and II at the 1951 census.

1 Szreter, *Fertility, Class, and Gender*, chs. 9–10, esp. 546–58 on 'communication communities', Garrett et al., *Changing Family Size*, chs. 4–7.

2 Kate Fisher, 'An Oral History of Birth Control Practice c.1925–50: A Study of Oxford and South Wales'. Unpublished D.Phil. thesis. Oxford: University of Oxford, 1998. See also Kate Fisher, 'Uncertain Aims and Tacit Negotiation: Birth Control Practices in Britain, 1925–50', *Population and Development Review* 26, no. 2 (2000): 295–317.

3 Michael R. Haines, *Fertility and Occupation: Population Patterns in Industrialization* (New York: Academic Press, 1979), Szreter, *Fertility, Class, and Gender*, Figure 7.1, 312.

4 Anne Hardy and Simon Szreter, 'Urban Fertility and Mortality Patterns', in *The Cambridge Urban History of Britain*, ed. Martin J. Daunton (Cambridge: Cambridge University Press, 2000), 629–72, Table 20.6.S.

It was also considered important to interview representatives of both the middle and the working classes in each of the two selected communities. Garrett et al. (2001) found that the fertility of middle-class couples in 1911 resident in heavily industrial communities was more like that of the working-class couples in those communities than like other middle-class couples living in predominantly middle-class environments. Similarly, working-class couples living in affluent 'white-collar' residential suburbs exhibited much lower fertility than those with similar occupations living in industrial towns.[5] Therefore, the attempt was made to include interviews with working-class respondents in the affluent, middle-class communities of north-west Hertfordshire and with middle-class respondents who had lived in or around the proletarian mill town of Blackburn. There are, therefore, four distinct social groups, whose recollections are examined here: a Blackburn working-class set, a Blackburn middle-class group, a Hertfordshire middle-class set and a Hertfordshire working-class group.[6] Altogether fifty married or previously married persons were interviewed in Blackburn (plus one spinster – see Chapter 1, note 2) and thirty-eight in Hertfordshire.[7]

The fifty-seven married women and thirty-one married men interviewed were all born between 1901 and 1931 (Figure 1 shows that 90% were born between 1905 and 1924). This is therefore a group of people who came of marriageable age at the end of the national, secular fertility decline. Most respondents were first married between 1930 and 1950 (Figure 2). The most fertile period of their marriages was from the early 1930s through to the late 1950s in most cases. This coincided both with the point at which the secular fall in fertility since the 1870s reached its lowest recorded levels in the 1930s and with the immediate post-war decades when fertility, though relatively low, was buoyed up somewhat above the level of the depressed 1930s; this occurred in the context of a nation enjoying the new benefits and securities of the innovative welfare state.[8] While two small sets of interviewees can only claim to be representative of their generation in a general sense, it is important to check that they are not clearly unrepresentative in terms of their fertility behaviour. The principal relevant check on this is provided by reviewing their marital fertility characteristics. As Figures 3 and 4 confirm, the childbearing characteristics of each of the two groups of interviewees do not exhibit any unexpected

[5] Garrett et al., *Changing Family Size*.

[6] See Appendix B for definitions of middle and working class adopted for this study.

[7] The majority were contacted through the non-residential day-care centres of Blackburn and Hertfordshire. Most interviews were conducted with individual widows and widowers. Two widowers who were neighbours were interviewed together and ten sets of couples were interviewed together. Interviewing was open-ended with a wide licence given to respondents to present their memoirs and stories at length in their own terms while interviewers had to hand a checklist of issues to be addressed. An average of approximately four hours of interviewing material was collected on each marriage, typically entailing two, and sometimes three or more, visits.

[8] OPCS *Population Trends* 48 (1987), 8, Table 1 'Age-specific fertility rates and TPFRs 1841–1986'.

features. Marriages producing two births constituted the most common pattern, as would be expected for these marriage cohorts, and there was a slight tendency for those marrying after 1940 to have produced a greater number of births per marriage than those marrying before 1940, which conforms with the national pattern of higher marital fertility after the Second World War.

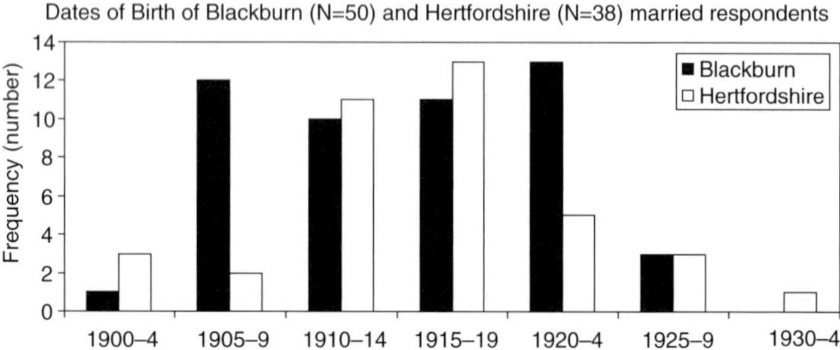

Figure 1

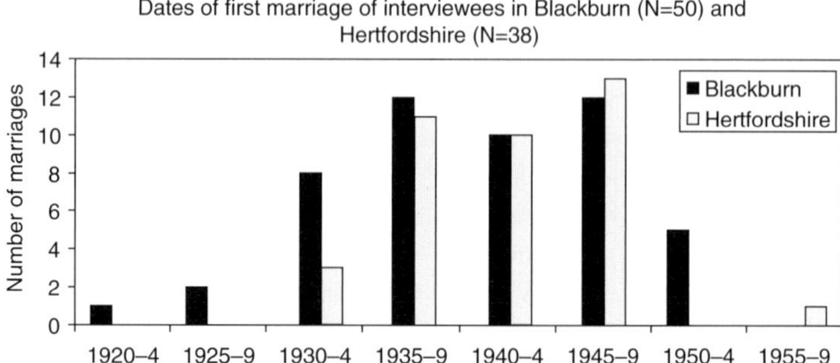

Figure 2

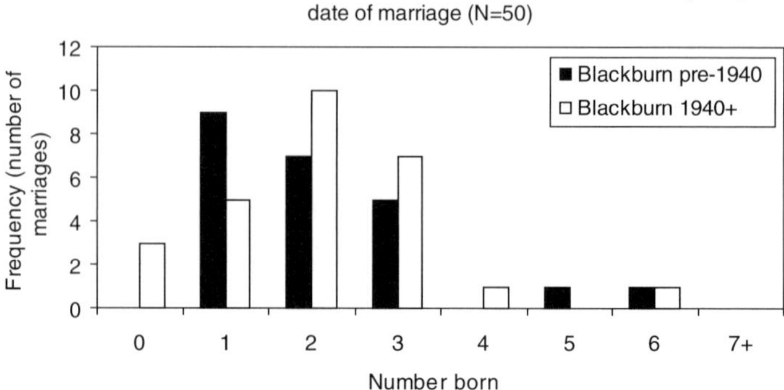

Figure 3

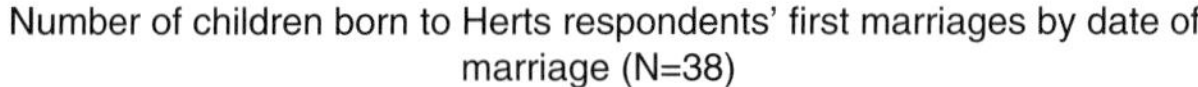

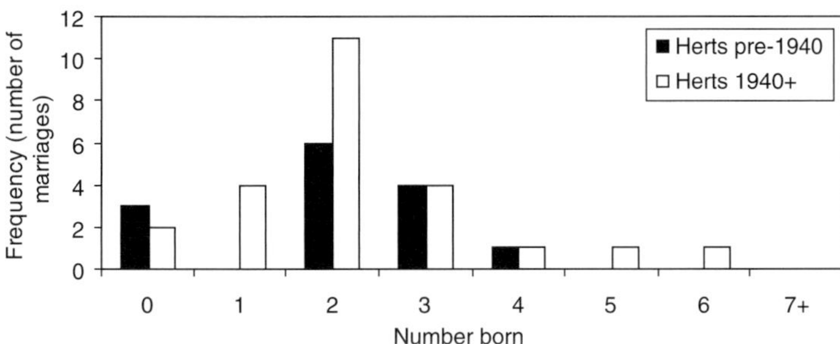

Figure 4

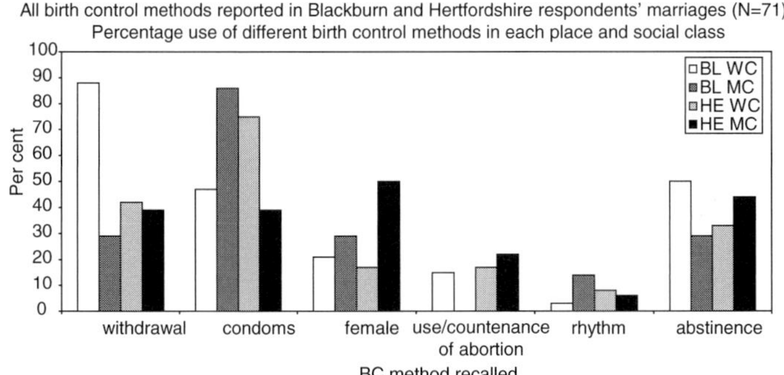

Figure 5

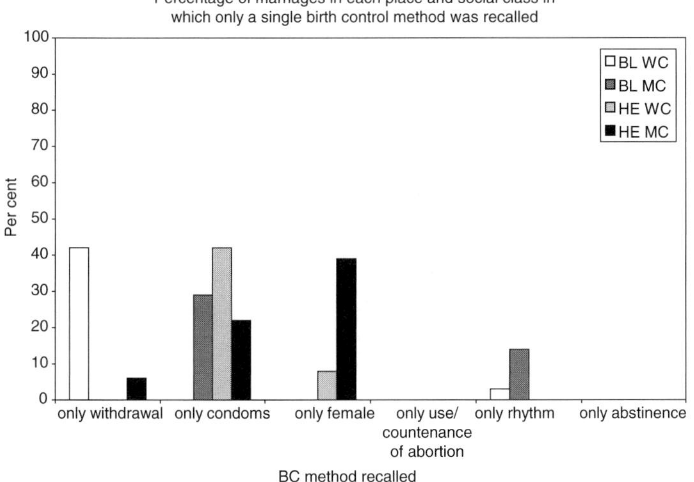

Figure 6

Appendix B: Note on social classification of the respondents

Respondents were assigned a social class status affiliation using an adapted version of the Registrar-General's social classification of male occupations – the official scheme that was in use throughout the period 1911 to 1991.[1]

The official scheme has changed little but the description and precise occupational contents of each of the six categories have gone through a number of modifications during its long existence. The descriptions below best fit the manner in which it has been used here:

Class I higher professional, administrative and managerial, those with inherited wealth
Class II lower professional, and middle administrative and managerial in large organisations
Class IIIN clerical workers
Class IIIM skilled manual workers
Class IV partly skilled manual workers
Class V unskilled manual workers

In this study the scheme's categories have been further modified by the creation of two additional 'social class' affiliations, 'II/IIIM' and 'IIIM/II'. This is to deal with a well-known weakness of the R-G's scheme: its failure to recognise the distinctive social significance of the private sector, small business community. The more substantial businessmen, such as directors, financiers, managers or owners of large enterprises, can be satisfactorily classified to Class I or Class II, on the basis of their professional qualifications, educational and family background, and wealth. But there remains a large number of small businessmen and independent, petit bourgeois traders, for whom the official classification is inadequate, since it is misleading to place these either in Class IIIN or IIIM. Class IIIM, of course, contains a range of skilled manual

[1] Simon Szreter, 'The Genesis of the Registrar-General's Social Classification of Occupations', *The British Journal of Sociology* 35, no. 4 (1984): 522–46; Simon Szreter, 'The Official Representation of Social Classes in Britain, the United States, and France: The Professional Model And "Les Cadres"', *Comparative Studies in Society and History* 35 (1993): 285–317.

workers, who are typically subordinate, waged employees. Class IIIN are also employees, but they are non-manual salaried employees, paradigmatically junior and middling clerical and administrative office workers in the corporate sector or government. The additional Class II/IIIM has therefore been created for the small-scale retailers and artisans with their own modest fixed capital in the form of a proprietary shop or premises, such as watchmakers, car repairers or grocers; while Class IIIM/II comprises the self-employed tradesmen with no fixed capital or premises, such as builders, painters and decorators. Thus, the classification used here is as follows:

Class I higher professional, administrative and managerial, those with inherited wealth
Class II lower professional, and middle administrative and managerial in large organisations
Class IIIN clerical workers
Class II/IIIM small-scale business proprietors
Class IIIM/II self-employed tradesmen
Class IIIM skilled manual workers (employees)
Class IV partly skilled manual workers
Class V unskilled manual workers

While occupation of husband was the principal criterion used to assign interviewees to a social class category, there are a well-known number of reservations with this method; indeed, all such classificatory exercises inevitably have an arbitrary element to them and involve making fine, ultimately subjective judgements in marginal cases. Of course, many men changed occupation during their working lives, so a judgement had to be made about which occupation reflected their overall social status most accurately. Also wife's occupation, both partners' social origins, housing status, personal educational history and preferences for their children were all additional criteria which were considered, at the margins, in making a classificatory judgement.

Only those classified to Class I, Class II or Class IIIN have been considered 'middle class' (including, therefore, the lower-middle class) throughout the discussions in this book. All others have been referred to as 'working class'. Undoubtedly there are some individuals whose classification in this way is less satisfactory than others. The inclusion throughout the chapters of relevant socio-biographical items of information on individuals cited in the text is there to enable readers to take in some of these nuances. Appendix C also reproduces much relevant information on the respondents in a more systematic fashion.

Appendix C

Hertfordshire Panel 1

	Name	ref. no.	sex	d.o.b	place of birth
1	Agatha	msf/kf/ht/#7	f	1910	Chesterfield
2	Angela	msf/kf/ht/#18	f	1924	Preston
3	Antonia	msf/kf/ht/#35	f	1928	London
4	Betty	msf/kf/ht/#31	f	1922	Peckham, Lon.
5	Catherine	msf/kf/ht/#1	f	1912	West Ham (Plaistow)
6	Clare	msf/kf/ht/#8	f	1912	Berkhamsted
7	Dora	msf/srss/ht/#38	f	1923	Bethnal Green
8	Emma	msf/kf/ht/#37	f	1906	Goole, South Yorks
9	Esme	msf/kf/ht/#9	f	1921	Edmonton, Lon.
10	Gay	msf/kf/ht/#13	f	1928	Highgate, Lon.
11	Grace	msf/srss/ht/#38	f	1922	Goole, South Yorks
12	Heather	msf/kf/ht/#14	f	1916	Chelsea, Lon.
13	Joanna	msf/kf/ht/#22	f	1915	High Wycombe
14	Judith	msf/kf/ht/#33	f	1931	Edinburgh
15	June	msf/kf/ht/#27	f	1914	Barnsley
16	Monica	msf/kf/ht/#11	f	1902	Tenby, S.W. Wales
17	Pam	msf/kf/ht/#19	f	1907	Kimpton, Herts
18	Penny	msf/srss/ht/#20	f	1916	Southend

no. of siblings	father's occupation	mother's occupation
8	not known	not known
8	iron moulder in Booths iron foundry	weaver at Horrocks cotton mill, gave up when 1st child born
1	solicitor	secretary, worked for voluntary associations, e.g. in WWII for single mothers
2	pay clerk for London Transport	never worked
1	carpenter and joiner	before marriage in a bakery
11	builder, journeyman	before marriage nursery schoolteacher
3 (2 d. infancy)	RN pensioner (chain injury), Inspector Naval Ordnance Woolwich Arsenal	boxmaker in East End in small Jewish factory
1	crane operator (fought through whole of WWI and survived)	ran post office, teacher before marriage, head of infant school
3	general managing director large retailing firm	WVS during WWII
1	tea salesman, owned furniture business	secretary in tea trade company before marriage
5 (1 illegit. half-sister)	chemical worker in alum works (died young in motorbike accident)	cleaning (to supplement relief payments after husband died in accident 1928)
5	(wounded in WWI) postman	worked in aunt's antique/bric-a-brac shop before marriage, nothing after marriage
2 (step-siblings)	chairmaker (killed in WWI)	none
none	GP (d. 1936); step-father head post-master, WWII high civil servant	WVS in WWII only
1	manager of Yorkshire Penny Bank	none
11	ran largish wallpapering firm	none
2	(illegitimate) step-father worked on Lord Hampden's estate, army in WWI	none
11	soldier (NCO), labouring work for War Dpt ('an army family')	none, took in Jewish families in the summer

Hertfordshire Panel 1

	Name	ref. no.	sex	d.o.b	place of birth
19	Pru	msf/kf/ht/#12	f	1911	Newbury
20	Rebecca	msf/kf/ht/#6	f	1903	East End, London
21	Vera	msf/kf/ht/#34	f	1917	County Down
22	Alf	msf/kf/ht/#14	m	1915	Fulham, Lon.
23	Bryan	msf/kf/ht/#25	m	1918	Caerphilly
24	Dennis	msf/kf/ht/#15	m	1915	Wheathampstead, Herts
25	Dougie	msf/kf/ht/#5	m	1919	Rickmansworth
26	Edmund	msf/kf/ht/#23	m	1910	Harpenden
27	Gerald	msf/kf/ht/#9	m	1919	Sutton Coldfield
28	Horace	msf/kf/ht/#31	m	1915	Bermondsey, Lon.
29	Hubert	msf/kf/ht/#32	m	1911	Limbury (nr Luton)
30	Hugh	msf/kf/ht/#18	m	1926	Trowbridge, Wilts
31	Humphrey	msf/kf/ht/#26	m	1914	Wansted, Lon.
32	Mark	msf/kf/ht/#22	m	1917	High Wycombe
33	Norman	msf/kf/ht/#17	m	1914	Islington
34	Patrick	msf/kf/ht/#16	m	1918	East Ham, Lon.
35	Reg	msf/kf/ht/#36	m	1919	Eastbourne
36	Roger	msf/kf/ht/#10	m	1910	Plymouth
37	Sam	msf/srss/ht/#28	m	1912	Rothbury, Northumberland
38	William	msf/kf/ht/#24	m	1902	Mortlake, W. Lon.

no. of siblings	father's occupation	mother's occupation
2	manager, building firm	none
4	self-employed tailor	none
3	worked in brick works	owned village grocer's
4	van driver for Harrods, sacked for illegal book keeping	cleaning at Harrods
3 (1 adopted war orphan)	miner, WWI veterinary corp, looked after race horses in Epsom	dressmaker before marriage, nothing after
3	building and agricultural labour, armaments worker in WWII	hat trade in Luton before marriage, domestic help when children at school
7	Watford bus conductor, also worked for London Transport	took in washing
3	gardener for nursery farm, jobbing gardener	took in washing
3	electrical engineer for City of Birmingham	none
2	Sgt Major Boer War to WWI, unemployed then worked on the buses	scrubbed floors
none	estate agent (owned own business)	nurse (died when Hubert aged 2)
1	cleaner for Great Western Railway, fireman, then finally promoted to driver	woollen weaver before marriage
2 (half-siblings)	sales representative for Lancaster firm 'Storey brothers' (d. 1920)	took in lodgers after husband's death
none	medical orderly in India, owned general stores in High Wycombe	district nurse, nurse during WWI, nothing after child born
3	London County Council	home-based piecework for London tie manufacturer
none	inspector for gas company	machinist clothes manufacture, council relief work WWII, social work
2	market gardener, hunting-dog breeder (grandfather was master-builder)	voluntary church maintenance, serving in a 'British Restaurant' (communal kitchen)
1	RN commander	none
1	bank manager (deputy manager)	none, butcher's shop during WWI
4	manager of Allen-Liversedge, Victoria St, supplier acetylene cylinders	doesn't know before marriage (died in childbirth when William aged 5)

Hertfordshire Panel 2

	Name	d.o.m	female AM	male AM	no. of children	d.o.b. of children
1	Agatha	1940	30	36	1	1946
2	Angela	1947	23	20	2	1950, 1956
3	Antonia	1949	21	35	6	1950, 1952, 1954, 1956, 1963, 1965
4	Betty	1948	26	33	2	1954, 1958
5	Catherine	1941	29	29	1	1948
6	Clare	1936	24; 35	24; 35	2	1940, 1947
7	Dora	1945	22	25	2	1947, 1949
8	Emma	1936	30	38	3	1937, 1944, 1947
9	Esme	1945	24	26	3	1947, 1950, 1953
10	Gay	1947	18	26	2	1949, 1951
11	Grace	1944	21	23	2	1946, 1950
12	Heather	1938	21	23	2	1940, 1949
13	Joanna	1947	32	30	0	n/a
14	Judith	1958	27	28	5	1959, 1960, 1961, 1966, 1969
15	June	1936	22	25	2	1937, 1947
16	Monica	1933	30	40	4	1936, 1937, 1940, 1946
17	Pam	1932	24	26	0	n/a
18	Penny	1938	21	23	3	1947, 1949, 1950
19	Pru	1935	24	27	2	1941, 1943
20	Rebecca	1943	40	35	1	1944
21	Vera	1949	32	33	2	1950, 1952
22	Alf	1938	21	23	2	1940, 1949
23	Bryan	1947	23	28	2	1949, 1958
24	Dennis	1940	24	25	2	1944, 1949
25	Dougie	1941	21	21	2	1948, 1949
26	Edmund	1938	27	28	0	n/a
27	Gerald	1945	24	26	3	1947, 1950, 1953
28	Horace	1948	26	33	2	1954, 1958
29	Hubert	1936	27	26	3	1940, 1942, 1945
30	Hugh	1947	23	20	2	1950, 1956
31	Humphrey	1938	25	24	1	1940, 1949 (second adopted)
32	Mark	1947	32	30	0	n/a
33	Norman	1944	31	30	1	1944, 1952 (second adopted)
34	Patrick	1941	23	23	3	1944, 1947, 1949

miscarriages/stillbirths/ infant deaths	main place of residence in marriage	religious affiliation
none	Surrey	C of E regular attendance until lately
none	Preston, Harpenden	strong Methodist
none	St Albans	C of E committed
miscarr. twins; med. abort.	Brighton, Harpenden	C of E regular throughout life
none	Berkhamsted	no attendance at church mentioned
1 stillbirth	Berkhamsted	C of E
1 miscarriage	Radlett, Herts	regular attendance at local church
none	Harpenden	atheist
1 miscarriage	Bexhill, E. Sussex	C of E, confirmed in teens
1 miscarriage	Tring, Herts	C of E, strong believer
1st born d. aged 5	Harpenden	not religious as adult
none	London	not religious
none	High Wycombe	Quakers, very committed
none	St Albans	C of E, non-attender
1 miscarriage	Yorkshire	C of E believer (children confirmed)
none	military postings around the world	C of E but not religious
1 miscarriage	Harpenden	Wesleyan as a child, then C of E
none	Harpenden	no religious attendance
none	Newbury	C of E, regular attender
1 miscarriage	London	Jewish and still Kosher
none	Harpenden	RC (husband not religious)
none	London	not religious
4 miscarriages	St Albans	C of E non-attender
1 miscarriage	Harpenden	Methodist, religious
none	Berkhamsted	C of E non-attender
none	Harpenden	C of E fairly devout
1 miscarriage	Bexhill, E. Sussex	C of E very irregular attender
miscarr. twins; med. abort.	Brighton and Harpenden	C of E regular, was Sidesman
none	Leighton Buzzard	C of E but not religious
none	Preston, Harpenden	C of E very rarely attends, Freemason
1 d. few hours old (1948)	North London and Hertfordshire	Anglican, quite regular attender
none	High Wycombe	Quakers, very committed
1 stillbirth	London	C of E sporadic attender
1 miscarriage (a twin)	East Ham	C of E church organist

Hertfordshire Panel 2

	Name	d.o.m	female AM	male AM	no. of children	d.o.b. of children
35	Reg	1942	18; 32	21; 38	4	1945, 1958, 1962, 1964
36	Roger	1938	21	27	1	1941
37	Sam	1941	27	29	1	1948
38	William	1931	34	29	0	n/a

Hertfordshire Panel 3

	Name	soc. class	sec. ed.?	main male occupation
1	Agatha	IV		gardener in stately home
2	Angela	IIIN		electrical engineer (Royal Engineers WWII)
3	Antonia	I	y	chartered accountant (army service WWII)
4	Betty	II	y	primary headteacher (RN Asdic op WWII)
5	Catherine	IIIM(II)		Self-employed watchmaker shop (army service WWII)
6	Clare	IV		1st husband milkman (RAF WWII – killed); 2nd – construction worker
7	Dora	IIIM		car mechanic (bomb disposal WWII)
8	Emma	I	y	research scientist
9	Esme	I	y	manager large public company (army signals WWII)

miscarriages/stillbirths/ infant deaths	main place of residence in marriage	religious affiliation
2nd wife 1 miscarriage	Manchester	rarely attends church
1 stillbirth	Hertfordshire	C of E, now agnostic
none	Harpenden	Christian but not religious
none	Dunstable, Herts	C of E (wife was strict RC)

female occupation – before marriage	female occupation – after marriage	spouse's b'place	spouse death
service in stately home	part-time service in stately home	not known	1970s
riveter WWII, clerk in NAAFI office, and in surgical manufacture	secretarial work from home when son aged 5–12, then clerk at local health centre	Trowbridge	n/a
none	ran home B&B from 1977; after husband died part-time admin/CAB work, took degree	London	1987
teacher	teacher, mainly sec. schools, retired at 54 because leg/hip disability	Bermondsey, Lon.	n/a
officework: shorthand and typing	helped husband in shop	London	1968
in domestic service	factory cleaning after 1st husb. died, no work during 2nd marriage or after	Aylesbury; Berkhamsted	1940, 1951
dressmaker West End, clothing machinist East End	clothing alterations from home, nanny, then various jobs incl. bar work	London	1998
teacher: London, Eastbourne,Worcester	teacher in sec. schools throughout marriage, retired at 70	Huddersfield	1988
bank clerk, cashier, secretary	bank work, interrupted for young children, school secretary, student counsellor	Sutton Coldfield	n/a

Hertfordshire Panel 3

	Name	soc. class	sec. ed.?	main male occupation
10	Gay	II	y	high-earning salesman
11	Grace	IIIM(II)		self-employed small car-repair business (army service WWII)
12	Heather	II(IIIM)		(WWII army amputee (leg)) nightshift phone operator 10 yrs, P. O. counters 15 yrs
13	Joanna	II	y	civil servant (conscientious objector WWII)
14	Judith	I	y	managing director of large retailing chain
15	June	II		Liptons-trained grocery store owner-manager (RAMC medical corps WWII)
16	Monica	I		RAF officer
17	Pam	IV		mouldmaker in tyre factory
18	Penny	IV		rubber factory labourer, became foreman (army N. Africa WWII)
19	Pru	I	y	bank securities (RN WWII)
20	Rebecca	IV		taxi driver (hospital driver during WWII)
21	Vera	IV		Vauxhall Motors worker
22	Alf	II(IIIM)		(WWII army amputee (leg)) nightshift phone operator 10 yrs, P. O. counters 15 yrs
23	Bryan	IIIM		trainee tailor, rubber factory operative, then foreman (army WWII – bad wound)
24	Dennis	IIIM(II)		printer and compositor (army WWII clerical sergeant)
25	Dougie	V		odd jobs, (eventually) chargehand (foreman) in chemicals factory (army WWII)
26	Edmund	IIIM		printer (Royal Artillery ack-ack gunner WWII)

female occupation – before marriage	female occupation – after marriage	spouse's b'place	spouse death
advertising agency West End	nothing till c.1961, accounts work, after divorce property valuation and town hall accounts	South London	(divorced)
factory work, munitions during the war	intermittent cleaning work and shop work	Harpenden	1986
various factory jobs in London	war work for Min. of Labour part-time when children young, then full-time lab technican	Fulham, Lon.	n/a
trained secretary in Quaker HQ at Euston	Philanth. social and housing work. Work for Quakers again from 1975	High Wycombe	n/a
qualified midwife, ward sister Edinburgh	stopped work after 1st pregnancy; clerical work after divorce 1975	Campbeltown	1999 (divorced)
helper at Dr Barnardos for 2 yrs	nothing after marriage, later some work for husband's grocery firm	Darton, S. Yorks	1983
amateur actress	amateur actress	Stubbington, Hants	1976
domestic work in Harpenden	none	Ware, Herts	1969
domestic service	stopped work on marriage, work in rubber factory after children left	Harpenden	1996
secretarial and typing in insurance office and banks	continued to work in banks until children, later worked in doctor's office	Scotland	1982
alteration hand in West End (Harvey Nichols), nurse	took part-time work when daughter school age	London	1990
shop work then trained as a nurse	not much, worked for a short while as home help to an elderly woman	Birkenhead	1984
various factory jobs in London	war work for Min. of Labour part-time when children young, then full-time lab technican	Chelsea, Lon.	n/a
shop assistant	none	Harpenden	1993
nurse in Luton	secretary and shorthand typing sometimes	London	1990
garment factory	break for children then back at garment factory part-time	Berkhamsted	1992
clerical work at Rothamsted research station	none	Mystole, Kent	1989

Hertfordshire Panel 3

	Name	soc. class	sec. ed.?	main male occupation
27	Gerald	I	y	manager large public company (army signals WWII)
28	Horace	II	y	primary headteacher (RN Asdic op WWII)
29	Hubert	II	y	journalist, then company director engineering firm (army NCO WWII)
30	Hugh	IIIN		electrical engineer (Royal Engineers WWII)
31	Humphrey	I	y	civil engineer, building surveyor (RAF Flt Lt runways engineer Middle East WWII)
32	Mark	II	y	civil servant (conscientious objector WWII)
33	Norman	II(IIIM)		pre-war labourer, teacher (Emerg. Teach. Train. Scheme after WWII service)
34	Patrick	IIIN	y	auditor and local govt official, then salesman (conscientious objector WWII)
35	Reg	II	y	film, documentary and commerical maker (Royal Marines Film Unit WWII)
36	Roger	I	y	chartered surveyor (Royal Engineers WWII)
37	Sam	II	y	articled clerk, large company secretary (official in army's Court Martial WWII)
38	William	II		factory works manager and entrepreneur (in aircraft prodn during WWII)

female occupation – before marriage	female occupation – after marriage	spouse's b'place	spouse death
bank clerk, cashier, secretary	bank work, interrupted for young children, school secretary, student counsellor	Edmonton, Lon.	n/a
teacher	teacher, mainly sec. schools, retired at 54 because leg/hip disability	Peckham, Lon.	n/a
nurse	none	Leighton Buzzard	1999
riveter WWII, clerk in NAAFI office, and in surgical manufacturer	secretarial work from home when son aged 5–12, then clerk at local health centre	Preston	n/a
Lloyd's insurance, office work	none	Hackney, Lon.	1994
trained secretary in Quaker HQ at Euston	philanthropic, social and housing work, work for Quakers again from 1975	High Wycombe	n/a
commerical company typist and shorthand	did patches as a typist throughout marriage	Tottenham, Lon.	1987
Post Office Saving Bank 1934–43	nothing 1943–50 then part-time clerical office work until 1967	East Ham, Lon.	1997
1st hairdresser; 2nd large-crane driver in Vickers Barrow shipyards and nightclub singer	2nd wife part-time for husband's company while children small, then TV stage manager	Portsmouth; Barrow-in-Furness	1992; (1st divorced)
hairdresser	none	Chatham, Kent	alive (Alzheimer's)
secretarial work	secretarial work till 4 months before 1st child born then nothing	Newcastle upon Tyne	1996
deputy headmistress of RC school	deputy headmistress	Dublin	1968

Blackburn Panel 1

	Name	ref. no.	sex	d.o.b	place of birth
1	Daphne	msf/jm/bl/#38	f	1912	Harwood, Lancs
2	Diana	msf/jm/bl/#45	f	1910	Oldham
3	Doreen	msf/kf/bl/#20	f	1922	Preston
4	Dorris	msf/ssrs/bl/#22	f	1921	Blackburn
5	Eileen	msf/kf/bl/#12	f	1913	Blackburn
6	Eleanor	msf/kf/bl/#11	f	1907	Blackburn
7	Elizabeth	msf/kf/bl/#26	f	1923	Blackburn
8	Elma	msf/jm/bl/#42	f	1909	Rotherham
9	Emily	msf/kf/bl/#13	f	1917	Blackburn
10	Enid	msf/kf/bl/#49	f	1909	Blackburn
11	Eva	msf/kf/bl/#9	f	1911	Blackburn
12	Felicity	msf/kf/bl/#37	f	1919	Accrington
13	Gill	msf/kf/bl/#48	f	1920	Market Drayton, Shrops
14	Glynnis	msf/kf/bl/#4	f	1901	Great Harwood
15	Hilda	msf/kf/bl/#50	f	1914	Swinton, Cheshire
16	Iris	msf/kf/bl/#2	f	1914	Darwen, Lancs
17	Jane	msf/kf/bl/#32	f	1925	Blackburn
18	Jennie	msf/kf/bl/#27	f	1908	Blackburn
19	Laura	msf/kf/bl/#6	f	1923	Blackburn
20	Lorna	msf/kf/bl/#25	f	1917	Blackburn
21	Lucy	msf/kf/bl/#10	f	1907	Blackburn
22	Lyn	msf/kf/bl/#1	f	1907	Blackburn
23	Maria	msf/kf/bl/#8	f	1917	Blackburn
24	Marian	msf/kf/bl/#28	f	1908	Blackburn
25	Marilyn	msf/kf/bl/#7	f	1914	Blackburn
26	Maud	msf/kf/bl/#18	f	1912	Blackburn
27	Maureen	msf/kf/bl/#46	f	1920	Blackburn
28	Mavis	msf/kf/bl/#29	f	1908	Blackburn
29	Mildred	msf/kf/bl/#41	f	1924	Ferndale, Glam
30	Molly	msf/ssrs/bl/#17	f	1913	Blackburn
31	Nora	msf/jm/bl/#47	f	1920	Blackburn
32	Olive	msf/jm/bl/#44	f	1915	West Bromwich

no. of siblings	father's occupation	mother's occupation
none	cotton overlooker (foreman)	weaver
none	manager of gas meter manufacturer	none
1	tea merchant (family business)	sewing work from home
3	bin man, street sweeper	fuse factory work during WWI, hospital cleaner later
4	accountant for Corporation, then ran boarding house	ran boarding house
1 (step-sister)	riveter on ships, step-father – drawer in	ring spinner
4	bakery	weaver before children born
5	shunter on railway (low-paid)	housewife (educated at boarding school), glovemaker before marriage
none	weaver (killed in WWI)	weaver
none	engineer in Scotland (grandfather Co-op supervisor)	not known (born out of wedlock and brought up by grandparents)
4	weaver (killed in WWI)	none
1	grocer at Co-op, became manager of a small shop	weaver all working life – part-time when children small
2	bank accountant before and after WWI (gassed badly)	never worked (went to Blackburn High School) – monied family
7	overlooker in the mill	none
1 (Down's)	qualified geologist – artesian well-boring family firm	none
1	plasterer (injured on scaffolding and incapacitated)	ran secondhand shop
2	clerk in town hall	weaver before marriage, then odd jobs: hat stall, sewing, shop work
7	doesn't know (d. before she was born)	took in washing, cleaning
1	mill worker	weaver throughout marriage (d. when respondent aged 12)
3	weaver, coal merchant	weaver before marriage, silk weaving during WWI
3	engine tenter and fitter	weaver
none	owned herbalist shop	weaver and winder before marriage, then helped out in shop
1	joiner, builder, and funeral director	none
1	drawer in cotton mill	winder before and after marriage until both children earning
1	engineer Northrop loom factory, then ran grocery	ran grocer's shop
none	engineer in steel works	weaving before childbirth and after, left work permanently in her 40s
2	ironmonger (owned shop)	weaver, then nothing when children born
10	antique dealer and rag-and-bone man	winder
3	miner	in service in Gloucester before marriage
7	labourer, bricklayer	carding room
2	motor engineer	dressmaker
4	manager of lock- and keysmiths	none

Blackburn Panel 1

	Name	ref. no.	sex	d.o.b	place of birth
33	Pearl	msf/kf/bl/#40	f	1915	Burnley
34	Phyllis	msf/kf/bl/#5	f	1921	Blackburn
35	Rose	msf/kf/bl/#21	f	1928	Oswaldtwistle, Lancs
36	Sally	msf/kf/bl/#31	f	1908	Blackburn
37	Sarah	msf/kf/bl/#30	f	1906	Preston
38	Alistair	msf/kf/bl/#33	m	1927	Scotland
39	Arthur	msf/ssrs/bl/#24	m	1918	Capetown, South Africa
40	Bernard	msf/jm/bl/#45	m	1907	Oldham
41	Christopher	msf/kf/bl/#34	m	1918	Barrow-in-Furness
42	Colin	msf/kf/bl/#36	m	1923	Blackburn
43	Dick	msf/kf/bl/#32	m	1920	Blackburn
44	Ed	msf/ssrs/bl/#23	m	1913	Blackburn
45	Frank	msf/ssrs/bl/#16	m	1919	Birkenhead
46	Jake	msf/ssrs/bl/#22	m	1922	Blackburn
47	Larry	msf/kf/bl/#20	m	1917	Blackburn
48	Merlin	msf/kf/bl/#35	m	1908	Blackburn
49	Peter	msf/kf/bl/#26	m	1921	Withnell, Lancs
50	Terence	msf/ssrs/bl/#15	m	1915	Blackburn
51	Tim	msf/ssrs/bl/#19	m	1917	Leyland, Lancs

Blackburn Panel 2

	Name	d.o.m	female AM	male AM	no. of children	d.o.b. of children
1	Daphne	1937	25	26	2	1939, 1947
2	Diana	1936	26	29	1	1939
3	Doreen	1946	24	29	2	1949, 1952
4	Dorris	1945	24	22	3	1948, 1951, 1954

no. of siblings	father's occupation	mother's occupation
1	clerical work then branch manager of Thomas Cook travel agent	weaver
3 (1 d. as infant)	canal wharf horse-drawn carter, fuse factory	nothing (had multiple sclerosis)
1	chip shop owner	took in washing, cleaner
1	engineering fitter, became foreman	winder, left after 1st child born
4	patternmaker, engineer	weaver (until premature death)
11	hawker, then steady job elec. board	local, unqualified midwife, odd jobs cleaning
10 (2 half-siblings)	step-father – boilermaker for S. African railways	none
1	superintendent for Refuge Assurance Company	none
7	publisher's clerk in local newspaper	only worked before marriage (details not known)
7	music hall performer (wounded WWI) (violent, Colin in care at age 8)	ran toffee shop, nothing after children born (children taken into care)
1	foreman then clerk in wood yard	nurse all her life: started in WWI then became works nurse
8	weaver, later warehouseman at same mill	winder before marriage only
1	riveter	weaver
1	poultry keeper	looked after grandfather
12	builder	weaver before marriage
7	army sergeant gassed in WWI – never worked again	weaver before marriage
2	platelayer (railways)	weaver (d. when respondent aged 13)
4	railway blacksmith	weaver until respondent aged 14
1	Crewe rail works, turner, inspector, union man (AEU)	worked before marriage only, in small factory

miscarriages/stillbirths/ infant deaths	main place of residence in marriage	religious affiliation
none	Great Harwood, Lancs	RC
none	Blackburn	Baptist then C of E
1 miscarriage	Blackburn	attends quite often, non-denom. allegiance
none	Blackburn	not religious

Blackburn Panel 2

	Name	d.o.m	female AM	male AM	no. of children	d.o.b. of children
5	Eileen	1943	30	30	1	*1938, 1942, 1944
6	Eleanor	1934	27	27	3	1937, 1939, 1949
7	Elizabeth	1947	24, 76	26, 74	1	1948
8	Elma	1933	24	26	1	1934
9	Emily	1938	21	23	2	1940, 1946
10	Enid	1939	30	27	3	1944, 1945, 1950
11	Eva	1932	21	31	2	1943, 1948
12	Felicity	1954	34	31	2	1957, 1959
13	Gill	1945	25	24	3	1947, 1949, 1950
14	Glynnis	1924	23	23	4	1933, 1934 (twins), 1936
15	Hilda	1935	21, 33	29, 37	1	1939
16	Iris	1938	24	30	3	1939, 1947, 1949
17	Jane	1953	28	33	2	1958, 1959
18	Jennie	1930	22	23	1	1930
19	Laura	1942	20	22	2	1944, 1946
20	Lorna	1939	21	27	2	1942, 1945
21	Lucy	1931	24	22	1	1937
22	Lyn	1931	24	22	1	1932
23	Maria	1940	23	25	1	1941
24	Marian	1939	30	28	1	1947
25	Marilyn	1940	23	32	3	1942, 1944, 1951
26	Maud	1934	21	25	1	1944
27	Maureen	1943	22	27	2	1944, 1946
28	Mavis	1929	21	22	6	1930, 1932, 1934, 1941, 1944, 1946
29	Mildred	1947	22	20	0	n/a
30	Molly	1930	17	18	2	1930, 1933
31	Nora	1945	25	25	2	1948, 1952
32	Olive	1951	36	35	0	n/a
33	Pearl	never married	n/a	n/a	0	n/a

miscarriages/stillbirths/ infant deaths	main place of residence in marriage	religious affiliation
none	Blackburn	C of E, father very devout, she less so
none	Blackburn (London WWII)	Methodist, then congregational – religious
none	Blackburn	moderately religious but no time to attend
none	Manchester	C of E, quite religious
none	Blackburn, briefly Hitchin	C of E, not strongly religious
none	Blackburn	C of E, quite religious
1 stillbirth (1934)	Blackburn	C of E, doesn't attend any more
none	Accrington	Methodist (husband RC)
none	Blackburn	Swedenborgian as a child, then C of E
1 d. aged 3 months (1925)	Blackburn	C of E, regular attender
none	Blackburn	atheist
none	Darwen	not religious
1 miscarriage	Blackburn	Congregational, United Reformed, then Methodist
none	Blackburn	RC
none	Blackburn	C of E and still attends
none	Blackburn	devout, C of E, then joined United Reformed
none	Blackburn	C of E, believer and attender
none	Blackburn	regular church goer but no denom. allegiance
none	Blackburn	C of E, believes but non-attender
1st child d. aged 12 months (1941)	Blackburn	C of E, regular attender and takes communion
1 stillbirth (1940)	Blackburn	RC as a child and then C of E
2 miscarriages	Blackburn	C of E as a child, then Presbyterian
none	Blackburn	very devout C of E
1 child d. aged 4	Blackburn	not as a child, became RC
none	Burnley	Methodist, gave up when in Huddersfield
none	Blackburn	C of E, no attendance (husband RC)
none	Blackburn	C of E
none	Standish, Lancs	C of E
none	Rochdale	C of E

Blackburn Panel 2

	Name	d.o.m	female AM	male AM	no. of children	d.o.b. of children
34	Phyllis	1943	22	24	2	1944, 1947
35	Rose	1948	19, 31, 45, 52	22, 36, 30, 55	6	1949, 1951, 1952, 1954, 1960, 1964
36	Sally	1934	26	24	1	1945
37	Sarah	1928	21	25	1	1934
38	Alistair	1952	25	24	2	1957, 1960
39	Arthur	1942	23	24	1	1943
40	Bernard	1936	26	29	1	1939
41	Christopher	1947	19	29	3	1948, 1950, 1952
42	Colin	1947	22, 58	24, 56	3	1947, 1950, 1964
43	Dick	1953	33	28	2	1958, 1959
44	Ed	1937	21	24	2	1938, 1939
45	Frank	1941	21	22	0	n/a
46	Jake	1945	24	22	3	1948, 1954, 1951
47	Larry	1946	24	29	2	1949, 1952
48	Merlin	1940	29	32	1	1949
49	Peter	1940	18, 27, 76	18, 24, 74	3	1941, 1948, 1951
50	Terence	1939	26	24	3	1940, 1945, 1946
51	Tim	1947	19	29	3	1948, 1949, 1952

Blackburn Panel 3

	Name	soc. class	sec. ed?	main male occupation
1	Daphne	II(IIIM)		shopkeeper (confectioner's), butcher before marriage (REME WWII)
2	Diana	I	y	journalist (local newspaper general manager)
3	Doreen	IIIM		builder and foreman bricklayer (mine defuser WWII)

miscarriages/stillbirths/ infant deaths	main place of residence in marriage	religious affiliation
none	Reading	RC only moderate attender
1 miscarriage (poss. more)	Blackburn	C of E, not regular today
1 miscarriage	Blackburn	C of E, pretty active
1 d. 10 days old, spina bifida (1932)	Bolton	C of E, only as a child
none	Blackburn	RC and C of E schooling, lost faith aged 55
none	S. Africa then Blackburn	not religious
none	Blackburn	Baptist then C of E
none	Cumbria and Lancashire	C of E, regular attendance
none	Blackburn	C of E, not regular
1 miscarriage	Blackburn	Congregational, United Reformed, then Methodist
1 miscarriage or early stillbirth	Blackburn	C of E, non-attender
2 miscarriages	Blackburn	C of E, only occasional attendance
none	Blackburn	not religious
1 miscarriage	Blackburn	C of E
none	Blackburn	C of E, lost faith when wife died
none	Blackburn	not religious
none	Blackburn	Congregationalist as a child, nothing today
none	Leyland	C of E, not religious but believes

female occupation – before marriage	female occupation – after marriage	spouse's b'place	spouse death
worked in confectioner's shop owned with husband	worked with husband in confectioner's shop	Blackburn	1982
switchboard for engineering firm	none	Oldham	n/a
sewing, domestic science training	nothing – husband wouldn't let her	Blackburn	n/a

Blackburn Panel 3

	Name	soc. class	sec. ed?	main male occupation
4	Dorris	IIIM		foreman in an engineering works
5	Eileen	IV		partly skilled factory work
6	Eleanor	IIIM		mechanic (coach builder) (aircraft production WWII)
7	Elizabeth	IV		1st husband factory worker, milkman, car repair work (mil. service WWII); 2nd – see Peter (49), below
8	Elma	IIIM		policeman in the courtesy squad, never promoted
9	Emily	IIIM		electrical engineer for 'phone company
10	Enid	IIIN	y	supervisor in textile mill (RN WWII, incl. Murmansk convoys)
11	Eva	II(IIIM)		owned shoe repair shop
12	Felicity	II	y	travelling claims assessor for British Rail
13	Gill	I	y	mill owner and manager (infantry major WWII)
14	Glynnis	IIIM		plumber at Mullards valve factory
15	Hilda	I	y	1st – sales director for pharmaceutical firm; 2nd – chartered accountant: snr partner
16	Iris	IV		railway porter (army in WWII)
17	Jane	IIIN	y	commerical clerk
18	Jennie	IV		sawmill worker
19	Laura	IV		partly skilled factory work (Northrop loom makers) (RAF g.c.*** WWII)
20	Lorna	IV		factory worker (valve tester), later school caretaker

female occupation – before marriage	female occupation – after marriage	spouse's b'place	spouse death
nursemaid, Mullards factory, Philips radio factory	Mullards then little part-time jobs only after children born	Blackburn	n/a
machinist (prison uniforms), shop assistant in large stores	nothing till after huband's death and youngest child aged 10: factory work	Blackburn	1969
weaver, Methodist mother's help, dentist's receptionist	confectioner's, laundry, cook but not after children born	Blackburn	1957
Mullards fuse factory worker	Marks & Spencer, winding, hand bag manufacture, laundry, cleaning	Rishton; Withnell (both Lancs)	1st – 1991; (2nd – n/a)
cook in engineering factory canteen	head cook in factory canteen, worked in food business throughout marriage	Birmingham	1972
weaver	after divorce weaver, then cleaner for county council	Blackburn	(divorced)
secretary for local firm (cleaners)	secretary for local firm, nothing when children small then part-time secretary	Accrington	1990
weaver	helped in husband's shoe shop	Knaresborough, Yorks	1993
none	started working as school secretary when youngest child was 5, worked 15 yrs	Bolton	1994
social work in welfare department of textile firms	unpaid voluntary work, none when children small, became magistrate aged 54	Blackburn	1997
tailoress	nothing after children	Blackburn	1989
none but did designs for fabrics	none	Blackburn (both)	(1st divorced) 2nd – 1987
winding (textiles), sales assistant Woolworths	worked on and off for mother's secondhand shop	Salford	1978
civil servant in tax office (CO**)	CO before children, part-time shop/clerical work when children at school	Blackburn	n/a
worked in spinning mill and various other low-paid jobs	work in gas-masks factory in war then in leather factory (became supervisor)	Blackburn	1986
weaver, valve inspector for Mullards fuse factory	continued work until husband demobbed	Blackburn	1971
weaver	weaver, later cleaner	Blackburn	1985

Blackburn Panel 3

	Name	soc. class	sec. ed?	main male occupation
21	Lucy	II(IIIM)		grocer then bus driver
22	Lyn	IIIM		reacher in mill before and during war; then Mullards factory
23	Maria	IV		painter for Blackburn Corporation, wrestling announcer
24	Marian	IV		colour mixer in dye factory until 1952 then Corporation bin man (Burma WWII)
25	Marilyn	II(IIIM)		hairdresser (owned a salon) (RAF g.c.*** WWII)
26	Maud	IIIM		1st – warehouseman and despatch foreman; 2nd – cobbler
27	Maureen	IIIN	y	sales representative in building trade (army batman WWII)
28	Mavis	IV		long-distance lorry driver
29	Mildred	II		draftsman at David Brown (Aston Martin), metal/woodwork teacher
30	Molly	IV		bricklayer
31	Nora	II	y	director electrical retail firm, expanded to motor trade (RAF production WWII)
32	Olive	II(IIIM)	y	undertaker embalmer (opened own business in 1960)
33	Pearl	II	y	n/a
34	Phyllis	IIIN	y	grocery business then paper mill export clerk (bomb disposal WWII)
35	Rose	V		1st – unemployed; 2nd – lorry driver; 3rd – bin man; 4th – foundry inspector
36	Sally	II(IIIM)		self-employed painter and decorator

female occupation – before marriage	female occupation – after marriage	spouse's b'place	spouse death
weaver	helped in husband's shop, weaver again for 10 yrs after children left	Blackburn	1980
winder, Woolworths Saturday girl	part-time in shops, left once son born, when son aged 5 returned to part-time jobs	Blackburn	1988
winder, book work for father's businesses	book work for father's businesses: garage, dog track, catering for nightclub 1960s	Blackburn	1993
weaver	continued to work in mill until 2nd birth, did cleaning work later	Blackburn	1982
bakery, in mother's grocery shop	took in sewing	Blackburn	1964
cashier at Saxone shoe company	nothing till son aged 5, then filing work in shoe shop, became office manager	Blackburn	1977
commerical clerical office work in various large companies	none until children at school then part-time for typing agency	Blackburn	1996
ring spinner	later worked a few yrs as kitchen staff in female mental hospital	Blackburn	1997
burling in mill	burling in mill till retirement	Bradford	in a home
worked in card room in Imperial mill until 2nd birth	none after 2nd birth	Darwen	1970s
bank work	none	Blackburn	1997
Woolworths, trained as nurse then head nurse at nursing home	1951 trained as embalmer to work with husband in his business	Leek, Staffs	1984
schoolteacher – became deputy head, then head	n/a	n/a	n/a
cashier and book keeper	cashier and book keeper and helped in grocery, later secretary for father-in-law	Reading	1995
winder	Prestige factory conveyor-belt work, dinner lady, office tea lady	Blackburn (all)	all divorced
shirtmaker; aged 18–26 in woollen mill; shop assistant	shop assistant, nothing while child under 5, factory work then hairdresser	Blackburn	1994

Blackburn Panel 3

	Name	soc. class	sec. ed?	main male occupation
37	Sarah	IIIM		upholsterer
38	Alistair	IIIM		cotton mill worker then paper mill supervisor (in army 1945–8)
39	Arthur	IV		S. Africa: print operative; UK: cricketer (semi-pro), JCB operator
40	Bernard	I	y	journalist (local newspaper general manager)
41	Christopher	IV		professional soldier 1937–52, building maintenance, then office work
42	Colin	IIIM		qualified plumber (RN WWII)
43	Dick	IIIN		commerical clerk
44	Ed	IIIM		carpenter (employee) (Royal Engineers in WWII)
45	Frank	IV		part-skilled jobs, ended as ambulance driver attendant (RN WWII)
46	Jake	IIIM		foreman in an engineering works (army WWII)
47	Larry	IIIM		builder and foreman bricklayer (mine defuser WWII)
48	Merlin	IV		Corporation bus/tram driver (RAF g.c.*** WWII)
49	Peter	IIIM		cotton mill (stripper and grinder) (Royal Marines WWII)
50	Terence	IIIM(II)		self-employed decorator (army – Far East, WWII)
51	Tim	II(IIIM)		owned watch repair shop

female occupation – before marriage	female occupation – after marriage	spouse's b'place	spouse death
weaver	returned to weaving briefly after marriage, other short-term, part-time jobs	Lincoln	1987
ring winder	ring winder until children born, later ran small corner shop	Blackburn	1980
looking after uncle's children, some office work	none	Capetown, South Africa	1995
switchboard for engineering firm	none	Oldham	n/a
Boots Chemist assistant	cleaning once children grown up	Kirkham, Lancs	1996
1st – Mullards valve testing	1st – nothing, domestic sewing when children older; 2nd – barmaid (in her 1st marriage)	Blackburn (both)	1977, 1993
civil servant in tax office (CO**)	CO before children, part-time shop/clerical work when children at school	Blackburn	n/a
none	nothing then winder when children at school	Sharpness, Gloucs	1993
greetings card factory worker	Park Brothers car electrics throughout marriage	Blackburn	1992
nursemaid, Mullards factory, Philips radio factory	Mullards, then little part-time jobs only after children born	Blackburn	n/a
sewing, domestic science training	nothing – husband wouldn't let her	Preston	n/a
Mullards, gas mask manufacture	Mullards factory then nothing after children born	Blackburn	1977
1st – daffer in ring room; 2nd – weaver; 3rd – fuse factory	1st – none; 2nd – none; 3rd – Marks & Spencer, winding, hand bag manufacture, laundry, cleaning	Blackburn (all)	1946; 1996; (3rd n/a)
ring spinner	ring spinner, stopped at 1st birth, part-time shop work when children older	Blackburn	1997
typist at Leyland Motors social club	did books for husband's watch repair shop	Peckham, Lon.	n/a

Notes on Definitions and Abbreviations used in Appendix C

F	female
M	male
d.o.b.	date of birth
d.o.m	date of ***first*** marriage
no. of children	final family size ***excluding*** stillbirths, step-children, adopted children, ***and*** children who died in their first year of life
female AM	age at ***first*** marriage; higher ages listed give age at subsequent marriages
male AM	age at ***first*** marriage; higher ages listed give age at subsequent marriages

Couples interviewed together:
Hertfordshire: Angela and Hugh; Betty and Horace; Esme and Gerald; Heather and Alf; Joanna and Mark.
* Eileen's two oldest children were her husband's by a previous deceased wife
** CO: clerical officer
*** RAF g.c.: RAF ground crew
Blackburn: Diana and Bernard; Doreen and Larry; Dorris and Jake; Elizabeth and Peter; Jane and Dick.

RN	Royal Navy
WVS	Women's Voluntary Service
NCO	Non-Commissioned Officer
RAMC	Royal Army Medical Corps
REME	Royal Electrical and Mechanical Engineers
RC	Roman Catholic
C of E	Church of England
WWI	First World War
WWII	Second World War
CAB	Citizens' Advice Bureau
PO	Post Office
AEU	Amalgamated Engineering Union

Details given for occupations are not exhaustive but indicate the main employments undertaken by respondents and their partners during their lives.
Work for Corporations refers to municipal bodies such as Blackburn Corporation.
Work for Councils refers to local governing bodies, such as Blackburn Borough Council, Harpenden Town Council.

Bibliography

Abbott, Mary. *Family Affairs: A History of the Family in 20th-Century Britain*. London: Routledge, 2002.

Addison, Paul. *The Road to 1945: British Politics and the Second World War*. London and New York: Quartet Books, 1982.

Adonis, Andrew, and Stephen Pollard. *A Class Act: The Myth of Britain's Classless Society*. London and New York: Hamish Hamilton and Penguin Books, 1997.

Alexander, Sally. 'The Mysteries and Secrets of Women's Bodies: Sexual Knowledge in the First Half of the Twentieth Century'. In *Modern Times: Reflections on a Century of English Modernity*, edited by Mica Nava and Alan O'Shea, 161–75. London: Routledge, 1996.

Allport, Alan. *Demobbed: Coming Home after the Second World War*. New Haven: Yale University Press, 2009.

Anderson, Gregory. *The White-Blouse Revolution: Female Office Workers since 1870*. Manchester and New York: Manchester University Press and St. Martin's Press, 1988.

Anderson, Michael. 'The Emergence of the Modern Life Cycle in Britain'. *Social History* 10, no. 1 (1985): 69–87.

Anderson, Stuart, and Virginia Berridge. 'The Role of the Community Pharmacist in Health and Welfare, 1911–1986'. Ch. 2 in *Oral History, Health and Welfare*, edited by Joanna Bornat, Robert Perks, Paul Thompson and Jan Walmsley, 48–74. London: Routledge, 2000.

Arai, Lisa. 'Low Expectations, Sexual Attitudes and Knowledge: Explaining Teenage Pregnancy and Fertility in English Communities. Insights from Qualitative Research'. *The Sociological Review* 51, no. 2 (2003): 119–27.

Atkinson, Paul. *Handbook of Ethnography*. London: Sage, 2001.

August, Andrew. *The British Working Class, 1832–1940*. Harlow and New York: Pearson Longman, 2007.

Babington, Bruce. *British Stars and Stardom: From Alma Taylor to Sean Connery*. Manchester and New York: Manchester University Press, 2001.

Bailey, Beth L. *From Front Porch to Back Seat: Courtship in Twentieth-Century America*. Baltimore: Johns Hopkins University Press, 1988.

Bailey, Peter. 'Glamour and Parasexuality: The Victorian Barmaid as Cultural Prototype'. *Gender & History* 2, no. 2 (1990): 148–72.

'"Will the Real Bill Banks Please Stand Up?" Towards a Role Analysis of Mid-Victorian Working-Class Respectability'. *Journal of Social History* 12, no. 3 (1979): 336–53.

Baines, Dudley, and Robert Woods. 'Population and Regional Development'. In *The Cambridge Economic History of Modern Britain*, edited by Roderick Floud and Paul Johnson, 25–55. Cambridge and New York: Cambridge University Press, 2003.

Banks, J. A. *Prosperity and Parenthood: A Study of Family Planning among the Victorian Middle Classes*. London: Routledge & Kegan Paul, 1954.

Barnes, Kenneth C., and Frances Barnes. *Sex, Friendship and Marriage*. London: G. Allen & Unwin, 1938.

Bashford, Alison, and Carolyn Strange. 'Public Pedagogy: Sex Education and Mass Communication in the mid-Twentieth Century'. *Journal of the History of Sexuality* 13 (2004): 71–99.

Bayly, Chris. *The Birth of the Modern World 1780–1914*. Oxford: Blackwell, 2004.

Beck, Ulrich, and Elisabeth Beck-Gernsheim. *The Normal Chaos of Love*. Cambridge, UK and Cambridge, MA: Polity Press and Blackwell, 1995.

Beier, Lucinda McCray. *For Their Own Good: The Transformation of English Working-Class Health Culture, 1880–1970*. Columbus: Ohio State University Press, 2008.

'"We Were Green as Grass": Learning About Sex and Reproduction in Three Working-Class Lancashire Communities, 1900–1970'. *Social History of Medicine* 16, no. 3 (2003): 461–80.

Benchoffer, Frank, John Harry Goldthorpe, David Lockwood and Jennifer Platt. *The Affluent Worker in the Class Structure*. Cambridge: Cambridge University Press, 1969.

Benson, John. *The Rise of Consumer Society in Britain 1880–1980*. London: Longman 1994.

Bernstein, George L. *The Myth of Decline: The Rise of Britain since 1945*. London: Pimlico, 2004.

Bibby, C. *Sex Education: A Guide for Parents*. London: Macmillan & Co. Ltd, 1944.

Bingham, Adrian. 'An Era of Domesticity? Histories of Women and Gender in Interwar Britain'. *Cultural and Social History* 1, no. 2 (2004): 225–33.

Family Newspapers?: Sex, Private Life, and the British Popular Press 1918–1978. Oxford and New York: Oxford University Press, 2009.

Gender, Modernity, and the Popular Press in Inter-War Britain. Oxford and New York: Clarendon and Oxford University Press, 2004.

Birchall, Jenny. '"The Carnival Revels of Manchester's Vagabonds": Young Working-class Women and Monkey Parades in the 1870s'. *Women's History Review* 15, no. 2 (2006): 229–52.

Bland, Lucy. *Banishing the Beast: English Feminism and Sexual Morality 1885–1914*. London: Penguin, 1995.

'Marriage Laid Bare: Middle-class Women and Marital Sex, c.1880–1914'. In *Labour and Love*, edited by Jane Lewis, 123–46. Oxford: Basil Blackwell, 1986.

Blewett, Mary H. 'Yorkshire Lasses and Their Lads: Sexuality, Sexual Customs, and Gender Antagonisms in Anglo-American Working-Class Culture'. *Journal of Social History* 40, no. 2 (2006): 317–36.

Blom, Ida. '"Master of Your Own Body and What Is in It" – Reducing Marital Fertility in Norway, 1890–1930'. In *Gendering the Fertility Decline in the Western World*, edited by Angélique Janssens, 59–84. Bern: Peter Lang, 2007.

Blood, Robert O., and Donald M. Wolfe. *Husbands and Wives: The Dynamics of Married Living*. New York: Free Press, 1960.

Booth, Alan, and Sean Glynn. *Modern Britain: An Economic and Social History*. London and New York: Routledge, 1996.

Booth, Meyrick. *Youth and Sex: A Psychological Study*. London: G. Allen & Unwin, 1932.

Bott, Elizabeth. *Family and Social Network: Roles, Norms, and External Relationships in Ordinary Urban Families*. London: Tavistock Publications, 1957.

Bourke, Joanna. *Working Class Cultures in Britain 1890–1960: Gender, Class, and Ethnicity*. London and New York: Routledge, 1994.

Branigan, Patrick, Kirsti Mitchell and Kaye Wellings. 'Discomfort, Discord and Discontinuity as Data: Using Focus Groups to Research Sensitive Topics'. *Culture, Health & Sexuality* 2, no. 3 (2000): 255–67.

Brannen, Julia. 'The Study of Sensitive Subjects'. *Sociological Review* 36, no. 3 (1988): 552–63.

Braun, Virginia, Nicola Gavey and Kathryn McPhillips. 'The "Fair Deal"? Unpacking Accounts of Reciprocity in Heterosex'. *Sexualities* 6, no. 2 (2003): 237–61.

Braybon, Gail. *Women Workers in the First World War: The British Experience*. London and Totowa, NJ: Croom Helm and Barnes & Noble, 1981.

Bristow, Edward J. *Vice and Vigilance: Purity Movements in Britain since 1700*. Dublin and Totowa, NJ: Gill and Macmillan and Rowman and Littlefield, 1977.

Bromley, Dorothy Dunbar, and Florence Haxton Britten. *Youth and Sex: A Study of 1300 College Students*. New York and London: Harper & Brothers, 1938.

Brooke, Stephen. 'Bodies, Sexuality and the "Modernization" of the British Working Classes, 1920s to 1960s'. *International Labor and Working-Class History* 69, no. 1 (2006): 104–22.

'Gender and Working Class Identity in Britain During the 1950s'. *Journal of Social History* 34, no. 4 (2001): 773–95.

Brookes, Barbara L. *Abortion in England, 1900–1967*. London and New York: Croom Helm, 1988.

Brown, Callum G. *The Death of Christian Britain: Understanding Secularisation, 1800–2000*. 2nd edn. London and New York: Routledge, 2009.

Brown, Peter. *The Body and Society: Men, Women, and Sexual Renunciation in Early Christianity*. New York: Columbia University Press, 1988.

Brundage, Anthony. *The English Poor Laws, 1700–1930*. Basingstoke and New York: Palgrave, 2002.

Buckland, Elfrida. *The World of Donald Mcgill*. Poole: Javeline Books, 1985.

Burgess, Ernest W., and Harvey J. Locke. *The Family, from Institution to Companionship*. New York: American Book Company, 1945.

Burnett, John. *A Social History of Housing, 1815–1985*. London and New York: Methuen, 1986.

Caine, Barbara. *Victorian Feminists*. Oxford and New York: Oxford University Press, 1992.

Call, Vaughn, Susan Sprecher and Pepper Schwartz. 'The Incidence and Frequency of Marital Sex in a National Sample'. *Journal of Marriage and the Family* 57, no. 3 (1995): 639–52.

Campbell, Patricia J. *Sex Education Books for Young Adults, 1892–1979*. New York: R. R. Bowker Co., 1979.

Carnevali, Francesca, Paul Johnson and Julie Marie Strange, eds. *Twentieth-Century Britain: Economic, Cultural and Social Change*. London: Longman, 2007.

Cartwright, Ann, and Joanna Moffett. 'A Comparison of Results Obtained by Men and Women Interviewers in a Fertility Survey'. *Journal of Biosocial Science* 6, no. 3 (1974): 315–22.

Chance, Janet. *The Cost of English Morals*. London: Douglas, 1931.

Charles, Enid. *The Practice of Birth Control: An Analysis of the Birth Control Experiences of Nine Hundred Women*. London: Williams and Norgate, 1932.

Chauncey, George. *Gay New York: Gender, Urban Culture and the Making of the Gay Male World, 1890–1940*. New York: Basic Books, 1994.

Chesser, Eustace. *Love without Fear*. London: Rich & Cowan, 1941.

Sexual Behaviour, Normal and Abnormal. London: Medical Publications Ltd, 1949.

Chesser, Eustace, Joan Maizels, Leonard Jones and Brian Emmett. *The Sexual, Marital and Family Relationships of the English Woman*. London: Hutchinson's Medical Publications, 1956.

Chinn, Carl. *They Worked All Their Lives: Women of the Urban Poor in England, 1880–1939*. Manchester: Manchester University Press, 1988.

Chow, Karen. 'Popular Sexual Knowledges and Women's Agency in 1920s England: Marie Stopes's Married Love and E. M. Hull's The Sheik'. *Feminist Review* 63, no. 1 (1999): 64–87.

Christ, Carol. 'Victorian Masculinity and the Angel in the House'. In *A Widening Sphere: Changing Roles of Victorian Women*, edited by Martha Vicinus, 146–62. Bloomington: Indiana University Press, 1977.

Clark, Anna. *Desire: A History of European Sexuality*. New York and London: Routledge, 2008.

Review of *The Gentleman's Daughter: Women's Lives in Georgian England*. Reviews in History review no. 57. www.history.ac.uk/reviews/review/57 (accessed 29 April 2010).

The Struggle for the Breeches: Gender and the Making of the British Working Class. Berkeley: University of California Press, 1995.

Cocks, Harry. *Classified: The Secret History of the Personal Column*. London: Random House, 2009.

'Review: The Growing Pains of the History of Sexuality'. *Journal of Contemporary History* 39, no. 4 (2004): 657–66.

Review of *Hera Cook, The Long Sexual Revolution: English Women, Sex and Contraception, 1800–1975*, December 2005. Available from www.h-net.org/reviews/showrev.cgi?path=164411141759612 (accessed 30 April 2010).

'Saucy Stories: Pornography, Sexology and the Marketing of Sexual Knowledge in Britain, c. 1918–70'. *Social History [London]* 29, no. 4 (2004): 465–84.

Cocks, Harry, and Matt Houlbrook, eds. *Palgrave Advances in the Modern History of Sexuality, Palgrave Advances*. Basingstoke and New York: Palgrave Macmillan, 2006.

Collini, Stefan. 'The Idea of "Character" in Victorian Political Thought'. *Transactions of the Royal Historical Society* 35 (1985): 29–50.

Collins, Marcus. *Modern Love: An Intimate History of Men and Women in Twentieth-Century Britain*. London: Atlantic Books, 2003.

ed. *The Permissive Society and Its Enemies: Sixties British Culture*. London: Rivers Oram, 2007.

Cominos, Peter T. 'Innocent Femina Sensualis in Unconscious Conflict'. *Suffer and Be Still: Women in the Victorian Age*, edited by Martha Vicinus, 155–72. Bloomington and Indianapolis: Indiana University Press, 1972.

Cook, Hera. 'The English Sexual Revolution: Technology and Social Change'. *History Workshop Journal* 59, no. 1 (2005): 109–28.

The Long Sexual Revolution: English Women, Sex, and Contraception 1800–1975. Oxford: Oxford University Press, 2004.

'Sexuality and Contraception in Modern England: Doing the History of Reproductive Sexuality'. *Journal of Social History* 40, no. 4 (2007): 915–32.

Coontz, Stephanie. *Marriage, a History: From Obedience to Intimacy, or How Love Conquered Marriage*. New York: Viking, 2005.

Costos, D., R. Ackerman and L. Paradis. 'Recollections of Menarche: Communication between Mothers and Daughters Regarding Menstruation'. *Sex Roles* 46, no. 1 (2002): 49–59.

Cowan, Ruth Schwartz. *More Work for Mother*. New York: Basic Books, 1983.

Cross, Gary S. *Worktowners at Blackpool: Mass-Observation and Popular Leisure in the 1930s*. London: Routledge, 1990.

Curtis, Bruce, and Alan Hunt. 'A Genealogy of the Genital Kiss: Oral Sex in the Twentieth Century'. *Canadian Journal of Human Sexuality* 15, no. 2 (2006): 69–84.

Daley, Caroline. '"He Would Know, but I Just Have a Feeling": Gender and Oral History'. *Women's History Review* 7, no. 3 (1998): 343–59.

Darby, Robert. 'The Masturbation Taboo and the Rise of Routine Male Circumcision: A Review of the Historiography'. *Journal of Social History* 36, no. 3 (2003): 737–57.

Dare, O. O., and J. G. Cleland. 'Reliability and Validity of Survey Data on Sexual Behaviour'. *Health Transition Review* 4, no. 2 (1994): 93–111.

Daston, Lorraine, and Fernando Vidal, eds. *The Moral Authority of Nature*. London: University of Chicago Press, 2004.

Daunton, Martin. *Wealth and Welfare: An Economic and Social History of Britain, 1851–1951*. Oxford and New York: Oxford University Press, 2007.

Davenport-Hines, Richard. *Sex, Death and Punishment: Attitudes to Sex and Sexuality in Britain since the Renaissance*. London: Collins, 1990.

Davey, Claire. 'Birth Control in Britain During the Interwar Years: Evidence from the Stopes Correspondence'. *Journal of Family History* 13, no. 1 (1988): 329–45.

David, Paul A., and Warren C. Sanderson. 'Rudimentary Contraceptive Methods and the American Transition to Marital Fertility Control, 1855–1915'. In *Long Term Factors in American Economic Growth*, edited by Stanley L. Engerman and Robert E. Gallmen, 307–79. Chicago: University of Chicago Press, 1986.

Davidoff, Leonore, Megan Doolittle, Janet Fink and Katherine Holden. *The Family Story: Blood, Contract, and Intimacy, 1830–1960*. London: Longman, 1999.

Davidoff, Leonore, and Catherine Hall. *Family Fortunes: Men and Women of the English Middle Class, 1780–1850*. London: Hutchinson, 1987.

Davie, Grace. *Religion in Britain since 1945: Believing without Belonging*. Oxford and Cambridge, MA: Blackwell, 1994.

Davies, Andrew. *Leisure, Gender, and Poverty: Working-Class Culture in Salford and Manchester, 1900–1939*. Buckingham and Philadelphia, PA: Open University Press, 1992.

'Youth, Violence, and Courtship in Late-Victorian Birmingham: The Case of James Harper and Emily Pimm'. *The History of the Family* 11, no. 2 (2006): 107–20.

Davis, Angela. '"Oh No, Nothing, We Didn't Learn Anything": Sex Education and the Preparation of Girls for Motherhood, c.1930–70'. *History of Education* 37 (2008): 661–77.

Dawson, Graham. *Soldier Heroes: British Adventure, Empire and the Imagining of Masculinities*. London and New York: Routledge, 1994.

D'Cruze, Shani. *Crimes of Outrage: Sex, Violence and Working Women in Victorian and Edwardian England*. London: UCL Press, 1998.

ed. *Everyday Violence in Britain 1850–1950: Gender and Class*. Harlow: Longman, 2000.

De Burger, James E. *Marriage Today: Problems, Issues, and Alternatives*. Cambridge and New York: Schenkman Pub. Co. and J. Wiley, 1977.

Degler, Carl N. 'What Ought to Be and What Was: Women's Sexuality in the Nineteenth Century'. *The American Historical Review* (1974): 1467–90.

Delap, Lucy, Ben Griffin and Abigail Wills. *The Politics of Domestic Authority in Britain since 1800*. Basingstoke: Palgrave Macmillan, 2009.

Dennis, Norman, Fernando Henriques and Clifford Slaughter. *Coal Is Our Life: An Analysis of a Yorkshire Mining Community*. London and New York: Tavistock Publications, 1969.

Dixon, Jay. *The Romance Fiction of Mills & Boon 1909–1990s*. London: UCL Press, 1999.

Dorr, Lisa Lindquist. 'The Perils of the Back Seat: Date Rape, Race and Gender in 1950s America', *Gender & History* 20, no. 1 (2008): 27–47.

Douglas, Mary. *Purity and Danger; an Analysis of Concepts of Pollution and Taboo*. New York: Praeger, 1966.

Drower, Jill. *Good Clean Fun: The Story of Britain's First Holiday Camp*. London: Arcadia Books, 1982.

Duncombe, Jean, and Dennis Marsden. 'Love and Intimacy: The Gender Division of Emotion and "Emotion Work": A Neglected Aspect of Sociological Discussion of Heterosexual Relationships'. *Sociology* 27, no. 2 (1993): 221–41.

Dworkin, Dennis L. *Class Struggles*. Harlow and New York: Pearson Longman, 2007.

Dyhouse, Carol. *Glamour: Women, History, Feminism*. London: Zed Books, 2010.

'Working-Class Mothers and Infant Mortality in England, 1895–1914'. *Journal of Social History* 12, no. 2 (1978): 248–67.

Elias, Norbert. *The Civilizing Process*. Transl. Edmund Jephcott, revised edition, edited by Eric Dunning, Johan Goudsblom and Stephen Mennell. Oxford: Blackwell, 2000 (first published in German 1939).

Elliott, B. Jane. 'Demographic Trends in Domestic Life, 1945–87'. In *Marriage, Domestic Life and Social Change: Writings for Jacqueline Burgoyne (1944–88)*, edited by David Clark, 85–108. London: Routledge, 1991.

England, L. R. 'Little Kinsey: An Outline of Sex Attitudes in Britain'. *Public Opinion Quarterly* 13, no. 4 (1950): 587–600.

Ericksen, Julia A., and Sally A. Steffen. *Kiss and Tell: Surveying Sex in the Twentieth Century*. Cambridge, MA: Harvard University Press, 1999.

Eyles, Leonora. *Commonsense About Sex*. London: Victor Gollancz, 1933.

The Woman in the Little House. London: G. Richards Ltd, 1922.

Farrell, Christine. *My Mother Said...: The Way Young People Learned about Sex and Birth Control*. London: Routledge & Kegan Paul, 1978.

Faulkner, Evelyn. '"Powerless to Prevent Him": Attitudes of Married Working-Class Women in the 1920s and the Rise of Sexual Power'. *Local Population Studies* 49 (1992): 51–61.

Featherstone, Simon. 'The Mill Girl and the Cheeky Chappie: British Popular Comedy and Mass Culture in the Thirties'. *Critical Survey* 15, no. 2 (2003): 3–24.

Felski, Rita. *The Gender of Modernity*. Cambridge, MA: Harvard University Press, 1995.

Fenton, Kevin A., Anne M. Johnson, Sally McManus and Bob Erens. 'Measuring Sexual Behaviour: Methodological Challenges in Survey Research'. *British Medical Journal* 77, no. 2 (2001): 84–92.

Fields, Jill. *An Intimate Affair: Women, Lingerie, and Sexuality*. Berkeley: University of California Press, 2007.

Finch, Janet. '"It's Great to Have Some-One to Talk to": The Ethics and Politics of Interviewing Women'. In *Social Researching: Politics, Problems, Practice*, edited by C. Bell and H. Roberts, 70–87. London: Routledge & Kegan Paul, 1984.

Finch, Janet, and Penny Summerfield. 'Social Reconstruction and the Emergence of Companionate Marriage, 1945–59'. In *Marriage, Domestic Life and Social Change: Writings for Jacqueline Burgoyne (1944–88)*, edited by David Clark, 7–32. London: Routledge, 1991.

Fink, Janet, and Katherine Holden. 'Pictures from the Margins of Marriage: Representations of Spinsters and Single Mothers in the Mid-Victorian Novel, Inter-War Hollywood Melodrama and British Film of the 1950s and 1960s'. *Gender & History* 11, no. 2 (1999): 233–55.

Fisher, Kate. 'An Oral History of Birth Control Practice c. 1925–50: A Study of Oxford and South Wales'. D. Phil. thesis. Oxford: University of Oxford, 1998.

Birth Control, Sex and Marriage in Britain, 1918–1960. Oxford and New York: Oxford University Press, 2006.

'"Didn't Stop to Think I Just Didn't Want Another One": The Culture of Abortion in Interwar South Wales'. In *Sexual Cultures in Europe: Themes in Sexuality*, edited by Franz Eder, Lesley A. Hall and Gert Hekma, 213–32. Manchester: Manchester University Press, 1999.

'"She Was Quite Satisfied with the Arrangements I Made": Gender and Birth Control in Britain 1920–1950'. *Past & Present* 169, no. 1 (2001): 161–93.

'Uncertain Aims and Tacit Negotiation: Birth Control Practices in Britain, 1925–50'. *Population and Development Review* 26, no. 2 (2000): 295–317.

'Women's Experiences of Abortion before the 1967 Act'. In *Abortion Law and Politics Today*, edited by Ellie Lee, 27–42. Basingstoke: Macmillan Press, 1998.

Fisher, Kate, and Simon Szreter. '"They Prefer Withdrawal": The Choice of Birth Control in Britain, 1918–1950'. *Journal of Interdisciplinary History* 34, no. 2 (2003): 263–91.

Fisher, Tim. 'Fatherhood and the British Fathercraft Movement 1919–39'. *Gender & History* 17, no. 2 (2005): 441–62.

Fitzgerald, Mike, Gregor McLennan and Jennie Pawson, eds. *Crime and Society: Readings in History and Theory*. London: Routledge & Kegan Paul, 1981.

Florence, Lella Secor. *Birth Control on Trial*. London: George Allen & Unwin Ltd, 1930.

Foucault, Michel. *The History of Sexuality*, 3 volumes. Transl. by Robert Hurley. Harmondsworth: Penguin, 1990 (first published in French 1976, 1984).

Fowler, David. *The First Teenagers: The Lifestyle of Young Wage-Earners in Interwar Britain*. London: Woburn, 1995.

Francis, Martin. 'The Domestication of the Male? Recent Research on Nineteenth- and Twentieth-Century British Masculinity'. *The Historical Journal* 45, no. 3 (2002): 637–52.

Frost, Ginger. '"The Black Lamb of the Black Sheep": Illegitimacy in the English Working Class, 1850–1939'. *Journal of Social History* 37, no. 2 (2003): 293–322.

Fryer, Peter. *The Birth Controllers*. London: Secker & Warburg, 1965.

Fussell, Paul. *The Great War and Modern Memory*. New York: Oxford University Press, 1975.

Gagnier, Regenia *Subjectivities: A History of Self-Representation in Britain, 1832–1920*. New York and Oxford: Oxford University Press, 1991.

Gagnon, John H. *An Interpretation of Desire: Essays in the Study of Sexuality, Worlds of Desire*. Chicago and London: University of Chicago Press, 2004.

Gallagher, Catherine, and Thomas Laqueur, eds. *The Making of the Modern Body: Sexuality and Society in the Nineteenth Century*. Berkeley: University of California Press, 1987.

Gallichan, Walter M. *A Textbook of Sex Education for Parents and Teachers*. London: Laurie, 1919.

Gardiner, Juliet. *The Thirties: An Intimate History*. London: Harper Press, 2010.

Garrett, Eilidh, Alice Reid, Kevin Shurer and Simon Szreter. *Changing Family Size in England and Wales: Place, Class, and Demography, 1891–1911*. Cambridge and New York: Cambridge University Press, 2001.

Garton, Stephen. *Histories of Sexuality*. New York: Routledge, 2004.

Gatrell, Caroline. 'Interviewing Fathers: Feminist Dilemmas in Fieldwork'. *Journal of Gender Studies* 15, no. 3 (2006): 237–51.

Gavey, Nicola, Kathryn McPhillips and Virginia Braun. 'Interruptus Coitus: Heterosexuals Accounting for Intercourse'. *Sexualities* 2, no. 1 (1999): 35–68.

Geppert, Alexander C.T. 'Divine Sex, Happy Marriage, Regenerated Nation: Marie Stopes's Marital Manual *Married Love* and the Making of a Best-Seller, 1918–1955'. *Journal of the History of Sexuality* 8, no. 3 (1998): 389–433.

Giddens, Anthony. *The Transformation of Intimacy: Sexuality, Love and Eroticism in Modern Societies*. Cambridge: Polity Press, 1992.

Giles, Judy. *The Parlour and the Suburb: Domestic Identities, Class, Femininity and Modernity*. Oxford: Berg, 2004.

'"Playing Hard to Get": Working-Class Women, Sexuality and Respectability in Britain, 1918–40'. *Women's History Review* 1, no. 2 (1992): 239–55.

Women, Identity, and Private Life in Britain, 1900–50. New York: St. Martin's Press, 1995.

'"You Meet 'Em and That's It": Working Class Women's Refusal of Romance between the Wars in Britain'. In *Romance Revisited*, edited by Lynne Pearce and Jackie Stacey, 279–92. London: Lawrence & Wishart, 1995.

Gillis, John R. *For Better, for Worse: British Marriages, 1600 to the Present*. New York: Oxford University Press, 1985.

A World of Their Own Making: Myth, Ritual, and the Quest for Family Values. New York: Basic Books, 1996.

Gittins, Diana. *Fair Sex: Family Size and Structure, 1900–39*. London: Hutchinson, 1982.

'Women's Work and Family Size between the Wars'. *Oral History* 5, no. 2 (1977): 84–100.

Goldsmid, J.A. *Companionate Marriage: From the Medical and Social Aspects*. London: William Heinemann, 1934.

Gorer, Geoffrey. *Exploring English Character*. London: Cresset Press, 1955.

Sex and Marriage in England Today: Study of the Views and Experience of the under-45s. London: Nelson, 1971.

Graves, Robert, and Alan Hodge. *The Long Weekend: A Social History of Great Britain 1918–1939*. London: McDonald & Co., 1991; first published 1940.

Gray, Arthur Herbert. *Sex Teaching, Every Teacher's Library*. London: The National Sunday School Union, 1930.

Green, T.L. 'Sex Education and Social Biology'. *Health Education Journal* 3 (1945): 39–44.

Griffin, Ben. 'Class, Gender and Liberalism in Parliament 1868–1882: The Case of the Married Women's Property Acts'. *The Historical Journal* 46, no. 1 (2003): 59–87.

Griffin, Ben, Lucy DeLap and Abigail Wills. 'Introduction: The Politics of Domestic Authority in Britain since 1800'. In *The Politics of Domestic Authority in Britain since 1800* edited by Lucy DeLap, Ben Griffin and Abigail Wills, 1–24. Basingstoke: Palgrave Macmillan, 2009.

Griffith, Edward F. *Modern Marriage and Birth Control*. London: Victor Gollancz, 1942 (first published 1935).

Groebner, Valentin. '*Complexio*/Complexion: Categorizing Individual Natures 1250–1600'. Ch. 14 in *The Moral Authority of Nature*, edited by Lorraine Daston and Fernando Vidal, 361–83. London: University of Chicago Press, 2004.

Gurney, Peter. 'Intersex and Dirty Girls: Mass-Observation and Working Class Sexuality in England in the 1930s'. *Journal of the History of Sexuality* 8, no. 2 (1997): 256–90.

Haag, Pamela S. 'In Search of "The Real Thing": Ideologies of Love, Modern Romance, and Women's Sexual Subjectivity in the United States, 1920–40'. *Journal of the History of Sexuality* 2, no. 4 (1992): 547–77.

Haines, Michael R. *Fertility and Occupation: Population Patterns in Industrialization*. New York: Academic Press, 1979.

Hajnal, John. 'The Marriage Boom'. *Population Index* 19, no. 2 (1953): 80–101.

Hall, Lesley A. 'Birds, Bees and General Embarrassment: Sex Education in Britain, from Social Purity to Section 28'. In *Public or Private Education?: Lessons from History*, edited by Richard Aldrich, 98–115. London: Woburn Press, 2004.

'Forbidden by God, Despised by Men: Masturbation, Medical Warnings, Moral Panic, and Manhood in Great Britain, 1850–1950'. *Journal of the History of Sexuality* 2, no. 3 (1992): 365–87.

Hidden Anxieties: Male Sexuality, 1900–1950. Cambridge: Polity, 1991.

'Impotent Ghosts from No Man's Land, Flappers' Boyfriends, or Crypto-Patriarchs? Men, Sex and Social Change in 1920s Britain'. *Social History* 21, no. 1 (1996): 54–70.

Outspoken Women: An Anthology of Women's Writing on Sex, 1870–1969, Women's and Gender History. London and New York: Routledge, 2005.

'Review of Hera Cook, *The Long Sexual Revolution: English Women, Sex, and Contraception 1800–1975*'. *Continuity and Change* 19, no. 2 (2004): 331–2.

Sex, Gender and Social Change in Britain since 1880. Basingstoke: Macmillan, 2000.

Hall, Ruth E., ed. *Dear Dr. Stopes: Sex in the 1920s*. London: Deutsch, 1978.

Halsey, Alfred H. *Change in British Society*. 4th edn. Oxford and New York: Oxford University Press, 1995.

Trends in British Society since 1900: A Guide to the Changing Social Structure of Britain. London and New York: Macmillan and St. Martin's Press, 1972.

Hammerton, A. James. *Cruelty and Companionship: Conflict in Nineteenth-Century Married Life*. London: Routledge, 1992.

'Pooterism or Partnership? Marriage and Masculine Identity in the Lower Middle Class, 1870–1920'. *The Journal of British Studies* 38 (1999): 291–321.

Hammill, Faye. *Women, Celebrity, and Literary Culture Between the Wars*. Austin: University of Texas Press, 2007.

Hampshire, James, and Jane Lewis. '"The Ravages of Permissiveness": Sex Education and the Permissive Society'. *Twentieth Century British History* 15, no. 3 (2004): 290–312.

Hardy, Anne. *The Epidemic Streets: Infectious Disease and the Rise of Preventive Medicine, 1856–1900*. Oxford: Oxford University Press, 1993.

Hardy, Anne, and Simon Szreter. 'Urban Fertility and Mortality Patterns'. In *The Cambridge Urban History of Britain*, edited by Martin J. Daunton, 629–72. Cambridge: Cambridge University Press, 2000.

Harris, Bernard. *The Health of the Schoolchild: A History of the School Medical Service in England and Wales, 1908–74*. Buckingham and Philadelphia, PA: Open University Press, 1995.

Harrison, Brian. *Drink and the Victorians: The Temperance Question in England, 1815–1872*. Keele: Keele University Press, 1994.

'The Public and the Private in Modern Britain'. Ch. 19 in *Civil Histories: Essays Presented to Sir Keith Thomas*, edited by Peter Burke, Brian Harrison and Paul Slack, 337–57. Oxford: Oxford University Press, 2000.

Hawkes, Gail. 'Liberalizing Sexuality?' In *The Sociology of the Family: A Reader*, edited by Graham A. Allan, 35–55. Oxford and Malden, MA: Blackwell, 1999.

Hazleden, Rebecca. 'The Pathology of Love in Contemporary Relationship Manuals'. *The Sociological Review* 52, no. 2 (2004): 201–17.

Heiss, Jerold S. 'Variations in Courtship Progress among High School Students'. *Marriage and Family Living* 22, no. 2 (1960): 165–70.

Herzog, Dagmar. 'Sexuality in the Postwar West'. *Journal of Modern History* 78 (2006): 144–71.

Heward, Christopher. *The Hidden Consumer: Masculinities, Fashion and City Life 1860–1914*. Manchester: Manchester University Press, 1996.

Higgs, E. 'Domestic Service and Household Production'. In *Unequal Opportunities: Women's Employment in England 1800–1918*, edited by A. V. John, 125–50. Oxford: Basil Blackwell, 1986.

Higgins, Natalie. 'The Changing Expectations and Realities of Marriage in the English Working Class, 1920–1960'. Unpublished Ph.D. thesis; Cambridge: University of Cambridge, 2003.

Higonnet, Margaret R., and Jane Jenson, eds. *Behind the Lines: Gender and the Two World Wars*. New Haven: Yale University Press, 1989.

Hilton, Matthew. *Consumerism in Twentieth-Century Britain: The Search for a Historical Movement*. Cambridge: Cambridge University Press, 2003.

Himes, Norman E., and Vera C. Himes. 'Birth Control for the British Working Classes: A Study of the First Thousand Cases to Visit an English Birth Control Clinic'. *Hospital Social Service* 19 (1929): 578–617.

Hirsch, Jennifer S. *A Courtship after Marriage: Sexuality and Love in Mexican Transnational Families*. Berkeley: University of California Press, 2003.

Hirsch, Jennifer S., and Holly Wardlow, eds. *Modern Loves: The Anthropology of Romantic Courtship and Companionate Marriage*. Ann Arbor: University of Michigan Press, 2006.

Hoggart, Lesley. 'The Campaign for Birth Control in Britain in the 1920s'. In *Gender, Health and Welfare*, edited by Anne Digby and John Stewart, 143–66. London and New York: Routledge, 1998.

Hoggart, Richard. *The Uses of Literacy*. London: Chatto & Windus, 1957.

Holden, Katherine. '"Nature Takes No Notice of Morality": Singleness and Married Love in Interwar Britain'. *Women's History Review* 11, no. 3 (2002): 481–504.

The Shadow of Marriage: Singleness in England, 1914–60. Manchester and New York: Manchester University Press and Palgrave, 2007.

Holmes, Ann Sumner. '"Fallen Mothers": Maternal Adultery and Child Custody in England, 1886–1925'. Ch. 3 in *Maternal Instincts: Visions of Motherhood and Sexuality in Britain, 1875–1925*, edited by Claudia Nelson and Ann Sumner Holmes, 37–57. London: Macmillan, 1997.

Holtzman, Ellen M. 'The Pursuit of Married Love: Women's Attitudes toward Sexuality and Marriage in Great Britain, 1918–1939'. *Journal of Social History* 16, no. 2 (1982): 39–51.

Horn, P. *The Rise and Fall of the Victorian Servant*. Dublin: Gill and Macmillan, 1975.

Horwood, Catherine. '"Girls who Arouse Dangerous Passions": Women and Bathing 1900–1939'. *Women's History Review* 9, no. 4 (2000): 653–72.

Houlbrook, Matt. '"Lady Austin's Camp Boys": Constituting the Queer Subject in 1930s London'. *Gender & History* 14, no. 1 (2002): 31–61.

Queer London: Perils and Pleasures in the Sexual Metropolis, 1918–1957. Chicago: University of Chicago Press, 2005.

'Sexing the History of Sexuality'. *History Workshop Journal* 60, no. 1 (2005): 216–22.

Hoy, Suellen M. *Chasing Dirt: The American Pursuit of Cleanliness*. New York: Oxford University Press, 1995.

Humble, Nicola. *The Feminine Middlebrow Novel, 1920s to 1950s: Class, Domesticity, and Bohemianism*. Oxford and New York: Oxford University Press, 2001.

Humphries, Steve. *A Secret World of Sex: Forbidden Fruit, the British Experience 1900–1950*. London: Sidgwick & Jackson, 1988.

'Married Love: Sex on Demand' [VHS videocassette; 60 min.]. London: Testimony Films for Channel 4, 2002.

Humphries, Steve, and Pamela Gordon. *A Man's World: From Boyhood to Manhood 1900–1960*. London: BBC Books, 1996.

Labour of Love: Experience of Parenthood in Britain, 1900–50. London: Sidgwick & Jackson, 1993.

Hunt, Alan. 'The Great Masturbation Panic and the Discourses of Moral Regulation in Nineteenth- and Early Twentieth-Century Britain'. *Journal of the History of Sexuality* 8, no. 4 (1998): 575–615.

Jackson, Louise A. '"The Coffee Club Menace": Policing Youth, Leisure and Sexuality in Post-War Manchester'. *Cultural and Social History* 5, no. 3 (2008): 289–308.

Jackson, Margaret. *The Real Facts of Life: Feminism and the Politics of Sexuality, 1850–1940*. London and Bristol, PA: Taylor & Francis, 1994.

Jackson, Stevi, and Sue Scott. 'Gut Reactions to Matters of the Heart: Reflections on Rationality, Irrationality and Sexuality'. *The Sociological Review* 45, no. 4 (1997): 551–75.

Jacobs Brumberg, J. '"Something Happens to Girls": Menarche and the Emergence of the Modern American Hygienic Imperative'. *Journal of the History of Sexuality* 4, no. 1 (1993): 99–127.

Jamieson, Lynn. *Intimacy: Personal Relationships in Modern Societies*. Cambridge and Malden, MA: Polity Press, 1998.

'Intimacy Transformed? A Critical Look at the "Pure Relationship"'. *Sociology* 33, no. 3 (1999): 477–94.

Jeffreys, Sheila. *Anticlimax: Feminist Perspective on the Sexual Revolution*. London: Women's Press, 1990.

Jephcott, Agnes Pearl. *Girls Growing Up*. London: Faber and Faber, 1942.

Rising Twenty: Notes on Some Ordinary Girls. London: Faber and Faber, 1948.

John, Angela V. *Unequal Opportunities: Women's Employment in England 1800–1918*. Oxford: Basil Blackwell, 1986.

Johnson, Paul, ed. *Twentieth-Century Britain: Economic, Social, and Cultural Change*. London and New York: Longman, 1994.

Johnson, Weldon T., and John D. Delamater. 'Response Effects in Sex Surveys'. *Public Opinion Quarterly* 40, no. 2 (1976): 165–181.

Jones, Geoffrey. 'Blonde and Blue-Eyed? Globalizing Beauty, c.1945–c.1980'. *Economic History Review* 61, no. 1 (2008): 125–54.

Joyce, Patrick. *Visions of the People: Industrial England and the Question of Class, 1848–1914*. Cambridge and New York: Cambridge University Press, 1991.

Work, Society and Politics: The Culture of the Factory in Later Victorian England. Brighton: Harvester Press, 1980.

Katz, Jonathan Ned. *The Invention of Heterosexuality*. New York: Dutton Books, 1995.

Kent, Susan Kingsley. *Sex and Suffrage in Britain, 1860–1914*. Princeton: Princeton University Press, 1987.

Kern, Stephen. *The Culture of Love: Victorians to Moderns*. London: Harvard University Press, 1992.

'When Did the Victorian Period End? Relativity, Sexuality, Narrative'. *Journal of Victorian Culture* 11, no. 2 (2006): 326–38.

Kerr, Madeline. *The People of Ship Street*. London: Routledge, 1958.

Kiernan, Kathleen. 'The Family: Formation and Fission'. In *The Changing Population of Britain*, edited by Heather Joshi, 27–41. Oxford: Basil Blackwell, 1989.

Klein, Joanne. 'Irregular Marriages: Unorthodox Working-Class Domestic Life in Liverpool, Birmingham, and Manchester, 1900–1939'. *Journal of Family History* 30, no. 2 (2005): 210–29.

Klein, Josephine. *Samples from English Cultures*. London: Routledge & Kegan Paul, 1965.

Kleinplatz, Peggy J. *New Directions in Sex Therapy: Innovations and Alternatives*. Philadelphia, PA and Hove: Brunner-Routledge and Accelerated Development, 2001.

Kling, Sophia. '"I Think I'd Rather Die Than Go through with a Pregnancy Again": Experiences of Childbearing and Birth Control in Sweden in the 1930s'. In *Gendering the Fertility Decline in the Western World*, edited by Angélique Janssens, 177–203. Bern: Peter Lang, 2007.

Klingender, F. D. *The Condition of Clerical Labour in Britain*. London: M. Lawrence Ltd, 1935.

Kuhn, Annette. *Cinema, Censorship and Sexuality, 1909–1925, Cinema and Society*. London: Routledge, 1988.

An Everyday Magic: Cinema and Cultural Memory. London: I. B. Tauris, 2002.

Kynaston, David. *Family Britain 1951–57*. London: Bloomsbury, 2009.

Laipson, Peter. '"Kiss without Shame, for She Desires It": Sexual Foreplay in American Marital Advice Literature, 1900–1925'. *Journal of Social History* 29, no. 3 (1996): 507–25.

Lambertz, Jan. 'Sexual Harassment in the Nineteenth Century English Cotton Industry'. *History Workshop Journal* 19, no. 1 (1985): 29–61.

Langford, Christopher M. 'Birth Control Practice in Great Britain: A Review of the Evidence from Cross-Sectional Surveys'. In Mike Murphy and John Hobcraft, eds. *Population Research in Britain*, Special Supplement to *Population Studies* 45, no. 1 (1991): 49–68.

Langford, Wendy. *Revolutions of the Heart: Gender, Power, and the Delusions of Love*. London and New York: Routledge, 1999.

Langhamer, Claire. 'Adultery in Post-War England'. *History Workshop Journal* 62, no. 1 (2006): 86–115.

'Love and Courtship in Mid-Twentieth-Century England'. *The Historical Journal* 50, no. 1 (2007): 173–96.

'The Meanings of Home in Postwar Britain'. *Journal of Contemporary History* 40, no. 2 (2005): 341–62.

Women's Leisure in England, 1920–60. Manchester and New York: Manchester University Press, 2000.

Laqueur, Thomas. *Making Sex: Body and Gender from the Greeks to Freud*. Cambridge, MA: Harvard University Press, 1990.

Laslett, B., and R. Rapoport. 'Collaborative Interviewing and Interactive Research'. *Journal of Marriage and the Family* 37, no. 4 (1975): 968–77.

Laslett, Peter. *Family Life and Illicit Love in Earlier Generations: Essays in Historical Sociology*. Cambridge: Cambridge University Press, 1977.

'Introduction, Comparing Illegitimacy over Time and between Cultures'. In *Bastardy and its Comparative History*, edited by Peter Laslett, Karla Oosterveen and Richard Michael Smith, 1–64. Cambridge, MA: Harvard University Press, 1980.

Laslett, Peter, Karla Oosterveen and Richard Michael Smith, eds. *Bastardy and Its Comparative History: Studies in the History of Illegitimacy and Marital Nonconformism in Britain, France, Germany, Sweden, the United States, Jamaica, and Japan*. Cambridge, MA: Harvard University Press, 1980.

Law, Cheryl. *Suffrage and Power: The Women's Movement, 1918–28*. London: I. B. Tauris, 1997.

Lawrence, Jon. 'The British Sense of Class'. *Journal of Contemporary History* 35, no. 2 (2000): 307–18.

Leap, Nicky, and Billie Hunter. *The Midwife's Tale: An Oral History from Handywoman to Professional Midwife*. London: Scarlet Press, 1993.

Leathard, Audrey. *The Fight for Family Planning: The Development of Family Planning Services in Britain, 1921–74*. London: Macmillan, 1980.

Lee, C. H. 'Regions and Industries in Britain'. Ch. 3 in *Twentieth-Century Britain: Economic, Social, and Cultural Change*, edited by Paul Johnson, 38–56. London and New York: Longman, 1994.

Lee, Raymond M. *Doing Research on Sensitive Topics*. London: Sage Publications, 1993.

Lees, Lynn Hollen. *The Solidarities of Strangers: The English Poor Laws and the People, 1700–1948*. Cambridge and New York: Cambridge University Press, 1998.

Lees, Sue. *Sugar and Spice: Sexuality and Adolescent Girls*. London: Penguin, 1993.

Levine, David. *Reproducing Families: The Political Economy of English Population History*. Cambridge: Cambridge University Press, 1987.

Lewis, Jane. *The End of Marriage?: Individualism and Intimate Relations*. Cheltenham: Edward Elgar, 2001.

'The Ideology and Politics of Birth Control in Inter-War England'. *Women's Studies International Quarterly* 2, no. 1 (1979): 33–48.

The Politics of Motherhood: Child and Maternal Welfare in England, 1900–1939. London and Montreal: Croom Helm and McGill-Queen's University Press, 1980.

'Public Institution and Private Relationship: Marriage and Marriage Guidance, 1920–1968'. *Twentieth Century British History* 1, no. 3 (1990): 233–63.

'Women and Late-Nineteenth Century Social Work'. In *Regulating Womanhood: Historical Essays on Marriage, Motherhood, and Sexuality*, edited by Carol Smart, 78–99. London and New York: Routledge, 1992.

Women in England 1870–1950. Brighton: Harvester, 1984.

Lewis, Jane, and Kathleen Kiernan. 'The Boundaries between Marriage, Nonmarriage, and Parenthood: Changes in Behavior and Policy in Postwar Britain'. *Journal of Family History* 21, no. 3 (1996): 372–87.

Lewontin, Richard C. 'Sex, Lies, and Social Science'. *New York Review of Books* 42, no. 7 (1995): 24–9.

Light, Alison. *Forever England: Femininity, Literature and Conservatism between the Wars*. London: Routledge, 1991.

Lindsey, Ben B., and Wainwright Evans. *The Companionate Marriage*. New York: Boni & Liveright, 1927.

Livesey, Ruth. *Socialism, Sex, and the Culture of Aestheticism in Britain, 1880–1914*. Oxford and New York: Oxford University Press, 2007.

Lloyd, Jennifer M. 'Conflicting Expectations in Nineteenth Century British Matrimony: The Failed Companionate Marriage of Effie Gray and John Ruskin'. *Journal of Women's History* 11, no. 2 (1999): 86–109.

Lockwood, David. *The Blackcoated Worker: A Study in Class Consciousness*. London: Allen & Unwin, 1958.

Lowe, Rodney. *The Welfare State in Britain since 1945*. 3rd edn. Basingstoke: Palgrave Macmillan, 2005.

Lynch, Katherine A. 'Theoretical and Analytical Approaches to Religious Beliefs, Values, and Identities During the Modern Fertility Transition'. In *Religion and the Decline of Fertility in the Western World*, edited by Renzo Derosas and Franz Van Poppel, 21–39. Dordrecht: Springer, 2006.

Mahood, Linda, and Barbara Littlewood. 'The "Vicious" Girl and The "Street-Corner" Boy: Sexuality and the Gendered Delinquent in the Scottish Child-Saving Movement, 1850–1940'. *Journal of the History of Sexuality* 4, no. 4 (1994): 549–77.

Malleson, Joan. *Any Wife or Any Husband: A Book for Couples Who Have Met Sexual Difficulties and for Doctors*. Harmondsworth: Penguin, 1962.

Marsh, David. *The Changing Social Structure of England and Wales, 1871–1961*. London: Routledge & Kegan Paul, 1965.

Martin, Emily. *The Woman in the Body*. Milton Keynes: Open University Press, 1993.

Marwick, Arthur. *The Sixties: Cultural Revolution in Britain, France, Italy, and the United States, c.1958–c.1974*. Oxford: Oxford University Press, 1998.

Mason, Michael. *The Making of Victorian Sexuality*. Oxford and New York: Oxford University Press, 1994.

Mass Observation Archive at the University of Sussex File Reports, 2495 'The State of Matrimony', June 1947.

3110 'General Attitudes to Sex', April 1949.

3150, 'Teenage Girls', August 1949.

Matthews, Jill Julius. 'Building the Body Beautiful'. *Australian Feminist Studies* 5, no. 1 (1987): 17–34.

'They Had Such a Lot of Fun: The Women's League of Health and Beauty between the Wars'. *History Workshop Journal* 30, no. 1 (1990): 22–54.

McConnachie, James. *The Book of Love: The Story of the Kamasutra*. New York: Metropolitan Books, 2008.

McGregor, Oliver Ross. *Divorce in England: A Centenary Study*. London: Heinemann, 1957.

McKeon, Michael. *The Secret History of Domesticity: Public, Private and the Division of Knowledge*. Baltimore: Johns Hopkins University Press, 2005.

McKibbin, Ross. *Classes and Cultures: England, 1918–1951*. Oxford: Oxford University Press, 1998.

McLaren, Angus. *A History of Contraception: From Antiquity to the Present Day*. Oxford and Cambridge, MA: B. Blackwell, 1990.

Impotence: A Cultural History. London: University of Chicago Press, 2007.

Twentieth-Century Sexuality: A History. Oxford: Blackwell, 1999.

McLeod, Hugh. *Religious Crisis of the 1960s*. New York: Oxford University Press, 2007.

Melman, Billie. *Women and the Popular Imagination in the Twenties: Flappers and Nymphs*. Basingstoke: Macmillan Press, 1988.

Mogey, John M. *Family and Neighbourhood: Two Studies in Oxford*. London: Oxford University Press, 1956.

Moore, Francesa P. L. 'Beyond the Ideal: Motherhood in Industrial Lancashire, 1860–1937'. Unpublished Ph.D. thesis; Cambridge: University of Cambridge, 2008.

Morgan, David. 'Ideologies of Marriage and Family Life'. In *Marriage, Domestic Life, and Social Change: Writings for Jacqueline Burgoyne (1944–88)*, edited by David Clark, 114–38. London: Routledge, 1991.

Morgan, Rosemarie. *Women and Sexuality in the Novels of Thomas Hardy*. London and New York: Routledge, 1988.

Morris, Robert J. 'Clubs, Societies and Associations'. In *The Cambridge Social History of Britain, 1750–1950*, edited by F. M. L. Thompson, 395–443. Cambridge and New York: Cambridge University Press, 1990.

Mort, Frank. *Capital Affairs: The Making of the Permissive Society*. London: Yale University Press, 2010.

Cultures of Consumption: Commerce, Masculinities and Social Space in Late Twentieth-Century Britain. London: Routledge, 1996.

Dangerous Sexualities: Medico-Moral Politics in England since 1830. London and New York: Routledge, 2000.

Moser, Claus Adolph, and Graham Kalton. *Survey Methods in Social Investigation*. New York: Basic Books, 1972.

Nelson, Claudia. '"Under the Guidance of a Wise Mother": British Sex Education at the Fin de Siecle'. Ch. 6 in *Maternal Instincts: Visions of Motherhood and Sexuality in Britain, 1875–1925*, edited by Claudia Nelson and Ann Sumner Holmes, 98–121. London: Macmillan, 1997.

Neuhaus, Jessamyn. 'The Importance of Being Orgasmic: Sexuality, Gender, and Marital Sex Manuals in the United States, 1920–1963'. *Journal of the History of Sexuality* 9, no. 4 (2000): 447–73.

Newcombe, Suzanne. 'A Social History of Yoga and Ayurveda in Britain, 1950–1995'. Unpublished Ph.D. thesis; Cambridge: University of Cambridge, 2007.

Nott, James J. *Music for the People: Popular Music and Dance in Interwar Britain*. Oxford: Oxford University Press, 2002.

Nye, Robert, 'Introduction'. In *Sexuality*, edited by R. Nye, 3–15. Oxford: Oxford University Press, 1999.

O'Connell, Sean. 'Motoring and Modernity'. In *Twentieth-Century Britain: Economic, Cultural and Social Change*, edited by Francesca Carnevali, Paul Johnson and Julie-Marie Strange, 111–26. London: Longman, 2007.

Offer, Avner. *The Challenge of Affluence: Self-Control and Well-Being in the United States and Britain since 1950*. Oxford and New York: Oxford University Press, 2006.

Oram, Alison. 'Repressed and Thwarted, or Bearer of the New World? The Spinster in Inter-War Feminist Discourses'. *Women's History Review* 1, no. 3 (1992): 413–33.

Packer, E.L. 'Aspects of Working-Class Marriage'. *Pilot Papers: Social Essays and Documents* 2, no. 1 (1947): 92–104.

Padfield, Maureen, and Ian Procter. 'The Effect of Interviewer's Gender on the Interviewing Process: A Comparative Enquiry'. *Sociology* 30, no. 2 (1996): 355–66.

Parker, Richard G., and John H. Gagnon, eds. *Conceiving Sexuality: Approaches to Sex Research in a Postmodern World*. New York and London: Routledge, 1995.

Parratt, Catriona M. *More Than Mere Amusement: Working-Class Women's Leisure in England, 1750–1914*. Boston: Northeastern University Press, 2001.

Peel, John. 'The Manufacture and Retailing of Contraceptives in England'. *Population Studies* (1963): 113–25.

Peiss, Kathy. 'Making Up, Making Over: Cosmetics, Consumer Culture, and Women's Identity'. Ch. 10 in *The Sex of Things: Gender and Consumption in Historical Perspective*, edited by Victoria Grazia with Ellen Furlough, 311–36. London: University of California Press, 1996.

Phillips, Roderick. *Untying the Knot: A Short History of Divorce*. Cambridge: Cambridge University Press, 1991.

Pilcher, Jane. 'Body Work: Childhood, Gender and School Health Education in England, 1870–1977'. *Childhood* 14, no. 2 (2007): 215–33.

'School Sex Education: Policy and Practice in England 1870 to 2000'. *Sex Education* 5, no. 2 (2005): 153–70.

Pini, Barbara. 'Interviewing Men: Gender and the Collection and Interpretation of Qualitative Data'. *Journal of Sociology* 41, no. 2 (2005): 201–16.

Polhemus, Ted, ed. *Social Aspects of the Human Body*. Harmondsworth: Penguin, 1978.

Pollock, Linda. *A Lasting Relationship: Parents and Children over Three Centuries*. London: Fourth Estate Ltd, 1987.

Pooley, Sian. 'Parenthood and Child-rearing in England, c.1860–1910'. Unpublished Ph.D. thesis; Cambridge: University of Cambridge, 2009.

Porter, Roy, and Lesley A. Hall. *The Facts of Life: The Creation of Sexual Knowledge in Britain, 1650–1950*. New Haven: Yale University Press, 1995.

Prochaska, Frank K. *Women and Philanthropy in Nineteenth-Century England*. Oxford and New York: Clarendon Press and Oxford University Press, 1980.

Pugh, Martin. *We Danced All Night: A Social History of Britain Between the Wars*. London: The Bodley Head, 2008.

Rapp, Dean. 'The Early Discovery of Freud by the British General Educated Public, 1912–1919'. *Social History of Medicine* 3, no. 2 (1990): 217–43.

Reay, Barry. *Microhistories: Demography, Society and Culture in Rural England, 1800–1930*. Cambridge: Cambridge University Press, 1996.

Reibstein, Janet, and Martin Richards. *Sexual Arrangements: Marriage and Affairs*. London: Heinemann, 1992.

Reiss, Ira L. 'The Scaling of Premarital Sexual Permissiveness'. *Journal of Marriage and the Family* 26, no. 2 (1964): 188–98.

Richards, Jeffrey. 'Cinemagoing in Worktown: Regional Film Audiences in 1930s Britain'. *Historical Journal of Film, Radio and Television* 14, no. 2 (1994): 147–66.

Films and British National Identity: From Dickens to Dad's Army. Manchester and New York: Manchester University Press, 1997.

The Age of the Dream Palace: Cinema and Society in 1930s Britain. London: I. B. Tauris, 2010.

Richards, Martin P. M., and B. Jane Elliott. 'Sex and Marriage in the 1960s and 1970s'. In *Marriage, Domestic Life and Social Change: Writings for Jacqueline Burgoyne (1944–88)*, edited by David Clark, 33–54. London: Routledge, 1991.

Richardson, Angélique. *Love and Eugenics in the Late Nineteenth Century: Rational Reproduction and the New Woman*. Oxford and New York: Oxford University Press, 2003.

Riesman, David. 'Review: *English Life and Leisure: A Social Study* by B. Seebohm Rowntree and G. R. Lavers'. *The American Journal of Sociology* 57, no. 6 (1952): 600–2.

Riley, Denise. *War in the Nursery: Theories of the Child and Mother*. London: Virago, 1983.

Roberts, Elizabeth. *A Woman's Place: An Oral History of Working-Class Women 1890–1940*. Oxford: Blackwell, 1984.

Women and Families: An Oral History, 1940–1970. Oxford and Cambridge, MA: Blackwell, 1995.

Roffman, Deborah. 'The Power of Language: Baseball as a Sexual Metaphor in American Culture'. *SIECUS Report* 19, no. 5 (1991): 1–6.

Roper, Michael. 'Re-Remembering the Soldier Hero: The Psychic and Social Construction of Memory in Personal Narratives of the Great War'. *History Workshop Journal* 50 (2000): 181–204.

Rose, Gillian. *Love's Work: A Reckoning with Life*. London: Chatto & Windus, 1995.

Rose, Jonathan. *Intellectual Life of the English Working Classes*. New Haven, CT: Yale University Press, 2001.

Rose, June. *Marie Stopes and the Sexual Revolution*. London and Boston: Faber and Faber, 1992.

Rose, Sonya O. *Limited Livelihoods: Gender and Class in Nineteenth-Century Britain*. London: Routledge, 1992.

'Respectable Men, Disorderly Others: The Language of Gender and the Lancashire Weavers' Strike of 1878 in Britain'. *Gender & History* 5, no. 3 (1993): 382–97.

Which People's War? National Identity and Citizenship in Britain, 1939–1945. Oxford and New York: Oxford University Press, 2003.

Rosenbloom, Nancy J. 'Between Reform and Regulation: The Struggle over Film Censorship in Progressive America, 1909–1922'. *Film History* 1, no. 4 (1987): 307–25.

Ross, Ellen. *Love and Toil: Motherhood in Outcast London, 1870–1918*. Oxford: Oxford University Press, 1993.

'"Not the Sort That Would Sit on the Doorstep": Respectability in Pre-World War I London'. *International Labour and Working-Class History* 27 (1985): 39–59.

Rosser, Colin, and C. C. Harris. *The Family and Social Change: A Study of Family and Kinship in a South Wales Town*. London and New York: Routledge & Kegan Paul and Humanities Press, 1965.

Rossi, Alice S., ed. *Sexuality across the Life Course*. Chicago and London: University of Chicago Press, 1994.

Rowbotham, Sheila. *A New World for Women: Stella Browne, Socialist Feminist*. London: Pluto Press, 1977.

'Revolt in Roundhay'. In *Truth, Dare or Promise: Girls Growing up in the 1950s*, edited by L. Heron, 189–211. London: Virago, 1985.

Rowntree, B. Seebohm, and G. R. Lavers. *English Life and Leisure: A Social Study*. London: Longmans, Green, 1952.

Russell, Bertrand. *Marriage and Morals*. London: George Allen & Unwin Ltd, 1930.

Santow, Gigi. 'Coitus Interruptus in the Twentieth Century'. *Population and Development Review* 19, no. 4 (1993): 767–92.

Sarsby, Jacqueline. *Missuses and Mouldrunners: An Oral History of Women Pottery-Workers at Work and at Home.* Milton Keynes: Open University Press, 1988.

Saunders, Andy. *Jane: A Pin-up at War*. London: Leo Cooper Ltd, 2004.

Savage, Mike. 'Trade Unionism, Sex Segregation, and the State: Women's Employment in "New Industries" in Inter-War Britain'. *Social History* 13, no. 2 (1988): 209–30.

'Women and Work in the Lancashire Cotton Industry, 1890–1939'. In *Employers and Labour in the English Textile Industries*, edited by Tony Jowitt and Arthur McVicor, 203–23. London: Routledge, 1988.

Scharlieb, Mary, Dame, and Frederic Arthur Sibly. *Youth and Sex*. London and Edinburgh: T. C. & E. C. Jack and T. Nelson & Sons Ltd, rev. edn 1919.

Schelling, Thomas. *Micromotives and Macrobehavior*. New York: Norton, 1978.

Schmeichen, J. A. *Sweated Industries and Sweated Labour: The London Clothing Trades, 1860–1914*. Urbana, IL: University of Illinois Press, 1984.

Schofield, George, and Central Council for Health Education (Great Britain). *The Sexual Behaviour of Young People*. Boston: Little, 1965.

Schwarzkopf, Jutta. 'Bringing Babies into Line with Mothers' Jobs: Lancashire Cotton Weavers' Fertility Regime'. In *Gendering the Fertility Decline in the Western World*, edited by Angélique Janssens, 309–34. Bern and New York: Peter Lang, 2007.

Unpicking Gender: The Social Construction of Gender in the Lancashire Cotton Weaving Industry, 1880–1914. Aldershot and Burlington, VT: Ashgate, 2004.

Scott, Jacqueline L., Judith Treas and Martin Richards, eds. *The Blackwell Companion to the Sociology of Families*. Malden, MA: Blackwell Publishers, 2004.

Scott, Joan. 'The Evidence of Experience'. *Critical Inquiry* 1, no. 7 (1991): 773–97.

Scott, Joseph E., and Jack L. Franklin. 'The Changing Nature of Sex References in Mass Circulation Magazines'. *The Public Opinion Quarterly* 36, no. 1 (1972): 80–6.

Scott, Peter. 'Consumption, Consumer Credit and the Diffusion of Consumer Durables'. In *Twentieth-Century Britain: Economic, Cultural and Social Change*, edited by Francesca Carnevali, Paul Johnson and Julie-Marie Strange, 162–79. London: Longman, 2007.

'Did Owner-occupation Lead to Smaller Families for Interwar Working-class Households?' *Economic History Review* 61, no. 1 (2008): 99–124.

Seccombe, Wally. *Weathering the Storm: Working-Class Families from the Industrial Revolution to the Fertility Decline*. London: Verso, 1995.

Segal, Lynne. 'New Battlegrounds: Genetic Maps and Sexual Politics'. In *Sexuality Repositioned: Diversity and the Law*, edited by Belinda Brooks-Gordon, Loraine Gelsthorpe, Martin Johnson and Andrew Bainham, 65–83. Oxford: Hart Publishing, 2004.

Straight Sex: The Politics of Pleasure. London: Virago, 1994.

Seymour-Ure, Colin. *The British Press and Broadcasting since 1945*. Oxford: Blackwell, 1996.

Sheail, John. *An Environmental History of Twentieth-Century Britain*. Basingstoke: Palgrave Macmillan, 2002.

Sheard, Sally. 'Profit is a Dirty Word: The Development of Public Baths and Wash-Houses in Britain 1847–1915'. *Social History of Medicine* 13, no. 1 (2000): 63–85.

Shorter, Edward. 'Illegitimacy, Sexual Revolution, and Social Change in Modern Europe'. *Journal of Interdisciplinary History* 2, no. 2 (1971): 237–72.

Written in the Flesh: A History of Desire. Toronto and Buffalo: University of Toronto Press, 2005.

Shumway, David R. *Modern Love: Romance, Intimacy, and the Marriage Crisis*. New York: New York University Press, 2003.

Simmons, Christina. *Making Marriage Modern: Women's Sexuality from the Progressive Era to World War Two*. Oxford and New York: Oxford University Press, 2009.

Simon, Brian. *Education and the Social Order, 1940–1990*. London: Lawrence & Wishart, 1991.

Slater, Eliot, and Moya Woodside. *Patterns of Marriage: A Study of Marriage Relationships in the Urban Working Classes*. London: Cassell and Co., 1951.

Smith, Janet, and Simon Inglis. *Liquid Assets: The Lidos and Open Air Swimming Pools of Britain*. London: English Heritage, 2006.

Smith, Virginia. *Clean: A History of Personal Hygiene and Purity*. Oxford and New York: Oxford University Press, 2007.

Søland, Birgitte. *Becoming Modern: Young Women and the Reconstruction of Womanhood in the 1920s*. Princeton: Princeton University Press, 2000.

Spencer, Stephanie. '"Be Yourself": *Girl* and the business of growing up in late 1950s England'. Ch. 7 in *Women and Work Culture in Britain c.1850–1950*, edited by Krista Cowman and Louise A. Jackson, 141–58. Aldershot: Ashgate Press, 2005.

Spurlock, John C., and Cynthia A. Magistro. '"Dreams Never to Be Realized": Emotional Culture and the Phenomenology of Emotion'. *Journal of Social History* 28, no. 2 (1994): 295–310.

Stacey, Margaret. *Tradition and Change: A Study of Banbury*. Oxford: Oxford University Press, 1960.

Stanley, Liz. *Sex Surveyed, 1949–1994: From Mass-Observation's 'Little Kinsey' to the National Survey and the Hite Reports*. London: Taylor & Francis, 1995.

Stearns, Carol Z., and Peter N. Stearns. 'Victorian Sexuality: Can Historians Do It Better?' *Journal of Social History* 18, no. 4 (1985): 625–34.

Stearns, Peter N., and Mark Knapp. 'Men and Romantic Love: Pinpointing a 20th-Century Change'. *Journal of Social History* 26, no. 4 (1993): 769–95.

Steele, Valerie. *Fashion and Eroticism: Ideals of Feminine Beauty from the Victorian Era to the Jazz Age*. New York: Oxford University Press, 1985.

Stopes, Marie Carmichael. *Contraception (Birth Control) Its Theory, History and Practice; a Manual for the Medical and Legal Professions*. London: J. Bale, Sons & Danielsson Ltd, 1923.

Married Love or Love in Marriage. London: Putnam, 1918.

Mother England, a Contemporary History. London: J. Bale, Sons & Danielsson Ltd, 1929.

Wise Parenthood, a Sequel to 'Married Love'; a Book for Married People. London: A. C. Fifield, 1918.

Married Love, edited by Ross McKibbin. Oxford: Oxford University Press, 2004.

Strange, Julie-Marie. 'The Assault on Ignorance: Teaching Menstrual Etiquette in England, c. 1920s to 1960s'. *Social History of Medicine* 14, no. 2 (2001): 247–65.

'Leisure'. In *Twentieth-Century Britain: Economic, Cultural and Social Change*, edited by Francesca Carnevali, Paul Johnson and Julie-Marie Strange, 197–213. London: Longman, 2007.

Summerfield, Penny. 'Dis/Composing the Subject: Intersubjectivities in Oral History'. In *Feminism and Autobiography: Texts, Theories, Methods*, edited by Celia Lury, Tess Cosslett and Penny Summerfield, 91–106. London and New York: Routledge, 2000.

'Women in Britain since 1945: Companionate Marriage and the Double Burden'. In *Understanding Post-war British Society*, edited by James Obelkevich and Peter Catterall, 58–72. London and New York: Routledge, 1994.

Sutherland, Gillian. 'Education'. In *The Cambridge Social History of Britain, 1750–1950,* edited by F. M. L. Thompson, 119–69. Cambridge and New York: Cambridge University Press, 1990.

Sutherland, Gillian, and Stephen Sharp. *Ability, Merit, and Measurement: Mental Testing and English Education, 1880–1940*. Oxford and New York: Clarendon Press and Oxford University Press, 1984.

Sutton, Maureen. *We Didn't Know Aught: Study of Sexuality, Superstition and Death in Women's Lives in Lincolnshire During the 1930's, 40's and 50's*. Stamford: P. Watkins, 1992.

Szreter, Simon. *Fertility, Class, and Gender in Britain, 1860–1940*. Cambridge and New York: Cambridge University Press, 1996.

'The Genesis of the Registrar-General's Social Classification of Occupations'. *The British Journal of Sociology* 35, no. 4 (1984): 522–46.

'The Official Representation of Social Classes in Britain, the United States, and France: The Professional Model and "Les Cadres"'. *Comparative Studies in Society and History* 35 (1993): 285–317.

'Victorian Britain, 1837–1963: Towards a Social History of Sexuality'. *Journal of Victorian Culture* 1 (1996): 136–49.

Szreter, Simon, and Kate Fisher. 'Love and Authority in Mid-twentieth Century Marriages: Sharing and Caring'. Ch. 6 in *The Politics of Domestic Authority in Britain since 1800*, edited by Lucy DeLap, Ben Griffin and Abigail Wills, 132–54. Basingstoke: Palgrave Macmillan, 2009.

'"We weren't the Sort that Wanted Intimacy Every Night": Birth Control and Assistence in England, c.1930–60'. *The History of the Family* 15, no. 2 (2002): 139–60.

Tebbutt, Melanie. *Women's Talk?: A Social History of Gossip in Working-Class Neighbourhoods, 1880–1960*. Aldershot: Scolar Press, 1995.

Thane, Pat, and Tanya Evans. *Unmarried Motherhood in Modern England* (Oxford: Oxford University Press, forthcoming).

Thompson, Derek. 'Courtship and Marriage in Preston between the Wars'. *Oral History* 3, no. 2 (1975): 39–44.

Thompson, Paul. *The Edwardians: The Remaking of British Society*. London: Weidenfeld & Nicolson, 1975.

The Edwardians: Remaking of British Society. 2nd edn. London: Routledge, 1992.

Thompson, Steven. *Unemployment, Poverty and Health in Interwar South Wales*. Cardiff: University of Wales Press, 2006.

Tiefer, Leonore. *Sex Is Not a Natural Act and Other Essays*. Boulder, CO and Oxford: Westview Press, 2004.

Tinkler, Penny. *Constructing Girlhood: Popular Magazines for Girls Growing up in England, 1920–1950*. London and Bristol, PA: Taylor & Francis, 1995.

Tizard, Leslie J. *Guide to Marriage*. London: Allen & Unwin, 1948.

Todd, Selina. 'Affluence, Class and Crown Street: Reinvestigating the Post-War Working Class'. *Contemporary British History* 22, no. 4 (2008): 501–18.

'Domestic Service and Class Relations in Britain 1900–1950'. *Past and Present* 203, no. 1 (2009): 181–204.

Young Women, Work, and Family in England, 1918–1950. Oxford and New York: Oxford University Press, 2005.

Tomes, Nancy. *The Gospel of Germs: Men, Women, and the Microbe in American Life*. Cambridge, MA: Harvard University Press, 1999.

Tosh, John. *A Man's Place: Masculinity and the Middle-Class Home in Victorian England*. New Haven: Yale University Press, 1999.

Tyler, Melissa. 'Managing between the Sheets: Lifestyle Magazines and the Management of Sexuality in Everyday Life'. *Sexualities* 7, no. 1 (2004): 81–106.

Van de Velde, Theodoor H. *Ideal Marriage: Its Physiology and Technique*. London: William Heinemann, 1947 (first published 1928).

Van de Velde, Theodoor H., and Stella Browne. *Ideal Marriage: Its Physiology and Technique*. London: William Heinemann, 1928.

Vickery, Amanda. 'Golden Age to Separate Spheres? A Review of the Categories and Chronology of English Women's History'. *The Historical Journal* 36, no. 2 (2009): 383–414.

Vincent, David. *The Culture of Secrecy: Britain 1832–1998*. Oxford: Oxford University Press, 1998.

Voigt, David Q. 'Sex in Baseball: Reflections of Changing Taboos'. *Journal of Popular Culture* 12, no. 3 (1978): 389–403.

Vostral, Sharra L. 'Making Menstruation: The Emergence of Menstrual Hygiene Products in the United States'. In *Menstruation: A Cultural History*, edited by Andrew Shail and Gillian Howie, 243–58. Basingstoke and New York: Palgrave Macmillan, 2005.

Wahrman, Dror. *The Making of the Modern Self: Identity and English Culture in the Eighteenth Century*. New Haven: Yale University Press, 2004.

Waites, Bernard. *A Class Society at War, England, 1914–1918*. Leamington Spa and New York: Berg and St. Martin's Press, 1987.

Walkowitz, Judith R. 'Science, Feminism and Romance: The Men and Women's Club 1885–1889'. *History Workshop Journal* 21, no. 3 (1986): 37–59.

Walton, John K. 'Blackpool and the Varieties of Britishness'. In *Relocating Britishness*, edited by Stephen Caunce, Ewa Mazierska, Susan Sydney-Smith and John K. Walton, 53–70. Manchester: Manchester University Press, 2004.

The British Seaside: Holidays and Resorts in the Twentieth Century. Manchester: Manchester University Press, 2000.

Warde, Paul. 'Facing the Challenge of Climate Change: Energy Efficiency and Energy Consumption', available from www.historyandpolicy.org/archive/policy-paper-65.html (accessed 15 April 2010).

Waters, Chris. 'Distance and Desire in the New British Queer History'. *GLQ-NEW YORK* 14, no. 1 (2008): 139–55.

'Sexology'. In *Palgrave Advances in the Modern History of Sexuality*, edited by Harry Cocks and Matt Houlbrook, 41–63. Basingstoke and New York: Palgrave Macmillan, 2006.

Weatherhead, Leslie D. *The Mastery of Sex: Through Psychology and Religion*. 17th edn. London: SCM Press, 1954.

Webb, Alisa. 'Constructing the Gendered Body: Girls, Health, Beauty, Advice, and the Girls' Best Friend, 1898–99'. *Women's History Review* 15, no. 2 (2006): 253–75.

Webster, Wendy. *Imagining Home: Gender, Race and National Identity, 1945–64*. London: UCL Press, 1998.

Weeks, Jeffrey. 'History, Desire, and Identities'. In *Conceiving Sexuality: Approaches to Sex Research in a Postmodern World*, edited by Richard G. Parker and John H. Gagnon, 33–49. New York and London: Routledge, 1995.

Sex, Politics, and Society: The Regulation of Sexuality since 1800. London: Longman, 1981.

Sexuality and Its Discontents: Meanings, Myths and Modern Sexualities. London: Routledge & Kegan Paul, 1985.

The World We Have Won: The Remaking of Erotic and Intimate Life. London and New York: Routledge, 2007.

Wellings, Kaye. *Sexual Behaviour in Britain: The National Survey of Sexual Attitudes and Lifestyles*. London and New York: Penguin Books, 1994.

Wellings, Kaye, Patrick Branigan and Kirsti Mitchell. 'Discomfort, Discord and Discontinuity as Data: Using Focus Groups to Research Sensitive Topics'. *Culture, Health & Sexuality* 2, no. 3 (2000): 255–67.

Welshman, John. '"Bringing Beauty and Brightness to the Back Streets": Health Education and Public Health in England and Wales, 1890–1940'. *Health Education Journal* 56, no. 2 (1997): 199–209.

'Physical Education and the School Medical Service in England and Wales, 1907–1939'. *Social History of Medicine* 9, no. 1 (1996): 31–48.

Whipp, Richard. *Patterns of Labour: Work and Social Change in the Pottery Industry*. London and New York: Routledge, 1990.

White, Kevin. *The First Sexual Revolution: Male Heterosexuality in Modern America*. New York and London: New York University Press, 1993.

Wile, Ira S. *Sex Education*. London: Andrew Melrose, 1913.

Wilkinson (now Hardy), Anne. 'The Beginnings of Disease Control in London: The Work of the Medical Officers of Health in Three Parishes, 1865–1900'. Unpublished Ph.D. thesis; Oxford: University of Oxford, 1980.

Williams, Raymond. *Keywords: A Vocabulary of Culture and Society*. New York: Oxford University Press, 1983.

Williams, Sarah C. *Religious Belief and Popular Culture in Southwark, c.1880–1939*. Oxford and New York: Oxford University Press, 1999.

Williamson, Margaret. 'Gender, Leisure and Marriage in a Working-Class Community, 1939–1960'. *Labour History Review* 74 (2009): 185–98.

'"Getting Off at Loftus": Sex and the Working-Class Woman, 1920–1960'. *Family and Community History* 3, no. 1 (2000): 5–18.

Willis, Paul E. *Learning to Labour: How Working Class Kids Get Working Class Jobs*. Farnborough: Saxon House, 1977.

Wilson, Dolly Smith. 'A New Look at the Affluent Worker: The Good Working Mother in Post-War Britain'. *Twentieth Century British History* 17, no. 2 (2006): 206–29.

Wolffe, John. 'Religion and Secularisation'. In *Twentieth-Century Britain: Economic, Cultural and Social Change*, edited by Francesca Carnevali, Paul Johnson and Julie-Marie Strange, 323–38. London: Longman, 2007.

Wood, Clive, and Beryl Suitters. *The Fight for Acceptance: A History of Contraception*. Guildford: Billing & Sons, 1970.

Woodruff, William. *The Road to Nab End: A Lancashire Childhood*. London: Abacus, 2002.

Worboys, Michael. *Spreading Germs: Diseases, Theories, and Medical Practice in Britain, 1865–1900*. Cambridge: Cambridge University Press, 2000.

Wright, Helena. *More About the Sex Factor in Marriage*. London: Williams & Norgate, 1954.

The Sex Factor in Marriage: A Book for Those Who Are or Are About to Be Married. London: N. Douglas, 1930.

Wrightson, Keith. *English Society, 1580–1680, Hutchinson Social History of England*. London: Hutchinson, 1982.

Young, Michael, and Peter Willmott. *Family and Kinship in East London*. Glencoe, IL: Free Press, 1957.

The Symmetrical Family. London: Routledge & Kegan Paul, 1973.

Yow, Valerie Raleigh. *Recording Oral History: A Practical Guide for Social Scientists*. Thousand Oaks, CA: Sage Publications, 1994.

Zavella, Patricia. '"Playing with Fire": The Gendered Construction of Chicana/Mexicana Sexuality'. In *The Gender/Sexuality Reader: Culture, History, Political Economy*, edited by R. N. Lancaster and M. D. Leonardo, 392–408. New York: Routledge, 1997.

Zimmeck, Meta. 'Jobs for the Girls: The Expansion of Clerical Work for Women, 1850–1914'. In *Unequal Opportunities: Women's Employment in England 1800–1918*, edited by Angela V. John. Oxford: Basil Blackwell, 1986.

Zweig, Ferdynand. *Women's Life and Labour*. London: V. Gollancz, 1952.

Zweiniger-Bargielowska, Ina. *Austerity in Britain: Rationing, Controls, and Consumption, 1939–1955*. Oxford and New York: Oxford University Press, 2000.

'The Body and Consumer Culture'. In *Women in Twentieth-Century Britain*, edited by Ina Zweiniger-Bargielowska, 183–97. Harlow: Longman, 2001.

'The Culture of the Abdomen: Obesity and Reducing in Britain, Circa 1900–1939'. *Journal of British Studies* 44, no. 2 (2005): 239–73.

'"Raising a Nation of Good Animals": The New Health Society and Health Education Campaigns in Interwar Britain'. *Social History of Medicine* 20, no. 1 (2007): 73–89.

ed. *Women in Twentieth-Century Britain*. Harlow: Longman, 2001.

Index

Index of interviewees

Note: References are to Interviewees' transcripts in the text and to significant discussion in footnotes